CROSSCURRENTS

INTERNATIONAL

RELATIONS

IN THE POST–COLD WAR ERA
THIRD EDITION

EDITED BY
MARK CHARLTON

THOMSON
™
NELSON

lia   Canada   Mexico   Singapore   Spain   United Kingdom   United States

THOMSON

NELSON

Crosscurrents: International Relations in
the Post–Cold War Era,
Third Edition
Edited by Mark Charlton

Editorial Director and Publisher:
Evelyn Veitch

Executive Editor:
Chris Carson

Senior Marketing Manager:
Murray Moman

Developmental Editor:
Joanne Sutherland

Production Editor:
Wendy Yano

Production Coordinator:
Helen Jager Locsin

Copy Editor:
Joan Rawlin

Proofreader:
Carol J. Anderson

Creative Director:
Angela Cluer

Cover Design:
Katherine Strain

Cover Image:
digitalvisiononline.com

Compositor:
Carol Magee

Printer:
Transcontinental Printing Inc.

National Library of Canada
Cataloguing in Publication Data

Main entry under title:

Crosscurrents: international
relations in the post–cold war era

3rd ed.
Includes bibliographical reference
ISBN 0-17-616965-2

1. World politics—1989–
2. International relations. I.
Charlton, Mark William, 1948–

D860.C76 2002   327'.09'049
C2001-904032-6

Contents

Contributors   vii

Introduction   x

PART ONE: UNDERSTANDING OUR CHANGING WORLD   1

1.   **Is War Becoming Obsolete?**   2

    YES: John Mueller, "The Obsolescence of Major War"   4

    NO: Michael O'Hanlon, "Coming Conflicts: Interstate War in the New Millennium"   14

2.   **Is Globalization Undermining the Power of the Nation-State?**   23

    YES: Susan Strange, "The Erosion of the State"   25

    NO: Martin Wolf, "Will the Nation-State Survive Globalization?"   33

3.   **Is the World Fragmenting into Antagonistic Cultures?**   45

    YES: Samuel Huntington, "The Clash of Civilizations? The Next Pattern of Conflict"   47

    NO: Douglas Ross, "Despair, Defeatism, and Isolationism in American 'Grand Strategy': The Seductive Convenience of Huntington's 'Civilizational Clash' Thesis"   67

PART TWO: FINDING A PLACE FOR CANADA IN A CHANGING WORLD ORDER   87

4.   **Should Human Security Be the Core Value of Canadian Foreign Policy?**   88

    YES: Lloyd Axworthy, "Human Security: Safety for People in a Changing World"   91

    NO: William W. Bain, "Against Crusading: The Ethics of Human Security and Canadian Foreign Policy"   97

5.   **Can Canada's Foreign Policy Be Best Understood by the Concept of "Middle Power"?**   114

    YES: Andrew Cooper, Richard Higgot, and Kim Richard Nossal, excerpt from *Relocating Middle Powers: Australia and Canada in a Changing World Order*   117

Contents

NO: Mark Neufeld, "Hegemony and Foreign Policy Analysis: The Case of Canada as a Middle Power"   134

6.   Should Canada Pursue a Strategy of Niche Diplomacy?   153

YES: Evan H. Potter, "Niche Diplomacy as Canadian Foreign Policy"   155

NO: Heather A. Smith, "Caution Warranted: Niche Diplomacy Assessed"   164

PART THREE: ENSURING PEACE AND SECURITY   181

7.   Should Terrorism Be Treated as an Act of Warfare?   182

YES: Caleb Carr, "Terrorism as Warfare: Lessons of Military History"   184

NO: Bruce Hoffman, "Terrorism: Who Is Fighting Whom?"   199

8.   Has the Concept of "Rogue State" Become Outdated?   211

YES: Michael Klare, "An Anachronistic Policy: The Strategic Obsolescence of the 'Rogue Doctrine'"   214

NO: Thomas Henriksen, "The Rise and Decline of Rogue States: Dividing Patrons from Rogue Regimes"   222

9.   Will a Ballistic Defence System Undermine Security?   231

YES: Ernie Regehr, "Missile Proliferation, Globalized Insecurity, and Demand-Side Strategies"   234

NO: Frank P. Harvey, "The International Politics of National Missile Defence: A Response to the Critics"   242

10.   Do Biological Differences Predispose Men to War?   260

YES: Francis Fukuyama, "Women and the Evolution of World Politics"   263

NO: J. Ann Tickner, "Why Women Can't Run the World: International Politics According to Francis Fukuyama"   275

11.   Is Peacekeeping Irrelevant?   286

YES: Charles Krauthammer, "Peacekeeping Is for Chumps"   288

NO: Peter Viggo Jakobsen, "Overload, Not Marginalization, Threatens UN Peacekeeping"   296

PART FOUR: INTERNATIONAL POLITICAL ECONOMY   311

12.   Does Globalization Cheat the World's Poor?   312

YES: Michel Chossudovsky, "Global Poverty in the Late 20th Century"   314

NO: Gautam Sen, "Is Globalisation Cheating the World's Poor?"   330

13. Should the WTO Be Abolished?   354

YES and NO: Walden Bello and Philippe Legrain, "Should the WTO Be Abolished?" An Exchange 356

14. Was the "Battle in Seattle" a Significant Turning Point in the Struggle against Globalization?   366

YES: Stephen Gill, "Toward a Postmodern Prince? The Battle in Seattle as a Moment in the New Politics of Globalisation"   368

NO: Jan Aart Scholte, "Cautionary Reflections on Seattle"   378

15. Will Debt Relief Address the Needs of Highly Indebted Countries?   387

YES: William Peters and Martin J. Dent, "Grass Roots Mobilization for Debt Remission: The Jubilee 2000 Campaign"   390

NO: Denise Froning, "Will Debt Relief Really Help?"   408

16. Would a Tobin Tax on International Trade Be Detrimental to the Global Economy?   421

YES: A.R. Riggs and Tom Velk, "The Tobin Tax: A Bad Idea Whose Time Has Passed"   424

NO: Alex C. Michalos, "The Tobin Tax: A Good Idea Whose Time Has Not Passed"   430

PART FIVE: GLOBAL COOPERATION AND HUMAN SECURITY   439

17. Do We Need an International Criminal Court?   440

YES: Douglas Cassel, "Why We Need the International Criminal Court"   442

NO: Alfred P. Rubin, "Some Objections to the International Criminal Court"   450

18. Can International Law Eliminate the Problem of Child Soldiers?   458

YES: Ross Snyder, "The Optional Protocol on the Involvement of Children in Armed Conflict"   461

NO: Ananda S. Millard, "Children in Armed Conflicts: Transcending Legal Responses"   469

19. Should States Pursue an Open Border Policy toward Migrants?   483

YES: Andrew Coyne, "The Case for Open Immigration: Why Opening Up Our Borders Would Be Good for the Country and Good for the Soul"   486

NO: G.E. Dirks, "Why States Are Justified in Limiting Their Entry of Migrants"   499

20. Should Political and Civil Rights Always Take Priority over Economic and Social Rights?   509

YES: George Weigel, "The New Human-Rights Debate"   512

NO: Ron Dart, "The New Human Rights Debate: A Reply to George Weigel"   525

21. Can Economic Sanctions Mitigate Conflict and Halt Human-Rights Abuses?   535

YES: Elizabeth Rogers, "Economic Sanctions and Internal Conflict"   538

NO: Kim Richard Nossal, "The False Promise of Economic Sanctions"   556

22. Does Africa Pose a Threat to Environmental Security?   563

YES: Robert D. Kaplan, "The Coming Anarchy: How Scarcity, Crime, Overpopulation, Tribalism, and Disease Are Rapidly Destroying the Social Fabric of Our Planet"   566

NO: Cyril Obi, "Globalised Images of Environmental Security in Africa"   581

Appendix   Lucille Charlton, "How to Write an Argumentative Essay"   602

Contributor Acknowledgments   609

Contributors

Lloyd Axworthy is director of the Liu Centre for the Study of Global Issues at the University of British Columbia and a former minister of Foreign Affairs of Canada.

William W. Bain is a Ph.D. candidate in Political Science at the University of British Columbia.

Walden Bello is director of Global South.

Caleb Carr is a contributing editor of *MHQ: The Quarterly Journal of Military History.*

Douglas Cassel is director of the Center for International Human Rights at Northwestern University School of Law in Chicago.

Michel Chossudovsky is a professor of economics and international development at the University of Ottawa.

Andrew Cooper is a professor of political science at the University of Waterloo.

Andrew Coyne is a journalist who writes for the *National Post.*

Ron Dart is an instructor in political science at the University College of the Fraser Valley.

Martin J. Dent is a fellow of Keele University and co-founder of Jubilee 2000.

G.E. Dirks is a professor of political science at Brock University.

Denise Froning is a policy analyst with the Center for International Trade and Economics at the Heritage Foundation, Washington, D.C.

Francis Fukuyama is a consultant with the Rand Corporation.

Stephen Gill is a professor of political science at York University.

Frank P. Harvey is Director of the Centre for Foreign Policy Studies, Dalhousie University.

Thomas Henriksen is a fellow at the Hoover Institution.

Richard Higgot is a professor of political science at the University of Manchester, England.

Bruce Hoffman is director of the Centre for the Study of Terrorism and Political Violence and chair of the Department of International Relations at St. Andrews University, Scotland.

Samuel Huntington is a professor of political science at Harvard University.

Peter Viggo Jakobsen is a professor in international relations at the University of Copenhagen, Denmark.

Robert Kaplan is an author and journalist.

Michael Klare is a professor of peace and world security studies at Hampshire College, Massachusetts.

Charles Krauthammer is a syndicated columnist.

Phillipe Legrain is an official with the World Trade Organization.

Alex C. Michalos is a professor and chair of the political science program at the University of Northern British Columbia.

Ananda S. Millard is a Researcher at the International Peace Research Institute (PRIO), Oslo, Norway.

John Mueller is a professor of political science and Director of the Watson Center for the Study of International Peace and Cooperation at the University of Rochester.

Mark Neufeld is a professor of political science at Trent Univesity.

Kim Richard Nossal is a professor of political science at McMaster University.

Cyril Obi is a fellow with the Nigerian Institute of International Relations.

Michael O'Hanlon is a Senior Fellow at the Brookings Institute.

William Peters is co-founder of Jubilee 2000.

Evan H. Potter is editor of Canadian Foreign Policy.

Ernie Regehr is Research Director for Project Ploughshares.

A.R. Riggs teaches in the department of history at McGill University.

Elizabeth Rogers is a fellow at the John F. Kennedy School of Government, Harvard University.

Douglas Ross is a professor of political science at Simon Fraser University.

Alfred P. Rubin is Distinguished Professor of International Law at the Fletcher School of Law and Diplomacy at Tuffs University.

Gautam Sen is Lecturer in the Politics of the World Economy, Department of International Relations, London School of Economics & Political Science.

Jan Aart Scholte is Reader in International Studies, University of Warwick.

Heather A. Smith is a professor of international studies at the University of Northern British Columbia.

Ross Synder has served as the deputy director of the Peacebuilding and Human Security Division of the Department of Foreign Affairs and International Trade, Canada.

Susan Strange, until her death in 1998, was professor of international political economics at the University of Warwick.

J. **Ann Tickner** teaches in the School of International Relations, University of Southern California.

Tom Velk teaches in the department of economics at McGill University.

George Weigel is president of the Ethics and Public Policy Center in Washington, D.C.

Martin Wolf is Associate Editor and Chief Economics Commentator at the *Financial Times*.

ACKNOWLEDGMENTS

I would like to express appreciation to the reviewers who provided many valuable suggestions and comments: Duane Bratt, University of Calgary; Chris Kukucha, Douglas College; Ron Dart, University College of the Fraser Valley; Michael Tucker, Mount Allison University; Alistair Edgar, Wilfrid Laurier University; Malcolm Grieve, Acadia University; Hevina Dashwood, University of Toronto; Sandra Whitworth, York University; Tom Keating, University of Alberta; and Mark Franke, University of Northern British Columbia. In addition, I would like to thank Jareed Kuehl for his help as a research assistant. Appreciation is also expressed to the authors and publishers who have given permission to include their work in this volume. At Nelson, I would like to acknowledge the excellent and patient support of Joanne Sutherland and other members of the staff. Finally, a word of thanks to Lucille, Daniel, and David for the sacrifices that they have made in the completion of this project.

Introduction

When the first edition of *Crosscurrents: International Relations in the Post-Cold War Era* was published in 1993, the introduction began with the following words from Charles Dickens: "It was the best of times: it was the worst of times." Dickens wrote those words in response to the tumult of revolutionary France in the 18th century. His words seem even more apt for the current situation than when I cited them nine years ago. For many, the past decade has been one of growing prosperity, expanding human rights, and progress towards democratization. The emergence of a global civil society and the "democratization" of foreign policy has enabled new actors on the global scene to achieve successes in promoting issues—such as a global ban on landmines and international debt relief—that were unheard of decades ago.

At the same time, others have experienced the 1990s as a period of increased impoverishment and alienation. Resistance to the forces of globalization intensified and took more violent forms. Genocidal warfare in the former Yugoslavia and Rwanda challenged the ability of the international community to respond. Conflicts and hatreds in the Middle East are more entrenched than ever. A series of terrorist attacks by radical Islamists, culminating in the deaths of nearly 3,500 civilians in a coordinated attack on Washington and New York city, gave new credence to talk of a "new world disorder." The scale of the attack on the World Trade Centers and the subsequent spread of anthrax made even the worst-case scenarios about chemical, biological, and nuclear terrorism suddenly seem real and credible. In an era of seemingly endless opportunities, North Americans suddenly felt less secure and certain about their futures. Indeed, "the best of times, the worst of times" is an apt description for our entry into the new millennium.

As we enter this new millennium, we are faced with a number of complex questions: Is war likely to become obsolete or is it being transformed into new and more virulent forms? Will cultural, ethnic, and religious differences become the basis for new "civilizational" conflicts? Do the forces associated with globalization threaten to undermine a more equitable distribution of resources and progress towards human rights?

Are new forms of global governance emerging that will enable the international community to better address issues of war crimes, weapons proliferation, international debt, and migration?

THE DEBATE FORMAT

In preparing the third edition of *Crosscurrents: International Relations in the Post-Cold War Era*, it is my hope that students will be challenged to wrestle with many of these questions. Students enrolling in introductory international relations courses generally do so in the hopes of gaining a better understanding of contemporary world issues and events. In contrast, many international relations texts focus on structures, abstract concepts, and theories that, while vital to the discipline, when taken alone fail to address students' interest in current world developments. The debate format in the *Crosscurrents* series, I believe, provides a structured way of relating topical information about current affairs to the broader concepts and theories of the discipline. By evaluating contending arguments concerning various global issues, students will be encouraged to analyze for themselves the relevance of different theories and concepts for explaining contemporary international developments.

While the debate format has its advantages, it sometimes limits the choice of readings. Thus, some of the more seminal pieces on particular topics were not included because they were not suitable to the debate format, or adequate companion pieces could not be found for them. In these cases, we have added them to the suggested reading list in the postscripts.

USAGE IN THE CLASSROOM

Crosscurrents: International Relations in the Post-Cold War Era is designed as a flexible pedagogical tool that can be incorporated into courses in several ways.

i. Perhaps the most effective use of *Crosscurrents: International Relations in the Post-Cold War Era* is to use the readings as a means of organizing weekly discussion sessions in a debate format. On each topic, two students may be asked to argue the case for the opposing sides, and these arguments could be followed by a group discussion. This format requires students to adopt a particular point of view and defend that position. Because the necessary background material is provided in the readings, this format is very easily adapted to large courses in which teaching assistants are responsible for weekly tutorial sessions.

ii. Some may wish to assign the chapters simply as supplementary readings reinforcing material covered in the lectures, and to use them as points of illustration in classroom lectures or discussions. In this way the text can be used as a more traditional course reader, with the instructor having the option of assigning only one of the readings under each topic.

iii. Others may wish to use the readings as a point of departure for essay assignments in the course. In some cases, the readings and the postscript with its suggestion of further readings could simply serve as a starting point for researching the topic under discussion. In other cases, the instructor might want to encourage students to develop their critical skill by having them write an assessment of the arguments and evidence presented by the writers in a particular debate. Alternatively, students could select one side of the debate and write a persuasive essay developing their own arguments in favour of that point of view. We have included, as an appendix, instructions on writing an argumentative essay that should be a useful guide to students.

NEW TO THE THIRD EDITION

Since the first edition of *Crosscurrents: International Relations in the Post-Cold War Era*, the manner in which students conduct research has changed dramatically. The availability of Internet resources and the use of electronic journals has significantly expanded the resources at the disposal of the student. To reflect these changes this third edition has two new features:

- **Website resources:** The postscripts in this edition have been shortened in favour of presenting both a list of suggested print resources and an annotated list of websites. The list of web resources will be available on the Nelson Thomson Learning Political Science (www.polisci.nelson.com) where students can connect directly to the recommended links. This list of web resources will be updated periodically as needed. Instructors may also wish to have their students purchase Grant Heckman, *Nelson Guide to Web Research* (Scarborough: Nelson Thomson Learning, 2001). This manual provides not only useful tips on conducting web research, but also includes information on citing web resources including MLA and APA formats.

- **Infotrac:** Students purchasing this edition of *Crosscurrents: International Relations in the Post-Cold War Era*, will receive a free four-month subscription to Infotrac College Edition. This is an online library containing full-text articles from a large number of scholarly journals and popular news magazines. In each postscript I have suggested useful keywords that students may wish to use in facilitating their research. A separate *User Guide for Instructors* is available from Nelson.

Mark Charlton
Trinity Western University
Langley, B.C.

About the Editor

Mark Charlton is professor of political science at Trinity Western University. He has written *The Making of Canadian Food Aid Policy* (1992) and has co-edited, with Paul Barker, *Crosscurrents: Contemporary Political Issues,* 4th edition (2002). He has also published a number of articles in *International Journal, Etudes Internationales, and The Canadian Journal of Development Studies.*

PART ONE

UNDERSTANDING OUR CHANGING WORLD

Is war becoming obsolete?

Is globalization undermining the power of the nation-state?

Is the world fragmenting into antagonistic cultures?

ISSUE**ONE**

Is War Becoming Obsolete?

✔ **YES**
JOHN MUELLER, "The Obsolescence of Major War," *Security Dialogue* 21, no. 3 (2001): 321–28

✗ **NO**
MICHAEL O'HANLON, "Coming Conflicts: Interstate War in the New Millennium," *Harvard International Review* 23, no. 2 (Summer 2000): 42–47

Few events symbolized the significant changes taking place in the last decade of the twentieth century more than the dismantling of the Berlin Wall. For those who remembered the tense and frightening circumstances that led to the building of the wall in the early years of the Cold War, its destruction seemed to confirm that a fundamental shift in modern human history had taken place.

For some observers this event marked the beginning of a new era of greater peace and stability in international politics, one in which war would no longer serve as a useful instrument of foreign policy. John Mueller, author of *Retreat from Doomsday: The Obsolescence of Major War* (Basic Books, 1989), shares this optimistic interpretation of recent trends. According to Mueller, we have reached the stage in history when the notion that war can be used to resolve conflicts has "been discredited and abandoned." This optimism does not stem just from a reading of events relating to the end of the Cold War. Instead, Mueller takes a longer historical perspective, arguing that war was already becoming obsolete by the First World War. Since then, the horrors of the Second World War and the tensions of the Cold War have served only to reinforce earlier lessons about the horrendous cast of modern warfare.

In arguing that war is becoming obsolete, Mueller challenges traditional realist views that have dominated the study of international relations. Proponents of the latter perspective argue that war is an inescapable feature of an anarchical international system in which states seek power and security. However, Mueller argues that war is neither an inevitable result of the human condition nor the byproduct of the structure of international power. Instead, he insists that war begins in the minds of humans and that this is where it will end. War is becoming obsolete, not because of any immediate changes provoked by the end of the Cold War, but due to a change in mental habits stemming from a long process of sociocultural evolution.

An initial look at the evidence would suggest that Mueller's argument has some basis. After all, there have been no *direct* wars between major world powers in over fifty years, the longest period of stable peace since the Treaty of Westphalia in 1648. While recent studies have shown that there are as many as thirty wars going on in any given year, the vast majority of these are internal civil wars or localized conflicts between neighbouring Third World states.

But if major powers have been successful in avoiding war for so long, does it necessarily mean that there has been a fundamental shift in values and norms relating to the use of force among industrialized states? Was it a mere coincidence that the Persian Gulf War, the largest mobilization of military power since the Korean War, took place so soon after the proclaimed end of the Cold War? Could it be that the Cold War, with its nuclear stalemate between the superpowers, had been responsible for the period of the "long peace"? Might the end of the nuclear standoff, which made the potential cost of war unthinkable, lead to a renewed use of force as an instrument of policy?

✔ YES
The Obsolescence of Major War
JOHN MUELLER

1. INTRODUCTORY REMARKS

In discussing the causes of international war, commentators have often found it useful to group theories into what they term levels of analysis. In his classic work, *Man, the State and War,* Kenneth N. Waltz organizes the theories according to whether the cause of war is found in the nature of man, in the nature of the state, or in the nature of the international state system. More recently Jack Levy, partly setting the issue of human nature to one side, organizes the theories according to whether they stress the systemic level, the nature of state and society, or the decisionmaking process.[1]

In various ways, these level-of-analysis approaches direct attention away from war itself and toward concerns that may influence the incidence of war. However, war should not be visualized as a sort of recurring outcome that is determined by other conditions, but rather as a phenomenon that has its own qualities and appeals. And over time these appeals can change. In this view, war is merely an idea, an institution, like dueling or slavery, that has been grafted onto human existence. Unlike breathing, eating, or sex, war is not something that is somehow required by the human condition, by the structure of international affairs, or by the forces of history.

Accordingly, war can shrivel up and disappear; and this may come about without any notable change or improvement on any of the level-of-analysis categories. Specifically, war can die out without changing human nature, without modifying the nature of the state or the nation-state, without changing the international system, without creating an effective world government or system of international law, and without improving the competence or moral capacity of political leaders. It can also go away without expanding international trade, interdependence, or communication; without fabricating an effective moral or practical equivalent; without enveloping the earth in democracy or prosperity; without devising ingenious agreements to restrict arms or the arms industry; without reducing the world's considerable store of hate, selfishness, nationalism, and racism; without increasing the amount of love, justice, harmony, cooperation, good will, or inner peace in the world; without establishing security communities; and without doing anything whatever about nuclear weapons.

Not only *can* such a development take place: it *has* been taking place for a century or more, at least within the developed world, once a cauldron of international and civil war. Conflicts of interest are inevitable and continue to persist within the developed world. But the notion that war should be used to resolve them has increasingly been discredited and abandoned there. War is apparently becoming obsolete, at least in the developed world: in an area where war was once often casually seen as beneficial, noble, and glorious, or at least as necessary or inevitable, the conviction has now become widespread that war would be intolerably costly, unwise, futile, and debased.[2]

Some of this may be suggested by the remarkable developments in the Cold War in the late 1980s. The dangers of a major war in the developed world clearly declined remarkably: yet this can hardly be attributed to an improvement in human nature, to the demise of the nation-state, to the rise of a world government, or to a notable improvement in the competence of political leaders.

2. TWO ANALOGIES: DUELING AND SLAVERY

It may not be obvious that an accepted, time-honored institution which serves an urgent social purpose can become obsolescent and then die out because many people come to find it obnoxious. But the argument here is that something like that has indeed been happening to war in the developed world. To illustrate the dynamic, it will be helpful briefly to assess two analogies: the processes by which the once-perennial institutions of dueling and slavery have all but vanished from the face of the earth.

2.1 Dueling

In some important respects, war in the developed world may be following the example of another violent method for settling disputes, dueling. Up until a century ago dueling was common practice in Europe and the USA among a certain class of young and youngish men who liked to classify themselves as gentlemen.[3] Men of the social set that once dueled still exist, they still get insulted, and they are still concerned about their self-respect and their standing among their peers. But they no longer duel. However, they do not avoid dueling today because they evaluate the option and reject it on cost-benefit grounds. Rather, the option never percolates into their consciousness as something that is available. That is, a form of violence famed and fabled for centuries has now sunk from thought as a viable, conscious possibility.

The Prussian strategist Carl von Clausewitz opens his famous 1832 book, *On War*, by observing that "War is nothing but a duel on a larger scale."[4] If war, like dueling, comes to be viewed as a thoroughly undesirable, even ridiculous, policy, and if it can no longer promise gains, or if potential combatants come no longer to value the things it can gain for them, then war can fade away as a coherent possibility even if a truly viable substitute or "moral equivalent" for it were never formulated. Like dueling, it could become unfashionable and then obsolete.

2.2 Slavery

From the dawn of prehistory until about 1788 slavery, like war, could be found just about everywhere in one form or another, and it flourished in every age.[5] Around 1788, however, the anti-slavery forces began to argue that the institution was repulsive, immoral, and uncivilized, and this sentiment gradually picked up adherents. Remarkably, at exactly the time that the anti-slavery movement was taking flight, the Atlantic slave economy, as Seymour Drescher notes, "was entering what was probably the most dynamic and profitable period in its existence."[6]

Thus the abolitionists were up against an institution that was viable, profitable, and expanding, and moreover one that had been uncritically accepted for thousands—perhaps millions—of years as a natural and inevitable part of human existence. To counter this powerful and time-honored institution, the abolitionists' principal weapon was a novel argument: it had recently occurred to them, they said, that slavery was no longer the way people ought to do things.

As it happened, this was an idea whose time had come. The abolition of slavery required legislative battles, international pressures, economic travail, and, in the United States, a cataclysmic war (but it did *not* require the fabrication of a functional equivalent or the formation of an effective supranational authority). Within a century slavery, and most similar institutions like serfdom, had been all but eradicated from the face of the globe. Slavery became controversial and then obsolete.

2.3 War

Dueling and slavery no longer exist as effective institutions; they have largely faded from human experience except as something we read about in books. While their re-establishment is not impossible, they show after a century of neglect no signs of revival. Other once-popular, even once-admirable, institutions in the developed world have been, or are being, eliminated because at some point they began to seem repulsive, immoral, and uncivilized: bear-baiting, bareknuckle fighting, freak shows, casual torture, wanton cruelty to animals, burning heretics, flogging, vendetta, deforming corsetting, laughing at the insane, the death penalty for minor crimes, eunuchism, public cigarette smoking.

War may well be in the process of joining this list of recently-discovered sins and vices. War is not, of course, the same as dueling or slavery. Like war, dueling is an institution for settling disputes; but it was something of a social affectation and it usually involved only matters of "honor," not ones of physical gain. Like war, slavery was nearly universal and an apparently inevitable part of human existence, but it could be eliminated area by area: a country that abolished slavery did not have to worry about what other countries were doing, while a country that would like to abolish war must continue to be concerned about those that have kept it in their repertory.

On the other hand, war has against it not only substantial psychic costs, but also obvious and widespread physical ones. Dueling brought death and destruction but, at least in the first instance, only to a few people who had specifically volunteered to participate. And while slavery may have brought moral destruction, it generally was a considerable economic success.

In some respects then, the fact that war has outlived dueling and slavery is curious. But there are signs that, at least in the developed world, it too has begun to succumb to obsolescence.

3. TRENDS AGAINST WAR BEFORE 1914

There were a number of trends away from war in the developed world before World War I. Two of these deserve special emphasis.

3.1 The Hollandization Phenomenon

As early as 1800 a few once-warlike countries in Europe, like Holland, Switzerland, and Sweden, quietly began to drop out of the war system. While war was still generally accepted as a natural and inevitable phenomenon, these countries found solace (and prosperity) in policies that stressed peace. People who argue that war is inherent in nature and those who see war as a recurring, cyclic phenomenon need to supply an explanation for these countries. Switzerland, for example, has avoided all international war for nearly 200 years. If war is inherent in human nature or if war is some sort of cyclic inevitability, surely the Swiss ought to be roaring for a fight by now.

3.2 The Rise of an Organized Peace Movement

While there have been individual war opponents throughout history, the existence of organized groups devoted to abolishing war from the human condition is quite new. The institution of war came under truly organized and concentrated attack only after 1815, and this peace movement did not develop real momentum until the end of the century.[7]

War opponents stressed various arguments against war. Some, like the Quakers, were opposed to war primarily because they found it immoral. Others stressed arguments that were essentially aesthetic: war, they concluded, was repulsive, barbaric, and uncivilized. Still others, such as the British liberals, stressed the futility of war: particularly from an economic standpoint, they argued, even the winners of war were worse off than if they had pursued a policy of peace. These protesters were joined by socialists and others who had concluded that war was a capitalistic device in which the working class was used as cannon fodder. Among their activities, the various elements of the anti-war movement were devoted to exploring alternatives to war such as arbitration and international law and organization, and to developing mechanisms, like disarmament, that might reduce its frequency or consequences.

Peace advocates were a noisy gadfly minority by 1900, and they had established a sense of momentum. Their arguments were inescapable, but, for the most part, they were rejected and derided by the majority, which still held to the traditional view that war was noble, natural, thrilling, progressive, manly, redemptive, and beneficial.[8] Up until 1914, as Michael Howard has observed, war "was almost universally considered an acceptable, perhaps an inevitable and for many people a desirable way of settling international differences."[9]

4. THE IMPACT OF WORLD WAR I

The holocaust of World War I turned peace advocates into a pronounced majority in the developed world and destroyed war romanticism. As Arnold Toynbee points out, this war marked the end of a "span of five thousand years during which war had been one of mankind's master institutions." Or, as Evan Luard observes, "the First World War transformed traditional attitudes toward war. For the first time there was an almost universal sense that the deliberate launching of a war could now no longer be justified."[10]

World War I was, of course, horrible. But horror was not invented in 1914. History had already had its Carthages, its Jerichos, its wars of 30 years, of 100 years. Seen in historic context, in fact, World War I does not seem to have been all that unusual in its duration, destructiveness, grimness, political pointlessness, economic consequences, breadth, or intensity. However, it does seem to be unique in that it was the first major war to be preceded by substantial, organized antiwar agitation, and in that, for Europeans, it followed an unprecedentedly peaceful century during which Europeans had begun, perhaps unknowingly, to appreciate the virtues of peace.[11]

Obviously, this change of attitude was not enough to prevent the wars that have taken place since 1918. But the notion that the institution of war, particularly war in the developed world, was repulsive, uncivilized, immoral, and futile—voiced only by minorities before 1914—was an idea whose time had come. It is one that has permeated most of the developed world ever since.

5. WORLD WAR II

It is possible that enough war spirit still lingered, particularly in Germany, for another war in Europe to be necessary to extinguish it there. But analysis of opinion in the interwar period suggests that war was viewed with about as much horror in Germany as any place on the continent.[12] To a remarkable degree, major war returned to Europe only because of the astoundingly successful machinations of Adolf Hitler, virtually the last European who was willing to risk major war. As Gerhard Weinberg has put it: "Whether any other German leader would indeed have taken the plunge is surely doubtful, and the very warnings Hitler received from some of his generals can only have reinforced his belief in his personal role as the one man able, willing, and even eager to lead Germany and drag the world into war."[13] That is, after World War I a war in Europe could only be brought about through the maniacally dedicated manipulations of an exceptionally lucky and spectacularly skilled entrepreneur; before World War I, any dimwit—e.g., Kaiser Wilhelm—could get into one.

The war in Asia was, of course, developed out of the expansionary policies of distant Japan, a country which neither participated substantially in World War I nor learned its lessons. In World War II, Japan got the message most Europeans had received from World War I.

6. THE COLD WAR, THE LONG PEACE, AND NUCLEAR WEAPONS

Since 1945 major war has been most likely to develop from the Cold War that has dominated postwar international history. The hostility of the era mostly derives from the Soviet Union's ideological—even romantic—affection for revolution and for revolutionary war. While this ideology is expansionistic in some respects, it has never visualized major war in the Hitler mode as a remotely sensible tactic.[14]

East and West have never been close to major war, and it seems unlikely that nuclear weapons have been important determinants of this—insofar as a military deterrent has been necessary, the fear of escalation to a war like World War I or II supplies it. Even allowing considerably for stupidity, ineptness, miscalculation, and self-deception, a large war, nuclear or otherwise, has never been remotely in the interest of the essentially contented, risk-averse, escalation-anticipating countries that have dominated world affairs since 1945. This is not to deny that nuclear war is appalling to contemplate and mind-concentratingly dramatic, particularly in the speed with which it could bring about massive destruction. Nor is it to deny that decisionmakers, both in times of crisis and in times of non-crisis, are well aware of how cataclysmic a nuclear war could be. It is simply to stress that the horror of repeating World War II is not all that much less impressive or dramatic, and that leaders essentially content with the status quo will strive to avoid anything that they feel could lead to either calamity. A jump from a fiftieth-floor window is probably quite a bit more horrible to contemplate than a jump from a fifth-floor one, but anyone who finds life even minimally satisfying is extremely unlikely to do either.[15]

In general the wars that have involved developed countries since World War II have been of two kinds, both of them declining in frequency and relevance. One of these concerns lingering colonial responsibilities and readjustments. Thus the Dutch got involved in (but did not start) a war in Indonesia, the French in Indochina and Algeria, the British in Malay and the Falklands.

The other kind relates to the Cold War contest between East and West. The communists have generally sought to avoid major war, not so much because they necessarily find such wars to be immoral, repulsive, or uncivilized, but because they find them futile—dangerous, potentially counter-productive, wildly and absurdly adventurous. However, for decades after 1945 they retained a dutiful affection for what they came to call wars of national liberation—smaller wars around the world designed to further the progressive cause of world revolution. The West has seen this threat as visceral and as one that must be countered even at the cost of war if necessary. Wars fought in this context, such as those in Korea and Vietnam, have essentially been seen to be preventive—if communism is countered there, it will not have to be countered later, on more vital, closer turf.

The lesson learned (perhaps overlearned) from the Hitler experience is that aggressive threats must be dealt with by those who abhor war when the threats are still comparatively small and distant; to allow the aggressive force to succeed only brings nearer the day when a larger war must be fought. Thus some countries that abhor war have felt it necessary to wage them in order to prevent wider wars.

7. CONSEQUENCES OF THE DEMISE OF THE COLD WAR

Because of economic crisis and persistent ideological failure, it now appears that the Cold War has ended as the Soviet Union, following the lead of its former ideological soulmate, China, abandons its quest for ideological expansion, questing instead after prosperity and a quiet, normal international situation. Unless some new form of conflict emerges, war participation by developed countries is likely to continue its decline.

As tensions lapse between the two sides in what used to be known as the Cold War, there is a natural tendency for the arms that backed that tension, and in a sense measured it, to atrophy. Both sides have begun what might be called a negative arms race. Formal arms negotiations will probably be only slow and pedantify this natural process, and might best be abandoned at this point. It may also be time to confederate the East–West alliances (rather than allowing them to fragment) with the combined organization serving to regulate the remarkable changes going on in Europe.[16]

The demise of the Cold War should also facilitate further expansion of international trade and interdependence. Trade and interdependence may not lead inexorably to peace, but peace does seem to lead to trade, interdependence, and economic growth—or, at any rate, it facilitates them. That is, peace ought to be seen not as a dependent but rather as an independent variable in such considerations. The 1992 economic unity of Europe and the building of a long-envisioned Channel tunnel are the consequences of peace, not its cause.

Left alone, enterprising business people will naturally explore the possibilities of investing in other countries or selling their products there. Averse to disastrous surprises, they are more likely to invest if they are confident that peace will prevail. But for trade to flourish, governments must stay out of the war not only by eschewing war, but also by eschewing measures which unnaturally inhibit trade.

Furthermore, if nations no longer find it sensible to use force or the threat of force in their dealings with one another, it may be neither necessary nor particularly desirable to create an entrenched international government or police force (as opposed to ad hoc arrangements and devices designed to meet specific problems). Indeed, an effective international government could be detrimental to economic growth since, like domestic governments, it could be manipulated to reward the inefficient, coddle the incompetent, and plague the innovative.

8. WAR IN THE THIRD WORLD

War has not, of course, become fully obsolete. While major war—among developed countries—seems to be going out of style, war obviously continues to flourish elsewhere. The demise of the Cold War suggests that the United States and the Soviet Union, in particular, are likely to involve themselves less in these wars. Moreover, it is possible that the catastrophic Iran-Iraq war will sober people in the Third World about that kind of war. And it does seem that much of the romance has gone out of the concept of violent revolution as Third World countries increasingly turn to the drab, difficult, and unromantic task of economic development.

Thus, it is possible that the developed world's aversion to war may eventually infect the rest of the world as well (international war, in fact, has been quite rare in Latin America for a century). But this development is not certain, nor is its pace predictable. As slavery continued to persist in Brazil even after it had been abolished elsewhere, the existence of war in some parts of the world does not refute the observation that it is vanishing, or has vanished, in other parts.

9. IMPERFECT PEACE

War, even war within the developed world, has not become impossible—nor could it ever do so. When it has seemed necessary, even countries like the United States and Britain, which were among the first to become thoroughly disillusioned with war, have been able to fight wars and to use military force—often with high morale and substantial public support, at least at first. The ability to make war and the knowledge about how to do so can never be fully expunged—nor, for that matter, can the ability or knowledge to institute slavery, eunuchism, crucifixion, or human sacrifice. War is declining as an institution not because it has ceased to be possible or fascinating, but because peoples and leaders in the developed world—where war was once endemic—have increasingly found war to be disgusting, ridiculous, and unwise.

The view presented in this article is based upon the premise that, in some important respects, war is often taken too seriously. War, it seems, is merely an idea. It is not a trick of fate, a thunderbolt from hell, a natural calamity, or a desperate plot contrivance dreamed up by some sadistic puppeteer on high. If war begins in the minds of men, as the UNESCO charter insists, it can end there as well. Over the centuries, war opponents have been trying to bring this about by discrediting war as an idea: the argument here is that they have been substantially successful at doing so. The long peace since World War II is less a product of recent weaponry than the culmination of a substantial historical process. For the last two or three centuries, major war has gradually moved toward terminal disrepute because of its perceived repulsiveness and futility.

It could also be argued that, to a considerable degree, people have tended to take *peace* too seriously as well. Peace is merely what emerges when the institution of war is neglected. It does not mean that the world suddenly becomes immersed in those qualities with which the word "peace" is constantly being associated: love, justice, harmony, cooperation, brotherhood, good will. People still remain contentious and there still remain substantial conflicts of interest. The difference is only that they no longer resort to force to resolve their conflicts, any more than young men today resort to formal dueling to resolve their quarrels. A world at peace would not be perfect, but it would be notably better than the alternative.

NOTES

1. Kenneth N. Waltz, *Man, the State and War* (New York: Columbia University Press, 1959); Jack S. Levy, "The Causes of War: A Review of Theories and Evidence," in Philip E. Tetlock, Jo L. Husbands, Robert Jervis, Paul C. Stern, and Charles Tilly, eds., *Behavior, Society, and Nuclear War*, vol. 1 (New York: Oxford University Press, 1989), pp. 209-333. See also J. David Singer, "The Levels of Analysis Problem in International Relations," in Klaus Knorr and Sydney Verba, eds., *The International System* (Princeton, NJ: Princeton University Press, 1961), pp. 77-92; and James N. Rosenau, "Pre-theories and Theories of Foreign Policy," in R.B. Farrell, ed., *Approaches to Comparative and International Policies* (Evanston, IL: Northwestern University Press, 1966), pp. 27-92.

2. For a further development of these arguments, see John Mueller, *Retreat from Doomsday: The Obsolescence of Major War* (New York: Basic Books, 1989).

3. For other observations of the analogy between war and dueling, see Bernard Brodie, *War and Politics* (New York: Macmillan, 1973), p. 275; Norman Angell, *The Great Illusion* (London: Heinemann, 1914), pp. 202-203; G.P. Gooch, *History of Our Time, 1885-1911* (London: Williams & Norgate, 1911), p. 249; J.E. Cairnes, "International Law," *Fortnightly Review*, vol. 2, 1 November 1865, p. 650 n.

4. Carl von Clausewitz, *On War* [1832] (Princeton, NJ: Princeton University Press, 1976), p. 75.

5. See Orlando Patterson, *Slavery and Social Death: A Comparative Study* (Cambridge, MA: Harvard University Press, 1982); Stanley Engerman, "Slavery and Emancipation in Comparative Perspectives: A Look at Some Recent Debates," *Journal of Economic History*, vol. 46, no. 2 (June 1986), pp. 318-339. For another comparison of the institutions of war and slavery, see James Lee Ray, "The Abolition of Slavery and the End of International War," *International Organization*, vol. 43, no. 3 (Summer 1989), pp. 405-439.

6. Seymour Drescher, *Capitalism and Antislavery: British Mobilization in Comparative Perspectives* (New York: Oxford University Press, 1987), p. 4. See also David Eltis,

Economic Growth and the Ending of the Transatlantic Slave Trade (New York: Oxford University Press, 1987); Engerman "Slavery and Emancipation," pp. 322–333, 339.

7. For a useful history, see A.C.F. Beales, *The History of Peace: A Short Account of the Organized Movements for International Peace* (New York: Dial, 1931).

8. For an excellent discussion, see Roland N. Stromberg, *Redemption by War: The Intellectuals and 1914* (Lawrence, KS: Regents Press of Kansas, 1982).

9. Michael Howard, *The Causes of Wars and Other Essays* (Cambridge, MA: Harvard University Press, 1984), p. 9.

10. Arnold J. Toynbee, *Experiences* (New York: Oxford University Press, 1969), p. 214; Evan Luard, *War in International Society* (New Haven, CT: Yale University Press), p. 365.

11. For a further development of this argument, see John Mueller, "Changing Attitudes Toward War: The Impact of World War I," *British Journal of Political Science*, forthcoming.

12. For a discussion of the antipathy felt by the German people toward war in the 1930s, see Ian Kershaw, *The "Hitler Myth"* (Oxford: Oxford University Press, 1987), pp. 122–147, 229, 241; Marlis G. Steinert, *Hitler's War and the Germans: Public Mood and Attitude During the Second World War* (Athens, OH: Ohio University Press, 1977), pp. 40–41, 315, 341.

13. *The Foreign Policy of Hitler's Germany* (Chicago: University of Chicago Press, 1980), p. 664.

14. For a valuable discussion, see Frederic S. Burin, "The Communist Doctrine of the Inevitability of War," *American Political Science Review*, vol. 57, no. 2, June, 1963, pp. 334–354.

15. For a further development of this argument, see John Mueller, "The Essential Irrelevance of Nuclear Weapons: Stability in the Postwar World," *International Security*, vol. 13, no. 2, Fall 1988, pp. 55–79.

16. On these two policy proposals, see John Mueller, "A New Concert of Europe," *Foreign Policy*, Winter 1989–90, pp. 3–16.

✘ NO
Coming Conflicts: Interstate War in the New Millennium
MICHAEL O'HANLON

Is interstate war becoming obsolete? Many thoughtful observers, including political scientists, now believe so. Six key arguments—not to mention the modest number of interstate wars in recent decades—support their thesis. The nuclear revolution has made such conflict between major powers far more foreboding. The memory of the world wars and an understanding of the destructiveness of industrial-age conventional weaponry have further chastened any global leader who might contemplate acts of aggression. The US-led Western alliance system has also made the international political environment less anarchic. The spread of democracies, which have tended not to fight each other, has added a further stabilizing element. Modern economics has made the acquisition of additional territory less important for enhancing national wealth than in previous eras. In any event, anti-colonial movements of the 20th century made imperial conquest far more difficult politically and militarily. These six major developments in human history suggest that the 21st century will involve far less violence between countries than did the 20th century—even if civil conflict, terrorism, and other nontraditional threats to security remain serious worries.

On the whole, these broad assessments about trends in human conflict seem correct. For the foreseeable future, international acts of violence appear much more likely to arise at the intrastate or nonstate level than between countries. Conflicts between major powers seem particularly unlikely.

However, it would be a major intellectual error—and quite possibly a tragic policy mistake—to discount the possibility of war between the international community's larger actors. Those who point to the declining frequency of interstate wars sometimes forget that such conflicts have rarely been numerous. Their prevalence matters less than their severity once they do unfold. In addition, there has been no continual decline in their frequency over the past half-century, and recent years have witnessed a slight upturn in their number, according to a recent analysis by Ted Gurr, Monty Marshall, and Deepa Khosla of the University of Maryland.

Of the six major factors listed above that make countries less apt to go to war with each other, not all are absolute. Memories of World War I, World War II, and the Korean and Vietnam conflicts will fade with the passing of the generations that waged them. The US-led alliance system, remarkably successful by the standards of human history and still quite strong today, could face severe challenges in the years ahead. Given the absence of a clear external threat, and in the face of disagreements between Washington and many allied capitals over issues such as Iraq, Iran, Taiwan, and national missile defense, the alliance system's cohesion cannot be presumed to last forever.

Of the remaining four global realities discouraging interstate war, each has its limitations. As for nuclear deterrence, it certainly reduces the risk that countries will march on each other's capitals. It is less obvious, however, that nuclear deterrence is reliable for preventing wars over more limited stakes such as Kashmir or Taiwan. Democracies do tend to fight each other less often—once they are constitutionally and politically consolidated, and once they fully perceive each other as democracies, as scholars such as Edward Mansfield, Jack Snyder, and John Owen have argued. Democracies in transition have far less stabilizing effects. Moreover, countries that become democratic may not always stay that way, as the example of Weimar Germany reminds us. Colonialism may be dead, but irredentism is not, and some countries still reserve the right to use force to defend or acquire disputed lands. Finally, modern high-technology market economics may reduce the need for large swaths of land to assure national power and prestige. But key resources remain as critical as ever to the success of nations' economic systems, and it is not difficult to imagine wars driven by governments' desires to secure such resources.

These general concerns may be fleshed out by thinking through several future conflict scenarios that seem plausible—or at least difficult to dismiss out of hand.

COLD WAR LEGACY: KOREA

It may only represent a small appendage to the giant Eurasian land mass, and the military confrontation it hosts may seem little more than a leftover conflict from the Cold War. But the Korean peninsula remains dangerous: any war there could have consequences transcending what is directly at stake.

Promising moves toward detente notwithstanding, the peninsula remains the most militarized place on earth. The density of forces on both sides of the demilitarized zone is greater than the concentration of the North Atlantic Treaty Organization's (NATO) and Warsaw Pact's armed units along the intra-German border during the Cold War. Worse, there are still plausible paths to violence. For example, if Pyongyang attempts to coerce more aid out of the West with its missile and nuclear programs, but Seoul, Washington, and Tokyo respond in a hardline fashion, the situation could deteriorate. That sequence of events could lead to a joint US-South Korean air strike against key North Korean nuclear or missile facilities. That in turn could provoke a North Korean response, up to and including another attempt to invade South Korea. Each of these steps is in itself unlikely, and together they are quite unlikely. But this scenario is one that is far from unthinkable.

The United States and South Korea would surely prevail in any such war. However, there could nonetheless be serious consequences for the broader international system. Notably, if thousands of US soldiers were killed in the conflict, and the war was seen in part as the result of bungling by Western leaders rather than that of blatant North Korean aggression, the US public could lose much of its interest in maintaining a global system of alliances underwritten by its tax dollars and by the lives of its troops. At present, the US public supports the United States' strong role in the world partly because it believes in it, but also because international engagement has not caused a massive loss of US troops for decades. Should that fact change in a post-Cold War setting, the effects upon the US public would be unpredictable and possibly harmful to sustaining a strong security community of allied democratic nations.

War in Korea could also cause severe tensions in the Sino-US relationship. Formally, the People's Republic of China (PRC) remains allied with North Korea, but it seems doubtful that China would directly intervene on North Korea's behalf again in a war on the peninsula. Still, that possibility cannot be dismissed entirely, especially if the United States fires the first shot in an attack on North Korean weapons facilities. More dangerously, China may (again) worry about a US-South Korean invasion of North Korea that approaches its borders. Since Seoul and Washington probably would elect to overthrow the North Korean regime in any major future war on the peninsula, this concern is very real. China would be unlikely to challenge the combined allied forces directly, but it might well occupy a swath of northern North Korea as a defensive cordon—or simply as a bargaining chip for future negotiations over how many US troops would be allowed to remain on the peninsula should the two Koreas reunify. Since South Korea and the United States would be unlikely to recognize China's right to coerce them into a particular post-reunification alliance relationship and force structure, the result could be a lingering military standoff. Combined with other potential tensions between the United States and China in the region, this is one route toward a Sino-US relationship that could remain tense and dangerous for decades to come.

TAIWAN'S DIRE STRAITS

The basic situation between China and Taiwan is delicate, to say the least. China insists that Taiwan is a part of its territory, Taiwan refuses to be ruled by Beijing, and neither side shows any signs of changing these core views. Taiwan's new president, Chen Shui-bian, was elected principally on a domestic-reform agenda, and although he pledged to avoid declaring independence from the PRC unless attacked, his Democratic Progressive Party has long called for just such a declaration of independence. Chen is willing to abstain from making one only on the grounds that it is unnecessary, given that Taiwan is already sovereign in his eyes. This attempt to have it both ways may or may not prove sustainable.

Beijing has offered an equivocal policy of its own. It has welcomed Chen's restraint, on the one hand, and even offered to view Taiwan as an equal partner in negotiations rather than as a local, renegade government. But it has also issued a defense white paper stating that it will not wait for reunification indefinitely. Beijing has demanded that Chen publicly renounce his party's stand on independence and explicitly reaffirm the "one China" principle, reminding the international community that it reserves the right to use force against Taiwan to "safeguard [China's] own sovereignty and territorial integrity."

One might hope that the leaders in Beijing will be deterred from any attack on Taiwan out of fear of the enormous political and economic consequences that would follow. Surely, global trade with and investment in China would suffer for years to come, regardless of the outcome of the battle. However, China may believe that Western countries are so focused on making money that they would soon forgive and forget any war that had only a limited direct effect on them. Failing that, they might feel that they had no choice but to attack Taiwan under certain circumstances, given the emotions that surround the Taiwan issue in China and the fear among some in Beijing that letting Taiwan go could encourage other separatist movements.

Any war between China and Taiwan could easily involve the United States. The 1979 Taiwan Relations Act stipulates that the United States will view any conflict over Taiwan with "grave concern," suggesting a possible US military response even if neither that act nor any other US law or treaty actually requires such a reaction. In fact, the ambiguity is deliberate: Washington wishes to convey to Beijing that it might well respond to any attack against Taiwan, but it also wishes to simultaneously signal Taipei that US military support should not be taken for granted, thus tempering Taipei's disposition toward declaring independence. The goal is to maximize deterrence of China while minimizing any risk of emboldening Taiwan to take provocative actions.

But if war in the Taiwan Straits did occur, a US military role would be more likely than not. In addition to providing for the security of Taiwan itself, there would be a broader strategic rationale for opposing any Chinese attack. If the United States stood by while a longstanding friend was in peril, the credibility of other US alliance commitments in the region, and indeed around the world, would be called into question. That could spur some allies to embark upon undesirable military buildups and to develop nuclear weapons to ensure their own security; it could also embolden potential aggressors to attack US interests overseas.

What this all means, in short, is that war between the world's current superpower and its chief rising competitor really is possible. Should it occur, in addition to the dangers of escalation during the war itself, the international system could easily revert to a protracted period of Cold Warlike tensions and dangers after hostilities were ended. Even if the chance of such a conflict is no more than five to ten percent, that probability is itself sufficient to repudiate any complacent notion that the United States can relax its vigilance about the dangers of interstate conflict.

THE EXPLOSIVE MIDDLE EAST

There is little need to revisit the matter of Saddam Hussein in any detail. However, those who would doubt his willingness to again cause conflict in the Persian Gulf region might consult, among other sources, an incisive column in early 2001 by Thomas Friedman in *The New York Times*, in which he noted that officials in Baghdad continue to depict Kuwait as an inherent part of Iraqi territory.

Even after Hussein departs from the scene, the Persian Gulf and Middle East regions will remain dangerous for years to come. First, Hussein's successor could easily have the same irredentist ambitions towards Kuwait, even if he might be more careful and less ruthless than Hussein in pursuing them. Indeed, it was Hussein's son, as well as his Deputy Prime Minister Tariq Aziz, whom Friedman quoted as making inflammatory comments about Kuwait. Second, the combination of oil resources, extremist governments, and national borders that cut across ethnic and religious groups is highly combustible. Iran could invade southern Iraq, purportedly to defend fellow Shi'a Muslims, when its real purpose would be to secure land from which oil resources could be extracted. Resources in the Gulf seabed itself could be subject to competing territorial claims.

Were this just one modest-sized region full of autocratic governments and potential conflicts, one might dismiss it as a bygone of yesteryear—a region oblivious to the end of the Cold War, the advent of globalization, and the claim made by Francis Fukuyama that history has ended. Given the fact that the Middle East holds two-thirds of all global oil reserves, however, it will remain important far beyond its size or demographic base.

Then there is the Israeli-Palestinian conflict, in which developments in recent months have been deeply distressing. Any tendencies toward violence could be intensified by the types of competing claims to resources discussed in greater detail below. Even if war began as an Israeli-Palestinian exchange, it could snowball and involve one or more front-line Arab states. Alas, the day in which interstate conflict within this region can be definitively ruled out is not yet at hand, and that day may not arrive for decades.

DANGEROUS SCARCITY

Persian Gulf oil may be the most valuable resource in the most volatile location, but it hardly represents the only valuable commodity over which countries could wage war in the future. One can also point to the pipeline issues involving petroleum resources in the Caucasus. Russia, Turkey, Armenia, Azerbaijan, and Georgia are all directly involved. Another key area of potential dispute involves the modest but not insignificant oil resources that lie below the South China Sea—with China apparently bent on claiming them for itself.

Leaving aside the diamonds and other valuable minerals that often fuel civil conflict in regions such as Africa, it is entirely plausible that water could be a source of conflict between Turkey and Syria (the Euphrates), Egypt and Sudan (the Nile), Kazakhstan and Uzbekistan (the Aral Sea), Israel and Palestine, or countries of the west African desert. Other flashpoints could easily be added to the list as global populations grow in the decades ahead. One need not view competition for such resources as inevitable in order to see its plausibility. Growing populations and growing economies in most of these regions will increase demands for water and thus the potential for conflict over scarce resources. A rational government would probably buy water from abroad before going to war for it—but not all such decisions in international politics are made rationally as a matter of strict cost-benefit optimization.

Ocean fisheries are another cause for concern. They are presently being exploited to their maximum sustainable potential, if not beyond. Disputes over exactly what that potential level is could lead different countries to define different sustainable levels of harvest. Even if countries agreed on the latter metric, they could easily disagree over how to apportion the total catch. For example, countries that suffer from global climate change might feel a legitimate claim to extract more ocean resources as a compensation of sorts. States with strong navies may feel tempted to set their own rules and their own quotas.

Then there is the matter of pollution, ranging from acid rain to contamination of ground water to carbon dioxide emissions to improper disposal of radioactive waste. To be sure, for most of these matters, one might argue that if the problems have not yet led to conflict between states, they are unlikely to do so in the future. However, some pressures may intensify considerably in the future. The most glaring worry may be global warming, which could threaten different countries in many different ways, making it a much more urgent matter in some places than in others. Industrializing countries may insist on having their turn to produce greenhouse-enhancing emissions, while developed countries may resist the steep price tag of funding the emission-reducing technologies demanded by such developing nations. One could even imagine actions such as air strikes against coal-fired power plants and similarly drastic measures—especially in a world in which global temperatures might be five degrees higher and a solution nowhere in sight.

A final category of conflict could result from terrorist acts leading to full-scale, cross-border interstate conflict. Israeli responses to terrorism have already had this dynamic in the Middle East. The United States could respond to a future attack by Osama bin Laden's Al-Qaeda network by invading Afghanistan through Iran or Pakistan, possibly causing further problems. It could also respond to Colombian drug cartels or Russian mafia groups in similar fashion, especially if the criminal organizations carried out terrorist actions or threatened to do so. More likely yet, India could invade Pakistan in response to the continued

Pakistani-backed insurgency in Kashmir. Unfortunately, the invaded countries might not see such anti-terrorist operations as legitimate; escalation and interstate war could result. These types of scenarios are so plausible that little more need be said about them.

PEACEFUL CONSOLIDATION

Noting the potential for future interstate war is not meant to predict its occurrence. Rather, it is designed to motivate continued attention to the elements of national and international policy that reduce the chances of future international conflict. The United States and its allies need to keep their alliances strong, in part by expanding membership to include as many democratic and peaceful countries as possible over time (though the enlargement of NATO to former Soviet states seems premature and unnecessarily provocative towards Russia). Military deterrence needs to remain robust, particularly in key regions of potential conflict. Whenever possible, resource disputes need to be solved before they bring countries to the brink of war; the United States can help by assisting other nations to develop their economies and reduce their dependencies on scarce commodities. Young democracies need help consolidating and strengthening their political systems, and we all need to keep learning and relearning our history, for as the cliché rightly observes, to forget history is to risk reliving it.

Postscript

In examining this debate, readers will note that Mueller is referring to a particular type of war—interstate war between major powers. One might agree with him on certain points, but argue that the nature of wars since the end of the Cold War has been undergoing a significant transformation. In light of the terrorist attack on the United States in September 2001 and the resulting response, it is interesting to note that O'Hanlon makes only passing reference near the end of his article to terrorism as a possible trigger for future wars. Those wishing to understand how the nature of war may be changing should consult the writings of Mary Kaldor and Michael Ignatieff cited below.

In making his case that norms regarding the use of war as an instrument of foreign policy are changing, Mueller uses the analogy to dueling and slavery to suggest that these institutions were abolished once it was seen that they served no real social purpose. This would suggest that "evil" institutions like slavery and war are not immutable parts of the international order. If slavery could disappear when international norms changed, then too international war might disappear. Such an assertion directly challenges those who see either human nature or biological factors as the root cause of war. But is the analogy an apt one? To purse this, students should consult the reading by James Lee Ray listed below.

Infotrac Keyword Search

"future war" or "future international conflict"

Suggested Additional Readings

Henriksen, Thomas C. "The Coming Great Powers Competition," *World Affairs*, 158, 2 (Fall 1995): 63ff.

Ignatieff, Michael. *Virtual War: Kosovo and Beyond*. Toronto: Penguin Books, 2000.

Kaldor, Mary. *New and Old Wars: Organized Violence in a Global Era*. Stanford: Stanford University Press, 1999.

Kaysen, Carl. "Is War Obsolete? A Review Essay," *International Security* 14 (Spring 1990): 42–64.

Ray, James Lee. "The Abolition of Slavery and the End of International War," *International Organization* 43, 3 (Summer 1989): 405–39.

Rapport, Anatol. *Peace: An Idea Whose Time Has Come*. Ann Arbor: University of Michigan Press, 1992.

Viorst, Milton. "The Coming Instability." *Washington Quarterly*, 20, 4 (Autumn 1997): 153–68.

Website Resources

INCORE   Described as "a global center for the study and resolution of conflict," INCORE maintains extensive data on conflicts, especially those of an ethnic nature.

Journal of Military and Security Studies, **University of Calgary**   See particularly the article by David Bercuson, "War and the New Global Order: Has Anything Really Changed?" in the Spring 1998 issue.

Project Ploughshares   Prepares an annual summary of ongoing wars and conflicts throughout the world.

Stockholm International Peace Research Institute   Publishes annual data on conflicts around the world.

Is Globalization Undermining the Power of the Nation-State?

✔ **YES**

SUSAN STRANGE, "The Erosion of the State," *Current History* 96, no. 613 (November 1997): 365–69

✘ **NO**

MARTIN WOLF, "Will the Nation-State Survive Globalization?" *Foreign Affairs* (January/February 2001): 178–90

In the readings for Issue One, the authors discuss the future of war within the context of war between states. In thinking about international relations the concept of the state has always been central. Scholars date the modern international system of states from the Peace of Westphalia in 1648. This agreement, designed to bring an end to the Thirty Years War, signified both the secularization of politics and the rise of the territorial state as the principal unit of political organization. The Peace redrew the map of Europe into a society of legally equal states. Each claimed to exercise sovereignty within fairly well-defined frontiers and acknowledged no authority above itself. Inherent in this notion is the claim that each state has the right to non-interference by others in its domestic affairs.

Since 1648, the territorial state has become the principal vehicle for organizing humankind into political communities. The composition of the international system has grown from a handful of European states in the seventeenth century to over 200 states and territorial entities today. States remain the highest level of political authority. Decisions made by bodies like the United Nations and the International Court of Justice in the Hague are adhered to by states only on a voluntary basis. There has yet to emerge anything like a global state or world government.

Given the power and importance of sovereign states, it is perhaps not surprising that scholars have traditionally focused on a "state-centric" approach to the study of international politics. According to this view, the focus of the study of international relations is really *interstate* relations. Although there may be many other "actors" on the global scene, states remain the dominant actors since they alone can claim monopoly of legal authority within their territory and of the use of military force within and beyond that territory.

Why have states emerged as the predominant form of political organization? John Herz argues that the strength of states lie in their capacity to perform two major functions: defend those citizens who live within their borders, and promote the economic well-being of their citizens. States have been successful to the extent that they have been able to build a "hard shell" of impermeability around themselves while ensuring a degree of self-sufficiency and autonomy.

In the twentieth century there have been frequent predictions that the notion of the sovereign, territorial state is in demise. Herz himself, in the aftermath of the Second World War, predicted the imminent end of the territorial state. The development of instruments of total war, especially nuclear weapons, demonstrated that no state could any longer claim to provide a hard shell of security for its citizens. Herz later retracted his gloomy prediction in the wake of post-war decolonization and the birth of dozens of new states. He pointed out the "synthetic" quality of these states and argued for an international role in their "hardening" over time. (John Herz, *The Nation-State and the Crisis of World Politics* [New York: David McKay, 1976]).

However, in the past decade, new concerns have arisen from those who argue that the forces of globalization now threaten the future of the nation-state. These analysts argue that since the early 1970s the international political economy has been experiencing a profound transformation. The idea of national economies, enclosed by national borders and controlled by national governments, is being rendered nearly meaningless by a globalized economy. As a result, the modern state is faced with an increasing inability to provide economic prosperity within its borders. In a global marketplace, few states can claim economic autonomy or self-sufficiency. The prosperity of citizens is to a large extent now determined beyond their national borders, rather than by any decisions taken by their national governments.

Those who believe that the state is in decline argue that students of international relations need to broaden their focus beyond an analysis of state behaviour, to the growing role played by transnational corporations, non-government organizations (NGOs), and international institutions. In addition, they suggest a need to shift the focus away from considerations of military power as the primary determinant in international politics to other forms of power and influence. However, while some see the state as in permanent decline, others are not so certain. They suggest that states are resilient and have many resources at their disposal to ensure their role as the principal influence in international relations.

In the readings below, we enter into this debate with two leading analysts of the modern state. In the first reading, Susan Strange, who until her recent death was a professor of international political economy at the University of Warwick, examines the pressures that are leading to a decline in the authority of states. She suggests that international relations analysts need to take these changes into account and shift away from a "state-centric" focus. In the second reading, Martin Wolfe, Chief Economics Commentator for the *Financial Times,* argues that globalization, if anything, has strengthened the role of states.

✔ YES
The Erosion of the State
SUSAN STRANGE

I hear two choruses of voices raised against the whole notion of globalization; I have some sympathy with one and none at all with the other. Explaining this requires me to say—briefly—what I understand the term to mean, and forms the first part of this essay. It also helps to make clear what I understand to be the root causes behind the process of globalization. This is the essay's second part. And, for the last part, I explain what I understand to be the main consequences of globalization for the state in the context of consequences for other political institutions and social and economic groups.

THE NAYSAYERS

The chorus of voices with whom I have no sympathy—or very little—is that which denies the reality of globalization and claims that nothing has really changed. According to this chorus it is all "globaloney," a great myth, an illusion, and therefore not to be taken seriously. Globalization, according to them, is an illusion because the state still exists; because enterprises still "belong" to one particular state in the sense that their headquarters are located in the territory of the state from which they sprang; because their directors are almost exclusively of one national origin; and because their corporate culture is markedly different from that of other "national" firms.

They are wrong, however: the fact that states still exist does not prove that globalization is not a part of the reality in which we all live. Nor does the fact that firms are referred to as "American," "British," or "Japanese" mean that the nature and behavior of firms, like that of states, has not been changed by globalization. Although it is hard to measure the process of globalization, it is no myth. It exists, and it changes things, on several levels. As an international political economist, I perceive these changes first of all in what the French historian Fernand Braudel called "material life"—the production structure that determines what material goods and services are produced by human societies for their survival and comfort. Instead of goods and services being predominantly produced by and for people living in the territory of a state, they are now increasingly produced by people in several states, for a world market instead of for a local market.

Second, globalization involves changes in the financial structure—the system by which credit is created to finance production and trade in goods and services. Where once the creation and use of credit mostly took place within the societies of territorial states, it now takes place across territorial frontiers, in global markets electronically linked into a single system. True, within that system there are local banks and markets creating credit for local use. But these are no longer autonomous; they are part of the larger system, more vulnerable to its ups and downs than it is to their ups and downs.

Finally, globalization takes place on a third level: the level of perceptions, beliefs, ideas, and tastes. Here, while cultural differences persist, the sensitivities and susceptibilities of individual human beings are increasingly being modified by the processes of global homogenization. While made easier and faster by the so-called information revolution and the falling costs of international communications, these are only channels, the means by which the processes of globalization take place. Although this third level of globalization is the hardest to quantify or monitor, it may in the long run be the most significant of all the changes brought by globalization.

Yet this level is the one most often overlooked by those economists and others who join the chorus denying the reality of globalization. While some merely question whether the extent of change attributable to globalization is being exaggerated, others call the whole concept of globalization into question, denying that there has been any real change.[1]

Many of these voices belong to my former colleagues in that branch of social science called international relations. It is a branch that did not exist before the First World War, and in America, not until after the Second World War. The terrible destruction and waste in both conflicts prompted intellectuals to ask the question, "Why do states wage war on each other?" The problematic of international relations, therefore, was the causes of interstate conflict and war, and whether, and how, war could be prevented and peace preserved. Always, the state was the primary focus of attention and was often habitually treated also as a unitary actor. Because discussion of globalization introduces other actors—markets and firms, and other forces of change, like technology, the media, and communications—such discussion implies the growing obsolescence of the study of international relations. On top of these longer-term secular changes, moreover, came the end of the cold war, removing one of the main dangers inherent in the international political system.

Like a stag at bay, the professor of international relations is apt to turn and hurl defiance at those who would bring him down. For myself, as an international political economist, I believe study of the world we live in should adapt to change, not resist it; I have little sympathy with those who deny the reality of globalization and cling to an obsolescing paradigm and a problematic superseded by others. As I have argued elsewhere, the danger of major wars between states has paled beside the danger of long-lasting economic depression resulting from flaws in the financial system and of irreversible environmental damage resulting from worldwide industrialization.[2]

THREE DILEMMAS AND AN EXPLANATION

With the other chorus that acknowledges the reality but urges resistance to it, I have more sympathy. Change always creates losers as well as winners. It is never painless for everyone. There are costs, and it can be (and is) argued that the costs are not worth the benefits: that the pace of change is so fast that the risks are greater than the opportunities. If globalization cannot be reversed or even resisted, it should at least be slowed down. For reasons that will be clearer when I come to the consequences of globalization, I think this may be a tenable view. It seems to be especially prevalent in Europe. A recent book, *The Global Trap*, by Harald Schumann and Hans-Peter Martin of *Der Spiegel*, proved an unexpected bestseller in Germany in 1996.[3] Germans generally prefer the deutsche mark to the euro, the national past to the globalized future.

Three dilemmas for the world political economy result from the effects of globalization on the state. One is economic. A market economy, whether global or national, needs a lender of last resort, an authority—call it hegemonic, though the term misleads—able to discipline but also to give confidence to banks and financial markets, and able to apply Keynesian logic in times of slow growth and recession. The dilemma is that neither former hegemons nor international organizations can be relied on for either task.

Another dilemma is environmental. The motivations of corporate players in the world market economy lead most of them to destroy and pollute the planet, while the necessary countervailing power of the states is handicapped by principles of international law, sovereignty, and the like.

The third dilemma is political. The long struggle for liberty and accountability gradually made at least some states accountable to the people, but globalization, by shifting power from states to firms, has allowed international bureaucracies to undermine that accountability. None of the new nonstate authorities are accountable; few are even transparent. There is a democratic deficit, not only in Europe, but in America, Japan—the entire globalized economy.

As to the underlying causes of globalization—and the consequential retreat of the state from its predominant position of authority in the economy and society—I would point first to the accelerating rate of technological change, and second to the accelerated mobility of capital, as the two indispensable factors affecting production in a modern economy.[4] Both are too often overlooked and neglected by social scientists. An appreciation of their importance surely requires a historical perspective. Their origins go back at least 200 years to the late eighteenth century—or in the case of technological change, as far back as Galileo and da Vinci. Both men believed that science held the answers to the great puzzles of life on the planet and had the potential to change the human condition for the better. That belief (reinforced by the competition of states for technical advantage in waging war) has sustained the pursuit of scientific discovery and technological innovation from the Industrial Revolution onward. Yet the application of the discoveries and the innovations beyond the place where they were made would have been impossible if capital had not been mobile enough to move from where credit was created to where it could be profitably invested. The international mobility of capital, in short, which began to be seen in small ways by the late eighteenth century, has been the sine qua non of twentieth-century globalization.

What must be additionally explained is why both technological change and capital mobility began to accelerate around the middle of this century. The two are interrelated but the cause of one was mainly economic, the other mainly political. Technological change has typically involved the substitution of capital for labor. That was the essence of Fordism: by installing a capital-intensive assembly line and the management to go with it at Willow Run, Henry Ford could employ cheap unskilled labor instead of skilled expensive labor. Afterward, even cheaper robots replaced the workers, once again involving higher capital costs as the price of lower running costs. In Marxist terms, technological change altered the organic composition of capital, thus increasing the demand for capital and lowering the demand for labor.

By mid-century, this substitution was fueling the expansion of international trade since newcomers like the Japanese could lower marginal costs by producing for export as well as the home market. In sector after sector, from steel to beer, production for the world market became imperative. Every technological innovation called for more capital investment. And as the pace of technological innovation accelerated under the pressure of competition between firms for market shares, it became less and less possible to survive on the basis of profits in a home market. Firms, in short, did not choose to produce for foreign markets; they were forced to do so or go under. The price of entry, in many cases but especially in developing countries with potentially large markets, was often relocation of manufacturing capacity inside the trade barriers against competitive imports.[5]

THE NEW DIPLOMACY

None of this would have been possible without the greater mobility of capital. For this, the Europeans and especially the British were responsible during the long nineteenth century to 1914, and the Americans thereafter. Mobility slowed almost to a standstill after the crash of 1929, but even then United States firms continued to invest in international production in Europe and Latin America. After 1945, successive American governments pushed for the reduction of exchange controls over capital movements. This, more than the reduction of tariffs and other barriers to trade, created the necessary and sufficient conditions for the internalization of production. Firms found it increasingly easy to borrow in one country or currency—not necessarily their own—and invest it in another. It could be done through banks or through stock markets, and the whole business was greatly aided by the creation of the unregulated, untaxed Eurocurrency markets.

First in the new postwar wave of foreign investment were the American multinationals. They soon overtook the British, Swiss, and Dutch as the major holders of the stock of foreign direct investment. The big enterprises were soon followed by much smaller firms. The American multinationals were soon joined by the Japanese, Koreans, Taiwanese, and others. Their spread into other markets was made easier by the concurrent change in the attitudes of host countries. Where these had initially been hostile to foreign firms, by the 1980s most had realized that the foreign firms held three keys to earning the foreign exchange so necessary for industrialization. These three keys were: command of technology; ready access to mobile capital; and (often the most important) the brand name and distribution network that gave ready access to the rich markets of America and Europe.

The significance of this "new diplomacy" (as John Stopford and I called it) has been largely lost on conventional writers on international relations. For it means that states are joined by firms as the authorities exercising power over the course of national and global economic development. The governments of states may still be the gatekeepers to the territory over which other states recognize their authority. But if no foreign firms want to go through their gate, their countries have a slim chance of keeping up with the competition from other, more welcoming governments for world market shares. Even if firms do seek entry, governments have to negotiate with them over terms. The balance of power between host and foreign firm then becomes an important field of study in comparative political economy, with much depending on the size of the host market and the firm's standing in the kind of business it is in.

Another aspect of the new diplomacy is also of growing importance in world politics and world economics. Corporate takeovers and strategic alliances between firms increasingly determine future trends in economic growth, employment, and trade. Recall the fuss in Europe over Boeing's takeover of McDonnell-Douglas. It created an aircraft manufacturer likely to dominate the world market, a competitor for Europe's Airbus even more formidable than before. Recall the alarm felt in Hong Kong last August when Li Ka-shing bought 3 percent of the shares in Jardine Mathieson, raising doubts over how long Beijing would allow non-Chinese interests to survive the new regime. Such questions—both political and economic in their implications—call for more serious study of firm-firm relations than exists at the moment. It is a new field where experts in international business and management have to work with those in international relations, and to listen carefully, too, to business historians.

Although neglected, the growing importance of state-firm and of firm-firm diplomacy is only one aspect of the rising power of firms and other non-state actors and the corresponding decline in the authority of the state in the world economy and society. But before attempting to demonstrate this decline in a more systemic manner, it should be pointed out that "decline" may have been preceded by "rise," and that it may be dangerous to extrapolate decline into the future. This is to say that the predominance of the nation-state as the foremost authority over society and economy may turn out to have been exceptional, not normal. In a longer historical perspective, multiple sources of authority were perhaps the norm, and the concentration of power in the hands of state governments in this century and the last may have been a deviation. Second, those of us who perceive decline in state authority in the last decade or two are not necessarily predicting that the decline will continue indefinitely into the future. We simply do not know.

ERODING THE STATE'S AUTHORITY

There are three main areas in which state authority has declined. Other aspects of decline are almost all subsidiary to these three. The first is defense: the security of society from violence. The second is finance: the preservation of money as a reliable means of exchange, unit of account, and store of value (this is especially necessary to a market, as opposed to a state-planned, economy). And the third is the provision of welfare: the assurance that some of the benefits of greater wealth go to the poor, the weak, the sick, and the old. This too is particularly necessary in a capitalist market economy, where the system tends to make the rich conspicuously richer and the gap wider between them and the disadvantaged. It can be quickly and easily shown that the power of most states in all three—and therefore the justification for their claims on society—has seriously declined. And it has done so as a result of the forces of globalization already described.

Defense against foreign invasion is no longer necessary if—as is now mostly the case—neighbors show no sign of wanting to invade for the sake of command over territory. There are now only three exceptional cases where neighbors may be so tempted. One is for command over oil or gas fields. Another is for control over water supplies. The third is irredentism, where societies or their governments feel a moral or emotional compulsion to incorporate territory inhabited by ethnic or religious groups into the state to safeguard their interests and security (there are more cases today where this might have happened but has not, than there are where it has).

For the most part, the obsolescence of major interstate war is implicit in state policies, for the very good reason that people recognize that success in gaining world market shares has replaced territorial acquisition as the means of survival. Armies and navies continue to exist—not least because of competition for world market shares in the arms trade—but more because they are needed to preserve civil order rather than to repel invaders. Where there is no risk of civil disorder, they are merely an ornamental anachronism. Where there is such a risk parts of society will regard national armed forces as a threat to their security, not as an impartial guardian of the peace. The decline of support for conscription in many countries is one indicator of this change.

The second justification for state authority–that it maintains the value of the currency–is also fast disappearing. With probably the sole exception of the United States (and possibly the Swiss Confederation), states are no longer able to resist the foreign exchange markets. It is not that speculators have run amok, but that the mobility of capital mentioned earlier means that flows of money in and out of currencies, not trade balances, trigger market responses, which in turn move exchange rates. And only a powerful coalition of major central banks led by the United States (as in the Mexican peso crisis in 1994) can stop a collapsing currency.

With one of the three legs of monetary stability so weak, what of the other two, interest rates and inflation rates? Governments can determine the first, but only within limits set by the markets. Too high an interest rate may keep money flowing in but–as in Germany recently, or Britain under Gordon Brown as finance minister–this will impose excruciating costs on small business and will push the exchange rate too high to make exports competitive.

As for inflation rates, governments pretend to control the money supply, and thus the value of money, mainly by varying interest rates. But technology is about to frustrate their efforts. Credit card spending is rising quickly in the United States and now in Britain. It is purchasing power over which the state has no control. Digital money and digital shopping on the Internet will be even less under state control and potentially even more disruptive. Much depends on the banks as major players in the money markets. Yet the central banks' Bank for International Settlements in Basel confessed just this past year that its concordats on bank regulation cannot be relied on to preserve the global financial system against the dangers besetting it. Rules of thumb on reserve requirements that used to limit growth in the money supply, and therefore the value of money, no longer work. Commercial banks therefore must be trusted (and helped) to regulate themselves. But trusting the bankers to discipline themselves is like asking poachers to see that there is no poaching. So far, so good...

The state as social safety net, redistributing resources and entitlements to make good the shortcomings of the market, has been a recent but important justification for its authority and one most powerfully appreciated by the Europeans. The superiority of "Rhenish capitalism" in the vocabulary of Michel Albert (over Anglo-Saxon capitalism) was precisely that it ensured a measure of social justice denied by the market.[6]

This justification is still made, but it lacks creditability. Globalization has opened tax-evading doors for multinationals and many individuals. As more tax havens open up and more use is made of them, states' revenues suffer; everywhere, welfare services are cut back (the age at which state pensions are paid will soon be raised in Italy, France, and probably Germany). In desperation, states raise money by selling off state-owned enterprises. The public sector that once—even in the United States in World War II—was an important lever of state power over the economy cannot survive the pressures of global competition. Even the power of the state to use trade protection as an economic weapon against foreign competition and a supplementary safety net for those (such as farmers, fishermen, miners, or steelworkers) in declining occupations is fast disappearing. The global consensus declares protectionism wrong, liberalization right. National experience is that it often protects the inefficient and uncompetitive and is therefore counterproductive.

The "globaloney" school is not only wrong, but by trying to persuade people that nothing has changed, is also encouraging an ostrich-like response to recent changes in the world economy. If, as I have argued, the state's power to provide economic and financial stability, to protect the vulnerable in society, and to preserve the environment has been weakened, society is at the mercy of big business. That is not a prospect I suspect most Europeans and many Americans really want for their children and their grandchildren in the years to come.

NOTES

1. See, for example, Paul Hirst and Grahame Thompson, *Globalization in Question: The International Economy and the Possibilities of Governance* (Cambridge: Polity Press, 1996).

2. See Susan Strange, *Statistics and Markets*, 2nd ed. (London: Pinter, 1994), pp. 60–63; and ibid., *The Retreat of the State: The Diffusion of Power in the World Economy* (Cambridge: Cambridge University Press, 1996), pp. 66–87.

3. Harald Schumann and Hans-Peter Martin, *The Global Trap* (London: Zed Books, 1997).

4. This argument is developed at greater length in *The Retreat of the State*, op cit.

5. See John Stopford and Susan Strange, *Rival States, Rival Firms: Competition for World Market Shares* (Cambridge: Cambridge University Press, 1991), pp. 1–64.

6. See Michel Albert, *Capitalism against Capitalism* (London: Whurr, 1993).

✗ **NO**
Will the Nation-State Survive Globalization?
MARTIN WOLF

DEFINING GLOBALIZATION

A specter is haunting the world's governments—the specter of globalization. Some argue that predatory market forces make it impossible for benevolent governments to shield their populations from the beasts of prey that lurk beyond their borders. Others counter that benign market forces actually prevent predatory governments from fleecing their citizens. Although the two sides see different villains, they draw one common conclusion: omnipotent markets mean impotent politicians. Indeed, this formula has become one of the cliches of our age. But is it true that governments have become weaker and less relevant than ever before? And does globalization, by definition, have to be the nemesis of national government?

Globalization is a journey. But it is a journey toward an unreachable destination—"the globalized world." A "globalized" economy could be defined as one in which neither distance nor national borders impede economic transactions. This would be a world where the costs of transport and communications were zero and the barriers created by differing national jurisdictions had vanished. Needless to say, we do not live in anything even close to such a world. And since many of the things we transport (including ourselves) are physical, we never will.

This globalizing journey is not a new one. Over the past five centuries, technological change has progressively reduced the barriers to international integration. Transatlantic communication, for example, has evolved from sail power to steam, to the telegraph, the telephone, commercial aircraft, and now to the Internet. Yet states have become neither weaker nor less important during this odyssey. On the contrary, in the countries with the most advanced and internationally integrated economies, governments' ability to tax and redistribute incomes, regulate the economy, and monitor the activity of their citizens has increased beyond all recognition. This has been especially true over the past century.

The question that remains, however, is whether today's form of globalization is likely to have a different impact from that of the past. Indeed, it may well, for numerous factors distinguish today's globalizing journey from past ones and could produce a different outcome. These distinctions include more rapid communications, market liberalization, and global integration of the production of goods and services. Yet contrary to one common assumption, the modern form of globalization will not spell the end of the modern nation-state.

THE PAST AS PROLOGUE

Today's growing integration of the world economy is not unprecedented, at least when judged by the flow of goods, capital, and people. Similar trends occurred in the late nineteenth and early twentieth centuries.

First, the proportion of world production that is traded on global markets is not that much higher today than it was in the years leading up to World War I. Commerce was comparably significant in 1910, when ratios of trade (merchandise exports plus imports) to GDP hit record highs in several of the advanced economies. Global commerce then collapsed during the Great Depression and World War II, but since then world trade has grown more rapidly than output. The share of global production traded worldwide grew from about 7 percent in 1950 to more than 20 percent by the mid-1990s; in consequence, trade ratios have risen in almost all of the advanced economies. In the United Kingdom, for example, exports and imports added up to 57 percent of GDP in 1995 compared to 44 percent in 1910; for France the 1995 proportion was 43 percent against 35 percent in 1910; and for Germany it was 46 percent against 38 percent in the same years. But Japan's trade ratio was actually lower in 1995 than it had been in 1910. In fact, among today's five biggest economies, the only one in which trade has a remarkably greater weight in output than it had a century ago is the United States, where the ratio has jumped from 11 percent in 1910 to 24 percent in 1995. That fact may help explain why globalization is more controversial for Americans than for people in many other countries.

Second, by the late nineteenth century many countries had already opened their capital markets to international investments, before investments, too, collapsed during the interwar period. As a share of GDP, British capital investments abroad—averaging 4.6 percent of GDP between 1870 and 1913—hit levels unparalleled in contemporary major economies. More revealing is that the correlation between domestic investment and savings (a measure of the extent to which savings remain within one country) was lower between 1880 and 1910 than in any subsequent period.

Historical differences exist, however. Although current capital mobility has precedents from the pre-World War I era, the composition of capital flows has changed. Short-term capital today is much more mobile than ever before. Moreover, long-term flows now are somewhat differently constituted than in the earlier period. Investment in the early twentieth century took the form of tangible assets rather than intangible ones. Portfolio flows predominated over direct investment in the earlier period (that trend has been reversed since World War II); within portfolios, stocks have increased in relative importance to roughly equal bonds today. And finally, before 1914, direct investment was undertaken largely by companies investing in mining and transportation, whereas today multinational companies predominate, with a large proportion of their investment in services.

Today's high immigration flows are also not unprecedented. According to economists Paul Hirst and Grahame Thompson, the greatest era for recorded voluntary mass migration was the century after 1815. Around 60 million people left Europe for the Americas, Oceania, and South and East Africa. An estimated 10 million voluntarily migrated from Russia to Central Asia and Siberia. A million went from Southern Europe to North America. About 12 million Chinese and 6 million Japanese left their homelands and emigrated to eastern and southern Asia. One and a half million left India for Southeast Asia and Southwest Africa.

Population movement peaked during the 1890s. In those years, the United States absorbed enough immigrants to increase the U.S. population from the beginning of the decade by 9 percent. In Argentina, the increase in the 1890s was 26 percent; in Australia, it was 17 percent. Europe provided much of the supply: the United Kingdom gave up 5 percent of its initial population, Spain 6 percent, and Sweden 7 percent. In the 1990s, by contrast, the United States was the only country in the world with a high immigration rate, attracting newcomers primarily from the developing world rather than from Europe. These immigrants increased the population by only 4 percent.

As all of this suggests, despite the many economic changes that have occurred over the course of a century, neither the markets for goods and services nor those for factors of production appear much more integrated today than they were a century ago. They seem more integrated for trade, at least in the high-income countries; no more integrated for capital—above all for long-term capital—despite important changes in the composition of capital flows; and much less integrated for labor.

So why do so many people believe that something unique is happening today? The answer lies with the two forces driving contemporary economic change: falling costs of transport and communications on the one hand, and liberalizing economic policies on the other.

THE TECHNOLOGICAL REVOLUTION

Advances in technology and infrastructure substantially and continuously reduced the costs of transport and communications throughout the nineteenth and early twentieth centuries. The first transatlantic telegraph cable was laid in 1866. By the turn of the century, the entire world was connected by telegraph, and communication times fell from months to minutes. The cost of a three-minute telephone call from New York to London in current prices dropped from about $250 in 1930 to a few cents today. In more recent years, the number of voice paths across the Atlantic has skyrocketed from 100,000 in 1986 to more than 2 million today. The number of Internet hosts has risen from 5,000 in 1986 to more than 30 million now.

A revolution has thus occurred in collecting and disseminating information, one that has dramatically reduced the cost of moving physical objects. But these massive improvements in communications, however important, simply continue the trends begun with the first submarine cables laid in the last century. Furthermore, distances still impose transport and communications costs that continue to make geography matter in economic terms. Certain important services still cannot be delivered from afar.

Diminishing costs of communications and transport were nevertheless pointing toward greater integration throughout the last century. But if historical experience demonstrates anything, it is that integration is not technologically determined. If it were, integration would have gone smoothly forward over the past two centuries. On the contrary, despite continued falls in the costs of transport and communications in the first half of the twentieth century, integration actually reversed course.

Policy, not technology, has determined the extent and pace of international economic integration. If transport and communications innovations were moving toward global economic integration throughout the last century and a half, policy was not—and that made all the difference. For this reason, the growth in the potential for economic integration has greatly outpaced the growth of integration itself since the late nineteenth century. Globalization has much further to run, if it is allowed to do so.

CHOOSING GLOBALIZATION

Globalization is not destined, it is chosen. It is a choice made to enhance a nation's economic well-being—indeed, experience suggests that the opening of trade and of most capital flows enriches most citizens in the short run and virtually all citizens in the long run. (Taxation on short-term capital inflows to emerging market economies is desirable, however, particularly during a transition to full financial integration.) But if integration is a deliberate choice, rather than an ineluctable destiny, it cannot render states impotent. Their potency lies in the choices they make.

Between 1846 and 1870, liberalization spread from the United Kingdom to the rest of Europe. Protectionism, which had never waned in the United States, returned to continental Europe after 1878 and reached its peak in the 1930s.

A new era of global economic integration began only in the postwar era, and then only partially: from the end of World War II through the 1970s, only the advanced countries lowered their trade barriers. The past two decades, by contrast, have seen substantial liberalization take root throughout the world. By the late 1990s, no economically significant country still had a government committed to protectionism.

This historical cycle is also apparent in international capital investments. Capital markets stayed open in the nineteenth and early twentieth centuries, partly because governments did not have the means to control capital flows. They acquired and haltingly solidified this capacity between 1914 and 1945, progressively closing their capital markets. Liberalization of capital flows then began in a few advanced countries during the 1950s and 1960s. But the big wave of liberalization did not start in earnest until the late 1970s, spreading across the high-income countries, much of the developing world, and, by the 1990s, to the former communist countries. Notwithstanding a large number of financial crises over this period, this trend has remained intact.

In monetary policy, the biggest change has been the move from the gold standard of the 1870–1914 era to the floating currencies of today. The long-run exchange-rate stability inherent in the gold standard promoted long-term capital flows, particularly bond financing, more efficiently than does the contemporary currency instability. Today's vast short-term financial flows are not just a consequence of exchange-rate instability, but one of its causes.

Yet governments' control over the movement of people in search of employment tightened virtually everywhere in the early part of the last century. With the exception of the free immigration policy among members of the European Union (EU), immigration controls are generally far tighter now than they were a hundred years ago.

The policy change that has most helped global integration to flourish is the growth of international institutions since World War II. Just as multinational companies now organize private exchange, so global institutions organize and discipline the international face of national policy. Institutions such as the World Trade Organization (WTO), the International Monetary Fund (IMF), the World Bank, the EU, and the North American Free Trade Agreement underpin cooperation among states and consolidate their commitments to liberalize economic policy. The nineteenth century was a world of unilateral and discretionary policy. The late twentieth century, by comparison, was a world of multilateral and institutionalized policy.

TRADEOFFS FACING STATES

Ironically, the technology that is supposed to make globalization inevitable also makes increased surveillance by the state, particularly over people, easier than it would have been a century ago. Indeed, here is the world we now live in: one with fairly free movement of capital, continuing (though declining) restrictions on trade in goods and services, but quite tight control over the movement of people.

Economies are also never entirely open or entirely closed. Opening requires governments to loosen three types of economic controls: on capital flows, goods and services, and people. Liberalizing one of the above neither requires nor always leads to liberalization in the others. Free movement of goods and services makes regulating capital flows more difficult, but not impossible; foreign direct investment can flow across national barriers to trade in goods without knocking them down. It is easier still to trade freely and abolish controls on capital movement, while nevertheless regulating movement of people.

The important questions, then, concern the tradeoffs confronting governments that have chosen a degree of international economic integration. How constrained will governments find themselves once they have chosen openness?

THREE VITAL AREAS

Globalization is often perceived as destroying governments' capacities to do what they want or need, particularly in the key areas of taxation, public spending for income redistribution, and macroeconomic policy. But how true is this perception?

In fact, no evidence supports the conclusion that states can no longer raise taxes. On the contrary: in 1999, EU governments spent or redistributed an average of 47 percent of their GDPS. An important new book by Vito Tanzi of the IMF and Ludger Schuknecht of the European Central Bank underlines this point. Over the course of the twentieth century, the average share of government spending among Organization for Economic Cooperation and Development (OECD) member states jumped from an eighth to almost half of GDP. In some high-income countries such as France and Germany, these ratios were higher than ever before.

Until now, it has been electoral resistance, not globalization, that has most significantly limited the growth in taxation. Tanzi claims that this is about to change. He argues that collecting taxes is becoming harder due to a long list of "fiscal termites" gnawing at the foundations of taxation regimes: more cross-border shopping, the increased mobility of skilled labor, the growth of electronic commerce, the expansion of tax havens, the development of new financial instruments and intermediaries, growing trade within multinational companies, and the possible replacement of bank accounts with electronic money embedded in "smart cards."

The list is impressive. That governments take it seriously is demonstrated by the attention that leaders of the OECD and the EU are devoting to "harmful tax competition," information exchange, and the implications of electronic commerce. Governments, like members of any other industry, are forming a cartel to halt what they see as "ruinous competition" in taxation. This sense of threat has grown out of several fiscal developments produced by globalization: increased mobility of people and money, greater difficulty in collecting information on income and spending, and the impact of the Internet on information flows and collection.

Yet the competitive threat that governments face must not be exaggerated. The fiscal implications of labor, capital, and spending mobility are already evident in local jurisdictions that have the freedom to set their own tax rates. Even local governments can impose higher taxes than their neighbors, provided they contain specific resources or offer location-specific amenities that residents desire and consume. In other words, differential taxation is possible if there are at least some transport costs—and there always are.

These costs grow with a jurisdiction's geographic size, which thus strongly influences a local government's ability to raise taxes. The income of mobile capital is the hardest to tax; the income of land and immobile labor is easiest. Corporate income can be taxed if it is based on resources specific to that location, be they natural or human. Spending can also be taxed more heavily in one jurisdiction than another, but not if transport costs are very low (either because distances are short or items are valuable in relation to costs). Similarly, it is difficult to tax personal incomes if people can live in low-tax jurisdictions while enjoying the amenities of high-tax ones.

Eliminating legal barriers to mobility therefore constrains, but does not eliminate, the ability of some jurisdictions to levy far higher taxes than others. The ceiling on higher local taxes rises when taxable resources or activities remain relatively immobile or the jurisdiction provides valuable specific amenities just for that area.

The international mobility of people and goods is unlikely ever to come close to the kind of mobility that exists between states in the United States. Legal, linguistic, and cultural barriers will keep levels of cross-border migration far lower than levels of movement within any given country. Since taxes on labor income and spending are the predominant source of national revenue, the modern country's income base seems quite safe. Of course, although the somewhat greater mobility resulting from globalization makes it harder for governments to get information about what their residents own and spend abroad, disguising physical movement, consumption, or income remains a formidable task.

The third major aspect of globalization, the Internet, may have an appreciable impact on tax collection. Stephane Buydens of the OECD plausibly argues that the Internet will primarily affect four main areas: taxes on spending, tax treaties, internal pricing of multinational companies, and tax administration.

Purely Internet-based transactions—downloading of films, software, or music—are hard to tax. But when the Internet is used to buy tangible goods, governments can impose taxes, provided that the suppliers cooperate with the fiscal authorities of their corresponding jurisdictions. To the extent that these suppliers are large shareholder-owned companies, which they usually are, this cooperation may not be as hard to obtain as is often supposed.

It is also sometimes difficult to locate an Internet server. If one cannot do so, how are taxes to be levied and tax treaties applied? Similar problems arise with multinational companies' ability to charge submarket prices to their subsidiaries abroad (so-called "transfer pricing" within multinationals), which leaves uncertain the question of how and in which country to levy the tax. This scenario suggests that classic concepts in the taxation of corporations may have to be modified or even radically overhauled.

The overall conclusion, then, is that economic liberalization and technology advances will make taxation significantly more challenging. Taxes on spending may have to be partially recast. Taxation of corporate profits may have to be radically redesigned or even abandoned. Finally, the ability of governments to impose taxes that bear no relation to the benefits provided may be more constrained than before.

Nevertheless, the implications of these changes can easily be exaggerated. Taxation of corporate income is rarely more than ten percent of revenue, whereas taxes on income and spending are the universal pillars of the fiscal system. Yet even lofty Scandinavian taxes are not forcing skilled people to emigrate in droves. People will still happily pay to enjoy high-quality schools or public transport. Indeed, one of the most intriguing phenomena of modern Europe is that the high-tax, big-spending Scandinavian countries are leading the "new economy."

Governments will also use the exchange of information and other forms of cooperation to sustain revenue and may even consider international agreements on minimum taxes. They will certainly force the publicly quoted companies that continue to dominate transactions, both on-line and off, to cooperate with fiscal authorities. But competition among governments will not be eliminated, because the powerful countries that provide relatively low-tax, low-spending environments will want to maintain them.

The bottom line is that the opening of economies and the blossoming of new technologies are reinforcing constraints that have already developed within domestic politics. National governments are becoming a little more like local governments. The result will not necessarily be minimal government. But governments, like other institutions, will be forced to provide value to those who pay for their services.

Meanwhile, governments can continue the practice of income redistribution to the extent that the most highly taxed citizens and firms cannot—or do not wish to—evade taxation. In fact, if taxes are used to fund what are believed to be location-specific benefits, such as income redistribution or welfare spending, taxpayers will likely be quite willing to pay, perhaps because they either identify with the beneficiaries, fear that they could become indigent themselves, or treasure the security that comes from living among people who are not destitute. Taxpayers may also feel a sense of moral obligation to the poor, a sentiment that seems stronger in small, homogeneous societies. Alternatively, they may merely be unable to evade or avoid those taxes without relocating physically outside the jurisdiction. For all these reasons, sustaining a high measure of redistributive taxation remains perfectly possible. The constraint is not globalization, but the willingness of the electorate to tolerate high taxation.

Last but not least, some observers argue that globalization limits governments' ability to run fiscal deficits and pursue inflationary monetary policy. But macroeconomic policy is always vulnerable to the reaction of the private sector, regardless of whether the capital market is internationally integrated. If a government pursues a consistently inflationary policy, long-term nominal interest rates will rise, partly to compensate for inflation and partly to insure the bondholders against inflation risk. Similarly, if a government relies on the printing press to finance its activity, a flight from money into goods, services, and assets will ensue—and, in turn, generate inflation.

Within one country, these reactions may be slow. A government can pursue an inflationary policy over a long period and boost the economy; the price may not have to be paid for many years. What difference, then, does it make for the country to be open to international capital flows? The most important change is that the reaction of a government's creditors is likely to be quicker and more brutal because they have more alternatives. This response will often show itself in a collapsing exchange rate, as happened in East Asia in 1997 and 1998.

THE CONTINUING IMPORTANCE OF STATES

A country that chooses international economic integration implicitly accepts constraints on its actions. Nevertheless, the idea that these constraints wither away the state's capacity to tax, regulate, or intervene is wrong. Rather, international economic integration accelerates the market's responses to policy by increasing the range of alternative options available to those affected. There are also powerful reasons for believing that the constraints imposed on (or voluntarily accepted by) governments by globalization are, on balance, desirable.

For example, the assumption that most governments are benevolent welfare-maximizers is naive. International economic integration creates competition among governments—even countries that fiercely resist integration cannot survive with uncompetitive economies, as shown by the fate of the Soviet Union. This competition constrains the ability of governments to act in a predatory manner and increases the incentive to provide services that are valued by those who pay the bulk of the taxes.

Another reason for welcoming the constraints is that self-imposed limits on a government's future actions enhance the credibility of even a benevolent government's commitments to the private sector. An open capital account is one such constraint. Treaties with other governments, as in the WTO, are another, as are agreements with powerful private parties. Even China has come to recognize the economic benefits that it can gain from international commitments of this kind.

The proposition that globalization makes states unnecessary is even less credible than the idea that it makes states impotent. If anything, the exact opposite is true, for at least three reasons. First, the ability of a society to take advantage of the opportunities offered by international economic integration depends on the quality of public goods, such as property rights, an honest civil service, personal security, and basic education. Without an appropriate legal framework, in particular, the web of potentially rewarding contracts is vastly reduced. This point may seem trivial, but many developing economies have failed to achieve these essential preconditions of success.

Second, the state normally defines identity. A sense of belonging is part of the people's sense of security, and one that most people would not want to give up, even in the age of globalization. It is perhaps not surprising that some of the most successfully integrated economies are small, homogeneous countries with a strong sense of collective identity.

Third, international governance rests on the ability of individual states to provide and guarantee stability. The bedrock of international order is the territorial state with its monopoly on coercive power within its jurisdiction. Cyberspace does not change this: economies are ultimately run for and by human beings, who have a physical presence and, therefore, a physical location.

Globalization does not make states unnecessary. On the contrary, for people to be successful in exploiting the opportunities afforded by international integration, they need states at both ends of their transactions. Failed states, disorderly states, weak states, and corrupt states are shunned as the black holes of the global economic system.

What, then, does globalization mean for states? First, policy ultimately determines the pace and depth of international economic integration. For each country, globalization is at least as much a choice as a destiny. Second, in important respects—notably a country's monetary regime, capital account, and above all, labor mobility—the policy underpinnings of integration are less complete than they were a century ago. Third, countries choose integration because they see its benefits. Once chosen, any specific degree of international integration imposes constraints on the ability of governments to tax, redistribute income, and influence macroeconomic conditions. But those constraints must not be exaggerated, and their effects are often beneficial. Fourth, international economic integration magnifies the impact of the difference between good and bad states—between states that provide public goods and those that serve predatory private interests, including those of the rulers.

Finally, as the world economy continues to integrate and cross-border flows become more important, global governance must be improved. Global governance will come not at the expense of the state but rather as an expression of the interests that the state embodies. As the source of order and basis of governance, the state will remain in the future as effective, and will be as essential, as it has ever been.

Postscript

The debate over the impact of globalization on the future of the nation-state has led to a growing interest in alternative forms of political community. Since states have little control over global markets and limited influence on decisions made by transnational corporations, some argue that we need to move toward some form of cosmopolitan democracy. Advocates of this view suggest that individuals need to think of themselves as transnational or world citizens and should join together to seek to democratize international institutions. Some have suggested that international institutions like the United Nations need to be reformed to permit direct popular participation. Perhaps citizens of individual countries could elect representatives to a Popular Assembly of the United Nations much like Europeans elect representatives to the European Parliament today.

Others see a different future. They suggest that we are entering a situation much like Europe in the Middle Ages. Individuals would be governed by a number of overlapping authorities. States would transfer some powers to international institutions to deal with global problems. At the same time, they would transfer some powers to more regional units where the sense of distinctive identities is stronger. States would occupy only one level of government among many. Citizens would divide their loyalty between states, sub-state entities, and transnational political authorities. Some believe that Europe is farthest along this path. Whether you accept either of these visions of the future, both suggest that the role of the nation-state in global governance will be significantly different than it has been in the past.

Infotrac Keyword Search

"nation-state" or "future" + "nation-state"

Suggested Additional Readings

Cerny, Philip G. "What Next for the State?" in Elenore Kafman and Gillian Youngs, eds., *Globalization: Theory and Practice*. London: Pinter, 1996.

Del Rosso, Jr., Stephen J. "The Insecure State (What Future for the State?)" *Daedalus*, 124, No. 2 (Spring 1995).

Evans, Peter. "The Eclipse of the State? Reflections on Statelessness in the Era of Globalization," *World Politics* 50 (October 1997): 62–87.

Holton, Robert J. *Globalization and the Nation-State*. London: MacMillan, 1998.

Ohmae, Kenichi. "The Rise of the Region State," *Foreign Affairs*, 72, 2 (Spring 1993).

Opello, Jr., Walter C and Rosow, Stephen J. *The Nation-State and Global Order: An Historical Introduction to Contemporary Politics*. Boulder, Col.: Lynne Rienner, 1999.

Rosenau, James. "The State in an Era of Cascading Politics," in James Caporaso, ed., *The Elusive State: International and Comparative Perspectives*. London: Sage, 1990.

Strange, Susan. *Retreat of the State: The Diffusion of Power in the World Economy.* Cambridge: Cambridge University Press, 1996.

Website Resources

Jurgen Habermas, "The European Nation-State: On the Past and Future of Sovereignty and Citizenship," *Public Culture* 10, no. 2 (Winter 1998)   This article looks at the more recent events related to the nation-state from an historical and philosophical perspective.

Murray N. Rothbard, "Nations by Descent: Decomposing the Nation-State," *Journal of Libertarian Studies,* 11, no 1 (Fall 1984)   This paper looks at the re-emergence of the nation from a libertarian perspective.

Nationalism: A Conceptual Study   This site offers in-depth applicable definitions of Nation, Nation-State, and Nationalism prepared by students in the politics department of the University of Sheffield.

ISSUE**THREE**

Is the World Fragmenting into Antagonistic Cultures?

✔ **YES**
SAMUEL HUNTINGTON, "The Clash of Civilizations? The Next Pattern of
Conflict," *Foreign Affairs* 72, no. 3 (Summer 1993): 22–28

✗ **NO**
DOUGLAS ROSS, "Despair, Defeatism, and Isolationism in
American 'Grand Strategy': The Seductive Convenience of
Huntington's 'Civilizational Clash' Thesis"

Francis Fukuyama's article "The End of History?" (*The National Interest* 16, 1989)
argued that we may be witnessing the end of humankind's ideological evolution
and the universalization of Western liberal democracy. One of the noted scholars
to respond to Fukuyama's thesis was Samuel Huntington, whose article "No Exit:
The Errors of Endism" (*The National Interest* 17, 1989) challenges the optimistic
assessments of the end of the Cold War. In particular, he was concerned about the
growing preoccupation with "endism," the view that "bad things are coming to an
end." Huntington was reacting not only to Fukuyama's optimistic scenarios, but
to those of other writers, such as John Mueller, who argue that in the late twentieth century, major war is becoming obsolete, just as slavery and dueling became
obsolete as social institutions in the nineteenth century (see Issue One).

Huntington argues that these optimistic analyses are patently wrong. He warns
his readers that we are entering an era not of expanding zones of peace and tranquillity but, rather, of "instability, unpredictability, and violence in international
affairs." What troubles Huntington is not simply that these analysts have their
interpretations wrong, but that the policy implications of their analysis would
have dire consequences, especially for the United States, if implemented. Endism
is "dangerous and subversive," Huntington argues, because it "presents an illusion
of well-being," invites "relaxed complacency," and gives credence to policies that
he believes will be disastrous for the West and the United States in particular.

In his article, Huntington seems to base his arguments on those of neorealist
analysts like John Lewis Gaddis and John Mearsheimer. Drawing on Gaddis,
Huntington notes that the structure of bipolarity and the presence of nuclear
weapons had both defined the nature of and placed constraints on U.S.–Soviet
rivalry. The end of the Cold War does not "mean the end of the struggle for power
and influence." In fact, the end of the Cold War bipolar structure and the "balance

of terror" between the two superpowers presages a slide into a more chaotic and troubling time.

In 1993 Huntington published an article in which he sought to identify in clearer terms what he sees as the sources of this increased instability and unpredictability. In doing so, Huntington claims to be presenting students of international relations with a new and more comprehensive paradigm for understanding world politics. Rather than simply thinking about the structure of world politics in terms of polarity and balance of power between nation-states, Huntington stresses the relevance of civilizations and cultures in shaping international conflict, a dimension that has often been ignored in traditional realist analyses of world politics. This "new paradigm," he argues, is necessitated by the evolution of history. According to Huntington, the modern world has evolved through three phases of conflict, progressing from conflicts between princes for power to conflicts between nation-states, and then to conflicts between ideologies. We are entering a new phase of human history in which conflict between civilizations will supplant ideological conflict as a dominant force in international politics.

In the future, Huntington contends, conflicts are most likely to develop between groups that are part of different civilizations. Thus, he argues that the cultural differences between the eight different civilizations he identifies will become more dangerous and entrenched than traditional ideological and economic clashes. Advances in communications technologies, and increased economic and social interaction, rather than create a globalized culture, will magnify "civilizational consciousness" and exacerbate future conflicts. Because questions of identity, culture, and religion are more fundamental to people, future conflicts will be less amenable to negotiation and compromise. As Islamic and Confucian states increasingly challenge Western political, economic, and cultural dominance, the possibility of conflict on a global scale—the "West against the rest"—becomes increasingly likely. Accordingly, Huntington warns, this is not the time for American policymakers to be complacent or isolationist.

Huntington's "clash of civilizations" thesis has received criticism from various sources. In the accompanying essay, Douglas Ross of Simon Fraser University argues that, rather than providing a useful framework for guiding U.S. policy in the post–Cold War era, Huntington's thesis represents "a very substantial and dangerous retreat into 'civilizational' isolationism when ... the world can least afford a collapse of international solidarity and cooperative reform of global institutions."

✔ YES
The Clash of Civilizations? The Next Pattern of Conflict
SAMUEL HUNTINGTON

World politics is entering a new phase, and intellectuals have not hesitated to pro-liferate visions of what it will be—the end of history, the return of traditional rivalries between nation states, and the decline of the nation state from the con-flicting pulls of tribalism and globalism, among others. Each of these visions catches aspects of the emerging reality. Yet they all miss a crucial, indeed a cen-tral, aspect of what global politics is likely to be in the coming years.

It is my hypothesis that the fundamental source of conflict in this new world will not be primarily ideological or primarily economic. The great divisions among humankind and the dominating source of conflict will be cultural. Nation states will remain the most powerful actors in world affairs, but the principal con-flicts of global politics will occur between nations and groups of different civi-lizations. The clash of civilizations will dominate global politics. The fault lines between civilizations will be the battle lines of the future.

Conflict between civilizations will be the latest phase in the evolution of conflict in the modern world. For a century and a half after the emergence of the modern international system with the Peace of Westphalia, the conflicts of the Western world were largely among princes—emperors, absolute monarchs, and constitu-tional monarchs attempting to expand their bureaucracies, their armies, their mer-cantilist economic strength and, most important, the territory they ruled. In the process they created nation states, and beginning with the French Revolution the principal lines of conflict were between nations rather than princes. In 1793, as R.R. Palmer put it, "The wars of kings were over; the wars of peoples had begun." This nineteenth-century pattern lasted until the end of World War I.

Then, as a result of the Russian Revolution and the reaction against it, the conflict of nations yielded to the conflict of ideologies, first among communism, fascism-Nazism, and liberal democracy, and then between communism and liberal democ-racy. During the Cold War, this latter conflict became embodied in the struggle between the two superpowers, neither of which was a nation state in the classical European sense and each of which defined its identity in terms of its ideology.

These conflicts between princes, nation states, and ideologies were primarily conflicts within Western civilization, "Western civil wars," as William Lind has labeled them. This was as true of the Cold War as it was of the world wars and the earlier wars of the seventeenth, eighteenth, and nineteenth centuries. With the end of the Cold War, international politics moves out of its Western phase, and its centerpiece becomes the interaction between the West and non-Western civiliza-tions and among non-Western civilizations. In the politics of civilizations, the peoples and governments of non-Western civilizations no longer remain the objects of history as targets of Western colonialism but join the West as movers and shapers of history.

THE NATURE OF CIVILIZATIONS

During the Cold War the world was divided into the First, Second, and Third Worlds. Those divisions are no longer relevant. It is far more meaningful now to group countries not in terms of their political or economic systems or in terms of their level of economic development but rather in terms of their culture and civilization.

What do we mean when we talk of a civilization? A civilization is a cultural entity. Villages, regions, ethnic groups, nationalities, religious groups, all have distinct cultures at different levels of cultural heterogeneity. The culture of a village in southern Italy may be different from that of a village in northern Italy, but both will share in a common Italian culture that distinguishes them from German villages. European communities, in turn, will share cultural features that distinguish them from Arab or Chinese communities. Arabs, Chinese, and Westerners, however, are not part of any broader cultural entity. They constitute civilizations. A civilization is thus the highest cultural grouping of people and the broadest level of cultural identity people have short of that which distinguishes humans from other species. It is defined both by common objective elements, such as language, history, religion, customs, and institutions, and by the subjective self-identification of people. People have levels of identity: a resident of Rome may define himself with varying degrees of intensity as a Roman, an Italian, a Catholic, a Christian, a European, a Westerner. The civilization to which he belongs is the broadest level of identification with which he intensely identifies. People can and do redefine their identities and, as a result, the composition and boundaries of civilizations change.

Civilizations may involve a large number of people, as with China ("a civilization pretending to be a state," as Lucian Pye put it), or a very small number of people, such as the Anglophone Caribbean. A civilization may include several nation states, as is the case with Western, Latin American, and Arab civilizations, or only one, as is the case with Japanese civilization. Civilizations obviously blend and overlap, and may include subcivilizations. Western civilization has two major variants, European and North American, and Islam has its Arab, Turkic, and Malay subdivisions. Civilizations are nonetheless meaningful entities, and while the lines between them are seldom sharp, they are real. Civilizations are dynamic; they rise and fall; they divide and merge. And, as any student of history knows, civilizations disappear and are buried in the sands of time.

Westerners tend to think of nation states as the principal actors in global affairs. They have been that, however, for only a few centuries. The broader reaches of human history have been the history of civilizations. In *A Study of History*,

Arnold Toynbee identified 21 major civilizations; only six of them exist in the contemporary world.

WHY CIVILIZATIONS WILL CLASH

Civilization identity will be increasingly important in the future, and the world will be shaped in large measure by the interactions among seven or eight major civilizations. These include Western, Confucian, Japanese, Islamic, Hindu, Slavic-Orthodox, Latin American, and possibly African civilization. The most important conflicts of the future will occur along the cultural fault lines separating these civilizations from one another.

Why will this be the case?

First, differences among civilizations are not only real; they are basic. Civilizations are differentiated from each other by history, language, culture, tradition and, most important, religion. The people of different civilizations have different views on the relations between God and man, the individual and the group, the citizen and the state, parents and children, husband and wife, as well as differing views of the relative importance of rights and responsibilities, liberty and authority, equality and hierarchy. These differences are the product of centuries. They will not soon disappear. They are far more fundamental than differences among political ideologies and political regimes. Differences do not necessarily mean conflict, and conflict does not necessarily mean violence. Over the centuries, however, differences among civilizations have generated the most prolonged and the most violent conflicts.

Second, the world is becoming a smaller place. The interactions between peoples of different civilizations are increasing; these increasing interactions intensify civilization consciousness and awareness of differences between civilizations and commonalities within civilizations. North African immigration to France generates hostility among Frenchmen and at the same time increased receptivity to immigration by "good" European Catholic Poles. Americans react far more negatively to Japanese investment than to larger investments from Canada and European countries. Similarly, as Donald Horowitz has pointed out, "An Ibo may be ... an Owerri Ibo or an Onitsha Ibo in what was the Eastern region of Nigeria. In Lagos, he is simply an Ibo. In London, he is a Nigerian. In New York, he is an African." The interactions among peoples of different civilizations enhance the civilization-consciousness of people that, in turn, invigorates differences and animosities stretching or thought to stretch back deep into history.

Third, the processes of economic modernization and social change throughout the world are separating people from longstanding local identities. They also weaken the nation state as a source of identity. In much of the world religion has moved in to fill this gap, often in the form of movements that are labeled "fundamentalist." Such movements are found in Western Christianity, Judaism,

Buddhism, and Hinduism, as well as in Islam. In most countries and most religions the people active in fundamentalist movements are young, college-educated, middle-class technicians, professionals and business persons. The "unsecularization of the world," George Weigel has remarked, "is one of the dominant social facts of life in the late twentieth century." The revival of religion, "la revanche de Dieu," as Gilles Kepel labeled it, provides a basis for identity and commitment that transcends national boundaries and unites civilizations.

Fourth, the growth of civilization-consciousness is enhanced by the dual role of the West. On the one hand, the West is at a peak of power. At the same time, however, and perhaps as a result, a return to the roots phenomenon is occurring among non-Western civilizations. Increasingly one hears references to trends toward a turning inward and "Asianization" in Japan, the end of the Nehru legacy and the "Hinduization" of India, the failure of Western ideas of socialism and nationalism and hence "re-Islamization" of the Middle East, and now a debate over Westernization versus Russianization in Boris Yeltsin's country. A West at the peak of its power confronts non-Wests that increasingly have the desire, the will and the resources to shape the world in non-Western ways.

In the past, the elites of non-Western societies were usually the people who were most involved with the West, had been educated at Oxford, the Sorbonne or Sandhurst, and had absorbed Western attitudes and values. At the same time, the populace in non-Western countries often remained deeply imbued with the indigenous culture. Now, however, these relationships are being reversed. A de-Westernization and indigenization of elites is occurring in many non-Western countries at the same time that Western, usually American, cultures, styles and habits become more popular among the mass of the people.

Fifth, cultural characteristics and differences are less mutable and hence less easily compromised and resolved than political and economic ones. In the former Soviet Union, communists can become democrats, the rich can become poor and the poor rich, but Russians cannot become Estonians and Azeris cannot become Armenians. In class and ideological conflicts, the key question was "Which side are you on?" and people could and did choose sides and change sides. In conflicts between civilizations, the question is "What are you?" That is a given that cannot be changed. And as we know, from Bosnia to the Caucasus to the Sudan, the wrong answer to that question can mean a bullet in the head. Even more than ethnicity, religion discriminates sharply and exclusively among people. A person can be half-French and half-Arab and simultaneously even a citizen of two countries. It is more difficult to be half-Catholic and half-Muslim.

Finally, economic regionalism is increasing. The proportions of total trade that were intraregional rose between 1980 and 1989 from 51 percent to 59 percent in Europe, 33 percent to 37 percent in East Asia, and 32 percent to 36 percent in North America. The importance of regional economic blocs is likely to continue to increase in the future. On the one hand, successful economic regionalism will reinforce civilization-consciousness. On the other hand, economic regionalism may succeed only when it is rooted in a common civilization. The European Community rests on the shared foundation of European culture and Western Christianity. The success of the North American Free Trade Area depends on the convergence now underway of Mexican, Canadian, and American cultures. Japan, in contrast, faces difficulties in creating a comparable economic entity in East Asia because Japan is a society and civilization unique to itself. However strong the trade and investment links Japan may develop with other East Asian countries, its cultural differences with those countries inhibit and perhaps preclude its promoting regional economic integration like that in Europe and North America.

Common culture, in contrast, is clearly facilitating the rapid expansion of the economic relations between the People's Republic of China and Hong Kong, Taiwan, Singapore, and the overseas Chinese communities in other Asian countries. With the Cold War over, cultural commonalities increasingly overcome ideological differences, and mainland China and Taiwan move closer together. If cultural commonality is a prerequisite for economic integration, the principal East Asian economic bloc of the future is likely to be centered on China. This bloc is, in fact, already coming into existence. As Murray Weidenbaum has observed,

> Despite the current Japanese dominance of the region, the Chinese-based economy of Asia is rapidly emerging as a new epicenter for industry, commerce and finance. This strategic area contains substantial amounts of technology and manufacturing capability (Taiwan), outstanding entrepreneurial, marketing and services acumen (Hong Kong), a fine communications network (Singapore), a tremendous pool of financial capital (all three), and very large endowments of land, resources and labor (mainland China)....
> From Guangzhou to Singapore, from Kuala Lumpur to Manila, this influential network—often based on extensions of the traditional clans—has been described as the backbone of the East Asian economy.[1]

Culture and religion also form the basis of the Economic Cooperation Organization, which brings together ten non-Arab Muslim countries: Iran, Pakistan, Turkey, Azerbaijan, Kazakhstan, Kyrgyzstan, Turkmenistan, Tadjikistan, Uzbekistan, and Afghanistan. One impetus to the revival and expansion of this organization, founded originally in the 1960s by Turkey, Pakistan, and Iran, is the realization by the leaders of several of these countries that they had no chance of admission to the European Community. Similarly, Caricom, the Central American Common Market and Mercosur rest on common cultural foundations. Efforts to build a broader Caribbean-American economic entity bridging the Anglo-Latin divide, however, have to date failed.

As people define their identity in ethnic and religious terms, they are likely to see an "us" versus "them" relation existing between themselves and people of different ethnicity or religion. The end of ideologically defined states in Eastern Europe and the former Soviet Union permits traditional ethnic identities and animosities to come to the fore. Differences in culture and religion create differences over policy issues, ranging from human rights to immigration to trade and commerce to the environment. Geographical propinquity gives rise to conflicting territorial claims from Bosnia to Mindanao. Most important, the efforts of the West to promote its values of democracy and liberalism as universal values, to maintain its military predominance, and to advance its economic interests engender countering responses from other civilizations. Decreasingly able to mobilize support and form coalitions on the basis of ideology, governments and groups will increasingly attempt to mobilize support by appealing to common religion and civilization identity.

The clash of civilizations thus occurs at two levels. At the micro-level, adjacent groups along the fault lines between civilizations struggle, often violently, over the control of territory and each other. At the macro-level, states from different civilizations compete for relative military and economic power, struggle over the control of international institutions and third parties, and competitively promote their particular political and religious values.

THE FAULT LINES BETWEEN CIVILIZATIONS

The fault lines between civilizations are replacing the political and ideological boundaries of the Cold War as the flash points for crisis and bloodshed. The Cold War began when the Iron Curtain divided Europe politically and ideologically: The Cold War ended with the end of the Iron Curtain. As the ideological division of Europe has disappeared, the cultural division of Europe between Western Christianity, on the one hand, and Orthodox Christianity and Islam, on the other, has reemerged. The most significant dividing line in Europe, as William Wallace has suggested, may well be the eastern boundary of Western Christianity in the year 1500. This line runs along what are now the boundaries between Finland and Russia and between the Baltic states and Russia, cuts through Belarus and Ukraine separating the more Catholic western Ukraine from Orthodox eastern Ukraine, swings westward separating Transylvania from the rest of Romania, and then goes through Yugoslavia almost exactly along the line now separating Croatia and Slovenia from the rest of Yugoslavia. In the Balkans this line, of course, coincides with the historic boundary between the Hapsburg and Ottoman empires. The peoples to the north and west of this line are Protestant or Catholic; they shared the common experiences of European history—feudalism, the Renaissance, the Reformation, the Enlightenment, the French Revolution, the Industrial Revolution; they are generally economically better off than the peoples to the east; and they may now look forward to increasing involvement in a common European economy and to the consolidation of democratic political systems. The

peoples to the east and south of this line are Orthodox or Muslim; they historically belonged to the Ottoman or Tsarist empires and were only lightly touched
by the shaping events in the rest of Europe; they are generally less advanced economically; they seem much less likely to develop stable democratic political systems. The Velvet Curtain of culture has replaced the Iron Curtain of ideology as
the most significant dividing line in Europe. As the events in Yugoslavia show, it
is not only a line of difference; it is also at times a line of bloody conflict.

Conflict along the fault line between Western and Islamic civilizations has been
going on for 1,300 years. After the founding of Islam, the Arab and Moorish surge
west and north only ended at Tours in 732. From the eleventh to the thirteenth
century the Crusaders attempted with temporary success to bring Christianity and
Christian rule to the Holy Land. From the fourteenth to the seventeenth century,
the Ottoman Turks reversed the balance, extended their sway over the Middle East
and the Balkans, captured Constantinople, and twice laid siege to Vienna. In the
nineteenth and early twentieth centuries as Ottoman power declined, Britain,
France, and Italy established Western control over most of North Africa and the
Middle East.

After World War II, the West, in turn, began to retreat; the colonial empires disappeared; first Arab nationalism and then Islamic fundamentalism manifested
themselves; the West became heavily dependent on the Persian Gulf countries for
its energy; the oil-rich Muslim countries became money-rich and, when they
wished to, weapons-rich. Several wars occurred between Arabs and Israel (created
by the West). France fought a bloody and ruthless war in Algeria for most of the
1950s; British and French forces invaded Egypt in 1956; American forces went
into Lebanon in 1958; subsequently American forces returned to Lebanon,
attacked Libya, and engaged in various military encounters with Iran; Arab and
Islamic terrorists, supported by at least three Middle Eastern governments,
employed the weapon of the weak and bombed Western planes and installations
and seized Western hostages. This warfare between Arabs and the West culminated in 1990, when the United States sent a massive army to the Persian Gulf to
defend some Arab countries against aggression by another. In its aftermath NATO
planning is increasingly directed to potential threats and instability along its
"southern tier."

This centuries-old military interaction between the West and Islam is unlikely
to decline. It could become more virulent. The Gulf War left some Arabs feeling
proud that Saddam Hussein had attacked Israel and stood up to the West. It also
left many feeling humiliated and resentful of the West's military presence in the
Persian Gulf, the West's overwhelming military dominance, and their apparent
inability to shape their own destiny. Many Arab countries, in addition to the oil
exporters, are reaching levels of economic and social development where autocratic forms of government become inappropriate and efforts to introduce
democracy become stronger. Some openings in Arab political systems have

already occurred. The principal beneficiaries of these openings have been Islamist movements. In the Arab world, in short, Western democracy strengthens anti-Western political forces. This may be a passing phenomenon, but it surely complicates relations between Islamic countries and the West.

Those relations are also complicated by demography. The spectacular population growth in Arab countries, particularly in North Africa, has led to increased migration to Western Europe. The movement within Western Europe toward minimizing internal boundaries has sharpened political sensitivities with respect to this development. In Italy, France, and Germany, racism is increasingly open, and political reactions and violence against Arab and Turkish migrants have become more intense and more widespread since 1990. On both sides the interaction between Islam and the West is seen as a clash of civilizations. The West's "next confrontation," observes M.J. Akbar, an Indian Muslim author, "is definitely going to come from the Muslim world. It is in the sweep of the Islamic nations from the Maghreb to Pakistan that the struggle for a new world order will begin." Bernard Lewis comes to a similar conclusion:

> We are facing a mood and a movement far transcending the level of issues and policies and the governments that pursue them. This is no less than a clash of civilizations—the perhaps irrational but surely historic reaction of an ancient rival against our Judeo-Christian heritage, our secular present, and the worldwide expansion of both.[2]

Historically, the other great antagonistic interaction of Arab Islamic civilization has been with the pagan, animist, and now increasingly Christian black peoples to the south. In the past, this antagonism was epitomized in the image of Arab slave dealers and black slaves. It has been reflected in the on-going civil war in the Sudan between Arabs and blacks, the fighting in Chad between Libyan-supported insurgents and the government, the tensions between Orthodox Christians and Muslims in the Horn of Africa, and the political conflicts, recurring riots, and communal violence between Muslims and Christians in Nigeria. The modernization of Africa and the spread of Christianity are likely to enhance the probability of violence along this fault line. Symptomatic of the intensification of this conflict was Pope John Paul II's speech in Khartoum in February 1993 attacking the actions of the Sudan's Islamist government against the Christian minority there.

On the northern border of Islam, conflict has increasingly erupted between Orthodox and Muslim peoples, including the carnage of Bosnia and Sarajevo, the simmering violence between Serb and Albanian, the tenuous relations between Bulgarians and their Turkish minority, the violence between Ossetians and Ingush, the unremitting slaughter of each other by Armenians and Azeris, the tense relations between Russians and Muslims in Central Asia, and the deployment of Russian troops to protect Russian interests in the Caucasus and Central Asia.

Religion reinforces the revival of ethnic identities and restimulates Russian fears about the security of their southern borders. This concern is well captured by Archie Roosevelt:

> Much of Russian history concerns the struggle between the Slavs and the Turkic peoples on their borders, which dates back to the foundation of the Russian state more than a thousand years ago. In the Slavs' millennium-long confrontation with their eastern neighbors lies the key to an understanding not only of Russian history, but Russian character. To understand Russian realities today one has to have a concept of the great Turkic ethnic group that has preoccupied Russians through the centuries.[3]

The conflict of civilizations is deeply rooted elsewhere in Asia. The historic clash between Muslim and Hindu in the subcontinent manifests itself now not only in the rivalry between Pakistan and India but also in intensifying religious strife within India between increasingly militant Hindu groups and India's substantial Muslim minority. The destruction of the Ayodhya mosque in December 1992 brought to the fore the issue of whether India will remain a secular democratic state or become a Hindu one. In East Asia, China has outstanding territorial disputes with most of its neighbors. It has pursued a ruthless policy toward the Buddhist people of Tibet, and it is pursuing an increasingly ruthless policy toward its Turkic-Muslim minority. With the Cold War over, the underlying differences between China and the United States have reasserted themselves in areas such as human rights, trade, and weapons proliferation. These differences are unlikely to moderate. A "new cold war," Deng Xaioping reportedly asserted in 1991, is under way between China and America.

The same phrase has been applied to the increasingly difficult relations between Japan and the United States. Here cultural difference exacerbates economic conflict. People on each side allege racism on the other, but at least on the American side the antipathies are not racial but cultural. The basic values, attitudes, and behavioral patterns of the two societies could hardly be more different. The economic issues between the United States and Europe are no less serious than those between the United States and Japan, but they do not have the same political salience and emotional intensity because the differences between American culture and European culture are so much less than those between American civilization and Japanese civilization.

The interactions between civilizations vary greatly in the extent to which they are likely to be characterized by violence. Economic competition clearly predominates between the American and European subcivilizations of the West and between both of them and Japan. On the Eurasian continent, however, the proliferation of ethnic conflict, epitomized at the extreme in "ethnic cleansing," has not been totally random. It has been most frequent and most violent between groups belonging to different civilizations. In Eurasia the great historic fault lines between civilizations are once more aflame. This is particularly true along the boundaries of the crescent-shaped Islamic bloc of nations from the bulge of Africa to central Asia. Violence also occurs between Muslims, on the one hand, and Orthodox Serbs in the Balkans, Jews in Israel, Hindus in India, Buddhists in Burma, and Catholics in the Philippines. Islam has bloody borders.

CIVILIZATION RALLYING: THE KIN-COUNTRY SYNDROME

Groups or states belonging to one civilization that becomes involved in war with people from a different civilization naturally try to rally support from other members of their own civilization. As the post–Cold War world evolves, civilization commonality, what H.D.S. Greenway has termed the "kin-country" syndrome, is replacing political ideology and traditional balance of power considerations as the principal basis for cooperation and coalitions. It can be seen gradually emerging in the post–Cold War conflicts in the Persian Gulf, the Caucasus, and Bosnia. None of these was a full-scale war between civilizations, but each involved some elements of civilizational rallying, which seemed to become more important as the conflict continued and which may provide a foretaste of the future.

First, in the Gulf War one Arab state invaded another and then fought a coalition of Arab, Western, and other states. While only a few Muslim governments overtly supported Saddam Hussein, many Arab elites privately cheered him on, and he was highly popular among large sections of the Arab publics. Islamic fundamentalist movements universally supported Iraq rather than the Western-backed governments of Kuwait and Saudi Arabia. Forswearing Arab nationalism, Saddam Hussein explicitly invoked an Islamic appeal. He and his supporters attempted to define the war as a war between civilizations. "It is not the world against Iraq," as Safar Al-Hawaii, dean of Islamic Studies at the Umm Al-Qura University in Mecca, put it in a widely circulated tape. "It is the West against Islam." Ignoring the rivalry between Iran and Iraq, the chief Iranian religious leader, Ayatollah Ali Khamenei, called for a holy war against the West: "The struggle against American aggression, greed, plans and policies will be counted as a jihad, and anybody who is killed on that path is a martyr." "This is a war," King Hussein of Jordan argued, "'against all Arabs and all Muslims and not against Iraq alone."

The rallying of substantial sections of Arab elites and publics behind Saddam Hussein caused those Arab governments in the anti-Iraq coalition to moderate their activities and temper their public statements. Arab governments opposed or distanced themselves from subsequent Western efforts to apply pressure on Iraq, including enforcement of a no-fly zone in the summer of 1992 and the bombing of Iraq in January 1993. The Western-Soviet-Turkish-Arab anti-Iraq coalition of 1990 had by 1993 become a coalition of almost only the West and Kuwait against Iraq.

Muslims contrasted Western actions against Iraq with the West's failure to protect Bosnians against Serbs and to impose sanctions on Israel for violating U.N. resolutions. The West, they alleged, was using a double standard. A world of clashing civilizations, however, is inevitably a world of double standards: people apply one standard to their kin-countries and a different standard to others.

Second, the kin-country syndrome also appeared in conflicts in the former Soviet Union. Armenian military successes in 1992 and 1993 stimulated Turkey to become increasingly supportive of its religious, ethnic, and linguistic brethren in Azerbaijan. "We have a Turkish nation feeling the same sentiments as the Azerbaijanis," said one Turkish official in 1992. "We are under pressure. Our newspapers are full of the photos of atrocities and are asking us if we are still serious about pursuing our neutral policy. Maybe we should show Armenia that there's a big Turkey in the region." President Turgut Ozal agreed, remarking that Turkey should at least "scare the Armenians a little bit." Turkey, Ozal threatened again in 1993, would "show its fangs." Turkish Air Force jets flew reconnaissance flights along the Armenian border; Turkey suspended food shipments and air flights to Armenia; and Turkey and Iran announced they would not accept dismemberment of Azerbaijan. In the last years of its existence, the Soviet government supported Azerbaijan because its government was dominated by former communists. With the end of the Soviet Union, however, political considerations gave way to religious ones. Russian troops fought on the side of the Armenians, and Azerbaijan accused the "Russian government of turning 180 degrees" toward support for Christian Armenia.

Third, with respect to the fighting in the former Yugoslavia, Western publics manifested sympathy and support for the Bosnian Muslims and the horrors they suffered at the hands of the Serbs. Relatively little concern was expressed, however, over Croatian attacks on Muslims and participation in the dismemberment of Bosnia-Herzegovina. In the early stages of the Yugoslav breakup, Germany, in an unusual display of diplomatic initiative and muscle, induced the other 11 members of the European Community to follow its lead in recognizing Slovenia and Croatia. As a result of the Pope's determination to provide strong backing to the two Catholic countries, the Vatican extended recognition even before the Community did. The United States followed the European lead. Thus the leading actors in Western civilization rallied behind their coreligionists. Subsequently Croatia was reported to be receiving substantial quantities of arms from Central European and other Western countries. Boris Yeltsin's government, on the other hand, attempted to pursue a middle course that would be sympathetic to the Orthodox Serbs but not alienate Russia from the West. Russian conservative and nationalist groups, however, including many legislators, attacked the government for not being more forthcoming in its support for the Serbs. By early 1993 several hundred Russians apparently were serving with the Serbian forces, and reports circulated of Russian arms being supplied to Serbia.

Islamic governments and groups, on the other hand, castigated the West for not coming to the defense of the Bosnians. Iranian leaders urged Muslims from all countries to provide help to Bosnia; in violation of the U.N. arms embargo, Iran supplied weapons and men for the Bosnians; Iranian-supported Lebanese groups sent guerrillas to train and organize the Bosnian forces. In 1993 up to 4,000 Muslims from over two dozen Islamic countries were reported to be fighting in Bosnia. The governments of Saudi Arabia and other countries felt under increasing pressure from fundamentalist groups in their own societies to provide more vigorous support for the Bosnians. By the end of 1992, Saudi Arabia had reportedly supplied substantial funding for weapons and supplies for the Bosnians, which significantly increased their military capabilities vis-à-vis the Serbs.

In the 1930s the Spanish Civil War provoked intervention from countries that politically were fascist, communist, and democratic. In the 1990s the Yugoslav conflict is provoking intervention from countries that are Muslim, Orthodox, and Western Christian. The parallel has not gone unnoticed. "The war in Bosnia-Herzegovina has become the emotional equivalent of the fight against fascism in the Spanish Civil War," one Saudi editor observed. "Those who died there are regarded as martyrs who tried to save their fellow Muslims."

Conflicts and violence will also occur between states and groups within the same civilization. Such conflicts, however, are likely to be less intense and less likely to expand than conflicts between civilizations. Common membership in a civilization reduces the probability of violence in situations where it might otherwise occur. In 1991 and 1992 many people were alarmed by the possibility of violent conflict between Russia and Ukraine over territory, particularly Crimea, the Black Sea fleet, nuclear weapons, and economic issues. If civilization is what counts, however, the likelihood of violence between Ukrainians and Russians should be low. They are two Slavic, primarily Orthodox peoples who have had close relationships with each other for centuries. As of early 1993, despite all the reasons for conflict, the leaders of the two countries were effectively negotiating and defusing the issues between the two countries. While there has been serious fighting between Muslims and Christians elsewhere in the former Soviet Union and much tension and some fighting between Western and Orthodox Christians in the Baltic states, there has been virtually no violence between Russians and Ukrainians.

Civilization rallying to date has been limited, but it has been growing, and it clearly has the potential to spread much further. As the conflicts in the Persian Gulf, the Caucasus and Bosnia continued, the positions of nations and the cleavages between them increasingly were along civilizational lines. Populist politicians, religious leaders, and the media have found it a potent means of arousing mass support and of pressuring hesitant governments. In the coming years, the local conflicts most likely to escalate into major wars will be those, as in Bosnia and the Caucasus, along the fault lines between civilizations. The next world war, if there is one, will be a war between civilizations.

THE WEST VERSUS THE REST

The West is now at an extraordinary peak of power in relation to other civilizations. Its superpower opponent has disappeared from the map. Military conflict among Western states is unthinkable, and Western military power is unrivaled. Apart from Japan, the West faces no economic challenge. It dominates international political and security institutions and with Japan international economic institutions. Global political and security issues are effectively settled by a directorate of the United States, Britain, and France, world economic issues by a directorate of the United States, Germany, and Japan, all of which maintain extraordinarily close relations with each other to the exclusion of lesser and largely non-Western countries. Decisions made at the U.N. Security Council or in the International Monetary Fund that reflect the interests of the West are presented to the world as reflecting the desires of the world community. The very phrase "the world community" has become the euphemistic collective noun (replacing "the Free World") to give global legitimacy to actions reflecting the interests of the United States and other Western powers.[4] Through the IMF and other international economic institutions, the West promotes its economic interests and imposes on other nations the economic policies it thinks appropriate. In any poll of non-Western peoples, the IMF undoubtedly would win the support of finance ministers and a few others, but get an overwhelmingly unfavorable rating from just about everyone else, who would agree with Georgy Arbatov's characterization of IMF officials as "neo-Bolsheviks who love expropriating other people's money, imposing undemocratic and alien rules of economic and political conduct and stifling economic freedom."

Western domination of the U.N. Security Council and its decisions, tempered only by occasional abstention by China, produced U.N. legitimation of the West's use of force to drive Iraq out of Kuwait and its elimination of Iraq's sophisticated weapons and capacity to produce such weapons. It also produced the quite unprecedented action by the United States, Britain, and France in getting the Security Council to demand that Libya hand over the Pan Am 103 bombing suspects and then to impose sanctions when Libya refused. After defeating the largest Arab army, the West did not hesitate to throw its weight around in the Arab world. The West in effect is using international institutions, military power, and economic resources to run the world in ways that will maintain Western predominance, protect Western interests, and promote Western political and economic values.

That at least is the way in which non-Westerners see the new world, and there is a significant element of truth in their view. Differences in power and struggles for military, economic, and institutional power are thus one source of conflict between the West and other civilizations. Differences in culture, that is basic values and beliefs, are a second source of conflict. V.S. Naipaul has argued that Western civilization is the "universal civilization" that "fits all men." At a

superficial level much of Western culture has indeed permeated the rest of the world. At a more basic level, however, Western concepts differ fundamentally from those prevalent in other civilizations. Western ideas of individualism, liberalism, constitutionalism, human rights, equality, liberty, the rule of law, democracy, free markets, the separation of church and state, often have little resonance in Islamic, Confucian, Japanese, Hindu, Buddhist, or Orthodox cultures. Western efforts to propagate such ideas produce instead a reaction against "human rights imperialism" and a reaffirmation of indigenous values, as can be seen in the support for religious fundamentalism by the younger generation in non-Western cultures. The very notion that there could be a "universal civilization" is a Western idea, directly at odds with the particularism of most Asian societies and their emphasis on what distinguishes one people from another. Indeed, the author of a review of 100 comparative studies of values in different societies concluded that "the values that are most important in the West are least important worldwide."[5] In the political realm, of course, these differences are most manifest in the efforts of the United States and other Western powers to induce other peoples to adopt Western ideas concerning democracy and human rights. Modern democratic government originated in the West. When it has developed in non-Western societies it has usually been the product of Western colonialism or imposition.

The central axis of world politics in the future is likely to be, in Kishore Mahbubani's phrase, the conflict between "the West and the Rest" and the responses of non-Western civilizations to Western power and values.[6] Those responses generally take one or a combination of three forms. At one extreme, non-Western states can, like Burma and North Korea, attempt to pursue a course of isolation, to insulate their societies from penetration or "corruption" by the West, and, in effect, to opt out of participation in the Western-dominated global community. The costs of this course, however, are high, and few states have pursued it exclusively. A second alternative, the equivalent of "bandwagoning" in international relations theory, is to attempt to join the West and accept its values and institutions. The third alternative is to attempt to "balance" the West by developing economic and military power and cooperating with other non-Western societies against the West, while preserving indigenous values and institutions; in short, to modernize but not to Westernize.

THE TORN COUNTRIES

In the future, as people differentiate themselves by civilization, countries with large numbers of peoples of different civilizations, such as the Soviet Union and Yugoslavia, are candidates for dismemberment. Some other countries have a fair degree of cultural homogeneity but are divided over whether their society belongs to one civilization or another. These are torn countries. Their leaders typically wish to pursue a bandwagoning strategy and to make their countries members of the West, but the history, culture, and traditions of their countries are non-Western. The most obvious and prototypical torn country is Turkey. The late-twentieth-century leaders of Turkey have followed in the Attaturk tradition and defined Turkey as a modern, secular, Western nation state. They allied Turkey with the West in NATO and in the Gulf War; they applied for membership in the European Community. At the same time, however, elements in Turkish society have supported an Islamic revival and have argued that Turkey is basically a Middle Eastern Muslim society. In addition, while the elite of Turkey has defined Turkey as a Western society, the elite of the West refuses to accept Turkey as such. Turkey will not become a member of the European Community, and the real reason, as President Ozal said, "is that we are Muslim and they are Christian and they don't say that." Having rejected Mecca, and then being rejected by Brussels, where does Turkey look? Tashkent may be the answer. The end of the Soviet Union gives Turkey the opportunity to become the leader of a revived Turkic civilization involving seven countries from the borders of Greece to those of China. Encouraged by the West, Turkey is making strenuous efforts to carve out this new identity for itself.

During the past decade Mexico has assumed a position somewhat similar to that of Turkey. Just as Turkey abandoned its historic opposition to Europe and attempted to join Europe, Mexico has stopped defining itself by its opposition to the United States and is instead attempting to imitate the United States and to join it in the North American Free Trade Area. Mexican leaders are engaged in the great task of redefining Mexican identity and have introduced fundamental economic reforms that eventually will lead to fundamental political change. In 1991 a top adviser to President Carlos Salinas de Gortari described at length to me all the changes the Salinas government was making. When he finished, I remarked: "That's most impressive. It seems to me that basically you want to change Mexico from a Latin American country into a North American country." He looked at me with surprise and exclaimed: "Exactly! That's precisely what we are trying to do, but of course we could never say so publicly." As his remark indicates, in Mexico as in Turkey, significant elements in society resist the redefinition of their country's identity. In Turkey, European-oriented leaders have to make gestures to Islam (Ozal's pilgrimage to Mecca); so also Mexico's North American–oriented leaders have to make gestures to those who hold Mexico to be a Latin American country (Salinas's Ibero-American Guadalajara summit).

Historically Turkey has been the most profoundly torn country. For the United States, Mexico is the most immediate torn country. Globally the most important torn country is Russia. The question of whether Russia is part of the West or the leader of a distinct Slavic-Orthodox civilization has been a recurring one in Russian history. That issue was obscured by the communist victory in Russia, which imported a Western ideology, adapted it to Russian conditions and then challenged the West in the name of that ideology. The dominance of communism

shut off the historic debate over Westernization versus Russification. With communism discredited, Russians once again face that question.

President Yeltsin is adopting Western principles and goals and seeking to make
Russia a "normal" country and a part of the West. Yet both the Russian elite and
the Russian public are divided on this issue. Among the more moderate dissenters,
Sergei Stankevich argues that Russia should reject the "Atlanticist" course, which
would lead it "to become European, to become a part of the world economy in
rapid and organized fashion, to become the eighth member of the Seven, and to
put particular emphasis on Germany and the United States as the two dominant
members of the Atlantic alliance." While also rejecting an exclusively Eurasian
policy, Stankevich nonetheless argues that Russia should give priority to the protection of Russians in other countries, emphasize its Turkic and Muslim connections, and promote "an appreciable redistribution of our resources, our options,
our ties, and our interests in favor of Asia, of the eastern direction." People of this
persuasion criticize Yeltsin for subordinating Russia's interests to those of the
West, for reducing Russian military strength, for failing to support traditional
friends such as Serbia, and for pushing economic and political reform in ways
injurious to the Russian people. Indicative of this trend is the new popularity of
the ideas of Petr Savitsky, who in the 1920s argued that Russia was a unique
Eurasian civilization.[7] More extreme dissidents voice much more blatantly
nationalist, anti-Western, and anti-Semitic views, and urge Russia to redevelop its
military strength and to establish closer ties with China and Muslim countries. The
people of Russia are as divided as the elite. An opinion survey in European Russia
in the spring of 1992 revealed that 40 percent of the public had positive attitudes
toward the West and 36 percent had negative attitudes. As it has been for much
of its history, Russia in the early 1990s is truly a torn country.

To redefine its civilization identity, a torn country must meet three requirements. First, its political and economic elite has to be generally supportive of and
enthusiastic about this move. Second, its public has to be willing to acquiesce in
the redefinition. Third, the dominant groups in the recipient civilization have to
be willing to embrace the convert. All three requirements in large part exist with
respect to Mexico. The first two in large part exist with respect to Turkey. It is
not clear that any of them exist with respect to Russia's joining the West. The
conflict between liberal democracy and Marxism-Leninism was between ideologies which, despite their major differences, ostensibly shared ultimate goals of
freedom, equality, and prosperity. A traditional, authoritarian, nationalist Russia
could have quite different goals. A Western democrat could carry on an intellectual debate with a Soviet Marxist. It would be virtually impossible for him to do
that with a Russian traditionalist. If, as the Russians stop behaving like Marxists,
they reject liberal democracy and begin behaving like Russians but not like
Westerners, the relations between Russia and the West could again become distant and conflictual.[8]

THE CONFUCIAN–ISLAMIC CONNECTION

The obstacles to non-Western countries joining the West vary considerably. They are least for Latin American and East European countries. They are greater for the Orthodox countries of the former Soviet Union. They are still greater for Muslim, Confucian, Hindu, and Buddhist societies. Japan has established a unique position for itself as an associate member of the West: it is in the West in some respects but clearly not of the West in important dimensions. Those countries that for reasons of culture and power do not wish to, or cannot, join the West compete with the West by developing their own economic, military, and political power. They do this by promoting their internal development and by cooperating with other non-Western countries. The most prominent form of this cooperation is the Confucian–Islamic connection that has emerged to challenge Western interests, values, and power.

Almost without exception, Western countries are reducing their military power; under Yeltsin's leadership so also is Russia. China, North Korea, and several Middle Eastern states, however, are significantly expanding their military capabilities. They are doing this by the import of arms from Western and non-Western sources and by the development of indigenous arms industries. One result is the emergence of what Charles Krauthammer has called "Weapon States," and the Weapon States are not Western states. Another result is the redefinition of arms control, which is a Western concept and a Western goal. During the Cold War the primary purpose of arms control was to establish a stable military balance between the United States and its allies and the Soviet Union and its allies. In the post–Cold War world the primary objective of arms control is to prevent the development by non-Western societies of military capabilities that could threaten Western interests. The West attempts to do this through international agreements, economic pressure, and controls on the transfer of arms and weapons technologies.

The conflict between the West and the Confucian–Islamic states focuses largely, although not exclusively, on nuclear, chemical, and biological weapons, ballistic missiles and other sophisticated means for delivering them, and the guidance, intelligence, and other electronic capabilities for achieving that goal. The West promotes nonproliferation as a universal norm and nonproliferation treaties and inspections as means of realizing that norm. It also threatens a variety of sanctions against those who promote the spread of sophisticated weapons and proposes some benefits for those who do not. The attention of the West focuses, naturally, on nations that are actually or potentially hostile to the West.

The non-Western nations, on the other hand, assert their right to acquire and to deploy whatever weapons they think necessary for their security. They also have absorbed, to the full, the truth of the response of the Indian defense minister when asked what lesson he learned from the Gulf War: "Don't fight the United States unless you have nuclear weapons." Nuclear weapons, chemical weapons, and missiles are viewed, probably erroneously, as the potential equalizer of superior Western conventional power. China, of course, already has nuclear weapons; Pakistan and India have the capability to deploy them. North Korea, Iran, Iraq, Libya, and Algeria appear to be attempting to acquire them. A top Iranian official has declared that all Muslim states should acquire nuclear weapons, and in 1988 the president of Iran reportedly issued a directive calling for development of "offensive and defensive chemical, biological and radiological weapons."

Centrally important to the development of counter-West military capabilities is the sustained expansion of China's military power and its means to create military power. Buoyed by spectacular economic development, China is rapidly increasing its military spending and vigorously moving forward with the modernization of its armed forces. It is purchasing weapons from the former Soviet states; it is developing long-range missiles; in 1992 it tested a one-megaton nuclear device. It is developing power-projection capabilities, acquiring aerial refueling technology, and trying to purchase an aircraft carrier. Its military buildup and assertion of sovereignty over the South China Sea are provoking a multilateral regional arms race in East Asia. China is also a major exporter of arms and weapons technology. It has exported materials to Libya and Iraq that could be used to manufacture nuclear weapons and nerve gas. It has helped Algeria build a reactor suitable for nuclear weapons research and production. China has sold to Iran nuclear technology that American officials believe could only be used to create weapons and apparently has shipped components of 300 mile-range missiles to Pakistan. North Korea has had a nuclear weapons program under way for some while and has sold advanced missiles and missile technology to Syria and Iran. The flow of weapons and weapons technology is generally from East Asia to the Middle East. There is, however, some movement in the reverse direction; China has received Stinger missiles from Pakistan.

A Confucian–Islamic military connection has thus come into being, designed to promote acquisition by its members of the weapons and weapons technologies needed to counter the military power of the West. It may or may not last. At present, however, it is, as Dave McCurdy has said, "a renegades' mutual support pact, run by the proliferators and their backers." A new form of arms competition is thus occurring between Islamic–Confucian states and the West. In an old-fashioned arms race, each side developed its own arms to balance or to achieve superiority against the other side. In this new form of arms competition, one side is developing its arms and the other side is attempting not to balance but to limit and prevent that arms build-up while at the same time reducing its own military capabilities.

IMPLICATIONS FOR THE WEST

This article does not argue that civilization identities will replace all other identities, that nation states will disappear, that each civilization will become a single coherent political entity, that groups within a civilization will not conflict with and even fight each other. This paper does set forth the hypotheses that differences between civilizations are real and important; civilization-consciousness is increasing; conflict between civilizations will supplant ideological and other forms of conflict as the dominant global form of conflict; international relations, historically a game played out within Western civilization, will increasingly be de-Westernized and become a game in which non-Western civilizations are actors and not simply objects; successful political, security, and economic international institutions are more likely to develop within civilizations than across civiliza-tions; conflicts between groups in different civilizations will be more frequent, more sustained, and more violent than conflicts between groups in the same civ-ilization; violent conflicts between groups in different civilizations are the most likely and most dangerous source of escalation that could lead to global wars; the paramount axis of world politics will be the relations between "the West and the Rest"; the elites in some torn non-Western countries will try to make their coun-tries part of the West, but in most cases face major obstacles to accomplishing this; a central focus of conflict for the immediate future will be between the West and several Islamic–Confucian states.

This is not to advocate the desirability of conflicts between civilizations. It is to set forth descriptive hypotheses as to what the future may be like. If these are plausible hypotheses, however, it is necessary to consider their implications for Western policy. These implications should be divided between short-term advan-tage and long-term accommodation. In the short term it is clearly in the interest of the West to promote greater cooperation and unity within its own civilization, particularly between its European and North American components; to incorpo-rate into the West societies in Eastern Europe and Latin America whose cultures are close to those of the West; to promote and maintain cooperative relations with Russia and Japan; to prevent escalation of local inter-civilization conflicts into major inter-civilization wars; to limit the expansion of the military strength of Confucian and Islamic states; to moderate the reduction of Western military capa-bilities and maintain military superiority in East and Southwest Asia; to exploit differences and conflicts among Confucian and Islamic states; to support in other civilizations groups sympathetic to Western values and interests; to strengthen international institutions that reflect and legitimate Western interests and values and to promote the involvement of non-Western states in those institutions.

In the longer term other measures would be called for. Western civilization is both Western and modern. Non-Western civilizations have attempted to become modern without becoming Western. To date only Japan has fully succeeded in this quest. Non-Western civilizations will continue to attempt to acquire the wealth, technology, skills, machines, and weapons that are part of being modern. They will also attempt to reconcile this modernity with their traditional culture and values. Their economic and military strength relative to the West will increase.

Hence the West will increasingly have to accommodate these non-Western modern civilizations whose power approaches that of the West but whose values and interests differ significantly from those of the West. This will require the West to maintain the economic and military power necessary to protect its interests in relation to these civilizations. It will also, however, require the West to develop a more profound understanding of the basic religious and philosophical assumptions underlying other civilizations and the ways in which people in those civilizations see their interests. It will require an effort to identify elements of commonality between Western and other civilizations. For the relevant future, there will be no universal civilization, but instead a world of different civilizations, each of which will have to learn to coexist with the others.

NOTES

1. Murray Weidenbaum, *Greater China: The Next Economic Superpower?* St. Louis: Washington University Center for the Study of American Business, Contemporary Issues, Series 57, February 1993, pp. 2–3.

2. Bernard Lewis, "The Roots of Muslim Rage," *The Atlantic Monthly*, vol. 266, September 1990, p. 60; *Time*, June 15, 1992, pp. 24–28.

3. Archie Roosevelt, *For Lust of Knowing*, Boston: Little, Brown, 1988, pp. 332–33.

4. Almost invariably Western leaders claim they are acting on behalf of "the world community." One minor lapse occurred during the run-up to the Gulf War. In an interview on *Good Morning America*, Dec. 21, 1990, British Prime Minister John Major referred to the actions "the West" was taking against Saddam Hussein. He quickly corrected himself and subsequently referred to "the world community." He was, however, right when he erred.

5. Harry C. Triandis, *The New York Times*, Dec. 25, 1990, p. 41, and "Cross-Cultural Studies of Individualism and Collectivism," *Nebraska Symposium on Motivation*, vol. 37, 1989, pp. 41–133.

6. Kishore Mahbubani, "The West and the Rest," *The National Interest*, Summer 1992, pp. 3–13.

7. Sergei Stankevich, "Russia in Search of Itself," *The National Interest*, Summer 1992, pp. 47–51; Daniel Schneider, "A Russian Movement Rejects Western Tilt," *Christian Science Monitor*, Feb. 5, 1993, pp. 5–7.

8. Owen Harries has pointed out that Australia is trying (unwisely in his view) to become a torn country in reverse. Although it has been a full member not only of the West but also of the ABCA military and intelligence core of the West, its current leaders are in effect proposing that it defect from the West, redefine itself as an Asian country and cultivate close ties with its neighbors. Australia's future, they argue, is with the dynamic economies of East Asia. But, as I have suggested, close economic cooperation normally requires a common cultural base. In addition, none of the three conditions necessary for a torn country to join another civilization is likely to exist in Australia's case.

✗ NO
Despair, Defeatism, and Isolationism in American "Grand Strategy": The Seductive Convenience of Huntington's "Civilizational Clash" Thesis
DOUGLAS ROSS

Samuel Huntington's "clash of civilizations" thesis, first published in 1993 in the most favoured journal of the American foreign policy elite, *Foreign Affairs*, has been celebrated by some as the defining analytical paradigm for the post–Cold War era. But many others have castigated this analysis as little more than bizarrely reactionary political necromancy. The civilization clash thesis is neither. The fundamental argument is complex and intellectually defensible even though it is expressed in a deceptively simple and at times highly provocative fashion. Otherwise, Huntington's argument would not have received such extensive national and international attention. While the article's international readership has been considerable, its greatest impact was felt in the United States, where its seductive appeal to an American political elite weary of the burdens of the Cold War, frightened by the deterioration of civil society in the United States mainland, and apprehensive about the relative decline of American society in world affairs was all too ready to have its exit from global hegemony rationalized and legitimated. In brief, the original "clash" article and the related auxiliary writings in support of its principal themes[1] amount to an elaborate intellectual justification for a new era of retrenchment, isolationism, and conservative, nationalist intolerance in American foreign policy.

Huntington's message and the policy recommendations that flow from it constitute a threat to the process of fostering a consensus on international security and environmental reform among the world's major powers. Widespread acceptance of the "clash" thesis threatens to make identity politics the leitmotif of American and European foreign relations and would only likely worsen the swelling chorus of anti-immigration hysteria that has swept Western Europe and the United States in the 1990s.

In essence, Huntington's thought promotes a willful turning away from the broader liberal-internationalist tradition in American foreign policy. During the Cold War the northeastern Atlanticist establishment fought the Soviet bloc through what was for the most part a patient, farsighted application of the containment doctrine: expensive overseas troop deployments, a global alliance network, and an immensely expensive nuclear infrastructure were at the core of the American security response. In the economic dimension, American and other Western leaders kept Soviet "defensive" expansionism at bay through other critically important measures: constructing the GATT system of ever freer trade; promoting development assistance flows from North to South to speed the "great ascent" by the world's poorest; and more or less successfully wooing the non-aligned states into the emerging global market economy. Despite periodic deep differences in policy among the Europeans, North Americans, and Japanese, a stable and prosperous world order was created and the foundations for an authentic world society were laid.

Americans discovered the limits to their Cold War internationalism through the many divisive controversies involved in "extending" their nuclear deterrent protection to their allies, and still more through the tragic and costly exigencies of interventionary warfare in Asia. But by the 1970s, following the most critical watershed of the Cold War era—Sino-American rapprochement—the framework for international institutional cooperation was fully established. The IMF, the World Bank, the UN and its agencies, the OECD, and Cold War levels of foreign aid were all supported by the liberal wing of the American elite as instruments of enlightened leadership in what was portrayed (and experienced) as an epic, historical struggle against communist tyranny and imperial expansion. Americans did not see themselves as imperialistic, even if others did. To successive American administrations foreign military entanglements and the American version of "defensive" expansionism had been forced on a reluctant American nation that someday would happily return home.

That time has now arrived. With the Soviet threat vanquished, with the brief burst of American celebratory triumphalism now played out, American national security planners and political leaders have sought rationales for retrenchment, for sharing the burden of world security "management" with the Europeans and Japanese, so as to thereby reduce the direct expense of global management for the U.S. treasury. With the clash thesis, Huntington has provided a highly dubious and provocative policy framework that may unfortunately fill the conceptual-doctrinal void that exists at the heart of contemporary American foreign policy.

By predicting a world of intensifying "civilizational" and cultural conflicts over which the United States is said to be comparatively powerless, Huntington has blessed the sharp cuts in American Official Development Assistance (ODA) of the past fifteen years. If much of Asia and Islam are going to become "enemies" or at least rivals for world dominance, why help them? His analysis has endorsed American politico-strategic disengagement from Asia, and extended approval for a policy of economic confrontation with Japan.[2] If the world is going to disintegrate into "civilizational" blocs, why try to discourage regional conflicts far from one's own territorial domains? And more immediately Huntington has cheered on the imprudent, ill-considered enlargement of NATO so as to encompass what Huntington terms the "kin countries" of Central and Eastern Europe. The flock must be fully gathered into the protective security fold of Western Christendom. Finally, and more irresponsibly, he has consigned Africa's troubled and desperate millions to foreign policy irrelevance and international economic and ecological oblivion. Black Africa is after all only a "possible" civilization, in Huntington's view, and is of negligible politico-strategic consequence. So let them rot and perish in their un-Christian, animist anarchy.

Curiously, Huntington has counselled relative strategic and economic disengagement from a world where the balance of population and economic and industrial strength is shifting away from the "West." Forging ties to potential allies would make more sense, and indeed in *The Remaking of World Order* he qualified his isolationism by asserting that the United States and the "West" should try to woo the so-called "swing" civilizations of the Russians, Hindus, and Japanese (with an assigned probability of success in descending order).[3] More predictably he has urged the American elite to prepare for a more violent and dangerous 21st century by continuing to arm to the teeth. On that point the American political elite needs little persuasion. American defence spending is currently equal to the combined defence expenditures of the next eight countries (in order: Russia, Japan, France, Germany, U.K., China, Italy, and South Korea).[4] For fiscal year 1995 American defence spending was twenty-seven times greater than total defence expenditures by the six countries most commonly cited as probable enemies (Iraq, Iran, North Korea, Syria, Libya, and Cuba).[5]

In his major statement of the "clash" argument, Huntington claimed that he had formulated nothing less than a philosophical-methodological alternative to "realism"—the dominant intellectual approach in the field of international relations in the Anglo-American world.[6] He claimed further that his civilizational clash "evolutionary paradigm" will be a far better predictor of the incidence and origins of conflicts in the early 21st century than prevailing schools of thought in government and academia. The quest for power alone, he asserts, cannot explain international state behaviour; cultural/civilizational urges must be factored into the analysis to explain the probable shifts in world politics in the 21st century. Civilizational "imperatives" derived from religion, language, and shared cultural artifacts will shape the behaviour of states. Unlike most of the past four centuries, states, he argues, will not control and shape civilizations.[7]

With respect to this second claim, he may be correct, but not quite in the way he expects. To the extent that the American policy elite listens to and acts upon his analysis, Huntington's thesis may well be borne out by events. For while the United States has declined relatively in power vis-à-vis Europe, Japan, and China (a point Huntington emphasizes at every opportunity), nevertheless it still possesses sufficient power to be the dominant shaper of world events for the next two decades. If American leadership accepts the profoundly conservative, pessimistic message purveyed by Huntington, the "clash" thesis might well become a self-fulfilling prophecy. If the United States were to decide to discriminate on the basis of alleged "civilizational" affiliations, imitation by other leading powers would no doubt spread, if only for reactive, defensive purposes. In such a context, global economic and political-security cooperation would most assuredly begin to break down.

In one respect Huntington's analysis is quintessentially American: it plays up to American frustration. A large part of the appeal of the "clash" thesis to national security planners derives from the residual but still onerous burden of Cold War alliance leadership and American resentment concerning "free riders" like Japan and Germany, who, in the view of many Americans, have exploited the U.S. treasury for the last thirty-five years. Now the Europeans are compounding this record of neglect and ingratitude by insisting on a post–Cold War "peace dividend." With the marginal cost of U.S. military deployments in and near the Persian/Arab Gulf at between $20 and 30 billion (US) per year, the cost of "protecting" Japanese and European fossil fuel supplies (and Israeli security) is increasingly irritating to American foreign policy planners. According to many annoyed American policy analysts, U.S. aerial intervention in Bosnia in 1995, which bombed the Serbs into accepting the Dayton Accord's armistice, almost did not occur: only Bill Clinton's need for a major foreign policy success in the run-up to the presidential elections of 1996 led to yet another American rescue of Western Europe. According to these disgruntled American burden bearers, the end of such self-sacrifice by the United States may be at hand. Any replay of internecine warfare in Bosnia or Iraqi aggression without a vastly increased military commitment by the Europeans might well see the United States refrain from action altogether, leaving the Europeans to defend their own interests—if they can.[8]

Huntington's clash thesis speaks to this frustration and world-weariness by implying that "civilizational" introversion is now both intellectually legitimate and politically and strategically desirable. The era of extensive American global power projection capability, with its massive and human costs, is drawing to a close in Huntington's schema. As the United States makes this transition to a new world of cautious, almost introverted, "grand strategy," it need not concern itself with genocide in Rwanda or Iraq, with tyranny and oppression in East Timor, Tibet, and Burma, or with the balance of military power in the South China Sea. Gone too is any deep concern for global institutions under the UN's direction, or for key pillars of international security such as the Nuclear Non-Proliferation Treaty regime. Arms control and disarmament are thought be more or less a hopeless cause. Trans-Atlantic civilizational "solidarity" will be the primary focus of foreign policy. The United States will turn its back on the quest for any "universal" set of values and norms for international behaviour. Westerners are advised to hunker down in their civilizational lifeboat and prepare for stormy weather.

For Huntington, the United States ought to move from a policy of global reach to one of protective "civilizational" crouch. Americans are being urged to stay at home, and therefore out of the "crossfire" of any future regional wars that might involve nuclear, chemical, or biological weapons. Huntington at various points implies that the proliferation of weapons of mass destruction in unstoppable. He asserts repeatedly that a global human rights regime is unattainable given deep "civilizational" differences about such concepts. The Sinic–Islamic "connection" (referred to as the Islamic–Confucian connection in the 1993 article) will be ever freer to pursue expansionary, assertive policies threatening all their neighbours— particularly on "Islam's bloody borders."[9] Although he is a bit ambivalent about this, Huntington finally predicts that the Japanese will be left to fend for themselves. They will have to pay far more for their own security and eventually will fall under the sway of the new regionally dominant leaders in Beijing. Huntington's blunt hostility to the Japanese demonstrated in his writings of the early 1990s was muted by 1996—possibly based on a quiet sense of satisfaction that America's economic threat from Japan was going to evaporate as the Japanese fell victim to the tender mercies of Asian hierarchical control by the butchers of Tiananmen.

Huntington paints a bleak and disturbing picture of the 21st century. But it is a perspective that is nevertheless infused with elements of traditional American optimism. While he can admit the grave challenge posed by the uncontrolled growth in population of the poor countries (and correlates youthful age structures of populations with "civilizational" bellicosity), Huntington has strongly resisted defining the next century in terms of a looming environmental and economic crisis. He in no way accepts the futurist scenarios of environmentally concerned analysts who foresee a century dominated by the politics of resource scarcity, famines, global warming, ozone depletion, toxic waste contamination of food and water, and unwanted mass migrations—in short, generalized environmental crisis. Instead, Huntington holds fast to the ideologically inculcated optimism of American liberalism: economic progress will not be stopped in the West or elsewhere; science, technology, and market economics can conquer, if given the chance, virtually all problems of famine, resource scarcity, and pollution; world politics in the 21st century will not be confronted by the limits to growth. In short, in this respect Huntington is a typical American technological cornucopianist.

The most critical foreign policy conclusions and recommendations that flow from the "civilizational clash" premises may be summarized as follows:

1. The United States should distance itself from past security commitments to countries in Asia—particularly Japan—while narrowing the American security umbrella to cover only "kin countries" in Western and Central Europe. Russia and much of Ukraine should be excluded. NATO must remain a collective defence treaty and not be transformed into a regional collective security organization.

2. In the long term, the United States, as the leading "core state" of the "West," should work to develop a cooperative relationship with the Russian and Hindu "civilizations," so that the bellicose and expansionary forces of

Islamic and Sinic societies can be contained and inhibited. Dual containment against Iraq and Iran is to be transformed into dual containment of the Sinic–Islamic (formerly Confucian–Islamic) threat.

3. American scientific and industrial leadership and military superiority should be maintained or widened over all other states for as long as economically sustainable—the better to safeguard and promote world order consonant with American and Western values.[10] The corollary to this idea is that there should be a better division of labour between Europeans and North Americans to ensure such scientific and industrial leadership in the techniques and technologies of war.

4. In future, the United States should intervene abroad very reluctantly and most selectively to advance American interests where and when required, and to contain intercivilizational "fault line wars" where appropriate. No unconditional political or strategic ties should be created except with civilizational "kin countries."[11] For Huntington, "promiscuous intervention" would only be a waste of resources and make relations with the other leading civilizations needlessly difficult.[12] In his view, an "abstention rule" under which "core states" will "abstain from intervention in conflicts in other civilizations is the first requirement of peace in a multicivilizational, multipolar world".[13]

5. The United States must do what it can to restore and safeguard the cultural, linguistic, and sociopolitical heritage of the West against subversive forces from other civilizations that threaten to reduce the coherence of its values, the stability of its core institutions, and, ultimately, its very survival.[14] Assimilationism should be a paramount objective of Western governments; multiculturalism is to be abhorred. "A multicivilizational United States will not be the United States; it will be the United Nations,"[15] and therefore, in Huntington's view, would lack coherence, a "cultural core," and survivability.

6. NATO, as "the security organization of Western civilization" whose "primary purpose is to defend and preserve that civilization," ought to be supported strongly by the United States, and all European societies culturally oriented toward the West should be brought into the organization "but not countries that have historically been primarily Muslim or Orthodox."[16] The Visegrad states and the Baltics are seen to be prime candidates for admission. (Expulsion of "Orthodox" Greece and Islamic Turkey is not discussed, although such action would seem to be a logical corollary.)

7. The frontiers of North America should be sealed against uncontrolled migration from countries belonging to the Latin American, African, Islamic, or Asian "civilizations"—"as every major European country has done and as the United States is beginning to do"—while "ensuring the assimilation into Western culture of the immigrants who are admitted."[17]

The temperature under the "melting pot" of American society would be raised. Intolerance would be officially embraced under the guise of cultural and "civilizational" protection.

8. The United States should support arms control and disarmament as a way of advancing American and Western interests by slowing the diffusion of advanced weapons technology to the rival "civilizations of tomorrow"— especially to those "Islamic" and Sinic states that are hostile to the United States or Europe. The "universalism" of past arms control measures, then, is to be jettisoned, and a blunt advocacy of arms control and disarmament as a way of containing the growth of rival centres of military power is to be publicly embraced by the "West."[18] The ABM Treaty preventing nationwide defence against ballistic missile attack is rejected as a Cold War anachronism.[19]

Despite Huntington's nominal renunciation of isolationism and unilateralism,[20] his practical policy conclusions are hardly reflective of a middle ground between disengagement and global interventionism to which he lays claim. Certainly in comparison with the approaches recommended by Paul Kennedy, Huntington's message calls for a very substantial and dangerous retreat into "civilizational" isolationism at a time when, according to Kennedy and many other writers, the world can least afford a collapse of international solidarity and cooperative reform of global institutions.[21]

Whatever one may make of Huntington's overall diagnosis and prescriptions for American international security policy, he is almost certainly correct in asserting that the broad foreign policy choices Americans made during the 1990s will have an impact on the international environment comparable in scale to the consequences of choices made by American leaders in 1898 and 1945.[22] At this the high tide of American hegemonic power in the international system, what the American elite chooses may well set the pattern of world politics for decades to come—just as American isolationism in the 1920s and 1930s set the world on course for World War II. Huntington's call for civilizationally "rallying," and for what might be termed "protective disengagement" by the United States and other "Western" countries, is in fact a threatening abdication of strategic leadership and political responsibility.

Huntington's critics are of course legion and many of their most telling comments deserve close attention. While space precludes an exhaustive review of the detailed criticisms,[23] a number of criticisms deserve statement or reiteration. Many commentators have disputed the "civilizational" categories that he has selected, suggesting that no such entities exist and are unlikely ever to coalesce. Islam, for example, is composed of many nation-states and, as Fouad Ajami asserted, nation-states run "civilizations," not the other way around. State structures have gone through four centuries of adaptation and change and are unlikely to disappear anytime soon—liberal pluralist speculative musings notwith-standing.[24] Despite being a nominal champion of the diffusion of liberal democratic process in the world—across cultures—Huntington's "clash" writings suggest that a "Fortress West" concept should be the guiding light of American foreign policy. Huntington is thus preaching an exclusionary approach to foreign policy, and is ranged directly opposite those who support "democratic enlargement" and a responsible exercise of international leadership (per Anthony Lake's formulation[25] while he was Clinton's first-term Assistant for National Security Affairs). And as George Modelski has noted, Huntington's approach owes less to Arnold Toynbee's optimistic reading of history and much more to the pessimism of Oswald Spengler. Furthermore, Huntington's notion of "civilizations" at war with each other has no historical precedent to back up such speculative musing.[26] Throughout recorded history, and in particular during the last 400 years, wars have been fought by nations or states, but never by "civilizations."[27] Finally, Huntington's analysis, while concurring in predictions by other futurists of a shift in the global balance of population, economic strength, and power away from Europe and North America, artfully but dubiously avoids the entire question of imminent global ecological and economic crises that will flow directly from the consequences of excessive and destabilizing population increase coupled with the cancerous spread of unregulated industrial capitalism.

Speculatively, one may attribute the success of Huntington's writings in attracting a large audience to widespread psychological denial in the American policy community who are ideologically and culturally predisposed to accept the tenets of "technological cornucopianism;" the deeply neoconservative tenor of American national politics may have more to do with the negative reception accorded to the ecological pessimism embodied in writings by Kaplan, Homer-Dixon, and Kennedy. Much of Huntington's popularity may derive strongly from the fact that his "clash" thesis and associated policy recommendations are remarkably free of implications that might necessitate major adjustments to current American defence spending or foreign policy.

HUNTINGTON'S BLINDNESS TO ENVIRONMENTAL CRISIS

Is the global environment likely to be able to accept the sustained recent growth rates in the industrial sectors of China, India, and other rapidly modernizing states in the global South? Huntington premises his forecast of new civilizational realpolitik on such sustainable growth. But certainly since the Brundtland report of 1987 and the data amassed for the 1992 Rio Conference, grave doubts have been cast on such a rosy scenario. China's future industrial growth is to be based on exploitation of its massive coal reserves. Such growth in fossil fuel burning will overwhelm whatever progress the existing northern states will be able to make in reducing greenhouse gas emissions. With the "holes" in the ozone layer worsening steadily at both poles (extending ever farther into the mid-latitudes), with global average temperatures continuing to climb (and recent evidence of potentially catastrophic warming in Antarctica), the imperative of reaching new binding (not merely hortatory) agreements on the emission of dangerous atmospheric gases is becoming ever clearer. How could this be accomplished in the world of competing, aggressive civilizations envisioned by Huntington?

THE THREAT OF UNCONTROLLED MIGRATION: WHAT STRATEGY WILL WORK?

How feasible is it to try to seal the borders of the "West" against uncontrolled migration induced by ecological collapse and environmental crisis? Surely the more sensible way to proceed is to try to help the peoples, nations, and states most threatened to cope with the challenges of worsening water scarcity, deforestation, desertification, and famine. Help in solving these crises through renewed development assistance surely makes far more sense than terminating all involvement in "alien" civilizational domains. Tangibly demonstrating the sympathy of the Western peoples by providing relief for the most desperate citizens of planet Earth is, one would think, a strategy much more likely to help bridge ethnolinguistic differences and reduce the risk of "intercivilizational" warfare. Consigning the so-called "failed societies" of Africa to misery, collapse, and death is a counsel of despair and deep moral confusion. It would be an outrageously callous act similar in kind and far worse in degree than the casually vicious abandonment of the Irish by the English during the potato famines of the 19th century.

Another prestigious American political scientist and a colleague of Huntington's at Harvard, Thomas C. Schelling, takes a far different view of the human prospect. The global condition is analogous to the condition of the peoples of South Africa under apartheid. For Schelling, the implications of widening income disparities, population growth, and the attempted migration by the poor to the rich states are deeply disturbing.[28] In his view new collective institutions for global governance are urgently needed. For Schelling, the "depressing" central truth of the human condition was summarized as follows:

> We live in a world that is one-fifth rich and four-fifths poor; the rich are segregated into the rich countries and the poor into the poor countries; the rich are predominantly lighter skinned and the poor darker skinned; most of the poor live in "homelands" that are physically remote, often separated by oceans and great distances from the rich. Migration on any great scale is impermissible. There is no systematic redistribution of income. While there is ethnic strife among the well-to-do, the strife is vicious and destructive among the poor.... we have defined national security as "preserving the U.S. as a free nation with our fundamental institutions and values intact."

"Values" is a wonderfully ambiguous word. I believe it must include what we *possess* as well as what we *appreciate*. It includes our material standard of living. We protect those institutions and values by, among other things, protecting our national boundaries.[29]

Regrettably but realistically, Schelling expressed virtually no hope at all that the American government could be expected to "play a leading role in elevating population growth to the status of a major threat to international peace and security." American "values," he wryly noted, are sufficiently "elastic" to accommodate a doubling of world population over the next two decades.[30] Nor is the United States likely to take any significant role in curbing CO_2 emissions—something that Schelling clearly views as critically important. The international policy activity on environmental reform during the 1990s, he believed, would be spent in erecting institutions, and not in achieving or even consensually setting significant goals for dealing with incipient climatic change, pollution, resource depletion, and the population crisis. Furthermore, he detected no political willingness among Americans to prevent further decreases in development assistance.[31] And such a shirking of commitment will occur at a time when the problem of climate change could be dealt with only by increasing Official Development Assistance (ODA) to "several times the magnitude of all current aid to the developing world."[32]

Schelling has a more candid and accurate assessment of our collective situation. There is no sign on the political horizon of any willingness by American political leaders or American public opinion to share the wealth. Greed and the protection of privilege seem to be at the root of our collective inability to deal with the compounded crises of late industrial capitalism.

An even more candid and troubling warning about the fate of the world and the inadequacies of American policy was published by historian and futurist Paul Kennedy. Kennedy and co-author Matthew Connelly have sketched out a grim warning of literal engulfment of the rich states by tens of millions of poor migrants by 2025 unless the rich northern states change their self-indulgent ways and act soon to mitigate the deteriorating conditions in the less developed countries (LDCs).[33] Kennedy and Connelly deplored the emerging "siege mentality" of the northern countries who are now frantically trying to reassert control of their borders. They also criticize the slashing of ODA flows of any consequence from the United States and other OECD countries, and the failure to redirect the scientific expertise developed during the Cold War toward creating pollution-free energy sources (solar and photovoltaic power). Kennedy and Connelly are, to say the least, cautious in their expressions of hope that a revolution in foreign policy thinking can be effected, noting that "we will have to convince a suspicious public and cynical politicians that a serious package of reform measures is not fuzzy liberal idealism but a truer form of realism." The climate of the time in the

United States is not propitious, they conclude. It may take "the collapse of continents rather than single states" before the peoples of the rich states can be awakened from their materialistic, foolish, self-indulgent, neoconservatively blinkered torpor.[34]

Huntington's analysis, of course, contributes nothing useful to the effort to forge a renewed, reformed commitment to addressing this troubled planet's worst ills. Indeed, it is only likely to worsen matters by reinforcing an ostrich-like, stay-the-course mentality in Washington and other NATO European capitals.

Even if steel walls can be built from Texas to California, the control of illegal migration will do nothing to block the entry of dangerous infectious diseases—a threat about which Huntington says nothing. Laurie Garrett has stressed that the arrival of the borderless world for business has created an identical condition for infectious diseases.[35] As does Ivan Head, she emphasizes the extraordinarily heightened risks of both new and mutated "old" infectious diseases. While the exploding populations of the poor states cannot migrate, bacterial and viral diseases that have been flushed from the newly penetrated forests can migrate easily. And in the appallingly unsanitary, crowded shantytown conditions of the new suburban slums around the major cities of the LDC zone, old diseases can rapidly mutate.[36] Inadequate or dangerously incomplete use of antibiotic drugs by the new very poor slum dwellers compounds the problem by helping to accelerate the evolution of drug-resistant strains of various diseases.

Diseases are therefore likely to become a great unifier of rich and poor—however distasteful and frightening that prospect may be for the affluent and those who hope to promote "civilizational" apartheid. "Lifeboat" fantasies by the rich about this problem are hopelessly naive. Over a million people a day crossed international borders each day during 1996. Surveillance at airports or other ports of entry is useless; the incubation of "hot" viruses is usually too long for readily identifiable symptoms to show up in infected travellers.[37] With respect to the incidence of infectious diseases in both the rich and poor zones, public health is thus fully, globally interdependent. And of course the opportunities for ingenious and inexpensive application of diseases to some of the manifold causes promoted by international terrorist networks is growing. The use of sarin nerve gas on the Tokyo subway in March 1995 may be the precursor of other such attacks. As Garrett noted:

> One hundred kilograms of a lethal sporulating organism such as anthrax spread over Washington, D.C., by a crop duster could cause well over two million deaths. Enough anthrax spores to kill five to six million people could be loaded into a taxi and pumped out its tailpipe as it meandered through Manhattan. Vulnerability to terrorist attacks, as well as to the natural emergence of disease, increases with population density.[38]

THE ABANDONMENT OF INTERNATIONAL ARMS CONTROL AND DISARMAMENT EXCEPT AS A TOOL FOR INTERCIVILIZATIONAL WARFARE

How rational is it for American policymakers to walk away from a generation of success in negotiating nonproliferation regimes for offensive nuclear weapons, horrendously expensive, technologically dubious, and strategically destabilizing missile defences, and chemical and biological terror weapons? For Huntington, the game is apparently already lost and the horses have fled the barn. Is such pessimism justifiable when over 185 state governments have signed the Nuclear Non-Proliferation Treaty? When the treaty has been converted to a commitment of indefinite duration in 1995? When the NPT conversion success was followed a year later by the successful conclusion of a Comprehensive Test Ban Treaty (held in abeyance only by the lingering dissent of India, but being observed by all the declared weapon states)? Surely the quest to eliminate such weapons of mass destruction should be at the heart of any search for authentic "commonalities" that Huntington allegedly supports. There is no convincing evidence or argument in Huntington's work to support the assumption that an emerging civilizational consciousness around the world (granting for the moment that it will coalesce) will in fact produce war.

SALVATION THROUGH THE SPREADING "DEMOCRATIC PEACE"?

Huntington argues that the evolving globalized economy will speed the withering away of many state capabilities in coming decades and that states are going to decline if not disappear. But are all states at risk of collapse and withering away (a proposition asserted but not substantiated in Huntington's "clash" writings), or are only authoritarian regimes at risk? For the first time in human history more than a majority of the world's populations are now living under more or less authentically democratic governance. Dictatorships have continued to fall on every continent. As a result, the growing academic literature that asserts that democratic states do not war with other states also perceived to be democratic has taken on new significance. Can we plausibly hope that the spread of democratic governance will eventually make war as unacceptable and as unthinkable as slavery, or duelling—or smoking?

This theory of the democratic peace has been incorporated into a broader theory of social and political evolution by Gwynne Dyer, who has argued that the communications revolution, rising literacy worldwide, the erosion and disintegration of patriarchy, and the collapse of militarism and the war system are all intimately interconnected.[39] Without delving too deeply into his argument, suffice it to say that he sees the advent of literacy and the communications revolution (television and other forms of rapid communication) as causing the collapse of authoritarian rule. Since the advent of urban civilization some five or six millennia ago, states have had to rule through terror and repression. Part of the mechanism for instituting centralized state control and viable armed communities was the almost universal subjugation of women. The communications revolution has changed all that. Nations of hundreds of millions can now make decisions collectively in ways that were physically impossible before the rise of literacy and the development of mass communication technologies. Accordingly, patriarchy is collapsing throughout the most educated countries. And so too is the willingness to go to war. As American military affairs analyst Edward Luttwak put it, we seem to have entered the era of the "no dead war": the prospect of any level of "friendly" casualties is enough to dissuade Western governments from thoughts of military intervention.

From Dyer's point of view, it would be profoundly mistaken to assume that war and civilization confrontations are the inevitable, unavoidable prospect for the 21st century. Quite the contrary—if leadership, foresight, and a spirit of realistic accommodation can be fostered between North and South. What is ultimately needed is a "grand compromise" between the rich, demographically stable northern countries and the poor, demographically exploding southern states. The compromise will necessarily entail a severe cut to the material standard of living of people in the rich northern states. No aspect of life will be unscathed. Everyone will be affected by:

- heavy taxes on automobiles and transportation;

- stiff carbon taxes on all other uses of fossil fuels for space heating or industrial processes;

- imposition of other appropriate "green taxes" to ensure the sustainability of renewable resources and the minimization of pollution;

- an internationally agreed upon and domestically legislated limited of something like one car for every ten people in each national population (to be kept on at least until solar or hydrogen propulsion systems are standard equipment);

- universal rationing of energy, meat, water, and possibly jobs among the world's population;

- job sharing and a legislated reduction of the work week to four days, to prevent social upheaval in a time of ever scarcer permanent employment.

Correspondingly, because of the fruits of such reforms, the standard of living of the poorest nations in the world would continue to rise and eventually converge with the level of material comfort enjoyed by the rich northerners—but within exactly the same resource consumption and pollution control constraints as applied to the wealthy. In Dyer's view, such sharing of the pain of conservation and preservation of the natural environment and the human habitat is unavoidable. And it is not charity. As he puts it bluntly: "this is not morality; it is the logic of survival." The alternative—a world without collective agreement and enlightened self-restraint—would be a global domain with three billion cars, permanently brown skies, a destabilized atmosphere and climate, and a dying biosphere: in other words, collective suicide. Dyer does not see salvation as guaranteed, but neither does he see disaster as certain. A global consensus may not emerge, he notes, until after some major environmental catastrophe occurs—possibly in the South, but more likely it will be needed in the North so as to generate the appropriate degree of sacrifice by the rich. The simultaneous loss of Miami, much of Holland, Venice, Cairo, Bangkok, and Calcutta to global warming—induced flooding might do the trick. The great compromise may take decades to achieve, but come it must. The exceptional affluence of the richest countries will have to be sacrificed, but, Dyer notes, even the reduced standard of living will be light years beyond what was experienced by royalty as late as the 18th century. So why moan about it? As Dyer put it: "It's been a great ride, but now it's time to grow up." If we do not, then exploring alternative scenarios for "the end of the world," certainly the end of civilization as we have come to understand it, will take on new relevance.

CONCLUSION

Huntington's work is challenging and provocative, but it is finally not persuasive. The West is not monolithic, and neither are the other "civilizations" that Huntington has attempted to reify. International economic trends are changing the face of the planet, but so too is the rise of the global poor to political articulateness. They will not be silenced and manipulated any longer. Only the foolishly shortsighted would attempt to ignore them.

The 21st century is likely to be all about the politics of global sharing and redistribution; if it is not, then we may have to revisit the idea of a coming clash—and impending global catastrophe. Perversely, at a time when the American government may be more open to the sharing of leadership burdens and international security responsibilities because of domestic difficulties, leadership in the governments allied to the United States are virtually opting out of any effective contribution to collective defence, collective security, and international development. By so doing they are only likely to accentuate the tendency in the United States toward unilateral decisionmaking and the sort of de facto isolationism that Samuel Huntington is pressing upon them. By sitting back and waiting for omnipotent America to make security decisions for them, they are at risk of validating Huntington's exclusionary approach to foreign policy through their very passivity. What is sorely needed among the NATO countries is political leadership in the great struggle for development and survival that will certainly be our collective lot in the 21st century. The end of war, militaristic oligarchy, and the subjection of women is generations away for most of the world's population even if one were to believe in the irresistible transforming power of literacy and mass communications.

The reality of the 1990s is one of unavoidable interdependence among the peoples of the world. Strategic and economic insecurity flow automatically from this reality. The rich cannot isolate themselves from the pain and suffering of the "wretched of the earth." To attempt to do so in pursuit of some truncated version of "civilizational" realpolitik would drastically increase the risk of an ultimate disaster for the human species. American analysts are at risk of losing their bearings in trying to grapple with the magnitude and diversity of the security challenges that have been made so starkly plain in the post-Soviet era. Fear has clouded their judgment and their ability to act. In the face of the immense challenges we now confront, the advice of Ivan Head and Pierre Trudeau is apposite: "Our future as humans will be influenced immeasurably by our definition of community and our acceptance of the common destiny of our species.... Conscience is much more than a guide for human behaviour; at the conclusion of the twentieth century, it is the elevated—and only certain—path towards the survival of civilization."[40] A hypothetical and speculative "clash of civilizations" must not dominate our thoughts about international security in the next century, but rather a determination to forge ever broader common standards of civilized and responsible behaviour for the troubled decades ahead.

NOTES

1. See Huntington's *The Clash of Civilizations and the Remaking of World Order* (New York: Simon and Schuster, 1996) for his full development of the argument (cited hereafter as *The Remaking of World Order*). Also relevant is his response to critics of the original article found at "If Not Civilizations, What? Paradigms of the Post–Cold War World," *Foreign Affairs*, vol. 72 n. 5 (November/December 1993). An additional article based on material from the 1996 book may be found in "The West Unique, Not Universal," *Foreign Affairs*, vol. 75 n. 6 (November/December 1996), 28–46; cited hereafter as Huntington, "West Not Universal."

2. In an article published before the "clash of civilizations" essay, Huntington argued bluntly that the American government should act to contain the growth of Japanese economic power and political influence. In his view the Japanese leadership had in effect been practising "economic warfare" against the United States for decades in pursuing dominance in key high-technology, high-value-added industries, in racking up financially destabilizing trade surpluses year after year, in systematically accumulating extensive ownership positions in U.S. industry, and by buying direct political influence in the U.S. electoral system. See "Why International Primacy Matters," *International Security*, vol. 17 n. 4 (Spring 1993), esp. pp. 73–81. In an earlier article, Huntington denounced the Japanese elite because of their threats to American interests, economic and geostrategic. He argued that "economic measures will be central to dealing with the Japanese challenge ... not only foreign and defense policy but also domestic policy on the budget, taxes, subsidies, industrial policy, science and technology,

child care, education." See "America's Changing Strategic Interests," *Survival*, vol. 33 n. 1 (January/February 1991), as reprinted in Richard K. Betts, *Conflict after the Cold War* (New York: Macmillan, 1994), p. 518.

3. *The Remaking of World Order*, pp. 241–45.

4. *The Military Balance 1996/97* (London: International Institute for Strategic Studies, 1996).

5. Seymour Melman, "Preparing for War (Against Ourselves)," *New York Times*, 26 June 1995.

6. See *The Remaking of World Order*, pp. 33–39.

7. Curiously, by the end of his book, Huntington engages in repeated speculation about the emerging regional power balances as the preeminent civilizational "core states" (apparently the United States and China only) engineer alliances and strategic collaboration with the weaker "swing" civilizations (Hindu, Japanese, and Russian). In short, he sketches out an only modestly amended balance-of-power system. Realism, it would seem, will live on. See *The Remaking of World Order*, pp. 240–45 (esp. the diagram on p. 245).

8. According to David Gompert, editor of an influential RAND Corporation report, *America and Europe: A Partnership for a New Era* (Cambridge University Press, 1997), the strategic status quo in which the United States pays a vastly disproportionate share of alliance security costs "can't last. U.S. public and political opinion won't stand for it. Remember, Bosnia was a close call. The crunch in the U.S. could come tomorrow if there's a crisis in the Persian Gulf and the Europeans duck. As an alliance we are living on borrowed time." As quoted in Martin Walker, "Home Truths for the White House," *Guardian Weekly*, 9 March 1997. Gompert has declared elsewhere that "the American public would rather share world leadership than fully bear its costs," or more simply, that "national power is 'out' and standard of living is 'in'." See "Sharing the Burdens of Global Security," *Occasional Paper 1* (Washington: Stimson Center/Overseas Development Council, August 1996), p. 10.

9. *The Remaking of World Order*, pp. 254–58.

10. "Why International Primacy Matters," pp. 70–71 and 82–83. Huntington wrote: "If the United States is unable to maintain security in the world's trouble spots, no other single country or combination of countries is likely to provide a substitute" (p. 82). Military superiority underwritten by continuing economic hegemony is clearly essential to perpetuating a constructive role for the world's most universalizing state. With the death of the USSR, Huntington argued, the United States is left as "the only major power whose national identity is defined by a set of universal political and economic values ... liberty, democracy, equality, private property, and markets" (p. 82). In the post–Cold War era, moreover, arms control has ceased to be a mechanism for fostering great-power détente and instead "the primary objective of arms control is to prevent the development by non-Western societies of military capabilities that could threaten Western interests." See "Clash of Civilizations", p. 46.

11. Huntington, "Clash of Civilizations," p. 49. Huntington specifically enumerates a goal for "the West" of limiting "the expansion of the military strength of Confucian and Islamic states" and maintaining Western "military superiority in the East and Southwest Asia."

12. As he noted in his most recent article: "As Asian and Muslim civilizations begin to assert the relevance of their cultures, Westerners will come to appreciate the connec-

tion between universalism and imperialism and to see the virtues of a pluralistic world.... The time has come for the West to abandon the illusion of universality and to promote the strength, coherence, and vitality of its civilizations. The *interests of the West are not served by promiscuous intervention into the disputes of other peoples.*" As in "West Not Universal," p. 41.

13. *The Remaking of World Order*, p. 316.

14. The promotion of "greater cooperation and unity within its own civilization" is seen to be crucial for the West, in particular deepening relations between the North American and Western European branches of this cultural complex. "Clash of Civilizations," pp. 48–49. Huntington wrote in a later article: "Maintaining the unity of the West, however, is essential to slowing the decline of Western influence in world affairs.... United, the West will remain a formidable presence on the international scene; divided, it will be prey to the efforts of non-Western states to exploit its internal differences by offering short-term gains to some Western countries at the price of long-term losses for all Western countries. The peoples of the West, in Benjamin Franklin's phrase, must hang together or most assuredly they will hang separately." As in Huntington, "West Not Universal," p. 44.

15. *The Remaking of World Order*, p. 206.

16. Huntington, "West Not Universal," p. 45. Russia and Ukraine would clearly be barred under the criterion for membership—contrary to Bill Clinton's statement on this issue at the 1997 Helsinki summit.

17. Huntington, "West Not Universal," p. 45.

18. Huntington, "Clash," p. 46.

19. *The Remaking of World Order*, p. 309.

20. Huntington, "West Not Universal," p. 46.

21. Paul Kennedy, *Preparing for the Twenty-First Century* (Toronto: HarperCollins, 1993).

22. Huntington, "America's Changing Strategic Interests," p. 520.

23. An initial set of criticisms may be found in comments by Fouad Ajami, Kishore Mahbubani, et al. in "Responses to Samuel P. Huntington's 'The Clash of Civilizations,'" *Foreign Affairs*, vol. 72 n. 4 (September/October 1993).

24. On the demise of the state and government as one possible future for North America, see David Elkins, *Beyond Sovereignty: Territory and Political Economy in the Twenty-First Century* (Toronto: University of Toronto Press, 1995).

25. Lake's views may be found in "Confronting Backlash States," *Foreign Affairs*, vol. 73 n. 2 (March/April 1994), pp. 45–55. He calls for "a genuine and responsible effort, over time, to protect American strategic interests, stabilize the international system and enlarge the community of nations committed to democracy, free markets and peace" (p. 55).

26. Modelski to the Pacific North West Colloquium on International Security seminar, University of Washington, in reply to lecture by Samuel Huntington, October 24, 1993.

27. As stressed by Ajami, "Responses," pp. 2–3, and Modelski, *ibid.*

28. See T.C. Schelling, "The Global Dimension," in Graham Allison and Gregory F. Treverton, *Rethinking America's Security* (New York, London: American Assembly/Council on Foreign Relations, W.W. Norton, 1992), pp. 196–210.

29. Schelling, "Global Dimension," p. 200. It is noteworthy that Gwynne Dyer began his *Human Race* series by highlighting South Africa as a microcosm of global reconciliation.

30. Schelling, "The Global Dimension," p. 202.

31. Schelling, "The Global Dimension," pp. 206–9.

32. Schelling, "The Global Dimension," p. 210.

33. Matthew Connelly and Paul Kennedy, "Must It Be the West against the Rest?" *Atlantic Monthly*, December 1994, 61–84; cited hereafter as "West against Rest?"

34. Connelly and Kennedy, "West against Rest?" p. 84.

35. Laurie Garrett, "The Return of Infectious Disease," *Foreign Affairs*, vol. 75 n. 1 (January/February 1996), pp. 66–79; and Garrett, *The Coming Plague: Newly Emerging Diseases in a World Out of Balance.*

36. Garrett, "Return of Infectious Disease," p. 71.

37. For an elaboration of the risk of the rapid, uncontrolled worldwide spread of "hot" viruses (those with no cure and a fatality rate in excess of 20 to 90 percent), see Richard Preston, *The Hot Zone* (New York: Random House, 1993). As Preston noted: "A hot virus from the rain forest lives within a twenty-four-hour plane flight from every city on earth. All of the earth's cities are connected by a web of airline routes. The web is a network. Once a virus hits the net, it can shoot anywhere in a day—Paris, Tokyo, New York, Los Angeles, wherever planes fly" (pp. 11–12). Civil aircraft at international airports are excellent means for spreading diseases given the dry recycled air on the planes and the congestion in the airports.

38. Garrett, "Return of Infectious Disease," p. 76.

39. See Gwynne Dyer's four-part film production *The Human Race* (Montreal: National Film Board of Canada/Green Lion Productions, 1994).

40. Ivan Head and Pierre Trudeau, *The Canadian Way: Shaping Canada's Foreign Policy, 1968–1984* (Toronto: McClelland and Stewart, 1995), pp. 318–19.

Postscript

The publication of Huntington's article and his subsequent book elicited a broad range of reactions. Many welcomed the focus on cultural analysis and the suggestion that large cultural units, not states, are becoming the new actors of international politics. At the same time many disagreed with Huntington's pessimistic view that the rising significance of cultural factors will necessarily lead to violence and conflict. In fact, writers like Robert Cox and Richard Falk, cited below, are concerned that Huntington's thesis may be used to tool for further exclusion of groups already feeling marginalized from the West.

However, not everyone accepted Huntington's focus on civilizational forces as a force in international politics. Fouad Ajami, writing in *Foreign Affairs*, criticized Huntington for underestimating the extent to which the concept of the state, along with the forces of modernization and secularism, has been internalized throughout the world. Ajami warns against assigning too much weight to the revival of fundamentalist religions or "detours into tradition." In the face of growing economic competitiveness, "men want Sony, not soil." In such a world, Ajami contends, the interests of states remain primary. "Civilization does not control states, states control civilizations. In testing Huntington's argument, it is useful to take several recent conflicts and ask to what extent his thesis is useful for understanding the nature of these conflicts.

Infotrac Keyword Search

"clash" + "civilizations"

Suggested Additional Readings

Ajami, Fouad. "The Summoning," *Foreign Affairs* (September/October 1993): 2–9.

Cox, Robert. "Civilizations: Encounters and Transformations." *Studies in Political Economy*, 47 (Summer 1995): 7–27.

Falk, Richard. "False Universalism and the Geopolitics of Exclusion: The Case of Islam," *Third World Quarterly* 18, no. 1 (1997): 7–23.

Huntington, Samuel. *The Clash of Civilisations*. New York: Simon and Schuster, 1996.

Jackson, Patrick Thaddeus. "'Civilization' on Trial," *Millennium: Journal of International Relations*, 28,1 (1999): 141–53.

Kurth, James. "The Real Clash," *The National Interest*, (Fall 1994): 3–15.

McKinnon, John. "The Clash of Civilizations," *New Zealand International Review*, 22, 3 (May-June 1997): 22–4.

Neckermann, Peter. "The Promise of Globalization or the Clash of Civilizations," *World and I*, 13, 12 (December 1998): 314.

Tranock, Adam. "Civilizational Conflict? Fighting the Enemy under a New Banner," *Third World Quarterly* 16, no. 1 (March 1995): 5–18.

Website Resources

The Clash of Civilizations Data Project   A data collection project established by Professors Errol Henderson and Richard Tucker to test hypotheses generated from Huntington's argument.

Global Education Associates: Felix Marti, "Clash of Civilizations or Intercultural Dialogue?" *Breakthrough News* **(January–August 1998)**   Questions whether cultural diversity necessarily leads to conflict and violence.

Okamoto International Affairs Research Institute: Seizaburo Sato, "The Clash of Civilizations: A View from Japan," *Institute for International Policy Studies,* **"Asian Pacific Review" (October 1997)**   A Japanese perspective on Huntington's thesis published by the Okamoto International Affairs Research Institute.

David Skidmore, "Huntington's Clash Revisited," *Journal of World-Systems Research* **4, No. 2 (Fall 1998)**   Contains a critical review of "Clash of Civilizations and the Remaking of World Order."

PART TWO

FINDING A PLACE FOR CANADA IN A CHANGING WORLD ORDER

Should human security be the core value of Canadian foreign policy?

Can Canada's foreign policy be best understood by the concept of "middle power"?

Should Canada pursue a strategy of niche diplomacy?

Should Human Security Be the Core Value of Canadian Foreign Policy?

✔ **YES**
LLOYD AXWORTHY, "Human Security: Safety for People in a Changing World," Ottawa: Department of Foreign Affairs and International Trade, 1999

✗ **NO**
WILLIAM W. BAIN, "Against Crusading: The Ethics of Human Security and Canadian Foreign Policy," *Canadian Foreign Policy* 6, no. 3 (Spring 1999): 85–98

During much of the twentieth century, most policy makers and academics had a common understanding of the concept of security as the basis for foreign policy. It was generally assumed that the study of security had to do with the ways in which the use of force, or threats to use force, was employed to ensure the physical safety of a country's citizens and the protection of that country's core values. Thus, security was closely associated with the state's role in providing "national security."

This approach is based on several realist assumptions:

1. The international system is characterized by a state of anarchy—that is, a lack of overarching authority. As a result, states must pursue their own self-interest, even if at times it conflicts with the larger collective interest.

2. The danger of a foreign attack is a constant and overriding threat to the physical well-being of the state and its inhabitants. States must therefore be vigilant to recognize threats as they emerge, and take appropriate action to counter them.

3. Ensuring national security is rooted in the effective management of military force and the balance of power.

4. Since the state is the ultimate guarantor of security, the security of individuals is subsumed in the broader quest for "national security."

In this traditional formulation, the notion of threat was primarily associated with military threats posed by other states, or in some cases threats posed by non-state actors such as terrorist groups. As policymakers and analysts assessed the changes taking place in the post-Cold War international order, there was growing dissatisfaction with the traditional concept of national security. Many began to question the definition of security itself. Analysts argue that we should move beyond some abstract notion of the state and "national interests" and focus on "security" as it affects the well-being of individual human beings and groups where they actually live.

Typical of this approach was the *Human Development Report*, 1994, issued by the United Nations Development Program. In this report a case is made for developing a concept of "human security" that is universal, human-centred, and multidimensional. Rather than being a military concept, the report maintains that security has many components: economic, nutritional, environmental, personal, community, and political. In reconceptualizing security, the report proposes that states move away from the unilateralism that typifies traditional national security policies, toward a more collective and cooperative approach. It also would give rise to a new form of diplomacy in which states would increasingly cooperate not only with other states and international governmental organizations but with non-governmental organizations (NGOs) and other civil society actors.

The "human security" agenda reflects what Nicholas Wheeler calls a "solidarist" approach to international society. Solidarists argue that a state's claim to sovereignty and non-intervention is limited by the duty of all states to maintain a minimal standard of humane treatment of all its citizens. Where such basic humane standards are not maintained, others have a responsibility, if not a duty, to come to the aid of those suffering.

When he became the minister of Foreign Affairs, Lloyd Axworthy took up the human security concept and made it the focal point of the Liberal government's foreign policy. As a result, a whole set of issues gained prominence on the Canadian foreign policy agenda: human rights and democratization, landmines, peacebuilding, and how the plight of war affected children, to name only a few. To Axworthy, the human security agenda builds naturally on the liberal internationalist principles that have long shaped Canadian foreign policy.

Although Axworthy has since left his government post, the human security agenda officially remains a key element in the Canadian foreign policy agenda. But how useful is the focus on human security? Should this continue to be the lens through which we view the world and shape our foreign-policy interests? In the readings, we get two perspectives on these questions. In the first reading, Lloyd Axworthy lays out his vision of human security and the role it should play in Canadian foreign policy.

In the second reading, William Bain presents a more skeptical perspective on human security. He argues for a more pluralist understanding of international society that gives greater priority to the notions of sovereignty and non-interference and respects the right of states to pursue their own vision of the good life. Bain doubts that the kind of moral principles that underlie the concept of human security have in fact become universally accepted. Instead, he fears that a foreign policy driven by a human security agenda could lead to an overly moralized policy. Such a crusading spirit could lead to charges of cultural imperialism abroad and cynicism at home if Canada cannot live up to its capacity to deliver. A more prudent approach to foreign policy, Bain argues, is more in keeping with the traditions of Canadian foreign policy than a crusading spirit.

✔ YES
Human Security: Safety for People in a Changing World
LLOYD AXWORTHY

I. THE NEED FOR A NEW APPROACH TO SECURITY

Since the end of the Cold War, security for the majority of states has increased, while security for many of the world's people has declined.

The end of the superpower confrontation has meant greater security for states touched by that rivalry. Yet during this decade we have seen new civil conflicts, large-scale atrocities, and even genocide. Globalization has brought many benefits, but it has also meant a rise in violent crime, drug trade, terrorism, disease, and environmental deterioration. It clearly does not follow that when states are secure, people are secure.

Security between states remains a necessary condition for the security of people. The principal objective of national security is the protection of territorial integrity and political sovereignty from external aggression. While declining in frequency, the threat of inter-state war has not vanished, and the potential consequences of such a war should not be underestimated. Technological advances and proliferation of weaponry mean that future wars between states will exact a horrific toll on civilians. At the same time national security is insufficient to guarantee people's security.

A growing number of armed conflicts are being fought within, rather than between, states. The warring factions in these civil wars are often irregular forces with loose chains of command, frequently divided along ethnic or religious lines. Small arms are the weapon of choice and non-combatants account for eight out of ten casualties. Once considered merely "collateral damage," civilians are being thrust into the epicentre of contemporary war.

Greater exposure to violence is not limited to situations of armed conflict. It is also directly related to the erosion of state control. This decline is most evident in failed states, where governments are simply incapable of providing even basic security for people threatened by warlords and bandits. Challenges to state control can also be seen in the expansion of organized crime, drug trafficking, and the growth of private security forces.

Security for people is also affected by a broadening range of transnational threats. In an increasingly interdependent world we routinely experience mutual, if unequal vulnerability. Opening markets, increased World trade, and a revolution in communications are highly beneficial, but they have also made borders more porous to a wide range of threats. A growing number of hazards to people's health—from long-range transmission of pollutants to infectious diseases—are global phenomena in both their origins and their effects. Economic shocks in one part of the world can lead rapidly to crises in another, with devastating implications for the security of the most vulnerable.

These broad trends are clearly not new to the 1990s; each has been intensifying over recent decades. During 40 years of superpower rivalry, however, nuclear confrontation and ideological competition dominated the security agenda. As a result, these other challenges have only been widely acknowledged in more recent years. Outside the confines of the Cold War, the opportunity exists to develop a comprehensive and systematic approach to enhancing the security of people.

II. BACKGROUND TO THE CONCEPT OF HUMAN SECURITY

While the term "human security" may be of recent origin, the ideas that underpin the concept are far from new. For more than a century—at least since the founding of the International Committee of the Red Cross in the 1860s—a doctrine based on the security of people has been gathering momentum. Core elements of this doctrine were formalized in the 1940s in the UN Charter, the Universal Declaration of Human Rights, and the Geneva Conventions.

The specific phrase "human security" is most commonly associated with the 1994 UNDP *Human Development Report*, an attempt to capture the post-Cold War peace dividend and redirect those resources towards the development agenda. The definition advanced in the report was extremely ambitious. Human security was defined as the summation of seven distinct dimensions of security: economic, food, health, environmental, personal, community, and political. By focusing on people and highlighting non-traditional threats, the UNDP made an important contribution to post-Cold War thinking about security.

The very breadth of the UNDP approach, however, made it unwieldy as a policy instrument. Equally important, in emphasizing the threats associated with underdevelopment, the Report largely ignored the continuing human insecurity resulting from violent conflict. Yet by the UNDP's own criteria, human insecurity is greatest during war. Of the 25 countries at the bottom of the 1998 Human Development Index, more than half are suffering the direct or indirect effects of violent conflict. The UNDP definition of human security was proposed as a key concept during the preparatory stages of the 1995 Copenhagen Summit on Social Development. But it was rejected during the Summit and has not been widely used thereafter.

Over the past two years the concept of human security has increasingly centred on the human costs of violent conflict. Here, practice has led theory. Two initiatives in particular, the campaign to ban landmines and the effort to create an International Criminal Court, have demonstrated the potential of a people-centred approach to security. Anti-personnel landmines are a clear example of a threat to the security of people. While contributing only marginally to the security of states, mines have a devastating impact on ordinary people attempting to rebuild their lives in war-torn societies. The International Criminal Court establishes a mechanism to hold individuals accountable for war crimes and crimes against humanity, and holds the promise of preventing the future abuse of people by governments and other parties to conflicts. Both measures are practical, powerful applications of the concept of human security.

III. DEFINING HUMAN SECURITY—A SHIFT IN THE ANGLE OF VISION

In essence, human security means safety for people from both violent and non-violent threats. It is a condition or state of being characterized by freedom from pervasive threats to people's rights, their safety, or even their lives. From a foreign policy perspective, human security is perhaps best understood as a shift in perspective or orientation. It is an alternative way of seeing the world, taking people as its point of reference, rather than focusing exclusively on the security of territory or governments. Like other security concepts—national security, economic security, food security—it is about protection. Human security entails taking preventive measures to reduce vulnerability and minimize risk, and taking remedial action where prevention fails.

The range of potential threats to human security should not be narrowly conceived. While the safety of people is obviously at grave risk in situations of armed conflict, a human security approach is not simply synonymous with humanitarian action. It highlights the need to address the root causes of insecurity and to help ensure people's future safety. There are also human security dimensions to a broad range of challenges, such as gross violations of human rights, environmental degradation, terrorism, transnational organized crime, gender-based violence, infectious diseases, and natural disasters. The widespread social unrest and violence that often accompanies economic crises demonstrates that there are clear economic underpinnings to human security. The litmus test for determining if it is useful to frame an issue in human security terms is the degree to which the safety of people is at risk.

IV. A NECESSARY COMPLEMENT TO NATIONAL SECURITY

Human security does not supplant national security. A human security perspective asserts that the security of the state is not an end in itself. Rather, it is a means of ensuring security for its people. In this context, state security and human security are mutually supportive. Building an effective, democratic state that values its own people and protects minorities is a central strategy for promoting human security. At the same time, improving the human security of its people strengthens the legitimacy, stability, and security of a state. When states are externally aggressive, internally repressive, or too weak to govern effectively, they threaten the security of people. Where human security exists as a fact rather than an aspiration, these conditions can be attributed in large measure to the effective governance of states.

From a human security perspective, concern for the safety of people extends beyond borders. Although broadening the focus of security policy beyond citizens may at first appear to be a radical shift, it is a logical extension of current approaches to international peace and security. The Charter of the United Nations embodies the view that security cannot be achieved by a single state in isolation. The phrase "international peace and security" implies that the security of one state depends on the security of other states. A human security perspective builds on this logic by noting that the security of people in one part of the world depends on the security of people elsewhere. A secure and stable world order is built both from the top down, and from the bottom up. The security of states, and the maintenance of international peace and security, are ultimately constructed on the foundation of people who are secure.

V. AN ENABLING ENVIRONMENT FOR HUMAN DEVELOPMENT

The two concepts of human security and human development are mutually reinforcing, though distinct. The UNDP report itself, while proposing a very broad definition of human security, was clear that the two concepts were not synonymous. Together, human security and human development address the twin objectives of freedom from fear and freedom from want.

People's freedom to act can be constrained by both fears; and for the poorest and most vulnerable members of society, poverty and insecurity are linked in a vicious circle. Breaking that cycle requires measures to promote human development, through access to reliable employment, education, and social services. But it also requires measures to promote human security by offering protection from crime and political violence, respect for human rights including political rights, and equitable access to justice. The absence of such guarantees of human security constitutes a powerful barrier to human development. Regardless of levels of income, if people lack confidence in society's ability to protect them, they will have little incentive to invest in the future. A development optic highlights this positive dimension of the concept—namely the opportunity that human security provides to liberate the potential for growth.

Human security provides an enabling environment for human development. Where violence or the threat of violence makes meaningful progress on the developmental agenda impractical, enhancing safety for people is a prerequisite. Promoting human development can also be an important strategy for furthering human security. By addressing inequalities which are often root causes of violent conflict, by strengthening governance structures, and by providing humanitarian assistance, development assistance complements political, legal, and military initiatives in enhancing human security.

VI. FOREIGN POLICY IMPLICATIONS

Human security provides a template to assess policy and practice for their effects on the safety of people. From a foreign policy perspective, there are a number of key consequences.

First, when conditions warrant, vigorous action in defence of human security objectives will be necessary. Ensuring human security can involve the use of coercive measures, including sanctions and military force, as in Bosnia and Kosovo.

At the same time, the human costs of strategies for promoting state and international security must be explicitly assessed. This line of argument dates back to the 19th-century movement to ban the use of inhumane weapons, but, as we have seen in the recent campaign to ban anti-personnel landmines, it continues to have contemporary relevance. Other security policies, such as comprehensive economic sanctions, should take into account the impact on innocent people.

Third, security policies must be integrated much more closely with strategies for promoting human rights, democracy, and development. Human rights, humanitarian, and refugee law provide the normative framework on which a human security approach is based. Development strategies offer broadly based means of addressing many long-term human security challenges. One of the dividends of adopting a human security approach is that it further elaborates a people-centred foreign policy.

Fourth, due to the complexity of contemporary challenges to the security of people, effective interventions involve a diverse range of actors including states, multilateral organizations, and civil society groups. As the challenges to the safety of people are transnational, effective responses can only be achieved through multilateral cooperation. This is evident in the array of new international instruments developed in the last decade to address transnational organized crime, drug trafficking, terrorism, and environmental degradation. These threats link the interest of citizens in countries which enjoy a high level of human security with the interests of people in much poorer nations, who face a wider range of threats to their safety.

Fifth, effective responses will depend on greater operational coordination. For example, successful peace-support operations are multi-dimensional, and depend on the close coordination of political negotiators, peacekeepers, human rights monitors, and humanitarian aid personnel among others. Furthermore, development agencies are now engaged in promoting security sector reform, while security organizations have helped channel development assistance in post-conflict countries. Managing these overlapping mandates and objectives is one of the principal challenges for a human security agenda.

Sixth, civil society organizations are seeking greater opportunity and greater responsibility in promoting human security. In many cases, non-governmental organizations have proven to be extremely effective partners in advocating the security of people. They are also important providers of assistance and protection to those in need of greater security. At the same time, the business sector, potentially a key actor in enhancing human security, could be more effectively engaged.

VII. TOWARDS AN AGENDA FOR HUMAN SECURITY

Human security offers a new angle of vision and a broad template for evaluating policies. It also yields a concrete set of foreign policy initiatives. Focusing systematically on the safety of people highlights the need for more targeted attention to key issues that are not yet adequately addressed by the international community. Current examples of such gaps include the unchecked proliferation of small arms and the inadequate protection of children in circumstances of armed conflict.

Human security is enhanced by reducing people's vulnerability and by preventing the conditions which make them vulnerable in the first place. Assisting people in highly insecure situations, particularly in the midst of violent conflict, is a central objective of the human security agenda. Refugees have long been the focus of international attention. The same focus on vulnerability highlights the immediate needs of the internally displaced, and demobilized combatants. At the same time, a human security agenda must go beyond humanitarian action, by addressing the sources of people's insecurity. Building human security, therefore, requires both short-term humanitarian action and longer-term strategies for building peace and promoting sustainable development.

Two fundamental strategies for enhancing human security are strengthening legal norms and building the capacity to enforce them. New standards are needed in areas such as restricting the illegal trafficking in small arms, banning the use and recruitment of children as soldiers, prohibiting exploitative child labour, providing greater protection for the internally displaced, and ensuring the applicability of legal standards to non-state actors and to violence below the threshold of armed conflict.

There is little point in defining new norms and rights, however, if societies have no capacity to enforce existing norms or to protect already recognized rights. For this reason, improving democratic governance within states is a central strategy for advancing human security. So is strengthening the capacity of international organizations, in particular the United Nations, to deliver on their agreed mandates. Yet the range of protection tasks assigned to UN-mandated operations is increasing, at the same time as the UN's capacity to organize and fund such operations is dwindling.

Building institutional capacity without strengthening respect for norms would undermine a human-centred standard of security. Strengthening norms without building the capacity to protect them only invites disillusionment with the possibility of constraining power by the rule of law. Both are essential strategies if we are to move towards a more humane world.

✗ NO

Against Crusading: The Ethics of Human Security and Canadian Foreign Policy
WILLIAM W. BAIN

Recent efforts to include the ethic of human security as one of the core objectives of Canada's foreign policy lack the necessary coherence required to be a useful guide for the conduct of statecraft. Canada's foreign policy seeks to achieve three key objectives: (1) to promote prosperity and employment; (2) to protect security within a stable international framework; and (3) to protect abroad Canadian values and culture (Canada 1995: 10). In the practice of statecraft these objectives are not always reconcilable and, consequently, they sometimes—though not always—demand conflicting action. Ottawa has traditionally emphasized its eco-nomic and security interests above other goals, even though Canada has been at the forefront of the effort to promote the global observance of human rights, the rule of law, and good governance. More recently, the discourse of Canada's for-eign policy, especially as it is articulated by Foreign Minister Lloyd Axworthy, may indicate a significant change in this order of priorities and in the moral sub-stance of Canada's interests abroad. But the practical implementation of Ottawa's emerging doctrine of human security may impede efforts to secure other equally fundamental, but conflicting, values and it may commit Canada to principles that it is not entirely prepared to fulfill.[1]

The ethic of human security challenges and possibly undermines the moral foundation of international society as it has existed for nearly four hundred years. Exponents of human security reject the sovereign state as the paramount moral community of international society; they do not believe that these communities ought to be the principal referents of security. Rather, the ethic of human security accords moral priority to the security of individual human beings. Therefore, the difference between human security and our traditional understanding of national security presupposes an important change in the moral character of world poli-tics; indeed, it may foreshadow a change which is nothing short of revolutionary. By investigating the ethical foundation of Ottawa's nascent doctrine of human security we can gain important insight into Canada's basic values and how these values impact its foreign policy and sense of purpose in world politics. It will become evident as a result of this investigation that Canada's doctrine of human security emphasizes certain norms which are often at odds with the prevailing norms of present-day international society, norms which also constitute an important part of Canada's traditional foreign policy objectives. Moreover, this doctrine may engender excessive moralism; that is, a tendency to encounter the world as if Canada were engaged in a moral crusade. Indeed, a foreign policy which is guided, at least in part, by a universal doctrine such as human security is difficult to reconcile with the practical realities and fundamentally pluralist nature of international society. In its effort to include human security as one of its core foreign policy objectives, Ottawa must recognize the circumstantial character of world politics and how this contingent condition affects the achievement of certain values. Recognizing this state of affairs entails relying upon prudent judgment, rather than indiscriminate universal principles, to guide Canada's foreign relations. An approach which carefully weighs competing and conflicting moral claims permits the greatest opportunity to criticize others for unjust practices, to stand in solidarity with those resisting oppression, to refrain from recklessly imposing our values on others, and to achieve the key objectives of Canada's foreign policy.

ALTERNATIVE ETHICS OF SECURITY IN THE POST-COLD WAR WORLD

The tremendous change brought about by the end of the cold war compelled scholars and practitioners of world politics to question and to reconceptualize the meaning of security. It is often said that focusing upon nuclear deterrence, military balances, zero-sum games, competing power blocs, and interstate relations is overly narrow or even out of date in the post-cold war world.[2] Replacing this cold war security discourse are several discourses which centre upon issues such as the environment, equity, human potential, multilateralism, religion, ethnicity, gender, identity, and cooperative and common security. Following from this ongoing process of critical reflection and redefinition is an approach which not only rejects the traditional cold war understanding of security, but proposes instead an ambitious set of principles that, if implemented fully, would signal a revolutionary change in the practice of diplomacy.

Given the lofty goals proposed by the advocates of human security, we might be inclined to view the concept as mere rhetoric or we might be tempted to dismiss it as unrealizable, albeit well-intentioned, ideals in much the same way as the aspirations of the inter-war idealists were disparaged by those who subscribed to a more "realistic" approach to world politics.[3] But human security is an idea which is much larger than Minister Axworthy and his aspirations for Canada's foreign policy. It is an idea which enjoys considerable support throughout the world. And the discourse of world politics indicates clearly that the idea of human security amounts to a great deal more expedient, idealistic, naïve, and foolish rhetoric. For example, the principles and imperatives of human security command a prominent place in the activities of the UN, they are at the centre of the Report of the Commission on Global Governance, and they are a pervasive theme in the discourse of global civil society.[4] Similarly, the purpose and value of global initiatives such as the Ottawa Treaty, which prohibits anti-personnel mines, the proposed International Criminal Court, efforts to define the rights of the child, and attempts to confront the global problem posed by the spread of AIDS are all intelligible and are frequently justified in the discourse of human security. These developments indicate that, far from being more rhetoric, at least some people associate human security with a set of ends which are good in themselves; that is, their enjoyment needs no further justification. And while advocates of human security often differ in areas of emphasis and in matters of prescription, they share a common belief that human security is a better way to engage the complexities of an emerging world that is challenged less by interstate threats than by threats which are contained within states or which transcend the jurisdiction of particular states.

The ethical foundation of human security differs in several important ways from the ethic of national security which has heretofore dominated both theoretical and practical understanding of security. The ethic of human security incorporates into the security discourse a cluster of values which broadens significantly the scope and substance of the word "security." In articulating the idea of human security, Minister Axworthy proposes an understanding which recognizes the elementary importance of "human rights and fundamental freedoms, the right to live in dignity, with adequate food, shelter, health and education services, and under the rule of law and good governance" (Axworthy 1996c: 3–7). In addition to these values, he suggests that human security also embraces a commitment to democratic development and ensuring quality of life and equity for all human beings. Collectively, these values are to form an integral part of a Canadian foreign policy, which is designed to confront the post-cold war world.

Human security has gained currency in large part because of the dilemmas presented by the practice of national security.[5] National security is concerned with the safety of particular political communities: sovereign states. Individual security is assumed to follow from national security by virtue of our membership in a particular political community. Thus, national security presupposes the assumption that states are worth preserving; that is, sovereign states are thought of as moral communities in their own right. In fact, preserving the fortunes of the political community is such a deeply held norm that national security is one of the few norms that, in certain circumstances, may justifiably pre-empt other fundamental norms of international society. But the practice of world politics reveals a more troubling side of national security: some states do not provide adequate security for their citizens and they fail to deliver the most basic social goods. Failed or unjust states, such as Somalia, Liberia, Rwanda, and the former Yugoslavia, are typically bastions of tyranny, sources of great misery, and are often themselves the most immediate threat to their citizens' security. In states such as these, the term "national security" is nothing more than a misnomer; it refers to a juridical entity rather than a sociological nation. Ironically, the constitutive norms of international society sustain this condition in a rather perverse way: the rights of sovereign equality, nonintervention, and political independence help to ensure the survival of what are otherwise unviable states.[6] That some states do not provide adequate security for their citizens, yet manage to ensure their own survival, casts doubt upon their worth as moral communities and upon the doctrine of national security.

Recognizing the principal difficulty of national security—individual security does not necessarily follow from the security of the political community—underscores the key normative difference between national security and human security. Whereas national security postulates states as the principal recipients of security, human security confers moral priority on the security of individual human beings. Human security, or what Minister Axworthy calls "real" security, is concerned foremost with the protection of the individual (1996b: 2). An ethic of human security does not permit us to remain detached from, or indifferent to, human suffering on account of deeply ingrained injunctions against interfering in the domestic affairs of sovereign states. For Canada, this means that a commitment to human security requires a "broadening of the focus of security policy form its narrow orientation of managing state-to-state relationships, to one that recognizes the importance of the individual and society for our shared security" (Canada 1995: 25). Thus, in a departure from the classical ethic of national security, human security discloses a cosmopolitan ethic which posits the community of humankind as resting above the society of states.

IS HUMAN SECURITY A SOUND FOUNDATION FOR CANADA'S FOREIGN POLICY?

A tension exists between the practical implications of a foreign policy which seeks to secure the values of human security and the prevailing moral disposition of the society of states. The moral substance of international society is disclosed in a constellation of constitutive norms which reflect the common values and interests of its constituent members. These norms are not given by any philosophical treatise; they are not discovered by power of human reason; and they are not theorized by the spectators of world politics in relation to how they think the world ought to be. The norms of international society are products of human activity: they are the distillation of centuries of diplomatic, military, economic, and other international practice. And because these norms are artifacts of human experience they are historically situated: over time they have varied in their incarnation, strength, importance, and interpretation.

Although international society is embedded in, and is a product of, history, it should not be confused with any purposive enterprise or any evolutionary view of human progress: international society is not justified by the achievement of specific ends, such as welfare or human dignity. The definite mark of international society "[lies] not in the shared purposes of its members states ... but in their acknowledgement of formal rules of mutual accommodation"(Nardin 1983: 309).

The constitutive norms of international society represent moral injunctions which circumscribe the exercise of power. And by imposing limits on the exercise of power these norms stand opposed to certain policies, even when they represent the most expedient way of fulfilling the requirements of the national interest. The constitutive norms of international society restrict the means that states may employ to obtain national advantage and the ends for which states may aspire (Morgenthau 1948: 80). Thus, in a key and basic way, the norms of international society provide the basis for mutual coexistence; collectively they admit that there are different conceptions of the "good life." In recognizing different conceptions of the good life, international society affords individual states the opportunity to pursue their own notion of the good life without being subject to interference on the part of others. Located at the heart of this notion of society is an ethic of pluralism: "the conception that there are many different ends that men may seek and still be fully rational, fully men, capable of understanding each other" (Berlin 1991: 11).

To argue that international society is fundamentally pluralist in its organization is not to say that the theory of pluralism is the only basis of human organization and association. For example, medieval Europeans ordered themselves on the principle that all European states constituted the *respublica Christiana*—the Christian Commonwealth of Europe. In this mode of association, human relations are intelligible in one universal pattern, a pattern which determines the place of all persons, their rights and duties, their function and purpose. It is a pattern which presupposes the acceptance of a singular common good, or common good life, to be shared by all. And while there is no logical or empirical reason not to believe that a universal association or commonwealth could again exist in contemporary world politics, the history and discourse of world politics suggest that large groups of human beings do not believe that they live in such a world today. In terms of foreign policy, we continuously debate the most profitable course of action; we complain that we give too much or not enough; we blame others for failing to fulfill their obligations and they, in turn, respond that they have done so; and in our relations with others, we are concerned to answer the question: to whom do we owe our primary obligations—to members of our own political community or to those persons who are not members?

These moral conversations may indicate that many of us do not properly understand the common good and purpose of our world or that perhaps we know too little or that we are too feeble-minded to comprehend its significance. These conversations may indicate also that the ends and purposes of human beings are many; that they speak to ends that are of the category "good" but which do not necessarily entail one another and are not reconcilable in one systematic, uniform, and all-encompassing patter.[7] We find that these different ends of human life may "come into conflict, and lead to clashes between societies, parties, individuals, and not least within individuals themselves; and furthermore that the ends of one age and county differ widely from those of other times and other out-looks" (Berlin 1969:102). And because the ends of human beings are many, the world in which they live is not intelligible in the context of a single moral theory. Rather we live in a world in which moral voices and perspectives coexist and sometimes conflict; over the course of history they advance and retreat; and we discern and evaluate their importance in the context of varying degrees of strength or weakness. Thus, it might be the case our present world discloses some degree of universalism and that our world may once again be ordered on princi-ples of a universalist ethic. However, it seems as if the ethic of pluralism, at least for the moment, best describes the dominant ethic of international society.

It is precisely this ethic of pluralism which potentially conflicts with human security. Human security does not allow full expression of different conceptions of the good life: it does not recognize that there are ways of organizing our lives which are both different and moral. The doctrine of human security imposes upon all a universal good life that is determined by values whose meaning is derived mainly from Canadian and western experience and which rest above the diversity and particularisms of individual political communities. Thus, a Canadian foreign policy based upon the doctrine of human security would not stop at securing the moral and material interests of Canadians; rather it would transcend this proper purpose in an attempt to secure the interests of humanity in its entirety. This uni-versal mission is revealed inasmuch as "Canadians hold deeply that we must pursue our values internationally. They want to promote them for their own sake, but they also understand that our values and rights will not be safeguarded if they are not enshrined throughout the international environment" (Canada 1995: 34). And in asserting that Canadians speak with one moral voice, Minister Axworthy suggests that "[i]t is critical that this voice be heard internationally as it both val-idates our worth as a country and promotes the value of human dignity around the globe" (1996a: 1). But in a society of states which values pluralism, this view wrongly identifies the aspirations of Canada with the aspirations of the world.

This excessive moralism which may infect Canada's sense of purpose in world politics is an unsuitable foundation for a nation's foreign policy. For a foreign policy of this type does not acknowledge the circumstantial nature of human rela-tions; and it is indicative of an attitude or mood which does not differ signifi-cantly from the indiscriminate cold war injunction, "stop communism," which led the US to oppose all communist regimes everywhere without assessing their origin or their specific character. And it was the pursuit of this (indiscriminate) univer-salist mission that entangled the US in the catastrophe of Vietnam. Like all realms of human relations, world politics is marked by contingency, chance, change, and unpredictability. But Minister Axworthy's notion of human security takes scant notice of this conditional state of affairs. Rather it is imbued with inchoate refer-ences and ill-considered commitments to a multitude of abstract ideals and uni-versal principles of which the implications have not been sufficiently thought through. A foreign policy which endorses abstract principles before appraising the circumstances which impose upon the statesperson, is bound to fail. The actions of the stateperson are bound by practical limits: "human activity, with whatever it may be concerned, enjoys a circumscribed range of movement. The limits which define this range are historic, that is to say, they are themselves the product of human activity" (Oakeshott 1996: 116). And that is why words such as "possibility," "necessity," "requirement," "likely," "compromise," "restraint," and "contingent," constitute the substance of the vocabulary of statecraft. But abstract principles are divorced from the practical world of statecraft. They are ahistorical, they take no notice of human experience, they are not susceptible to limitation, they are ignorant of circumstance, and they are not amenable to compromise. Indeed, human conduct which is guided wholly by abstract principle has difficulty recognizing that the achievement of one end may, in some circumstances, conflict with another desirable end (Mill 1988: 138).

The danger of permitting abstract principle to guide foreign policy is evident, for example, in Canada's human rights policy. Human rights are a central part of Canada's foreign policy agenda: they are accorded the status of a "threshold" issue which colours significantly Canada's international relations. Indeed, Minister Axworthy submits that "[r]espect for human rights is a critical component of the Canadian identity and therefore must play an important role in our foreign policy agenda" (1997: 1). But in these pronouncements it is difficult to find any moral reason to qualify how Canada's human rights policy is to be implemented. There is acknowledgement that Canada's "ability to effect change can be limited," and that its effort are sometimes construed as unjustified interference in the internal affairs of others (Axworthy 1997: 1–7). There is also recognition that Canada's ability to force change is limited by a paucity of economic leverage and international clout. However, these conditions speak to instrumental problems: they refer only to limitations of the means with which to achieve the end and not to the achievement of the end itself. Canada's foreign policy establishment, in its commitment to secure human rights, is noticeably silent on questions concerning moral conflict: it does not acknowledge that fundamental values sometimes clash. And it seems as if Canada's doctrine of human security does not recognize that the pursuit of human rights may sometimes impede securing other fundamental values; that obtaining the good of human rights may entail a loss of order, or of security, or some other value; and that an occasion may arise when human rights ought to be subordinated to the achievement of other fundamental values.

In the absence of these qualifications, Canada's stated human rights objectives are not the result of careful deliberation which weighs interest, power, obligations, rights, competing claims, and the circumstances in which they are embedded. A human rights policy which is guided wholly by abstract principle quickly transforms itself into a doctrine of universal human salvation. And it is in this spirit of universal salvation that Canada charts a course which asserts that: "it is important that we pursue the issue of human rights internationally. It is important as an extension of our own beliefs" (Axworthy 1997: 1). A foreign policy of this type is less about securing Canadian interests than it is about validation and affirmation of national righteousness. This is when the conduct of foreign policy ceases to be a useful instrument of statecraft: it becomes the servant of justice for the sake of doing justice.

A foreign policy which seeks justice, but is unaware of circumstance, rival claims, and conflicting obligations, can see no diversity or difference in human experience. Universalism and uniformity are all that is intelligible in a mission to extend our beliefs and to validate our worth as a country. It is at this point that we seek to repress difference, not because difference contributes to disorder or insecurity, but because it is identified with error. Thus, the chief duty of government and the purpose of foreign policy becomes one of suppressing as error all opposition to the enterprise of securing the greater justice of human rights for all.[8] And in its missions to secure a particular notion of justice for all of humanity, Canada runs the risk of inflicting injustice of a greater magnitude than that which it seeks to remedy. Instead of recognizing the circumstantial nature of world politics and the diversity of human existence, Canada seems intent on pursuing a universalist mission in an attempt to perfect the inherently imperfect nature of the human condition.

But we must be quick to note that recognizing and celebrating diversity does not require us to remain silent in the face of injustice. We are not required to accept an extreme relativist position which precludes all communication with members of other cultures and civilizations. We are not muted prisoners of our own cultural practices, unable to understand the practices of others. Because human beings are moral creatures, we are able to comprehend injustice, even when it occurs in circumstances quite different from our own. And because we are able to communicate with members of other cultures, we are able to criticize unjust practices and stand in solidarity with other human beings against injustice. Canada ought to criticize oppressive governments and it ought to stand in solidarity with those who are resisting oppression.

But in criticizing others for human rights abuses, for example, Canada must remain acutely aware of how this criticism affects the realization of other fundamental values, both for Canadians and for others. Occasion may arise when the achievement of order, security, or peace may be threatened by an overly progressive human rights policy. A foreign policy which is conscious of circumstances is aware of something which foreign policy guided by abstract principle is not: the norms of international society sometimes demand conflicting action. There is no predetermined was to disentangle these conflicting obligations. Good and right in international society are not derived from any particular norm such as order or justice. We can comprehend no universal and common chief good for which all the world's statespersons strive to secure. And we cannot resolve conflicting moral demands by appealing to a single authoritative norm; we cannot discern a definite and permanent hierarchy in which the norms of international society are arranged; nor is it evident that these norms are equal to each other at all times and in all circumstances. The norms of international society are an eclectic group which merely reflect the contradictions, tensions, and imperfections of the creatures that created them.

RECONCILING HUMAN SECURITY AND CANADA'S FOREIGN POLICY OBJECTIVES

The moral dilemmas and conflicts of world politics are not resolved in the abstract, but in the practice of statecraft. In the practice of world politics, the circumstances of our world, at times, oblige some norms to yield to others. The practice of statecraft suggests that, in extreme cases, the rights of sovereign states may be abrogated or suspended when it is in the interest of international society as a whole. Likewise, when human rights injunctions clash with the imperatives of national security, human rights usually lose. And in the absence of an authoritative norm to guide the practice of statecraft, the statesperson must rely upon a particular type of judgment, a type of judgment we call prudence, to resolve conflicting obligations.

Prudence, which is often described as the supreme virtue of politics, is a species of practical wisdom: it discloses a mode of common sense which is the antithesis of abstract intellectualism. Prudence is the name we give to that type of wisdom which is associated with careful consideration, deliberation, restraint, and foresight. It is a type of sound judgment which guides the statesperson through the difficult choices and which makes some sense of conflicting demands and obligations. And through all the complexity, mystery, and uncertainty of our world, it is the prudent statesperson who is able to choose the best course of action under these trying conditions. Thus, the prudent statesperson demonstrates the ability to make the right decision at the right time—the ability to solve real problems, to get things done, to select the most profitable course among the many possible paths on which to travel. However, prudence ought not to be mistaken for ordinary common sense; rather it is a kind of wisdom with which few are endowed. For prudence is not a technical subject: we do not become prudent simply by reading philosophy or by observing world politics from the sidelines. And prudence is not learned mechanically or by rote. The practice of statecraft, like human conduct in general, is indeterminate, uncertain, and susceptible to chance, and it is quite unlike exact sciences which require no deliberation (Aristotle 1963: 49). Therefore, it is not possible to stipulate in advance a prudential principle, apply it to our subject, and expect successful political action to follow. Rather, prudence is imparted and learned by way of practice and experience.

The prudent statesperson must consider a multitude of parties and circumstances in the conduct of statecraft. Prudential statecraft refuses to judge and solve problems in the abstract. In contrast, abstract principles know only absolute truth: they cannot discriminate between the circumstances which distinguish a problem's moral significance. The prudent statesperson is obligated to attend first to the interests of his/her own citizens—those to whom he/she is directly accountable. Performing this task is the chief duty of the stateperson. And in a democratic society, fulfilling this duty may sometimes require that the stateperson ignore popular opinion. But the stateperson's work is not finished after the requirements of the national interest have been satisfied. He/she must also consider the legitimate interests of other claimants and he/she must contemplate the interests of innocent third parties before deciding upon a particular course of action. Indeed, considering the legitimate interests of others is a basic and necessary ingredient of successful foreign policy; for a "nation that is too preoccupied with its own interests is bound to define those interests too narrowly. It will do this because it will fail to consider those of its interests which are *bound up in a web of mutual interests* with other nations. In short, the national interest when conceived only from the standpoint of the self-interest of the nation is bound to be defined too narrowly and therefore to be self-defeating [italics in original]"(Niebuhr, 1958: 40). The virtuous statesperson must assess all legitimate claims and decide which one, under the circumstances, appears to be closest to the truth. The prudent statesperson, in carefully weighing different claims and circumstances, adjusts to the contours of the problem (Vico 1965: 34). In contrast, the moral crusader applies to the problem a universal principle in the effort to obtain a solution.

It is not yet clear how Ottawa intends to reconcile its doctrine of human security with the circumstantial nature of human relations; for there appears to be little allowance for contingency, unpredictability, accident, and chance. Human security is a universalist doctrine which takes little notice of the pluralist nature of international society; instead it posits a community of humankind above the society of states. And this cosmopolitan commitment supposes that Canadian values are those of the entire world without ascertaining if this sense of right is a truth held by others. As such, human security is an unsuitable objective of Canada's foreign policy. However, this does not mean that Canada must abandon its commitment to issues concerning human rights, democracy, the rule of law, and good governance. Canada may legitimately, and ought to, criticize Indonesia's human rights record in East Timor, China's suppression of pro-democracy activists, child labour practices in India, military rule in Burma, war crimes in Yugoslavia, and genocide in Rwanda.

But caution must be exercised while expressing opposition to the practices of others. Canada must avoid undermining other constitutive norms of international society while pursuing these ends. This means that Canada may recognize injustice and may express solidarity with those who are resisting oppression; that is to say, that we can share with them an opposition to injustice and therefore "march in their parade" (Walzer 1994). This also means that purposive efforts to remedy injustice may be, in some cases, better left to those directly engaged. When we move from a position of moral solidarity to one of direct engagement, we inevitably retreat into our own particular morality (Walzer 1994). It is at this point that universalist schemes of human salvation manifest themselves and begin to erode the pluralist nature of international society. A prudent foreign policy allows us to "march in the parade" without indiscriminately imposing our values on others. A policy which abstains from moral crusading is important both for the moral development of others and for Canada. Canada has demonstrated that it is not always prepared to undertake the responsibilities that the ethic of human security entails. For example, when faced with choosing between human rights and economic interests, Canada has often demonstrated a willingness to secure the latter at the expense of the former. We see in the past that Canada has softened its human rights agenda in order to advance its economic interests abroad.[9] But in the absence of a willingness to consistently fulfill the requirements of a policy of human security, and in the absence of a forthright acknowledgment that the fundamental objectives of Canadian foreign policy may sometimes conflict, any ongoing commitment to a policy sustained by self-righteousness invites charges of hypocrisy and threatens to fray the moral fabric that is distinctly Canadian.

Surely this advice will meet profound dissatisfaction, and even indignation, from the prophets of human security and other similar universalist doctrines. They will criticize the prudent course as being conservative and slow to work. They are right. But Canada ought to be most reticent and cautious before it begins to subvert international society as it presently exists. International society has provided the basis for some countries—Canada among them—to strive for and achieve some notion of the good life. And enshrined in international society is an ethic that permits Canada to pursue an understanding of the good life which is distinctly its own. Thus, Canada ought to pursue its foreign policy objectives in such a way that it preserves and, indeed, sustains the pluralism of international society. However, a Canadian foreign policy based upon the principles of human security would not be favourably disposed toward securing this good. Rather it would likely to suffer from an unacknowledged contradiction which may hinder the practical conduct of statecraft by infusing Canada's international relations with excessive moralism. And insofar as Ottawa fails to acknowledge that Canada's foreign policy objectives may sometimes demand conflicting action, it invites allegations of hypocrisy which threaten to undermine Canada's credibility, both at home and abroad.

The potential danger of a foreign policy which does not acknowledge that conflicting demands may confound the best attempts to secure basic values is evident in recent events concerning Canada and the Asia-Pacific region. Canada's efforts to increase its economic presence in the region are often met with strident criticism because of Indonesia's human rights record in East Timor, China's treatment of pro-democracy activists, and child labor practices in India and Pakistan. Likewise, attempts to pursue Canada's human rights agenda regularly provoke attitudes of apathy and skepticism at home, and accusations of cultural imperialism from abroad. Canada's leaders are likely to evoke feelings of uncertainty and disbelief when, on the one hand, Minister Axworthy openly questions the value and relevancy of APEC because it does not address human rights issues and, on the other hand, Prime Minister Jean Chrétien emphasizes that APEC "means business" by indicating that it is primarily a free-trade group in which human rights concerns are to be raised "on the margin in private bilateral talks" (Sallot 1997). And we are apt to encounter confusion when foreign policy statements are less about Canada's interests abroad than with concerns at home. Canada may do harm to its international reputation and credibility, and it may unnecessarily complicate its foreign relations, to the extent that human security "must play a important role in our foreign policy agenda" because it "validates our worth as a country" and affirms Canada's national identity. The inevitable contradictions and hypocrisies of a foreign policy which is not grounded in the substance of international affairs, but is directed toward fostering national unity or some other domestic concern, is likely to breed mistrust, doubt, and suspicion. Thus, we should not be surprised that demonstrators protesting the recent APEC summit in Vancouver accused Ottawa of putting "profits before people," "indulging murderers," and being "indifferent to human suffering." The anti-APEC protesters, in their anger, passion, and skepticism, are pointing to the principal difficulty of committing Canada to a policy of human security: Canada is not always prepared to achieve the ambitious set of ideals that human security entails.

In abandoning its moralist pretensions and in tempering its aspirations with regard to human security, Ottawa need not abandon its commitment to human rights, democracy, the rule of law, and good governance. Canada ought to pursue these objectives in such a way that the statesperson, after carefully deliberating over competing and conflicting moral claims, determines a course of action which is most appropriate given the particular circumstances that distinguish the problem. This means that we ought to pursue human rights, democracy, the rule of law, and good governance when the circumstances permit us to do so. It is this middle ground, that area between relativism which accords validity to all truth claims and a universalism which imposes one pattern of life on all, for which Canada's foreign policy ought to aim. This area is, admittedly, difficult to find; it is something which is constantly shifting: its boundaries are blurred and uncertain and its content is always open to change, challenge and revision. However, the substance of this middle ground is sufficiently stable so that we are able to speak of it in a meaningful way. The middle ground of which we speak is that area in which we secure the greatest possible amount of the many obtainable goods, but which does not permit injustice of a magnitude that would be rightly called intolerable. We ought to aim at achieving those goods which are associated with human security insofar as the circumstances permit us to do so; but in doing so, we ought to aim also at maintaining values such as political independence and noninterference—goods which are essential to the maintenance of the society of states. Thus, we see that the middle ground between relativism and universalism is an area whose procedural basis rests upon the virtue of compromise.

But in aiming for this middle ground, we ought to be forthright in acknowledging that occasions may arise when we ought not pursue certain policies for the sake of other fundamental values. Recognizing that fundamental values clash; that it may not be possible to secure all things considered to be good at all times and in all places; and that sometimes it is best to accept a state of affairs which does not satisfy all the requirements of justice, is only to realize that finding the middle ground is often difficult. And it is difficult to maintain ourselves in this area precisely because our values may clash and because our moral injunctions may demand conflicting action. That is why a foreign policy which is based upon prudential ethics does the greatest justice to Canada and to its neighbors. Thus, in the effort to secure these goods while, at the same time, preserving the good of pluralism, Canada's foreign policy toward Asia Pacific, and elsewhere, ought to be guided by the wisdom of Vico's learned sage, "who through all the uncertainties of human action keeps his eye steadily focused on eternal truth, manages to follow in a roundabout way whenever he cannot travel in a straight line so as to be as profitable as the nature of things permit" (Vico 1965: 35).

REFERENCES

Annan, Kofi (1998). *Annual Report of the Secretary-General on the Work of the Organization* The Fifty-Third Session of the General Assembly (New York: United Nations).

Aristotle (1963). *Ethics* John Warrington ed. & trans. (London: J.M. Dent and Sons).

Axworthy, Lloyd (1997). *Notes for an Address by the Honourable Lloyd Axworthy, Minister of Foreign Affairs, at the Consultations with Non-Governmental Organizations in Preparation for the 53rd Session of the United Nations Commission on Human Rights* (Ottawa: February 5).

_____(1996a). *Notes for an Address by the Honourable Lloyd Axworthy, Minister of Foreign Affairs, at the Consultations with Non-Governmental Organizations in Preparation for the 52nd Session of the United Nations Commission on Human Rights* (Ottawa: February 13).

_____(1996b). *Notes for an Address by the Honourable Lloyd Axworthy, Minister of Foreign Affairs, to the 52nd Session of the United Nations Commission on Human Rights* (Geneva, Switzerland: April 3).

_____(1996c). *Notes for an Address by the Honourable Lloyd Axworthy, Minister of Foreign Affairs, to the 51st General Assembly of the United Nations* (New York, NY: September 24).

Baldwin, David (1997). "The Concept of Security" *Review of International Studies* 23: 1–26.

Berlin, Isaiah (1969). "Historical Inevitability" *Four Essays on Liberty* (Oxford: Oxford University Press).

_____ (1991). "The Pursuit of the Ideal" *The Crooked Timber of Humanity* Henry Hardy ed. (London: Fontana Press).

Canada, (1995). *Canada in the World* (Ottawa: DFAIT).

Carr, E. H. (1946). *The Twenty Year Crisis: 1919–1939* (London: Macmillan).

Commission on Global Governance (1995). *Our Global Neighbourhood* (Oxford: Oxford University Press).

Gilles, David (1996). *Between Principle and Practice: Human Rights in North-South Relations* (Montreal: McGill-Queen's University Press).

Jackson, Robert H. (1990). *Quasi-States: Sovereignty, International Relations and the Third World* (Cambridge: Cambridge University Press).

_____ (1995). *Human Security in a World of States* Paper Presented at the Annual Conference of the International Studies Association (Toronto: March 18–22).

Krause, Keith and Michael Williams (1996). "Broadening the Agenda of Security Studies: Politics and Methods" *Mershon International Studies Review* 40: 229–54.

Lipschutz, Ronnie D. ed. (1995). *On Security* (New York: Columbia University Press).

Mill, John Stuart (1988). *The Logic of the Moral Sciences* (La Salle, IL: Open Court).

Morgenthau, Hans J. (1948). "The Twilight of International Morality" *Ethics* 58:2.

Nardin, Terry (1983). *Law, Morality, and the Relations of States* (Princeton: Princeton University Press).

Niebuhr, Reinhold (1958). "America's Moral and Spiritual Resource" in Earnest W. Lefever ed. *World Crisis and American Responsibility* (New York: Association Press).

Oakeshott, Michael (1996). *The Politics of Faith and the Politics of Scepticism* Timothy Fuller ed. (New Haven: Yale University Press).

Roberts, Adam and Benedict Kingsbury eds. (1993). *United Nations, Divided World: The UN's Role in International Relations* (Oxford: Clarendon Press).

Sallot, Jeff (1997). "Axworthy Warns APEC of Irrelevancy" *The Globe and Mail* (24 November): A1, A6.

Vico, Giambattista (1965). *On the Study Methods of Our Time* Elio Gianturco trans. (Indianapolis: Bobbs-Merrill Company, Inc.).

Waltzer, Michael (1994). *Thick and Thin: Moral Argument at Home and Abroad* (Notre Dame: University of Notre Dame Press).

NOTES

This essay was first presented at the Annual Meeting of the International Studies Association, Washington DC, February 16–20, 1999. The author would like to thank Barbara Arneil, Megan Gilgan, K.J. Holsti, Robert Jackson, Brian Job, Samuel LaSelva, Heather Owens, Hamish Telford, Mark Zacher, and the two anonymous reviewers for their helpful comments and suggestions.

1. The category "human rights," unless indicated otherwise, refers to the restrictive civil and political conception rather than the more permissive conception which includes economic, social, and cultural rights. The more inclusive category "fundamental values" refers to a cluster of issues such as peace, order, security, and justice.

2. For example see Lipschutz (1995); Krause and Williams (1996); and Baldwin (1997).

3. For example see Carr (1946).

4. For example see Roberts and Kingsbury (1993); Annan (1998); Commission on Global Governance (1995). It should be noted that global civil society, or transnational society, performs a very important role in promoting human security and shaping the content of national and international security discourse. But the importance and significance of this role does not indicate a parallel foreign policy which exists apart from state activity. Rather global civil society and states are part of the same process of foreign relations, although they serve different purposes and functions. For the purpose of this article it is most appropriate to focus upon states and the issues that affect them because the ultimate authority to conduct foreign relations is endowed in states and it is states, in spite of role and influence of global civil society, who bear ultimate responsibility for the success or failure of foreign policy.

5. The following discussion on security is derived from and heavily influenced by Jackson (1990) and Jackson (1995).

6. For a detailed explication of this argument see Jackson (1990).

7. This discussion is derived from Berlin (1969).

8. This thought is derived from Oakeshott (1996: 60–64).

9. For example, see Gillies (1996).

Postscript

It is worth noting that Canada has taken a lead role in promoting the "human security" agenda among other states. Following a bilateral meeting between Lloyd Axworthy and the Foreign Minister of Norway in 1998 to launch the idea, a larger forum was held which included foreign ministers from Austria, Chile, Ireland, Jordan, the Netherlands, Slovenia, South Africa, Switzerland, and Thailand.

Although Bain questions whether the concept of human security is in keeping with Canadian foreign policy traditions, one can certainly argue that Canada's promotion of the idea follows its traditional role as a middle power. Axworthy, a former political scientist and university professor, has long been an advocate of the notion of "soft power." According to this view, Canada's power in the international community lies not in its military power, but in its ability to promote powerful ideas. Thus, Canadian efforts to build an international coalition of "like-minded" states around humanitarian issues in the 1990s can be seen a perpetuation of Canada's traditional role as middle power. What it means to be a middle power and whether this is still a relevant concept will be taken up on the next issue.

In his critique of human security, Bain is fearful that Canada may pursue a moralistic and interventionist foreign policy. In examining cases where Canada has pursued human security as goal is there evidence that it has tried to impose its claims on other states?

It is worth noting that Bain also suggests that "abandoning its moralist pretensions and ... tempering its aspirations" does not mean that Ottawa "abandon[s] its commitment to human rights, democracy, the rule of law, and good governance." But, it should pursue these objectives only "when the circumstances permit us to do so." If Bain's advice had been taken during the past decade, how different would Canadian foreign policy be? What issues might Canadian foreign policy makers have chosen not to promote?

Infotrac Keyword Search
"human" + "security"

Suggested Additional Reading

Axworthy, Lloyd. "Human Security and Global Governance: Putting People First," *Global Governance*, 7, 1 (January 2001).

Hampson, Fen Osler and Dean F. Oliver. "Pulpit Diplomacy: A Critical Assessment of the Axworthy Doctrine" *International Journal* 54, 3, (1998): 379–406.

_____. *Madness in the Multitude: Human Security and World Disorder,* Don Mills: Oxford University Press, 2002.

Jockel, Joe and Joel Sokolsky, "Lloyd Axworthy's Legacy: Human Security and the Rescue of Canadian Defence Policy," *International Journal,* 56, 1 (Winter 2000–2001): 1–18.

Khong, Yuen Foong, "Human Security: A Shotgun Approach to Alleviating Human Misery?" *Global Governance,* 7, 3 (July–Sept 2001).

McRae, Robert and Don Hubert. *Human Security and the New Diplomacy: Promoting People, Promoting Peace.* Montreal: McGill-Queen's University Press, 2001.

Nef, Jorge. *Human Security and Mutual Vulnerability: An Exploration into the Global Political Economy of Development and Underdevelopment.* Ottawa: International Development Research Centre, 1995.

Suhrke, Astri. "Human Security and the Interests of States." *Security Dialogue,* 30, 3 (1999): 265–76.

Website Resources

The Canada–Israel Committee: David H. Goldberg, "Foreign Minister Lloyd Axworthy's Concept of 'Human Security' and Canada's Contribution to Peacemaking in the Middle East" This paper examines the concept of human security as it applies to Canada's role in the Middle East.

Government of Canada, Department of Foreign Affairs and International Trade: Human Security This site offers a definition of human security and discusses Canada's role in human security.

Harvard University, Centre for Basic Research in Social Sciences: Program on Human Security This site offers a number of papers relating to human security.

Human Security Network The Human Security Network supports and encourages initiatives that protects human security.

United Nations Association Canada: George MacLean, "The Changing Perception of Human Security: Coordinating National and Multilateral Responses" This paper defines and illustrates how human security can create a more peaceful global climate. The paper also looks at modern threats to human security.

Can Canada's Foreign Policy Be Best Understood by the Concept of "Middle Power"?

✔ **YES**
ANDREW COOPER, RICHARD HIGGOT, AND KIM RICHARD NOSSAL, excerpt from
Relocating Middle Powers: Australia and Canada in a Changing World Order
(Vancouver: University of British Columbia Press, 1993), pp. 16–32

✘ **NO**
MARK NEUFELD, "Hegemony and Foreign Policy Analysis: The
Case of Canada as a Middle Power," *Studies in Political Economy*
48 (Autumn 1995): 7–29

In assessing the dramatic changes brought about by the end of the Cold War, many analysts have been concerned about how these developments affect the leading military power in the world, the United States. But the breakup of the Soviet Union, the expansion of the European Community and of the North Atlantic Treaty Organization (NATO), the emergence of the Asia-Pacific region as a new centre of economic activity, and other developments have forced other states, including Canada, to undertake a rethinking of their international roles as well.

Andrew Cooper, Richard Higgot, and Kim Richard Nossal have studied how Canada, along with similar powers such as Australia, has sought to adapt to the changing international system. They argue that the concept of "middle power" provides a useful concept for understanding Canada's changing role in the world. The concept of "middle power" has a long history in the study of Canadian foreign policy. But its meaning and application as a guide for policymaking have frequently been the subject of disagreement.

The concept of Canada as a middle power emerged after the Second World War. Before that time, Canadian policymakers largely accepted the prevailing assumption that the international system was divided into two categories of states: the great powers, who dominated the decisionmaking in international politics; and the minor powers, including Canada. As a result of Canada's contribution to the war effort, and its expanded international activities after the war, Canadian officials devoted more attention to defining Canada's place in the world. As early as 1944 Lionel Gelber wrote:

Under the impact of war, Canada has moved up from her old status to a new stature. With her smaller population and lack of colonial possessions, she is not a major or world power like Britain, the United States or Russia. But with her natural wealth and human capacity she is not a minor power like Mexico or Sweden. She stands in between as a Britannic Power of medium rank. Henceforth in world politics, Canada must figure as a Middle Power. (Quoted in Kim R. Nossal, *The Politics of Canadian Foreign Policy* [Toronto: Prentice-Hall, 1997], p. 54)

By the late 1940s, Canadians increasingly saw themselves as a middle power—less "powerful" than the United States, Russia, or Great Britain, but more powerful than most other nations.

Although the concept of middle power became virtually synonymous with Canadian foreign policy, its precise definition has long been contested. Some scholars have associated middle power with specific attributes that can be used to rank Canada in the hierarchy of states. By such criteria as size, resources, and geographical location, Canada is said to be a "middling state." Others have associated middle power with a particular style of foreign policy. Generally used in conjunction with the concept of liberal internationalism, "middlepowermanship" was seen to be associated with support for international organizations, promotion of international negotiation and dialogue, and multilateral peacekeeping. Still others have rejected the notion of middle power altogether, arguing that other concepts such as principal power or dependent power are more helpful for understanding Canada's role in the world.

Despite the contested nature of the concept of middle power, Cooper, Higgot, and Nossal argue that it is still useful for analyzing Canada's role in the world. Rather than trying to identify specific criteria for measuring middle-power states, such as size, power, or geographical location, the authors associate middle power with a "particular style of behaviour in international politics." Middle powers are identified by "their tendency to pursue multilateral solutions to international problems, their tendency to embrace compromise positions in international disputes, and their tendency to embrace notions of 'good international citizenship' to guide their diplomacy" (p. 19). Cooper, Higgot, and Nossal apply their framework to a number of case studies comparing how Canada and Australia have adapted to a changing international environment. They conclude that, with the demise of the Cold War and the withdrawal of American leadership in some key areas of international politics, "the 1990s will be an era in which the technical innovation and entrepreneurship in the international diplomacy of middle powers could, if effectively coordinated, play an important role in shaping the future" (p. 180).

In the second essay, Mark Neufeld provides a contrasting interpretation of Canada as a middle power. Neufeld is interested in developing a critical analysis that focuses more directly on the connection between the social and economic structures of the capitalist economic system and the exercise of power in the international system. In developing this critique, Neufeld draws on Cranford Pratt's "dominant class" perspective on Canadian foreign policy, which argues that the policies of the state reflect the interests of the dominant class, which in a capitalist society is the capital-owning class. At the same time, Neufeld goes beyond Pratt to draw on the work of Antonio Gramsci, an Italian Marxist of the interwar period, and Robert Cox, of York University, who has attempted to apply Gramsci's insights to contemporary international political economy.

In developing his analysis, Neufeld argues that the development of the concept of middle power, rather than being a guide to direct Canadian policy in a more independent direction, was "an elite attempt to succeed ... in garnering widespread public support for government foreign policy initiatives while retaining sufficient flexibility to work in the service of dominant class interests." Nor does he think that the concept of middle power will serve as a useful guide for future foreign policymaking. Instead, he notes, "it would seem more likely that the issue of Canada's behaviour on the world stage will remain strongly contested, and a potential flash-point within the larger debate surrounding the proper role of the Canadian state in an era of globalization."

✔ **YES**

Excerpt from *Relocating Middle Powers: Australia and Canada in a Changing World Order*
ANDREW COOPER, RICHARD HIGGOT, AND KIM RICHARD NOSSAL

TOWARDS A TYPOLOGY OF MIDDLE POWER BEHAVIOUR

The changing nature of leadership and followership in the contemporary international system is one of the key reasons for wishing to reconsider middle power behaviour in international politics in general, and middle power leadership initiatives in particular, in a way that "relocates" the idea of middle powers in the contemporary international system. Accompanying the hiatus in structural leadership in the international order, there would appear to be a growing awareness on the part of some of the smaller players of the need to substitute for this omission.[1] Such an awareness emanates from a recognition of both constraints and opportunity in the international order in the 1990s. While the increasing exposure of the United States economy to the vagaries of globalization demonstrates the degree to which the growth of interdependence in the international system has had an impact on even the largest of states,[2] there was another category of states which felt, even more acutely, the impact of increased interdependence–the secondary but still highly developed countries in the international system. Often thought of as quintessential middle powers, two of these–Canada and Australia–provide some empirical support upon which we attempt to reformulate middle powers as a useful conceptual category in international politics.

This [excerpt] briefly reviews the evolution of the middle power concept in the postwar international politics literature, following which some of the applications of the concept are examined. Moving from a critique of the earlier literature, we then propose a reformulated model of the concept. This reformulation focuses on state activity and behaviour in given issue areas and suggests the relevance of an egoistic definition of interest rather than a structural definition. It thus differs from traditional analysis of middle power foreign policy, which has tended to focus on aspects of aggregate state power, "location" in the hierarchy of states, or idealist normative influences. Above all, this approach–drawing on several examples of "middle power" behaviour in the latter part of the 1980s–offers both an analysis of, and prognosis for, potentially significant innovation and initiative on the part of secondary, but not insignificant, players in the management of various aspects of the international agenda in the 1990s.

Although the term middle power has long been used in discourse about Australian and Canadian foreign policy in the post-1945 era, there is little agreement on what constitutes a middle power in international politics. We can identify at least four general approaches to the definitional problem.

It is most common to define a middle power by its *position* in the international hierarchy. In this view, middle powers are said to be those states occupying the "middle" point in a range of bigness to smallness—usually measured by reference to such quantifiable attributes as area, population, size, complexity and strength of economy, military capability, and other comparable factors. Such an approach has its problems, particularly its dependence on quantifiable measures of power, but it does satisfy the intuitive desire to differentiate between those states which clearly are not great powers but are not minor powers either.[3]

Others, by contrast, have suggested that middle power derives from a state's *geography*. A middle power, it is asserted, is a state physically located "in the middle" between the system's great powers.[4] The geographic approach has at least two variants. One suggests that states which are powerful within their geographic regions might usefully be thought of as middle powers. Another, common in the bipolar Cold War period, suggests that middle powers occupy a "middle" position, ideologically, between polarized great powers.[5]

A third approach is the *normative* view of middle powers. In this view, middle powers are seen as potentially wiser or more virtuous than states positioned either "above" them (the great powers) or "below" them (the minor powers). Middle powers have been thought to be potentially more trustworthy because they can exert diplomatic influence without the likelihood of recourse to force. In addition, because of their past roles—for example, the participation of Australia and Canada in the First and Second World Wars·and the Korean War—they are thought to have earned certain rights, at least from their hegemonic ally, the United States. Because of this, countries located "in the middle" are portrayed as taking their responsibilities to the creation and maintenance of global order seriously; indeed, they have as a result often appeared less selfish than other states.[6]

Although buttressed by a long historical and philosophical pedigree, especially in Canada,[7] the limitations inherent in this emotionally centred view are numerous and significant. Viewed using normative lenses, middle power behaviour takes on a certain smugness, occupying the moral high ground of the politics of the "warm inner glow." Such a position, however, is often difficult to substantiate when the actual details of middle power foreign policy are examined more closely. Contrast, for example, Australian and Canadian rhetoric on Kuwait's sovereignty in the Gulf conflict of 1990–1 with their silence on Indonesia's invasion and annexation of East Timor in 1975. Likewise, Canada's reputation as an aid-giver in international emergencies can be contrasted with the hands-off approach adopted by Ottawa during the Nigerian civil war in the mid-1960s. These cases demonstrate the dangers of advocating a normative approach to middle power behaviour: middle powers can be asked to back their fine rhetoric with concrete actions or be susceptible to the charge of the "arrogance of no power."[8]

A more difficult problem with the normative approach is that it tends to exclude a wide variety of states which might reasonably claim membership in the ranks of the middle power tier according to other criteria. This problem is most clearly seen in the attempts of Cranford Pratt and his colleagues to examine "humane internationalism" as it has been practised by middle powers.[9] Their "middle powers," in fact, comprise only a small selection of international actors, mainly states that are "like-minded" developed northern states of middle size—Canada, the Netherlands, Norway, and Sweden—rather than a broader range of states that might include such countries as Argentina, Australia, Brazil, Hungary, India, Indonesia, Malaysia, Nigeria, or Poland.

Yet another problem with this normative approach relates to the demanding standards set for middle-power statecraft—standards which are difficult to meet even by the like-minded countries which have traditionally been opinion-leaders on North–South and development issues. The result, it may by suggested, is undue pessimism concerning the current direction of middle power diplomacy in the international arena. Instead of capturing the dynamism of middle power leadership in a variety of specific issue areas in the 1980s and 1990s, the present role (and future potential) of the middle powers appears to be in retreat, largely because of the uneven response of those countries to extremely broad and multi-layered topics with little hope of establishing workable agendas such as the New International Economic Order (NIEO).[10]

The central premise of this book is that the essence of middle power diplomatic activity is best captured by emphasizing not what this group of countries should be doing but what type of diplomatic behaviour they do, or could, display in common. This fourth approach, the *behavioural*, pays less attention to whether states remain on consistently high moral ground and more attention to a particular style of behaviour in international politics—a style that John W. Holmes termed, with considerable irony, "middlepowermanship."[11] According to this approach, middle powers are defined primarily by their behaviour: their tendency to pursue multilateral solutions to international problems, their tendency to embrace compromise positions in international disputes, and their tendency to embrace notions of "good international citizenship" to guide their diplomacy.[12] Certainly, the foreign ministers of both Australia and Canada tended to embrace such notions in their public statements,[13] even when they did not use the words "middle power."[14]

Such middle power behaviour, it should be noted, is guided by healthy doses of enlightened self-interest: as Gareth Evans, the Australian minister for foreign affairs and trade, once stated, good international citizenship is not "the foreign policy equivalent of boy scout good deeds."[15] It is also guided by a belief in the technical and entrepreneurial ability to fulfil such a role—what Holmes saw as the functional resources for effective performance.[16]

Moreover, middle power behaviour has been far from static in nature. As the international system has changed, we have seen dramatic modification in the behaviour of these states. Middle power statecraft in the immediate post-1945 era was very much in support of that order established and underwritten by American hegemony. In particular, these states were especially active participants in, and supporters of, international organizations spawned by that order. Yet, constrained by the parameters imposed by tight bipolarity and the Cold War conflict, middle power diplomacy tended to manifest a reactive quality. With the international agenda dominated by geopolitical-security issues, middle powers had little room for manoeuvrability. For the most part, their diplomatic efforts were directed towards easing global tensions and, through peacekeeping and arms control, trying to avert the possibility of the outbreak of another world war. As Bernard Wood put it, "For much of the post war period most of the middle powers may have felt themselves to be by-standers (or as basically acted upon rather than acting in these matters), with the implicit recognition that their role consisted in anticipating these external pressures and adjusting to them as swiftly as possible."[17]

In certain circumstances, the role adopted by middle powers encompassed mediatory activity between two antagonistic Cold War blocs. This idea of middle powers acting as "lynchpins" or "bridges" between East and West gained some prominence in the 1950s and 1960s. In particular, countries such as India (particularly under Jawaharlal Nehru) and Sweden frequently engaged in this type of inter-bloc diplomatic activity, but it was not limited to non-aligned or neutral states, as Canada's initiatives towards the Soviet Union in October 1955 indicate. More commonly, however, the statecraft of aligned middle powers tended to focus on intra-bloc relations: attempting to defuse tensions between bloc powers (during the Suez crisis of 1956, for example), or urging restraint on the alliance leader (during the Korean and Vietnam wars, for instance), or resisting renewed tendencies towards isolationism on the part of the bloc leader. Finally, a considerable amount of attention was paid by the middle powers to mediation and conflict resolution with respect to regional "brushfires," which had the potential of escalating into more widespread conflicts.

To say that the middle powers were highly reactive in their diplomatic activity in the 1950s and 1960s[18] is not to suggest that this group of countries did not have an impact on the international system generally or on the hegemonic leader specifically. To use Keohane's analogy, many of these non-great powers were, indeed, "able to lead the elephant" on occasion.[19] Cases of this type, however, remained, for the most part, atypical and were restricted to instances in which the United States was basically willing to be reined in. The overall impression one gets of middle power behaviour in that period, then, is not that of leadership but of what we term "first followership"—a form of activity in which those actors loyally support the norms and rules of the international system and perform certain tasks to maintain and strengthen that system.

By contrast, adapting to new circumstances in the late 1980s and early 1990s, middle powers became increasingly quick and flexible in responding not only to some new conditions and circumstances but in taking different forms of initiatives in policy terms. While growing interdependence threw up more challenges and exposed these states to greater vulnerabilities, particularly in the international economic system, it also provided new windows of opportunities (or, perhaps more accurately, new windows of necessity) for middle powers. It seems clear that middle powers had greater freedom of action thrust upon them in terms of their diplomacy. Because of the gap in the power base, resulting from the relative decline of American resources (and, hence, the umbrella of structural leadership and willingness to lead), these actors were provided with an opportunity to take on greater—albeit selective—forms of responsibility. As part of a more general shift towards burden sharing, followers from the post-1945 era were well positioned to take advantage of the added available space in which to operate: as Puchala and Coate put it, "numerous middle powers are now looking for ways to assert themselves in the context of the ... leadership void."[20] Indeed, research in the field of organizational behaviour suggests that committed and able members "in the ranks" tend to adopt new forms of creative action when confronted with altered circumstances or demands: over time, there is the possibility that followers may adopt leadership roles.[21]

Two other factors worked to reinforce the ability and willingness of middle powers to adopt a more activist, initiative-oriented approach in the international arena. The first is the change in the global agenda. Whereas "high" policy issues—the first agenda of international relations—were dominant in the 1950s and 1960s, "low" policy issues were ascendant in the 1970s, the 1980s, and the early 1990s. Concerns about economic security comprise the second agenda of contemporary international politics; this has been joined by a third agenda of social concerns such as environmental policy and human rights. This shift has, in turn, altered perceptions and definitions of national interest. The "security agenda," for example, took on a wider meaning in international relations generally.[22] For middle powers in particular, the search for national economic well-being and the maximization of economic sovereignty became as important as traditional conceptions of security, which fixed on physical or territorial conceptions of integrity.

A second significant factor impelling middle power activism is the accentuated intermeshing of domestic politics with foreign policy. With low issues increasingly in command, internal societal forces have been more involved in "domestic" issues having international ramifications and in those "international" issues which spill over into the national arena—ineluctably, as Putnam would have it, a two-level game.[23] In many cases, of course, this heightened form of internal pressure introduces a strong element of constraint on policy formulation and implementation. Despite high international expectations with respect to its role on an issue, for example, a given middle power may pull back from "doing something," because that action might cause pain to interest groups at home by making them more vulnerable to the exigencies of the changing international economic order. As Cutler and Zacher argue, the result is that, although middle powers such as Canada tend to be portrayed as having a firm attachment to multilateralism and international institution-building, their actual policy behaviour reveals that they have, at best, an uneven commitment to multilateralism.[24]

A classic case of this dynamic was the protectionism on textiles practised by a number of industrialized middle powers, Australia and Canada among them. While the government of Pierre Trudeau put a high priority on global economic development, it was also sensitive to the local needs and interests of Canadian industries—largely concentrated in Ontario and Quebec. With the political sensitivity of the issue heightened by the election of the Parti Québécois government in November 1976, and the run-up to the referendum on sovereignty-association in 1980, bilateral quotas were imposed on imports of clothing and footwear from low-cost sources.[25] Resistance to trade liberalization in this set of domestic industries was even stronger (and more effective) in the Australian case. Despite the cost imposed by such actions in terms of its economic and diplomatic relations with its neighbours in the Association of Southeast Asian Nations (ASEAN), the Liberal government of Malcolm Fraser responded to pressure by both manufacturers and trade unions to save jobs by imposing tougher new restrictions on imports of textiles, clothing, and footwear in the late 1970s.

If they can be a constraint on some issues, however, internal societal forces may push for stronger action or the exploration of more innovative options on other issues. Numerous examples of this pattern can be found in such areas as the environment, human rights, and development assistance—where non-state actors in general, and nongovernmental organizations in particular, can move out in front and provide pay-offs for governments that act expeditiously.... In Canada, the issue that stands out as a case in which societal forces led and government followed was the Ethiopian famine crisis, which took place between 1984 and 1985. Galvanized by television images of the catastrophe, the public responded en masse in Canada. While established nongovernmental organizations (NGOs), such as Inter Pares, Oxfam Canada, Care Canada, and the Canadian University Services Overseas, played an important role, one of the distinctive features of this campaign was the high degree of mobilization of ad hoc groupings such as Ethiopian Airlift and the Ethiopian Famine Relief Fund. Another was the scope of this type of activity, which ranged from high-profile campaigns of popular singers to create a "Northern Lights" trust fund to widespread grass roots endeavours.[26] These public campaigns, in turn, prompted the government in Ottawa to accelerate its own efforts. Less than a year after the government had rejected a proposal for massive relief operations as unnecessary, a special fund for Africa was initiated, and an emergency coordinator of African relief was appointed. As Joe Clark, Canada's secretary of state for external affairs, admitted, "Governments, particularly democratic governments, are affected by public priorities."[27]

What emerged in the 1980s and 1990s was not only a more segmented but a more multifaceted type of behaviour. Middle powers did not move to share structural leadership with the United States; nor, generally speaking, did they have the ability or the aspiration to move into a position of joint leadership on this basis. The leadership behaviour of middle powers was not of the classical type identified by James MacGregor Burns and other students of the phenomenon—that is, leadership based on coercion by brute strength.[28] Nor is it based on economic capability of the sort possessed by the country viewed by many as the "incipient leader of tomorrow"—Japan.[29] Rather, middle power leadership and initiative-taking have been based on non-structural forms of power and influence associated with the imaginative and energetic use of their diplomatic capabilities. The skills they have utilized are not those of a giant but of a good dancer—what, in a plea for more deft American leadership, David Abshire referred to as "persuasion, coalition-building, and the art of the 'indirect approach.'"[30] These are skills that the United States tended to underestimate in the late 1980s; by the early 1990s, Japan was still learning them. Although Japan, as the world's largest creditor and aid giver, had tremendous economic power, there was little sign that Tokyo was prepared to exercise agenda-based leadership. Japan's priority was primarily that of avoiding risks and danger. In contrast to the activism displayed by more skilful middle powers, its diplomatic approach remained exceedingly cautious and reactive in nature.[31] Far from taking the lead on specific issues, it tended to hang back and let other actors do the running.

In attempting to schematize the emergent pattern of middle power behaviour, we suggest that the dimensions highlighted by Oran Young serve as a useful starting point for mapping out categories of action.[32] A middle power approach to diplomacy (for this is what we are trying to demonstrate) emphasizes entrepreneurial flair and technical competence in the pursuit of diplomatic activities. Not only is this diplomacy devoted to building consensus and cooperation on issue-specific agendas, it is invariably differentiated and has an important temporal element as well. Consequently, an itemized pattern of middle power behaviour—changing over time—can be set out:

Catalyst: Entrepreneurial middle powers may act as a catalyst with respect to a diplomatic effort, providing the intellectual and political energy to trigger an initiative and, in that sense, take the lead in gathering followers around it.

Facilitator: In the early and middle stages the focus would be on agenda setting. The actor (or actors) would be a facilitator for some form of associational, collaborative, and coalitional activity. As we will show in our discussion of both Canada and Australia, coalition-building on issue-specific questions is a central technique of leadership for middle powers, which do not have the structural sources of power available to the great powers. Instead, as Sylvia Ostry has rightly observed, "Coalitions are a means of leveraging power."[33] This type of work invariably entails the planning, convening, and hosting of formative meetings, setting priorities for future activity, and drawing up rhetorical declarations and manifestos.

Manager: A third stage would be that of a manager, with a heavy emphasis on institution-building. Institution-building is used here in its broadest sense to include not only the creation of formal organizations and regimes but also the development of conventions and norms.[34] Central to institution-building is a work program that establishes a division of labour, the development of monitoring activity, and, possibly (but not necessarily), the establishment of a secretariat or bureaucracy. This managerial stage also requires the development of confidence-building measures and facilities for dispute resolution, in which trust and credibility are built up. Confidence-building also seeks to alleviate misunderstandings and misperceptions through liaison efforts, shuttle diplomacy, the use of alternative formal and informal fora, the creation of transparency, and other means to push a given process forward. In addition, this activity can be complemented by a push to demonstrate the relevance or importance of the initiative by operationalizing some of the more practical (and de-politicized) proposals and programs.

These roles depend on a small, core group of public officials and on the collection of data, which often requires the technical skills of specialists in the national bureaucracy or outside experts. It is often the case that specialists have been involved in the process for a considerable time and have had continuing input into the genesis of a given proposal. This represents a substantial departure from past behaviour, which was premised on the belief that this activity was the exclusive "turf" of diplomats.

Such activities are, of course, not the sole preserve of middle powers. Often the great powers have larger bureaucracies, more technical specialists, and greater resources in general at their disposal. However, they also invariably have larger agendas and a wider range of pressures and preoccupations than do middle powers, for whom one international issue may loom so large on their respective political agendas that they devote a larger proportion of their time, energy, and resources to it. In this regard, it is possible that there may be a considerable disjuncture between the overall structural capabilities of a given middle power on the one hand and its technical and entrepreneurial abilities and desires in a given policy area on the other.

This is what Gareth Evans, Australia's minister for foreign affairs and trade in the late 1980s and early 1990s, has called "niche diplomacy." It involves "concentrating resources in specific areas best able to generate returns worth having, rather than trying to cover the field."[35] How and why middle powers choose to allocate their technical resources to particular international policy issues is one of the more interesting and important questions for students of international relations to pursue in the 1990s. Several general comments may be made here. Concentration on the second and third agendas of international relations arises, in part, because, beyond the general question of potential global nuclear war, many of the developed middle powers do not feel themselves threatened by the issues on the first agenda of international politics—for example, the territorial integrity of the Scandinavian states, Australia, or Canada is not threatened from outside. On the other hand, technical and complex questions on the second and third agendas are threatening traditional high standards of living—for example, the Australian economy being hurt by a subsidy war between the United States and the European Community or the quality of the environment in Canada being under jeopardy from American pollution.

Significantly, these are not discrete foreign policy questions. Nor are they simply political questions manageable from within foreign ministries, using the traditional instruments of diplomacy. Invariably, they are technical questions, although no less political for that. They require not only international negotiators but also specialists from within and outside government to lay the knowledge basis for cooperative problem-solving activity on these matters at the international level. This required both countries to reassess their bureaucratic structures for the conduct of foreign policy....

There is, thus, a potentially important role for capable middle powers, with appropriate skills, to build transgovernmental and transnational coalitions to facilitate policy coordination in important issue areas on the international agenda "after hegemony." Needless to say, we are not trying to overestimate the magnitude of this form of initiative in international relations. The influence of middle powers in agenda setting and policy coordination will be constrained by structural pressures; their influence will vary issue by issue, by institutional arena, and by the openness and receptivity to initiatives from other sources. In addition, early initiatives from middle powers in a given issue area are always likely to be easier than they will be in the later stages of any particular piece of policy implementation. Enforcing compliance to agreements will invariably require structural power and institutional support as well as technical and entrepreneurial innovation.

But the general approach to understanding middle power leadership activity as identified above has a number of advantages. First of all, by focusing less on positional attributes and more on the tasks performed on specific issues, a more systematic (and less arbitrary) assessment of the range of middle power leadership activities can be achieved. Rather than concentrating on the behaviour of a narrow group of "like-minded" countries, for example, this mode of analysis opens up the possibility of studies on a wider range of middle-sized countries. While it is more inclusive, this approach does not devalue the currency of middle power leadership. To be included in the category of middle powers, countries have to act as middle powers. Further, this typology opens the way for a more nuanced portrayal of the diplomatic behaviour of individual middle powers—through a greater scrutiny of stylistic differences within this common middle power approach to diplomacy.

ISSUE-SPECIFIC BEHAVIOUR: AUSTRALIA AND CANADA COMPARED

To operationalize the model of middle power behaviour laid out above, we use Australia and Canada as useful test cases.[36] Historically, both of these countries may be characterized as committed "first followers" of the post-1945 international order. Australia and Canada accepted (and indeed, "internalized") the norms and values of that system; they self-consciously accepted what Paul Painchaud called a middle power "ideology,"[37] or what MacKay termed the "doctrine of the middle powers."[38] They also participated to a high degree in many of the diplomatic activities designed to support that order (especially at the founding of the United Nations in San Francisco in 1945), taking on a variety of functional responsibilities in areas in which they had some expertise or capacity.[39]

Australia and Canada have long had the potential to take initiatives on specific issues. Notwithstanding the traditional reactive nature of much of their diplomacy in such areas as peacekeeping and crisis management, both Australia and Canada were at the forefront of building international institutions (such as the Food and Agriculture Organization (FAO), for example), the strengthening of regimes such as the General Agreement on Tariffs and Trade (GATT), and economic development in the South (with schemes like the Colombo Plan of the early 1950s). Nor were Australia and Canada reluctant to criticize the United States or other major powers in the Cold War era, when they believed that the behaviour of the great powers ignored or subordinated the rights of middle powers. It might be noted that, in such efforts, these middle powers frequently spoke for other countries as well.

At the same time, however, Australia and Canada are useful to study because they appear to epitomize different styles of contemporary middle power behaviour.[40] To illustrate these differences, we characterize foreign policy behaviour on two intersecting axes, illustrated in Figure 1. One axis indicates the intensity of the initiatives undertaken: at one pole, we locate what the public policy literature calls the "heroic" approach to policymaking;[41] at the other pole are located "routine" approaches. The other axis represents the scope of international initiatives. At one pole we identify initiatives that are diffuse in focus; at the other end are discrete initiatives—those that are more narrowly defined and more separate.

On the intensity axis, Australia generally took a more heroic approach to leadership in international affairs. Australian initiatives tended to be ambitious exercises involving a great deal of effort and risk-taking. They were also highly politicized, in the sense that activity in this form tended to require a high degree of assertiveness and political will. Thus, Australian initiatives were exemplified both by a tendency towards personal diplomacy and an effort to mobilize domestic societal forces behind the initiatives.[42]

FIGURE 1
CHARACTERIZING MIDDLE POWER BEHAVIOUR

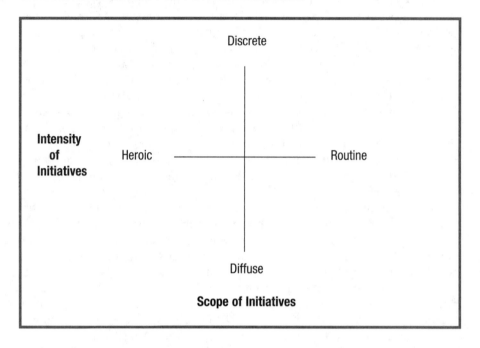

Canada, by contrast, has long been viewed as a practitioner of a more "routine" form of middle power leadership, with a great deal of emphasis on external mediation and internal consensus-seeking. Heroic initiatives, such as Trudeau's North–South initiative of 1980–1 and his peace initiative of 1983–4 were the exception and not the rule of Canadian diplomacy.[43] Certainly, both of these high-profile initiatives received considerable criticism at home: such forays into personal diplomacy were viewed by many commentators as contributing to counterproductive swings in Canadian diplomacy.[44] If successful in focusing domestic societal (and media) attention on important international issues for a brief period of time, these efforts lacked the political impetus and bureaucratic backup to be effective in the long run. Facilitated by the debate generated after the report of the Commission on International Development Issues (the Brandt Report), Trudeau did get North–South issues onto the agenda at the July 1981 Group of Seven (G-7) Summit he hosted at Montebello, Quebec. But after the Cancún North–South conference—at which he served as co-chair—failed to achieve any agreement on future strategy, Trudeau appeared to lose interest in the issue.

A similar, even more exaggerated, illustration of this pattern may be discerned in Trudeau's peace initiative of 1983–4. This initiative was launched in response to the deepening East–West tensions that followed the shooting down of Korean Air Lines flight 007 in September 1983 and the widespread fear that war was imminent.[45] Trudeau chose to launch the initiative with a major speech at Guelph, Ontario, in October 1983. Key officials from the Department of External Affairs, the Prime Minister's Office, and the Privy Council Office devoted considerable time and resources to developing concrete proposals for negotiation. A heavy emphasis was placed on shuttle diplomacy by the prime minister: Trudeau carried his peace initiative to the Commonwealth Heads of Government Meetings in New Delhi and also to Washington, Moscow, various Western European capitals, Eastern Europe (including East Berlin), and Beijing. This initiative did appear to have some calming effect on the tenseness of the East–West relationship. But its impact was lessened considerably, because, as J.L. Granatstein and Robert Bothwell noted, "his unilateral initiative had been hurriedly cobbled together ... and no effort had been made to build support for the initiative through patient low-level diplomatic discussions."[46]

If we turn to the other axis—the scope of international initiatives—it is clear that Australian leadership tended to be discrete rather than diffuse. If Australian diplomacy tended to be deep, it was not broad. Insecure, and becoming more and more marginalized within the international political economy,[47] Australia tended to focus its activity on a small number of issues, where stakes were particularly high. Initiatives tended to be linked to attempts to reform the rules of the game in the international order. For all of the declaratory statements concerning Australia's relationship with the Third World as a whole, few initiatives were directed outside the Asia-Pacific region. Indeed, a concern with over-stretching Australian capabilities limited and curtailed these non-regional initiatives, even in situations in which Australia wanted to act as the archetypal "good international citizen." Nothing better illustrates the point than the failure of Australian aid initiatives in Africa.[48]

Conversely, initiatives in Canadian diplomacy were more diffuse. Being alone with the United States of America in North America tended to make Canadian governments fearful of excessive regionalism.[49] Instead, governments in Ottawa tended to concentrate on initiatives of a global or functional orientation. While overshadowed by the prime minister's personal diplomacy, Canadian diplomatic initiatives were characterized by their variety and diversification during the Trudeau period. Canada found itself having both the will and the means to take the lead on second and third agenda items, galvanized by both a desire to protect parochial national interests as well as a sense of international stewardship. Canada moved well out in front of both the United States and the major Western European countries on a number of environmental and resource issues in the 1970s. For example, the voyages of the American supertanker *Manhattan* in the Canadian Arctic in 1969 and 1970 and the *Arrow* oil spill off Nova Scotia in February 1970 catalyzed the Canadian government into enacting legislation in 1970 that was to provide an important stimulus for global action against ocean pollution.[50] Likewise, Canada was instrumental in helping to launch a new environmental regime through the United Nations Conference on the Human Environment held in Stockholm in 1972. Distancing itself from both the United States and Britain in these endeavours, Canadian diplomacy concentrated on building support for action along these lines among both other middle powers and the developing countries. A particular emphasis was placed on institution-building. At the administrative level, Canada pushed successfully for the creation of a new international agency within the UN. At the normative level, the Canadian priority was for the development of uniform anti-pollution standards or a universally accepted code of ethics.

These efforts, in turn, formed a component of Canada's wider approach to the Law of the Sea negotiations. Canadian behaviour on this complex and multifaceted issue area epitomized the global and functional orientation of Canadian diplomacy. Avoiding a high-profile campaign on the claims of sovereignty, Canadian diplomacy focused on low-key, detailed, sustained activity over a broad range of issues, extending from pollution control, fishing protection, international straits, and mining in the deep seabed. Usually its coalition-building skills (through the Group of Twelve, and the Land-Based Producers' Group), and its reputation as a long-standing supporter of the development of international law in multilateral settings, the Canadian government was able to exert considerable influence over the outcome of these negotiations.[51]

It should be added in this context that Canadian officials played a prominent and diverse role in these types of initiatives. For example, Maurice Strong served as secretary-general of the Stockholm conference and was a strong and persistent advocate of the establishment of the United Nations Environment Program (UNEP). Likewise, the Department of External Affairs (DEA) showed certain adaptability in its willingness to acquire and disseminate technical knowledge in the environment issue area. Not only did the DEA establish a Scientific Relations and Environmental Problems Division and an Environmental Law Section in 1970 (to complement the work of the newly formed Department of the Environment), the department also relied heavily on the Legal Division (headed first by Allan Gotlieb and then by Alan Beesley) within the DEA for specialized advice. Externally, this combination of "diplomacy, law and science" facilitated on-going forms of technical collaboration between Canada and personnel from other countries.[52]

CONCLUSIONS

The purpose of this chapter has been to establish a framework for reassessing and, indeed, relocating the nature and role of middle powers. We have been at pains to make clear that we are not entirely comfortable with this concept as it has evolved over the postwar period. Historically, the concept has tended to be a somewhat blunt instrument for "locating" states such as Australia and Canada in an increasingly complex and interdependent world. Indeed, as it tended to be used in the postwar period, the concept of middle power came to lack definitional clarity. While some might be inclined to discard the concept altogether, we argue that the notion of middle power retains both validity and usefulness. The key, we suggest, is to try to move beyond the level of generality usually associated with discussions about middle powers. We argue that the notion of middle power becomes useful to the scholar and practitioner of international politics when we begin to consider the international agenda in an issue-specific manner and when we look at the behaviour of states rather than their positional or normative location in the international system....

NOTES

1. For one critique of structuralism that argues that it limits our understanding of leadership politics in Europe, see Stanley Hoffmann, "The Case for Leadership," *Foreign Policy* 81 (Winter 1990–1): 20–38.

2. Robert O. Keohane and Joseph S. Nye, Jr., *Power and Interdependence*, 2nd edition (Boston: Scott Foresman, 1989).

3. The work of Bernard Wood is indicative. In *The Middle Powers and the General Interest*, no. 1 in the series *Middle Powers in the International System* (Ottawa: North–South Institute, 1990), table 1, p. 18, Wood uses a positional approach to identify a "loose tier" of thirty-three states, which he asserts "would likely be proposed as middle power candidates according to any criterion."

4. In the nineteenth century, German theorists sought to analyze the role of the German states as *Mittelmachten*, located between the great powers of continental Europe. Interestingly, a century later, a study of West German foreign policy attributed middle power status to Germany on similar grounds. See Carsten Holbraad, *Middle Powers in International Politics* (London: Macmillan, 1984), 72.

5. For a discussion and critique of such an argument, see Kim Richard Nossal, *The Politics of Canadian Foreign Policy*, 2nd edition (Scarborough, ON: Prentice-Hall, 1989), 50.

6. Holbraad, *Middle Powers in International Politics*.

7. For example, see the essays in J. King Gordon, ed., *Canada's Role as a Middle Power* (Toronto: Canadian Institute of International Affairs, 1966). Also see the writings of John W. Holmes, particularly his *Canada: A Middle-Aged Power* (Toronto: McClelland and Stewart, 1976). Two very useful reviews of the literature on middle powers in a Canadian context are to be found in: Michael K. Hawes, *Principle Power, Middle Power, or Satellite?* (North York, ON: York Research Programme in Strategic Studies, 1984); and Maureen Appel Molot, "Where Do We, Should We, or Can We Sit? A Review of Canadian Foreign Policy Literature," *International Journal of Canadian Studies* 1–2 (Spring/Fall 1990): 77–96.

8. Paul Keal, ed., *Ethics and Australian Foreign Policy* (Sydney: Allen and Unwin, 1992), 16.

9. Cranford Pratt, ed., *Middle Power Internationalism: The North–South Dimension* (Kingston and Montreal: McGill-Queen's University Press, 1990); Pratt, ed.,

Internationalism under Strain: The North–South Policies of Canada, the Netherlands, Norway, and Sweden (Toronto: University of Toronto Press, 1989).

10. Robert Rothstein, "Regime Creation by a Coalition of the Weak: Lessons from the NIEO and the Integrated Program for Commodities," *International Studies Quarterly* 28 (Summer 1984): 307–28.

11. John W. Holmes, "Is There a Future for Middlepowermanship?" and Paul Painchaud, "Middlepowermanship as an Ideology," both in Gordon, ed., *Canada's Role as a Middle Power*, 13–36.

12. Wood, *Middle Powers and the General Interest*, 20.

13. For Australia, see Gareth Evans, "Australia's Place in the World," *Australian Foreign Affairs Review* 59 (December 1988): 526–30; "Australia's Foreign Policy: Responding to Change," *ibid.*, 61 (September 1990): 586–94; "Australia's Place in the World: The Dynamics of Foreign Policy Decision-Making," in Desmond Ball, ed., *Australia and the World: Prologue and Prospects* (Canberra: Strategic and Defence Studies Centre, Australian National University, 1990); Gareth Evans and Bruce Grant, *Australia's Foreign Relations in the World of the 1990s* (Melbourne: Melbourne University Press 1991), 322–6. For Canada: Joe Clark, "Canada's New Internationalism," in John Holmes and John Kirton, eds., *Canada and the New Internationalism* (Toronto: Canadian Institute of International Affairs, 1988), 3–11.

14. For example, in December 1991, Barbara McDougall, Canada's secretary of state for external affairs, described Canadian policy in precisely these middle power terms but studiously avoided using the words "middle power." See Barbara McDougall, "Introduction," in John English and Norman Hillmer, eds., *Making a Difference? Canada's Foreign Policy in a Changing World Order* (Toronto: Lester, 1992), ix–xvi.

15. *Department of Foreign Affairs and Trade—The Monthly Record* (hereafter *DFAT Monthly Record*) 61 (September 1990): 592.

16. John W. Holmes, *The Shaping of Peace: Canada and the Search for World Order, 1943–1957*, vol. 1 (Toronto: University of Toronto Press, 1979).

17. Bernard Wood, "Towards North–South Power Coalitions," in Pratt, ed., *Middle-Power Internationalism*, 69–107.

18. T.B. Millar, *Australia in Peace and War* (Canberra: Australian National University Press, 1978); Nossal, *Politics of Canadian Foreign Policy*.

19. Robert O. Keohane, "Big Influence of Small Allies," *Foreign Policy* (Spring 1971): 161–82.

20. Donald Puchala and R.A. Coate, *The State of the United Nations, 1988* (Hanover, NH: Academic Council on the United Nations System, 1988).

21. W. Litzinger and T. Schaefer, "Leadership through Followership," in William E. Rosenbach and Robert L. Taylor, eds., *Contemporary Issues in Leadership* (Boulder: Westview 1989); also Robert E. Kelly, "In Praise of Followers," *Harvard Business Review* 66 (November–December 1988): 142-8.

22. The best formulation may be found in Barry Buzan, *People, States and Fear: An Agenda for International Security Studies in the Post Cold War Era* (London: Harvester Wheatsheaf, 1991).

23. Robert Putnam, "Diplomacy and Domestic Politics: The Logic of Two-Level Games," *International Organization* 42 (Spring 1988): 427–60.

24. A. Claire Cutler and Mark W. Zacher, "Introduction," in A. Claire Cutler and Mark W. Zacher, eds., *Canadian Foreign Policy and International Economic Regimes* (Vancouver: UBC Press, 1992), 4.

25. For example, Glenn P. Jenkins, *Costs and Consequences of the New Protectionism: The Case of Canada's Clothing Sector* (Ottawa: North–South Institute, 1980).

26. *The African Famine and Canada's Response, A Report by the Honourable David MacDonald, Canadian Emergency Coordinator–African Famine, for the Period from November 1984 to March 1985* (Hull, PQ: Canadian International Development Agency, 1985).

27. Cited in James Travers, "Ethiopia: Is It a Fad or Step to Solution?" *Ottawa Citizen* (10 November 1984).

28. Burns, *Leadership*, 4.

29. Richard Rosecrance and Jennifer Taw, "Japan and the Theory of International Leadership," *World Politics* 42 (January 1990): 290.

30. David Abshire, "The Nature of American Global Economic Leadership in the 1990s," in William Brock and Robert Hormats, eds., *The Global Economy: America's Role in the Decade Ahead* (New York: Norton for the American Assembly, 1990), 175–8.

31. Kenneth Calder, "Japanese Foreign Economic Policy Formation: Explaining the Reactive State," *World Politics* 40 (July 1989): 517–41.

32. Young, "International Regime Formation," 349–75; "Political Leadership and Regime Reform," 1–42.

33. Sylvia Ostry, "Changing Multilateral Institutions: A Role for Canada," in Cutler and Zacher, eds., *Canadian Foreign Policy and International Economic Regimes*, 337.

34. Robert O. Keohane, *Institutions and State Power: Essays in International Relations Theory* (Boulder: Westview, 1990), 1–20.

35. Gareth Evans and Bruce Grant, *Australia's Foreign Relations in the World of the 1990s* (Melbourne: Melbourne University Press, 1991), 323.

36. Indicative would be Annette Baker Fox, "The Range of Choice for Middle Powers: Australia and Canada Compared," *Australian Journal of Politics and History* 26 (1980): 193–203.

37. Painchaud, "Middlepowermanship as an Ideology," argued that the belief systems of those who practised this kind of middle power role had all the features of a political ideology.

38. R.A. MacKay, "The Canadian Doctrine of the Middle Powers," in H.L. Dyck and H.P. Krosby, eds., *Empire and Nations: Essays in Honour of Frederic H. Soward* (Toronto: University of Toronto Press, 1969), 133–43; reprinted in J.L. Granatstein, ed., *Towards a New World: Readings in the History of Canadian Foreign Policy* (Toronto: Copp Clark Pitman, 1992), 65–75.

39. Examples would include Escott Reid, *On Duty: A Canadian at the Making of the United Nations, 1945–1946* (Kent, OH: Kent State University Press 1983); and Paul Hasluck, *Diplomatic Witness: Australian Foreign Affairs 1941–1947* (Melbourne: Melbourne University Press, 1980).

40. For an exploration of some differences in the issue area of agriculture, see Andrew F. Cooper, "Like-Minded Nations/Contrasting Diplomatic Styles: Australian and Canadian Approaches to Agricultural Trade," *Canadian Journal of Political Science* 25 (June 1992): 349–70.

41. On the concept of "heroic" leadership, see Stanley Hoffmann, "Heroic Leadership: The Case of Modern France," in Lewis J. Edinger, ed., *Political Leadership in Industrialized Societies: Studies in Comparative Analysis* (New York: John Wiley, 1967), 108–54; and J. Hayward, "National Aptitudes for Planning in Britain, France and Italy," *Government & Opposition* 9 (1974): 397–410.

42. For example, Richard A. Higgot, "International Constraints on Labor's Economic Policy," in Brian Galligan and Gwyn Singleton, eds., *How Labor Governs: The Hawke Government and Business* (Melbourne: Longman Chesire, 1991); and "The Politics of Australia's International Economic Relations: Adjustment and the Politics of Two-Level Games," *Australian Journal of Political Science* 26 (March 1991): 2–28; and Andrew Fenton Cooper, "Australia: Domestic Political Management and International Trade Reform," in Grace Skogstad and Andrew Fenton Cooper, eds., *Agricultural Trade: Domestic Pressures and International Trade* (Halifax, NS: Institute for Research on Public Policy, 1990), 113–34.

43. On the peace initiative, see Richard and Sandra Gwyn, "The Politics of Peace," *Saturday Night* (May 1984), 19–32. On the North–South initiative, see Kim Richard Nossal, "Personal Diplomacy and National Behaviour: Trudeau's North–South Initiatives," *Dalhousie Review* 62 (Summer 1982): 278–91.

44. For example, Stephen Lewis, the former leader of the Ontario New Democratic Party, whom Brian Mulroney had appointed as Canada's permanent representative to the UN, was scathing in his attack on this approach: "When the prime minister was engaged in an issue it was the centrepiece of Canadian public policy. But when Prime Minister Trudeau lost interest in or was not engaged in an issue, it was no longer the centrepiece." Quoted in the *Toronto Star* (26 November 1987), A3.

45. For a discussion of Soviet fears of war at this time, see Michael McGwire, *Military Objectives in Soviet Foreign Policy* (Washington: Brookings Institution, 1987), esp. ch. 13.

46. J.L. Granatstein and Robert Bothwell, *Pirouette: Pierre Trudeau and Canadian Foreign Policy* (Toronto: University of Toronto Press, 1990), 375.

47. Richard A. Higgot, "The Dilemmas of Interdependence: Australia and the International Division of Labor in the Asia Pacific Region," in James Caporaso, ed., *The New International Division of Labor: International Political Economy Yearbook,* vol. 1 (Boulder: Lynne Reinner, 1987), 147–86.

48. D. Porter, B. Allen, and G. Thompson, *Development in Practice: Paved with Good Intentions* (London: Routledge, 1991); and C. Gertzel and D. Goldsworthy, "Australian Aid to Africa," in P. Eldridge, D. Forbes, and D. Porter, eds., *Australian Overseas Aid* (Canberra: Croom Helm, 1986).

49. See, for example, Molot, "Where Do We, Should We, or Can We Sit?"

50. John Kirton and Don Munton, "The Manhattan Voyages and Their Aftermath," in Franklyn Griffiths, ed., *Politics of the Northwest Passage* (Montreal and Kingston: McGill-Queen's University Press, 1987), 67–97.

51. Elizabeth Riddell-Dixon, *Canada and the International Seabed: Domestic Determinants and External Constraints* (Kingston and Montreal: McGill-Queen's University Press, 1989).

52. Michael Tucker, *Canadian Foreign Policy: Contemporary Issues and Themes* (Toronto: McGraw-Hill Ryerson, 1980), 33.

✗ NO
Hegemony and Foreign Policy Analysis: The Case of Canada as a Middle Power
MARK NEUFELD

INTRODUCTION

It has become commonplace in the discipline of international relations to observe that changing conditions in the global order demand new analyses of that order. The dissolution of the Soviet bloc and the lingering global economic downturn are both touted as developments requiring new appraisals and prognoses. Equally important, this realization has its parallel at the (meta-)theoretical level; it is increasingly accepted that the failure of students of world politics to anticipate and account for the sea-changes of the past few years cannot be divorced from a discussion of the way in which world politics has been studied. Simply put, what is required is not just new analysis, but new ways of analyzing; not merely re-examination of global structures and processes, but critical exploration of alternatives to the dominant theoretical traditions and analytical frameworks that have guided our thinking about world politics.[1]

It is the intent of this paper to pursue this theme with regard to the analysis of Canadian foreign policy in the context of a changing global order. The alternative tradition that will be the focus is one which is derivative of neo-Marxist theories of the state—an approach to foreign policy which Pratt has termed "dominant class theory."[2] It will be argued that the "dominant class theory" approach to the study of Canadian foreign policy, as articulated by Pratt and others, can be strengthened and enhanced through the integration of Gramscian-inspired theorizing—in particular, the notion of "hegemony." I will illustrate this point in terms of the notion of Canada as a "middle power." Before moving to a discussion of the relevance of the Gramscian notion of hegemony, and to its usefulness in conceptualizing discourse around the notion of "middlepowermanship," however, I will briefly examine recent developments in the theoretical mainstream which also take up the question of new ways of analyzing in relation to the notion of Canada as a "middle power."

RELOCATING CANADA AS A MIDDLE POWER: NEOREALIST DIRECTIONS

In a review of scholarly literature on Canadian foreign policy, Molot has argued that what distinguishes that literature is a preoccupation with Canada's "location" in the international system.[3] Typical has been the notion of Canada as a "middle power" which informed traditional analyses of Canada's place in the world in terms of diplomatic practice and influence, and, more recently, with reference to Canada's position within the global economy.[4]

With reference to the wider academic literature, Molot identifies two liabilities attached to this approach. First, in concentrating analysis on Canada's middle power status, and the attendant "selfless" character of Canadian foreign policy, this approach has "tended to ignore considerations of national interest in Canadian action, despite emphasis in the larger international relations literature on precisely this issue."[5] Furthermore, argues Molot, given the centrality of the analysis of international regimes during the 1980s,

> It is noteworthy that there has been no analysis of Canada's behaviour in international and other institutions as what Lake describes as a "system supporter," particularly given the liberal internationalist tradition in Canadian scholarship.... Does the regime paradigm of analytical utility have a Canadian perspective, or does it exemplify a theoretical preference at variance with Canadian interests?[6]

In this regard, it is significant that recent works coming out of the theoretical mainstream have attempted to address both these issues. Of particular note is Cooper, Higgot, and Nossal's *Relocating Middle Powers: Australia and Canada in a Changing World Order,*[7] where an effort is made to relate Canadian foreign policy initiatives during the 1980s to the issue of "national interest." More importantly, the authors frame the question of Canada as middle power not in terms of its location, but rather in terms of an approach to diplomacy, "geared to mitigating conflict and building consensus and cooperation."[8] Drawing heavily upon the very regime literature highlighted by Molot, they argue that middle power diplomacy

> will fix on mediatory and consensus-building activities, especially such activities as building reformist coalitions ... to bring about change within existing regimes or creating "foundational coalitions" to establish new regimes.[9]

It must be recognized that, in terms of the mainstream study of Canadian foreign policy, *Relocating Middle Powers* represents important progress. In emphasizing the centrality of Canada's "national interest," this approach demonstrates that power and interest cannot be ignored; as such, it provides an effective counter to the idealist-inspired myth of Canadian "exceptionalism" in foreign policy practice. Furthermore, by drawing on the regime literature the approach makes several important contributions. First, by integrating the concept of international regimes[10] it becomes possible to take a more differentiated view of the international context in which foreign policy is made and implemented.[11] Secondly, the notion of regimes opens the door to the integration of interpretive methodologies and explicitly normative concerns.[12] And finally, it allows for the conceptualization of greater autonomy for international actors—of particular relevance when the object of foreign policy analysis is a non-superpower.

It must be acknowledged, however, that the neorealist/regime-oriented approach represented by *Relocating Middle Powers* suffers from important liabilities as well. First, neorealism's neglect of the important role played by social forces and societal structures in determining state action leads to an exaggeration of the autonomy of the state bureaucracy in foreign policy making.[13] Furthermore, neorealism's focus on the "national interest" lends legitimacy to policies in place, obscuring the degree to which state policy may serve some parts of the "nation" better than others. A parallel critique can be directed at regime theory, where the clear predilection to support the basic principles of the Liberal International Economic Order (LIEO) obscures the degree to which that order serves the interests of some individuals and groups better than others.

As a consequence, it must be recognized that the neorealist/regime-oriented approach to the study of foreign policy is not a neutral one. In every case, the object of analysis—i.e., the liberal-capitalist state, or the LIEO—becomes something to be accommodated and not challenged. In short, despite its strengths, the neorealist/regime-oriented approach to the study of Canadian foreign policy can be understood as a form of "traditional theory," seeking to facilitate the smooth working of existing social and political arrangements.[14] Accordingly, here the focus will be on the development of a more "critical" form of foreign policy analysis—an approach that, instead of accepting the status quo, seeks to challenge the "ideologically frozen relations of dependence"[15] that sustain it.

THE DOMINANT CLASS MODEL AND CANADIAN FOREIGN POLICY

Although marginalized within mainstream foreign policy analysis, it is important to note that effects to develop a critical approach to the study of foreign policy have been made. One of the most important is Cranford Pratt's exploration of the relevance of the "dominant class model." Following Pratt, the defining characteristics of the dominant class model can best be understood in terms of an alternative answer to the question "How can one best conceptualize theoretically the interaction of government and society in the making of Canadian foreign policy?" In contrast to neorealism's emphasis on the autonomy of the bureaucracy in constructing policies in the "national interest," the dominant class approach suggests that

> the capital-owning class in any capitalist state is the dominant class and that the policies of the state reflect and perpetuate that dominance.[16]

Accordingly, notes Pratt, dominant class theory approaches the study of foreign policy by concentrating on the widely pervasive bias in policy towards the interests of the dominant class. Sometimes this bias operates through the structural constraints identified by the structural theorists and sometimes through the network of linkages identified by the so-called instrumental theorists. Through the power which the dominant class has to shape social attitudes and values, its influence extends far beyond those cases where structural determinant or direct class influence can be demonstrated. It can thus claim to be a powerful theory even while abandoning any aspiration to reduce to class terms the whole range of internal factors which influence policy formation.[17]

The dominant class theory approach has a number of strengths. First, dominant class theory, like neorealism, is able to attribute a considerable degree of autonomy to the state; unlike neorealism, however, which must be content to affirm the universal pursuit of power, dominant class theory is able to identify the specific goals pursued by the state apparatus: the reproduction of the capitalist relations of production. Second, dominant class theory acknowledges the crucial legitimizing function of an accepted dominant ideology that "provides a rationale for the private and severely unequal ownership of capital."[18]

At the same time, it must be conceded that the dominant class approach suffers from some lacunae. First, the dominant class approach as articulated by Pratt is limited to being a theory of "foreign policy," thus leaving largely unanswered the question of how its emphasis on class society at the domestic level relates to the larger global context. Secondly, to the degree that dominant class theory is derivative of structuralist Marxist theories of the state, it is prone to the same weaknesses as structuralist Marxism itself, the most serious of which is the over-emphasis on determining structures, and the corresponding neglect of human agency.

Accordingly, this paper will seek to build upon the strengths of dominant class theory by means of Gramscian-inspired theorizing at two specific levels. To begin, I will draw upon the Gramscian approach to the study of world order to sketch out the global politico-economic setting of Canadian foreign policy. This is necessary for two reasons. First, a focus on the global setting makes clearer how the emphasis on class society at the domestic level relates to the larger global context. Secondly, attentiveness to the material context of Canadian foreign policy is vital if the discursively oriented analysis which follows is not to descend into linguistic idealism.[19]

Consistent with the Gramscian emphasis on the importance of ideas, I will analyze the public discourse surrounding Canadian foreign policy at the domestic level. Specifically, I will focus on the regulative ideal of "middle power." It is important to stress that no fixed meaning is attached to this term. "Middle power" (and the attendant notion of "middlepowermanship") will be approached as an "essentially contested concept," whose definitional content in any given context is a product of efforts by societal agents to define key terms in public discourse in a way consistent with the political project they support. In certain contexts, those articulating a vision corresponding to the interests of the dominant class (e.g., government leaders, mainstream intellectuals) may enjoy a relatively free hand in defining key terms. In others, the understanding of key terms in public discourse may be hotly contested by oppositional forces within society as part of the larger effort to give voice to political aspirations directly contradictory to the interests of societal elites. Accordingly, while the particular definitional content of the notion of "middle power/middlepowermanship" must be seen in relation to its material context, it should not be seen as merely the "effect" of that context; rather, its politico-normative content is the product of creative social agents in pursuit of concrete political projects.

CONCEPTUALIZING THE GLOBAL CONTEXT OF CANADIAN FOREIGN POLICY

It is necessary to distinguish the Gramscian notion of hegemony from that of (neo)realism. In the neorealist framework, states are understood to be the principal actors in the international realm. Given a context of "anarchy"—that is, an absence of a central authority with a monopoly on the legitimate use of force—states compete with one another in an ongoing struggle for power. The distribution of capabilities (power) across the units (states) is the key variable in explaining outcomes in the international system.

Accordingly, in neorealist terms international orders may be understood as hegemonic or non-hegemonic. They are hegemonic to the degree that a preponderance of power on the part of one state (the hegemon) allows it to dominate other states, thereby serving as a rough approximation of a central authority. Hegemonic international orders in this sense have been seen as the necessary precondition for a liberal international economy embodying the norms of openness and nondiscrimination.[20]

In contrast, the Gramscian notion of hegemony assumes a capitalist world economy in which relations between classes is a key explanatory variable.[21] The role and activities of social structures, from firms to states to international organizations, are understood in terms of class relations. As in the case of neorealism, hegemony can be applied to an analysis of the international realm. In this case, however, hegemony is understood to involve not dominance of one state by another, but rather the institution and maintenance of a world order which serves the interests of the dominant class of the dominant state while at the same time it serves the interests of the dominant classes of other states as well.[22]

As such, a hegemonic order is characterized by the fact that the dominant power presents that order as consistent with the common interest. As Cox notes, in a hegemonic world order "A leading nation's conception of the world becomes universalized to the point where its own leaders stand by the universalized principles when they conflict with particularist domestic interests."[23]

Thus, in contrast to the neorealist approach, the Gramscian notion of hegemony allows us to conceptualize not two but three distinct categories of world order: (i) a hegemonic world order, defined by a duly recognized leader whose actions are understood to serve the "common interest" (i.e., those of the dominant social classes at home as well as associated elements in other states); (ii) a non-hegemonic order in which a single state dominates other actors in pursuit of its own "national" interests; and (iii) a non-hegemonic order in which power is sufficiently diffused so that no single state dominates all others.

The Gramscian-derived notion of hegemony is not limited to the level of the international order, however. In terms of core states, at least, hegemony at the international level has its parallel in hegemony at the domestic level, where dominant classes make real concessions (always within limits) to subordinate classes to achieve broad societal consent for their leadership.

A hegemonic world order, then, implies relations of hegemony in the international/interstate realm coupled with hegemonic relations at the level of civil society in core states. Such an order, moreover, has important consequences in terms of the understanding of the behavioural norms and institutions established to regulate the world order, whether it be a question of inter-state conflict or forces of civil society acting across borders. Significantly, these norms and institutions are not identified with the narrow interests of specific states or social classes, but rather take on a semblance of universality and, therewith, an aura of legitimacy.[24]

In terms of the post-war period, one can speak of a hegemonic world order extending from the end of the Second World War to the mid-1960s. In this period, the United States established a world order built around norms and institutions that Ruggie has termed the "compromise of embedded liberalism"—i.e., a Keynesian welfare state combined with a liberal(izing) international economic order—all stabilized under the overarching structure of the cold war.

By the end of the 1960s, however, the bases for a stable American-led hegemony were beginning to erode. The expectation of continuing economic growth and rises in productivity, which had been central to the stability of the hegemonic order as the means of moderating both inter- and intra-state conflict, proved more and more questionable. Indeed, the very components of the "compromise of embedded liberalism" came increasingly into conflict one with another.[25] Finally, the rise of East–West détente robbed the Soviet threat of much of its mobilizing efficiency.

As a consequence, hegemony began to dissolve not only at the international level, but also in domestic terms. In the United States, for example, hegemony began to unravel as the legitimacy of the American state and the order it represented came to be seen as open to question, a process clearly visible in the growing public opposition to US government policy in South-East Asia, as well as the increasingly vocal civil rights movement.[26]

Given the centrality of the leading state in the maintenance of any hegemonic order, the nature of the foreign policy of that state is a good indicator of the robustness of hegemony. As Cox notes, "The evidence of the decline of hegemony is to be sought less in loss of power than in a tendency towards unilateralism in furtherance of specific interests."[27]

In point of fact, by the 1980s the change in the nature of the global order was clearly visible in the shift in US foreign policy. Specifically, the Reagan administration's response to the undermining of American moral superiority and universalism took the form of "nationalist assertiveness," most clearly evident in the abandonment of multi-lateral consultative leadership, typifying hegemony, in favour of an unrepentant unilateralism—a trend which, arguably, remains very much present in US foreign policy into the present. Thus, the US remains dominant in the system at present. However, it must be remembered that, in contrast with neorealist notions of hegemony, in Gramscian terms US dominance is a sign of a *non*-hegemonic world order qualitatively different from the hegemonic pax-Americana which preceded it.

CANADA AS A MIDDLE POWER: THE HISTORY OF A CONCEPT

The early successes of Canada as a middle power were attributable to our skill in producing sound ideas for the general rather than just the Canadian interest. This is the way to be listened to.

John Holmes[28]

It was in the context of the American-led hegemonic order that the character of post-war Canadian foreign policy first took shape. Given Canada's status as a core state, the Canadian capitalist class enjoyed clear benefits in its association with American-led efforts toward liberalization in trade and investment regimes. Domestically, of course, concessions were extended to subaltern classes—in the form of the welfare state—to provide a stable basis for capitalist class hegemony within Canadian society.

It was also in this context that the regulative ideal of Canada acting in the world as a "middle power" first came into prominence. To begin, it is important to note that as a regulative ideal guiding state action, middlepowermanship was nested in a complex set of assumptions about the global order shared by Canada's politico-economic elite. Pratt identifies the following two assumptions as key:

i. the most serious threat to international peace and global human welfare was international communism and the strength of the United States was the primary bulwark against its spread;

ii. the international economic order and its major institutions operate to the substantial advance of all participants therein, that consequently no significant injustices or indefensible inequalities were due to the international economic relationships.[29]

It was these assumptions which provided "the underlying unity to such seemingly disparate policies as Canada's membership in the North Atlantic Treaty Organization, its close military and defence productions links with the United States, its expanding aid programme, its active role in peacekeeping, and its effective participation in international institutions ..."[30]

Upon the foundation of these assumptions, then, the notion of "middle power" was erected. As a regulative ideal, "middle power" must be understood in terms of both levels of the global order. In terms of the international level, middle-powermanship directed by the Canadian state to play a prominent role in multilateral fora, particularly in terms of international organizations associated with the North Atlantic community, and the Bretton Woods and UN systems. In this way, the notion of "middle power" oriented the Canadian state to a role supportive of the hegemonic global order in two critical senses: (i) by fulfilling an important role of facilitator and mediator, Canada helped to defuse potential conflicts which, if not addressed, might have undermined the stability of the global order;[31] and (ii) by showing itself willing to sacrifice short-term national interests for the greater good, Canada helped to reinforce the notion that the global order was in fact not a narrowly "American" order, but one which truly represented the "common interest."[32]

In terms of the construction of hegemony at the domestic level the notion of "middle power" played an important function as well. First, in its stability-reinforcing role of facilitator at the international level noted above, the Canadian state helped to create an environment conducive to economic growth. It was upon this growth that the compromise of the liberal welfare state—the cornerstone of hegemony within core states like Canada—depended. Secondly, the image of "middle power," with its attendant emphasis on Canada as a responsible member of the international community, was crucial in creating a domestic consensus in support of extensive involvement in the maintenance of the international order. As Holmes has noted, in the immediate post-war context the notion of "middle power" served the important function of "encouraging a wallflower people to get responsibly involved in keeping the peace and unleashing the world economy ..."[33] Finally, in representing Canada's selfless activism in the international realm as the natural expression of Canadian society as a whole, middlepowermanship reinforced the notion that the social order within Canada's borders was an essentially just one, and deserving of widespread public support.

It is clear, then, that in its original formulation, the regulative ideal of "middle power" was framed in terms of dominant class interests and in tune with a hegemonic global order. Nor is it surprising, given such an understanding of the origins of this formulation, that in a context of declining hegemony (both internationally as well as within core states) already discernible during the 1960s, this definition of middle power would progressively lose its value both as a guide for action and as a source of legitimacy....

Accordingly, as the 1960s came to an end, a growing dissatisfaction with the regulative ideal of "middle power" could be discerned within government circles. And since that time, efforts to find an alternative formulation, which would both safeguard dominant class interests as well as achieve public acceptance, have been a regular feature of Canadian political discourse.

The first such effort was made by the newly elected Trudeau government, which initiated a review of foreign policy, the result of which was a series of papers, collectively entitled *Foreign Policy for Canadians*.[34] There is no question that this report was designed to revise the terms in which foreign policy was understood.

What is most notable about *Foreign Policy for Canadians* was the explicit rejection of the essence of "middlepowermanship." "Public disenchantment" [read, "elite dissatisfaction"] with Canada's foreign policy, stated the report, was directly attributable to "an over-emphasis on role and influence" [read "middlepowermanship"] resulting in an "obscuring [of] policy objectives and actual interests."[35] It was "misleading," argued the report, "to base foreign policy on an assumption that Canada can be cast as the 'helpful fixer' in international affairs," a role which "no longer corresponds with international realities ..."

> There is no natural, immutable or permanent role for Canada in today's world, no constant weight of influence. Roles and influence may result from pursuing certain policy objectives ... but they should not be made the aims of policy. To be liked and to be regarded as good fellows are not ends in themselves; they are a reflection of but not a substitute for policy.[36]

It can be argued that the effort to redefine the regulative ideal for Canada's foreign policy away from the image of selfless internationalism to an explicitly self-focused pursuit of "national aims and interests in the international environment" was a logical response to a changing international environment marked by a hegemonic order in decline. The erosion of hegemonic pax-Americana allowed increasingly little scope for a middle power foreign policy characterized, at least in part, by a stance of "loyal opposition."[37]

Significantly, the break with "middlepowermanship" promoted by *Foreign Policy for Canadians* met with considerable resistance in many parts of the attentive public. In some quarters this resistance was motivated by a continuing allegiance to the traditional notion of "middle power," and the attendant "selfless" character of Canadian foreign policy. For others, however, the rejection of the alternative promoted by *Foreign Policy for Canadians* was grounded in a deeper-level dissatisfaction with the basic assumptions common both to the notion of a self-interested foreign policy as well as to the traditional practice of "middlepowermanship."

Indeed, it was public questioning of the traditional assumptions about the international order by emerging oppositional social groupings which led, outside of official circles, not to an abandonment, but to a substantive redefinition of the notion of "middle power." Pratt has referred to this social grouping, which arose in the context of declining hegemony, and remains active into the present context, as the "counter-consensus."[38] What distinguished the members of the counter-consensus was their rejection of the principal assumptions informing elite discourse about the global order, voicing criticism, in explicitly ethical terms, of both the militarism associated with the cold war as well as the workings of the international economy which they saw as systematically disadvantageous to the Third World.

Indeed, radicalization and expansion of the social base of the "counter-consensus" through the 1970s and 1980s, most recently in the context of anti-free trade struggles, led to increased emphasis on the links between disarmament, economic development and wealth redistribution, environmental policy, and democratization at the global level with radical change at the domestic level. In this respect the "counter-consensus" can be understood as forming part of an emerging "counter-hegemonic bloc."

Of particular importance for the discussion here is the fact that the counter-discourse of the "counter-consensus" gave new life to the regulative ideal of Canada as a "middle power." Significantly, the links of the earlier notion of "middle power" to support for an American-led hegemonic order were severed. Rather, "middle power" was recast to signify the influence enjoyed by a country like Canada, and the potential such influence offers to effect radical progressive change in terms of disarmament, economic development and wealth redistribution, environmental policy, and democratization of the foreign policy-making process:

> The outline of the global community, in which the planet's resources could be managed by institutions practising fairness and stewardship, is coming into view.... People who sense the power and creativity of our time now demand a safer, saner world in which governments, using the levers in hand, generate the production of the goods of life, not the weapons of death.
>
> As this constitutes an enormous challenge to Canada, this land so blessed in space, resources, technology, ability and reputation throughout the world. *The rise of middle-power influence* with the end of superpower enmity provides Canada with an unprecedented opportunity to work for the development of global security structures.[39]

It is not hard to appreciate how this oppositional understanding of "middle power," were it to achieve widespread acceptance, could pose a serious threat to dominant class interests at both the domestic and international level. Accordingly, it is not surprising to observe that the regulative ideal of "middlepowermanship"—if not the term itself[40]—resurfaced in the reviews of foreign policy conducted by the Mulroney government beginning in the latter half of the 1980s. What is equally noteworthy, however, is that the definitional content of the revived notion of "middle power" in official discourse differed significantly, not only from that of the counter-consensus, but also from the traditional notion of "middle power" associated with the heyday of pax-Americana. No longer was the notion of "middle power" designed to motivate "a wallflower people" to active participation in the management of a hegemonic global order. Rather, now "middlepowermanship" was defined in a way consistent with Holmes' observation, made in the 1980s, that if there was still a point in seeing Canada as a middle power, it was "to discipline ourselves":

> we still need guidelines to cling to and knowing one's strength remains a sound principle. If we are now more discriminating and calculating in our estimates of our own as well as others' powers, so much the better. Scepticism about spreading our good offices too wide may have induced a sense of proportion about the number of rescue missions, crusades, or moral interventions a country of twenty-five million can conduct at one time.
>
> Our moral majority may want the government to pass judgement on every misbehaviour in the world, and no doubt they will feel better if we do so, but it is the surest way to undermine the beneficient role of the middle power.[41]

In this regard, it is striking that beginning with the 1985 review of Canadian foreign policy, *Competitiveness and Security*, through the report of the Special Joint Committee on Canada's International Relations (*Independence and Internationalism*), the response of the government of Canada to the report of the Special Joint Committee (*Canada's International Relations*), and to the Defence White Paper of 1988–89, concessions to the "counter-consensus" that Canada must work in multi-lateral fora in the interests of peace and justice[42] were consistently twinned with observations about the limits to Canada's power and influence, and about the restrictions the international environment places on Canada's latitude of action. Accordingly, and notwithstanding the fact that "our values dictate that we help the poor, the hungry and the politically abused,"[43] Canadians were admonished to discipline their expectations, and accept the simple and unavoidable truth: "We do not have the resources to do all we would like in international affairs."[44] In short, the "limitationist" conception of "middle power" was a call to abandon exactly the kind of progressive activism entailed by the definition of "middle power" proffered by the counter-consensus (even while paying it lip service), in favour of an orientation more in keeping with existing power and privilege in Canadian society and in the global order.

CONCLUSION

The limitationist notion of "middle power" was an elite attempt to succeed—as the image of Canada as a self-interested, utility maximizer had not—in garnering widespread public support for government foreign policy initiatives while retaining sufficient flexibility to work in the service of dominant class interests. Accordingly, the limitationist notion of "middle power," which first achieved prominence in the Mulroney years, has also become a regular feature of official discourse since the election of the Chrétien government in 1993.[45] The Liberal government statement, *Canada in the World,* for example, repeats the pattern established in the 1980s by twinning affirmations of "exceptionalism" in Canada's foreign policy record

> Canada's history as a non-colonizing power, champion of constructive multilateralism and effective international mediator, underpins an important and distinctive role among nations as they seek to build a new and better order....

with thinly veiled admonishments to limit expectations of progressive action in the future:

> While Canadians strongly support an active foreign policy, they also have a realistic view about the challenges ahead and the constraints—especially financial constraints—that we face.... [Accordingly] we will not do everything we have done in the past, nor shall we do things as we have done before.[46]

In a similar vein, renewed enthusiasm in policy circles for peacekeeping, often represented as the quintessential expression of the Canadian tradition of "middle-powermanship,"[47] can be seen as a strategy to appeal to public sentiment while dampening expectations for progressive action. Specifically, a focus on peacekeeping (i) appeals to public sentiments which support a progressive role for Canada in the international realm, while (ii) serving as a justification for high levels of military spending, thereby deflecting calls for a "peace dividend." In terms of the international order, middle power as peacekeeper makes Canadian military forces available to serve the larger agenda of "global riot control" increasingly important in a non-hegemonic world order marked by US dominance.[48]

At the same time, it is far from certain that these efforts will be successful. For while government pronouncements in favour of peacekeeping and multilateralism may be more effective in garnering public support than the notion of a self-interested foreign policy in the national interest associated with *Foreign Policy for Canadians*, it is doubtful whether such a limited conception of middle power will, in the long run, satisfy the demands of the counter-consensus. Nor is it all clear in what sense even a limitationist notion of "middle power" can serve as an effective guide for policy-making in a post-hegemonic world order marked by

(i) American unilateralism; (ii) the lack of a unifying external threat (absent the Soviet menace); and (iii) increasing economic insecurity derivative of an unregulated global economy. Accordingly, it would seem much likely that the issue of Canada's behaviour on the world stage will remain strongly contested, and a potential flash-point within the larger debate surrounding the proper role of the Canadian state in an era of globalization.

Ironically, recent events would suggest that political leaders are finding even the limitationist notion of "middle power" too prone to incite expectations of progressive policy initiatives. It is noteworthy that, despite the call for the promotion of Canadian values such as human rights in *Canada and the World*, more recent statements have sought to distance government policy from that orientation by down-playing the importance of human rights records in determining Canada's trade relations.[49] Ultimately, political leaders may be tempted to distance themselves from even the limitationist notion of "middle power" to ensure sufficient latitude for the defence of dominant class interests, much as they have broken with the basic tenets of the welfare state. What is not clear is how public acceptance of the former can be achieved any more easily than the latter.

Finally, although too cursory an overview to be more than suggestive, the exploration of Canada and middlepowermanship effected here lends support to the argument that Gramscian theorizing—and in particular, the notion of hegemony—is a valuable adjunct to the dominant class approach to foreign policy analysis. To begin, it is compatible with—and, indeed, reinforces—dominant class theory's inherently critical orientation. Additionally, it provides a means of relating the global context to foreign policy-making, as well as a space for agency in terms of the construction of meaning through discourse. As such, the Gramscian approach is a viable alternative to realist-oriented theorizing, and deserves serious consideration in the search for analytical frameworks adequate to the contemporary world order.

NOTES

I would like to thank Leo Panitch, Fred Judson, Harriet Friedman, and, especially, Tony Porter for their comments on earlier drafts, as well as the Social Science and Humanities Research Council of Canada for financial support. An earlier version of this paper was prepared for the conference "Canada and the World," held in May 1993, at the Centre for International and Strategic Studies, York University.

1. For a discussion of this theme in relation to theorizing about world politics more generally, see Mark Neufeld, *The Restructuring of International Relations Theory* (Cambridge: Cambridge University Press, 1995).

2. Cranford Pratt, "Dominant Class Theory and Canadian Foreign Policy: The Case of the Counter-Consensus," *International Journal* 39 (Winter 1983–4), pp. 99–135.

3. Maureen Appel Molot, "Where Do We, Should We, or Can We Sit? A Review of Canadian Foreign Policy Literature," *International Journal of Canadian Studies* 1–2 (Spring-Fall 1990), pp. 77–96.

4. As a counter-position within the mainstream literature, see the literature on Canada as a principal power, in particular, David Dewitt and John Kirton, *Canada as a Principal Power* (Toronto: John Wiley & Sons, 1983).

5. Molot, "Where Do We ...," p. 80.

6. *Ibid.*, pp. 86–87.

7. (Vancouver: UBC Press, 1993). See also A. Clair Cutler and Mark W. Zacher (eds.), *Canadian Foreign Policy and International Economic Regimes* (Vancouver: UBC Press, 1992).

8. Cooper et al., *Relocating Middle Powers*, p. 174.

9. *Ibid.*, p. 174.

10. The classic definition is that of Krasner, where regimes are defined as "implicit or explicit principles, norms, rules, and decision-making procedures around which actors' expectations converge in a given area of international relations." Stephen D. Krasner, "Structural Causes and Regime Consequences: Regimes as Intervening Variables," in S. Krasner (ed.), *International Regimes* (Ithaca, N.Y.: Cornell University Press, 1983), p. 2.

11. For example, by distinguishing between economic and strategic contexts.

12. On this point, see Friedrich Kratochwil and John Gerard Ruggie, "International Organization: A State of the Art on the Art of the State," *International Organization* 40/4 (1986), pp. 753–75.

13. Critiques of the propensity of neorealist theorizing to reify the state, and thereby underplay (if not negate completely) the role of social forces are, of course, standard within critical theorizing about world politics. One of the best remains Richard Ashley, "The Poverty of Neorealism," in Robert Keohane (ed.), *Neorealism and Its Critics* (New York: Columbia University Press, 1986), pp. 255–300. For a parallel critique which targets Kirton and Dewitt's neorealist re-conceptualization of Canadian foreign policy, see Pratt, "Dominant Class Theory ...," pp. 108–15.

14. On the distinction between "traditional" and "critical" theory, see Max Horkheimer, "Traditional and Critical Theory ...," in Horkheimer, *Critical Theory: Selected Essays* (New York: Continuum, 1989), pp. 188–243.

15. Jürgen Habermas, *Knowledge and Human Interests*, trans. Jeremy J. Shapiro (Boston: Beacon Press, 1971), p. 310.

16. Pratt, "Dominant Class Theory ...," p. 104.

17. *Ibid.*, p. 116.

18. *Ibid.*, p. 105.

19. In this I follow Fredric Jameson in affirming that while history "is inaccessible to us except in textual form," history is nonetheless "*not* a text, nor a narrative, master or otherwise." Rather, "history is what hurts," and "its alienating necessities will not forget us, however much we might prefer to ignore them." See Jameson, *The Political Unconscious* (New York: Cornell University Press, 1981), pp. 35, 102.

20. The most developed formulation of this position is that of "hegemonic stability theory." See Robert Keohane, *International Institutions and State Power* (Boulder: Westview Press, 1989), esp. chapter four. See also David Lake, "Leadership, Hegemony, and the International Economy: Naked Emperor or Tattered Monarch with Potential?" *International Studies Quarterly* 37/4 (December 1993), pp. 459–89.

21. The pioneer in this regard is, of course, Robert Cox. For a good overview of the relevance of Gramscian theorizing for the study of world politics, see Stephen Gill (ed.), *Gramsci, Historical Materialism, and International Relations* (Cambridge: Cambridge University Press, 1993).

22. One of the outcomes of such a global order is the internationalization of what were, originally, domestic forces. As Cox notes, such an order "would most likely give prominence to opportunities for the forces of civil society to operate on the world scale (or on the scale of the sphere within which hegemony prevails)." See R. Cox, "Gramsci, Hegemony and International Relations: An Essay in Method," in Gill, *Gramsci, Historical Materialism, and International Relations*, p. 61. General agreement between representatives of the dominant classes of core states on politico-economic arrangements and strategies is often achieved by means of a semi-formal, institutionalized bargaining process located within Northern-controlled international organizations. In this regard, one can also speak of an internationalization of the dominant classes of core states not only in material terms, but also in terms of class-consciousness. See Stephen Gill, *American Hegemony and the Trilateral Commission* (Cambridge: Cambridge University Press, 1990).

23. Robert Cox, "Middlepowermanship, Japan, and Future World Order," *International Journal* 44 (1989), p. 829.

24. As Cox has noted: "The rules and practices and ideologies of a hegemonic order conform to the interests of the dominant power while having the appearance of a universal natural order of things which gives at least a certain measure of satisfaction and security to lesser powers." "Middlepowermanship ...," p. 825.

25. As Cox notes, the crisis of hegemony "became apparent at the level of the world economy in the conjunction of oil shocks, disarray in the international monetary system, the international transmission of inflation, and the downturn in growth in the advanced capitalist countries that also had consequential negative effects for Third World trading partners." See "Middlepowermanship ...," p. 829.

26. *Ibid.*, pp. 829–31.

27. *Ibid.*, p. 829.

28. John Holmes, "Most Safely in the Middle," *International Journal* 39 (Spring 1984). Reprinted in J.L. Granatstein (ed.), *Towards a New World: Readings in the History of Canadian Foreign Policy* (Toronto: Copp Clark Pitman, 1992), p. 100.

29. See Cranford Pratt, "Dominant Class Theory ...," pp. 120–21. To these two assumptions, shared by leading decision-makers both north and south of the 49th parallel, can be added a third, more distinctly Canadian notion, deriving from Canada's status as a non-superpower, namely that the national interest is best served by "an orderly and predictable world environment that embod[ies] some limits to the ambition and the reach of dominant powers." See Robert Cox, "Middlepowermanship ...," p. 824.

30. Pratt, "Dominant Class Theory," p. 121. For a discussion of the seamier side of Canadian diplomacy in the service of Pax Americana, see Noam Chomsky, "The Drift Towards Global War," *Studies in Political Economy* 17 (Summer 1985), pp. 5–31.

31. It will be remembered that the Pearsonian innovation of "peacekeeping" was prompted by the desire to regulate a conflict between core states during the Suez crisis. Specifically, the Canadian peacekeeping contribution allowed for a resolution of the potentially destabilizing rift between France and Great Britain, on the one hand, and the United States on the other. In short, it can be argued that from the beginning the principal function of peacekeeping has been to contribute to the maintenance of order and stability within the hegemonic sphere—a goal very much in keeping with the "national interest" of a non-superpower.

32. It can be argued that Canada's political leadership was not always completely consistent in this regard. One of the corollaries of middlepowermanship was the principle of functionalism, according to which countries, such as Canada, should be allotted a seat at the table in international organizations to the degree to which they contributed. This principle, while achieving some success in deterring the great powers from appropriating all decision-making power to themselves, clearly contradicted liberal international principles of global governance (i.e., the formal equality of all states) by arguing, in effect, that there should be a further differentiation between secondary and lesser powers. The cost of advocating a principle of global governance which hardly lent itself to the claim of representing the "common interest" was that at the first meeting of the UN General Assembly, Australia, and not Canada, won a seat on the Security Council. See Tom Keating, *Canada and World Order* (Toronto: McClelland & Stewart, 1993), chapter one.

33. Holmes, "Most Safely in the Middle," p. 90.

34. (Ottawa: Secretary of State for External Affairs, 1970).

35. *Foreign Policy for Canadians*, p. 8.

36. *Ibid.*, p. 8.

37. See Mark Neufeld and Sandra Whitworth, "Imag(in)ing Canadian Foreign Policy," in Glen Williams and Wallace Clement (eds.), *Building on the New Canadian Policy Economy* (Montreal: McGill-Queen's University Press, forthcoming).

38. Pratt defines the "counter-consensus" as "internationally minded public interest groups," which exist in substantial number, and which have traditionally been "peripheral to decision-making in Canadian public life." Within this group, Pratt includes church-related organizations like Project Ploughshares, the Canadian Council for International Co-operation, Oxfam, the Canadian Catholic Organization for Development and Peace, Ten Days for World Development, the Inter-Church Committee on Human Rights in Latin America, the Taskforce on the Churches and Corporate Responsibility, as well as secular organizations such as disarmament, peace, or Third World solidarity groups. One should also include organized labour, as well as extra-parliamentary opposition groups such as the National Action Committee.

39. *Transformation Moment: A Canadian Vision of Common Security*, The Report of the Citizen's Inquiry into Peace and Security (co-published by Project Ploughshares and the Canadian Peace Alliance, March 1992), p. 6, emphasis added.

40. As Cooper *et al.* note, in December 1991, Barbara McDougall, Canada's secretary of state for External Affairs, described Canada's foreign policy in middle power terms without, however, employing the term itself. See *Relocating Middle Powers*, p. 184, note 37.

41. Holmes, "Most Safely in the Middle," p. 102.

42. Now refurbished with the new title of "constructive internationalism."

43. *Competitiveness and Security*, p. 43.

44. Joe Clark, "Foreword," *Competitiveness and Security*.

45. Interestingly, under the Liberals, the term "middle power" itself has been resurrected. In early November, 1993, for example, the new Foreign Affairs minister, André Ouellet, promised a foreign policy review with explicit reference to the tradition of "middlepowermanship": "It's clear Canada's foreign policy must be reviewed in the context of the end of the Cold War.... It also has to be reviewed in the context of Canada's capacity, as a *middle* power, to play an important role at the United Nations ..." *The Toronto Star,* Friday, November 5, 1993, emphasis added.

46. *Canada in the World* (1995), pp. 8, 9.

47. A recent discussion of Canadian peacekeeping under the rubric of "middlepower-manship" is to be found in *Meeting New Challenges: Canada's Response to a New Generation of Peacekeeping*, Report of the Standing Senate Committee on Foreign Affairs (February 1993). For a critical look at the use of the image of Canada as peace-keeper, see Stephen Dale, "Guns N' Poses," *This Magazine* 26/7 (1993), pp. 11–16.

48. See Michael T. Klare, "The Pentagon's New Paradigm," in Micah Sifry and Christopher Cerf (eds.), *The Gulf War Reader* (New York: Random House, 1991), pp. 466–76.

49. In this regard, note Foreign Affairs Minister André Ouellet's insistence that "to try to be a Boy Scout on your own, to impose your own rules on others when indeed nobody else is following it is absolutely counterproductive and does not lead to any successful future." *The Globe and Mail,* Tuesday, May 16, 1995, p. A11.

Postscript

In entering into this debate it is important to note that, although the two articles both use the term hegemony, it is given quite different meanings in each. Cooper, Higgot, and Nossal use the term hegemony in the realist sense of the word, associating it with the unequal distribution and mobilization of material power resources. A state is considered a hegemonic power when it has a predominance of power resources, enabling it to exert dominance over subordinate actors. Subordinate states, fearing what the hegemonic power may do, will modify their behaviour in anticipation of the hegemon's reaction. Because of such anticipated reaction, hegemonic power may not always be exerted overtly. Cooper, Higgot, and Nossal are concerned with the implications of what they see as a decline in American hegemony because of the "relative decline of American resources" and less willingness on the part of the United States to take the lead. This decline has provided an opportunity for middle powers to adopt a larger and more activist role in some areas of foreign policy.

In contrast, Mark Neufeld draws on a Gramscian concept of hegemony. Gramscian analysis places more emphasis on the role of ideas and culture and the way that they shape preferences and constrain perceptions of possible courses of action. This perspective gives less attention to the role of the state as the dominant international actor and more emphasis on transnational social forces, thus shedding more light on the class dimension of international politics. According to this analysis, the preferences of the dominant classes become internalized in the sense that they become perceived as a shared set of values, ideas, and material interests. As a result, hegemonic power is exercised less overtly and coercively as its preferences become embedded in the ideas and institutions of a society. Thus, Neufeld argues that, rather than giving Canada a more independent role, middle-powermanship conferred on it a "role supportive of the hegemonic global order."

Suggested Additional Readings

Chapnick, Adam. "The Middle Power," *Canadian Foreign Policy*, 7, 2 (Fall 1999).

——. "The Canadian Middle Power Myth," *International Journal*, 55, 2 (Spring 2000): 188–206.

Holbraad, Carsten. *Middle Powers in International Politics*. London: Macmillan Press, 1984.

Keating, Thomas. *Canada and World Order: The Multilateralist Tradition in Canadian Foreign Policy*. Toronto: Oxford University Press, 2002.

Nossal, Kim Richard. *The Politics of Canadian Foreign Policy*. Scarborough: Prentice-Hall, 1997.

Pratt, Cranford. "Dominant Class Theory and Canadian Foreign Policy: The Case of the Counter-Consensus," *International Journal* 39 (Winter 1983–84): 99–135.

_____. *Middle Power Internationalism: The North-South Dimension.* Montreal: McGill-Queen's University Press, 1990.

Website Resources

Laurence Baxter and Jo-Ann Bishop, "Uncharted Ground: Canada, Middle Power Leadership, and Public Diplomacy" *Journal of Public and International Affairs* **(1998)** This piece examines Canada's role, as a "middle power," in the establishment of the Ottawa Treaty.

Government of Canada, Department of Foreign Affairs and International Trade: Foreign Policy The site offers a comprehensive display of Canada's current foreign policy in a number of issues. There are also a number of DFAIT publications, as well as archives.

The Middle Powers Initiative An organization that lobbies Middle Power states on nuclear weapons issues.

Should Canada Pursue a Strategy of Niche Diplomacy?

✔ **YES**
EVAN H. POTTER, "Niche Diplomacy as Canadian Foreign Policy" *International Journal* LII (Winter 1996–7): 25–38

✗ **NO**
HEATHER A. SMITH, "Caution Warranted: Niche Diplomacy Assessed," *Canadian Foreign Policy* 6, no. 3 (Spring 1999) 57–72

Following the September 11, 2001 attack on the United States, Prime Minister Chrétien visited President Bush in the White House to offer support for the president's newly declared war on terrorism. When the meeting finished, the two leaders faced the cameras outside as President Bush thanked the Canadian prime minister for his offer of support. Both leaders were vague about what such support might entail. But press reports made one thing clear—the president had not asked for an immediate commitment of military troops.

Shortly after the prime minister's visit to the White House, the Conference of Defence Associations released a report indicating that the Canadian Armed Forces has serious shortfalls in meeting its commitments to help the United States defend North American territory and participate in overseas commitments. Equipment and force levels have fallen to such a level that Canada could only send token forces to NATO, the United Nations, and other coalition operations. Even the capability to adequately carry out surveillance of Canadian territory was called into question.

For some commentators, these events symbolized not only a weakness in Canadian defense preparedness, but a broader problem in Canada's foreign policy as well. After years of budget slashing and cutbacks, Canada's ability to project an active and credible presence abroad has been seriously eroded. At the same time, Canada's desire to undertake international obligations as a middle power and to participate in a major forum like the G-8 summit has not diminished. As a result, some have wondered if there is a serious gap between Canadian commitments and its capabilities.

The growing commitment-capability gap in Canadian foreign policy has already been a debate for some time among analysts. In 1994, Janice Gross Stein wrote, "Canada cannot be everywhere and do everything. If it attempts to do so, it risks dissipating its resources and sliding into mediocrity."

However, if it can no longer pretend to be both a "global boy scout" and a committed and active alliance and coalition partner, what can it do to address the commitment-credibility gap? Stein suggests: "Canada must define its priorities, identify areas of comparative advantage, develop 'niche' policies, and focus its resources so that Canada contributes distinctively across the broad spectrum of common security."

In many ways, this is not a new debate in Canadian foreign policy. After World War II, Canada was anxious to define a role for itself in discussions regarding the post-war world order. In that period, the concept of functionalism became the primary organizing principle for Canadian foreign policy. It was argued that the power and influence of a state should be determined by its ability to bring key resources and skills into play in the context of specific issues. Instead of relegating middle powers to a permanent second-tier status, countries like Canada used their unique capabilities to play a significant role in particular areas of international policy. Thus, the principle of functionalism helped to define a role for Canada in such key areas as peacekeeping, conflict mediation, and multilateral cooperation.

In the 1990s, the functional concept was essentially reborn under the label of 'niche' diplomacy. In the face of consecutive years of budgeting and diminishing capabilities, a growing number of analysts began asking how Canada could still pursue an activist, internationalist foreign policy while maintaining its credibility. Analysts like Janice Gross Stein, Andrew Cooper, and Evan Potter took up the concept of "niche diplomacy" as one solution to the commitment-capability gap.

These analysts suggest that niche diplomacy, while in part a repackaging of an old concept, is especially suited to the changing circumstances of international politics. On the one hand, American leadership on key international issues appears more uncertain and erratic. While taking up a leadership role on issues like the war in Kosovo, it has appeared to retreat from international obligations in other areas like global warming when the Bush administration rejected the Kyoto Protocol. At the same time, issues like human security, global poverty, human rights, and the environment have risen to the fore of the international agenda in the past decade. These are the kinds of issues that require multilateral cooperation and broad-based coalition building suitable to the skills of traditional middle powers.

While the concept of niche diplomacy may make good sense, how does a country like Canada go about selecting the "niches" it will pursue? What criteria will guide the selection of niches? Should selection be guided by concerns about economic benefit and comparative advantage? Or should such selection be guided by concepts such as human security?

In the first selection Evan Potter sets the case for a niche diplomacy that is more narrowly focused on pursuing Canadian interests. He argues that a more scaled-down, less emphatic foreign policy is needed in the future. Heather Smith provides a critique of the niche diplomacy concept and outlines some of its limitations.

✔ YES
Niche Diplomacy as Canadian Foreign Policy
EVAN H. POTTER

Few observers of Canadian foreign policy would deny that the number and complexity of foreign policy issues is increasing, yet the resources available to manage them are decreasing.[1] If we assume that "old" foreign-policy concerns—non-proliferation, economic diplomacy, alliance politics, and multilateralism—will continue to be important, Canada is left with three choices: increase the foreign policy budget to reflect the expanding agenda, do more things less well, or assign a lower priority to some issue-areas. This last choice implies a shift in Ottawa's focus away from some traditional functional concerns and geographic areas and towards those areas in which there is a clear and identifiable Canadian interest and where Canada's international policy decisions and programmes can have maximum impact. The operative term here is maximum impact because the millions of public dollars spent to keep Canadian peacekeepers in the former Yugoslavia may have satisfied the criterion of identifiable interest but have surely fallen short of maximum impact.

In this article I argue that to maximize its influence in an era of fiscal austerity, Canada will have to be more selective about the many international spheres in which it plays. In the search for niches, Ottawa must not only use its resources more efficiently; it must look increasingly to the under-utilized and under-appreciated non-governmental and philanthropic sectors. Moreover, Canada's pent up "soft" power that comes from knowledge and ideas, and the information technologies that transmit them further, faster, and with greater effect around the world, must be allowed to flourish.[2] A greater exercise of such power—in effect, energizing the cultural pillar of the foreign policy agenda of Jean Chrétien's government rather than, for example, trying to achieve a greater naval presence in the Pacific in support of Canada's commercial interests in the region (as the 1994 defence white paper advocates[3])—is consistent with niche diplomacy.

Foreign policy reviews over the past two years have emphasized that Canada's national interests dictate a global rather than a regional foreign policy and hence a widespread and effective diplomatic presence. [...] Growing domestic fiscal pressures have highlighted a fundamental tension in the conduct of Canada's international relations between a more engaged global player in an age of globalization and interdependence and a more disengaged actor. Despite the conclusions of the parliamentary reviews, this debate is not likely to abate. On the one hand, some (notably members of the Reform party) have questioned how long Canada can enhance its prestige in a number of expensive spheres of influence—the United Nations, North Atlantic Treaty Organization, Commonwealth, la francophonie, Asia Pacific Economic Co-operation (APEC), and the Group of Seven

(G-7), to name just a few—simultaneously.[4] On the other hand, powerful forces reinforce this internationalism.

As noted by the minister of foreign affairs, Lloyd Axworthy, before the House of Commons Standing Committee on Foreign Affairs and International Trade in April 1996,[5] it is anachronistic to try to draw a clear distinction between international and domestic. Because of economic and post–Cold War security globalization, problems are no longer East-West or North-South in scope. For example, unemployment, transportable diseases (for example, HIV), environment degradation (for example, global warming) affect both South and North. As nation-states realize that they cannot respond to these challenges alone, increased multilateralism appears to be the only answer.

From a narrower Canadian perspective, one need look no further than Canada's growing economic dependence on the rest of the world: in 1995 exports accounted for 37 per cent of national income compared to 17 per cent in 1960. Each billion of the $250 billion in total exports represented 11,000 domestic jobs, and overall foreign direct investment totalled $150 billion. Changing demographics have increased the heterogeneity of Canada's population: five million Canadians are foreign-born and it is anticipated that another one million will reside in Canada by the turn of the century. Finally, there is the searing collective experience of Canadian participation in two world wars on European soil—a continent which, despite the push towards the Asia Pacific region in government and business circles, should not yet be seen as a residual part of Ottawa's foreign-policy calculus.

What this indicates is that Canada is not a typical middle power. The development of a more selective middle-power diplomacy is complicated by the pressures of globalization and Canada's dual status: it has international obligations through its G-7 membership and middle-power commitments in other forums. There need not, however, be any inconsistency between internationalism and selectivity. Some scholars have suggested that Ottawa should veer away from "diffuse internationalism" of the past towards a more entrepreneurial approach within internationalist foreign policy.[6] More recently, Andrew Cooper has asserted that Canada's G-7 membership can reinforce the tendency to concentrate on specific issues, particularly when Ottawa plays host to the G-7 summit (as witnessed by the focus on North-South relations at Montebello in 1981, agricultural trade reform at Toronto in 1988, and the reform of international financial institutions at Halifax in 1995). He concedes, however, that this form of membership can overextend Canada's diplomatic resources, as, for example, when it wants to be at the forefront of issues such as terrorism and the interdiction of drug trafficking, in which a number of other countries have greater interests and expertise.[7]

The challenge for Ottawa's foreign policy bureaucracy, especially the Department of Foreign Affairs and International Trade (DFAIT), in the coming years will be to provide services to a growing multicultural population more affected by and interested in Canada's external relations, while still maintaining quality research and policy advice on an expanding and more complex international policy agenda—and all with fewer dollars. Efficiency, cost-effectiveness, and accountability are not necessarily incompatible with the management of such an agenda. In fact, greater control over an expanding foreign policy agenda and a shrinking budget can be achieved through organizational changes, such as the creation at DFAIT of a Global and Human Issues Bureau and the amalgamation in the summer of 1996 of its various geographic and functional bureaux that reduced by almost half the number of assistant deputy ministers in the department. Other changes include the application of information technologies to make DFAIT more responsive and efficient[8]; co-location agreements between Canada and other countries abroad; greater cost-recovery in Canada's international business-promotion programmes; and the closure of some foreign missions. Without doubt, the responses to date by the federal government's foreign-policy planners to fiscal realities have been imaginative, needed, and flexible. But they are not sufficient.

Implicit in the parliamentary foreign policy review and the government's response to it, as in DFAIT's response to the two programme reviews, was that savings in departmental operations would reduce the likelihood of compromising Canada's liberal international impulse in its foreign policy. The problem is that budgetary cutbacks in Canada's external affairs (DFAIT and the Canadian International Development Agency [CIDA]) and national defence will be on-going and deeper that those that could be offset by existing and potential future operational savings. For example, those federal departments on the frontlines of the growing international agenda are seeing dramatic budget cuts. CIDA will have its budget cut by $309 million to $1.9 billion by Fiscal Year 1998–9—the lowest level since the mid-1960s as a share of gross national product (estimated to be .27 per cent) and down 29 per cent from just two years ago. Meanwhile, DFAIT's budget has been cut ten times since 1988–9; cumulative cuts will amount to $292 million by 1998–9.[9] The Department of National Defence should not be forgotten. In recent years, while attempting to reposition the Canadian military so that it is equally capable of fighting a "hot" war and responding to "global" and so-called emerging security challenges to Canadian sovereignty (illegal or harmful overfishing, drug trafficking, illegal immigration, and the intentional release of pollutants off Canadian coasts[10]), it has faced the biggest cuts of all. Its budget is expected to fall to $8.7 billion by 1998–9 from a 1994–5 level of $11.4 billion.[11] Consequently, hard political choices will have to be made if Canada's international efforts are to remain creditable.

First, the closing or downsizing of Canada's missions in countries where Canadian economic and political interests are not paramount must continue. At the same time, a number of official representatives abroad (especially the high proportion of officials from federal departments other than DFAIT) must be reduced and others must be replaced by locally engaged staff. The consequences in actual dollars is not insignificant: it costs about $100,000 in addition to salary for every Canadian government official posted abroad (in 1996 there were 1,429 officials, excluding soldiers on active duty). Nevertheless, seen alongside the total external affairs budget, these savings are relatively small. For this reason, more fundamental changes are needed.

Second, the Canadian government should withdraw completely from business promotion in Western Europe and the United States. The private sector has repeatedly asked that the government move away from a focus on the member countries of the Organisation for Economic Co-operation and Development (OECD) in its trade-promotion programmes and provide greater assistance in emerging markets in Latin America and the Asia Pacific or more esoteric and difficult markets in the Middle East and North Africa. Third, it is expensive and highly inefficient to use soldiers as peace-builders. When Canada responds to intrastate conflict, there must be more discipline in the in the division of labour among Canada's non-governmental organizations, the military, and other governmental agencies and departments. Fourth, foreign aid to developing countries on the threshold of joining the First World must be reduced. Finally, and most significantly, there must be a shift away from military alliances such as NATO and towards international economic (for example, the World Trade Organization and the G-7) and social institutions.

The Canadian response to the above proposals to date has been decidedly piecemeal, with cabinet ministers succumbing to pressure from interest groups, fierce resistance within DFAIT to even partial privatization of the Trade Commissioner Service, and the inevitable impulse to tinker rather than embark on more radical institutional changes that are the hallmarks of the Australian and New Zealand responses to changing geographical realities of the post–Cold War world. Part of the reason for this halting response, as already noted, is Canada's dualistic status. There is also the legacy of the Golden Age (1947–57) of Canadian diplomacy—not only in the corporate culture of Canada's current crop of foreign-policy practitioners but also in the minds of many Canada-watchers abroad. The non-Canadian view of Canada's international role—as exemplified by praise for Canada's leadership in the humanitarian relief mission to aid Rwandan refugees in Zaire in November 1996—continues to be that of a country highly valued for its diplomacy of ideas in service to international justice, fairness, and the rule of law. We are still seen as do-gooders. (Yet not since Prime Minister R.B. Bennett in the 1930s has Canadian foreign policy been so dominated by trade, a trend that will likely continue given Prime Minister Chrétien's embrace of so-called Team Canada trade missions to enhance Canada's profile abroad.) Canadian diplomats have expressed both pride in the past and sadness at no longer being able to live up to the high expectations of their foreign colleagues. The prime minister's general disinterest in peace and security matters (with the exception of his personal involvement in pushing for a humanitarian mission to central Africa) has made reconciling competing images of Canada's international role and living within growing financial constraints even more difficult. That having been said, a greater reconciliation between Canada's foreign-policy capacities and the perception of Canada abroad may be achieved under the stewardship of Lloyd Axworthy, who, since he became foreign minister in early 1996, has sought to reinsert the social pillar in Canada's foreign policy by emphasizing such issues as human rights and especially the welfare of children.

THE PRIVATIZATION OF CANADA'S INTERNATIONAL RELATIONS

The fundamental problem, then, is that Canada no longer has the government capacity to be as broadly engaged as it was in decades past. This does not mean that Canada should not be engaged globally; rather, the means of this global engagement will have to change. Less and less will Canada's international face be that of a diplomat, soldier, and aid official; more and more it will be the staff of Canadian-based non-governmental organizations—academic, philanthropic, and business. The financing needed to support this non-official Canadian presence abroad will, in the short term, come mostly from public coffers. In other words, the government will become more of a facilitator and less of a doer. Over time, Canada's private and philanthropic sectors will be forced either to support this Canadian presence or to let it die. It is unlikely that the Canadian state, through institutions such as CIDA and DFAIT, will be able to move back into these domains once it has withdrawn from them.

This potential "privatization" of Canada's foreign policy is worth examining more closely. While there is extensive literature on the relationship between the state and non-governmental organizations in development assistance, there is comparatively little written on the role of philanthropic organizations. There are some high-profile examples, most notably in the United States, of contributions from this sector to the international objectives of other countries. The Open Society Institute (OSI) is a New York-based, tax-exempt charitable foundation organized and funded by the philanthropist George Soros. It and its affiliated foundations, also funded principally by Soros to promote the goals of democratic participation, free expression, human rights, and the rule of law in some thirty countries, have been most active in eastern Europe and the former Soviet Union where they are responsible for, among other things, the founding of two universities. Annual charitable spending for the network of foundations at approximately US$350–400 million makes it one of the largest foundations in terms of total charitable expenditures. In recent years, the OSI has been an active funder of projects related to landmines, including humanitarian assistance, rehabilitation, and prosthetics in the war in the former Yugoslavia.

While I would not suggest that it is either feasible or appropriate for private or philanthropic organizations to replace a state's diplomacy, the success of the OSI nevertheless points to the potential for greater public-private co-operation in areas of security and the projection abroad of democratic practices and good governance. In Canada, even accounting for the size differential with the United States, foundations have not played such a proactive role. There are exceptions of course. The Toronto-based Walter and Duncan Gordon Charitable Foundation has invested, over the course of the last seven years, in excess of $1 million in the development of an Arctic Council. It was also the major funder of the Canada 21 report, which, in advance of the parliamentary reviews, provided a non-governmental blueprint for Canada's security objectives into the next century.[12] The Montreal-based CRB Foundation has for many years been active in fostering greater understanding between Arabs and Jews in the Middle East.

There are a number of drawbacks in pursuing international objectives through philanthropic foundations. A particular concern, of course, is that foreign-policy initiatives approved by a foundation's governing board may reflect the whims of its board members rather than a pressing, national foreign-policy concern. In a worst-case scenario, foundation objectives could undermine the carefully calibrated diplomatic initiatives of the state. In Canada, given the limited funds to be dispensed by most charitable organizations, when one donor assumes the bulk of funding on a particular internationally oriented project in the hope of acting as a magnet for other donors it has not necessarily led to a critical mass of support. Perhaps even more disturbing is the difficulty in persuading some of Ottawa's foreign-policy planners to take such private initiatives seriously. Still, we should not be too pessimistic. The contributions of charitable foundations to Canada's international interests are real and auger well for an increasingly active role in helping to augment Canadian capacities in certain specific areas. These are the subjects of the concluding section.

A NEW APPROACH FOR A NEW FOREIGN-POLICY AGENDA

In the coming century, the values (multiculturalism, civility, and tolerance), innovative ideas (legislative reform, Canada's proposal for a standing United Nations rapid-reaction force), and the solid research capacities of Canada's public and private sectors will set Canada's foreign policy apart. Given Canada's history of mediation, participation in major and international agreements and regimes, and solid performance in assisting the developing world, the new post–Cold War landscape is ready-made for it to flex its soft power muscle. Canada's position, recognized internationally, as an innovator in information technology and communications means that it can disseminate its ideas further and faster than other countries. It has taken some time for Canadians to realize that they have been making the most of this power. Now there are signs that this untapped potential is being recognized.

Before describing some niches for Canada's international relations in the years ahead, it is useful to reiterate that Canada has a greater comparative advantage in the international economic and social policy-making arenas than it does in the security domain. For example, Canada's traditional comparative advantage in the business of peacekeeping is slowly being eaten away by budgetary constraints, Ottawa's unwillingness to participate in enforcement missions, and the nascent international involvement of countries such as Germany and Japan. Not to be forgotten is Ottawa's acute embarrassment at having been excluded in 1994 from the Contact Group (France, Russia, Britain, the United States, and the European Union) in former Yugoslavia where 1,000 Canadian soldiers were on the ground. A signal was sent that Canada would likely be unable to join similar great-power talking shops in the future. However, Canada *is* a member of all the most exclusive economic forums, such as the G-7, the Quadilateral Group, and the OECD. In a world characterized more by geoeconomics than geopolitics, Canada should be able to play an important role in setting international agenda, whether establishing a global investment regime or protecting intellectual property rights.[13]

We must also make use of the experience and influence of Canadians in important international portfolios—Stephen Lewis, a former ambassador to the United Nations, as deputy executive director of UNICEF; Donald Johnston, former Liberal cabinet minister who is now secretary-general of the OECD; Maurice Strong, who is special adviser to the secretary-general of the United Nations; Elisabeth Dowdswell, who heads the United Nations Environment Program; and Bill O'Neil, who heads the International Maritime Organization. The leadership positions of these Canadians touch on issues that are gaining a higher profile on the Canadian foreign-policy agenda. For example, the OECD is well-placed to provide research on the economic and social effects of exploitive workplace conditions (including child labour), and UNICEF was created to protect the rights of children.

A brief discussion first about the need for a more cohesive international communications presence and second about the challenge of international migration indicates areas in which Canada could be more selective in its international relations. It also demonstrates the tremendous capacity that Canada has at its disposal.

As a leader in the development of information technology, as a major producer of television programming, and as a country whose broadcasters are held in high regard, Canada has all the components in place to develop a formidable international communications presence. Few people realize that New Brunswick is one of the most "wired" regions in the world and a showcase for Canada's communications know-how. Already, there have been calls for Canada to increase its use of information and communications technology to support its foreign trade, aid, and diplomatic objectives. [...]

There can be no doubt that, because of increasing intrastate strife and the social and economic distress that is a by-product of globalization, one of the most pressing problems of the post–Cold War era is the large number of refugees and internally displaced persons. Of the estimated 100 million migrants in the world, it has been calculated that in 1996 about 14.5 million were refugees (in 1980 there were 8.2 million) and another 23 million were internally displaced persons fleeing mostly from intrastate conflicts.[14] Countries of preferred destination such as Canada must consider how to prevent situations which produce refugees and which may lead to costly humanitarian intervention; how to protect refugees in need of resettlement, without creating incentives for illegal immigration; and how to manage immigration so as to maintain effective control over organized crime, security threats, and communicable diseases. The question concerns the specific contribution Canada can make to the challenges posed by international migration. As I have noted elsewhere, Canada has a number of options.[15] It can help to set the international policy agenda on migration now that it chairs the OECD's Working Party on Migration and through its investment in university centres of research on the effects of immigration; it can use its influence within the Organization for Security and Co-operation in Europe to involve the OSCE directly in promoting dialogue between Eastern and Western Europe on cross-border population flows; it should try to place a representative on the executive board of the International Organization for Migration because of that institution's important operational role. Given the connections between the internal displacement of people and crossborder migration, Canada could make a significant difference by bolstering the woefully under-resourced United Nations Office of the Special Representative of the Secretary-General for Internally Displaced People. As well, Canada is in a position of influence to push for permanent, rather than only renewable, funding for an over-stretched organization such as the United Nations High Commissioner for Refugees, especially since the problem of population displacement is likely to be a permanent feature of international relations.[16] These proposals are all potentially low-cost initiatives that could reap large dividends by enabling the international community to anticipate future migration crises more accurately. One has only to consider the far higher costs of dispatching Canadian troops, either on humanitarian grounds or for the purposes of enforcement actions, to flashpoints abroad.

These are just two examples of a growing range of more selective types of Canadian diplomatic initiatives. Such approaches maximize Canada's inherent advantages, are cognizant of growing financial constraints in the public sector, recognize the utility of non-governmental actors, and still allow Ottawa to maintain a high profile on the international stage. They should constitute a niche diplomacy for the next century.

NOTES

1. This article draws on and amplifies arguments previously expressed in Evan Potter, "Redesigning Canadian diplomacy in an age of fiscal austerity," in Fen Osler Hampson and Maureen Appel Molot, eds. *Canada Among Nations 1996: Big Enough to be Heard* (Ottawa: Carleton University Press 1996), 23–56.

2. Joseph Nye defines soft power as "rest[ing] on the appeal on one's ideas or the ability to set the agenda in ways that shape the preference of others." See Joseph S. Nye, Jr,

and William A. Owens, "America's Information Edge," *Foreign Affairs* 75 (March/April 1996), 21. For an application of this idea to the Canadian experience see Ann Medina, "Canada's Information Edge," *Canadian Foreign Policy* 4 (forthcoming 1997).

3. *1994 Defence White Paper* (Ottawa: Minister of Supply and Services/Canada Communications Group, 1994).

4. On the Reform party's dissenting voice on the future directions of Canadian foreign policy, see the Report of the Special Joint Committee of the Senate and the House of Commons Reviewing Canada's Foreign Policy, *Canada's Foreign Policy: Dissenting Opinions and Appendices* (Ottawa: Publications Service, Parliamentary Publications Directorate, 1994).

5. Department of Foreign Affairs and International Trade, "Foreign Policy at a Crossroad," Notes for an Address by the Honourable Lloyd Axworthy, Minister of Foreign Affairs, to the Standing Committee on Foreign Affairs and International Trade, *Statement* 96/12, 16 April 1996, 1.

6. See Andrew F. Cooper, Richard A. Higgott, and Kim R. Nossal, *Relocating Middle Powers: Australia and Canada in a Changing World Order* (Vancouver: University of British Columbia Press, 1993).

7. Andrew F. Cooper, "In Search of Niches: Saying 'Yes' and saying 'No' in Canada's International Relations," *Canadian Foreign Policy* 3 (Winter 1995): 4.

8. See Gordon Smith, deputy minister, DFAIT, on the impact of information technology on the conduct of diplomacy in "Cyber-Diplomacy," speaking notes for speech delivered to the Technology in Government Forum, Ottawa, 18 September 1996.

9. Between 1988–9 and 1998–9 the percentage of spending for core programmes—that is, "discretionary spending"—will decline from 70 to 36 per cent of total expenditures because assessed contributions—that is, Canada's share of costs for United Nations membership, UNESCO, the International Labour Organization, and other international organizations—grew by 66 per cent from $137 million to $227 million, while peacekeeping assessments jumped from $7 million to $134 million, an increase of 1,814 per cent. Axworthy, "Foreign Policy at a Crossroad," 3.

10. "Review of defence policy guidance document to the Defence Policy Review Committee from the minister of national defence." *Canadian Defence Quarterly* 23 (March 1994), 40–2.

11. On the impact of budget cuts to the Department of National Defence, see Claire Turenne Sjolander, "Cashing in on the 'peace dividend': National Defence in the post-Cold War world," in Gene Swimmer, ed, *How Ottawa Spends 1996–97: Life Under the Knife* (Ottawa: Carleton University Press, 1996), esp. 268–74.

12. *Canada 21: Canada and Common Security in the Twenty-First Century* (Toronto: Centre for International Studies, University of Toronto, 1994).

13. Cooper, "In search of niches," 2.

14. Alan Dowty and Gil Loescher, "Refugee flows as grounds for international action," *International Security* 21 (Summer 1996): 46.

15. Potter, "Redesigning Canadian diplomacy."

16. Evan H. Potter, "The challenge of international migration," *Canadian Foreign Policy* 4 (Spring 1996): 19.

✗ NO
Caution Warranted: Niche Diplomacy Assessed
HEATHER A. SMITH

Coined by Andrew Cooper (1995) and further by Evan Potter (1996–7), niche diplomacy calls for selectivity in areas of foreign activity. The Minister of Foreign Affairs, Lloyd Axworthy, has rejected the specific term "niche diplomacy" in favour of the phrase "selective foreign policy" (Potter 1997:1). Nonetheless, he has identified niches embedded in broader issue areas such as human rights, peace-building, and international communications (DFAIT 1996c; 1996f; 1997c). Niche diplomacy is a concept that has been promoted by academics and used by practitioners. We should not, however, accept this concept uncritically.

It is the aim of this article to offer a critique of niche diplomacy. The critique is theoretically informed by critical theory and begins with the premise that "theory is always for someone and for some purpose" (Cox 1986:207). This premise may seem to be a truism to some who might argue that obviously theory is never neutral. Yet, Robert Cox's words provide a worthwhile reminder of the power inherent in any academic project. All scholarship has a "politico-normative content" (Neufeld 1995b:41) and all policy is informed by a set of ethical and philosophical assumptions. It is essential that we consider the ideas driving Canadian foreign policy (CFP). As Denis Stairs (1994–5:19) has argued, perhaps it is time that we think about the philosophies and not just the theories that inform CFP. With regard to niche diplomacy, careful consideration is necessary because it comes with a political agenda that legitimizes the narrowing of CFP in such a way that the credibility of foreign policy initiatives could be undermined.

[...]

NICHE DIPLOMACY DESCRIBED

Niche diplomacy is premised on the view that in an era of fiscal restraint Canada must make some hard choices if our foreign policy is to remain credible. Cooper (1995:1) argues that we are faced with a commitment-credibility gap and that it is in our national interest to adopt a discrete rather than a diffuse approach to CFP. Potter (1996–7:25) also points to the need to ensure that our policy choices are made with a "clear and identifiable Canadian interest" in mind.

The end of the cold war coupled with fiscal crisis in the Canadian state means that while there are new opportunities in the international system we must, at the same time, rationalize, be selective, and draw on areas of Canada's comparative advantage. Foreign policy must be effective and we must select areas where we have "maximum impact" (Potter: 1996–7:25).

The areas of specialization identified are numerous. Cooper (1995:1) cites Janice Stein's call for the selection of areas of comparative advantage in the field of security. In her comments to the 1994 Special Joint Committee Reviewing Canadian Foreign Policy (Special Joint Committee 1994:16) she identifies peace-keeping as an area of comparative advantage, but this "niche" is dismissed by Potter. Both Cooper and Potter tend to focus on non-traditional areas of foreign policy primarily encompassed by the social pillar and including issues such as human rights broadly, but more specifically women's and children's rights. Cooper also identifies comprehensive security, reform of financial institutions, protection of natural resources, and peacebuilding. Potter highlights soft power that comes from knowledge and ideas, and links soft power to information technologies and the "energizing of the cultural pillar of the foreign policy agenda" (1996–7:26). The latter part of his assessment focuses on international communications and international migration as areas worthy of niche selection. Cooper also stresses global communications and intellectual entrepreneurship.

Specialization is one component of niche diplomacy. The possible devolution of foreign policy responsibility to non-governmental organizations (NGOS), academic philanthropic organizations, and business is another element. According to Cooper, "while the expression and target of Canada's diplomatic activity will vary consider-ably, a common theme that will link its disparate parts together will be its ability to be a 'Facilitator' for the increasing number of NGOs, private voluntary organizations, and international NGOs involved in international relations" (1995:13). Consistent with Cooper, Potter suggests "the government will be a facilitator and less of a doer" (1996–7:13). Potter (1996–7:33-34), however, is cautious in his advocacy of this route because such devolution could undermine Canadian diplomacy if organiza-tions pursue their own concerns, rather than the concerns of the government.

[...]

Neither author considers niche diplomacy a fait accompli. Both articles advo-cate the approach with the recognition that there are obstacles to its full realiza-tion. Cooper (1995:4) concedes that the practice of niche selection is likely to be highly contentious and that critics are likely to see it as "part of the problem; as a component of a domestic political agenda imposing disciplines and limitations." He responds by saying that sophisticated critics, referring in particular to Mark Neufeld, have recognized that "it is precisely this sense of discipline and limita-tions that informed so much of the understanding of the practitioners of Canada's immediate post-1945 diplomacy." Cooper also identifies possible bureaucratic obstacles. Potter observes that there is a tension "in the conduct of Canada's inter-national relations between a more engaged global player in an age of globaliza-tion and interdependence and a more disengaged actor" (1996–97:26).

Cooper does not regard his work as "niche-picking," rather, he views it as pro-viding a "contextual groundwork for making this type of targeted exercise possible"

(1995:5). In this vein, we are informed that a complex international agenda demands that we practice niche diplomacy. By making the necessary choices we will close the commitment-credibility gap and more importantly, we can continue to play a leading role in the world. But, we are cautioned by Cooper in his conclusion, that to continue to play this leading role "Canada must make its priorities clear and effectively marshall its talents and resources by developing responsibilities to other countries and societal actors" (1995:13). Potter concludes by stating that selective diplomatic initiatives "maximize Canada's inherent advantages, are cognizant of growing financial constraints in the public sector, recognize the utility of non-governmental actors, and still allow Ottawa to maintain a high profile on the international stage. They should constitute a niche diplomacy for the next century" (1996–97:38).

At the heart of niche diplomacy is the protection and promotion of the state's interests. Terms such as maximum impact bring to mind the words of Hans Morgenthau who, in his classic *Politics Among Nations*, advocates a rational foreign policy that "minimizes risks and maximizes benefits" (1967:7). An emphasis on national interest is not unique to either American political realists or 1990s CFP scholars. John Holmes, one of the central figures of the study of CFP has been careful to remind us that "internationalism ... was based on a very hard-boiled calculation of Canadian national interest rather than on woolly-minded idealism" (1976:6). Combined with key realist concepts, niche diplomacy also adopts the language of liberal economics as is evident in the terms of "niche" and "comparative advantage." The predominance of fiscal restraint in the niche literature represents the practical concerns and priorities of the Liberal government. Ultimately, niche diplomacy is about the management of power, largely defined as soft power, in a changing world order. It offers a template, almost a self-help guide, to practitioners in their quest for Canadian leadership on the international scene.

NICHE DIPLOMACY IN PRACTICE

The niche diplomacy lexicon and its philosophical underpinnings have been adopted by the various ministers responsible for Canada's foreign relations. Parallels between the language of Cooper and Potter and government pronunciations can be identified.

[...]

The government's use of the term "niche" is different from the way Cooper and Potter use it. In practice, niche diplomacy does not appear to have been used to suggest the end of some vision of internationalism; rather, government statements seem to merge tenets of niche diplomacy with concepts such as human security, which have, at least rhetorically, a strong streak of internationalism. For example, built into human security is a set of non-traditional threats such as poverty, human rights abuses, terrorism, and environmental degradation (Axworthy 1997a;

1997b; DFAIT 1997h). Within the subset of human rights is a set of priority issues such as children's rights, particularly child labour (DFAIT 1996b; 1997e; 1997g). Niches are then identified with the issues given priority status. Canada's niche or area of specialization in the context of human rights is defined as "working from within" (DFAIT 1997i; 1997j). A similar pattern can be identified when we refer to peacebuilding. Peacebuilding, like human rights, is embedded in human security. Peacebuilding is then linked to niches. Recognizing the enormity of the concept of peacebuilding, Axworthy seems to suggest that we build niches within peacebuilding. This is inferred when he states that we must ask ourselves a number of questions, one of which includes: "what our peacebuilding priorities are, both geographically and in terms of niches in which to establish Canadian expertise" (DFAIT 1996c:5).

As noted in the beginning of the section, there are striking parallels between government pronouncements and the work of Cooper and Potter. For example, the 1995 government response to the Canadian foreign policy review clearly emphasizes the need to function effectively in a time of fiscal restraint. "More effective and less costly will have to be the watchwords guiding our approach to international relations.... We will not do everything we have done in the past, nor shall we do things as we have done before" (Government of Canada 1995:9). Art Eggleton, former Minister for International Trade, expressed the spirit of niche diplomacy in a 1996 speech to the Pacific Basin Economic Council when he declared that we "need to focus our energy and resources and not try to be all things to all people" (DFAIT 1996d:3). Axworthy, in a speech on de-mining, states that "we must work together, each contributing in our own area of strength" (DFAIT 1997b:6). Comparative advantage, a term used by Cooper and Potter, is also used in government statements. Strengths identified by Eggleton, in a May 1996 speech include "agriculture and agri-food, telecommunications, transportation, energy and environmental protection" (DFAIT 1996a:1). Four areas of focus, identified by Axworthy in a January 1997 speech made in India, are "telecommunications and information technology; power and energy equipment and services; oil and gas; and environmental products and services" (DFAIT 1997a:2).

Maximum impact, an objective stressed by Potter, has also been used by Axworthy with reference to targeting resources with the aim of "maximum impact" in the area of Canadian cultural relations with the Asia Pacific, Europe, and the Americas (DFAIT 1997d:5). In a similar vein, the concept of effective influence has arisen in Axworthy's speech to human rights non-governmental organizations (NGOs) in 1997 (DFAIT 1997c:1) and more recently in a speech to an American audience where he stated: "I like to think that Canada is a nation that adds value internationally by exercising effective influence" (DFAIT 1998c:2).

The use of soft power, particularly as related to telecommunications and intellectual entrepreneurship, both identified as potential niches by Potter and Cooper, has also been highlighted in government statements. For example, in a December

1996 speech and again in a February 1997 speech Axworthy uses the language of soft power in relation to knowledge and information (DFAIT 1996e; 1997c). In this context he observes that "the mouse, if not mightier than, is at least as mighty as the missile" (DFAIT 1996e:1). In a more recent statement Axworthy has linked the use of soft power with human security noting that the use of soft power is "an effective means to pursue the human security agenda" (DFAIT 1998j: 3). A quick survey of statements by the Minister of Foreign Affairs clearly reveals that soft power is a concept that has become integral to the practice of CFP.[1] This observation is further supported by the recent analysis by Hampson and Oliver (1998).

Also similar to the analyses of Cooper and Potter is the evidence in the foreign policy makers' speeches of greater efforts at consultation with NGOs. Speeches (DFAIT 1996c; 1997c; 1998i) on peacebuilding and human rights stress the importance of consultation and the inclusion of NGOs in the policy-making process. For example, when speaking on the rights of children, Axworthy said that dealing with human rights generally required a multi-disciplinary response, a response; that included NGOs—both Canadian and international (DFAIT 1997g: 1 and 4). Inclusiveness is also part of the approach to international environmental issues. In April 1997 Axworthy, introducing the Sustainable Development Strategy, declared that "we are starting to sketch out a new approach on international environmental issues: one that is anticipatory, inclusive and integrated" (DFAIT 1997f:5).

What this analysis shows, in combination with the previous section, is that there are parallels between the statements of Cooper and Potter and those of various federal ministers. The government has gone so far as to identify a number of niches. [...] The fact that the term has been used in a recent high profile analysis (Hampson and Oliver 1998:388) of CFP, thus signalling at least some degree of integration into the mainstream CFP lexicon, makes it even more important for us to consider the limitations of the concept. Do we really want to promote the concept of niche diplomacy? As the next section will show, niche diplomacy is a problematic concept.

LIMITATIONS OF NICHE DIPLOMACY

In this section three sets of limitations are identified. First, the term niche diplomacy is conceptually vague. The criteria for niche selection are vacuous concepts and there is no discussion of niche inception or niche deselection. Second, in theory and practice, rather than being democratic, it appears to have an elitist streak. Third, the language obscures the personal and perpetuates a balance sheet mentality in practice. Each of these limitations will be discussed further below.

The conceptual vagueness of niche diplomacy is readily apparent when one considers what seem to be the criteria for niche selection. We are told that it must be in Canada's national interest and it should be an identifiable interest. What are the authors really saying when they suggest that niches should be areas of national interest? The obvious question is: whose interest? Is it in our interest if we have effective influence and if the policy has maximum impact? If these are criteria for niche selection then a problem arises. We can only measure impact and influence after the fact and therefore as criteria for selection they offer little guidance. Comparative advantage can be measured by trade statistics but the other criterion and objectives lack the same immediate quantifiability. Or is the key whether or not our foreign policy promotes Canadian prosperity and employment—an objective noted in the federal government's response to the foreign policy review? This certainly seems to be one of the criteria for niche selection. Or is the primary criterion cost-efficiency—the greatest gain at the least cost?

The problem is that the terms suggested by Cooper and Potter as criteria for niche selection are almost all essentially contested concepts, open to multiple interpretations. While the very elasticity of the terms may be seen to provide flexibility, they may be so elastic that they provide no policy guidance whatsoever. This translates, effectively, into an absence of criteria.

The conceptual vagueness of niche diplomacy is not isolated to selection criteria. Questions about niche inception, equally applicable to both theory and practice, can also be raised. When does an issue area or strategy become a niche? If niches are areas in which Canada excels—areas of leadership—then surely we have practiced niche diplomacy previously, although perhaps under a different label such as functional internationalism, a link made by Cooper. Cooper, however, suggests that the selectivity of functional internationalism disappeared from the 1960s to the late 1980s only to now reemerge. If we accept Cooper's argument then areas of leadership in the 1980s, climate change for example, did not constitute niches because they were not selected under the rationale of niche diplomacy. We would then expect niches, and niche diplomacy, to herald a new era of CFP. Yet, niche diplomacy does not seem to mark any great departure from the past.

A prime example of a niche identified by the government that is not at all different from past behaviour is "working from within." This niche, as noted earlier, relates to Canada's human rights policies. The government argues that it is not necessary to choose between trade and human rights, believes that trade might lead to the internal democratization of developing states, and contends that maintaining trade links and working from within the states is the best approach because it doesn't "have the economic leverage or international clout to force change" (DFAIT 1997j:8). This so-called niche, however, is little more than a 1990s version of constructive engagement.

One need only to consider CFP towards Indonesia to support this point. There has been fairly consistent support for the Indonesian government by successive Canadian governments, in spite of the atrocities committed in East Timor. The exception in this case is the imposition of sanctions by the Mulroney government after the Dili Massacre of 1991 (Nossal 1994). The Chrétien government, however, has pursued a business as usual approach. Military exports were resumed in 1994 when Minister of Foreign Affairs André Ouellet gave permission to Canadian Marconi to sell communications technology to the Indonesian military and in 1995 over $300 million worth of military export permits were granted to Canadian companies intent on exporting to Indonesia (East Timor Alert Network 1996).

It remains unclear when a niche becomes a niche but it is clear that adopting the niche of "working from within" does not separate present behaviour from that of the past. By raising these questions we challenge the claim of difference and newness implicit in this suggested redirection of CFP. It is not redirection at all.

It is also necessary to raise questions about the longevity and sustainability of niches. One element that seems remarkably absent from the analyses of Potter and Cooper is deselection. What happens if a niche no longer provides maximum impact? What happens when our policy is no longer effective? Do we have the flexibility to switch niches when they no longer fulfil our objectives? What happens when a niche, in a time of fiscal restraint, becomes too economically costly?

A prime example of niche deselection is the Canadian policy on climate change. In the late 1980s the Mulroney government claimed a position of moral leadership in the area of climate change. Now, almost ten years later, Canada can be viewed as laggard on this policy issue (Smith 1998). The Chrétien government's 1993 election *Red Book* committed Canada to an aggressive emissions reduction target but as the third Conference of Parties (COP3) to the Framework Convention on Climate Change approached the federal government waffled on its international position finally settling on a three percent reduction of greenhouse gas emissions from 1990 levels by 2010 (Government of Canada 1997:1).[2] While the federal government is constrained by a variety of factors in its ability to implement more aggressive policies, it nonetheless remains committed to only voluntary initiatives that are seen as not having an adverse effect on economic growth and international competitiveness. One may argue that it is not an area where Canada can have maximum impact because we only emit two percent of the world's carbon dioxide, in spite of our high per capita emissions. But to make that argument absolves the government of its inaction and obscures the fact that at the heart of this policy is not the environment but concerns about perceived economic costs and the need to maintain a level playing field with our largest trading partner, the US. Concerted and focused effort on climate change does not merit the label niche, if we adopted the criteria identified by Cooper and Potter.

The implications of the evolution from climate change leader to climate change laggard are, at minimum, a reduction in international credibility on climate change and a challenge to Axworthy's recent claim that "one of DFAIT's strengths is its international advocacy on sustainable development issues" (DFAIT 1997f:4). The implications of this may run deeper than simply in climate change and could have spillover effects, as Canadian international credibility, on a variety of areas is undermined, while at the same time environmental degradation continues apace. Ironically, the commitment-credibility gap that niche diplomacy is designed to counter reemerges. It reemerges because in an attempt to mark a new era of foreign policy niche diplomacy appears blind to previously made commitments, in spite of the apparent nostalgia for Pearsonian internationalism. Implicit in niche diplomacy is an assumption about beginnings and endings (Walker 1995) that overlooks elements of continuity. We are not in a position to undo all previously made commitments and thus leadership claims for the future must be mindful of leadership claims in the past.

Furthermore, it should be recognized that cost cannot and should not be defined in economic terms alone. Canadian inaction on climate change shows us that cost can be defined in many ways. Besides the challenge to cost assumptions the case of climate change challenges the contention that a holistic vision of security guides CFP. Human security cannot be achieved by disregarding the environmental pillar—an argument supported by the public statements of the Minister of Foreign Affairs.

The second problem with niche diplomacy is that it is elitist both in practice and theory. On the practical side, we can turn to the question of national interest and address the question of whose interest. From the vantage point of one concerned with internal democratization, it is clear from Potter's assessment that while the devolution of Canada's international relations to NGOs or private interests seems advisable, we do not want them to pursue their own interests. We do not want them to define their own perspectives because they might undermine CFP. In Potter's words "a particular concern, of course, is that the foreign policy initiatives approved by a foundation's governing board may reflect the whims of its board members rather than a pressing, national foreign policy concern" (1996-97:34). Potter seems to be voicing the concerns of the policy makers when he notes that some foreign policy makers do not take private initiatives seriously. There is an assumption that there can be devolution of policy, of some sort, but that the direction of initiatives by NGOs, academics, and business must support the whims of the federal government who have defined what constitutes a "pressing, national foreign policy concern." In all fairness to Potter, one could easily make a case that there are NGOs and private interest groups that promote values and practices that are completely incommensurate with Canadian traditions and we would not want such groups speaking for Canada. The problem is that Potter's statement does not discriminate between different kinds of groups (perhaps a contentious endeavour) and thus it is argued here that Potter's argument can be seen as antithetical to the notions of academic freedom, espoused by the scholarly community, and it undermines the independent thought and action of some NGOs. If the policy is not in keeping with the interests (whatever they are) of the federal government, they are regarded with a sceptical eye. What then happens to the critical voice of outsiders? Are they of no value?

We have, unfortunately, some evidence of what happens to those who step out of the "accepted" boundaries, a dangerous place even for well established mainstream scholars. The disciplining of ideas is evident in the foreign minister's (Axworthy 1998:B6) castigation of Kim Nossal (1998:A19) for his observations in the *Ottawa Citizen* regarding soft power. As Hampson and Oliver state: "such ad hominem attacks suggest an official smugness and lack of introspection over critical policy issues" (Hampson and Oliver 1998:382). More than a lack of introspection, the minister's statement imposes an unnecessary closure on academic debate and inquiry, making non-questions out of critical analyses.

The contradiction lies in the attempt to somehow foster a more democratic foreign policy—a stated and much lauded initiative of the Chrétien government—through the devolution of Canadian foreign policy and through the growth of partnerships with the NGOs and other stakeholders while at the same time ensuring that the "appropriate" policy outcome is realized. This resembles Sandra Whitworth's (1995) observation that the foreign policy review process was politically managed. Critical voices were marginalized in the foreign policy review process and assumptions articulated by Potter clearly support that kind of marginalization. As constructed by Potter, the foreign policy process appears at first glance more democratic but at its heart are elite assumptions about national interest.

Finally, we turn to the concern that niche diplomacy obscures the personal and legitimates balance sheet diplomacy. We are told that foreign policy should aim to achieve maximum impact. Cooper and Potter speak to us in terms of economics: comparative advantage, efficient, effective, fiscal restraint, entrepreneurial, selective. Potter goes so far as to say that "hard political choices will have to be made if Canada's international efforts are to remain creditable" (1996-97:30). Not credible—creditable. The language of the balance sheet infuses this argument. Not only do these terms appear to define criteria for the selection of priorities and niches, they completely abstract any sense of the individual from the foreign policy equation. If we accept the language of niche diplomacy, are we not equally as complicit in making people simply numbers on a balance sheet? Care must be used when we adopt language such as this. It is not without implications. Comparative advantage serves the same function in CFP as the concept of countervalue targeting in strategic theory—it obscures the political. It nullifies the personal—perhaps the economic being. It completely decontextualizes and in the name of objectivity and rationality associated with a balance sheet mentality we are made immune to much of humanity. It is Canada's version of Ken Booth's "international relations Prozac." "International relations Prozac consoles in some areas, and energizes in others, but its overall effect is to obstruct its takers from facing up to and dealing with what the great mass of humanity, and the rest of the natural world, need to survive passably well" (Booth 1995:104).

THE LONGEVITY OF NICHE DIPLOMACY

In order to assess the longevity of niche diplomacy two essential questions must be addressed. First, what are the implications for the theoretical and practical longevity of niche diplomacy given the recent shift in the foreign policy statements of the Minister of Foreign Affairs? Second, what are the practical implications for the continuation of some variation of niche diplomacy given the recent fiscal surplus?

The response to the first question is based on the observation that one is hard pressed to find references to niches in foreign policy statements throughout much of 1998. The term, used sparingly in previous statements, seems no longer in use. Even the term "selective foreign policy" seems absent. But does this mean Canada is no longer pursuing niche diplomacy?

Practically, it serves to note that the market oriented term niche has been replaced by the innocuous term "priorities." The priorities identified include small arms, children's rights, and child labour. These priorities are not incommensurate with the call for making choices that is central to niche diplomacy. We can also still identify references to "more focus and activism in Canadian foreign policy" (DFAIT 1998d:3). Similarly, the promotion and use of soft power, consultation with NGOs, and the selection of areas for Canadian leadership—all elements of niche diplomacy—continue to be mainstays of CFP.

In addition, the liberal economic bias of our foreign policy has not altered. In spite of the Minister's advocacy of human security it is difficult to associate CFP with the holistic quality characteristic of a human security that recognizes the interconnectedness between environmental protection, human dignity, economic well-being, and the eradication of poverty. Instead, and consistent with Canford Pratt's new dominant consensus, there exists an emphasis on the economic pillar, to the detriment of the other pillars of human security. Climate change is a case in point. Our human rights policies, in many instances, privilege the economic pillar over human dignity.

The absence of the term niche does not spell the end of the liberal economic and realist tenets that inform niche diplomacy. The absence may be explained as simply as a new speech writer in the Minister's office, or as cynically as the desire to soften Canada's image to make it more consistent with the desire to be seen as part of the international "moral minority"—that select group of states that call for the "creation of a just and more equitable world order" (Hampson and Oliver 1998:381).

We are not, however, witnessing a fundamental shift in CFP. This being the case, the concerns raised within this article continue to have merit. We could delete "niches" and insert "priorities" and still raise questions about the selection, inception and deselection of priorities. The concerns expressed regarding consultation with NGOs and the democratization of CFP stand regardless of the use of the word niche. Balance sheet diplomacy designed to serve Canadian interests is made more obvious by the use of the term niche, but the decontextualizing of the individual remains even if the Minister claims that the individual is at the heart of human security. Individuals may matter but the ones that seem to matter most live within Canadian borders. [...]

Turning to the second question posed at the beginning of this section, perhaps if DFAIT had more resources our present foreign policy orientation would change, thus challenging the charges made above and those of Hampson and Oliver (1998:388) who refer to Canada's behaviour as "nickel diplomacy." Given the financial surpluses in the last two years and the predicted surpluses for the next two years (Finance Canada 1998) one may speculate that more resources will flow into the DFAIT coffers. If DFAIT had more resources it could provide more substantive support for its present initiatives but funding foreign policy initiatives does not appear to be high on the federal government's financial priority list. In fact, any kind of massive spending seems unlikely given statements by the Prime Minister that there would be "no more political quick fixes. No more spending sprees" (Office of the Prime Minister 1998c:3). The Prime Minister has further stated that "our overriding objective has been, is, and will be to do whatever it takes to produce more jobs, higher incomes, and a higher standard of living for Canadians" (Office of the Prime Minister 1998b:1). The emphasis for the federal government is relief of the debt burden and the reduction of taxes. In terms of spending initiatives, public pronouncements target education and health care, not foreign aid or the eradication of child labour. This is not to suggest that there is no recognition of issues such as human rights and environmental degradation but they are not areas targeted for significant spending. Trade, and the drive for more liberalized trade, is very much a government priority because it is integral to Canada's economic well-being.[3] Ultimately, the projected financial surplus is likely to have little impact on the orientation and practice of CFP. Niche diplomacy or some variation thereof will continue to define CFP into the 21st century.

CONCLUSION

Niche diplomacy counsels us to make choices. This advice is certainly sound. Choices must be made about the future direction of CFP. The question is: what will be the foundation for these choices? Will the criteria be efficiency, maximum impact and comparative advantage? Will we privilege economic gain over human dignity? If we adopt the liberal and realist tenets of niche diplomacy expressed by Cooper and Potter that is the likely direction. The one thing this direction has in its favour is that the philosophy that drives it is explicit. Potter, for example, has declared: "Is there anything inherently wrong with equating our national interest with the fact that, according to Ottawa's calculations, $1 billion in exports represents approximately 12,000 jobs in Canada? And is the Government supposed to *pretend* in its declaratory foreign policy that unilateral—mostly futile—grand-standing on human rights must greatly outweigh the need to reverse Canada's declining global market share?" (1994:1). It would be hard to claim that these statements are wrapped in flowery rhetoric.

There is the option of maintaining business as usual. In this instance we find ministers' speeches full of references to soft power, human security, and Canadian leadership. Unfortunately, the fiscal reality is such that many of our initiatives are simply that—initiatives. We do not have the resources to back up our words. The budget of the Canadian International Development Agency (CIDA) is slashed (Draimin and Tomlinson 1998:144–146) while trade promotion with China takes precedence.[4] This does not speak to interconnectedness between issues but rather the importance of trade competitiveness. Balance is difficult to identify but the gap between declaratory policy and practice is not. The commitment-credibility gap, accurately identified by Cooper and Potter, exists and grows as the Minister insists on making claims of Canadian leadership. Such claims are shallow.

Finally, there is a third option. It builds on some already existing strengths such as Canada's role in agenda setting and coalition building. And Axworthy is cor-rect in believing that ideas are important. Our strengths should not be underesti-mated but neither should they be underfunded. The federal government must recognize that narrowly conceived national interests will ultimately undermine the legitimacy and credibility of CFP. It is, however, more than simply funding initiatives. If our advocacy of human security is to be taken seriously then we must make our activities commensurate with the philosophy of connectedness that human security gives expression to. If individuals matter and not just Canadian citizens then our practitioners need to adopt a slightly more cos-mopolitan view of the world, one that is not incommensurate with the notion of human security as presently expressed by Axworthy. Canada cannot be all things to all people. This is not a call for massive spending but rather a call for targeted spending in less self-interested ways.

Richard Falk has argued that in an era of globalization "humane or compas-sionate state is being phased out"(1997:130). The Canadian choice should be for the compassionate state, not one dominated by niche diplomacy or similar concepts that promote a balance sheet mentality, nor one that makes shallow commitments.

NOTES

An earlier version of this paper was presented at the workshop on Human Rights, Ethics and Canadian International Security, sponsored by the York Centre for International and Security Studies, November 1997. The author would like to thank Claire Turenne Sjolander, Lawrence T. Woods, and Cameron Ortis for their insightful comments on earlier drafts.

1. In most of the statements noted already soft power is a key phrase. For more recent examples see DFAIT (1998a; 1998b; 1998c).
2. The Canadian government ultimately accepted six percent reductions at the Kyoto Conference.
3. See Office of the Prime Minister (1998a:3).
4. International Trade Minister Sergio Marchi recently witnessed the signing of "46 commercial agreements worth $720.8 billion during the Canada-China Forum"(DFAIT 1998f:1).

REFERENCES

Axworthy, Lloyd (1997a). "Between Globalization and Multipolarity: The Case for a Global, Humane Canadian Foreign Policy" *Revue Etudes Internationales* 28:1 [http://www.dfait-maeci.gc.ca/english/foreignp/humane.html].

_____ (1997b). "Canadian and Human Security: The Need for Leadership" *International Journal* [http://www.dfait-maeci.gc.ca/english/foreignp/sehume.html].

_____ (1998). "Why Soft Power is the Right Policy for Canada" *Ottawa Citizen* 25 (April): B6.

Black, David R. and Heather A. Smith (1993). "Notable Exceptions? New and Arrested Directions in Canadian Foreign Policy Literature" *Canadian Journal of Political Science* 26:4, 745–774.

Booth, Ken (1995). "Human Wrongs and International Relations" *International Affairs* 71:1, 103–126.

Canada, Finance Canada (1998). Statement Prepared for the Interim Committee of the International Monetary Fund, the Honourable Paul Martin, Minister of Finance for Canada (April 16).

Canada, Department of Foreign Affairs and International Trade (DFAIT) (1996a). Notes for an Address by the Honourable Art Eggleton, Minister of International Trade, on the Occasion of the Canada China Business Council's Business Opportunities in the Yangtze Delta Region Seminar.

_____ (1996b). Notes for an Address by the Honourable Lloyd Axworthy, Minister of Foreign Affairs, at the World Congress Against the Sexual Exploitation of Children (August 27).

_____ (1996c). "Building Peace to Last: Establishing a Canadian Peacebuilding Initiative." Notes for an Address by the Honourable Lloyd Axworthy, Minister of Foreign Affairs, at York University (October 30).

_____ (1996d). Notes for an Address by the Honourable Art Eggleton, Minister for International Trade on the Occasion of the Pacific Basin Economic Council Luncheon (November 1).

_____ (1996e). Notes for an Address by the Honourable Lloyd Axworthy, Minister of Foreign Affairs, "Foreign Policy in the Information Age" (December 6).

_____ (1996f). "Canadian Foreign Policy in a Changing World" Notes for an Address by the Honourable Lloyd Axworthy, Minister of Foreign Affairs, to a Meeting of the National Forum on Foreign Policy (December 13).

____ (1997a). "Canada-India Partnership: Prosperity and Security" Notes for an Address by the Honourable Lloyd Axworthy, Minister of Foreign Affairs, to the Partnership Summit of the Confederation of Indian Industry (January 10).

____ (1997b). Notes for an Address by the Honourable Lloyd Axworthy, Minister of Foreign Affairs, to the Canadian Conference of Humanitarian Demining and Landmine Victim Assistance (January 31).

____ (1997c). Notes for an Address by the Honourable Lloyd Axworthy, Minister of Foreign Affairs, at the Consultations with Non-Governmental Organizations in Preparation for the 53rd Session of the United Commission on Human Rights (February 5).

____ (1997d). Notes for an Address by the Honourable Lloyd Axworthy, Minister of Foreign Affairs, at the Harbourfront Centre on the Launch of Canada's Year of Asia Pacific Cultural Program (February 8).

____ (1997e). Notes for an Address by the Honourable Christine Stewart, Secretary of State (Latin America and Africa) at the Amsterdam Child Labour Conference (February 26).

____ (1997f). Notes for an Address by the Honourable Lloyd Axworthy, Minister of Foreign Affairs on Sustainable Development in Canadian Foreign Policy (April 17).

____ (1997g). Notes for an Address by the Honourable Lloyd Axworthy, Minister of Foreign Affairs before the Standing Committee on Foreign Affairs and International Trade on Child Labour (April 23).

____ (1997h). Notes for an Address by the Honourable Lloyd Axworthy, Minister of Foreign Affairs to the 52nd Session of the United Nations General Assembly (September 25).

____ (1997i). "Canadian Foreign Policy in an Ever-Shrinking World," Notes for an Address by the Honourable David Kilgour, Secretary of State (Latin America and Africa) at the October Meeting of the Diplomatic Press Attache Network, National Press Club (October 15).

____ (1997j). "Human Rights and Canadian Foreign Policy," Notes for an Address by the Honourable Lloyd Axworthy, Minister of Foreign Affairs at McGill University (October 16).

____ (1998a). Notes for an Address by the Honourable Lloyd Axworthy, Minister of Foreign Affairs to the United Nations Commission on Human Rights (March 30).

____ (1998b). "The New Diplomacy: The UN, the International Criminal Court and the Human Security Agenda," Notes for an Address by the Honourable Lloyd Axworthy, Minister of Foreign Affairs to a Conference on UN Reform at the Kennedy School, Harvard University (April 25).

____ (1998c). "Global Action, Continental Community: Human Security in Canadian Foreign Policy," Notes for an Address by the Honourable Lloyd Axworthy, Minister of Foreign Affairs to Meeting of the Mid-America Committee (September 9).

____ (1998d). Notes for an Address by the Honourable Lloyd Axworthy, Minister of Foreign Affairs to the Canadian Institute of International Affairs 1998 Foreign Policy Conference (October 16).

____ (1998e). "A Blueprint for Peace, Justice and Freedom," Notes for an Address by the Honourable Lloyd Axworthy, Minister of Foreign Affairs to the International Conference on Universal Rights and Human Values (November 27).

_____ (1998f). "Canadian Business Deals in Beijing Strengthen Canada-China Business Relationship," *News Release* 20 (November).

Canada, Office of the Prime Minister. (1998a). Notes for an Address by Prime Minister Jean Chrétien on the Occasion of the 69th Annual General Meeting of the Canadian Chamber of Commerce (September 13).

_____ (1998b). Keynote Address to the 1998 Biennial Convention of the Liberal Party of Canada (March 20).

Cooper, Andre F. (1995). "In Search of Niches: Saying "Yes" and Saying "No" in Canada's International Relations," *Canadian Foreign Policy* 3:3, 1–13.

_____ ed. (1997). *Niche Diplomacy: Middle Powers After the Cold War* (New York: St. Martin's Press).

_____ and Geoffrey Hayes eds. (forthcoming). *Worthwhile Initiatives? Canadian Mission-Oriented Diplomacy* (Toronto: Irwin Publishing).

Cox, Robert W. (1986). "Social Forces, States and World Orders: Beyond International Relations Theory," in Robert O. Keohane ed., *Neorealism and Its Critics* (New York: Columbia University Press).

Draimin, Tim and Brian Tomlinson (1998). "Is there a Future for Canadian Aid in the Twenty First Century?" in Fen Osler Hamspon and Maureen Appel Molot, eds. *Leadership and Dialogue: Canada Among Nations 1998* (Toronto: Oxford University Press).

East Timor Alert Network (1996). "Canadian Military Sales to Indonesia," *Information/Action Kit*.

Government of Canada (1995). *Canada in the World* (Ottawa: Supply and Services Canada).

_____ (1997). "Canada Proposes Targets for Reductions in Global Greenhouse Gas Emissions," (December 1). [http://canada.gc.ca.cc.position_n_e.html].

Hampson, Fen Osler and Dean F. Oliver (1998). "Pulpit Diplomacy: A Critical Assessment of the Axworthy Doctrine," *International Journal* 54:3, 379–406.

Head, Ivan and Pierre Trudeau (1995). *The Canadian Way: Shaping Canada's Foreign Policy, 1968–1984* (Toronto: McClelland and Stewart).

Hocking, Brian (1997). "Finding Your Niche: Australia and the Trials of Middle-Powerdom" in Andrew F. Cooper ed. *Niche Diplomacy: Middle Powers After the Cold War* (New York: St. Martin's Press).

Know, Paul (1998). "Canada's Refugee Policy Assailed" *Globe and Mail* (November 10): A17.

Morgenthau, Hans J. (1967). *Politics Among Nations: The Struggle for Power and Peace* 4th ed. (New York: Alfred A. Knopf).

Neufeld, Mark (1995a). "Hegemony and Foreign Policy Analysis: The Case of Canada as a Middle Power," *Studies in Political Economy* 48 (Autumn): 7–29.

_____ (1995b) *The Restructuring of International Relations Theory* (Cambridge: Cambridge University Press).

Nossal, Kim Richard (1994). *Rain Dancing: Sanctions in Canadian and Australian Foreign Policy* (Toronto: University of Toronto Press).

_____ (1998). "Foreign Policy for Wimps," *Ottawa Citizen* (April 23): A19.

Potter, Evan H. (1994). "Ottawa's New Dollar Diplomacy and the Role of Economic Intelligence," *Canadian Foreign Policy* 2:3, I-III.

_____ (1996-7). "Niche Diplomacy as Canadian Foreign Policy," *International Journal* 101:1, 25-38.

_____ (1997). "An Interview with the Minister of Foreign Affairs, Hon. Lloyd Axworthy," *Canadian Foreign Policy* 4:3.

Pratt, Cranford (1983-84). "Dominant Class Theory and Canadian Foreign Policy: The Case of Counter-Consensus," *International Journal* 39:1, 99-135.

Rudner, Martin (1996). "Canada in the World: Development Assistance in Canada's New Foreign Policy Framework," *Canadian Journal of Development* 17:2, 193-220.

Smith, Heather A. (1998). "Stopped Cold," *Alternatives* 24:4, 10-16.

Special Joint Committee of the Senate and the House of Commons Reviewing Canadian Foreign Policy (1994). *Canada's Foreign Policy: Principles and Priorities for the Future* (Ottawa: Public Works and Government Services).

Stairs, Denis (1994-5). "Will and Circumstance and the Postwar Study of Canada's Foreign Policy," *International Journal* 50:1, 9-39.

Walker, R.B.J. (1995). "International Relations and the Concept of the Political," in Ken Booth and Steve Smith eds., *International Relations Theory Today* (University Park: Pennsylvania State University Press).

Whitworth, Sandra (1995). "Women and Gender, in Canadian Foreign Policy," in Maxwell A. Cameron and Maureen Appel Molot eds., *Democracy and Foreign Policy: Canadian Among Nations, 1995*. (Ottawa: Carleton University Press).

Postscript

In her concluding paragraph, Smith suggests that the selection of niches should be shaped by the values and principles that underlie the human security agenda. Certainly, the Canadian government has chosen to pursue specific issues such as landmines, war-affected children, and human rights. Many of these issues reflect the human security agenda discussed in Issue Four. Some would say that the selection of these issues provides a good example of niche diplomacy at work. How successful have these efforts been? Do they provide a model for how niche diplomacy should work in the future?

The above readings do not so much question Canada's diminishing capability, as ask how we should adjust to this situation. As noted in the introduction, the events of September 2001 triggered a renewed debate over Canadian capabilities. Polls taken after the attacks suggest that Canadians may be more willing to spend more on defence, even if taxes go up, in order to ensure a sense of security. As attention shifts towards questions of domestic physical security, how has this influenced the way that Canadians view niche diplomacy?

Infotrac Keyword Search

"Canadian" + "foreign policy"

Suggested Additional Readings

Cooper, Andrew F. "In Search of Niches: Saying 'Yes' and Saying 'No' in Canada's International Relations," *Canadian Foreign Policy* 3:3 (1995), 1–13.

_____ ed. *Niche Diplomacy: Middle Powers After the Cold War* (New York: St. Martin's Press, 1997).

_____ and Geoffrey Hayes eds. (forthcoming). *Worthwhile Initiatives? Canadian Mission-Oriented Diplomacy* (Toronto: Irwin Publishing).

Nossal, Kim Richard. "Foreign Policy for Wimps," *Ottawa Citizen* (April 23, 1998): A19.

Stein, Janice Gross, "Canada 21: A Moment and a Model," *Canadian Foreign Policy* 2 no. 1 (Spring 1994).

Website Resources

Government of Canada, Department of Foreign Affairs and International Trade, Info Canada: Niche Diplomacy: Canada Makes a Difference The site offers a brief report on how Canada has made a difference with niche diplomacy.

Shannon-Marie Soni, "A Lighter Shade of Blue: Japan's Role in UN Peacekeeping Operations," *Periscope* 2, no. 1 (1999) An article looking at the application of niche diplomacy to Japanese foreign policy.

PART THREE

ENSURING PEACE AND SECURITY

Should terrorism be treated as an act of warfare?

Has the concept of "rogue state" become outdated?

Will a ballistic defence system undermine security?

Do biological differences predispose men to war?

Is peacekeeping irrelevant?

Should Terrorism Be Treated as an Act of Warfare?

✔ **YES**
CALEB CARR, "Terrorism as Warfare: Lessons of Military History," *World Policy Journal* (Winter 1996–97)

✗ **NO**
BRUCE HOFFMAN, "Terrorism: Who Is Fighting Whom?" *World Policy Journal* 14, no. 1 (Spring 1997): 97–105

September 11, 2001, will long be remembered by North Americans as a day that changed their perceptions of the world forever. On a normal, sunny morning as many were still arriving at work, the unthinkable happened. Hijackers commandeered four domestic commercial airplanes and diverted them on suicide missions. Two crashed into the twin towers of the World Trade Center in New York City and a third slammed into the Pentagon building in Washington, D.C. A fourth plane crashed in Pennsylvannia after passengers and crew apparently struggled with the hijackers for control of the aircraft. The death toll on that morning of terror was nearly 3,500 civilians.

The attack came as a great shock to Americans. Certainly, American targets have been attacked before, often with hundreds of casualties. But these were generally against overseas targets and had seemed remote to the average American. While the Oaklahoma City bombing had been a shock, the capture, trial, and execution of Timothy McVeigh seemed to give credence to the belief that such attacks were the work of an isolated, deranged person. American soil still seemed relatively invincible from attack by foreign terrorists. Now, for the first time, the heartland of American wealth and power seemed starkly vulnerable.

In a speech to Congress following the attack, President George W. Bush noted that the attack was an act of war and that the United States was now engaged in the first war of the new millennium. He warned that it was not the kind of war that Americans were used to. It would be a war with an invisible enemy and no obvious battle lines. It would be a protracted war, without the kind of large-scale battlefield victories that traditional warfare affords. President Bush also warned that his government would not only target terrorists, but any states that provided support and safe sanctuary for them to operate. As he called on Americans and allies to rally to support this new war, he ensured them that they would prevail.

In the days that followed, writers and pundits debated the best way to respond to terrorism. Some suggested that only swift, strong military action would send the right message to the terrorists. A few even suggested that, given the nature of the enemy, tactics such as selectively targeted assassinations of terrorist organizers should be used. But others argued that a military response should be avoided altogether: a democratic state can best fight terrorism by keeping the rule of law and working within existing diplomatic and legal channels to bring the perpetrators to justice. This itself would be a witness to fundamental values that democracies stand for.

At the heart of this debate was the question: should terrorism be treated as an act of war or as a criminal act? If it is an act of war, then it should be responded to primarily through military force. If it is a criminal act, then a military response should take a back seat to more traditional investigative processes and court proceedings.

Before examining this debate in more detail, it is useful to ask what we mean by terrorism. It is a term which, like many political concepts, is often used for propaganda purposes. Terrorism is a special form of political violence that has been used by both states and non-state organizations to achieve a variety of political purposes. Unlike conventional military force, terrorism has several distinctive characteristics. First, terrorism is a premeditated use of violence to create a climate of extreme fear or terror. Second, it usually targets a wider audience than the immediate victims of the attack. Third, it generally involves random attacks against civilians and targets that have a high symbolic value. Fourth, the attacks violate fundamental social norms and cause widespread outrage within society. Fifth, terrorist attacks are usually intended to influence political behaviour in some way. The intention may be to force a concession of some key demands, publicize a cause, or provoke a wider-scale conflict.

While the attacks of September 11th may fit the classic definition of terrorism, the scale and boldness of the attacks took terrorism to a new level. If terrorists were willing to hijack loaded commercial flights and crash them into crowded office buildings, would they also be willing to use biological, chemical, or even nuclear weapons to inflict large-scale damage on civilians? How is such a threat to be countered?

In the readings that follow, Caleb Carr and Bruce Hoffman debate the appropriate response to terrorism. Although written before the recent events, their debate focuses on the question of whether terrorism should be treated as an act of war or a criminal act. How one answers that question is critical to the kind of strategy that is adopted in dealing with future terrorist threats.

✔ YES
Terrorism as Warfare: Lessons of Military History
CALEB CARR

Throughout the proliferation of international terrorism as a form of political expression and coercion over the past 25 years, American and other world leaders, in an effort to rally global indignation against the agents of such mayhem and deny them the status of actual belligerent soldiers, have taken to referring to the actions of terrorists as "crimes." To be sure, typical terrorist behavior—whether it be assassination, bombing, or kidnapping—is often indistinguishable from the actions of common criminals, and terrorist causes frequently attract individuals who simply use philosophical or political rationalizations to veil their more fundamental greed and bloodlust.

Yet there has always been a central problem with insisting that terrorists are criminals rather than soldiers: this generally limits to reactive and defensive measures the range of responses that the American and other governments can justifiably employ. The burden of combating terrorism too often falls on law enforcement and intelligence agencies, whose job becomes one of careful detection and individual apprehension. The recent proposals of the Clinton administration for countering terrorism reflect exactly this attitude: more than a billion dollars are being requested for programs that are targeted entirely at intelligence and detective work.

In other words, we continue to treat terrorists as if they were smugglers, drug traffickers, or, at most, some kind of political mafiosi, rather than what they have in fact become: organized, highly trained paramilitary units who are conducting an offensive campaign against a variety of nations and social systems. In truth, terrorism *is*, as its perpetrators so often insist, a form of warfare, and only when we recognize it as such will we be able to formulate a comprehensive and meaningful response to its threat.

The basic elements of that response will not be hammered out in legalistic debates or extrapolated from the pronouncements of international tribunals, however; instead, they will flow from the same discipline that has served as a wellspring for all progressive advances in international conflict: military history. By studying terrorism's place in the development of modern warfare we can not only begin to see it as something more than simple criminal activity, we can also begin to outline countermeasures to be taken by the only organizations that will ultimately be able to reduce and perhaps eradicate the terrorist menace: our armed forces.

If such a suggestion seems either alarmist or overly ambitious, consider the nature of the animal that is modern terrorism. True, there are some small-scale, isolated terrorist groups at work in the world whose behavior is characterized by limited goals and crude methods: the bizarre gassing of a Japanese subway station by religious zealots in 1995, the sporadic efforts of North Korean saboteurs, and the recent Chechen bombings of Russian train stations are just a few examples of the work of terrorist movements that either do not aspire to or have failed to achieve the status of significant threats to world security.

But these cases have by now become exceptions rather than the rule. Most of the terrorist havoc being wrought in today's world is the work of men and women who have been financed and supplied through international (and in some cases private) sources, heavily trained in the construction and use of often sophisticated weapons as well as in personal combat, and who are capable of striking at major *international* targets with deadly accuracy—all in the name of affecting the policy deliberations and even the stability of established governments.

This description is, of course, most true of the various groups serving the cause of fundamentalist Islam; but it is also applicable, to an only slightly lesser extent, to some purely nationalistic organizations, such as the militant wing of the Irish Republican Army (IRA), and it may even be true of domestic terrorist movements within the United States (it is still unclear how closely allied certain American militia groups are to similar organizations in other countries, especially Germany). The killing potential of such groups alone justifies their reclassification from criminals who disrupt daily life to soldiers mounting an assault on America's citizens, values, and interests, as well as those of other nations: in the last two decades, for example, more American lives were lost to terrorists than to the soldiers of Saddam Hussein during the Gulf War. Yet America has never developed a large-scale, carefully orchestrated, and sustained military response to terrorism.

This may well be because terrorists are not the acknowledged agents of any national government. But while they may not wear any one country's uniform, they consider themselves—and have in many cases become—armies, who have in their own way declared war on their enemies. Being first on the list of those enemies, America must respond appropriately, not merely with detective work and arrests, but with offensive military operations.

Of course, in formulating those operations, the United States must examine the nature of its opponents and their tactics. Here, we cannot help but use some of the tools of the modern criminologist, primarily psychological research. Terrorism in its current form grew primarily out of two relatively recent sociopsychological developments: first, the dramatically decreased ability of small interest groups (and in some cases small nations) to affect the policies of the major powers and their client states following the Second World War and, second, the emotional susceptibility of the citizens of those more powerful nations to images—eventually and especially television images—of devastating terrorist attacks in locales usually thought safe and secure.

The psychodynamics of the terrorist are very similar to those of the sociopathic killer: feeling that their voices go unheard in an uncaring world, the perpetrators use ritualistic violence against unsuspecting strangers to command attention and create widespread insecurity, subsequently rationalizing their actions with long harangues about injustice and past wrongs. As in the case of a sociopathic killer, such rationalizations reduce the victims of terrorism to dehumanized objects, and often have a taunting air intended to impress society with the virility and power of the perpetrators.

To this analytical extent, the tools of criminology and psychology are useful in dealing with terrorism; but we must be careful not to allow the identification of terrorists as essentially neurotic or even psychotic to minimize the magnitude of the threat that their activities pose. An army of deluded neurotics, as those of Hitler, Mao Zedong, and similar characters in history have shown us, is nonetheless an army. Therefore, if America hopes to defeat terrorism's various attempts to frustrate its national policies, Washington must not stop at identifying the tactics of terror as crimes; nor should it spend more time than is necessary psychoanalyzing terrorists. Rather, the United States should move on to place those tactics within the context of military history and thereby formulate a military solution to what is, in larger terms, a military rather than a criminological problem.

TERRORISM AS MILITARY STRATEGY

The primary goal of terror as a military strategy and tactic, more than to kill enemy soldiers, is to destroy the will of enemy citizens to support the policies of the enemy government. This goal is nothing new: it is as old as warfare itself and fits entirely into the category that has come to be called "total war."

Many military scholars maintain that total war is a modern phenomenon: it is generally thought to have come into being in the late nineteenth century. Such an estimate, however, is unrealistic. In ancient times, when armies slaughtered and raped civilian populations in conquered city-states and sowed their territories with salt; in the medieval era, when armies starved civilians through lengthy sieges; during the seventeenth century, when mercenary forces roamed Europe undermining the authority of princes by preying on their subjects; during the golden age of "privateering," when roving ships threatened the ability of civilians to travel safely and of private corporations to conduct international business securely; throughout human history, in short, total warfare has been as constant as famine and pestilence. Why, then, do so many analysts think of it as having originated during the late nineteenth century?

Perhaps because it was at that time that warfare against civilians stopped being viewed as an unfortunate and dishonorable side-effect of conflict and began to be consciously expounded as a military tool—when it began to be seen, in other words, not as a grim consequence of war but as one of its most effective techniques. In this sense, historians are right to assert that the great philosopher of total war (a rather dubious distinction) was the American general William Tecumseh

Sherman. When Sherman declared that "war is cruelty" and that there was no sense in trying to "reform" it, he was doing more than merely acknowledging that civilian populations suffered outrages during conflicts; he was arguing that, since such outrages were inevitable, the modern general ought to carefully orchestrate them to produce not only the maximum *military* effect (Sherman himself admitted that a mere 20 percent of the destruction he wrought in the South was of any real military value), but the maximum *psychological* and *emotional* effect, as well. Sad and angry as the statement may make many students of the American Civil War, Sherman can in this sense be seen as the godfather of modern terrorism. True, he preferred starvation to murder and rape as the instrument of that terror, but he openly believed himself to be at war with every "man, woman, and child" in the South, and his army conducted itself accordingly.

Technology and the changing morality of highly populated industrial societies soon led to the spread of such tactics of terror throughout the world. Sherman himself presided over the development of his methods by such generals as Philip Sheridan during campaigns in the American West that were designed not to defeat but to exterminate the various Indian tribes. Prussian chancellor Otto von Bismarck's bombardment of Paris during the Franco-Prussian War of 1870–71 (undertaken over the vehement objections of Prussia's chief of the General Staff and guiding military light, Helmuth von Moltke) can be classified as terrorism, if we adhere to the definition of terrorism as the victimization of unarmed civilians in an attempt to affect the policies of the government that leads those civilians.

The First World War found Great Britain attempting to starve German civilians into submission through a naval blockade, and the Germans answering with unrestricted submarine warfare, which cost thousands of civilians—many of them neutrals—their lives. And by the time of the Second World War, all parties had entered the terrorist fray: the Japanese rape of China, the Luftwaffe's blitzing of London, the Allied strategic and fire-bombing campaigns against Germany and Japan, and, most obviously, the nuclear destruction of Hiroshima and Nagasaki, all demonstrated that every nation on earth had come to consider civilian populations legitimate targets during time of war.

The objection may at this point be raised that all these conflicts *were* wars— formally declared conflicts between nations—but this is simply not accurate. The American Civil War—whatever the pretensions of the Confederacy and those who still rhapsodize about it—was just what the name implies, an internecine and not an international conflict. And one would have to look hard to find formal declarations of belligerency on either side between the Indian nations of the American West and the government of the United States. German U-boat commanders such as Lt. Walther Schwieger, who sank the *Lusitania*, killed American civilians long before there was a declaration of war between Germany and the Unites States, while the German government exploited legal and moral loopholes that were far from internationally accepted to rationalize the U-boats' actions. The Empire of

Japan attacked Pearl Harbor—an assault that caused many civilian casualties—before declaring war on the United States.

And, finally, one of the greatest examples to date of warfare waged against a civilian population in an effort to change the policies of that population's government—the American campaign in Vietnam—went undeclared for its duration. We cannot delude ourselves about the nature of modern conflict by clinging to legalistic niceties: the only things that separate "terrorism" from "warfare" in the modern age are the scope of operations and the fact that "terrorists" most often do not represent established national governments.

In their own eyes, however, they may represent much more. The members of such groups as Hezbollah and the Islamic Jihad believe themselves the defenders of the "nation" or "kingdom" of Islam generally, and they certainly consider themselves to be "at war" with the United States. The fact that they do not follow the protocols for organized conflict first ratified in Geneva in 1906 does not change their beliefs, and moralistic castigations rooted in nineteenth-century liberal humanist thinking will not mitigate either the terrorists' determination or their sense of self-righteousness.

Nor will it blind them to the fact that many of the signatories to the various Geneva Accords—including the United States—have often failed to abide by them. The terrorists are aware of the historical contradictions inherent in the Western condemnation of terrorism, even if we are loathe to acknowledge those contradictions ourselves, and they consider themselves every bit as much "soldiers" as the men and women who fill the ranks of Western armies.

Furthermore, their opinions in this regard have been confirmed by the very people who now seek to label their behavior immoral. It was the United States, after all, that helped create the monster of present-day Afghanistan, which has been the largest and most effective training ground for terrorists in the world. It is doubtful that while "advising" the Afghan *mujahidin* in their war against the Soviets, the American CIA spent much time telling those hardened fighters that they were not true soldiers or that their tactics were illegitimate.

Thus, military history reveals terrorism to be an almost inevitable product of the evolution of warfare throughout the ages, and especially during the modern era. And just as military history can afford us this insight into the origins and nature of terrorism, it can help us outline a response to terrorism's threat by answering the crucial question of how effective, as a military tactic, terrorism has been.

THE FALLACIES OF TERROR

The answer may surprise many: for in fact terror, as a *lone* military strategy (that is, when unaccompanied by other types of organized conventional military effort), has been remarkably unsuccessful. Even a cursory look at the tactics of terror reveals that reliance on such conduct alone, while it may succeed in psychologically gratifying its perpetrators, almost never coerces an enemy nation into complying with the political wishes of the agents of terror. Indeed, in some cases terror has proved so detrimental to the cause of its agents that even large-scale supportive military actions cannot correct the damage.

Consider the above set of historical examples, beginning with General Sherman's march of destruction through Georgia and the Carolinas during the American Civil War. The campaign itself was brilliantly conceived in purely military terms, representing perhaps the only truly inspired strategic stroke of the entire war, and anticipates the "indirect approach" that the German army would use with such devastating effect in the early years of the Second World War. But the widespread civilian destruction that characterized the tactical campaign represented an *entirely separate* component of the episode, and careful analysis raises the question of whether it was desirable or even necessary.

Starving and robbing civilians did little to change the *military* outcome of the war, and the most perceptive and honest Union officers—including Sherman himself—either directly or indirectly admitted as much. Sherman's military job was to cut the Confederate lines of supply and communication to the Southern forces that were fighting Gen. Ulysses Grant to the north; once that goal was accomplished—as it was—any further destruction became punitive, as Sherman intended, and thus something even worse: it made the postwar Union policy of pacifying the South, of making Southerners feel once again a part of the United States, far more difficult. In other words, *Sherman's tactics were ultimately counterproductive to the policies of the government that put them into effect.* Sherman as a military thinker and leader was a genius; Sherman as a political and social thinker was a failure.

One might argue that the strategy and tactics of waging war against civilians were more successful in the post-Civil War American West, but one must first ask: what was the policy of the United States government at the time? If it was in fact to exterminate the Indian tribes, then the campaign was a failure; if it was to reduce those tribes to the status of a disaffected minority within the United States who would in the future continue to pose difficult political and moral problems for the federal and various state governments, then it was a success.

The Indian tribes of North America could have been accommodated without being ruthlessly assaulted by the tactics of terror. The Canadian experience demonstrates as much. What happened in the American West may have made white Americans *feel* more powerful and confident (just as blowing up airplanes makes today's terrorists feel superior); but we cannot say that it was a successful policy, whereas we can point to definite areas where it has posed subsequent problems for the American government.

The list of failures goes on. Helmuth von Moltke bitterly opposed bombarding Paris at the end of the Franco-Prussian War because he felt that it would not serve Bismarck's purpose of hastening French capitulation, but would in fact only stiffen French resistance and prolong the war. He was correct, and in recognizing this eventuality he defined the central fallacy of the tactics of terror: rather than frightening the designated enemy into compliance, terrorist tactics tend to harden that enemy's resolve to resist. When the German empire that Moltke helped create engaged in unrestricted submarine warfare during the First World War, for example, the strategy may or may not have come close to breaking Great Britain's ability to prosecute the conflict (the point has always been argued by naval historians); what it most certainly did was play a crucial, and perhaps determining, role in bringing the industrial might of the formerly neutral United States crashing down on the German fatherland.

Moving on to the Second World War, few would argue that the Japanese surprise attack on Pearl Harbor galvanized the American people into fighting back. In the war's European theater, meanwhile, an even more cogent example of the failure of terror as a tactic was the London blitz of 1940–41, when British determination to fight the Nazi Reich was only stiffened by the attendant enormous loss of civilian life and property. When the Allies turned the tables and began their own "strategic bombing" (one of the great euphemisms for the tactics of terror) of Germany, arguments over the campaign's effectiveness erupted immediately and continue to this day. Certainly, those bombing raids that were aimed at purely military targets helped to shorten the war; but the punitive raids that reached their vicious crescendo with the fire-bombing of Dresden in 1945 arguably did nothing but allow Hitler to convince more old men and young boys to get into uniform during the last months of the war to avenge their slaughtered families and countrymen.

As to whether the atomic bombs dropped on Hiroshima and Nagasaki represented the most successful way for the United States to bring the war against Japan to a speedy conclusion, debate, again, continues to rage. But one thing may be safely said: had Japan not already been tremendously weakened by conventional Allied military assaults, the effect of Hiroshima and Nagasaki would have been far less profound. America had spent almost four years (and its allies far longer) determinedly battling and then turning back Japanese aggression. U.S. efforts on the high seas, particularly the American submarine campaign against Japanese shipping, had already drastically sapped Japanese strength. Had the reverse been true, and had the bombs been dropped when Japan's armies and navy were triumphant throughout Asia and the Pacific, one wonders if the destruction of Hiroshima and Nagasaki would have had any greater effect on Japanese policy than did the Doolittle bombing raids on Tokyo in April 1942.

But it is Vietnam that should serve as the clearest example of the failure of the tactics of terror. During the Vietnamese conflict, the United States engaged in every conceivable form of warfare against civilians, including such infamous undertakings as the Phoenix assassination program. Indiscriminate fire and strategic bombing, the widespread use of antipersonnel devices incapable of distinguishing an enemy soldier from a civilian child, and antiguerrilla efforts that resulted in such tragedies as My Lai lead one to wonder if even General Sherman would not have hung his head at the tactics employed by his countrymen in Vietnam. And yet, what effect did all this violence and devastation produce above all? An increased determination on the part of the Vietnamese Communists to resist the American aggressors.

MISCONCEPTIONS OF TERRORISM

An awareness of their own history should have prevented, and should still prevent, Americans being surprised at this. When, during the American Revolution, British soldiers and sailors roamed through the countryside and towns of New England, Virginia, and the Carolinas committing rapacious depredations against civilians, they did not help the Loyalist cause; indeed, their behavior drove many ambivalent colonists into the revolutionary ranks. And when British soldiers and sailors gratuitously burned the new American capital of Washington during the War of 1812, it only engendered a bitterness that caused most Americans to view Britain as their greatest potential enemy for the rest of the century—long after the actual probability of further conflicts between the two nations had passed. (Similarly, polls in recent years have shown that most Japanese citizens feel that if Japan were ever to get into another large-scale war, it would be with the United States.) The self-defeating nature of warfare against civilians has been demonstrated time and again in America's national experience, and yet Washington has continued to engage in such tactics; perhaps that is one reason why the United States cannot now seem to formulate an effective response to terrorism.

More recent international developments drawn from military history only further support the assertion that terrorism is a misconceived and misguided method of trying to influence international political affairs: modern terrorist tactics have done little or nothing to advance the causes of those groups that employ them. For example, Palestinian terrorists for years murdered innocent citizens of third-party nations without forcing the United States or the international community to exert any significant pressure on Israel to accommodate Palestinian demands. Indeed, it was only when the Palestinians began to adopt the far different tactic of confronting Israeli soldiers openly—and when, critically, the Israelis themselves responded by employing tactics that were effectively terrorist (assaulting civilian refugee camps suspected of harboring activists, brutally repressing Palestinian demonstrations, and so on)—that the Palestinian cause was appreciably advanced internationally.

On another continent, Great Britain certainly shows no sign of withdrawing from Northern Ireland as a result of the terrorist tactics of the Irish Republican Army, and every IRA bomb that explodes in England—like the V-1 and V-2 rockets that Hitler launched from France—only seems to increase British resolve to frustrate the IRA's goals. Domestic terrorism in the United States may draw a few additional souls into the ranks of local militias, but its more profound effect has been to identify those militias in the popular consciousness not as bastions of liberty and Americanism but as gathering places for the deluded and the deranged.

If terrorism is such a bankrupt, failed strategy, one might reasonably ask, why should we bother formulating an offensive response to it at all? Why not just ride out the storm and let terrorism defeat itself? Because a deeper problem regarding the goals and actions of today's terrorists, as distinct from those of past generations, has arisen. It has often been said—perhaps most eloquently by David Fromkin in his seminal article, "The Strategy of Terrorism," published in *Foreign Affairs* in July 1975—that the guiding principle of our response to terrorism must be a refusal to submit to its demands.

But we live now in a world in which terrorist acts are often not linked to specific demands, a world in which many powerful terrorist groups consider themselves at war with the United States and have no goal more specific than America's destruction. In such a world, America can no longer say simply that it will never give in to terrorism, because terrorism is no longer holding a gun to American heads and seeking compliant behavior—it is firing that gun without warning or ultimatums.

Analyses like Fromkin's were made at a time when in dealing with terrorists Washington was still operating roughly within the realm of negotiation; but one cannot negotiate, for example, with such simplistic "demands" as "We want the Koran to triumph throughout the globe," a statement made recently by a member of the Taliban, an organization of highly trained and well-equipped Islamic terrorists at this writing effectively in control of the capital of Afghanistan.

In confronting today's terrorists, the United States has moved from negotiation and into diplomacy's second domain—military force—and must formulate a new response accordingly. Economic sanctions, trade restrictions, and coercive diplomacy should not be abandoned, but they cannot suffice on their own. Armies must be met with armies, warfare with warfare.

THE STRATEGIC EDGE

With this end in mind, we return to the lessons of military history. As should be clear from this brief survey, the first and most unshakable military guideline in responding to terrorism should be a refusal to employ terrorism's own tactics, no matter how great the desire for revenge or the urge to fight fire with fire. Warfare against unsuspecting civilians is not only morally reprehensible but self-defeating, and it will not move America closer to the goal of destroying the terrorist threat.

It is perhaps unreasonable to expect unbalanced extremists who spend their time immersed in fundamentalist religious tracts, political dogma, and bomb schematics to take the time to learn even so elementary a lesson of military history—Americans have no such excuse. Washington ought to have known, for example, that when the United States struck at civilian in addition to military infrastructure in and around Baghdad during the Gulf War it was sowing the seeds of disease, starvation, and dehydration, and thus alienating the Iraqi people and prompting them to give Saddam Hussein an extended lease on power. If America's quarrel was not with the Iraqi people but with their leader, as President George Bush maintained, then why did so many Iraqi civilians die, while Saddam remained rather conspicuously alive?

In order to answer this question, we must pose another. Military history teaches us that in the modern era, the strategic edge has always resided in the offensive. While, for example, Ronald Reagan's dream of a "Star Wars" defensive shield against nuclear weapons remains a fantasy, the offensive threat implied by the doctrine of mutually assured destruction continues to be the determining law of international nuclear behavior.

In dealing with terrorism, therefore, America cannot hide behind a Maginot Line of tightened airport security, regional diplomatic maneuvering, and trade punishments against foreign companies that do business with nations that sponsor terrorism. Rather, Washington must formulate a standing military strategy that, like mutually assured destruction, will pose a perpetual offensive threat, to be implemented quickly and resolutely whenever an American life is lost to terrorism. But if the United States rejects civilian targets, against whom or what should such an offensive threat be directed?

Examples from military history can serve us again. As we have noted, when General Sherman marched through the South, he destroyed many installations and objectives that were of military value; but the overwhelming amount of destruction that his army wrought was against civilian property. This was—by his own admission—militarily useless. The result: generations of bitterness on the part of Southerners against the North. In contrast, when the German army invaded France in May 1940, it made a deliberate effort to concentrate its destructive activities against targets that would cut the British and French military lines of supply and communication and create political panic while simultaneously limiting collateral civilian damage.

This was not a humanitarian decision, of course: the Germans were conquerors bent on making military and recreational use of their conquests and their vanquished enemies. (The Nazi element within the German army also reminded rank-and-file German soldiers that it would be ethnically beneath them to rape women in France and the Lowlands.) But the point is that the German campaign in France was characterized by far fewer depredations against civilians and their property than, somewhat surprisingly, the Allied liberation would be four years later. The result was a French resistance effort during the German occupation that involved only a tiny fraction of the French populace.

From such examples, we can formulate our third guideline in responding to terrorism. It has been stated, first, that the United States must refuse to intentionally target civilian installations, and second, that it must stay ever on the offensive rather than shrinking behind reactionary defensive measures. The logic of these two principles produces the third: the United States must carefully but thoroughly direct its offensive planning against *military* targets. But when dealing with terrorists—who, again, may not be the uniformed soldiers of any specific nation—what ought such targets to be?

WHAT IS TO BE DONE

There are two answers in this regard, the first more apparent and, perhaps, predictable, the second calling for innovation of a type to which the American military is new but toward which it seems to be slowly moving.

The first involves military action against nations known to sponsor international terrorism. President Clinton's declaration that the United States will impose trade sanctions on foreign companies doing more than $40 million worth of business with Iran, Libya, Syria, and Sudan is morally laudable. But this is being resisted by the typically pusillanimous (on the subject of terrorism, at any rate) governments of Europe, and will doubtless have little real effect. Much more significant is the fact that President Clinton feels confident in openly declaring these four *countries* to be sponsors of terrorism (they supply terrorists, either directly or indirectly, and allow them to train within their borders) and therefore deserving of punishment. Such being the case, however, why is Washington stopping at trade sanctions against third-party corporations?

The answer usually given is that there is little more that can be done since trade sanctions against the sponsor states themselves are already in place. Moreover, it would be almost impossible, given the penchant of terrorist groups to hide their activities among civilian populations, to attack their training camps without killing civilians. All this may be true, but it leaves another enormous and more accessible target off the list of offensive objectives: the conventional military forces of the sponsor nations themselves.

We do not want to see American planes launching attacks against refugee camps in Lebanon or Syria, a tactic that recently proved so disastrous for Israel. But Syria's President Hafiz al-Assad takes great pride in his conventional military might; he has always acted as if the Syrian military were and is immune from great-power reprisals for terrorist acts. Inexplicably, the great powers have consented to and preserved this immunity. Why?

In the Cold War era, the explanation was that Syria, along with most other terrorist sponsors, was an important Soviet client. It is past time to allow U.S. antiterrorist efforts to catch up with post-Cold War international realities. With the Soviet Union gone and Russia's future ever more uncertain, Syria's ties to

Moscow—whatever may be left of them—should be even less of a deterrent to forceful, decisive action than were Russian attempts to mitigate Western responses to the Serbian atrocities in Bosnia. (It should be noted that Moscow eventually—and wisely—chose to effectively abandon the Serb cause).

If America were to announce that the conventional military forces of states that sponsor terrorism were to be held accountable for the actions of those terrorist groups that train and are equipped within their borders or even, as in the cases of those groups that base themselves in anarchic Lebanon but are supplied by other sponsor states, outside their borders, we may be sure that a host of such groups would suddenly be looking for new homes. Men like the leaders of Iran may be devoted to Islam, but they are even more devoted to maintaining both their power bases at home and their powerful positions within their regional balances of power.

Attacks against the military forces and installations of states that sponsor terrorism would revolutionize the struggle against terrorism and be in keeping with the priorities of avoiding civilian installations, staying on the offensive, and attacking purely military targets. The Clinton administration has tried to follow at least some of these guidelines during its recent attacks on Iraq. But (putting aside for the moment the fact that those attacks were not responses to terrorism, but to assaults on the protected Kurdish factions in northern Iraq, and therefore lie outside the strict boundaries of this discussion) any future attacks of this kind would have to target military units more effectively and military installations more stringently, so as to avoid damaging infrastructure (water systems, electrical plants, and the like) whose destruction only causes further disaffection among the civilian population.

That such measures would be effective, few can doubt. Terrorist groups would be forced to scurry from nation to nation seeking safe havens. But as those havens were shut down one by one by the sponsor states themselves out of self-interest, there would gradually be nowhere for the terrorists to go save underground (or to such no man's lands as Lebanon) where, without the kind of training, equipment, and funding that they are securing in the sponsor states, their operations would be dramatically curtailed and eventually choked off altogether.

TARGETING THE TERRORISTS

In order for such a scheme to work, of course, the list of potential targets for American attacks would have to grow beyond the four countries cited by President Clinton. Afghanistan, if its past behavior holds true in the future, might well top the list. Most of the American public is by now familiar with the fact that in arming and training the Afghan *mujahidin* for their war against Russia the United States was creating a force that might one day turn against America itself. At least until the takeover of the government in Kabul by the Taliban, which is led by militant Islamic clerics, the scale of terrorist training activities that was occurring in

Afghanistan was shocking. Disaffected Muslims from all over the world, many of them little more than violent misfits, were welcomed in Afghanistan and taught the use of sophisticated weapons of terror. At the same time, they were told that anyone who opposes the spread of Islam is a worthy target. (In a very real sense, as Israeli prime minister Benjamin Netanyahu has written, these new fighters are not the inheritors of such groups as the Palestine Liberation Organization, but of the Muslim warriors who battled Christian Europe during the Crusades.)

The American nation, of course, is seen as the principle obstacle to the triumph of Islam, but there are many secondary targets. After receiving their training, indoctrination, and equipment with some of the best weapons that can be had on the international arms market (or that are left over from the war with Russia), these fanatics are sent out into the world, and at the present time there is not a corner of the globe where their presence is not felt. As Said Ibrahim, chairman of the Ibn Khaldoun Center for Development Studies in Cairo, recently put it, "Fundamentalism has globalized. It is as global as the Sixth Fleet."

Yet while the weapons of fundamentalist terror are being fired, the weapons of the Sixth Fleet remain silent. It is no great secret where most of the terrorist training camps in Afghanistan have been located: Russian military and intelligence officers, many with firsthand experience in Afghanistan, have openly stated that in the provinces of Paktia, Zabul, Nangarhar, Takhar, and Badakhshan, anxious volunteers from all over the world go through their paces in large, well-organized encampments funded by other Islamic states, by wealthy Muslim businessmen sympathetic to the cause, and even by some international fundraising groups that masquerade as humanitarian charities.

Washington would be well advised to warn whoever holds power in Kabul that from this time forward military installations in Afghanistan will be considered legitimate targets of offensive military action, should Afghan rulers pursue a policy of supporting international terrorists. No specific, demonstrable links to actual terrorist acts need precede such a statement or such operations. Since we know that a large percentage of the world's terrorists have been trained in Afghanistan, the country has forfeited its right to feel immune from assault.

Afghanistan should be but the first country to be made aware that it is under the perpetual threat of attack: Syria, Iran, Libya, and Sudan, along with any other nations that are found to be sponsoring terrorists, should also be warned. Faced with the prospect of becoming regional military cripples for the sake of their terrorist "guests," we may feel fairly sure that these governments will turn those guests out.

As Secretary of State George Shultz said in 1984, "From a practical standpoint, a purely passive defense does not provide enough of a deterrent to terrorism and the states that sponsor it. It is time to think long, hard, and seriously about more active means of defense—defense through appropriate preventive or preemptive actions against terrorist groups *before* they strike." To this statement Shultz might have added, just as we can and should now add, "actions against terrorist groups *and the armed forces of the nations that sponsor them.*"

Shultz and the president he served, Ronald Reagan, were as good as their word, in this regard: in April 1986, after Libya had openly declared itself to be at war with the United States, attacked American aircraft, and aided in the terrorist bombing of a West Berlin nightclub known to be frequented by American servicemen, the Reagan administration unleashed an air strike against various military targets in Libya. The attack caused significant damage and badly rattled Libyan strongman Muammar al-Qaddafi, who narrowly escaped death. More important, the raid, and other similarly strong measures, sent a message to both terrorist groups and their sponsors that was taken seriously: by the end of the 1980s, international terrorism appeared to be on the wane. Unfortunately, this forceful response to terrorism was not sustained, so Qaddafi and other sponsors resumed dabbling in terrorism.

THE "COMMANDO" OPTION

The second component of the American offensive military response to terrorism—commando raids—is somewhat trickier to accomplish than the first, although there are rumblings that the American military is already considering this option. Commando raids into foreign countries to seize and perhaps even to execute enemy leaders has generally been considered a wartime-only tactic. But if the United States acknowledges itself to be at war with all nations connected to terrorism it must also adopt this tactic on a continuing basis. There have been reports in the British press that the United States has in place a plan to "kidnap" (the wrong word, given the objective) Bosnian war criminal Radovan Karadzic, by means of an airborne raid on the mountain town of Pale.

Admittedly, Karadzic is not an international terrorist who has specifically targetted U.S. assets; and the job of entering hostile territory to seize a local leader is one requiring precise intelligence and flawless execution. Nevertheless, the tactical concept, if it can be realized, is a sound and useful one.

Typically, the United States is being urged by its European allies to restrain from so forceful—and effective—a method of bringing Karadzic to justice before the U.N. war crimes tribunal at the Hague. But were it to be successful, such a move could herald a new age in dealing with war criminals. Were the United States to create a commando force capable of crossing foreign borders and removing specific key players in the spread of terrorism—whether government leaders, would-be heads of state (like Karadzic), mid-level officers, or simple foot-soldiers—then even safe havens in a sponsor country would no longer be a guarantee of safety for such individuals. Above all, it would further reduce the probability that the United States, in attempting to apprehend terrorist leaders or combat terrorist forces, would cause the deaths of foreign civilians.

If talk of commando abduction or execution seems too Machiavellian, we should remind ourselves again that in time of war civilian leaders assume the status of commanders-in-chief of armed forces, and as such are legitimate targets of military action. Why should Saddam Hussein have been allowed to feel safer during the Gulf War than the average citizen of Baghdad, or than the soldiers of his Republican Guard? Why should Hafiz al-Assad sleep more soundly at night than the terrorists whose work he sponsors, or than one of his own soldiers? The real reason is that the United States has not yet created the kind of units that could make such leaders uneasy, or, if it has, those units remain leashed. American efforts remain reactive: Washington investigates, it protests, it pursues, sometimes it even apprehends and convicts. But America does not do what its enemies are doing. It does not wage war.

None of this, to repeat, is to say that the United States should dispense with its criminological and intelligence work, only that it should substantially augment it. It is as unreasonable to expect law enforcement to deal with the problem of international terrorism on its own as it is to expect the Coast Guard and the Border Patrol to stop the flow of drugs and illegal aliens into the country without the help of the navy and army. Terrorism is a problem requiring a far more expansive and coherent *military* effort.

If Americans look to the lessons of military history, they will find hope that such an effort will be successful and that modern-day terrorists can be put out of business, just as eighteenth-century pirates—like those that the U.S. navy battled off the Barbary Coast in America's early years—were eventually subdued and neutralized. Only the efforts of American conventional forces made the victory over the Barbary pirates possible; only the intervention of American armed forces will put an end to terrorism.

✗ **NO**

Terrorism: Who Is Fighting Whom?
BRUCE HOFFMAN

Caleb Carr eloquently expresses the frustration and anger felt by many Americans over their inability to deter, much less defeat, the menace of terrorism. Recent events such as the massive explosion outside a U.S. Air Force housing complex in Saudi Arabia (which killed 19 persons and wounded nearly 500 others), the unsolved bombing at last summer's Olympic Games and the still unexplained crash of TWA Flight 800 into the sea off Long Island just weeks earlier, and the 1995 bombing of a federal office building in Oklahoma City (which claimed the lives of 168 persons) have appreciably heightened this sense of victimization, prompting renewed debate over how the United States can best respond to the terrorist threat and thus better safeguard the lives of its citizens and its vital interests.

To Carr, a contributing editor of *MHQ: The Quarterly Journal of Military History*, the answer to America's terrorist problem is obvious: "Americans should look to the lessons of military history" and realize that "only the intervention of American armed forces will put an end to terrorism." Accordingly, since terrorist groups often have no known permanent bases for the United States to target and are themselves inherently numerically small, clandestine, and elusive, Carr instead advocates offensive military action against their state-sponsors. "Armies must be met with armies, warfare with warfare," he declares. The advantages of such an approach are allegedly manifold: it would specifically punish the actual governmental entities upon whom terrorists depend while deliberately avoiding the infliction of civilian casualties among the targeted state's population, and thus reverse what Carr sees as America's current defensive state of mind so far as terrorism is concerned while sending a powerfully effective deterrent message to perpetrator and supporter alike. "Attacks against the military forces and installations of states that sponsor terrorism," he claims, "would revolutionize the struggle against terrorism" and therefore succeed decisively where other, nonmilitary measures—such as trade sanctions and other diplomatic initiatives—have failed.

It is a seductively sweeping argument that will appeal as much to Pentagon flag officers seeking new opportunities and new enemies to justify their vast arsenals as to ordinary citizens and their elected representatives who may already have begun to wonder why the United States needs to maintain so lavish a defense establishment if it is to remain idle in the face of such threats. But, as enticing as Carr's simple prescription for America's terrorist ills may appear, it is seriously flawed: he does not take into account more germane historical lessons of failed U.S. counterterrorist policies identical to the ones he proposes and thereby advocates previously tried remedies that have already demonstrated that the cure may be worse than the disease. Carr's greatest misconception, however, is his notion that terrorism is a military problem that therefore can not only be solved—but defeated—through the direct application of military force. Indeed, while terrorism is a form of warfare, Carr's claim that it is therefore amenable or susceptible to military solutions does not necessarily follow. He perhaps arrives at this conclusion from an imprecise definition of terrorism that lays too much emphasis on its use as a tactic rather than properly seeing it as a strategy.

MISPERCEIVING TERRORISM

In this respect, it is not sufficient to define terrorism simply as "the victimization of unarmed civilians in an attempt to affect the policies of the government that leads those civilians." Such a definition, as Carr himself acknowledges, applies equally to the violence inflicted by the armed forces of established nation-states as to that perpetrated by small cells of enigmatic nonstate or substate entities (for example, terrorists). But this is confusing apples with oranges. There is a critical distinction between the deliberate "terrorizing" of civilians by military forces (the "scorched earth policy" of General Sherman and attendant historical examples of the rape of Nanking, the London blitz, and the nuclear destruction of Hiroshima and Nagasaki described by Carr) and the acts of far more limited, but also far more deliberate and selective, violence that characterizes terrorism and indeed differentiates it from other forms of violence.

Carr's analysis is ill served by his resurrection of the popular misconception of terrorists as "neurotic or even psychotic...sociopathic killers" and as nothing more than an "army of deluded neurotics." His implication is that a few sharp, well-aimed blows—administered by a muscular American military establishment—will bring these persons to their senses and either remedy their intolerable behavior or dissuade them from further transgressions. The checkered history of military retaliation either in deterring or positively affecting terrorist—and their state-supporters'—behavior will be discussed below. Of greater relevance in this context is Carr's misinformed claim that terrorist causes "frequently attract individuals who simply use philosophical or political rationalizations to veil their more fundamental greed and bloodlust."

There are countless examples that both challenge this oversimplification and provide convincing evidence of how terrorism for many is often a rational choice, in many instances reluctantly embraced after considerable thought and debate. Certainly, Nelson Mandela's frank account of how he concluded in the early 1960s that the African National Congress had no choice but to move from nonviolent militancy to terrorism if it were ever to achieve its goals in the face of South African intransigence and repression belies Carr's claim. Similarly, the logic applied by Menachem Begin, another head of state who was once branded a terrorist, to the revolt he led against British rule in pre-independence Israel defies categorization as "neurotic," "psychotic," or "sociopathic." In perhaps one of the most famous exegeses of the rationale behind terrorism (which Mandela himself cites as a major influence on the ANC's decision to use violence), Begin recalled in his memoir, *The Revolt: Story of the Irgun* (1977), "History and our observation persuaded us that if we could succeed in destroying the government's prestige in Eretz Israel, the removal of its rule would follow automatically. Henceforward, we gave no peace to this weak spot. Throughout all the years of our uprising, we hit at the British Government's prestige, deliberately, tirelessly, unceasingly." Indeed, the strategy defined by Begin for the Irgun fails to evoke images of mindless, fanatical, or wanton violence.

Carr's description may admittedly have some relevance to the rank-and-file members of terrorist groups: the triggermen and bombers, hijackers, and getaway drivers who are the foot soldiers—and cannon fodder—of many types of organizations (including established military forces) with a violent purpose and orientation. Indeed, both terrorist and military recruits are trained in remarkably similar ways. They are taught to regard hitherto abhorrent lethal and destructive behavior as both personally and socially acceptable. Their respective individual value systems are "recalibrated" so that previously independent-minded persons are now taught to follow orders without question or hesitation and to adopt zealously the ethos of the organizations to which they belong.

Thus, just as it would be misleading to infer that all soldiers by dint of their vocation are "neurotic," "psychotic," or "sociopathic killers," it is similarly unhelpful to apply such a generalization to all terrorists. In sum, while treating terrorists as irrational fanatics and mindless killers may satisfy one's own sense of moral indignation and personal abhorrence over their "cowardly" tactics and frequently "innocent" targets, it nonetheless undermines the ability to understand the terrorists' motivations and rationale and, in turn, to effectively counter them and their violence.

In line with his belief in the fundamental irrationality of terrorism, Carr also regards it as a conspicuously failed strategy. As "a lone military strategy (that is, when unaccompanied by other types of organized conventional military effort)" terrorism, Carr judges, "has been remarkably unsuccessful." Although governments, throughout history and throughout the world have—not surprisingly—always made the same claim, the examples of Menachem Begin in Israel, Archbishop Makarios in Cyprus, Jomo Kenyatta in Kenya, Ahmed Ben Bella in Algeria, and, more recently, Gerry Adams in Northern Ireland, Yasir Arafat in the autonomous Palestine National Authority, and Nelson Mandela in South Africa provide firm evidence to the contrary.

Indeed, the tactical "successes" and political victories won through violence by groups like the Palestine Liberation Organization (PLO) and the ANC, alongside the new statesman-like status accorded to former terrorists, such as Nobel Peace Prize winners Yasir Arafat and Nelson Mandela, have demonstrated how long-standing—even often ignored or forgotten—causes or grievances can be resurrected and thrust onto the world's agenda through a series of well-orchestrated and attention-riveting acts.

More important, perhaps, the recent "successes" of the PLO, the ANC, and even the Irish Republican Army (IRA) until the ceasefire between the IRA and the British government collapsed last year (it is claimed by some that the IRA "bombed its way" to the conference table, pressuring the British government into negotiating with its aboveground political party, Sinn Fein) have also demonstrated to other terrorists and/or would-be terrorists that, contrary to the repeated denials of the governments they confront, terrorism does "work." Even if this "success" is not defined in terms of acquiring power in government, the respectability accorded to terrorist organizations hitherto branded as "criminal" and their success in attracting attention to themselves and their causes, and perhaps even in compelling governments to address issues that, if not for the terrorists' violence, would have largely been ignored, cannot be discounted.

In support of his argument that the dimensions of the terrorist threat are vast enough to warrant military action, Carr writes that the "killing potential of such groups alone justifies their reclassification from criminals who disrupt daily life to soldiers mounting an assault on American's citizens, values, and interests, as well as those of other nations: in the last two decades, for example, more American lives were lost to terrorists than to the soldiers of Saddam Hussein during the Gulf War."

While this is true, it is neither a complete nor accurate depiction of the dimensions of the threat posed by terrorism to Americans. For example, since the advent of what is considered the era of contemporary international terrorism in 1968, terrorists have killed fewer than 800 Americans: a number that pales in comparison to the 20,000 or so homicides recorded annually in the United States over the past decade or more. Accordingly, even if more American civilians have been killed by terrorists than Americans in uniform by Saddam's forces, an average of fewer than 28 fatalities per year can hardly be construed as representing a salient threat to either America's national security or citizenry.

Finally, Carr argues that "we live now in a world in which terrorist acts are often not linked to specific demands, a world in which many powerful terrorist groups consider themselves at war with the United States and have no goal more specific than America's destruction." Such a view is as patently false today as when similar theories of monolithic, global terrorist conspiracies were peddled to receptive presidential administrations at the height of the Cold War. At the time, such books as *The Terror Network* (1981) by Claire Sterling claimed that the Soviet Union was behind most, if not all, of the world's terrorism. Carr resurrects this same argument today, hinting at a network primarily of Islamic organizations arrayed against the United States.

A review of at least some of the most significant terrorist incidents directed against or in the United States in recent years disproves this contention. The intent of the World Trade Center bombers—at least according to the letter claiming credit for the blast they sent to the *New York Times*—was not the destruction of the United States per se, but to affect American policy toward, and support of, the terrorists' stated enemies: Zionist Israel and the Mubarak regime in Egypt.

Similarly, the bombings of the U.S. Air Force barracks in Dhahran, Saudi Arabia, last June and of a joint Saudi-American training center in Riyadh the previous November were designed less to destroy the United States than to undermine American support for the ruling Saudi royal family. Other parallels can be drawn with the 1983 bombing of the U.S. Marine barracks in Lebanon, where the goal was to force Washington to withdraw its troops from the multinational peace force then deployed in Lebanon. With the departure of the American forces, the multinational effort—precisely as the terrorists predicted—collapsed, thus precipitating the end of international efforts to stabilize Lebanon and the creation of a power vacuum that was filled by the terrorists' state-sponsors.

THE FALLACY OF MILITARY SOLUTIONS

But Carr's main argument is his contention that "terrorism is a problem requiring a more expansive and coherent military effort." Like many others, he too cites the 1986 U.S. airstrike against Libya as proof of the effectiveness of military retaliation. "The attack caused significant damage," Carr enthuses, "and badly rattled Libyan strongman Muammar al-Qaddafi, who narrowly escaped death. More important, the raid and other similarly strong measures sent a message to both terrorist groups and their sponsors that was taken seriously: by the end of the 1980s, international terrorism appeared to be on the wane."

But those who tout military response and reprisal as the ultimate panacea for the terrorist problem, and particularly those who embrace Libya as the shining exemplar of its successful application, base their arguments on self-satisfying assumptions and popular myth, ignoring empirical evidence to the contrary.

First, rather than deterring the Qaddafi regime from sponsoring terrorism, the U.S. airstrike in fact goaded the Libyan dictator to undertake even more serious and heinous acts of terrorism against the United States and its citizens. Indeed, after a brief lull, Libya not only resumed—but actually increased—its international terrorist activities. For example, according to the RAND-St. Andrews University Chronology of International Terrorism, at least 15 identifiable state-sponsored terrorist incidents in 1987 and eight in 1988—including the 1987 attacks on the American embassies in Madrid and Rome, the bombing of a USO club in Naples (that killed five persons and wounded 17 others) the following year, and the attempted bombing of a navy recruiting office in downtown Manhattan by a Japanese terrorist—have been conclusively linked to Libya.

The latter incident is especially noteworthy in that not only did Qaddafi continue his terrorist campaign against the United States in the airstrike's aftermath but the dispatch of a veteran Japanese Red Army terrorist to carry out the bombing mission on American soil represented a significantly undesirable escalation of that campaign.

However, perhaps the most incontrovertible refutation of "the myth of military retaliation" is the 1988 in-flight bombing of Pan Am Flight 103, in which 278 persons perished. After what has been described as the "most extensive criminal investigation in history," the joint FBI and British investigation resulted in the indictment of two Libyan employees of that country's national airline, who are alleged to have been agents of Qaddafi's intelligence service.

Nor was America the only country to suffer continued acts of Libyan-sponsored international terrorism. In retaliation for Britain's role in allowing the U.S. warplanes that bombed Libya to take off from bases in that country, Qaddafi deliberately increased his supply of weapons to the IRA. In the wake of the American airstrike, the Irish terrorist group reportedly took delivery of some five to ten tons of Semtex-H plastic explosive (investigators believe that about eight ounces of Semtex-H was used in the bomb that exploded on board Pan Am Flight 103), in addition to 120 tons of other arms and explosives, including 12 SAM-7 ground-to-air missiles, RPG-7 rocket-propelled grenades, and anti-aircraft and anti-tank guns. British authorities largely credit the Libyan weapons shipments with having appreciably facilitated the IRA's terror campaign to this day.

Even the oft-repeated claims of the attack's surgical precision and the immense technological sophistication of American precision-guided air-delivered ordnance fall flat. Despite the particularly careful selection of military targets for the U.S. fighter-bombers, 36 civilians were killed and 93 others wounded in the airstrike. The death and injuries caused to these civilians were not only tragic but deprived Americans of the moral high ground they claim to occupy above terrorists and terrorism, and thereby opened them up to domestic and international criticism.

Finally, the evidence that the airstrike sent a powerful deterrent message to other terrorists is similarly wanting. Indeed, more terrorist attacks against American targets occurred during the three-month period following the U.S. airstrike (53) than during the three months preceding it (41). All this is not to say that military force should never be used, only that its efficacy and impact are often exaggerated and its less-comfortable consequences and potentially counterproductive outcomes often ignored.

IF NOT MILITARY FORCE, WHAT?

The "jumping off" point for Carr's essay was the argument that the Clinton administration's recent billion-dollar initiatives to strengthen America's counterterrorist intelligence and law enforcement capabilities are misguided and inappropriate—and therefore doomed to failure. In this respect, Carr may indeed be correct but—as the preceding analysis has attempted to demonstrate—for all the wrong reasons.

America has historically taken a largely piecemeal approach to terrorism. For example, over the past quarter century, in the wake of every terrorist crisis, new measures have been successively grafted onto a counterterrorist structure that may already have been rendered obsolete or anachronistic by some of the fundamental changes in the nature of terrorism now occurring, which Carr correctly identifies. Indeed, missing from the reports of the blue-ribbon presidential commissions appointed to study terrorism, the successive congressional hearings that have examined this issue from every conceivable dimension, and the televised comments and published analyses of experts both in and outside government is a fundamental baseline assessment of the current terrorist threat, alongside a bottom-up review of current American counterterrorist capabilities.

If the United States is truly to come to grips with terrorism, the nature of the threat itself and what capabilities America can bring to bear in fighting it—military as well as diplomatic, economic, and psychological—must be systematically reconsidered. Indeed, nearly three decades of experience in counterterrorism shows that the selective application of individual tactics and policies outside a cohesive strategic framework or coherent multinational plan can not only render these specific efforts ineffective, but counterproductive as well.

One final point remains. Terrorism can never be completely eliminated or suppressed by any society, much less a liberal-democratic country such as the United States. Accordingly, it is perhaps far more helpful to view terrorism as a problem akin to domestic organized crime: while the Justice Department and state and local law enforcement attempt to suppress and curtail it, no one entertains the unrealistic expectation that organized crime can ever be completely eliminated. Nor can Washington expect to eliminate terrorism. By finally accepting this fact, America will be able to react coolly and calmly to terrorist attack and provocation and not feel driven to dramatic—and possibly pointless and counterproductive—military reprisals. Rather, America will be able to more prudently, effectively, and productively marshal its resources where and against whom they will have the greatest positive effect.

CALEB CARR RESPONDS:

Mr. Hoffman claims that I believe the "answer to America's terrorist problem is obvious." Yet, at no point do I or would I make such an assertion. I do maintain that America has moved into a new era in dealing with terrorists, one that makes it necessary to look harder for military solutions; and I further assert that those military solutions should spring out of the discipline of military history. But there is nothing "obvious" in such logic, as ought to be demonstrated by the fact that it has thus far eluded most American and foreign leaders.

Similarly, Mr. Hoffman's labeling of my ideas as a "simple prescription to America's terrorist ills" is a mischaracterization. Given their unfamiliarity to most readers, as well as the forum in which they appear, my proposals are necessarily broad; but I can assure Mr. Hoffman that I am under no illusion as to the difficulty and the complexity of the type of military operations I suggest.

I certainly find Mr. Hoffman's argument that a military solution is not the best answer to what even he acknowledges to be a military problem rather difficult to follow. He surely misrepresents my views. I do not label all terrorists "sociopathic killers," as he claims; I do say that "the psychodynamics of the terrorist are very similar to those of the sociopathic killer." Meaning that the reaction terrorists seek from the public at large is very similar to that sought by sociopaths, whether or not the terrorists themselves fit into that category. Nor do I at any point even imply anything so simpleminded as the statement that "a few sharp, well-aimed blows—administered by a muscular American military establishment—will bring these persons to their senses and either remedy their intolerable behavior or dissuade them from further transgressions." Indeed, one of my main points in suggesting that America target the conventional forces of terrorism's sponsor states is that terrorists themselves cannot be dissuaded; therefore their supplies of arms must be cut off and their refuges closed down.

But Mr. Hoffman's historical assertions shock me far more than anything he has to say about my own suggestions. To claim that terrorism is "often a rational choice," and to support that claim with the example of Menachem Begin's activities as leader of the Irgun before and during the Israeli war for independence, is shocking. One can argue whether Begin was "neurotic" or "sociopathic"; but to say that "the strategy defined by Begin for the Irgun fails to evoke images of mindless, fanatical, or wanton violence" is to ignore the historical record.

Begin's campaign of terror against the British culminated in one of history's most infamous acts of terror: the bombing of Jerusalem's King David Hotel in July 1946, in which 91 Britons, Arabs, and Jews alike—many if not most of them innocent civilians—were killed. This was most assuredly a wanton and fanatical act, though far too coldly calculated, it is true, to be considered mindless. And if Begin's terrorist strategy was so effective in advancing the Israeli cause, then why did David Ben-Gurion eventually find it necessary to order him to stop killing civilians—including, again, Jews whom Begin considered fainthearted—and to focus the Irgun's attacks strictly on military targets?

I will pass quickly by the statement that my characterization of terrorists "may admittedly have some relevance to the rank-and-file members of terrorist groups" but not, apparently, to those commanders who dispatch such soldiers on their missions; I pause only to say that such logic would have been of some use to high Nazi officials at Nuremburg. And Mr. Hoffman's argument that there are often sociopathically violent soldiers to be found in regular armies does nothing save support my point that terrorists can and should, in fact, be considered soldiers. (I would certainly never argue that America's armies are not a magnet for such personalities, especially today). This, however, is also a lesser objection.

Legitimizing terrorism

But Mr. Hoffman's final historical assertion that modern terrorism is somehow legitimate because such leaders as Nelson Mandela, Yasir Arafat, and Gerry Adams have advocated it demands a more detailed response. The example of Mandela is obfuscation: Mandela did not become an international hero because he was a terrorist but because he spent much of his life in prison—as punishment for that terrorism, among other things. In reality, one important result of the African National Congress's terrorist activities was to breed such bitterness and hatred among other black South Africans (most notably the Zulu-based Inkatha party) that sectarian violence still threatens South Africa's future.

And the fact that Yasir Arafat received the Nobel Peace Price ought not to rationalize his murderous terrorist activities any more than Henry Kissinger's reception of the same prize ought to make us forgive the part he played in such illegal and reprehensible actions as the bombing of Cambodia during the Vietnam War.

Finally (while we are speaking of Kissinger), the assertion that Gerry Adams's IRA "bombed its way" to the peace table holds approximately as much water as did the Nixon administration's claim that it "bombed" the North Vietnamese into the Paris peace talks: at the time of this writing, the British government—which, historically, has often been willing to talk to Irish radicals but rarely willing to make concessions to them—shows no sign of giving in to Adams's demands, any more than the North Vietnamese ultimately gave into the United States.

As to the notion that the American raid on Libya in 1986 discouraged international terrorism, this is apparently an assertion that Mr. Hoffman feels the need to refute with the most nebulous basis of all arguments: statistics. To say that the raid was a failure because terrorism continued to exist after it took place is misleading, and to further claim that the raid increased the level of international terrorist activity is unprovable. I cannot say that terrorism might not have tapered off faster than it did had the raid never happened; nor can Mr. Hoffman know that it would have, and to try to support such a hypothetical claim by drawing a circumstantial line from the raid (which was against Libya) to the downing of Pan Am Flight 103 (which may have been the work of Libyans) is, again, unprovable logic. What many experts, like Israel's Benjamin Netanyahu, do find supportable is the assertion that, whatever the specific incidence of terrorist activity after the raid, by 1987, "the growing understanding of the nature of terrorist methods, combined with the very real threat of further American operations against terrorist bases and terrorist states around the world, undermined the foundations on which international terror had been built" (*Fighting Terrorism*, 1995).

True, America and other terrorist target nations became more complacent about the terrorist menace after the raid, but that overconfidence was arguably more responsible for the revival of the terrorist menace than was any desire on the part of the terrorists for revenge.

Ultimately, Mr. Hoffman has what I can only call the temerity to compare terrorist casualties to domestic homicides and to go on to say that "an average of fewer than 28 fatalities per year can hardly be construed as representing a salient threat to either America's national security or citizenry." Leaving aside the fact that no such comparison can legitimately be drawn (terrorist acts are political crimes, homicides almost always acts of domestic violence or acts committed in conjunction with robbery), this seems to me a shockingly callous statement—not to mention a poor excuse for a solution to the problem.

There was a time when the loss of any American life to political fanatics, especially abroad, was considered reason enough for forceful American military action: 100 years ago, a single act of (at the time unproven) terrorism in Havana harbor was held to be a sufficient cause for war. America's various domestic police forces are constantly searching for new ways to combat both individual and organized domestic crime. The U.S. armed forces should be constantly looking for new ways to combat international terrorism. It is my contention that such methods exist and should be tried: to do anything less—to accept terrorism as something akin to drive-by shootings, or, worse, to morally rationalize it, as Mr. Hoffman frequently seems willing to do—is to insult the victims, as well as their families, of this modern barbarism.

Postscript

Following the September 11th attacks, commentators in the American media frequently stated that the world was forever changed. Is this simply journalistic hyperbole or had something fundamentally different occurred? As the readings remind us, terrorism has been a part of politics for a very long time. However, some of the rules in dealing with terrorism in past decades seem no longer to apply. In the past, a group of hijackers may have taken passengers hostage in hopes of obtaining the release of a colleague being held in jail. Hence governments made it clear that they would adopt a "no-deals" strategy to discourage such tactics. However, in the case of the September 11th attacks, the old rules for dealing with terrorism no longer seem relevant. How does one respond to a terrorist who makes no demands and is willing to commit suicide to make his point?

It is useful to read this issue in relation to Samuel Huntington's article in Issue Three. In statements following the attack, President Bush was careful to argue that the "war against terrorism" should not be seen as a war against Islam, but as a war against the radical Islamists who carried out that terrorism. But it is clear that Islamist leaders like Osama bin Laden see their terrorist attacks as part of a *jihad* against a decadent West. By triggering a vigorous military response from the West, it is hoped that Muslims everywhere will rally to the defense of Islam. In these circumstances, how do Western countries develop a counterterrorist strategy against radical Islamists without contributing to an escalating "clash of civilizations"?

Infotrac Keyword Search

"terrorism" or "counterterrorism"

Suggested Additional Readings

Charter, David. A. *Democratic Responses to International Terrorism.* Ardsley-on-Hudson, NY: Transnational Publishers, 1991.

Derian, James Der. *Antidiplomacy: Spies, Terror, Speed, and War.* Cambridge, MA: Blackwell, 1992.

Falkenrath, Richard A., Robert D. Newman, and Bradley A. Thayer. *America's Achilles Heel: Nuclear, Biological, and Chemical Terrorism and Covert Attack.* Cambridge, MA: MIT Press, 1998.

Gerecht, Reuel Marc. "The Counterterrorist Myth." *Atlantic Monthly,* Jul./Aug. 2001, 38–42.

Guelke, Adrian. *The Age of Terrorism and the International Political System.* London: Tauris, 1995.

Harmon, Christopher C. *Terrorism Today.* London and Portland, OR: Frank Cass, 2000.

Hoffman, Bruce. *Inside Terrorism.* New York: Columbia University Press, 1998.

Taylor, Max, and John Horgan, eds. *The Future of Terrorism.* London and Portland, OR: Frank Cass, 2000.

Website Resources

Council on Foreign Relations   Following the attack on the World Trade Center on September 11, 2001, the prestigious Council for Foreign Relations, which publishes the journal *Foreign Affairs,* established a Terrorism Resource Center on this website.

Federation of American Scientists, Intelligence Resource Program: Terrorism Contains background material on terrorism and risk assessment.

National Security Institute, Security Resource Net: Counter Terrorism   Contains links to extensive resources on terrorism.

The Terrorism Research Center   This an independent institute dedicated to the research of terrorism, information warfare, critical infrastructure protection and other issues of low-intensity political violence and grey-area phenomena.

U.S. State Department: *Patterns of Global Terrorism* **(yearly)**   Contains annual reports on patterns of terrorism around the world.

ZGram Terrorism Resources   Contains a detailed list of governmental, academic, and non-governmental sites relating to terrorism.

Has the Concept of "Rogue State" Become Outdated?

✔ **YES**
MICHAEL KLARE, "An Anachronistic Policy: The Strategic Obsolescence of the 'Rogue Doctrine'," *Harvard International Review* 22, no. 2 (Summer 2000): 46–52

✗ **NO**
THOMAS HENRIKSEN, "The Rise and Decline of Rogue States: Dividing Patrons from Rogue Regimes," *Vital Speeches* 67, 10 (March 1, 2001): 292ff

The term "rogue states" came into popular usage in the United States during the post-Cold War period to describe those states that American officials believed posed a threat to American and western security interests. Although what exactly constitutes a "rogue state" has never been entirely clear, the concept has nevertheless played an important role in shaping American foreign policy over the past decade. However, by the year 2000, there was growing criticism of the concept and its usefulness as a guide for policy making. Partly in response to this criticism, State Department officials dropped the usage of the term, replacing it with references to "states of concern." Nevertheless, many analysts have suggested that, while the label has changed, American foreign policy has still been shaped by the Rogue State Doctrine. In his address to the American Congress in the wake of the September 11th attacks on the United States, President Bush made it clear that the "new war on terrorism" would be directed not only at terrorist organizations but also toward any states that gives them "safe harbor." While the term "rogue states" may have been officially dropped, references to the term "rogue" continued to pop up in media analysis of the kinds of threats that the West faces.

What does "rogue state" mean? Is it still a useful concept for understanding international politics and current security threats? In addressing this question, it is useful to examine the roots of the term more closely.

Following the end of the Cold War, analysts sought to identify what new threats might be posed to American security. Writing in the Winter 1990–91 issue of *Foreign Affairs*, Charles Krauthammer identified "weapons states" as the new threat to international security. Krauthammer describes a weapons state as having a strong, coercive state apparatus that enables it to dominate civil society and exploit the wealth of the state, such as oil, in order to generate the capital to import high-technology weapons. According to Krauthammer, "the current Weapons States have a deep grievance against the West and the world order that it has established and enforces. They are therefore subversive of the international status quo, which they see as a residue of colonialism. These resentments fuel an obsessive drive to high-tech military development as the only way to leapfrog history and to place themselves on a footing from which to challenge a Western-imposed order" ("The Unipolar Moment," *Foreign Affairs* 10, no. 1 (Winter 1990–91:33).

Four years later, former national security advisor Anthony Lake, writing in the same journal, invoked a broader definition identifying "rogues" or "backlash states as "nations (which) exhibit a chronic inability to engage constructively with the outside world" ("Confronting Backlash States," *Foreign Affairs*, (March/April 1994:45–55).

As the term "rogue" came into more common usage, it became generally associated with four basic assumptions. First, "rogue' states are vocally antagonistic to American interests and values. Second, they have repressive governments in power with poor human rights records. Third, they have been known to sponsor international terrorism either through funding or serving as a safe haven and training ground. Fourth, they are actively developing weapons of mass destruction, including biological, chemical, and nuclear weapons.

Inherent in the notion of "rogue states" is the belief that as states which challenge the status quo or are not "constructively engaged" they must be isolated or contained much like Soviet communism was contained during the Cold War. As a result, the United States has employed a variety of strategies to isolate regimes so identified. Military support has been provided to opposition forces of these regimes. Covert operations and military actions have been undertaken to destabilize the government. Support has been given to treaties and conventions that will prohibit export of military technologies to these states. And economic sanctions have been employed to further isolate these countries while weakening their social and economic infrastructures.

Critics of a defence policy based on the concept of "rogue states" have put forward two basic arguments. First, the concept itself is vague and lacks any clear criteria for placing states in this category. It has generally been applied to states like Iran, Iraq, North Korea, and Cuba. But Cuba has no program for developing weapons of mass destruction and has not been in the business of funding terrorism abroad. Countries have been added and dropped from the list as prevailing political winds shift. (Interestingly, the Taliban regime in Afghanistan had not been on the usual list of "rogue states" cited by American officials as a threat.) Second, critics have suggested that a strategy of isolation, especially through the use of economic sanctions, has done little to change the policies of these regimes while only driving their populations further into poverty and hardship.

In his article, Michael Klare sets out the main criticisms brought against the concept of rogue states. A long-time military analyst who has written a book on the subject, Klare traces the history of the rogue concept, arguing that it served as a useful device for officials to "construct" a new threat in the post-Cold War era and justify military spending policies. He argues that the concept is outmoded and no longer appropriate to address the threats facing the United States. In contrast, Thomas Henriksen argues that the rogue state poses a very real and increasing threat. He argues that while in the past rogues tended to be isolated and acted alone, they now are cooperating with each other and acting as a "pack," making them even more dangerous.

✔ YES

An Anachronistic Policy: The Strategic Obsolescence of the "Rogue Doctrine"
MICHAEL KLARE

It has been ten years since General Colin Powell, then Chairman of the Joint Chiefs of Staff, manufactured the "Rogue Doctrine" as the basic template for US military strategy in the post–Cold War era. With the Soviet Union in irreversible decline and no other superpower adversary in sight, Powell elected to focus US strategy on the threat allegedly posed by hostile Third World powers–the so-called "rogue states." Although intended largely as an interim measure–a means of maintaining defense spending at near–Cold War levels until a more credible threat appeared on the horizon–the anti-rogue strategy has become the defining paradigm for American security policy. But while immensely popular on Capitol Hill, the Rogue Doctrine has become increasingly irrelevant to the security environment in which American forces operate.

Under current US military policy, the Department of Defense is required to maintain sufficient strength to simultaneously fight and defeat two Iraq-like regional adversaries. These adversaries–generally assumed to include Iraq, Iran, Libya, and North Korea–are said to be dangerous because of their potent military capabilities, history of antagonism toward the West, and their pursuit of weapons of mass destruction (WMD). Although not linked by treaty or formal alliance, these states are said to pose a threat because of their common disregard for the accepted norms of international society.

The Rogue Doctrine is presently the main guiding principle for the structure, orientation, and disposition of US military forces. Other tasks are, of course, assigned to the armed forces on a regular basis, as demonstrated most recently by the air war against Serbia. But these other missions, including multilateral peace-keeping operations, are considered "add-ons" to the primary mission of fighting the rogues; they do not govern the basic organization of the Armed Services. Just as US forces were once trained and equipped for the overriding task of resisting a Warsaw Pact invasion of Western Europe–the "Fulda Gap mentality"–they are now trained and equipped to repeat Operation Desert Storm again and again.

The Rogue Doctrine also significantly influences US foreign policy. For instance, much effort has been put into isolating Iran from the international community, despite the fact that most of the United States' allies do not share Washington's views on the necessity of doing so. The United States also expends great political capital in trying to maintain economic sanctions on Iraq–even though a growing number of states have concluded that the sanctions have outlived their usefulness.

Unfortunately, the Rogue Doctrine has been subjected to very little critical analysis. Few in Congress have questioned the rationale behind the "two war" policy that now governs US strategy, or its US$275 billion per year cost (soon to rise to US$300 billion). The mass media has not behaved any better; references to the "rogue state threat" are common, but are rarely accompanied by any analysis of political and military developments in the states involved or of the changing nature of the security environment. If we are to adopt a realistic approach to future perils, therefore, it is essential to look more critically at the dominant US security paradigm.

THE RISE OF THE ROGUE DOCTRINE

The origins of the Rogue Doctrine can be traced to the final weeks of 1989, when General Colin Powell commenced a search for a new, post-Soviet military doctrine. Recognizing that the threat of a US-Soviet clash had lost all plausibility in the wake of the Berlin Wall's collapse, Powell sought to construct a new threat scenario that would justify the preservation of America's superpower capabilities in a world with no Soviet-like opponent. Working closely with General Lee Butler, then Director of the Strategic Plans and Policy Directorate (J-5) of the Joint Staff, Powell conceived of a strategy in which regional threats, not the monolithic threat of the Soviet Union, would govern US military planning in the years to come.

In constructing this strategy, Powell was fully aware that identifying a credible successor to the USSR was essential if the Pentagon was to avert a major military downsizing at the hands of Congress. Within days of the Wall's collapse, many members of Congress and other prominent figures began talking of a substantial "peace dividend" that would be made possible through a sizable reduction in US military spending. Fearful that precipitous congressional action would also deprive the Department of Defense of any sense of strategic coherence, Powell sought to establish a new strategic paradigm that could be used to argue against deep cuts in military spending and at the same time imbue the armed forces with a new sense of purpose.

Powell did not waste any time starting this project. Just one week after the Berlin Wall's collapse, on November 15, 1989, he presented his initial ideas to then President George Bush. According to an official record of this meeting (which concerned the Pentagon's five-year planning document for Fiscal Years 1990–1994), Powell argued, "The drastically different strategic environment projected for 1994 called for a major restructuring of US security policy, strategy, force structure, and capabilities. With a diminished Soviet threat and sharply reduced resources, the focus of strategic planning should shift from global war with the Soviet Union to regional and contingency responses to non-Soviet threats."

To address this threat, Powell contended that the United States would require sufficient military strength to fight and win two regional conflicts simultaneously.

This need, in turn, established the requirement for a "Base Force" of 1.6 million active-duty personnel (down by about one-fourth from the 1989 level of 2.1 million), with a standing complement of 12 active Army divisions, 16 active Air Force tactical fighter wings, and 450 warships.

In advancing the Base Force concept, Powell did not use the term "rogue state," or any comparable expression. Nevertheless, the basic outlines of the Pentagon's current, anti-rogue posture were already present in his November briefing to the President. In the weeks that followed, senior Pentagon officials began speaking more frequently of the threat posed by well-armed, antagonistic Third World powers. In April 1990, for instance, Army Chief of Staff General Carl E. Vuono discussed this threat in *Sea Power* magazine and contends, "The proliferation of military power in what is often called the 'Third World' presents a troubling picture. Many Third World nations now possess mounting arsenals of tanks, heavy artillery, ballistic missiles, and chemical weapons . . . The United States cannot ignore the expanding military power of these countries, and the Army must retain the capability to defeat potential threats wherever they occur. This could mean confronting a well-equipped army in the Third World." Aside from its prophetic character—at this time the Iraqi invasion of Kuwait and the onset of Operation Desert Shield was but five months away—this article is striking because of its vivid portrayal of what would later be termed the rogue state threat.

General Powell and his aides continued to marshal support for the new strategy throughout the spring of 1990, and, on June 26, they presented the fully developed Base Force concept to President Bush and Secretary of Defense Richard Cheney. After much discussion, Bush gave his formal approval to Powell's plan and instructed his staff to prepare a speech outlining its general parameters. A scheduled appearance by the President at the Aspen Institute in Colorado on August 2, 1990 was then selected as a suitable occasion to deliver this address.

In his speech at the Aspen Institute, Bush reiterated many of the themes first articulated by Generals Powell and Vuono. "In a world less driven by an immediate threat to Europe and the danger of global war," he declared, "the size of our forces will increasingly be shaped by the needs of regional conflict." In line with this new posture, "America must possess forces able to respond to threats in whatever corner of the globe they may occur."

Bush's speech at the Aspen Institute in August was given more attention than might otherwise have been the case because a few hours earlier, on the night of August 1, Iraqi troops began pouring into Kuwait. Bush made reference to the Kuwait situation in his comments, leading many commentators to view the speech as a spontaneous response to the Iraqi invasion. Certainly the president's harsh attacks on Saddam Hussein, along with the announcement of Operation Desert Shield on August 7, led most people to telescope all of these events together. But from a historical point of view it is essential to remember that the "regional strategy" announced by Bush on August 2 was a response not to the Iraqi invasion of Kuwait but rather to the collapse of the Berlin Wall in November 1989 and the growing enfeeblement of the Soviet Union.

THE DOCTRINE'S GOLDEN AGE

The period from August 1990 to February 1998 constitutes what might be called the "golden age" of the Rogue Doctrine. When Iraqi forces rolled into Kuwait, Congress discontinued its discussion of the "peace dividend" and abandoned all plans for a significant reduction in military strength. Although some in Congress bemoaned the early decision to rely on force instead of economic sanctions to drive Iraq out of Kuwait, most Americans supported Operation Desert storm once US forces were committed to battle. Furthermore, as news of the elaborate Iraqi preparations for nuclear, chemical, and biological warfare became widely known, the "rogue state" concept took hold in the think tanks and the media, driving out all competing strategic paradigms.

The 1991 Gulf conflict also legitimized the view, first articulated by Generals Powell and Vuono, that America's most likely future adversaries would be well-armed regional powers like Iraq. On March 19, 1991, less than three weeks after the fighting in the Gulf had ended, Cheney told Congress that "the Gulf War presaged very much the type of conflict we are most likely to confront again in this new era—major regional contingencies against foes well-armed with advanced conventional and unconventional munitions." Other senior officials quickly agreed, giving the rogue doctrine an almost canonical status.

The potency of the rogue state model became especially evident in 1993, when President Clinton entered the White House. During the 1992 campaign, Clinton had promised to adopt a new foreign and military policy in response to the dramatic changes at the end of the Cold War era. Seeking to make good on this promise, Clinton's first Secretary of Defense, Les Aspin, ordered a "bottom-up review" (BUR) of US military policy. But while Aspin implied that the BUR would produce a dramatic transformation of US strategy, the final product looked a great deal like the Base Force concept originally developed by Colin Powell in 1989. As in the Powell plan, the BUR called for maintenance of sufficient forces to fight and win two major regional conflicts (MRCs) at more or less the same time. The only discernible difference between the two plans is that Aspin spoke of fighting two MRCs "nearly simultaneously," not all at once as in the Powell plan.

In presenting the BUR to the public, Aspin and Powell articulated the Rogue Doctrine in its mature form. Development of the new strategy, Aspin declared, was driven by a need to contain "rogue leaders set on regional domination through military aggression while simultaneously pursuing nuclear, biological, and chemical weapons capabilities." In meeting these threats, the Pentagon's principal objective would be "to project power into regions important to our interests and to defeat potentially hostile regional powers, such as North Korea and Iraq."

Opposition to rogue states also became a defining theme in the foreign policy of the Clinton administration. This opposition was communicated in a variety of ways. Continuous pressure was brought to bear on Iraq through non-stop air patrols and periodic missile attacks. Libya was subjected to UN-imposed economic sanctions in 1992, when Libyan strongman Colonel Muammar Qaddafi refused to extradite two government officials accused of complicity in the 1988 Lockerbie airline bombing. North Korea was threatened with similar sanctions in 1994, when it refused access to its nuclear sites by inspectors from the International Atomic Energy Agency in accordance with the Nuclear Non-Proliferation Treaty. And Iran was subjected to a unilateral US ban on trade and investment in 1995 in response to its alleged proliferation activities.

The popularity of the Rogue Doctrine was demonstrated again in 1997, when the Department of Defense conducted yet another review of American military posture. This study, known as the Quadrennial Defense Review (QDR), was expected to move beyond the BUR in addressing the emerging challenges of the post–Cold War era. As in 1993, however, the Department of Defense chose to embrace the status quo: a two-war posture aimed at defeating hostile Third World states.

CHALLENGES TO THE ROGUE DOCTRINE

Today, the Rogue Doctrine appears thoroughly entrenched in US military thinking. None of the presidential candidates has expressed any disagreement with the Doctrine's basic premises, and no one in Congress or in the major think tanks has proposed an alternative vision. In all likelihood, then, this policy will continue to govern US strategic planning when a new administration takes office in 2001.

The Rogue Doctrine remains popular in Washington because it points to a clearly identifiable set of enemies—no easy feat in this time of ambiguous threats and shifting loyalties—and because it can be used to justify the preservation of the existing military establishment, which no one in authority would like to alter. In addition, special interests, including the military think tanks and organizations, the manufacturers of high-tech weaponry, and so on, share a common interest in maintaining the status quo. So entrenched has this strategy become that none of its proponents feel the need to subject it to any sort of systematic reassessment based on a considered analysis of the existing world security environment; instead, the Doctrine is treated as unshakable wisdom, sufficient onto itself.

The fact that senior American officials have endorsed this Doctrine in such a dogmatic fashion should set off alarm bells all over the country. History suggests that the unquestioning embrace of a given strategy year after year can spell disaster when objective conditions no longer coincide with the strategy's basic assumptions. And in this case, there are many signs that the Rogue Doctrine is seriously out of touch with existing world conditions. In particular, I see five significant problems with the Doctrine:

Lack of Support From America's Allies

Although President Bush was able to organize a truly extraordinary coalition to fight Saddam Hussein in 1990–91, his successors have not been able to preserve that alliance or to employ it against other hostile states. In fact, no US ally has yet accepted the proposition that there is an identifiable category of "rogue" states, and few appear willing to join the United States in efforts to punish the regimes in question. Iraq remains under UN economic sanctions, but many countries seek to lift the sanctions and end Baghdad's total isolation from the world community. North Korea continues to be viewed as a pariah state by many, but the government of Kim Dae Jung in South Korea has made clear its desire to effect a rapprochement with the North. And no states have agreed to copy the stringent economic sanctions imposed on Iran by Washington. The lack of allied backing for the Rogue Doctrine became especially evident in February 1998, when President Clinton sought to mobilize international support for military action against Iraq in response to its failure to open certain weapons sites to UN inspection. While the British government did agree to provide some military forces for joint action against Baghdad, most US allies provided only token support or none at all. Particularly striking was the lack of support from long-term American allies in the Gulf, including Saudi Arabia. When Washington initiated the bombing of Iraq in December of 1998, the lack of international support for such action stood in sharp contrast to the situation in 1990–91.

Insufficiently Menacing Rogues

To be successful over the long run, the Rogue Doctrine requires that the "rogues" act like the outlaws they are said to be. But none of the nominal rogues has engaged in unambiguously aggressive behavior since 1991, and most seem determined to establish good—or at least businesslike—relations with the Western world. Saddam Hussein has continued to defy the world community with respect to weapons inspections, but he has not precipitated a replay of the 1990 invasion of Kuwait, or anything remotely like it. North Korea has also refrained from overtly aggressive moves, and in 1994 agreed to dismantle its nuclear weapons program. Libya has rebuilt its ties with other African nations and has turned over the two suspects in the Lockerbie case for a trial in the Netherlands. Iran has gone even further, offering lucrative oil- and gas-development concessions to prominent Western firms.

Also significant is the fact that the military capabilities possessed by the rogues have not grown appreciably since 1990, and in some cases have deteriorated. Bear in mind that both the BUR and the QDR assume that America's future regional adversaries will resemble the Iraq of 1990—that is, a force of nearly one million soldiers equipped with thousands of tanks, artillery pieces, and armored personnel carriers. At present, however, the Iraqi military is only one-third of its pre-Desert Storm strength, and none of the other rogue states is significantly better off. Only North Korea comes close to prewar Iraq in actual numbers, but its military hardware is thought to be markedly inferior to that possessed by South Korea. As a result, it is very difficult to portray the rogues in the same menacing tones used to describe Iraq in 1990.

Political Ferment in Iran

American rhetoric has always portrayed Iran, like the other rogues, as an authoritarian state dominated by anti-American tyrants. "While their political systems vary," presidential security advisor Anthony Lake wrote of such states in 1994, "their leaders share a common antipathy toward popular participation that might undermine the existing regimes." But while this image might convincingly be used to describe Iran in the 1980s, when the Ayatollah Khomeini exercised paramount power, it is less persuasive today, given the growing pluralism in the Iranian political system. While it is clear that conservative clergy still exercise enormous power in Tehran, their dominance has been challenged through popular elections, mass demonstrations, and an increasingly vociferous press.

By far the most striking development in this regard was the election of Mohammad Khatami—an outspoken advocate of reform—as President of Iran. Although it is clear that Khatami faces a strong challenge from conservative clerics in the Iranian parliament, he has significantly diminished the anti-American tenor of Iranian public discourse and has sought new openings to the West. Khatami has also traveled to Saudi Arabia and improved relations with Iran's other neighbors in the Persian Gulf area. All this has made it harder to characterize Iran as an unrepentant "rogue" that must be isolated from the world community.

The Indian and Pakistani Nuclear Tests

Perhaps the greatest blow to the Rogue Doctrine occurred on May 11, 1998, when the Indian government detonated the first of five nuclear devices and declared itself a nuclear power. This event, coupled with the Pakistani nuclear tests a few weeks later, shattered the claim that the threat of proliferation was essentially interchangeable with the rogue state threat. (In 1996, for instance, Secretary of Defense William Perry declared that the illicit demand for nuclear and missile technology comes primarily from a group of nations some call the Rogues Gallery.) Since then, it has become increasingly apparent that India and Pakistan have progressed much further down the road of proliferation than any of the nominal rogues.

It is true, of course, that the rogues continue to pose a threat of proliferation. But Iraq's WMD capabilities were severely damaged by Operation Desert Storm and the subsequent activities of UNSCOM, and North Korea agreed to abandon its nuclear weapons program under the Agreed Framework of 1994. Iran is suspected of pursuing a nuclear weapons program, but its main nuclear facilities are subject to periodic International Atomic Energy Agency (IAEA) inspection; progress—if any—is thought to be slow. By contrast, it is clear that India and Pakistan have jumped far ahead in the development of both nuclear weapons and ballistic missiles. It is also evident that other friendly states, including South Korea and Taiwan, have acquired ballistic missiles or are seeking to build them. To be successful, therefore, America's nonproliferation efforts will have to shift their focus from the rogues to these other, supposedly friendly states.

The Emergence of Other Types of Security Threats

Finally, it is abundantly clear that the world security environment harbors a wide variety of threats to global stability, many of which lie far beyond the terrain of the rogue state threat. These include, but are not limited to, the proliferation of ethnic and internal conflict, "state collapse" in areas of social and political upheaval, growing competition over scarce resources, and severe environmental degradation. All of these dangers have begun to place significant burdens on the attention of US policymakers, and all have required the deployment of significant American resources, including, in some cases, military resources. Yet none of these problems is explained by the rogue-state paradigm, nor can they be successfully addressed by using the responses developed to combat the rogues.

Of course, it can be argued the forces developed to defeat the rogue states in full-scale combat can also be used to perform other missions, including peacekeeping operations and humanitarian intervention of the sort conducted in Kosovo. To some degree this is true. But the strategy and tactics of peacekeeping and other unconventional missions are not the same as those employed in major regional conflicts. In many cases, American troops have been found to be ill trained and ill equipped for the sort of missions they have been obliged to perform. As new threats emerge, moreover, this problem is likely to prove even more common.

All of these developments have significantly diminished the Rogue Doctrine's utility in providing guidance for US security policy. It is still necessary to pay close attention to the military behavior of the rogues, just as it is necessary to monitor the behavior of other regional powers. But a continued reliance on the rogue state model as the paramount source of military guidance will leave US leaders and US forces increasingly ill prepared for the wider range of challenges the United States is sure to face in the years ahead. If the United States is to face successfully the security threats of the 21st century, it must conduct the sort of "bottom-up" review that was promised twice in the 1990s yet was never really performed. The security environment has changed substantially from that of 1990, yet we cling to the same strategic paradigm adopted in that year by General Colin Powell. A comprehensive review of those changes would indicate that the rogue state threat has been accorded disproportionate attention in comparison to other security threats. The time has come to abandon the Rogue Doctrine in favor of a more realistic and prudent policy.

✗ NO
The Rise and Decline of Rogue States: Dividing Patrons from Rogue Regimes
THOMAS HENRIKSEN

For the past decade, rogue states, such as North Korea or Iraq, appeared unpredictable, irrational, and free of larger patron support. Pundits viewed them as solitary menaces that could be engaged or confronted one-on-one by the United States. But this political picture fails to capture the evolving realities of rogue states. They now cooperate with one another, seek and receive aid and arms from more powerful states, and calculatingly pursue rational objectives. The former lone wolves have joined a pack, declining their go-it-alone course.

The incoming George W. Bush Administration must be cognizant of the changes and fashion its policies according to the new geopolitical environment.

The first official application of the term rogue state to refer to unsavory regimes (now dubbed "states of concern" by the U.S. Department of State), occurred when, in January 1994, President Clinton spoke in Brussels about the "clear and present" danger of missiles aimed at Europe from "rogue states such as Iran and Libya." This designation evoked an image of a rogue elephant, threatening a village by its vicious behavior.

The end of the Cold War witnessed the emergence of rogue states on the world stage. The four-decade East-West confrontation actually spawned the rogue states. But the former Soviet Union kept them on a short leash. When the Soviet empire collapsed, these militant, pariah states seemed to burst suddenly on the world scene. In reality, their gestation has been a long time in coming.

During the Cold War, Moscow resorted to proxy states to expand its influence and weaken the West. It was these former Soviet surrogates that surfaced to challenge international harmony in the 1990s.

Cuba became Moscow's archetype proxy state, instigating or supporting insurgencies in Africa and Central and South America. Havana first sent Ernesto "Che" Guevara to lead a failed rural insurgency in the Congo and next on a fatal effort in Bolivia. It dispatched arms and instructors to Ethiopia, Guatemala, El Salvador, and Nicaragua to spread communism. It even deployed thousands of ground troops in Angola during the mid-1970s to take part in the Soviet-sponsored military intervention. North Korea kept tens of thousands of U.S. troops tied down on the peninsula after the Korean War.

The Soviet Union also turned to other Third World regimes to sponsor terrorism against Western states or interests. Not all these governments embraced Marxism, as Cuba and North Korea had. Instead, this second group of proxies included garden-variety dictatorships like Iraq, Libya, and Syria. As such, their strongmen had little affinity with Marxism. Their game was antipathy to the United States and its allies. But their actions served Soviet strategic goals. Terrorism was often their weapon of choice.

The incidence of terrorism has steadily increased from the late 1950s and involved kidnapping, bombings, assassinations, and the hijacking of airplanes and ships. Muammar Qadaffi, for example, underwrote vigorous terrorist exploits soon after he ousted the Libyan monarch in 1969. Libya's deadly subversion reached such proportions that by the 1980s Qadaffi had become viewed by the Reagan administration as the center of global terrorism.

In time the U.S. Department of State placed eight countries on its terrorist listing and imposed sanctions on each to combat their state-directed violence. The list is currently made up of Cuba, Iran, Iraq, Libya, North Korea, Syria, Sudan, and South Yemen. South Yemen, whose seaport was the scene of the bombing of the USS Cole, had been removed in 1990 after it unified with the northern Yemen Arab Republic. States breeding terrorism during the Cold War became virtually synonymous with the future rogue states.

The 1991 collapse of the Soviet Union cast its former client states adrift. It was at this historical juncture that rogue states dramatically made their reappearance, evoking surprise in political circles despite many historical precedents of rogue states, including Nazi Germany.

The presence of rogue regimes confounded hopes for a harmonious world based on economic integration and the peaceful resolution of disputes. Rejecting international norms, rogue rulers in Iraq, Iran, and North Korea sponsored terrorism, pursued the acquisition of mega-death weapons, and threatened the peace in their neighborhoods.

Others, in fact, became outwardly quiescent. Deprived of Moscow's largesse, Libya, Cuba, and Syria became less extroverted in their practice of terrorism. They still offered their territory to terrorist cells as sanctuary. For their part, Libya and Syria continued to pursue the development of weapons of mass destruction and missile systems. Cuba kept up its shrill anti-U.S. diatribe, sent instructors to Latin American countries, and facilitated the shipment of narcotics onto American shores.

Like North Korea, Cuba found itself high and dry without Soviet aid. But unlike North Korea, it did not attempt to build nuclear weapons or export rockets. However, it did imitate its Asian counterpart by looking to China for selective support. Fidel Castro dropped his formerly anti-Chinese rhetoric, and Beijing stepped into the political vacuum left by Moscow. During the early 1990s, Castro and President Jiang Zemin reciprocated each other's visits, and Chinese defense minister Chi Haotian headed a military delegation to Cuba in 1997. China furnished military equipment and defense technology along with economic aid and selective investment. Beijing, in return, gained an eavesdropping post near the United States with its financing of the Terrena Caribe Satellite Tracking Base and other facilities.

After decades of being a hotbed of terrorism, Libya courted favorable international opinion. In 1999, Qaddafi turned two suspects in the 1988 downing of Pan American flight 103 over for trial in the Netherlands. Additionally, Qaddafi gave financial compensation to families of the French victims killed when their airliner was blown up over Africa in 1989. Libya also agreed to pay a $1 million ransom for each of the twelve foreign hostages held by Muslim rebels in the southern Philippines in mid-2000. Qaddafi's reversal, in part, stemmed from Libya's need to lift sanctions so as to salvage its depressed economy and export oil for hard currency. Nevertheless, the change in outward appearance was dramatic. But it paled in comparison with North Korea.

During the 1990s, North Korea loomed as the quintessential rogue state. A rusting relic of the Stalin period, North Korea preached its own brand of Marxism, or juche, which called for self-reliance. In reality, it depended greatly on Soviet subsidies, since the partition of the peninsula at the end of WWII. The Soviet Union's end deprived Pyongyang of its chief benefactor. Subject to a cycle of drought and floods, the North stood at the brink of calamity by the mid-1990s. It appeared as a lone-wolf player, since no state, not even China, claimed influence over Pyongyang's menacing policies.

North Korea's rogue status was confirmed by its threats to build nuclear weapons as the Clinton Administration took office and then in 1998 by launching a multi-stage rocket that traversed Japanese territory before crashing into the Pacific. North Korean officials claimed that the solid-fuel missile was fired in an attempt to place a satellite in orbit. This explanation failed to allay fears in Japan, South Korea, and even the United States where observers concluded that the North Korea was on the road to building ICBMs capable of hitting the American continent. Suddenly, it reversed course.

Pyongyang announced a suspension in missile launches in return for continued foreign aid from Japan, South Korea, and the United States. In 2000 after a series of meetings with William J. Perry, former U.S. Secretary of Defense, as well as the historic June summit between the North and South Korean leaders, Washington engaged Pyongyang.

China's influence on North Korea's pariah posture became a topic of interest along with Pyongyang's kinder and gentler image. Despite Beijing's long protestations to the contrary, outsiders held that China's voice carried more impact than any other state. After all, China had spent blood and treasure to repel the U.S. intervention into the North during the Korean War. The two continually trade with each other across their common border, and China exports goods through the North's ports to third countries.

In March 2000, the reclusive Kim Jong II made an unprecedented visit to the Chinese embassy in Pyongyang, signaling North Korea's subordination to China. The North Korean leader next visited Beijing for talks with President Jiang Zemin. The North Korean leader then agreed to the dramatic about-face in policy by announcing his willingness to meet with the South Korean president. The coincidence could hardly be more telling. Soon afterwards, another event cast further doubt on Chinese denials. Hours before U.S. Secretary of State Madeline Albright arrived in Pyongyang in October, China's defense minister, Chi Haotian, preceded her for a five-day visit to improve the existing friendship and cooperation. Beijing gains from an externally moderating North Korea by eroding the rationale for a U.S. troop presence on China's doorstep.

Most outside observers drew the conclusion by the late 1990s that the North Korean leadership desired survival instead of nuclear war. Its once-risky ventures gradually became interpreted as calculating but entirely rational. Diplomatically astute, they managed to insinuate themselves into American consciousness by nuclear blackmail in one of the most audacious stratagems imaginable. Breaking out of the U.S.-imposed containment, they circumvented South Korea and achieved direct contact with Washington. They gained U.S. shipments of food through the U.N.'s World Food Program and ended most sanctions. They played a weak hand with commensurate skill.

Appearing in public at the North-South summit and later the same year with Albright during her visit, Chairman Kim shed his stern visage for one of affability. The outgoing Kim matched the changed perceptions of North Korea's new quiescence. None of these diplomatic initiatives or public gestures even slightly modified the regime's apparatus of power, however. Nor did the North pull back its military units from the DMZ, including the forward-based artillery that threatens Seoul. Neither did the Kim Jong II government repudiate terrorism. It just appeared less dangerous, and the U.S. media fostered this benign image.

North Korea remains the chief entrepôt for missile technology shipments to other rogue states. This trade has become a distinguishing feature of intra-rogue cooperation. The North's export of missile technology to states like Iraq, Iran, Pakistan, and Syria, provoked consternation among neighbors and the United States. Sales raised much needed hard currency for a state with few commercial goods. Efforts to curb this arms trade either encountered a stonewall or unpalatable counteroffers such as a request for an annual $1 billion bribe in exchange for ending missile exports.

Iraq's trajectory from extreme rogue to leader of the "Arab street" and to being embraced by three members of the U.N. Security Council—China, France, and Russia—shares parallels with North Korea. Rather than licking its wounds in the wake of the Persian Gulf war, Baghdad redoubled its exertions to develop weapons of mass destruction. Without Soviet patronage, Iraq's reputation as a free-lance rogue solidified. At the close of hostilities, Iraq stood internationally isolated not only from the West but also from much of the Muslim world.

After the conflict, the United Nations imposed sanctions on Iraq, dispatched weapons inspection teams, pressed for reparations for the Iraqi invasion of Kuwait, and authorized no-fly zones in the north and the south. Later, after the four-day bombing operation, called Desert Fox, in December 1998, Washington continued airstrikes on Iraqi-antiaircraft sites. This no-war, no-peace formula persists today. But in time major cracks occurred in the anti-Hussein coalition as former enemies traded with and traveled to Iraq.

International attention shifted from Iraqi weapons violation to sympathy for the plight of Iraq's poor. Undermining the legitimacy of sanctions, nongovernmental organizations claimed that the U.N. embargo denied food and medicines to ordinary Iraqis. Meanwhile Saddam Hussein lavished oil revenues on palaces and resorts for his family and cronies.

The renewal of Israeli-Palestinian fighting in late 2000 also lessened Iraq's isolation, since Baghdad moved to embrace the Palestinian cause. The heightened anti-Americanism throughout the Muslim world played into the hands of Iraq. For the first time since the Gulf war, the Arab League invited Iraq to attend the October summit. The United Emirates, Bahrain, Oman, and Qatar resumed diplomatic relations with the Iraqis. Even Kuwait favored reconciliation, if its conditions on the return of missing citizens could be met by Baghdad.

Like North Korea, Iraq was no longer judged a genuine threat in several capitals.

In Beijing, Moscow, and Paris, Iraq represented an oil-rich trading partner. Even Washington failed to move decisively. The Clinton Administration temporized on implementing the Iraq Liberation Act of 1998, which called for the removal of the Saddam Hussein regime. This legislation authorized $97 million in equipment and arms for Iraqi opposition forces. At the conclusion of the Clinton presidency precious little had been expended.

The early post–Cold War period saw other brutal and dictatorial regimes come to power that eschewed weapons of mass destruction. Among them, Rwanda, Serbia, and the Congo practiced domestic terrorism, murdering large numbers of their countrymen. These governments escaped a branding as rogue states, because they did not cross the line by acquiring nuclear or biological weapons and exporting terror internationally.

Afghanistan, for example, enjoys a somewhat anomalous status among rogues. The Department of State has avoided listing it as a terrorist state. Yet, Washington diplomatically isolated and embargoed its Taliban regime for harboring America's most-wanted terrorist for his alleged role in U.S. embassy bombings in East Africa. Afghanistan bestows a safe haven for Osama bin Laden, the Saudi businessman-turned-master perpetrator of violence, whose terrorist network has been held responsible for hundreds of deaths.

Because of their disparity in ideological, political, and economic makeup, rogues were classified as distinct and treated on a case-by-case basis. The logic for this policy was—and is—sound. There is a galaxy of difference between, say, North Korea and Iraq. But this strategy must not blind policymakers to the fact to that rogue states cooperate with one another. Nor should the rogues' differing circumstances obscure the fact that they have increasingly reconnected to either former parent states or other major powers for material and diplomatic support. This collusion demonstrates all the signs of a bulwark against the spread of Western influence, globalization, and democratic values.

Anthony Lake, then-Assistant for National Security Affairs to President Clinton, wrote in 1994 that ties between these states are growing and called attention to the limited cooperation between Baghdad and Tehran. Since Lake's assessment, inter-rogue linkages have multiplied.

Despite the deep cultural cleavages among rogues, they increasingly collude. They practice a form of gangster fraternization that refutes the notion that these mavericks operate alone or are bereft of great-power patronage.

Even implacable enemies collaborated with each other. In spite of a bloody war between Iran and Iraq during the 1980s and continued animosity, the two cooperated. Iraq's oil smuggling, abetted by Iran's complicity, brought substantial profits to Iraq, which channeled the funds into arms coffers. Baghdad dispatched officials to help Serbia weather the Kosovo bombing campaign. China assists Sudan's oil exploitation and deploys security personnel to protect the oil-carrying pipelines. Iran, arguably the most independent of rogue states, has entered into cooperation with Russia. Despite official denials, Middle East rogues purchase missile components and technological know-how from North Korea.

China and Russia now sponsor rogues for commercial and geopolitical reasons rather than ideological objectives. They pursue arms sales for cash and reactivation of old Cold War relationships for diplomatic leverage to counter American influence. The linkages facilitate a proliferation of missile and nuclear-weapons capability from advanced industrial economies to renegade Third World regimes. The scale and destination of these transfers portend a frightening world in the near future. Unlike the symmetry of the Soviet-American nuclear standoff, today's security environment is a crazy quilt of "proliferators" and weapons-amassing states.

China, India, Russia, and even the European Union aspire to play major roles on the international stage. Even though their unilateral influence is well short of American power, their competition engenders political currents that will draw smaller states to their side. As the outcast states and major powers re-establish loose affiliations, the anomaly of solitaire rogues is fading.

A return to age-old patterns signals a failure for Washington's policy to isolate Iraq as well as its attempt at the "dual containment" of Iraq and Iran. In fact, the Clinton Administration abandoned its hands-off policy toward Iran in hopes of rapprochement.

Clinton's engagement of reclusive states like Iran, North Korea, and Libya was predicated on modifying and pacifying them. Yet their de-isolation has not produced genuine changes in any regime. Thus, the capacity and propensity for state-directed terrorism is still in place. Moreover, U.S. efforts to engage rogues provided "cover" for other states to do the same. Moscow can claim legitimacy in dealing with Iran and Iraq, for instance.

The return of rogues to parent-state orbits carries inconvenient implications for U.S. defense doctrine based on waging limited military engagements against sealed-off pariahs. Combat operations take on greater complexity against unpopular states if they have friends. As one illustration, the Kosovo air campaign damaged relations with Moscow and Beijing, for both were lending diplomatic support to Serbia.

Global chess envisions a return to great power tactics that compel concessions without head-on confrontation with the world's most powerful state. China and Russia, for example, can export advanced ballistic missile or nuclear technology to North Korea, Iran, or Iraq. These transfers threaten U.S. interests and friends in their respective regions. They fall short of a direct challenge to Washington but do put it on notice. Russia can even the political score for U.S. bombing of its ally Serbia during the Kosovo air campaign or for NATO expansion eastward. China, in another example, can exact a price for U.S. interference over its claim to Taiwan.

What options does this leave U.S. policy makers? First and foremost, the incoming Bush Administration must recalibrate its policies to take account of the changing realities of rogue states. Since nonproliferation of weapons of mass destruction is the single most pressing foreign policy issue, we must acknowledge that arms control treaties will not be effective against big-power supplied rogues, which ignore international legal codes.

Second, rogue and patron proliferation sustains the debate on the need for an American national missile defense and for smaller theater systems to protect U.S. forces in the field or safeguard allies. The spread of missiles with lengthening range makes the need more imperative, whether it be a new boost-phase interceptor, laser, or some other information-age innovation. Otherwise, the United States will be vulnerable to blackmail, if not outright attack.

Third, the United States must redouble its diplomatic exertions to halt the patronage of rogue dictators when dealing with Russia and China. It is not enough merely to engage Moscow and Beijing commercially in hopes that over time this will nudge them toward peaceful pursuits. Washington ought to build into its multifaceted negotiations the cessation of missile and nuclear technology exports to dangerous states.

Finally, Washington must pursue astute diplomacy that divides patrons from rogue regimes as well as rogues from one another. Since circumstances differ with each rogue, the steps taken to neutralize them can vary from covert actions for undermining a dictator to forms of economic and diplomatic engagement. But whatever the course of action, it must be sustained or we face certain peril.

Postscript

Some critics of the Rogue State Doctrine have tried to turn the concept on the United States itself. In a recent book, Noam Chomsky argues that rogue states are those who do not regard themselves as bound by international norms. If applied literally, he argues, then the United States should be considered a rogue state. Using examples from various American interventions abroad, Chomsky argues that every President since 1945 could be considered guilty of war crimes. Given the changed political climate in the United States since September 2001, it is doubtful that Chomsky will receive a very wide hearing for this interpretation. Nevertheless, it demonstrates the flexibility of "rogue state" as a concept. To what extent do you believe that the United States could also be characterized as a "rogue state"? What are the weaknesses of using the term in this way?

In working through this debate, it is possible to reject "rogue states" as a useful term while also calling attention to the threats that some of these states pose to international security. In an article cited below, Richard Falkenrath agrees that the term "rogue state" should be dropped since it confuses issues rather than clarifies them. Nevertheless, he argues that many of these states do pose a real threat because of their efforts to develop weapons of mass destruction, a concern that "will never become unfashionable." This leads us to the next issue to be debated: the threat of weapons of mass destruction and missile defense systems.

Infotrac Keyword Search
"rogue states"

Suggested Additional Readings

Chomsky, Noam. *Rogue States: The Rule of Force in World Affairs.* Cambridge: South End Press, 2000.

Falkenrath, Richard. "Weapons of Mass Reaction: Rogue States and Weapons of Mass Destruction," *Harvard International Review* 22, no. 2 (Summer 2000): 52–56.

Klare, Michael. *Rogue States and Nuclear Outlaws: America's Search for a New Foreign Policy.* New York: Hill & Wang, 1995.

Litwak, Robert S. *Rogue States and U.S. Foreign Policy.* Baltimore: Johns Hopkins University Press, 2000.

Mueller, John and Karl Mueller, "Sanctions of Mass Destruction," *Foreign Affairs* 78, no. 3 (May 1999): 43ff.

Sigal, Leon V. "Rogue Concepts: Misperceptions of North Korea," *Harvard International Review* 22, no. 2 (Summer 2000), 62–67.

Website Resources

Brookings Institution: Scholars—Meghan L. O'Sullivan   Contains several articles by Meghan O'Sullivan on "rogue states."

Hoover Institution: Essays in Public Policy   Contains a lengthy document on "Using Power and Diplomacy to Deal with Rogue States," by Thomas H. Henriksen.

Hampshire College, Peace and World Security Studies: Michael Klare   Contains a number of Michael Klare's articles dealing with "rogue states" and other military issues.

ISSUE**NINE**

Will a Ballistic Defence System Undermine Security?

✔ **YES**
ERNIE REGEHR, "Missile Proliferation, Globalized Insecurity, and Demand-Side Strategies," Waterloo: Project Ploughshares, Ploughshares Briefing, 01/4 (March 2001)

✗ **NO**
FRANK P. HARVEY, "The International Politics of National Missile Defence: A Response to the Critics," *International Journal* 55, no. 4 (Autumn 2000): 545–66

In July 2001, the Bush Administration signalled its clear intent to push forward with its plans to develop and deploy a ballistic missile defence (BMD) system by requesting an increase in funding for its program to $8.3 billion for the fiscal year 2002. This represented an increase of 57 percent from the previous year's spending. The administration also made it clear that it would go ahead with expanded testing of BMD systems, even if it meant abrogating the thirty-year-old Anti-Ballistic Missile (ABM) Treaty. In addition, the Defense Department announced that it would begin construction on a site in Alaska that could be functional as a first BMD site by 2004. Even as American attentions shifted towards the "war on terrorism" in late 2001, the Bush administration reiterated its pressing need for an effective BMD system.

The desire to develop a system for providing defence against missile attacks has been uppermost in the minds of defence planners ever since the Germans launched V-2 rockets against civilian populations in London. The advent of nuclear weapons and the subsequent development of long-range missiles only gave more urgency to the idea. In the 1960s, both the Americans and the Soviets were working on plans to develop missile defence systems.

But technologies were still at an early stage then, and relied on the development of small missiles carrying nuclear-tipped warheads that could intercept an incoming missile. The Americans begin deploying such a system in Grand Forks, ND; it was aimed primarily at defending their Inter-Continental Ballistic Missile (ICBM) sites. However, there were still many doubts about the effectiveness of such a system. Thus, the Americans supported the signing of the ABM Treaty in 1972 that limited both the Americans and the Soviets to the development of only two ABM sites. (This was later reduced by agreement to one.) The Americans eventually abandoned their BMD site in Grand Forks. Instead, the United States concentrated on deterring a nuclear attack by supporting treaties aimed at limiting the proliferation of nuclear weapons and ballistic missile technology. At the same time, they continued to rely on a strategy of deterrence by pursuing a doctrine of "mutually assured destruction" (MAD), which guaranteed an attack of devastating proportions on anyone who attacked the United States with nuclear weapons.

Nevertheless, the concept of a BMD defence system was reborn under Ronald Reagan. As tensions rose between the Soviets and the Americans in the early years of his presidency, defence analysts warned that the USSR appeared to be capable of launching both a first strike and a second retaliatory strike against American soil.

As part of his response, in 1983 President Reagan called for the building of a comprehensive defensive shield around the United States that would make nuclear weapons obsolete. Called the Strategic Defense Initiative (SDI), but popularly known as Star Wars, the plan called for the development of emerging technologies, such as laser weapons, to build a more effective BMD system. Although many were skeptical of the feasibility of such a system, the Reagan administration spent some $85 million on SDI research.

By the end of the 1980s, however, the strategic environment was changing. The USSR was in a state of collapse, democratization was spreading throughout Eastern Europe, and the Cold War had effectively come to an end. The threat of a massive nuclear attack from the Soviet Union was no longer a possibility. But studies carried out for the new administration of George Bush cautioned against complacency. In a review of the SDI program, analysts warned that the new threat would more likely come from an unauthorized use of nuclear weapons, or by terrorist groups using stolen nuclear devices. In addition, a growing number of states hostile to the United States were acquiring ballistic missile technology. The use of SCUD missiles against Israel and Saudi Arabia seemed to give credence to these new concerns. As a result, the Bush administration announced that SDI would be refocused on the development of a GPAL (Global Protection against Limited Strikes) system, which would have three components: ground-based national missile defence (NMD); ground-based theatre missile defence (TMD); and space-based missile defence.

Although the Clinton administration continued work on the BMD, the program's budget was cut from $39 billion to $18 billion over five years. Intelligence reports in the mid-1990s downplayed the danger of a nuclear attack on the United States in the next fifteen years. Enthusiasm for BMD seemed to be waning.

In 1998, Donald Rumsfeld was asked to lead an independent commission examining US security needs. The Rumsfeld Commission warned that a number of nations overtly hostile to the United States were pushing ahead with weapons programs and could develop the capability to use longer-range ballistic missiles, armed with biological or nuclear warheads, in the very near future. In the same year, both India and Pakistan carried out nuclear tests, while Iran and North Korea tested new, longer-range ballistic missiles. These events seemed to confirm the warnings of the Rumsfeld Commission and stimulated renewed interested in ballistic missile defence. Nevertheless, President Clinton decided to defer the deployment of a BMD system in 2000.

But newly elected President George W. Bush expressed much more enthusiasm for the concept of BMD. In fact, his administration announced dramatic increases in spending on BMD research and announced that it would press forward with deployment of such a system even if it meant violating the ABM Treaty.

These debates are of special relevance to Canadians. As a nation, Canada must consider the global-security implications of missile defence. But it must also respond to the possibility of participating in operating any BMD system that the US deploys. US officials have made it clear that the United States would like Canada to participate once such a system is operational.

If Canada did agree to participate, the missile defence system would be operated by the joint US-Canadian North American Aerospace Defence Command (NORAD) as a Ballistic Missile Defence of North America (BMD-NA). Although Canada's contributions, monetary or otherwise, may be minimal, its participation would be valuable in helping legitimize the program in the eyes of US allies and other countries around the world that remain skeptical about the wisdom of BMD.

In the readings below, we find two contrasting Canadian interpretations of BMD. Ernie Regehr, of Project Ploughshares, examines the problems with BMD and counsels against Canadian participation in the program. Frank Harvey examines the arguments made against BMD and sets out to refute them.

✔ YES
Missile Proliferation, Globalized Insecurity, and Demand-Side Strategies
ERNIE REGEHR

For the moment, demand for weapons of mass destruction remains significant, though not overwhelming. There are at least four prominent elements to reducing demand for weapons of mass destruction (WMD) and long-range ballistic missiles: promoting accountable governance, ameliorating regional insecurities, blocking ballistic missile defence, and challenging the double standard of non-proliferation.

Recent comments out of Ottawa, by the Prime Minister[1] as well as the Defence[2] and Foreign[3] ministers, have allowed that the proposed American national missile defence (NMD) "system has to be developed in a way that will not be offensive to the Russians and the Chinese," and should not be pursued without consultation with allies, with the implication that if direct Russian, Chinese, and NATO opposition can be forestalled, NMD will be acceptable. The most generous (and perhaps even correct) interpretation of that approach is that it amounts to a de facto Canadian "no" to NMD inasmuch as it makes Canada's approval conditional on that of two of the international community's most vociferous opponents of NMD (Russia and China).

But what if the main nuclear weapon states were to arrive at mutual acceptance of, or acquiescence to, ballistic missile defence, accompanied by European acceptance?[4] In other words, if a key focus of popular opposition to ballistic missile defence were to be removed, namely the fear that it would upset the fragile stability of the US/Russian/Chinese nuclear relationships and re-start the arms race, should that make NMD acceptable to Canadians?

An obvious reason why it should not is that NMD represents a commitment to the long-term retention of nuclear arsenals. American NMD proponents insist and assume that Russia and China will and must indefinitely maintain enough nuclear weapons and long-range delivery systems to overwhelm any defence system that the Americans might mount. That this posture calls into question the NPT-related "unequivocal undertaking to accomplish the total elimination of their nuclear arsenals" hardly needs further comment.

Less obvious, but no less real, is the contribution of NMD's nuclear retentionist assumptions to pressures toward the horizontal proliferation of weapons of mass destruction and long-range missiles to deliver, or threaten, them. The effective mitigation of that threat will be undermined by the pursuit of unilateral or monopolist high-cost, hi-tech protection efforts. NMD will add to the proliferation pressures, and it is only through collective international attention to the political and security issues that generate proliferation pressures—that is, through attention to the demand side of proliferation—that the threat that is said to be animating NMD interests will be successfully addressed.

HORIZONTAL PROLIFERATION PRESSURES

Even though NMD assumes continued nuclear threats from Russia and China, NMD advocates say that the focus of defence is not protection against those immediate and major threats. Rather, the focus of NMD is said to be on the few intercontinental-range ballistic missiles, tipped with nuclear, chemical, or biological warheads, that might one day be aimed at America from states nurturing a persistent hostility towards the US.

Whether such states are defined as "rogues," or "states of concern," or simply as states with a will and a capacity to acquire ballistic missiles (threshold states), they exist and represent a hard reality of current and potential missile proliferation that the international community will have to confront sooner or later—namely, the reality that neither ballistic missile technology nor the capacity to build weapons of mass destruction will indefinitely be confined to only a few major military powers under what they regard as the discipline of mutual deterrence.

And if Washington's public worrying about the likes of North Korea is indeed just a cover, as for some key American leaders it no doubt is, for its more ambitious pursuit of a robust NMD system coupled to offensive deployments in support of America's pursuit of terrestrial and space military domination, the WMD and missile proliferation pressures, horizontal and vertical, will only intensify accordingly.

GLOBALIZED VULNERABILITY

Even though the overwhelming majority of states that could become proliferators decide not to, the very fact that they could makes intercontinental or long-range ballistic missiles (ICBMs) one of the more tangible demonstrations of the globalization of insecurity. Like instantaneous currency transfers, ICBMs can erase national boundaries and cause the weak and the powerful to shudder with equal trepidation. Surface-to-surface intercontinental ballistic missiles are designed for only one payload, weapons of mass destruction, and no corner of the world from the corridors of Washington to the savannahs of Africa can elude their reach.

It is this shared vulnerability that ultimately renders "national" defence an oxymoron. ICBMs are inimical to the military protection of national territory—a stark reality that renders the American unilateral pursuit of "national" missile defence (NMD) a costly case of collective denial. The world is irrevocably interdependent, and unilateral national military responses to globalized insecurity are unlikely to be any more effective in protecting national territory than, say, strictly Canadian pollution-control regulations in protecting the Arctic environment.

NMD enthusiasts regard the struggle against proliferation as already lost. The missile threat cannot be eliminated, they say, so it's time to build our own impenetrable fortress. But the fact that there is no such thing as an impenetrable fortress, a fact confirmed by psychology as well as physics, rests on the first principle of globalized insecurity, which is that security is not amenable to national or unilateral arrangement. It is a principle that the United States, given its continuing ambitions for unilateral "space control and space superiority,"[5] does not find compelling. The rejection of unilateralism and the acceptance of mutual vulnerability are not the habits of superpowers, but it remains the case that only when the major powers join in re-inventing interdependence as a source of shared strength are they likely to set about building mutual global security regimes instead of trying to protect monopolies.

DEMAND AND NON-PROLIFERATION

A growing list of states does or could have access to those technologies of instant intercontinental destruction, and whether or not they act on that capacity depends finally on their own perceptions of self-interest and of the common interest. Israel, India, and Pakistan have thus decided to acquire both nuclear weapons and missiles of expanding range. South Africa, on the same grounds of self-interest and the common interest, has only recently decided the opposite, that is, to forgo the pursuit of such a capacity.

The proliferation or non-proliferation of weapons of mass destruction and the ballistic missiles to deliver them to distant targets depends finally on the voluntary decisions of states. States with expanding technical capabilities—and there are many of them—will in the end not be prevented, against their will, from acquiring WMD and long-range missile technologies in a world in which there continues to be a powerful demand for them.

For the moment, demand remains significant, though not overwhelming. States with grievances against, or that regard themselves as vulnerable to interventions by, distant powers, are likely to look with considerable interest at long-range missiles with which to pose a convincing counter-threat. That interest is powerfully present in all current nuclear weapon states (NWS). And, for example, it is clear that repeated military attacks on Iraq do not serve to reduce that regime's interest in acquiring WMD and extending the range of its missiles. And what guarantee is there that other countries, with the capability but no current interest in acquiring WMD and long-range ballistic missiles, will not change in ways that could produce conditions of intense demand for such weapons?

In arms control, demand tends to trump control. Efforts to control access to weapons that are not accompanied by measures to mitigate strong demand for them are in the long run not likely to be successful. The central insight of peace-building is that peace and disarmament (from small arms to WMD) do not endure through enforcement but through the building of political, social, and economic conditions conducive to restraint and stability. Regulatory and control regimes are important elements of stable security conditions, but as long as conditions produce a strong demand for weapons, it will be impossible to prevent the proliferation of WMD and ballistic missiles. And their spread to any new states promises a serious escalation of global insecurity.

There are at least four prominent elements to reducing demand for WMD and long-range ballistic missiles: promoting accountable governance, ameliorating regional insecurities, blocking ballistic missile defence, and challenging the double standard of non-proliferation.

1. Governance

It is too often overlooked, but one indispensable element of the effort to reduce the demand for ballistic missiles by states now in pursuit of them is support for the emergence of democratically accountable governments. The greatest current demand for ballistic missiles outside the acknowledged nuclear weapon states is in unaccountable repressive regimes that ignore the security of their citizens in favour of provocative policies aimed at regime aggrandizement or survival.

Strategies to isolate and demonize threshold states tend to reinforce the very vulnerabilities that produce the demand for weapons of mass destruction and the intercontinental ballistic missiles to deliver them. Regimes out of step with both the international community and their own citizens are usually inclined to try to intimidate both with increasingly threatening postures and practices, internationally and domestically. While direct engagement[6] of "outlaw" states holds the danger of rewarding threat with cooperation, the aim of diplomacy must obviously be to draw them into compliance with international norms and to encourage internal democratization. And a particular focus of engagement must be the strengthening of civil society and the impetus toward public participation and democracy.

In the end, the only credible long-term hedge against demand for weapons of mass destruction and the means of delivering them is an emboldened civil society that claims the right and acquires the capacity to give direct expression to alternative national interests and aspirations. States eschew extremism, not in response to external military threats, but in response to the emergence of an internal civil society that supports moderation and seeks a place of respect within the international community. In any state in which the people define public need, the demand is less likely to be for the acquisition of strategic missiles than for schools and hospitals.

That does beg the question of just who is defining national and collective needs in the United States and NATO. Some obviously think you can have it both ways—not only missiles and schools, but missiles for us and not for them, which gets us to the double standard problem (see The Double Standard).

2. Regional Insecurity

To date, nuclear weapons and advanced, if not yet intercontinental, missile capacity have spread beyond the traditional nuclear weapon states only in regions of intractable regional conflict. The Israel/Palestine and India/Pakistan conflicts both date back to the end of World War II and both have remained hot conflicts and involved hot wars. A call for new approaches to regional security and conflict resolution in instances such as these is both relevant and urgent, but unfortunately making the call for change is a lot easier than actually delivering alternatives. Nevertheless, the extent to which the international community and its security and peacemaking institutions can credibly address enduring regional conflicts is the extent to which we can expect real reductions in the demand for WMD and the means of their delivery.

3. NMD and Demand

Any American ballistic missile defence effort promises to increase both vertical and horizontal proliferation pressures (demand). Vertical proliferation pressures will grow in Russia and China as a result of NMD, even if they were to agree to it. As the public debate on NMD regularly points out, NMD will threaten current arms control agreements and lead both Russia and China to take escalatory steps they consider necessary to maintain a credible deterrent (e.g., maintain or shift to high alert status, and increase missile numbers to overwhelm any NMD capacity to intercept them). From there the vertical proliferation pressures will cascade to India and then Pakistan.

Horizontal proliferation pressures are also destined to increase in response to NMD deployment inasmuch as NMD signals the intention of current NWS to retain their nuclear arsenals indefinitely, while insisting that everyone else disavow them. NMD, in other words, exacerbates the problem of the double standard.

4. The Double Standard

Even if some measure of strategic stability among the NWS were to be re-established in a strategic environment that included an NMD system, the pressures toward horizontal proliferation would still have increased. The double standard, enshrined in the Nuclear Non-Proliferation Treaty, not in principle but in practice, and solemnly repeated in NATO strategic doctrine that says that in our hands nuclear weapons are agents of security, while in all others they are instruments of terror, is not sustainable.

Any state's policies towards acquiring or forgoing WMD and ballistic missiles are likely to be varied, complex, and focussed on their own perceptions of self-interest. In other words, it's not likely that any state will seek ballistic missiles just because the major powers have them, but the international community's effort to preserve a double standard in these matters is not an aid to restraint or compliance. Any state that believes it is in its interests to pursue provocative, attention-getting strategies is more likely to pursue nuclear weapons and missile capability if these enjoy some level of respectability and legitimacy in the international community by virtue of the retentionist policies of major powers. The international community cannot credibly say it is illegitimate for Iraq to acquire a ballistic missile capability if others claim that right and if Iraq is not party to any international agreement that prohibits it from acquiring them. Of course, the only point of having ballistic missiles is to deliver a weapon of mass destruction. Iraq, as a signatory to the NPT and to the biological weapons convention, and by Security Council action, is bound by international laws against any WMD acquisition. However, states like Iraq, and like the US on the matter of the first use of nuclear weapons, may find it useful to pursue a policy of provocative ambiguity.

The challenge to the international community is thus clear: to hold all states to the same standard of behaviour, and thus to reinforce principles of interdependence and mutual security with unambiguous commitments to reduce and eventually eliminate the ballistic missiles (as well as the nuclear weapons) of the major powers.[7] In the meantime, the disquietingly long meantime, during which current NWS are tasked to reduce and eventually eliminate their arsenals of long-distance mass destruction, means have to be found to make it attractive for other states to reject all WMD and long-distance delivery systems.

MULTILATERAL MISSILE MONITORING

Just as missile control measures are destined to failure unless they are complemented by vigorous demand reduction efforts, demand reduction efforts can only be sustained and harvested through control mechanisms designed to consolidate and institutionalize an international consensus of restraint leading finally to the prohibition of WMD and their means of delivery. Current and welcome discussions within the Missile Technology Control Regime (MTCR) are trying to encourage both supply and demand restraint by exploring a "set of principles, commitments, confidence-building measures and incentives that could constitute a code of conduct against missile proliferation."[8] These are not currently public discussions, but the fact that they are taking place should be understood as some movement towards an international consensus to reduce the number and limit the spread of ballistic missiles.

Russia's proposal for a global missile monitoring system (GMS) is a further effort to take advantage of, and to build on, that emerging consensus. The GMS would, among other things, incorporate the MTCR's focus on restricting technology transfers, provide security guarantees for states eschewing the pursuit of long-range ballistic missiles, and monitor missile launches.

Any mechanism to control long-range ballistic missiles faces the daunting political challenge of recognizing the current de facto, but ultimately unsustainable, monopoly on missiles, and then solidifying a commitment from all non-nuclear weapon states to themselves reject the acquisition of ballistic missiles in exchange for a commitment from the states that do have them to take discernable steps toward eliminating their long-range military ballistic missile arsenals. Sustained confidence in any arrangement by which most states agree not to acquire ballistic missiles while those with ballistic missiles for military purposes agree to reductions and movement toward their elimination[9] (and, significantly, agree not to link their offensive capabilities to missile defences) will depend on the emergence of a reliable global ballistic missile monitoring mechanism with four basic roles:

- to monitor, assess, and share information on the ballistic missile development programs of all states;

- to provide surveillance and monitoring of the pre-launch status of missiles in nuclear weapon states to facilitate and verify de-alerting measures;

- to receive and share pre-launch notification of missile launches for accepted purposes, such as satellite launches; and

- to detect and track ballistic missile launches and flights and share the information in real time.

The latter two functions are central to the proposed US/Russian Joint Data Exchange Center[10] (JDEC), which too should gradually be globalized.

Protection from weapons of mass destruction delivered across oceans and continents by ballistic missiles is not a national prerogative. It is a global imperative that will not be met through military defence. Protection is a common global responsibility that in this instance depends on eliminating the threat, and that in turn requires as much attention to removing the demand for such weapons as it does to restricting access to them.

NOTES

1. On Feb. 7, 2001, Prime Minister Chrétien told the House of Commons that he had indicated to President Bush that the NMD "system has to be developed in a way that will not be offensive to the Russians and the Chinese."

2. Paul Koring (Washington) and Jeff Sallot (Ottawa) (2001) report that Minister of Defence Art Eggleton says Canada is "open-minded" on the NMD question.

3. On Feb. 14, 2001, Foreign Affairs Minister John Manley, in response to a question from MP Svend Robinson, told the House of Commons that "it is appropriate to give the United States ... time to define what the project is that is being described as national missile defence—it has indicated that it has not done that yet—and the time it has asked for to take up what its plans are, not only with its allies but with the Russians and the Chinese."

4. According to Michael Gordon (2001), "European officials now seem to accept, grudgingly, the fact that the new American team is determined to move ahead.... The debate is entering a new phase in which the issue is more how the United States should go about developing missile defenses, than whether it should try."

5. On the occasion of the January 2001 Space Commission report to the US Congress, the Commander in Chief of NORAD and US Space Command and the Air Force Space Command, Gen. Ralph E. Eberhart, added to the inventory of US military leaders calling for the US to control space when he counselled increased "attention to the sensitive issues of space control and superiority."

6. See, for example, Haass and O'Sullivan 2000.

7. The Nuclear Non-Proliferation Treaty states pledged their commitment to "the elimination from national arsenals of nuclear weapons *and the means of their delivery*" (emphasis added; see preamble to the Treaty).

8. The MTCR is an export control arrangement (voluntary guidelines among a suppliers' group) designed to limit the spread of ballistic and cruise missile technologies. The MTCR group has begun discussions with other states on the viability of developing a broader, formal multilateral instrument to prevent missile proliferation.

9. One proposed deal would include a worldwide missile warning system accessible to all states, the provision by missile states of satellite launch facilities and other space probes for peaceful purposes for other states, permission for other countries to build missiles for space exploration and satellite launches, and a multilateral verification agency (Dean 1998).

10. The Joint Data Exchange Center is to be established under a June 2000 agreement between Presidents Clinton and Putin and will facilitate "the exchange of information derived from each side's missile launch warning systems on the launches of ballistic missiles and space launch vehicles."

REFERENCES

Dean, Jonathan (1998), "Step-by-Step Control Over Ballistic and Cruise Missiles," *Disarmament and Diplomacy*, Issue 31, October, pp. 2–11.

Gordon, Michael R. (2001), "News Analysis: Allies' Mood on 'Star Wars' Shifts," *New York Times*, February 5.

Haass, Richard N. and Meghan L. O'Sullivan (2000), "Terms of Engagement: Alternatives to Punitive Policies," *Survival* 42, No. 2, pp. 113–35.

Koring, Paul and Jeff Sallot (2001), Feb. 2, *The Globe and Mail*.

✗ NO
The International Politics of National Missile Defence: A Response to the Critics
FRANK P. HARVEY

INTRODUCTION

To encourage more informed discussion of national missile defence (NMD) and to widen a dangerously narrow public debate on the subject, this article challenges critics of NMD to confront the logical and factual errors in their arguments against deployment. Because the American programme has important implications for Canadian foreign and security policies (and Canadian-American relations more generally), critics should be prepared to defend their positions beyond simply reiterating the same superficial criticisms. The Canadian public should expect nothing less from the academic community (not to mention our elected officials) than a sophisticated exchange of ideas on such an important issue.

[...]

THE DEMISE OF THE NPT AND ABM

The most common criticisms of NMD are associated with warnings about the demise of the Non-Proliferation treaty (NPT) and Anti-Ballistic Missile (ABM) treaty. Signed in 1968 and 1972, respectively, these treaties are two pillars of nuclear disarmament and arms control that, according to proponents, were responsible for slowing the pace of proliferation during the cold war and stabilizing the longest nuclear rivalry in history. Because they continue to be essential for controlling proliferation and maintaining a stable nuclear environment, it is imperative that their underlying principles and fundamental logic should not be undermined.

What critics fail to point out is that the worst abuses of horizontal and vertical proliferation of nuclear weapons and technology occurred after the treaties were signed. Regardless of the indicator used to track nuclear proliferation—overall nuclear stockpiles, numbers of strategic warheads in submarine launched ballistic missiles, inter-continental ballistic missiles, strategic bombers,[1] production and stockpiles of weapons' grade plutonium, thefts of fissile material, trade in dual use technology tied to the atomic energy industry, trade in ballistic missile technology, and so on—the evidence of an increase in the pace of proliferation is clear. Recent nuclear tests by India and Pakistan are but the latest illustration of the same pattern. To claim that the NPT and the ABM treaty are essential parts of the international arms control structure doesn't say much for the treaties or for the prospects for serious arms control and disarmament in the future.[2]

Some critics—those who claim that the more relevant measure of the treaty's effectiveness is the number of nuclear weapons states in the world today—will reject my criteria for judging the NPT's success. These critics argue that there were five nuclear weapon's states when the NPT was signed in 1968, and there were still five at the beginning of 1998. There are now seven with India and Pakistan. If the undeclared states (Israel) and the "wannabes" (Iraq, Iran, and North Korea) are included, the number rises to eleven. The expectation when the NPT was negotiated was that there would be far more nuclear weapons states, but that prediction was obviously wrong. The NPT would, therefore, seem to be an overwhelming success.

Applying the same logic, perhaps the success of the New York Police Department (NYPD) should be judged on the basis of how many millions of New Yorkers do not commit murder or rob liquor stores, regardless of whether they ever intended to commit those (or other) crimes.[3] Similarly, an overwhelming majority of non-nuclear states are not interested in acquiring nuclear weapons, not because their leaders find the weapons repulsive and morally reprehensible (although some probably do) but primarily because nuclear weapons provide no added security (at this time), or because security guarantees from allies are more than sufficient (as is the case in Canada). Most states, in other words, have the luxury of being able to say "no" to nuclear weapons. The success of the NPT must be measured instead by (a) how many aspiring nuclear states (signatory and non-signatory) are prevented from acquiring or developing the technology to deploy nuclear weapons and/or their delivery vehicles, and (b) how many states (signatory and non-signatory) continue to provide the requisite technology to aspiring nuclear powers. It takes only one nuclear weapon to produce the catastrophe the NPT was designed to prevent, and the capability to deliver and inflict that kind of damage is spreading.

The fate of the NPT (and perhaps its ultimate demise) will not depend upon NMD deployment. It will continue to depend upon political, military, and security environments in places such as India, Iran, Iraq, Israel, Libya, North Korea, Pakistan, and Syria. Officials in these states are convinced that ballistic missiles and nuclear weapons technology serve their security and national interests and are more than willing to accept related technology transfers from China, Russia, France, the United States, and Canada to accommodate their concerns. Critics in the arms control community refuse to acknowledge that these states will continue to be perceived as threatening whether or not the United States has a defensive shield. [...]

Leaders of "new" and "aspiring" nuclear weapons states are perceived by many critics as passive observers who learn from established nuclear powers and, in true Pavlovian fashion, respond accordingly. The best way to control proliferation and maintain a stable nuclear environment, critics assume, is for established nuclear powers to "teach" officials in other states to adhere to the principles, logic, and moral (read "civilized") standards entrenched in the treaties. That assumption is not only naïve but also dangerously superficial when it comes to understanding the proliferation puzzle and the myriad factors that explain most (if not all) proliferation decisions. It is particularly insulting to officials in, for example, India and Pakistan to be told that their capacity to make informed decisions about their own global and regional security interests is limited. The notion that established nuclear powers or the international arms control community command the intellectual high ground on these issues and, by extension, have a moral obligation to "guide" other cultures and peoples toward the enlightened path of nuclear sanity is reminiscent of the worst extremes of Manifest Destiny and its associated policies. While this obviously is not the intention of the arms control community, it is precisely how their pronouncements are perceived in some states.

Finally, it is particularly ironic for critics in the arms control and disarmament community to embrace the ABM treaty as the cornerstone of non-proliferation and nuclear sanity when the same critics vehemently criticized the treaty throughout the 1970s and 1980s for entrenching the logic of mutually assured destruction (MAD) in United States-Soviet rivalry. That logic was used by both sides to justify huge defence expenditures, ever-increasing nuclear stockpiles, and an exponential increase in the number of nuclear targets—all with reference to the benefits of maintaining a robust, stable, and credible second-strike capability. The rationale underlying the ABM treaty remains the same: as long as the United States and Russia have enough weapons to survive and retaliate after a pre-emptive first-strike, neither side will be tempted to launch first. Given their new-found concern for protecting the sanctity of the ABM treaty, it seems NMD critics in the arms control community have now fully embraced a thesis that was so obvious to many in the defence community during the cold war—large stockpiles of nuclear weapons on high alert can serve the global desire for nuclear stability and peace.[4] If that is not the point these critics are trying to make, perhaps they should acknowledge the logical implications (and unintended consequences) of supporting the ABM treaty and/or rejecting NMD.

NMD WILL LEAD TO NUCLEAR PROLIFERATION BY RUSSIA AND CHINA

Building on claims about the impending demise of decades of disarmament negotiations, critics predict that China and Russia will respond to NMD with a major build-up and deployment of more sophisticated weapons as they attempt to regain their security by re-establishing (or, in the case of China, strengthening) their second-strike capability. This automatic action-reaction sequence will, in turn, create security threats for officials in India and Pakistan, who will retaliate with greater numbers of nuclear weapons for their own security. A huge spiral in defence spending and arms protection will result and propel the international community back to square one of the arms control and disarmament agenda—all because of a relatively minor investment of about two per cent of the United States defence budget (or 0.3 per cent of its federal budget). Three interrelated assumptions underlie these predictions: proliferation by Russia and China is directly related to (and will be a primary consequence of) American NMD deployment; Russian and Chinese warnings convey a "real" fear that the United States is attempting to gain a first-strike advantage; and the fear of an impending American first-strike advantage justifies Russian and Chinese proliferation. Each assumption reveals logical inconsistencies and factual errors.

First, the casual chain cited by critics to predict almost automatic proliferation by Russia and China ignores evidence compiled over years of research on why states proliferate. Without exception, the research points to a complex set of political, economic, and military-strategic prerequisites.[5] If the findings and patterns identified in this body of work are correct, China can be expected to acquire and deploy more advanced systems if and when the technology becomes available and affordable, and as long as Chinese officials perceive as unfair the imbalance between their nuclear capabilities and those of the United States, Russia, Europe, and the North Atlantic Treaty Organization (NATO). Although the United States and Russia have the luxury as major nuclear powers to disarm to START II, III, or IV levels, China will continue to build up the levels befitting an ascending major power. In other words, the real incentive for China to upgrade its nuclear capabilities is Beijing's perception that its nuclear deterrent is unstable, for the same reason American and Soviet officials worried in the 1960s and 1970s—China's retaliatory capability is not sufficiently potent (or credible) in "second-strike" terms. Whether or not the United States deploys NMD is irrelevant; Chinese officials will continue to see a capability/credibility gap, at least until their stockpiles approach parity with those in Europe. Even if the United States were to decide to scrap NMD tomorrow, China would continue to upgrade its systems on the basis of worst-case scenarios and assumptions about surreptitious NMD development. I suspect that as defence technologies become available and affordable, Russia and China will do precisely the same thing, regardless of what the Americans do today.[6]

Because Russia has already deployed advanced weapons designed to circumvent missile defence systems, critics' fears of this kind of proliferation following NMD deployment are moot. The new SS-X-27 ballistic missile, for example, has an accelerated boost phase of 100 seconds (down from 180 seconds, making it harder to detect on launch), can carry three warheads, and is highly manoeuvrable. It is particularly interesting that this combination of technologies serves as an effective countermeasure not only to NMD but to the alternative missile defence system that Vladimir Putin, the Russian president, offered the Europeans in June 2000.[7] Critics predict that Russia will accelerate the pace of proliferation in retaliation for NMD, but they should at least explain what Russia would gain and why its leaders are likely to ignore the political, military, and, especially, economic costs of returning to a cold war footing.

[...]

Second, Russian and Chinese fears of losing second-strike capabilities are based, in part, on a basic and fundamental cold war concern that effective defences will give the United States first-strike advantage. NMD deployment, therefore, will force Russia and China to acquire additional missiles to augment their retaliatory capability and, by extension, the credibility of their nuclear deterrent threat. Those critics who use such warnings to establish a case against NMD should be prepared to explain why their fears are legitimate. The only way to do so would be to explain how NMD provides the United States with a first-strike capability, and, more importantly, why the United States would sometime in the future threaten or launch a massive first-strike attack against Russia and/or China. [...]

Third, critics should explain why they are willing to accept current threats by China and Russia to proliferate in retaliation for NMD when they rejected as logically absurd the identical strategy when it was used by the United States and the Soviet Union to increase nuclear stockpiles throughout the cold war. Their arguments included the fact that most of the 30,000 missiles on each side were redundant and entirely useless; a few missiles were more often more than sufficient to inflict unacceptable damage, and this "minimum" deterrence was more than sufficient to provide effective security from a pre-emptive strike. After all, who would be foolish enough to risk provoking even one retaliatory missile? But critics in the arms control community today refuse to apply the same logic and criticism to Russia and China because it undermines the rationale tied to warnings about automatic proliferation. As an unintended consequence, nuclear proliferation becomes a reasonable and logical response to NMD.

TECHNOLOGICAL LIMITATIONS OF NMD

Two main assertions underpin the "technological limitations" critique: current defence technologies don't work; and simple decoys and countermeasures can overcome any shield. But if NMD is indeed plagued by these incredible technological hurdles, and if simple countermeasures can easily offset any investment in defence, then, aside from wasting money (see section four) what exactly is the problem for China and Russia? After all, only an effective NMD shield would justify an arms race to re-establish a stable second-strike capability. Conversely, if NMD does not (or will not) work, then any security concerns expressed by Russia or China about maintaining the credibility of their nuclear deterrent are misplaced and mistaken, as are related decisions by these states proliferate in retaliation for a useless defensive system. Juxtaposed against the previous criticisms, the technological critique is, in many ways, mutually exclusive—the stronger the arguments and evidence about the deficiencies of NMD, the weaker the claims about automatic and justifiable proliferation by Russia and China because they have no reason to feel compelled to compensate for losses in security. Notwithstanding this obvious logical inconsistency, which critics rarely acknowledge and almost never attempt to address, the limits of interceptor technology are offered as sufficient reason to scrap the entire programme.

With respect to NMD architecture, the scope of the proposed project will evolve through four stages, beginning with 20 interceptors in 2005 and growing to a larger system by 2011. As William Broad points out, "the shield would require at least 2 launching sites, 3 command centers, 5 communication relay stations, 15 radar, 29 satellites, 250 underground silos and a total of 250 missile interceptors (by 2011). It would be based in Hawaii, Alaska, California, Colorado, North Dakota, Massachusetts, Greenland, Britain and possibly Maine. Two radar would be set up in Asia, possibly in Japan and South Korea. Building it would cost at least $60 billion and running it would take at least 1,455 people, and probably hundreds more."[8] According to the critics, an investment of US$60 billion simply cannot be justified on the basis of recent tests or the prospects for success in the future. The technology is not capable of satisfying even the most basic requirements for success and, according to critics among scientists and engineers, it is unlikely ever to be robust enough to deal with decoys and simple countermeasures.

Consider the argument put forward by Burton Richter (winner of the 1976 Nobel Prize for physics): "Assume for the sake of argument that an attack is composed of five missiles (the massive attack we used to worry about from the Soviet Union would have involved hundreds or thousands) and suppose that the chance of one interceptor finding and destroying the real warhead from one of the attacking missiles is four out of five, or 80 percent. Then, the chance of killing all five incoming warheads with five interceptors would be calculated this way: 0.8 for the first interceptors on the first warhead, multiplied by 0.8 for the second on the second, and so on for all five. Work it out, and the probability of getting all five is about 33 percent, or a two-out-of-three chance that at least one of the incoming warheads will get through. Since one warhead can kill hundreds of thousands of people, that is not good enough."[9]

There are several problems with this argument. First, even if we acknowledge the incredible technological hurdles that remain, and even if we accept the fact that the current system is far from perfect, the more relevant questions for policy-makers are: how close to perfect does the technology have to be to be useful; and how prudent is deployment today if interceptor technology, speed, and precision will continue to evolve and improve? Critics have never clarified how close to perfect a defence system has to be to be useful and worthy of funding. Even the staunchest critics of NMD assign at least some probability of success. The question is whether that probability is worth an investment of two per cent of the United States defence budget.

Second, most critics in the scientific community intentionally side step the link between the number of interceptors launched at a single target and the probability of a successful hit. Current plans are to use three or four interceptors per target, applying a "hit-move-hit" strategy. According to congressional testimony by General Robert T. Kadish, director of the Pentagon's Ballistic Missile Defence Organization, if interceptors approach 80 per cent accuracy, two or three attempts would increase the probability of a successful hit to 96 per cent and 99 per cent, respectively.[10] For the sake of argument, accept the most pessimistic assessment of the technology in 2005–2008—say, about a 30 per cent probability of any given interceptor hitting its target. Critics will no doubt cite this as the fairest evaluation of contemporary interceptor technology—one out of three interceptor tests in 1999–2000 was successful. With 30 per cent accuracy, and assuming precision will not improve through trial and error, the second, third, and fourth attempts increase the probability of a successful hit to 51 per cent, 66 per cent, and 76 per cent, respectively.

Third, even if overall success rates remain as low as 30 per cent, the question American policy-makers are facing is whether to deploy a system that protects the population from three out of ten missiles (that is, eight out of ten missiles using four interceptors), or scrap the entire programme and, in so doing, face a 100 per cent probability that the population will suffer the effects of all ten missiles if attacked?[11] The technological case in favour of deployment is even stronger when one considers that 30 percent is far lower than the estimates offered by critics and proponents in the scientific community and significantly lower than estimates cited by scientists involved in all aspects of the NMD testing programme. Moreover, the 250 interceptors planned for deployment by 2011 will certainly compensate for limitations of current technology, even if they remain constant. Since that is highly unlikely, the investment of two per cent of the defence budget is a bargain.

Many critics suffer from static impressions of progress and overlook constant improvements in interceptor and decoy identification technology. That NMD has not yet reached 100 per cent accuracy is irrelevant. What is relevant is whether the pace of innovation is such that NMD will, at some future point, produce a "high enough" probability of success to warrant deployment (even 30 per cent is arguably high enough), whether the current programme provides sufficient security to offset the costs and potential risks, and whether alternatives (such as constructive engagement, transparency, economic sanctions, and so on) are cheaper and more likely to accomplish the same security objectives. Current and future decisions regarding research, development, and deployment should depend on these calculations; they should not (and mostly probably will never) depend on the status and limitations of present-day technology, especially if the technology is evolving at a rapid pace.

[...]

The greatest technological challenge for NMD is the system's capacity to disregard countermeasures and decoys. According to some critics, decoys are extremely hard to detect and cheaper to produce than interceptors. Thus, NMD will always be a waste of time and money. There are at least two problems with this argument.

First, critics tend to downplay the problems developing countries face when incorporating countermeasures into a well-functioning ballistic missile programme. They are also quick to acknowledge the enormous costs and limitations the world's richest and most scientifically advanced country faces when developing interceptor technology. The only states with the capability to develop and deploy decoys "easily" are the very states that don't need them; they already have a stable and credible retaliatory threat. Not true, claim the critics. Developing countries also have the technology to build and deploy decoys to circumvent NMD interception. If that is true, then they most certainly have the capacity to produce ballistic missiles as well. If ballistic missile threats are real, then it makes perfect sense for the United States to increase the costs incurred by "states of concern" by forcing them to deploy decoys and countermeasures when developing their ballistic missile programmes. Just because countermeasures can be deployed does not mean the United States should accept defeat, scrap NMD, and give potential adversaries the option of disregarding those added costs. Scrapping NMD simply means that the ballistic missile threat will continue to proliferate in ways that are more affordable. The harder it is for potential opponents to threaten (implicitly or explicitly) the use of these weapons, the better. On the other hand, if ballistic missile threats are indeed fabrications to justify military expenditure on NMD, and if there is no reason to be worried about the pace of ballistic missile proliferation, then critics should be prepared to provide a more comprehensive and detailed defence of that position.[12]

A second and related set of criticisms focuses on controversies surrounding the NMD testing programme and the standards used by the Pentagon to evaluate success and failure. Some critics have accused the Pentagon of fixing the tests in order to facilitate a successful hit and, therefore, congressional funding. I'm not a ballistic scientist and do not presume to understand the physics involved in the programme, but it seems perfectly reasonable to develop and improve technology through stages by first identifying NMD's limitations; the system's maximum potential is irrelevant at this time. If the initial tests were designed to assess an interceptor's capacity to hit hundreds of targets and 20–30 different decoys, and it fails, the results provide virtually no useful information about what went wrong, why certain decoys may have been missed, or what has to be improved to move the technology forward. On the other hand, if a single interceptor misses/hits a single target, or misses/hits a simple decoy, the information obtained from that test is far more useful and relevant. [...]

The same critique also tends to underplay the incredible scientific achievements associated with even a very simple test. Obviously, the system cannot achieve its maximum potential today, but we should not evaluate the performance of current technology based on the requirements for a system envisioned in five, eight, or ten years—interceptor technology, like any technology, will continue to improve. Again, the question for policy-makers is whether deployment today makes sense considering the probability of success, the probability of improving future systems through trial and error, and the costs and benefits to overall security when compared to alternative strategies.[13]

NMD: A COLOSSAL WASTE OF MONEY OR A MINOR AND PRUDENT INVESTMENT?

The most straightforward way to evaluate the quality of any significant defence expenditure is to estimate the money involved in the programme (financial costs); the contribution the programme makes to state security (benefits); the probability those benefits will be realized (technology); the potential dangers associated with deployment (risks); and the probability those costs will be incurred (security costs). The results should then be compared to other security programmes that promise to accomplish the same objectives, for the same (or lower) costs, with the same (or higher) probability of success. Finally, the estimates should be compared to those for alternative programmes designed to address a different set of equally or more important security objectives. All things considered, programmes with higher utility for a state's security should be funded.

With respect to the financial costs, the proposed United States investment in NMD is approximately US$60 billion over ten years, or about $6 billion per year between 2001 and 2011. That is about two per cent per annum of a defence budget of approximately US$300 billion (or approximately 0.3 per cent of the total federal budget of $2 trillion). The numbers are likely to be lower as the defence budget increases to $317 billion in 2005 and $349 billion in 2010, but the average yearly expenditure of two per cent serves as a useful benchmark to make a few important points.

For critics, two per cent of the defence budget is a waste of money (high financial costs) for a system aimed at non-existent threats (no benefits) that will not work (technological limitations) and will probably create a host of other problems (security costs) as Russia and China automatically retaliate by proliferating nuclear weapons (high risks). I have already responded to many of these assertions by outlining important flaws and inconsistencies in the critics' case. I would like to now turn to three items I have not yet addressed: financial investment, alternative programmes that are perhaps more suited to the task, and other programmes designed to address a different set of security objectives.

How cost effective is the American investment in NMD? With the preceding analysis in mind, and for the sake of argument, accept an optimistic estimate of evolving threats tied to the proliferation of ballistic missile technology—say, only a ten-per-cent probability that by 2005–2008 one or more "states of concern" will have developed and deployed one or more medium- to long-range ballistic missiles capable of reaching the United States (even critics would find this number very low). The current annual investment is quite a bargain, especially when one looks at where the remaining 98 per cent of the defence budget ends up and the correspondingly limited contribution much of that investment makes to United States security.

Moreover, a ten-per-cent probability of a ballistic missile threat is a far more significant and relevant concern when viewed in terms of the overall defence profile; that is, all American security, defence, and threat scenarios the government considers relevant and the consequences in damage and lives should those threats become real. If only those threats the United States can tackle with at least some likelihood of success are included, then the ten-per-cent probability of a ballistic missile threat becomes even more relevant. Put differently, a 99-per-cent probability of a terrorist attack in the next three years resulting in 100 deaths is not as relevant as a ten-per-cent threat with the potential to produce tens if not hundreds of thousands of casualties. The question policy-makers are confronting is whether the strategy designed to address the ten-per-cent threat has a higher probability of success than corresponding funds and programmes to stop, for example, terrorism. Would another $60 billion invested in anti-terrorism provide an equal (or better) return in security than stopping even a single missile with NMD?

Most critics agree that the rogue-state threat is exaggerated, but few are prepared to argue that there is nothing to worry about. The real debate, then, is about time and the pace and evolution of the threat. Critics must estimate the appropriate amount of funding for their preferred solution to the problem, even if their estimate of the probability of a ballistic missile threat in 2005–2008 is, say, one per cent. How much of the United States defence budget would critics be willing to allocate to address a one-per-cent threat, using whatever programme they prefer? If they conclude that one per cent (or $3 billion) of the defence budget would be enough to implement their preferred solution, then they have an obligation to explain what the money buys, how the proposed investment enhances United States security, how likely it is that the programme will succeed, and so on. Ultimately, critics should be prepared to evaluate their alternatives using the same standards they apply to NMD, with reference to the same criteria for assessing costs, risks, and probabilities for success or failure.

The "alternatives" proposed by critics usually include some combination of improved transparency, weapons verification, monitoring, import/export controls and a host of other diplomatic (for example, constructive engagement) and coercive diplomatic (for example, economic sanctions, bombing Iraq) strategies. Presumably these methods are more constructive because they address the proliferation problem from the demand and supply side and, in the process, produce none of the costs associated with NMD. But these popular policy pronouncements rarely include the details policy-makers need to compare them to NMD.

If one were to look at the money already invested, not only by the United States but also globally, on programmes tied to transparency, monitoring, verification, and economic sanctions, I suspect the total far exceeds the proposed investment in NMD. What exactly do we have to show for all these efforts, strategies, and investments? Even the most optimistic take on the proliferation record is not particularly encouraging—witness the recent failure of inspection, monitoring, verification, and sanctions regimes in Iraq, North Korea, India, and Pakistan. Where exactly is the proof that another $60 billion invested in these strategies is more cost-effective, or more likely to address (prevent) ballistic missile threats circa 2005–2008? How exactly will diplomatic efforts to "engage" Iraq, Iran, or North Korea prevent them from developing their nuclear programmes, and what is the probability of success—76 per cent? 30 per cent? Wouldn't improved economic relations provide the same capital required for these states to augment their receptive nuclear and ballistic weapons facilities? How probable is that outcome? Ah, ask the critics, but isn't it time we took the risk? Based on the evidence so far, no it is not!

Critics in the "human security" community are fond of claiming that there are so many other, more relevant threats—drug trafficking, environmental degradation, world hunger and disease, AIDS, intrastate ethnic conflict, refugees, terrorism, chemical and biological weapons proliferation—that should receive the bulk of security-related expenditures. But the existence of a threat says nothing about how the problems can be addressed, whether transferring NMD's $60 billion from the defence budget is a better and more cost-effective investment in security, or whether the transfer will do anything to address evolving ballistic missile threats (however remote they may be). Like NMD, decisions about which programme to fund, or which security threats to solve, must be based on a balanced evaluation of the costs, risks, and the probability of accomplishing objectives.

Consider the combined investments in "human security" by some of the largest United States or European aid agencies over the last ten years (the same time frame for NMD's $60 billion procurement). Now, track the trends in drug trafficking, environmental degradation, AIDS, ethnic conflict, etc., during the same period. Notwithstanding the billions of dollars invested globally by several countries, international agencies, and non-governmental organizations, the problems have arguably become worse. How would another $60 billion help resolve these or similar "human security" problems, and are the benefits (and attendant probabilities of realizing them) likely to make an equal (or greater) contribution to United States security than $60 billion on NMD?

Obviously, I am not suggesting that we should stop funding programmes to combat other serious problems. But critics should acknowledge the fact that many of these "other" problems and related solutions are incredibly complex, perhaps even more complex than interceptor technology, because their success depends on the support, sacrifice, and sponsorship of political and military officials within developing countries. In many cases solutions are made even more difficult by ruling elite who have other priorities—environmental security and controlling child labour, for example, are not likely to be priorities in a country whose leaders are trying to encourage foreign investment through cheap labour and low production costs. In addition, many human security threats are highly interconnected and interdependent, which further complicates the search for cost-effective solutions. Critics will continue to make reference to these "other" security concerns when criticizing expenditures on NMD, but they should be honest about the costs and success rates associated with resolving their preferred security threats.

In sum, if the relative importance of these "other" threats is debatable to begin with, and if they are complex, interdependent, and very difficult to resolve because of existing international and domestic impediments, and if investing in them instead of in NMD does absolutely nothing to resolve ballistic missile threats, then how exactly does transferring $60 billion in defence funds to "human security" problems make any practical sense? The specifics remain elusive, for obvious reasons.

NMD AND CANADIAN POLICY OPTIONS

Critics have warned Canadians that NMD will be costly. What they fail to point out is that little if any of the costs will be placed on the shoulders of Canadian taxpayers. Ottawa has not been asked to contribute a red cent to the project, and, unfortunately, Canadian companies are unlikely to compete for the larger defence contracts. Some critics will continue to mention "costs" at every opportunity, but they should admit that the United States is more than willing to pay for (and develop) the technology in-house—for all of the reasons outlined above.

The failure in July 2000 of the last three crucial interceptor tests will have no significant effect on the project—scientists (and United States senators) acquired no new information about components central to the functioning of NMD.[14] The kill vehicle failed to separate from the booster rocket, but the technology has been functioning successfully for decades in particularly every major space mission, satellite launch, and shuttle project in the history of the National Aeronautical Space Administration (NASA).[15] Ironically, the only clear failure, aside from booster separation, was the balloon designed as a basic countermeasure. This is likely to be far more upsetting to those critics who offer the simplicity of countermeasure technology as a reason to scrap the programme—if the United States is having a hard time deploying a decoy, what does that suggest about the capacity of developing countries to accomplish the same task?

In the end, Canada's position on NMD will have very little to do with the costs of the programme, the success or failure of interceptor technology, the relative merits of NMD versus boost-phase strategies, the implications for arms control and disarmament, or the warnings from China or Russia. These are issues at the heart of debates in the United States—Canada's position will depend on how they are resolved south of the border. Whether or not Canadian officials accept as valid the logic and utility of NMD, Ottawa will drop the subject if the United States decides to scrap the programme (regardless of its merits). The real choice during and after the 2000 presidential campaign is not "whether" NMD will be developed but "how" it will move forward—as a Democratically sponsored NMD or as a Republican version of the Strategic Defense Initiative (SDI)? The technology has matured to the point where United States policies will continue to shift to accommodate it, especially given the prospects for improvements. More specific predictions about the system's architecture, therefore, will depend primarily on domestic politics in the United States.

Many critics in Canada claim that a decision by Ottawa to reject NMD would have little, if any, effect on Canada-United States relations. But those who make that argument never explain in detail why the United States would accept such a decision without responding, or why Canada's relations with the United States in North American Aerospace Defence (NORAD) would be unaffected. There are few, if any, historical precedents to defend that position. The critics' response is that we do not need cold war relics like NORAD. But just what is the argument here: that there will be no consequences if Canada rejects NMD, or that the consequences will be irrelevant? Few, if any, details are offered to defend either position. Ironically, a break with NORAD would have a direct effect on Canada's access to the very satellite technology required for information on transparency, verification, and monitoring—all of which are more cost-effective alternatives to the proliferation problem, according to critics.

The dilemma for Canadian policy-makers is NMD's departures from principles and precedents embedded in the ABM treaty. For a variety of domestic political reasons, it makes perfect sense for Canadian officials to hold off on major policy statements until the United States makes a definitive move. But because the United States is unlikely to scrap NMD, Canada will have to consider its support for the programme sometime. Perhaps the most effective (and politically acceptable) approach would be for Canadian officials to emphasize the benefits of NMD in comparison to a full-blown SDI programme—ironically, by using many of the arguments put forward by critics of NMD. While the arguments are not particularly relevant (or persuasive) when applied to NMD, they are useful as criticisms of SDI—a more robust system that will depend on significantly more expensive space-based lasers, none of which is essential for addressing current or short-term threats from "states of concern." NMD, in other words, is the most balanced, stable, and affordable alternative today. Canada's decision to support the programme is the right one, not because the United States favours it, but because, all things considered, NMD makes sense for Canadian security and defence.

NOTES

I am very grateful to Brian Buckley and David Mutimer for their helpful comments on an earlier draft of the paper.

1. Relevant charts can be obtained from the Natural Resources Defense Council web page: http://www.nrdc.org/nuclear/nudb/datainx.asp.

2. Note 12 lists resources that highlight the threats tied to ballistic missile proliferation and fissile material theft.

3. The analogy is less than ideal, of course, because the NYPD has the capacity and authority to arrest criminals—police can credibly threaten a myriad of punishments to prevent criminal activity. There are no parallel international institutions that can effectively monitor, prevent, or reverse proliferation by states that decide to acquire the technology or successfully sanction those who break laws or other treaty obligations.

4. This logic is used today by American nuclear strategists to justify increasing the number of targets from 2,500 (in 1995) to 3,000 today, mostly to address threats from China, Iran, Iraq, and North Korea. See Hugo Young, "Secrets of Washington's nuclear madness revealed," *Guardian Weekly*, 22 June 2000.

5. For an excellent collection of articles summarizing these patterns, see Zachary S. Davis and Benjamin Frankel, eds, *The Proliferation Puzzle: Why Nuclear Weapons Spread and What Results* (London: Frank Cass 1993). See also William C. Potter and Harlan W. Jencks, eds., *The International Missile Bazaar: The New Suppliers' Network* (Boulder, CO and London: Westview, 1994).

6. For a detailed analysis of China's evolving nuclear policy see Brad Roberts, Robert A. Manning, and Ronald N. Montaperto, "China: the forgotten nuclear power," *Foreign Affairs 79* (July/August 2000). For an interesting discussion of China's position on bombing or invading Taiwan see http://www.washingtonpost.com/wp-dyn/articles/A7467-2000Jul8.html.

7. For additional details about Russia's SS-X-27 missile programme, see http://www.softwar.net/SS27.html, which claims that: "The first deployment was reported to be in a SS-19 silo complex located at Tatishchevo in January of 1998 ... The mobile Russian SS-27 also raises serious proliferation questions since the Moscow Institute of Thermal Technology is providing the SS-27 design to China. China intends to produce the TOPOL-M missile under the designation 'Dong Feng' (East Wind) DF-41. The DF-41 is expected to be deployed with Chinese manufactured nuclear warheads also designed with the aid of U.S. super computers."

8. The overview is from William Broad, "A missile defence with limits: the ABC's of the Clinton plan," http://www10.nytimes.com/library/world/americas/063000missile-plan.html (30 June 2000). Additional details of NMD architecture can be found at: http://www.acq.osd.mil/bmdo/bmdolink/html.

9. Burton Richter, "It doesn't take rocket science," *Washington Post*, 23 July 2000, BO2. http://www.washingtonpost.com/wp-dyn/articles/A25940-2000Jul22.html.

10. Ibid.

11. Why would any leader be foolish enough to launch an attack on the United States in the first place, critics will ask. But that popular question overlooks the other objective of NMD: to prevent opponents from believing that they can deter the United States (or NATO) from launching a conventional attack. Protecting United States (and

Canadian/European) bargaining leverage in Bosnia, Kosovo, Iraq, Taiwan, and North Korea is as relevant to NMD as protecting North America from a missile attack. Critics may be right in claiming the North Korean leaders are not likely to launch an attack (or even issue a nuclear threat) unless some crisis (for example, one that involves the United States over South Korea) escalates out of control. But the key question for United States policy-makers is whether, in the midst of this hypothetical conventional war, the probability of confronting an explicit nuclear threat from North Korea increases or decreases with/without NMD. In earlier stages of this crisis, does the probability of confronting a conventional war initiated by North Korea increase or decrease with/without NMD? And, to step even further back, does the probability of confronting crisis escalation by North Korea increase or decrease with/without NMD? And in terms of the initial stage of the crisis, are the incentives for crisis management and resolution higher or lower for the North Korean leadership with/without NMD? At each stage of the crisis United States NMD is likely to be more stabilizing, unless North Korean leaders are irrational. The critics respond that that is precisely the problem—North Korean leaders may be irrational and completely upset the logic associated with the simplistic, "rational choice" interpretation of the scenario offered by proponents of NMD. Fair enough, but in addition to defending the culturally insensitive assertion that North Korean leaders are less rational than Western leaders, critics are now faced with having to explain why North Korea would contemplate launching a ballistic missile, an action they previously concluded was highly unlikely and a fabrication of the military industrial complex. See Harvey, "Proliferation, rogue-states and national missile defence" (*Canadian Military Journal*, forthcoming, 2000).

12. A simple web search for keywords "nuclear proliferation" or "ballistic missile proliferation" should provide the optimists with sufficient information to reconsider their position. Here is a small sample:
http://www.fas.org/irp/threat/bm-threat.htm;
http://www.fas.org/nuke/guide/iran/missile/;
http://www.stimson.org/policy/nucleardangers.htm;
http://www.cia.gov/cia/publications/nie/nie99msl.html;
http://www.editors.sipri.se/pubs/pressre/akbk.html;
http://www.cato.org/pubs/fpbriefs/fpb-051es.html;
http://www.ceip.org/programs/npp/bmtestimony.htm;
http://www.defenselink.mil/news/Jan1999/to1201999_to120md.html;
http://www.cns.miis.edu/pubs/npr/moltz975.htm (Center for NonProliferation Studies);
http://www.nuclearfiles.org/prolif/;
http://www.aph.gov.au/library/pubs/cib/1999-2000/2000cib01.htm.

13. The "technological limitations" arguments has now shifted from debates about whether a defence system should be deployed at all to debates about which system is better: NMD or the alternative offered by Putin during the Clinton-Putin summit in June 2000. Now that Russia has acknowledged United States concerns about ballistic missile proliferation, the key question is whether a theatre missile defense system (based on boost phase interceptor technology) is more likely than NMD to succeed. Russia has so far been unclear on specifics.

14. One week after the second of three failed interceptor tests, the United States Senate approved a $1.9 billion expenditure for the next stage of the NMD programme. Audrey Hudson, "Senate approves $1.9 billion for missile defense," *Washington Times*, 14 July 2000.

15. A failure with booster separation was not even considered among the thousands of potential problems, for obvious reasons. For commentary by Kadish immediately following the failed test, see http://www.cnn.com/2000/US/07/08/missile.defense.04/index.html.

Postscript

In the introduction, mention was made of the Rumsfeld Commission's report in 1998 which highlighted the need to respond to the ballistic missile threat. Since then, Donald Rumsfeld has been appointed Secretary of Defense in the Bush Administration and is a key figure in the "war on terrorism." Given the events of September 11, 2001 and the resulting military action, attention has shifted to threats posed by terrorist organizations. The preoccupation is now focused on the dangers of biological or chemical weapons that might be delivered by terrorist groups rather than by ballistic missiles. What impact do these developments have on perspectives around the need for a BMD defense? In the future, will the American administration be more or less likely to pursue the idea? Harvey notes that Canadian critics argue that Canada could reject a BMD without hurting American-Canadian relations. With the renewed emphasis on the need for more cooperation on continental security, would it be harder now for Canada to opt out of a BMD program?

Infotrac Keyword Search

"BMD" or "ballistic missile defense"

Suggested Additional Reading

Cirincione, Joseph and Frank von Hippel. *The Last Fifteen Minutes: Ballistic Missile Defense in Perspective*, Washington D.C.: Coalition to Reduce Nuclear Dangers, 1996.

Cirincione, Joseph. "Why the Right Lost the Missile Defense Debate." *Foreign Policy*, (Spring 1997).

Dean, Jonathon. "Step-by-Step Control Over Ballistic and Cruise Missiles." *Disarmament and Diplomacy*, 31 (October 1998): 2–11.

Fitzgerald, Francis. *Way Out There in The Blue*. New York: Simon & Schuster, 2000.

Gronland, Lisbeth and David Wright. "Missile Defense: The Sequel." *Technology Review*, (May–June 1997): 29–36.

Handberg, Roger. *Ballistic Missile Defense and the Future of American Security: Agendas, Perceptions, Technology, and Policy*. Westport, Conn.: Praeger Publishers, 2001.

Karp, Aaron, *Ballistic Missile Proliferation: The Politics and Technics*, Stockholm: Stockholm International Peace Research Institute, 1995.

Lewis, George et al. "Why National Missile Defense Won't Work." *Scientific American*, (August, 1999): 36–41.

Mendelsohn, Jack. "Missile Defense: And It Still Won't Work." *Bulletin of the Atomic Scientists*, (May–June 1999): 29–31.

Website Resources

Carnegie Endowment for International Peace   Very extensive list of resources on missile defense issues.

Center for Security Policy   A conservative think-tank with an extensive collection of publications on BMD.

Council for a Livable World   A lobby opposed to BMD provides a range of resource materials. Check its detailed briefing book on MND.

The Heritage Foundation   Noted conservative think-tank with many pro-BMD resources. Note its materials suggesting that terrorist attacks show why BMD is needed now more than ever.

Project Ploughshares   Canada's leading peace-research institute has a large archive of resources on BMD from all perspectives.

ISSUE**TEN**

Do Biological Differences Predispose Men to War?

✔ **YES**

FRANCIS FUKUYAMA, "Women and the Evolution of World Politics," *Foreign Affairs* 77: 5 (September–October 1998): 24–40

✘ **NO**

J. ANN TICKNER, "Why Women Can't Run the World: International Politics According to Francis Fukuyama," *International Studies Review* 1: 3 (Fall 1999): 3–11

In a recent article in a leading international relations journal, Martin van Creveld writes: "From North America through Europe to Australia, the military of developed countries are in retreat" ("The Great Illusion: Women in the Military," *Millennium: Journal of International Studies* 29, no. 2, 2000: 429). He notes that during the last decade, "scarcely a day goes by in any developed country without some military program being cancelled, a procurement decision postponed, or personnel being made redundant" (Ibid.).

In examining this trend, van Creveld notes several critical factors. The proliferation of nuclear weapons after World War II made serious conflict between major states virtually unthinkable. With the end of the Cold War, there was less justification for maintaining military budgets. During the past decade, a preoccupation with deficits and a desire to reduce financial costs has made development of new weapons systems unattractive politically.

But Van Creveld notes that something else appears to be happening. The decline of western militaries is taking place at the same time that there has been an unprecedented influx of women into the military. Before 1914, very few women took active part in wars and no military force included them as a regular part of its establishment. The two world wars, and the unprecedented demands for personnel, led to a rethinking of the role for women. For the first time, nations established women's auxiliary corps. In World War I, some 150,000 women served. In World War II this number increased to 1.5 million women, 800,000 from the Soviet Union alone. Despite the increasing number of women in uniform, however, they still primarily played a support role. Most served in clerical positions or as doctors and nurses. Even in the Soviet Union, where the communist ideology placed more emphasis on the equality of women, few women participated in actual combat roles. Less than one percent of Soviet pilots were women.

This situation began to change in the late 1960s. As the Vietnam War lost popular support in the United States, it became more difficult to recruit men to the military. As a result, military planners became more willing to open the doors to female recruits. By the late 1970s, women made up about seven percent of the American armed forces. Soon other European countries joined in, recruiting larger numbers of women into their armed forces. Once in the military, women insisted that they have the same opportunities for advancement as their male counterparts. Since advancement in the military is limited to those with combat experience, women demanded that all roles be open to them, not just nontraditional, non-combat positions. Thus, the 1980s and 1990s saw not only an expansion in the number of women serving in the military, but their growing presence in combat positions. In recent war efforts in the Persian Gulf, Kosovo, and Afghanistan, it is not unusual to see press pictures of young mothers in combat fatigues kissing a baby goodbye as they are shipped out to the front.

How should this changing role of women in the military be interpreted? Does it represent a victory for the feminist movement and an indicator of the progress that women are making in competing with men more successfully in all endeavours? Van Creveld claims that the growing role of the women in the military is not a gain for the equality of women. The reason women are enlisting in larger numbers is not to enter into combat as equals with men, but because "they hope that they will not be obliged to fight." Thus, for Van Creveld, the "feminization" of the military is not so much a sign of the advancement of women as it is a symptom of the continuing decline of militaries in the West. In fact, Creveld argues that in countries where wars continue to be fought, women rarely play key leadership and combat roles and instead are involved "overwhelmingly as eggerson, camp followers, and victims" (441).

Van Creveld's article raises intriguing questions about the relationship between gender and war. Traditionally, war and military service have been the most gendered forms of human activity. Yet they have rarely received sustained attention from international relations scholars. Long dominated by males who largely work within a realist framework, the gendered nature of war has largely been taken for granted. In the past fifteen years, a growing feminist literature on war has tried to address these issues; mainstream international-relations scholarship, however, has largely ignored these findings. Joshua Goldstein, in analyzing this situation, notes that a recent major survey of the literature on war and peace showed that only one-tenth of one percent of the writings were devoted to the issue of gender and war.

The gender blinders in mainstream international-relations studies carry over to the foreign-policy establishment. The influential monthly *Foreign Affairs* did not carry a single article about gender issues between 1990 and 1996. In 1998, however, *Foreign Affairs* carried an article on gender and war that attracted considerable debate. Written by Francis Fukuyama, the article addresses the issues raised by van Creveld—what should one make of the "feminization" of the military? Fukuyama argues that biological differences make women more peaceful. As a result, he says, the "feminization of world politics" over the last century (since the suffrage movement) has been a significant contributor to today's "democratic zone of peace."

Although the article was entitled "Women and the Evolution of World Politics," the editors of *Foreign Affairs* chose the more sensational title "What If Women Ran the World?" to run on the front cover. Fukuyama's response appears at first to be largely in sympathy with feminist perspectives. If women ran the world, he says, it would likely be more peaceful and less violent. But Fukuyama bases his argument on an appeal to sociobiology and the inherited biological characteristics of men and women. Thus, he critiques those feminists who argue that war is largely a socially constructed cultural institution that reflects the values of a patriarchal society. In drawing out the implications of his argument, he comes to conclusions that could be used as a basis for arguing against the continued feminization of world politics.

In the second reading, J. Ann Tickner, a leading feminist scholar, critiques Fukuyama's argument. She warns of the dangers of debating the merits of Fukuyama's appeal to sociobiology, arguing that this approach deflects attention away from the real issues about gender and war that need to be addressed.

✔ **YES**
Women and the Evolution of World Politics
FRANCIS FUKUYAMA

World politics has become increasingly feminized in the 20th century as women have gained political power and exercised it. This evolution in the sexual basis of politics should be reflected in changes in international relations as the correlation between gender and antimilitarism decreases the use of force to solve international problems.

CHIMPANZEE POLITICS

In the world's largest captive chimp colony at the Burger's Zoo in Arnhem, Netherlands, a struggle worthy of Machiavelli unfolded during the late 1970s. As described by primatologist Frans de Waal, the aging alpha male of the colony, Yeroen, was gradually unseated from his position of power by a younger male, Luit. Luit could not have done this on the basis of his own physical strength, but had to enter into an alliance with Nikkie, a still younger male. No sooner was Luit on top, however, than Nikkie turned on him and formed a coalition with the deposed leader to achieve dominance himself. Luit remained in the background as a threat to his rule, so one day he was murdered by Nikkie and Yeroen, his toes and testicles littering the floor of the cage.

Jane Goodall became famous studying a group of about 30 chimps at the Gombe National Park in Tanzania in the 1960s, a group she found on the whole to be peaceful. In the 1970s, this group broke up into what could only be described as two rival gangs in the northern and southern parts of the range. The biological anthropologist Richard Wrangham with Dale Peterson in their 1996 book *Demonic Males* describes what happened next. Parties of four or five males from the northern group would go out, not simply defending their range, but often penetrating into the rival group's territory to pick off individuals caught alone or unprepared. The murders were often grisly, and they were celebrated by the attackers with hooting and feverish excitement. All the males and several of the females in the southern group were eventually killed, and the remaining females forced to join the northern group. The northern Gombe chimps had done, in effect, what Rome did to Carthage in 146 B.C.: extinguished its rival without a trace.

There are several notable aspects to these stories of chimp behavior. First, the violence. Violence within the same species is rare in the animal kingdom, usually restricted to infanticide by males who want to get rid of a rival's offspring and mate with the mother. Only chimps and humans seem to have a proclivity for routinely murdering peers. Second is the importance of coalitions and the politics that goes with coalition-building. Chimps, like humans, are intensely social creatures whose lives are preoccupied with achieving and maintaining dominance in status hierarchies. They threaten, plead, cajole, and bribe their fellow chimps to join with them in alliances, and their dominance lasts only as long as they can maintain these social connections.

Finally and most significantly, the violence and the coalition-building is primarily the work of males. Female chimpanzees can be as violent and cruel as the males at times; females compete with one another in hierarchies and form coalitions to do so. But the most murderous violence is the province of males, and the nature of female alliances is different. According to de Waal, female chimps bond with females to whom they feel some emotional attachment; the males are much more likely to make alliances for purely instrumental, calculating reasons. In other words, female chimps have relationships; male chimps practice realpolitik.

Chimpanzees are man's closest evolutionary relative, having descended from a common chimp-like ancestor less than five million years ago. Not only are they very close on a genetic level, they show many behavioral similarities as well. As Wrangham and Peterson note, of the 4,000 mammal and 10 million or more other species, only chimps and humans live in male-bonded, patrilineal communities in which groups of males routinely engage in aggressive, often murderous raiding of their own species. Nearly 30 years ago, the anthropologist Lionel Tiger suggested that men had special psychological resources for bonding with one another, derived from their need to hunt cooperatively, that explained their dominance in group-oriented activities from politics to warfare. Tiger was roundly denounced by feminists at the time for suggesting that there were biologically based psychological differences between the sexes, but more recent research, including evidence from primatology, has confirmed that male bonding is in fact genetic and predates the human species.

THE NOT-SO-NOBLE SAVAGE

It is all too easy to make facile comparisons between animal and human behavior to prove a polemical point, as did the socialists who pointed to bees and ants to prove that nature endorsed collectivism. Skeptics point out that human beings have language, reason, law, culture, and moral values that make them fundamentally different from even their closest animal relative. In fact, for many years anthropologists endorsed what was in effect a modern version of Rousseau's story of the noble savage: people living in hunter-gatherer societies were pacific in nature. If chimps and modern man had a common proclivity for violence, the cause in the latter case had to be found in civilization and not in human nature.

A number of authors have extended the noble savage idea to argue that violence and patriarchy were late inventions, rooted in either the Western Judeo-Christian tradition or the capitalism to which the former gave birth. Friedrich Engels anticipated the work of later feminists by positing the existence of a primordial matriarchy, which was replaced by a violent and repressive patriarchy only with the transition to agricultural societies. The problem with this theory is, as Lawrence Keeley points out in his book *War Before Civilization*, that the most comprehensive recent studies of violence in hunter-gatherer societies suggest that for them war was actually more frequent, and rates of murder higher, than for modern ones.

Surveys of ethnographic data show that only 10–13 percent of primitive societies never or rarely engaged in war or raiding; the others engaged in conflict either continuously or at less than yearly intervals. Closer examination of the peaceful cases shows that they were frequently refugee populations driven into remote locations by prior warfare or groups protected by a more advanced society. Of the Yanomamo tribesmen studied by Napoleon Chagnon in Venezuela, some 30 percent of the men died by violence; the !Kung San of the Kalahari desert, once characterized as the "harmless people," have a higher murder rate than New York or Detroit. The sad archaeological evidence from sites like Jebel Sahaba in Egypt, Talheim in Germany, or Roaix in France indicates that systematic mass killings of men, women, and children occurred in Neolithic times. The Holocaust, Cambodia, and Bosnia have each been described as a unique, and often as a uniquely modern, form of horror. Exceptional and tragic they are indeed, but with precedents stretching back tens if not hundreds of thousands of years.

It is clear that this violence was largely perpetrated by men. While a small minority of human societies have been matrilineal, evidence of a primordial matriarchy in which women dominated men, or were even relatively equal to men, has been hard to find. There was no age of innocence. The line from chimp to modern man is continuous.

It would seem, then, that there is something to the contention of many feminists that phenomena like aggression, violence, war, and intense competition for dominance in a status hierarchy are more closely associated with men than women. Theories of international relations like realism that see international politics as a remorseless struggle for power are in fact what feminists call a gendered perspective, describing the behavior of states controlled by men rather than states per se. A world run by women would follow different rules, it would appear, and it is toward that sort of world that all postindustrial or Western societies are moving. As women gain power in these countries, the latter should become less aggressive, adventurous, competitive, and violent.

The problem with the feminist view is that it sees these attitudes toward violence, power, and status as wholly the products of a patriarchal culture, whereas in fact it appears they are rooted in biology. This makes these attitudes harder to change in men and consequently in societies. Despite the rise of women, men will continue to play a major, if not dominant, part in the governance of postindustrial countries, not to mention less-developed ones. The realms of war and international politics in particular will remain controlled by men for longer than many feminists would like. Most important, the task of resocializing men to be more like women—that is, less violent—will run into limits. What is bred in the bone cannot be altered easily by changes in culture and ideology.

THE RETURN OF BIOLOGY

We are living through a revolutionary period in the life sciences. Hardly a week goes by without the discovery of a gene linked to a disease, condition, or behavior, from cancer to obesity to depression, with the promise of genetic therapies and even the outright manipulation of the human genome just around the corner. But while developments in molecular biology have been receiving the lion's share of the headlines, much progress has been made at the behavioral level as well. The past generation has seen a revival in Darwinian thinking about human psychology, with profound implications for the social sciences.

For much of this century, the social sciences have been premised on Emile Durkheim's dictum that social facts can be explained only by prior social facts and not by biological causes. Revolutions and wars are caused by social facts such as economic change, class inequalities, and shifting alliances. The standard social science model assumes that the human mind is the terrain of ideas, customs, and norms that are the products of man-made culture. Social reality is, in other words, socially constructed: if young boys like to pretend to shoot each other more than young girls, it is only because they have been socialized at an early age to do so.

The social-constructionist view, long dominant in the social sciences, originated as a reaction to the early misuse of Darwinism. Social Darwinists like Herbert Spencer or outright racists like Madsen Grant in the late nineteenth and early twentieth centuries used biology, specifically the analogy of natural selection, to explain and justify everything from class stratification to the domination of much of the world by white Europeans. Then Franz Boas, a Columbia anthropologist, debunked many of these theories of European racial superiority by, among other things, carefully measuring the head sizes of immigrant children and noting that they tended to converge with those of native Americans when fed an American diet. Boas, as well as his well-known students Margaret Mead and Ruth Benedict, argued that apparent differences between human groups could be laid at the doorstep of culture rather than nature. There were, moreover, no cultural universals by which Europeans or Americans could judge other cultures. So-called primitive peoples were not inferior, just different. Hence was born both the social constructivism and the cultural relativism with which the social sciences have been imbued ever since.

But there has been a revolution in modern evolutionary thinking. It has multiple roots; one was ethology, the comparative study of animal behavior. Ethologists like Konrad Lorenz began to notice similarities in behavior across a wide variety of animal species, suggesting common evolutionary origins. Contrary to the cultural relativists, they found that not only was it possible to make important generalizations across virtually all human cultures (for example, females are more selective than males in their choice of sexual partners) but even across broad ranges of animal species. Major breakthroughs were made by William Hamilton and Robert Trivers in the 1960s and 1970s in explaining instances of altruism in the animal world not by some sort of instinct towards species survival but rather in terms of "selfish genes" (to use Richard Dawkins' phrase) that made social behavior in an individual animal's interest. Finally, advances in neurophysiology have shown that the brain is not a Lockean tabula rasa waiting to be filled with cultural content, but rather a highly modular organ whose components have been adapted prior to birth to suit the needs of socially oriented primates. Humans are hard-wired to act in certain predictable ways.

The sociobiology that sprang from these theoretical sources tried to provide a deterministic Darwinian explanation for just about everything, so it was perhaps inevitable that a reaction would set in against it as well. But while the term socio-biology has gone into decline, the neo-Darwinian thinking that spawned it has blossomed under the rubric of evolutionary psychology or anthropology and is today an enormous arena of new research and discovery.

Unlike the pseudo-Darwininsts at the turn of the century, most contemporary biologists do not regard race or ethnicity as biologically significant categories. This stands to reason: the different human races have been around only for the past hundred thousand years or so, barely a blink of the eye in evolutionary time. As countless authors have pointed out, race is largely a socially constructed category: since all races can (and do) interbreed, the boundary lines between them are often quite fuzzy.

The same is not true, however, about sex. While some gender roles are indeed socially constructed, virtually all reputable evolutionary biologists today think there are profound differences between the sexes that are genetically rather than culturally rooted, and that these differences extend beyond the body into the realm of the mind. Again, this stands to reason from a Darwinian point of view: sexual reproduction has been going on not for thousands but hundreds of millions of years. Males and females compete not just against their environment but against one another in a process that Darwin labeled "sexual selection," whereby each sex seeks to maximize its own fitness by choosing certain kinds of mates. The psychological strategies that result from this never-ending arms race between men and women are different for each sex.

In no area is sex-related difference clearer than with respect to violence and aggression. A generation ago, two psychologists, Eleanor Maccoby and Carol Jacklin, produced an authoritative volume on what was then empirically known about differences between the sexes. They showed that certain stereotypes about gender, such as the assertion that girls were more suggestible or had lower self-esteem, were just that, while others, like the idea that girls were less competitive, could not be proven one way or another. On one issue, however, there was virtually no disagreement in the hundreds of studies on the subject: namely, that boys were more aggressive, both verbally and physically, in their dreams, words, and actions than girls. One comes to a similar conclusion by looking at crime statistics. In every known culture, and from what we know of virtually all historical time periods, the vast majority of crimes, particularly violent crimes, are committed by men. Here there is also apparently a genetically determined age specificity to violent aggression: crimes are overwhelmingly committed by young men between the ages of 15 and 30. Perhaps young men are everywhere socialized to behave violently, but this evidence, from different cultures and times, suggests that there is some deeper level of causation at work.

At this point in the discussion, many people become uncomfortable and charges of "biological determinism" arise. Don't we know countless women who are stronger, larger, more decisive, more violent, or more competitive than their male counterparts? Isn't the proportion of female criminals rising relative to males? Isn't work becoming less physical, making sexual differences unimportant? The answer to all of these questions is yes: again, no reputable evolutionary biologist would deny that culture also shapes behavior in countless critical ways and can often overwhelm genetic predispositions. To say that there is a genetic basis for sex differences is simply to make a statistical assertion that the bell curve describing the distribution or a certain characteristic is shifted over a little for men as compared with women. The two curves will overlap for the most part, and there will be countless individuals in each population who will have more of any given characteristic than those of the other sex. Biology is not destiny, as tough-minded female leaders like Margaret Thatcher, Indira Gandhi, and Golda Meir have proven. (It is worth pointing out, however, that in male-dominated societies, it is these kinds of unusual women who will rise to the top.) But the statistical assertion also suggests that broad populations of men and women, as opposed to exceptional individuals, will act in certain predictable ways. It also suggests that these populations are not infinitely plastic in the way that their behavior can be shaped by society.

FEMINISTS AND POWER POLITICS

There is by now an extensive literature on gender and international politics and a vigorous feminist subdiscipline within the field of international relations theory based on the work of scholars like J. Ann Tickner, Sara Ruddick, Jean Bethke Elshtain, Judith Shapiro, and others. This literature is too diverse to describe succinctly, but it is safe to say that much of it was initially concerned with understanding how international politics is "gendered," that is, run by men to serve male interests and interpreted by other men, consciously and unconsciously, according to male perspectives. Thus, when a realist theorist like Hans Morganthau or Kenneth Waltz argues that states seek to maximize power, they think that they are describing a universal human characteristic when, as Tickner points out, they are portraying the behavior of states run by men.

Virtually all feminists who study international politics seek the laudable goal of greater female participation in all aspects of foreign relations, from executive mansions and foreign ministries to militaries and universities. They disagree as to whether women should get ahead in politics by demonstrating traditional masculine virtues of toughness, aggression, competitiveness, and the willingness to use force when necessary, or whether they should move the very agenda of politics away from male preoccupations with hierarchy and domination. This ambivalence was demonstrated in the feminist reaction to Margaret Thatcher, who by any account was far tougher and more determined than any of the male politicians she came up against. Needless to say, Thatcher's conservative politics did not endear her to most feminists, who much prefer a Mary Robinson or Gro Harlem Brundtland as their model of a female leader, despite—or because of—the fact that Thatcher had beaten men at their own game.

Both men and women participate in perpetuating the stereotypical gender identities that associate men with war and competition and women with peace and cooperation. As sophisticated feminists like Jean Bethke Elshtain have pointed out, the traditional dichotomy between the male "just warrior" marching to war and the female "beautiful soul" marching for peace is frequently transcended in practice by women intoxicated by war and by men repulsed by its cruelties. But like many stereotypes, it rests on a truth, amply confirmed by much of the new research in evolutionary biology. Wives and mothers can enthusiastically send their husbands and sons off to war; like Sioux women, they can question their manliness for failing to go into battle or themselves torture prisoners. But statistically speaking it is primarily men who enjoy the experience of aggression and the camaraderie it brings and who revel in the ritualization of war that is, as the anthropologist Robin Fox puts it, another way of understanding diplomacy.

A truly matriarchal world, then, would be less prone to conflict and more conciliatory and cooperative than the one we inhabit now. Where the new biology parts company with feminism is in the causal explanation it gives for this difference in sex roles. The ongoing revolution in the life sciences has almost totally escaped the notice of much of the social sciences and humanities, particularly the parts of the academy concerned with feminism, postmodernism, cultural studies, and the like. While there are some feminists who believe that sex differences have a natural basis, by far the majority are committed to the idea that men and women are psychologically identical, and that any differences in behavior, with regard to violence or any other characteristic, are the result of some prior social construction passed on by the prevailing culture.

THE DEMOCRATIC AND FEMININE PEACE

Once one views international relations through the lens of sex and biology, it never again looks the same. It is very difficult to watch Muslims and Serbs in Bosnia, Hums and Tutsis in Rwanda, or militias from Liberia and Sierra Leone to

Georgia and Afghanistan divide themselves up into what seem like indistinguishable male-bonded groups in order to systematically slaughter one another, and not think of the chimps at Gombe.

The basic social problem that any society faces is to control the aggressive tendencies of its young men. In hunter-gatherer societies, the vast preponderance of violence is over sex, a situation that continues to characterize domestic violent crime in contemporary postindustrial societies. Older men in the community have generally been responsible for socializing younger ones by ritualizing their aggression, often by directing it toward enemies outside the community. Much of that external violence can also be over women. Modern historians assume that the Greeks and Trojans could not possibly have fought a war for ten years over Helen, but many primitive societies like the Yanomamo do exactly that. With the spread of agriculture 10,000 years ago, however, and the accumulation of wealth and land, war turned toward the acquisition of material goods. Channeling aggression outside the community may not lower societies' overall rate of violence, but it at least offers them the possibility of domestic peace between wars.

The core of the feminist agenda for international politics seems fundamentally correct: the violent and aggressive tendencies of men have to be controlled, not simply by redirecting them to external aggression but by constraining those impulses through a web of norms, laws, agreements, contracts, and the like. In addition, more women need to be brought into the domain of international politics as leaders, officials, soldiers, and voters. Only by participating fully in global politics can women both defend their own interests and shift the underlying male agenda.

The feminization of world politics has, of course, been taking place gradually over the past hundred years, with very positive effects. Women have won the right to vote and participate in politics in all developed countries, as well as in many developing countries, and have exercised that right with increasing energy. In the United States and other rich countries, a pronounced gender gap with regard to foreign policy and national security issues endures. American women have always been less supportive than American men of U.S. involvement in war, including World War II, Korea, Vietnam, and the Persian Gulf War, by an average margin of seven to nine percent. They are also consistently less supportive of defense spending and the use of force abroad. In a 1995 Roper survey conducted for the Chicago Council on Foreign Relations, men favored U.S. intervention in Korea in the event of a North Korean attack by a margin of 49 to 40 percent, while women were opposed by a margin of 30 to 54 percent. Similarly, U.S. military action against Iraq in the event it invaded Saudi Arabia was supported by men by a margin of 62 to 31 percent and opposed by women by 43 to 45 percent. While 54 percent of men felt it important to maintain superior world wide military power, only 45 percent of women agreed. Women, moreover, are less likely than men to see force as a legitimate tool for resolving conflicts.

It is difficult to know how to account for this gender gap; certainly, one cannot move from biology to voting behavior in a single step. Observers have suggested various reasons why women are less willing to use military force than men, including their role as mothers, the fact that many women are feminists (that is, committed to a left-of-center agenda that is generally hostile to U.S. intervention), and of partisan affiliation (more women vote Democratic than men). It is unnecessary to know the reason for the correlation between gender and antimilitarism, however, to predict that increasing female political participation will probably make the United States and other democracies less inclined to use power around the world as freely as they have in the past.

Will this shift toward a less status- and military-power-oriented world be a good thing? For relations between states in the so-called democratic zone of peace, the answer is yes. Consideration of gender adds a great deal to the vigorous and interesting debate over the correlation between democracy and peace that has taken place in the past decade. The "democratic peace" argument, which underlies the foreign policy of the Clinton administration as well as its predecessors, is that democracies tend not to fight one another. While the empirical claim has been contested, the correlation between the degree of consolidation of liberal democratic institutions and interdemocratic peace would seem to be one of the few nontrivial generalizations one can make about world politics. Democratic peace theorists have been less persuasive about the reasons democracies are pacific toward one another. The reasons usually cited—the rule of law, respect for individual rights, the commercial nature of most democracies, and the like—are undoubtedly correct. But there is another factor that has generally not been taken into account: developed democracies also tend to be more feminized than authoritarian states, in terms of expansion of female franchise and participation in political decision-making. It should therefore surprise no one that the historically unprecedented shift in the sexual basis of politics should lead to a change in international relations.

THE REALITY OF AGGRESSIVE FANTASIES

On the other hand, if gender roles are not simply socially constructed but rooted in genetics, there will be limits to how much international politics can change. In anything but a totally feminized world, feminized policies could be a liability.

Some feminists talk as if gender identities can be discarded like an old sweater, perhaps by putting young men through mandatory gender studies courses when they are college freshmen. Male attitudes on a host of issues, from child-rearing and housework to "getting in touch with your feelings," have changed dramatically in the past couple of generations due to social pressure. But socialization can accomplish only so much, and efforts to fully feminize young men will probably be no more successful than the Soviet Union's efforts to persuade its people to work on Saturdays on behalf of the heroic Cuban and Vietnamese people. Male tendencies to band together for competitive purposes, to dominate status hierarchies, and to act out aggressive fantasies toward one another can be rechanneled but never eliminated.

Even if we can assume peaceful relations between democracies, the broader world scene will still be populated by states led by the occasional Mobutu, Milosevic, or Saddam. Machiavelli's critique of Aristotle was that the latter did not take foreign policy into account in building his model of a just city: in a system of competitive states, the best regimes adopt the practices of the worst in order to survive. So even if the democratic, feminized, postindustrial world has evolved into a zone of peace where struggles are more economic than military, it will still have to deal with those parts of the world run by young, ambitious, unconstrained men. If a future Saddam Hussein is not only sitting on the world's oil supplies but is armed to the hilt with chemical, biological, and nuclear weapons, we might be better off being led by women like Margaret Thatcher than, say, Gro Harlem Brundtland. Masculine policies will still be required, though not necessarily masculine leaders.

The implications of evolutionary biology for the hot-button issue of women in the military is not as straightforward as one might think. The vast majority of jobs in a modern military organization are in the enormous support tail that trails behind the actual combat units, and there is no reason that women cannot perform them as well if not better than men. While men have clearly evolved as cooperative hunters and fighters, it is not clear that any individual group of women will perform less well than any individual group of men in combat. What is much more problematic is integrating men and women into the same combat units, where they will be in close physical proximity over long periods of time. Unit cohesion, which is the bedrock on which the performance of armies rests, has been traditionally built around male bonding, which can only be jeopardized when men start competing for the attention of women. Commanders who encourage male bonding are building on a powerful natural instinct; those who try to keep sexual activity between healthy 20-year-old men and women in check through "zero tolerance" policies and draconian punishments are, by contrast, seeking to do something very unnatural. Unlike racial segregation, gender segregation in certain parts of the military seems not just appropriate but necessary.

THE MARGARET THATCHERS OF THE FUTURE

The feminization of democratic politics will interact with other demographic trends in the next 50 years to produce important changes. Due to the precipitous fall in fertility rates across the developed world since the 1960s, the age distribution of countries belonging to the Organization of Economic Cooperation and Development will shift dramatically. While the median age for America's population was in the mid-20s during the first few decades of the twentieth century, it will climb toward 40 by 2050. The change will be even more dramatic in Europe and Japan, where rates of immigration and fertility are lower. Under the UN Population Division's low-growth projections, the median age in Germany will be 55, in Japan 53, and in Italy 58.

The graying of the population has heretofore been discussed primarily in terms of the social security liability it will engender. But it carries a host of other social consequences as well, among them the emergence of elderly women as one of the most important voting blocs courted by mid-21st century politicians. In Italy and Germany, for example, women over 50, who now constitute 20 percent of the population, will account for 31 percent in 2050. There is no way, of course, of predicting how they will vote, but it seems likely that they will help elect more women leaders and will be less inclined toward military intervention than middle-aged males have traditionally been. Edward Luttwak of the Center for Strategic and International Studies has speculated that the fall in family sizes makes people in advanced countries much more leery of military casualties than people in agricultural societies, with their surpluses of young, hotheaded men. According to demographer Nicholas Eberstadt, three-fifths of Italy's offspring in 2050 will be only children with no cousins, siblings, aunts, or uncles. It is not unreasonable to suppose that in such a world tolerance of casualties will be even lower.

By the middle of the next century, then, Europe will likely consist of rich, powerful, and democratic nations with rapidly shrinking populations of mostly elderly people where women will play important leadership roles. The United States, with its higher rates of immigration and fertility, will also have more women leaders but a substantially younger population. A much larger and poorer part of the world will consist of states in Africa, the Middle East, and South Asia with young, growing populations, led mostly by younger men. As Eberstadt points out, Asia outside of Japan will buck the trend toward feminization because the high rate of abortion of female fetuses has shifted their sex ratios sharply in favor of men. This will be, to say the least, an unfamiliar world.

LIVING LIKE ANIMALS?

In Wrangham and Peterson's *Demonic Males* (said to be a favorite book of Hillary Rodham Clinton, who has had her own to contend with), the authors come to the pessimistic conclusion that nothing much has changed since early hominids branched off from the primordial chimp ancestor five million years ago. Group solidarity is still based on aggression against other communities; social cooperation is undertaken to achieve higher levels of organized violence. Robin Fox has argued that military technology has developed much faster than man's ability to ritualize violence and direct it into safer channels. The Gombe chimps could kill only a handful of others; modern man can vaporize tens of millions.

While the history of the first half of the twentieth century does not give us great grounds for faith in the possibility of human progress, the situation is not nearly as bleak as these authors would have us believe. Biology, to repeat, is not destiny. Rates of violent homicide appear to be lower today than during mankind's long hunter-gatherer period, despite gas ovens and nuclear weapons. Contrary to the thrust of postmodernist thought, people cannot free themselves entirely from biological nature. But by accepting the fact that people have natures that are often evil, political, economic, and social systems can be designed to mitigate the effects of man's baser instincts.

Take the human and particularly male desire to dominate a status hierarchy, which people share with other primates. The advent of liberal democracy and modern capitalism does not eliminate that desire, but it opens up many more peaceful channels for satisfying it. Among the American Plains Indians or the Yanomamo, virtually the only way for a man to achieve social recognition was to be a warrior, which meant, of course, excelling at killing. Other traditional societies might add a few occupations like the priesthood or the bureaucracy in which one could achieve recognition. A modern, technological society, by contrast, offers thousands of arenas in which one can achieve social status, and in most of them the quest for status leads not to violence but to socially productive activity. A professor receiving tenure at a leading university, a politician winning an election, or a CEO increasing market share may satisfy the same underlying drive for status as being the alpha male in a chimp community. But in the process, these individuals have written books, designed public policies, or brought new technologies to market that have improved human welfare.

Of course, not everyone can achieve high rank or dominance in any given status hierarchy, since these are by definition zero-sum games in which every winner produces a loser. But the advantage of a modern, complex, fluid society is, as economist Robert Frank has pointed out, that small frogs in large ponds can move to smaller ponds in which they will loom larger. Seeking status by choosing the right pond will not satisfy the ambitions of the greatest and noblest individuals, but it will bleed off much of the competitive energy that in hunter-gatherer or agricultural societies often has no outlet save war. Liberal democracy and market economies work well because, unlike socialism, radical feminism, and other utopian schemes, they do not try to change human nature. Rather, they accept biologically grounded nature as a given and seek to constrain it through institutions, laws, and norms. It does not always work, but it is better than living like animals.

✗ NO
Why Women Can't Run the World: International Politics According to Francis Fukuyama
J. ANN TICKNER

Feminist perspectives on international relations have proliferated in the last ten years, yet they remain marginal to the discipline as a whole, and there has been little engagement between feminists and international relations (IR) scholars. As I have suggested elsewhere, I believe this is largely due to misunderstandings about feminist IR scholarship that are reflected in questions that feminists frequently are asked when presenting their work to IR audiences.[1] Many of these misunderstandings reflect considerable ontological and epistemological differences, which are particularly acute with respect to mainstream IR approaches. In other words, feminists and IR scholars frequently talk about different worlds and use different methodologies to understand them.[2]

A different kind of misunderstanding, also prevalent, arises from the fact that talking about gender involves issues of personal identity that can be very threatening, even in academic discourse. Feminists are frequently challenged by their critics for seeming to imply (even if it is not their intention) that women are somehow "better" than men. In IR, this often comes down to accusations that feminists are implying that women are more peaceful than men or that a world run by women would be less violent and morally superior. Critics will support their challenges by reference to female policymakers, such as Margaret Thatcher, Golda Meir, or Indira Gandhi, who, they claim, behaved exactly like men.[3]

Most IR feminists would deny the assertion that women are morally superior to men. Indeed, many of them have claimed that the association of women with peace and moral superiority has a long history of keeping women out of power, going back to the debates about the merits of female suffrage in the early part of the century. The association of women with peace can play into unfortunate gender stereotypes that characterize men as active, women as passive; men as agents, women as victims; men as rational, women as emotional. Not only are these stereotypes damaging to women, particularly to their credibility as actors in matters of international politics and national security, but they are also damaging to peace.

As a concept, peace will remain a "soft" issue, utopian and unrealistic, as long as it is associated with femininity and passivity.[4] This entire debate about aggressive men and peaceful women frequently comes up when issues about women and world politics are on the table. Moreover, it detracts from what feminists consider to be more pressing agendas such as striving to uncover and understand the disadvantaged socioeconomic position of many of the world's women and why women are so poorly represented among the world's policymakers.

A current version using the claim that women are more peaceful than men to women's disadvantage, and the types of agenda-deflecting debates it may engender, can be found in Francis Fukuyama's recent article, "Women and the Evolution of World Politics," in *Foreign Affairs*, as well as in the commentaries on it in the subsequent issue.[5] Unlike the type of criticism mentioned above that, often mistakenly, accuses feminists of claiming the morally superior high ground for women, Fukuyama boldly asserts that indeed women *are* more peaceful than men. But, as has so often been the case, Fukuyama deploys his argument to mount a strong defense for keeping men in charge. Not only does this type of reasoning feed into more strident forms of backlash against women in international politics, but it also moves our attention further away from more important issues. Hypothesizing about the merits or disadvantages of women in charge, or debating the relative aggressiveness of men and women, does little to address the realities of a variety of oppressions faced by women worldwide. Fukuyama's views not only deflect from important feminist agendas, but they also support some disturbing trends in IR more generally, which are reinforcing polarized views of the world in terms of civilization clashes and zones of peace versus zones of turmoil.[6]

Foreign Affairs chose to publish Fukuyama's article under the cover title (in red) "What If Women Ran the World?" This title was surely designed to provoke (and perhaps frighten) its readers, most of whom are probably unfamiliar with IR feminist scholarship. More problematically, it is likely that this will be the only article that mentions feminist IR scholarship to which readers of *Foreign Affairs* will be exposed.[7] Responses in the subsequent issue of *Foreign Affairs* were, for the most part, quite hostile to Fukuyama's position, and asked what was wrong with his argument. Katha Politt asserts, "just about everything."[8] Nevertheless, by focusing on the need to rebut Fukuyama's sociobiological and over-generalized portrayal of warlike men and peaceful women, these responses, like the article itself, refocus conversations in unproductive ways that do little to clarify many of the issues with which IR feminists are concerned.

Fukuyama's article is not overtly antifeminist. Indeed, he cites what he calls "a vigorous feminist subdiscipline within the field of international relations" (p. 32) quite favorably, albeit chastising postmodernism for its commitment to social constructionism and radical feminism for its misguided utopianism (p. 40).[9] Curiously, in light of his misgivings about utopianism, Fukuyama offers a seemingly optimistic, even radical vision of a different, relatively peaceful, "feminized" world (in the West at least), where men's aggressive animal instincts have been tamed and channeled into productive activities associated with liberal democracy and capitalism. Fukuyama supports his central claim—that men have "naturally" aggressive instincts—by comparing their behavior to the aggressive and even Machiavellian behavior of male chimpanzees in Gombe National Park in Tanzania. This type of aggression, which, Fukuyama argues, is atypical of most intraspecies behavior, is as true of male humans as it is of their nearest evolutionary relatives, male chimpanzees.

Fukuyama notes that, as with chimps, violence in all types of human societies has been perpetrated largely by men. He develops this claim by documenting recent discoveries in the life sciences and evolutionary psychology that find profound differences between the sexes, especially in areas of violence and aggression. Whereas he is careful to say that culture also shapes human behavior, Fukuyama believes that this line of thinking will replace social constructionist views of gender differences that came about as a reaction to the misuse of Darwinism to reinforce racial superiority and class stratification. In other words, these findings have profound implications for all the social sciences.

Fukuyama also notes that feminists prefer to see such behavior as a product of patriarchal culture rather than rooted in human biology because biologically rooted behavior is harder to change: therefore, they will not be happy with his claims. Fukuyama goes on to hypothesize about a feminized world that would follow different rules. He sees the realization of such a world as a distinct possibility, at least in the West, as women gain more political power. What he calls the "feminization" of world politics has been taking place gradually as women have won the right to vote. The right to vote, along with a relative increase in numbers of elderly women, has resulted in a gender gap with respect to voting on issues of foreign policy and national security, with women being less supportive of national defense spending and involvement in war than men. In spite of these trends, Fukuyama predicts that men will continue to play an important role, particularly in international politics where toughness and aggression are still required.

Given the difficulties of changing genetically programmed behavior and presuming that this new world would have to include socially constructed feminized men, this hypothetical picture seems like a considerable leap from reality. Even though Fukuyama's portrait of this feminized world is seemingly sympathetic, I believe that his message is, in fact, deeply conservative—offering one more iteration of the well-established argument that a "realistic" view of international politics demands that "real" men remain in charge. Accepting its premises actually silences, rather than promotes, feminist agendas and women's equality. Although many of his claims can be successfully challenged on empirical grounds, as his critics demonstrated by their rebuttals in *Foreign Affairs*, his views feed into a conservative agenda that serves not to put women in control, but to keep them out of positions of power.

Why is this the case? Because Fukuyama tells us that no matter how attractive it may seem, we should not move further toward this feminized world; instead, we must keep things the way they are—with strong men at the helm. He argues that women are not able to deal with today's threats that come from violent leaders, such as Slobodan Milosevic, Saddam Hussein, and Mobutu Sese Seko. On the horizon are threats from states in the Middle East, Africa, and South Asia, led by aggressive younger men unsocialized in the ways of mature democracies.

Fukuyama claims that people in agricultural societies, presumably outside the zone of peace, with their surpluses of young, hotheaded men, are less concerned with military casualties and therefore more prone to pick fights (p. 38), an assertion that appears to have disturbingly racist overtones.

Closer to home, citing the necessity for combat readiness in the face of these dangers, Fukuyama, by advocating separation of men and women in single-sex military units, effectively advises against women in combat positions. Although he does not deny that women could do as well in combat as men (which was indeed demonstrated in the Gulf War), he claims that their presence destroys combat units' cohesion, which he believes is built on male bonding (p. 37). This "false necessity," together with the need to channel what he calls biologically rooted male desire to dominate into successful competition in universities, corporations, and political arenas, seems to imply fewer rather than more opportunities for women in both military and civilian life.[10]

And what of men's biological or naturally aggressive tendencies?[11] As feminists have pointed out, one of the main reasons why today's military is recruiting women is because not enough "aggressive" men are joining up. Much of basic training involves overcoming men's reluctance to kill. Advances in military technology have depersonalized warfare so that the problems associated with the long-standing reluctance of men in combat to fire their weapons have been lessened.[12] Violence inside states, which is more prevalent in the United States than in many states outside the western democratic "zone of peace," about which Fukuyama speaks so favorably, stems at least as much from lack of economic opportunities as it does from innate male aggression.[13] Tenure in universities and corporate success are not just about satisfying the need for social recognition of alpha males; they are much-needed guarantees of income and job security, important to both men *and* women.

If we were to accept that men do have aggressive tendencies, the leap from aggressive men to aggressive states is problematic, as many international relations scholars have pointed out.[14] Do men's aggressive tendencies really get channeled into international war, thus leading to the possibility of domestic peace between wars? The high homicide rate in the United States makes one skeptical of this possibility, whereas Switzerland, a country with one of the lowest homicide rates in the world, is rarely an international aggressor. If most men, particularly young men, have violent tendencies, as Fukuyama claims, why is it that some states are so much more peaceful than others? Statesmen do not choose war lightly. Nor is war generally decided at the ballot box where, according to Fukuyama, significant numbers of women are voting for peace. It has often been older men who send young men off to war to fight for what they see as legitimate national interests. Would American policymakers in the 1960s or today's Vietnam veterans be satisfied with the explanation that America fought in Vietnam as an outlet for the aggressive tendencies of its young men?

Now to turn to some of the real feminist agendas for international politics—agendas that are completely silenced by Fukuyama's article. I know of no international relations feminists who hypothesize about or advocate women running the world, as the cover title of Fukuyama's article and the turn-of-the century illustration depicting a woman in boxing gloves "flooring her beau" (p. 29) suggest. Although Fukuyama includes socially feminized men (who must have overcome their aggressive genes) in the ruling coalitions of his feminized world, such a world is unappealing and sure to threaten, or perhaps amuse, those presently in charge, as well as reinforce culturally defined gender stereotypes about international politics and women.

What IR feminists *have* argued for is getting rid of idealistic associations of women with peace. Associations of women with peace, idealism, and impracticality have long served to disempower women and keep them in their place, which is out of the "real world" of international politics.

When Fukuyama claims that sociobiology was misused at the turn of the century, with respect to race and ethnicity, he too, is misusing it. He does this under the guise of evidence about profound genetically rooted differences between the sexes by inferring that these differences predetermine men's and women's different (and unequal) roles with respect to contemporary international politics.[15] Of course, feminists want women to participate more fully in global politics and contribute to making the world a less dangerous place. But, rather than killing each other, haven't many men been working toward this goal also?

Wherever men's genes may have pointed, they founded the discipline of international relations by trying to understand why states go to war and trying to devise institutions to diminish its likelihood in the future. Preferred futures are not feminized, but ones in which women *and* men participate in reducing damaging and unequal hierarchical social structures, such as gender and race.

Many feminists would agree that biology may indeed be a contributing factor to certain aggressive behaviors. Yet understanding and working to lessen various insecurities that women face can only be achieved if we acknowledge a need for diminishing socially constructed gender hierarchies that result in the devaluation of women's lives and their economic and social contributions to society. In spite of Fukuyama's assertion that social constructionism is being effectively challenged by new findings in evolutionary biology, the fact that the majority of subsistence farmers in Africa are women, while men are more frequently found in the more prosperous cash crop sector, can hardly be explained by biology alone. Culturally assigned roles, which have little to do with biology, diminish women's socioeconomic position in most societies. Speculating about women in charge, whether their boxing gloves are on or off, seems far removed from the lived reality of the vast majority of the world's women. Katha Pollitt states that even in the United States, where Fukuyama claims that women are fast gaining political power, women constitute only 12 percent of Congress and, after 80 years of female suffrage, have not even won the right to paid maternity leave or affordable day care.[16] Running foreign policy, she concludes, seems like a fantasy.[17] Nevertheless, by focusing on these unlikely futures, Fukuyama effectively silences more pressing agendas and deflects investigations away from trying to understand why the world's women are so often disempowered and even oppressed.

Of course, IR feminists are concerned with issues of war and peace. But rather than debating whether men are aggressive and women peaceful, they are asking new questions about conflict, as well as trying to expand conventional agendas. Feminist agendas include human rights issues such as rape in war, military prostitution, refugees (the majority of whom are women and children), and more generally issues about civilian casualties.[18] Even though civilians now account for well over 80 percent of wartime casualties, understanding the reasons for and consequences of these disturbing trends has not been at the center of international relations investigations. Feminists have also joined the debate about whether security should be defined more broadly to include issues of structural and ecological violence. With this question in mind, feminists are investigating the often negative effects of structural adjustment and economic globalization on women, as well as problems associated with the degradation of the environment.[19] All of these issues seem closer to women's lived realities than debates about their likelihood of running the world.

By asserting that developed democracies tend to be more feminized than authoritarian states, and by linking this to the popular claim about the relative peacefulness of democracies, Fukuyama obscures deeper truths and hides more progressive practical possibilities.

Kal Holsti has suggested that a better explanation for "zones of peace," which actually extend well beyond Western democracies, is the diminished likelihood of war between strong states with governments seen as legitimate by their populations.[20] There are very few states where some have reached a critical mass in political decisionmaking, which makes any link between the democratic peace and the political participation of women tenuous at best. A more fruitful line of investigation is one that is illustrated by a study outlining the results of survey data collected in several Middle Eastern countries, democratic and otherwise. The data show that in the case of the Arab-Israeli dispute, women are not less militaristic than men, but both women and men who are more supportive of gender equality are also more favorably disposed to compromise.[21] A cluster of such attitudes could be the building blocks not for a more feminized world, whatever that may mean, but for a more just and peaceful world in which gender and other social hierarchies of domination, which have resulted in the subordination of women, are diminished.

The debate surrounding Fukuyama's article appears to have stimulated a race to demonstrate who can be more aggressive than whom. Marshaling evidence of women's participation in wars, with pictures of female soldiers on parade and documenting women's violence in matters of abuse of children and servants, Ehrenreich and Pollitt assure us that women can be every bit as aggressive as men.[22]

Are these the debates we should be having? Surely they deflect from the real issues with which international relations scholars are struggling—namely to try to understand the roots of war and what can be done to prevent it. Investigating the enormous variations in levels of conflict across history and societies is surely a more promising place to begin than in deterministic, biologically rooted theories about the aggressive nature of men. International relations feminists have added a new and important dimension to these investigations.

Rather than joining debates about aggressive men and peaceful women, IR feminists are striving to better understand unequal social hierarchies, including gender hierarchies, which contribute to conflict, inequality, and oppression. Evidence suggests that war is more likely in societies with greater gender inequality. Intentionally or not, Fukuyama's musings about women running the world deflect attention away from this more pressing agenda of working toward a world with increased gender equality. Such a world could, I believe, be a less conflictual one for both women and men. Let us turn our attention to more productive conversations between feminist and international relations scholars about the evolution of world politics, conversations that strive to better understand how such a world could be realized.

NOTES

1. J. Ann Tickner, "You Just Don't Understand: Troubled Engagements Between Feminists and IR Theorists," *International Studies Quarterly* 41, No. 4 (1997), pp. 611–632.

2. The symposium in *International Studies Quarterly* 42, No. 1 (1998), pp. 193–209 is an exception to the lack of engagement. It also demonstrates some of the conversational difficulties to which I refer.

3. Tickner, "You Just Don't Understand," p. 613.

4. For elaboration on this claim, see Jean B. Elshtain, "The Problem with Peace," in Jean Elshtain and Sheila Tobias, eds., *Women, Militarism and War* (Savage, Md.: Rowman and Littlefield, 1990), pp. 255–266; and Christine Sylvester, "Some Dangers In Merging Feminist and Peace Projects," *Alternatives* 12, No. 4 (1987), pp. 493–509.

5. Francis Fukuyama, "Women and the Evolution of World Politics," *Foreign Affairs* 77, No. 5 (1998), pp. 24–40; and Barbara Ehrenreich, Katha Pollitt, et al., "Fukuyama's Follies: So What If Women Ran the World?" *Foreign Affairs* 78, No. 1 (1999), pp. 118–129.

6. See, for example, Samuel Huntington, *The Clash of Civilizations and the Remaking of World Order* (New York: Simon and Schuster, 1996); and Max Singer and Aaron Wildavsky, *The Real World Order: Zones of Peace, Zones of Turmoil* (Chatham, N.J.: Chatham House Publishers, 1993). Fukuyama also draws on the democratic peace argument to support his global polarization view. For further discussion of this point,

see Miriam Fendius Elman, "The Never-Ending Story: Democracy and Peace," in this issue of *International Studies Review*.

7. Indeed, Fukuyama's article has received much worldwide attention in the press, as well as in the foreign policy community. See, for example, Katie Grant, "Why We Need Men in Our New Feminine World," *Glasgow Herald*, January 11, 1999, p. 13.

8. Katha Pollitt, "Father Knows Best," *Foreign Affairs* 78, No. 1 (1999), p. 123.

9. Since *Foreign Affairs* does not allow footnotes, it is often difficult to know to which specific literature Fukuyama refers when making such criticism.

10. This type of argument has shown up in more virulent forms. See, for example, Harvey Mansfield, "Why a Woman Can't Be More Like a Man," *Wall Street Journal*, November 3, 1997, p. A22. Mansfield accuses feminists of "feminizing America." He argues that women are not cut out for war and that men must be allowed to fulfill their traditional role as protectors, a role that is being undermined as women gain equal access to jobs outside the home. Fukuyama also addresses some of these issues in his new book *The Great Disruption: Human Nature and the Reconstitution of Social Order* (New York: Free Press, 1999).

11. R. Brian Ferguson, "Perilous Positions," *Foreign Affairs* 78, No. 1 (1999), p. 125 claims that chimpanzees' naturally aggressive tendencies are also questionable. He contends that the Gombe chimps became aggressive only after human-induced changes in their feeding patterns.

12. While there has been evidence documenting soldiers' reluctance to kill, I realize this is a controversial argument. For further discussion of this issue, including positions that refute this hypothesis, see Joanna Bourke, *An Intimate History of Killing: Face to Face Killing in Twentieth Century Warfare* (London: Granta Books, 1999).

13. The recent dramatic drop in the crime rate in the United States seems to support this position.

14. For examples, see Kenneth Walz, *Theory of International Politics* (Reading, Mass.: Addison Wesley, 1979), Chap. 2; and Jane Jaquette, "States Make War," *Foreign Affairs* 78, No. 1 (1999), pp. 128–129.

15. The popularity of sociobiological arguments about sex differences is evidenced by a cover story in *Time*, March 8, 1999, p. 57, by Barbara Ehrenreich entitled "The Real Truth about the Female." Ehrenreich's position is much more sympathetic to women— she cites feminist scholars who are doing serious work in this area—but it is indicative of a trend toward emphasizing the sociobiological roots of human behavior and its appeal to wider audiences. Many feminists would probably argue that biology and culture are mutually constitutive of each other.

16. Pollitt, "Father Knows Best," p. 125.

17. Katie Grant points out that if, as Fukuyama claims, men can become feminized, we do not necessarily need women to run things, even in this new gentler world. Grant, "Why We Need Men."

18. Ruth Seifert, "The Second Front: The Logic of Sexual Violence in Wars," *Women's Studies International Forum* 19, No. 1–2 (1996), pp. 35–43; Cynthia Enloe, *Bananas, Beaches and Bases: Making Feminist Sense of International Politics* (Berkeley: University of California Press, 1990); Katharine Moon, *Sex Among Allies: Military Prostitution in US-Korean Relations* (New York: Columbia University Press, 1997); and Susan Forbes Martin, *Refugee Women* (London: Zed Books, 1992).

19. Eleonore Kofman and Gillian Youngs, eds., *Globalization: Theory and Practice* (London: Pinter, 1996); Maria Mies and Vandana Shiva, *Ecofeminism* (London: Zed Books, 1993); and Rosi Braidotti et al., *Women, the Environment and Sustainable Development: Towards a Theoretical Synthesis* (London: Zed Books, 1994).

20. Kalevj Holsti, *The State, War, and the State of War* (Cambridge, U.K.: Cambridge University Press, 1996).

21. Mark Tessler and Ina Warriner, "Gender, Feminism, and Attitudes Toward International Conflict: Exploring Relationships with Survey Data from the Middle East," *World Politics* 49, No. 2 (1997), pp. 250–281.

22. Barbara Ehrenreich, "Men Hate War Too," *Foreign Affairs* 18, No. 1 (1999), pp. 120–121; and Katha Pollitt, "Father Knows Best," p. 123.

Postscript

In discussing this issue it is useful to note that feminists do not take a single approach to the issue of war and peace. Some feminists believe that women's experiences are fundamentally different from men's. According to this view, the problem is not that men and women are different but that sexist cultures devalue "feminine" qualities instead of celebrating and promoting them. Women, because of their greater experience with nurturing and human relations, are generally more effective than men in conflict resolution and group decision-making. But they are less effective than men in combat. Such feminists see these gender differences as partly biologically based, as Fukuyama claims. But others see them as entirely culturally constructed. Many of these feminists see the role of women as primarily to oppose the male-constructed war system and all the symptoms of male dominance that go with it.

Other feminists argue that women are in fact equal to men in ability and that biological differences are not important. The gendering of war reflects male discrimination against women, like other forms of sexism. Women have the right to participate in all social and political roles (including military ones) without facing discrimination. The exclusion of women from positions of power in international relations is unfair and prevents women from making important contributions to society. However, such feminists do not believe that the inclusion of women in the military will fundamentally change the international system, a given country's foreign policy, or war itself. Unlike Fukuyama, they see no hidden dangers in the "feminization" of world politics.

Infotrac Keyword Search

"Gender + war" or "women + war" or "women + military"

Suggested additional Readings

Damousi, Joy and Marilyn Lake, eds. *Gender and War.* Cambridge: Cambridge University Press, 2001.

Elshtain, Jean Bethke. *Women and War.* New York: Basic Books, 1987.

Enloe, Cynthia. *Bananas, Beaches and Bases: Making Feminist Sense of International Politics.* Berkeley: University of California Press, 1989.

Pierson, Ruth Roach, ed. *Women and Peace: Theoretical, Historical and Practical Perspectives.* New York: Croom Helm, 1987.

Tickner, J. Ann. *Gender in International Relations: Feminist Perspectives on Achieving Global Security.* New York: Columbia University Press, 1992.

Van Der Dennen, J. and V. Falger. *Sociobiology and Conflict: Evolutionary Perspectives on Competition, Cooperation, Violence and Warfare.* New York: Chapman & Hall, 1990.

Weinstein, Laurie and Christie White. *Wives and Warriors: Women and the Military in the United States and Canada.* Westport, CT: Bergin & Garvey, 1997.

Whitworth, Sandra. *Feminism and International Relations: Towards a Political Economy of Gender in Interstate and Non-Governmental Institutions.* New York: St. Martin's, 1994.

Wicks, Stephen. *Warriors and Wildmen: Men, Masculinity, and Gender.* Westport, CT: Bergin & Garvey, 1996.

Wrangham, Richard and Dale Peterson. *Demonic Males: Apes and the Origins of Human Violence.* New York: Houghton Mifflin, 1996.

York, Jodi. "The Truth(s) about Women and Peace." *Peace Review* 8, no. 3 (1996): 323–29.

Website Resources

Feminist Theory Website (Virginia Tech University)   Provides research materials and information on a range of gender issues.

Feminist Theory and Gender Studies (International Studies Association)   A section of the International Studies Association, this site provides a variety of resources and links on feminist theory and international relations.

H-Net, H-Minevera: Women and War   A discussion network devoted to the study of women in war and in the military, worldwide and in all historical areas. This site also has links to related journals, announcements, and other websites.

War and Gender   This site is maintained by Joshua Goldstein and includes materials and discussions relating to his book, *War and Gender: How Gender Shapes the War System and Vice Versa.* Includes full text of chapter one of this book.

ISSUE**ELEVEN**

Is Peacekeeping Irrelevant?

✔ **YES**
CHARLES KRAUTHAMMER, "Peacekeeping Is for Chumps," *Saturday Night* (November 1995): 73–76

✘ **NO**
PETER VIGGO JAKOBSEN, "Overload, Not Marginalization, Threatens UN Peacekeeping," *Security Dialogue* 31, no. 2 (June 2000): 167–178

Monitoring elections in Namibia, El Salvador, Angola, Cambodia, and Mozambique. Protecting designated "safe areas" in Bosnia-Herzegovina from attack. Providing military protection for the delivery of humanitarian assistance in Somalia and the former Yugoslavia. Assisting in the reconstruction of governmental and police functions in Haiti and Cambodia. Aiding in the demilitarization of particular regions and parties in Bosnia and Angola. These are just some of a long list of "peacekeeping" activities that the United Nations has undertaken since the end of the Cold War. As the stature and popularity of the United Nations has increased in early 1990s, so too have the expectations and demands made of it. As of mid-1997, UN peacekeeping forces inlcuded more than 70,000 troops, observers, and civilian police.

Despite the key role that peacekeeping has come to play in the UN's mission, nowhere in the UN Charter are there provisions for peacekeeping operations. Nonetheless, they are one of the UN's most creative innovations and serve as an example of how the organization has attempted to adapt to meet changing global needs. Peacekeeping may be defined as "the prevention, containment, moderation and termination of hostilities between or within states through the medium of a peaceful third party intervention organized and directed internationally, using multilateral forces of soldiers, police and civilians to restore and maintain peace" (*International Peace Academy, Peacekeeper's Handbook,* International Peace Academy, New York: Permagon Press, 1984, p. 22). Traditionally, the primary objective of peacekeeping has been to prevent violence, thereby creating an environment conducive to peace.

The terms peacekeeping and peacemaking are not synonymous, however. The latter refers to the use of such methods as negotiation, mediation, arbitration, conciliation, and judicial settlement to resolve a dispute. Peacekeeping is premised on the idea that the warring states or factions will be reluctant to use violence against an impartial peacekeeping force backed by the international community. Thus, U.N. peacekeepers are not combatants and may use their weapons only in self-defence. Furthermore, during the Cold War, most forces have not included personnel from the major powers, but instead have relied on the support of middle powers. No state has contributed more to UN peacekeeping than Canada, which has participated in more operations and provided more personnel than any other country in the world.

Since 1947, when the first force was sent to monitor violation of the Greek border, the United Nations has launched over twenty peacekeeping operations. The UN's responsibilities have ranged from maintaining a cease-fire to restoring order to supervising troop withdrawal to overseeing national elections. Between 1947 and 1975, the United Nations established fourteen peacekeeping missions that, with few exceptions, were successful in preventing violence and minimizing bloodshed. Then came a period of marked decline, during which only one new operation (the UN Interim Force in Lebanon) was created. It was far from effective, although much of the blame for its failure rests with the warring parties that refused to cease hostilities. The tide turned in the late 1980s when, for the first time, the five permanent members of the Security Council began to cooperate to promote international peace and security. In 1988, four important peacekeeping forces were established, for which the United Nations was awarded the Nobel Peace Prize. Since May 1989, more than thirty peacekeeping operations have been approved by the United Nation's Security Council.

While this new era of UN peacekeeping has seen some notable successes, it has also witnessed a string of embarrassments and failures. Peacekeeping operations in Cambodia and Angola have been followed by renewed fighting. Responses to humanitarian crises in Somalia in 1992 and Rwanda in 1994 have been criticized for being too slow and ill-planned. In particular, the UN operations in Somalia led to scandals within the Canadian, Belgian, and Italian militaries. Bosnia exposed the weakness of the UN in carrying out peacekeeping operations in conflicts where the belligerents have little desire to cooperate.

While some critics have focused on identifying ways to improve the effectiveness of UN peacekeeping, others have questioned the very conceptual basis of peacekeeping itself. One such skeptic is Charles Krauthammer, a noted American journalist and editor. In his article, Krauthammer questions whether peacekeeping, or any other form of collective security action, can ensure international stability and order. In particular, he criticizes peacekeeping as "perhaps the most widely accepted illusion at work in today's 'Utopianism.'" In the second article, Peter Viggo Jakobsen examines some of the recent criticisms of peacekeeping, particularly from those who believe that it has become increasingly marginalized. Jakobsen argues that any weaknesses in peacekeeping arise from UN efforts to do too much, thus leading to an overreach in their resources. He discusses ways in which the UN's capacity can be strengthened.

✔ YES
Peacekeeping Is for Chumps
CHARLES KRAUTHAMMER

It is now the third time this century that we have come under the illusion of having found a new way to reorder the world. These illusions invariably come in the immediate aftermath of a great war. And, though we are hardly conscious of it, our time, marked by victory in the Cold War, is a classically postwar time.

The period immediately after the First World War, the heyday of U.S. President Woodrow Wilson, was characterized by an extraordinary belief in the power of parchment and goodwill, harnessed to an apparatus of collective security, to preserve the peace. The U.S. Senate rejected the League of Nations, but the American people and, indeed, much of the world, generally embraced the spirit of Wilsonianism. Its apotheosis was the 1928 Kellogg-Briand Pact, solemnly signed by sixty-four nations (including Germany, Japan, and Italy), declaring war outlawed. So seriously was this exercise in naivety taken that its author, Secretary of State Frank Kellogg, received the 1929 Nobel Peace Prize.

As another secretary of state, Henry Stimson, explained, this piece of parchment would protect against aggression "by the sanction of public opinion which can be made one of the most potent sanctions of the world.... Those critics who scoff at it have not accurately appraised the evolution in world opinion since the Great War."

This staggering belief in opinion and reason and dialogue ended not just in tragedy but in parody when Senator William Borah, the Idaho Republican, upon hearing that war had broken out in Europe in September, 1939, said: "Lord, if only I could have talked with Hitler, all this might have been avoided."

The second bout of Utopianism came with victory in the Second World War. Franklin Roosevelt's secretary of state, Cordell Hull, upon returning from the Moscow conference of 1943, declared that soon "there will no longer be need for spheres of influence, for alliances, for balance of power, or any other of the special arrangements through which, in the unhappy past, the nations strove to safeguard their security or to promote their interests."

This time we would have the United Nations, a real League of Nations with the United States at its centre, with real enforcement provisions, with an active Security Council. This time we would create Tennyson's parliament of man.

By 1947, the West had become disabused of this Utopianism. The Truman Doctrine, the Marshall Plan, and then the military alliance of NATO, all of them bulwarks against the Soviet Union, announced the end of our second innocence. Throughout the Cold War, it was these institutions, exactly the ones Hull said we would not need, that safeguarded our security and promoted our interests.

And now Round Three. In the 1990s, we have been told, indeed by such ostensible political realists as George Bush, that a New World Order is dawning, an order based on global community, international law, collective security, peace-keeping, the United Nations, and true multilateralism.

This is nonsense, dangerous nonsense, as dangerous as the nonsense that followed the first two great wars of this century. Marx said that all great events in world history reappear in one fashion or another, the first time as tragedy, the second time as farce. And I would add: the third time as hallucination. In plain truth, international relations remains in precisely the same state it was one and two and five centuries ago. As Henry Kissinger put it, "In the end, peace can be achieved only by hegemony [the leadership of one power] or by balance of power. There is no other way."

(Kissinger, incidentally, is said to have once had an unusual hiatus in his diplomatic career when, after being secretary of state, he took the unlikely job of director of the Biblical Zoo in Israel. An American reporter heard about this, went to the scene to find out what all the commotion was about, and found a huge crowd gathered around a most amazing exhibit: a cage in which a lion and lamb were lying down together. The reporter rushed to Kissinger and said: "Dr. Kissinger, for three thousand years people have been trying to make the lion and the lamb lie down together and you are the first to have ever succeeded. How did you do it?"

"Every day a new lamb," replied Kissinger.)

I, too, am from the lamb-a-day school of international relations. Peace can only achieved by hegemony or balance of power. It is achieved not by reason, not by dialogue, not by peacekeeping, not by the UN, not by multilateralism.

Peacekeeping is perhaps the most widely accepted illusion at work in today's Utopianism. It is important that this be understood here in Canada—here, where faith in peacekeeping is unabated. Canada has participated in almost every UN mission undertaken since its own Lester Pearson, then minister of external affairs, invented peacekeeping in 1956. Pearson proposed the creation of what became UNEF, the United Nations Emergency Force, to help extract the British and French from the Suez fiasco. The insertion of UNEF, in place of British and French troops, did help save face. But anyone who thought that it really preserved the peace was rudely disabused of that notion when it was put to the test almost exactly a decade later.

In May, 1967, Egyptian President Gamal Abdel Nasser decided to force a showdown with Israel, closing the Strait of Tiran, choking off Israel's access to the south, and ordering UNEF out of the Sinai. UN Secretary-General U Thant immediately agreed. The war that UNEF was supposed to prevent followed.

What made this episode doubly memorable and doubly painful for Canadians was the fact that Canadian peacekeepers were among the UNEF forces expelled. That expulsion, as York University historian J.L. Granatstein has written, "amounted almost to a national humiliation."

Well, a quarter of a century later in Croatia, we had an eerie replay of this same scenario. In 1991, at the beginning of the Balkan war, the Serbs swept into Croatia and captured about a third of the region. UN forces were then inserted as peace-keepers between Croatia and the Serb territories in the Krajina.

This summer, the Croatians decided it was time for war again. Unlike the Egyptians, however, they did not even bother with the formality of ordering the UN out. They simply rolled their tanks through and around UN positions, and conquered the Krajina within three days, leaving the UN peacekeepers in their wake, cruelly exposed as utterly helpless and pointless. They have since been withdrawn.

These episodes highlight the fundamental truth of peacekeeping: if you already have peace, you don't really need peacekeepers. Today, for example, there is peace between Israel and Egypt. The peacekeeping forces in the Sinai are a nice symbol of that peace. That is a good thing. But it is a very minor thing.

On the other hand, where there is no peace—as in Croatia in August, as in the Sinai in May and June, 1967, or as in Bosnia this fall—then peacekeepers are use-less. They can stand by or withdraw.

Well, you might say: haven't the peacekeepers in Bosnia actually woken up and done something real now? Hasn't the strategic-bombing campaign really made a difference, relieving the siege of Sarajevo, pushing the Serbs towards a negotiated settlement?

Yes, the strategic-bombing campaign has had some effect. But that is precisely because it was not peacekeeping. It is war-making, delivered by a war-making machine called NATO, a military alliance of the sort Cordell Hull once decried and declared obsolete, an alliance that kept the peace—the UN did not—during the Cold War and is now trying to impose a peace in Bosnia. With its air strikes, NATO is taking sides militarily on the side of the weaker in the hope of creating a new equi-librium—a new balance of power—because that is how peace comes about: either through hegemony or through balance of power, not the urging of blue helmets.

In the United States, one says this at some risk. Congressional Republicans have proposed cuts in the UN and peacekeeping budgets. Arthur Schlesinger, echoing the Clinton administration, denounced these Republican attacks on peacekeeping as a blow to "collective security." This is a wilful misuse of the term. UN blue-helmet operations, like the one in Bosnia, are not instruments of collective security. They roll back no aggressors. They are quite the opposite. They are handholding and temporizing operations, means by which the great powers pretend to do something in a place where they do not really want to be doing anything.

Real collective security, on the other hand, is what happened in the Gulf War. There, great powers got together to use military force to repel aggression—the one true example of collective security in the postwar era, and one, I might note, that Schlesinger and other purported champions of collective security vigorously opposed.

Note that this real kind of collective security, with the great powers banding together ad hoc to repel aggression, can occur with UN blessing or without. The UN is quite irrelevant.

Which brings us to the second great post–Cold War illusion—the UN itself.

In August, Canada's minister of national defence, David Collenette, addressing the National Forum on Canada's International Relations, said that "Canada sees the United Nations as our best hope for achieving global security."

Now I admit that the UN has a building, a budget, and bureaucrats. I admit that it has fine service organizations like UNICEF and the UN High Commissioner for Refugees. And I admit that it does good works in things like fisheries law. But when it comes to war and peace, to international security, in other words, to the mission for which it was originally established, it is an empty vessel.

It is a guarantor of nothing. The guarantor of security and peace today is, as it has been for five hundred years, the great powers, and, most specifically, given the unipolar structure of today's international system, the sole remaining super-power, the United States.

Again, that was demonstrated with stunning clarity in the Gulf War. The liberation of Kuwait was attended by all kinds of UN resolutions and declarations and proclamations. It has led to a lot of pious talk about the UN as the guarantor of collective security in some new post–Cold War order. But this is to confuse cause and effect, the U.S. with the UN. The UN guaranteed nothing. In the Gulf, without the U.S. leading and prodding, bribing and blackmailing, no one would have stirred. Nothing would have been done: no embargo, no threat of force, no Desert Storm. The world would have written off Kuwait the way the last body pledged to collective security, the League of Nations, wrote off Ethiopia when Mussolini rolled through in 1935.

Indeed, the entire apparatus of UN resolutions and declarations was a conscious product of American diplomacy, a conscious effort to give the Gulf War the air of international legitimacy. The UN was to be the flag of convenience under which the U.S. and its sundry friends would liberate Kuwait.

Contrast this with Croatia, a situation precisely the opposite, where the U.S. consciously absented itself and indeed gave the green light for Croatia to defy and sweep by the UN and conquer the Krajina. UN resolutions and reservations and protests came to nothing.

The debate over the UN is usually portrayed as between liberals who support it and believe in its promise, and conservatives who oppose it and fear its reach. The fact is, both sides of this debate are wrong. The UN is not a panacea and it's not a threat. It is merely irrelevant. It does not matter.

Indeed, on issues of war and peace, to speak of the UN as having some kind of separate, independent existence, some kind of will of its own, is spooky. It does not. The UN is, at most, a creature of the Security Council. When American diplomacy manages to neutralize the Russians and the Chinese, as in the Gulf War, the Security Council becomes a creature of the United States. And when, on the other hand, the great powers cannot agree, which generally means when the U.S. is either stymied by opposition by the other great powers or simply not interested in an issue, as with Bosnia until very, very recently, nothing gets done. It simply does not matter what UN Secretary-General Boutros Boutros-Ghali thinks. It matters what Bill Clinton thinks.

This is not to say that the UN could never be, in theory or in principle, an independent actor on the stage. It could be, but it would, like all other independent actors with any influence on the world, need an army. And not an army made up of units of the Italian and Canadian and Pakistani armies. We have seen how such an army operates in Somalia and it was a catastrophe. In Somalia, the different units were calling their capitals to ask whether or not to follow the orders of the local UN commander. This was not an army. This was group therapy in fatigues.

The UN would need more than that. In a speech to the UN General Assembly last month, Canada's foreign-affairs minister André Ouellet proposed that the UN develop a rapid-reaction force of 5,000 military and civilian personnel, ready at a moment's notice to fly into areas of unrest and prevent full-scale war from breaking out. These troops would report to an "operational-level headquarters," a mobile squad of between thirty and fifty UN personnel.

Fine. But if we were serious about the UN, as we are not today, these forces would constitute a real army consisting of soldiers *recruited as individuals*. It would be a kind of foreign legion for desperadoes, mercenaries, and idealists from around the world. They would come to New York to swear allegiance to Boutros-Ghali and the blue flag. It is a good idea and it would make an even better movie. But I doubt it will ever come to pass.

The great powers are simply not going to stand for another independent actor pushing them around in the world. They have enough trouble with the other countries of the world as it is. Nonetheless, I repeat: in the absence of an army, the UN—with no general staff, no military expertise, no command structure—is a fiction when it comes to war and peace. A meeting room.

The other reason the great powers do not want an armed UN is that an unarmed, fictional UN actually serves their purposes. It is a favourite dumping ground for messy and minor operations that they, and especially the United States, do not want to undertake on their own. After over fifty years of heroic struggle against Nazism and Communism, the American people are not particularly enthusiastic about mopping up the messes left behind. Accordingly, they are happy to assign thankless police work to the UN.

The situation puts one in mind of a story about W.C. Fields. A friend found him on his deathbed reading the Bible. "You?" he asked. "What are you doing reading the Bible?" Fields looked up and said: "Looking for loopholes." In the post–Cold War world the UN is the ultimate loophole, the perfect dodge for a reluctant America.

During the latter part of the Cold War, when the UN was corrupt and deeply anti-Western and served none of our interests, I was for sinking it. And yet now, after the Cold War, I would argue that we have an interest in preserving its largest fictional existence. Because in a dangerous world, dodges and loopholes have their uses.

The UN, as hand-holder and temporizer, achieves two things: it helps keep the number-one superpower out of some regional conflicts by providing moral cover in places like Bosnia, and it helps keep the other great powers out, too, thus reducing the chances of regional conflict going global.

Thus, in the Balkans, the UN has not kept the Yugoslavs from killing each other, but it has kept the Americans and the Russians and perhaps the Turks and the Greeks and others from coming in on any threatening scale. In other words, it helped keep Sarajevo 1995 from becoming Sarajevo 1914.

Bosnia demonstrates the UN's real role, as a cover for inaction. So too does Rwanda. That unfortunate country saw the worst genocide perpetrated on the globe since the Second World War. But the great powers—for reasons of exhaustion, indifference, distance—did not want to get involved (with the brief exception of France). So we handed it all over to the blue helmets. Similarly in Somalia, where the UN became the cover for an American retreat. By the time we had gotten to the Haiti operation, the UN-as-exit strategy had been planned even before the U.S. entry.

But let's not mistake what is going on here. The UN involved itself in Rwanda and Somalia and Haiti only because the great powers deemed them of insufficient importance to their national interest, of insufficient threat to real international peace. Hence the UN. It is not an agency. It is an excuse.

Let's now deal with a third post–Cold War illusion, the whole principle of multilateralism. Multilateral action is one of the great shibboleths of international relations. Multilateral action is always considered morally superior to unilateral action. Unilateral is a word used almost exclusively as a pejorative.

Why? After all, Britain's finest hour was the Battle of Britain, unilateral resistance to Nazi Germany. As the political theorist Ernest Lefevre writes, "The morality of state behavior is determined by its purpose and consequences, not by whether the state acts alone."

But most Americans and Canadians disagree. They believe deeply that there is something almost morally tainted about unilateral action.

Take Grenada. When the U.S. invaded in 1983, even the conservative Reagan administration felt that it could not admit to naked unilateralism. What did it do? On the day of the invasion, the prime minister of a tiny neighbouring Caribbean island was flown to Washington, where she issued a claim on behalf of an ad hoc, highly dubious alliance of very tiny islands, that it had invited the U.S. to invade Grenada.

Now, I am not saying that the U.S. should not welcome the support of even the tiniest nation for any of its actions. But I am saying that the U.S. should not have to depend on it. In American foreign-policy debates, it should not be necessary for one side or the other to claim the backing of Dominica. And yet it is.

If Grenada was the most farcical example of the multilateral myth, the Gulf War was the most elaborate. It was hailed, universally and enthusiastically, as an example of a much celebrated multilateralism of a new world order. The only people unconvinced were those on the receiving end of the multilateralism, the Iraqis. They charged that the entire multilateral apparatus—UN resolutions, Arab troops, European Community pronouncements, etc.—established in the Gulf by the U.S. was nothing but a transparent cover for what was essentially an American challenge to Iraqi regional hegemony.

And of course the Iraqis were right. The Gulf War was essentially an American operation. Others joined the U.S. effort precisely because President Bush had demonstrated that he was quite prepared to act unilaterally if necessary. Under those circumstances, lesser powers, convinced of American will, joined up. It was a classic example of an apparently multilateral effort hinging entirely on the fact of American unilateralism.

There is a sharp distinction to be drawn between real and apparent multilateralism. True multilateralism involves a genuine coalition of co-equal partners of comparable strength and stature—the Big Three wartime anti-Nazi coalition of the Second World War, for example. What we have today is pseudo-multilateralism: a dominant great power acts essentially alone, but, embarrassed at the idea and still worshipping at the shrine of collective security, recruits a ship here, a brigade there, and blessings all around to give its unilateral actions a multilateral sheen. The Gulf was no more a collective operation than was Korea, still the classic case study in pseudo-multilateralism.

Why the pretence? Because a large segment of public opinion doubts the legitimacy of unilateral American action but accepts quite readily actions undertaken by the "world community" acting in concert. Why it should matter to Americans that their actions get a Security Council blessing from, say, Deng Xiaoping and the butchers of Tiananmen Square is beyond me. But to many Americans it matters. It is largely for domestic reasons, therefore, that American political leaders make sure to dress unilateral action in multilateral clothing. The danger, of course, is that they might come to believe their own pretence.

But the greatest illusion of all is not peacekeeping. It is not the UN. It is not multilateralism. The greatest illusion of all is the one underlying all the others, the one concerning the very nature of the international system: the woolly Wilsonianism that plagued us after the two world wars and now plagues us again in the period of exhaustion and exhilaration that follows the end of the Cold War, the belief in sweet reason and perpetual peace.

The 1992 American presidential campaign was heavily under the influence of this illusion. It saw less foreign-policy debate than any campaign in the last fifty years. That is because it was run on the shared assumption that the U.S. had entered this era of perpetual peace, and that Americans could therefore safely turn their attention to domestic affairs.

The campaign merely confirmed that the U.S. had indeed entered its third period this century of postwar Utopianism. As before, it is an era marked by the belief that peace is the norm, that peace is something to be kept, that all that it requires is for the unrulies of the world to be civilized by compromise and reason, Western-style, and that we do this with talk—Vance-Owen plans, UN resolutions— and blue helmets.

In fact, however, the natural state of the world is not perpetual peace but per- petual conflict. Liberia, Rwanda, Somalia, Bosnia remind us of that. They remind us also that when we really want to end these wars, we must use overwhelming force to alter the balance. As was once said: "When there is no agreement on what cards are trumps, clubs are always trumps."

NATO jets drop bombs and kill people. Euphemize all you want. But that is not peacekeeping. That is war-making.

And war-making works. Things are moving in Bosnia not because of some change in the UN, or the British, French, or even the Russians, but because the United States has finally decided to do something serious about Bosnia. The rea- sons, I might note, are almost entirely domestic: Clinton needs to get this mess off his plate before the presidential campaign begins. But no matter the reason, the fact remains: America moves, the world moves.

"History is creative but not redemptive," said the American theologian Reinhold Niebuhr. It is important for us to recognize that the post–Cold War world is not new. It is as old as the international system. The reality of that system is that peace depends, as it has since the Peloponnesian wars, on balance of power. And the structure of the world being what it is today, with the United States over- whelmingly dominant, that means American power and the will to use it.

Ask the Bosnians.

✗ NO
Overload, Not Marginalization, Threatens UN Peacekeeping
PETER VIGGO JAKOBSEN

INTRODUCTION

In recent years "marginalization" has become a popular term in descriptions of the role of the United Nations (UN) in peacekeeping. According to former UN Secretary-General Boutros Boutros-Ghali: "The marginalization began in 1993 with the Somalia intervention and the subsequent change of majority in [the US] Congress."[1] Feelings of marginalization have been fed by the fall in the number of UN troops in the field and by the practice of delegating enforcement operations permitted to use force beyond self-defence (Chapter VII operations) to regional organizations and coalitions of the willing. However, concerns that the world organization was heading for irrelevance were brought to a head in the spring of 1999 by the North Atlantic Treaty Organization's (NATO) use of force in Kosovo without a UN mandate. Several high-ranking UN officials and observers sympathetic to the organization sounded the alarm,[2] and—in early June 1999—a troubled UN Secretary-General invited UN Security Council members to an informal, closed-door meeting to discuss the problem and ways of overcoming it.[3]

However, adding the Blue Helmets to the list of endangered species would be premature. What we have been witnessing in recent years, I would argue, is not a marginalization of the UN, but the emergence of a new division of labour that will stretch UN capabilities to the limit in the 21st century.

THE MARGINALIST ARGUMENT

The term *marginalist* is one I employ for the sake of convenience. It does not refer to a particular school of thought or a coherent position within the UN debate. Nor will it necessarily be possible to associate it with particular individuals. I have constructed the marginalist argument by collecting the standard arguments that a large and (so it seems) growing number of analysts and commentators have used in recent years to make the case that the UN is headed for extinction unless drastic reform measures are implemented. I have not found one person making all the arguments discussed below, meaning that an individual associated with one marginalist argument will not necessarily agree with other arguments that I refer to as marginalist.

At first sight the marginalist argument has a lot going for it: the number of military personnel under UN command has fallen from a high of 76,000 in September 1994. The total combined number of UN soldiers, civilian police and observers as of 31 March 2000 was 29,286, made up of 22,211 military, 5,712 police and 1,363 observers. The Security Council practice of delegating Chapter VII enforcement operations to regional organizations and "coalitions of the willing" meant at the time of writing (February 2000) that NATO and the Economic Community of West African States (ECOWAS) were conducting larger peace operations than the UN; the delegation of the Chapter VII operation in East Timor to an Australian-led force in September 1999 provides yet another indication that this practice is here to stay; and it is even conceivable that the Security Council may start contracting out operations to private security firms in Africa. This is advocated by an increasing number of scholars, and UN Secretary-General Kofi Annan considered hiring a private firm to separate refugees from Hutu soldiers in the Rwandan refugee camps in Goma when no member states proved willing to do so.[4]

To the marginalists, the practice of delegating enforcement operations to groups of member states is a recipe for marginalization. They argue that it will leave the UN without a job, because a large majority of future operations will involve enforcement. In addition, they believe that delegation will result in the neglect of Third World conflicts, great power abuse and a return to a world divided by spheres of influence, all of which will undermine UN legitimacy.[5] These concerns are not unfounded. After Somalia, Western powers with the capability to intervene effectively have proved highly reluctant to support new enforcement operations in Africa, and all but one of the delegated interventions carried out after the Cold War can be classified as "spheres-of-influence interventions." The US-led intervention in Somalia is the only exception to the rule. Similarly, the risk of abuse was highlighted by Operation Turquoise in Rwanda, where the French forces reportedly allowed the perpetrators of the genocide to escape with their weapons.[6]

From the marginalist perspective, NATO's decision to use force in the Kosovo conflict without a UN mandate is the final nail in the UN's coffin, representing the culmination of a trend that has been visible for a while. Again, there is a basis for such a claim. Operation Desert Fox, the bombing of Iraq by Britain and the USA in December 1998, took place without UN authorization, and in Africa the number of unauthorized interventions undertaken by (members of) regional organizations is growing. ECOWAS has undertaken unauthorized interventions in Liberia and Sierra Leone, and members of the South African Development Community (SADC) have intervened in the Democratic Republic of Congo (DRC) and in Lesotho.[7]

MARGINALIST SOLUTIONS

The solutions offered by the marginalists to overcome the threat of marginalization generally fall in two categories. In the first, we find a variety of proposals to give the UN an enforcement capacity of its own. They range from proposals to beef up the institutional capacity of the UN to calls for the establishment of a standing UN army. In the second category we find calls for fundamental UN Security Council reform, suggesting that the number of permanent seats be expanded to reflect a wider geographic representation and/or that the right to veto be abolished.[8]

These proposals could solve many of the operational problems that have hampered UN operations in recent years, and enhance the legitimacy of the UN in the Third World, where it is increasingly perceived as a vehicle for Western interests. They have, however, one problem in common: they stand no chance of implementation in the foreseeable future. Proposals to give the UN a modest enforcement capacity (like the 1995 Dutch proposal to establish a 5,000-strong rapid deployment brigade) have all become stranded on the lack of political will, and the negotiations to reform the Security Council are deadlocked, with no one close to the process willing to put the money on substantive progress any time soon.[9] So if the marginalists were right, the future of UN peacekeeping would be very bleak indeed. Fortunately, they are not.

WHY THE MARGINALISTS ARE WRONG

The decline in the number of UN peacekeepers in the field is no proof of marginalization, especially as the signs are that the numbers will rise again through involvement in Africa. The current level of UN troops and military observers (18,000) is much higher than the number deployed during the Cold War era—the "golden age" of peacekeeping. (The only exception is 1960–64, where the 20,000-strong Congo operation boosted numbers to an exceptionally high level.) The UN was thus more marginalized during the "golden age" of peacekeeping than at any time during the 1990s, and to expect the UN to be able to sustain the record force levels of 1993–94 was always unrealistic in an anarchic world where the organization depends entirely on great power consensus and support.

Another reason why it is wrong to view falling troop levels as a sign of marginalization is that the nature of peacekeeping has changed. After the Cold War, civilian personnel and non-military tasks have become just as important as soldiers, and the decline in UN troops is offset by a marked increase in the number of civilian UN personnel and non-military activities in the field. Civilian police, electoral assistance, humanitarian relief, demining, human rights monitoring and training assistance can all be described as "growth industries" within UN peace operations.

The number of UN civilian police (UNCIVPOL) has been steadily growing since 1988, when 35 could be found in the field. By February 2000 the number had risen to 4,700, and it would have been significantly higher if the UN had been able to find all the police officers it needed for the operations in Kosovo (UNMIK) and East Timor (UNTAET);[10] the number of requests for UN electoral assistance has risen from 7 in the 1988–92 period to 143 in the 1992–August 1997 period;

22 new human rights field presences have been set up in the last few years alone; demining activities are growing; the "big four" in the UN family–the United Nations Development Programme, the UN High Commissioner for Refugees, the UN Children's Programme and the World Food Programme–have become major players in the entire spectrum of peace operations; and the UN added a new task to its growing list of civilian activities when the first Child Protection Advisor (CPA) was deployed in Sierra Leone in February 2000. CPAs will also be deployed with the UN peacekeeping operation in the DRC.[11]

Training is another area in which UN involvement continues to grow. In 1993 the General Assembly established a Training Unit at the UN Department of Peacekeeping (DPKO) to coordinate and standardize training among member states that contribute to peacekeeping operations. Since then the Training Unit has played a central role with respect to enhancing the quality of civilian and military personnel involved in peace operations. Initiatives have included the development and distribution of training materials, the conducting of regional training work-shops on a regular basis, the development of codes of conduct, the creation of Training Assistance teams that provide specialized training–upon request and at short notice–to member states and the establishment of a UN Staff College in Turin.[12] In 1998 the Training Unit began developing a database on peacekeeping training and initiatives in Africa. The database is intended to facilitate the overall exchange of information on peacekeeping training and initiatives, and to assist in the coordination of future peacekeeping training objectives and activities in Africa.

Since the number of UN civilian personnel involved in these activities in the field exceeds the number of troops, using a decrease in numbers of the latter as proof of UN marginalization is–to say the least–misleading, as it obscures the changing and much more demanding role that the UN is playing in contemporary operations. That the UN has been put in charge of the interim administrations of Kosovo and East Timor and is expected to play a similar role in Sierra Leone fur-ther underscores this point.

PEACEKEEPING HAS A FUTURE

The marginalist belief that enforcement operations will crowd out consent-based Chapter VI operations in the 21st century is also wrong. Inability to carry out enforcement operations will not marginalize the UN, because traditional peace-keeping and multifunctional (Chapter VI) operations with consent remain as important as ever. Thirty-nine Chapter VI operations were launched in the 1990s, and 1999 alone witnessed the initiation of five new operations: a 1,000-strong civilian UN mission which monitored the referendum on autonomy in East Timor (UNAMET), a 5,000-strong civilian mission in Kosovo (UNMIK), a 10,790-strong peacekeeping operation authorized to take over from the Australian-led interven-tion force in East Timor (UNTAET), a 90-strong military observer mission in the

DRC (MONUC) and a 6,000-strong peacekeeping operation in Sierra Leone (UNAMSIL).[13] In February 2000, the Security Council expanded the Congo operation to 5,537 personnel and increased the one in Sierra Leone to 11,110 personnel.[14] The latter force was given limited Chapter VII authority in the areas of deployment to protect civilians under imminent threat of physical violence.

All in all, the launch of new UN operations, the successful UN operations in El Salvador, Macedonia and Mozambique and the 17 ongoing UN operations demonstrate the continued relevance of UN-controlled Chapter VI operations, and that the UN remains the only serious Chapter VI player.

FEAR OF GREAT POWER ABUSE EXAGGERATED

Marginalists exaggerate the risk of Great Power abuse because they tend to equate self-interest with abuse and underestimate the effectiveness of the measures that the Security Council introduced in the 1990s to enhance its ability to monitor and support operations delegated to groups of member states. Critics of the delegation practice complain that Italy led the intervention in Albania in order to stop the flow of refugees and boost Italian chances of acquiring a permanent seat on the Security Council, that France's intervention in Rwanda was driven by strategic considerations and that Canada's willingness to lead an intervention in the African Great Lakes region in 1996 was motivated by an interest in enhancing its international prestige.[15] Complaints that Australia was driven by economic interests and not humanitarian sentiment are bound to be made now that the UN administration in East Timor has signed a $1.4 billion gas exploration accord with the Australian government.[16]

These complaints are no doubt partially correct, but they are also irrelevant since self-interest does not automatically mean abuse. On the contrary, respecting UN guidelines and mandates is often a sine qua non for interveners wishing to realize their underlying agendas. Indeed, in each of the four cases mentioned above, the interveners could only further their national interests by adhering strictly to their UN mandates. Put differently, interveners acting on UN mandates have a strong incentive to respect UN guidelines and restrictions, and if they do so their self-interest motives become irrelevant.

The ability of the Security Council to ensure that interveners play by the rules hinges on its ability to monitor delegated operations. Significant progress has been made in this respect in the nineties. Measures introduced include:

- specific rules of engagement and time limits to the mandates;

- inclusion of civilian elements within delegated operations;

- attachment of UN liaison officers to delegated operations;

- regular submission of reports to the Security Council;

- regular briefing meetings between the Security Council and those states conducting the operations;

- co-deployment of UN observers and other personnel with delegated operations;

- joint operations conducted with other regional operations; and

- handover to the UN as soon as the conditions for a consent-based Chapter VI operation have been created.

Different combinations of these measures have been employed to monitor delegated operations. Specified rules of engagement, time limits and the inclusion of civilian UN personnel have been standard practice: eight UN military liaison officers assisted the ECOWAS force in Sierra Leone in planning its future objectives in 1998;[17] the Gabon-led Inter-African Mission to Monitor the Implementation of the Bangui Agreements (MISAB) in Central African Republic, the Italian-led Operation Alba in Albania and the Australian-led International Force for East Timor (INTERFET) were required to submit reports to the Security Council every two weeks;[18] UN observers have been co-deployed with Commonwealth of Independent States (CIS) forces in Georgia and Tajikistan and with ECOWAS forces in Liberia, Sierra Leone and Guinea-Bissau; a joint civilian mission has been conducted together with the Organization of American States (OAS) in Haiti (MICIVIH) since 1993; and UN peacekeepers have taken over from delegated Chapter VII operations in Rwanda, Haiti, the Central African Republic and East Timor.

A first step towards formalizing these measures was taken by the Security Council in 1998,[19] and the Lessons Learned Unit in the DPKO subsequently produced a report about peacekeeping cooperation between the UN and the regional organizations/arrangements, offering suggestions for further improvements.[20]

The record of such cooperation to date is mixed and it would be naïve to expect UN control measures to eliminate (Great Power) abuse. In an anarchic society, no rules or intergovernmental organizations can do that. But, by setting clear standards for acceptable behaviour that all interveners must meet to obtain international support for their interventions, they do not limit the scope for abuse. Generally considered the clearest example of Great Power abuse to date,[21] the French intervention in Rwanda can be said to provide a "hard" test of the effectiveness of UN control measures. It is indisputable that the French motives were less than pure, and that Hutu sympathizers within the French military and intelligence services continued to deliver weapons to the Hutus after the genocide had begun and helped their leaders and some of their troops to escape with their weapons. Nevertheless, the UN guidelines had a real impact on French behaviour as the French government and the force commander did their utmost to respect them in order to enhance the legitimacy of the operation. France reported regularly to the Council, stuck to the humanitarian mission and left

Rwanda when the UN mandate expired. Moreover, some disarmament of Hutu forces was carried out and the French force commander made a whole-hearted attempt to weed out Hutu sympathizers from the force in order to minimize the risk of a clash with the Tutsi army.[22]

The most reliable estimates suggest that the French intervention saved 13,000–14,000 lives and–although it obviously came to late to stop the genocide[23]–the argument that Rwanda would have been better off without it is open to question. There is little basis for arguing that the French intervention is to blame for all the problems that followed, and that it undermined regional peace and stability by saving the Hutu extremists: the advancing Tutsi forces could not have prevented the Hutu extremists from fleeing to neighbouring countries and taking control of refugee camps even if the French had not intervened.

KOSOVO: THE EXCEPTION TO THE RULE

The ability to monitor and control delegated operations is obviously irrelevant if Kosovo is the way of the future and the permanent members (P-5) of the UN Security Council will begin from now on to launch unauthorized interventions into other sovereign states on a regular basis. Fortunately, all indications are that unauthorized interventions led by P-5 will remain the exception to the rule. Internal security problems (Tibet and Chechnya) significantly reduce the risk of unauthorized interventions by China and Russia. The probability of a Chinese attack on Taiwan–generally considered the most likely scenario–remains very small, due to strong Taiwanese defences and US deterrence. Therefore, the greatest threat to unauthorized intervention is posed by the Western permanent members, who have led most of the interventions after the Cold War, and their handling of the Kosovo war suggests that the risk of new (unauthorized) Western interventions is also very small.

Although NATO's intervention in Kosovo violated the UN Charter, Alliance behaviour nevertheless revealed a strong commitment to the UN and its principles: NATO tried hard to obtain a UN mandate before using force, and all NATO members supporting the use of force–with the partial exception of the USA–legitimized the decision to use force on the basis of UN principles, going to great lengths to emphasize the exceptional nature of the intervention. The European NATO members defeated the USA's attempt to give NATO the right to intervene at will on the global scene in the new Strategic Concept, and Madeleine Albright, the US Secretary of Sate, accepted that Kosovo must not been seen as a precedent and that NATO should restrict its activities to Europe.[24]

NATO governments also went out of their way to ensure that the Kosovo war did not damage beyond repair their relationship with China and Russia, and hence the UN Security Council. They stayed in close contact with the Russians throughout the war and close cooperation with respect to finding a diplomatic solution to the conflict between Russia and the Western members of the Contact Group continued uninterrupted throughout the war.[25] Western damage control worked: less than a year after the war ended, Russia–NATO relations are almost back to normal and the Chinese have resumed high-level military contacts with the USA.[26]

However, the most powerful constraint on future (unauthorized) NATO interventions is the current Western obsession with avoiding casualties. The Western, and particularly US, zero-casualty culture–so evident in the reluctance displayed by NATO on the road to and in its actual conduct of the air campaign in Kosovo– provides a strong guarantee against new interventions in the foreseeable future. NATO was a reluctant warrior, and the Alliance would have done nothing to stop the Serb forces if Kosovo had not been situated in Europe–a fact admitted by a senior NATO spokesman.[27]

The greatest problem facing the UN today is therefore not unauthorized P-5 interventions, but P-5 reluctance to undertake or support enforcement operations when required to stop massive human rights violations. Thus, the UN failure to act in Rwanda is more likely to be repeated than NATO's unauthorized operation in Kosovo. In short, the marginalists are making the same mistake of generalizing from one case as the optimists who declared the New World Order in the wake of the Gulf War.

Of course, that the P-5 are unlikely to carry out unauthorized interventions will not prevent regional actors from doing so, and–as mentioned already–a number of such interventions took place in Africa in the nineties. These interventions are, however, more of a reflection of Security Council inaction in Africa than a lack of respect for the UN. This means that the number of unauthorized interventions in Africa is also likely to fall, if the Security Council's renewed interest in Africa, signalled by the unauthorization of the operations in the DRC and Sierra Leone, can be sustained.

DIVISION OF LABOUR

What we are witnessing, then, is not the marginalization of the UN but the emergence of a new division of labour in the field of peace operations which will stretch existing UN capabilities to the limit. This division of labour limits the role played by the UN in Chapter VII operations to authorization, monitoring and civilian support, but leaves the UN in the driver's seat with respect to Chapter VI activities. UN responsibilities, in other words, range from the simple deployment of a handful of military observers along borders or ceasefire lines to full-scale state building, as in the case of Kosovo.

This arrangement has great potential. It leaves operational responsibility for the military aspects of enforcement to coalitions with a capacity and a willingness to carry them out. As a consequence, operational effectiveness will increase and, while success will reflect positively on the UN, failures will do little to harm the reputation and economy of the organization. As indicated above, the danger of Great Power abuse is not as great as the marginalists fear because the UN has strengthened its ability to monitor and control delegated enforcement operations and, more importantly, because Great Powers display very little interest in undertaking such operations.

This lack of interest is the Achilles' heel of the emerging division of labour. Enforcement operations will be few in number and selective in nature owing to the reluctance of the Western permanent members to lead or support them outside their own spheres of influence. This selectiveness has already weakened UN legitimacy considerably in the Third World: African elites feel, not surprisingly, the Western powers are applying a double standard by supporting enforcement operations in former Yugoslavia while at the same time refusing to do so in Africa.[28] It also gives them little choice but to intervene themselves without UN mandates. The launch of two major operations in the DRC and Sierra Leone signals a change for the better, but the Western involvement in these operations is very limited and their success is far from guaranteed. If these operations fail, the renewed Security Council interest in Africa will be next to impossible to sustain.

Another problem is that the UN will have trouble playing its part effectively. In spite of all the progress that has been achieved in recent years, UN effectiveness remains wanting in peacekeeping, humanitarian assistance and civilian support. The reforms aimed at enhancing coordination among the UN humanitarian agencies, including the recent creation of the Office for the Coordination of Humanitarian Affairs (OCHA), have thus far failed to deliver and the jury is still out as the whether they signify a real improvement;[29] as the UN capacity to manage civilian police operations was overstretched even before Kosovo overwhelmed it; recent progress is threatened by new cutbacks in the UN DPKO; and efforts to provide the UN with a rapid reaction peacekeeping capability have also been hampered by half-hearted support from most member states. As of 1 March 2000, only 32 members had signed the Memorandum of Understanding on Stand-by Arrangements with the UN, and shortages in the areas of logistics, air- and sea-lift and civilian police prevent the system from functioning with "optimal" efficiency. Similarly, efforts since 1996 to establish a Rapidly Deployable Mission Headquarters to accelerate the deployment of peacekeeping missions have thus far become stranded owing to lack of funds. The good rapid reaction news is that the 4,500-strong UN Stand-by Forces High Readiness Brigade (SHIRBRIG) became operational by the end of 1999. This is available for deployment at short notice (15–30 days) for peacekeeping (Chapter VI) operations for a maximum period of six months.[30]

REALISTIC REFORMS

The marginalists have got one thing right: the UN desperately needs strengthening to play an effective role in the new millennium. Yet the danger is overload, not marginalization. Enabling the UN to play an effective role in the emerging division of labour will require a significant strengthening in the areas of rapid reaction, logistics, civilian police and coordination. Considering the current hostility towards the UN in the US Congress and the general Great Power unwillingness to strengthen the UN too much, it will be up to the group of traditional peacekeepers and similar informal groupings of like-minded member states to ensure that these reforms are implemented.[31] Moreover, sustained pressure and persuasion must be employed to induce the P-5 to limit their use of the veto to matters of vital interest. Since fundamental reform of the Council and revisions to the Charter are unrealistic, informal and procedural changes are what reform-minded states must aim for.[32]

Institutional reforms at the UN, however, will not suffice. To avoid a further weakening of UN legitimacy, efforts to enhance non-Western peace enforcement capabilities must be strengthened as well. Current initiatives in Africa and elsewhere certainly represent a step in the right direction, but their effectiveness suffers greatly from lack of coordination among Western donors. The Western initiatives should reinforce rather than overlap or supplant local African initiatives to a far greater extent than is the case at present.[33]

These reforms will not be easy to accomplish, but—unlike unrealistic demands for a UN army, fundamental Security Council reform and abolition of the veto right—they are within the realm of the possible in the foreseeable future.

NOTES

The author would like to thank Espen Barth Eide, Anthony McDermott and Georg Sørensen for useful comments on an earlier draft.

1. Cited in Judith Miller, "U.N. Security Council Relegated to Sidelines," *New York Times*, 14 March 1999.

2. See for instance Halvor Elvik, "FN på sidelinjen" [UN on the Sideline], *Dagbladet*, 21 April 1999; Michèle Griffin, "Blue Helmet Blues: Assessing the Trend Towards 'Subcontracting' UN Peace Operations," *Security Dialogue*, vol. 30, no. 1, March 1999, pp. 43–60; Giandomenico Picco, "Keeping the U.N. Relevant by Appealing to the Young," *Los Angeles Times*, 11 July 1999; "Kosovo: Former General Ass'y Chiefs Fear UN Is Marginalized", *UN Wire*, 14 May 1999.

3. "Security Council: Annan Calls Informal Retreat," *UN Wire*, 8 June 1999.

4. Kevin O'Brien, "Military-Advisory Groups and African Security: Privatized Peacekeeping?" *International Peacekeeping*, vol. 5, no 3, Autumn 1998, pp. 78–105; David Shearer, "Private Armies and Military Intervention," *Adelphi Paper* 316 (Oxford: Oxford University Press, 1998); UN Press Release SG/SM/6613.

5. Roland Paris, "The End of the UN as a Security Organization?" *Washington Quarterly*, vol. 20, no. 1, Winter 1997, pp. 191–206; Terry Terriff & James F. Keeley, "The United Nations, Conflict Management and Spheres of Interest," *International Peacekeeping*, vol. 2, no. 4, Winter 1995, pp. 510–35.

6. Eric Berman, "The Security Council's Increasing Reliance on Burden-Sharing: Collaboration or Abrogation?" *International Peacekeeping*, vol. 5, no. 1, Spring 1998, p. 10.

7. Cedric de Coning, "African Perspectives on Intervention: The Rising Tide of Neo-Interventionism," in Anthony McDermott, ed., *Sovereign Intervention* (Oslo: International Peace Research Institute, 1999), pp. 171–90; Espen Barth Eide, "Intervening Without the UN: A Rejoinder," *Security Dialogue*, vol. 30, no. 1, March 1999, pp. 91–94.

8. Mohamed Sid-Ahmed, "Restructuring the UN," *Al-Ahram Weekly*, no. 437, 8–14 July 1999; "Peacekeeping: Security Council Reform May Be Needed," *UN Wire*, 28 May 1999.

9. Michèle Griffin, "Retrenchment, Reform, and Regionalization: Trends in UN Peace Support Operations," *International Peacekeeping*, vol. 6, no. 1, Spring 1999, p. 13; Peter Lehmann Nielson, "Great Powers, Institutions and Legitimacy: An Analysis of the Negotiations on UN Security Council Reform after the Cold War" (MA thesis, Institute of Political Science, University of Copenhagen, 1999).

10. In late February 2000, only 2,300 police officers out of an authorized 4,718 had arrived in Kosovo. In East Timor only 480 out of 1,640 had arrived by 31 January 2000. See "United Nations Peacekeeping Operations," *Background Note*, February 2000 (UN Department of Public Information).

11. "UN Announces Deployment of Child Protection Advisers, Groundbreaking Development in UN Peacekeeping," UN Press Release HR/4463 PKO/85, 22 February 2000.

12. John Otte, "UN Concept for Peacekeeping Training," *Military Review*, vol. 83, no. 4, July–August 1998, pp. 25–30.

13. S/1999/595, 22 May 1999, para. 9; S/RES/1246, 11 June 1999; S/RES/1270, 22 October 1999; S/RES/1272, 25 October 1999; "UN Team To Set Up Bases Inside Congo,"*New Vision* (Kampala), 13 October 1999.

14. S/2000/1289, 7 February 2000; S/2000/1291, 24 February 2000.

15. Griffin (note 2, above), p. 47.

16. "Australia, UN Mission in East Timor Sign $1.4 Billion Gas Exploration Accord", *UN Newservice*, 23 February 2000.

17. S/RES/1162, 17 April 1998; S/1998/486, 9 June 1998, paras 19–20.

18. S/RES/1101, 28 March 1997; S/RES/1125, 6 August 1997; S/RES/1264, 15 September 1999.

19. S/PRST/1998/35, 30 November 1998.

20. This report is available at http://www.un.org/Depts/dpko/lessons/regcoop.htm.

21. Berman (note 6 above), p. 10; Griffin (note 9 above), p. 22; Nicholas J. Wheeler & Justin Morris, "Humanitarian Intervention and State Practice at the End of the Cold War," in Rick Fawn & Jeremy Larkins, eds, *International Society After the Cold War* (London: Macmillan, 1996), p. 160.

22. David Millwood, ed., *The International Response to Conflict and Genocide: Lessons from the Rwanda Experience. Study 3: Humanitarian Aid and Effects* (Copenhagen, Danida, 1996), pp. 42–43, 48: note 40; Gérard Prunier, *The Rwanda Crisis 1959-1994: History of Genocide* (London: Hurst & Company, 1995), p. 293.

23. Millwood (see note 22, above), p. 154.

24. Madeleine K. Albright, "After Kosovo: Building a Lasting Peace,"remarks and Q&A session with the Council on Foreign Relations, New York, 28 June 1999.

25. The Contact Group is made up of France, Germany, Great Britain, Italy, Russia and the USA. For an analysis of Contact Group cooperation during the Kosovo crisis, see Peter Viggo Jakobsen, "Kontaktgruppen i Kosovo: Koncert trods mislyde" [The Contact Group in Kosovo: Concert Despite Dissonances], *Politica*, vol. 32, no. 2, 2000 (forthcoming).

26. See "Russian–NATO Relationship Mending", *Associated Press*, 7 February 2000; Steven Lee Myers, "Chinese Military To Resume Contacts With The Pentagon," *New York Times*, 6 January 2000.

27. See Randall Richard, "NATO Official Justifies Use of Force in Talk at Brown," *Providence Journal-Bulletin*, 26 March 1999, p. A16.

28. UN Secretary-General Boutros Boutros-Ghali famously voiced this critique in July 1992 when he accused the Western powers of fighting "the rich man's war" in Yugoslavia while ignoring the collapse of Somalia. NATO's Operation Allied Force in Kosovo in 1999 has reinforced this perception among African elites. See Lynne Duke, "In Africa, Frustration and Envy Over the West's Rapid Response," *Washington Post*, 7 May 1999.

29. John Mackinlay, "UN Peacekeeping: Ready for Kosovo?" *World Today*, vol. 55, no. 6, June 1999, pp. 4–6; Thomas G. Weiss, "Humanitarian Shell Games: Whither UN Reform?" *Security Dialogue*, vol. 29, no. 1, March 1998, pp. 9–23.

30. As of 27 April 1999, 12 countries were members of SHIRBRIG's executive body, the steering committee: Argentina, Austria, Canada, Denmark, Finland, Italy, the Netherlands, Norway, Poland, Romania, Spain and Sweden. Six countries had status as observers: The Czech Republic, Hungary, Ireland, Jordan, Portugal and Slovenia. See http://www.shirbrig.dk.

31. The main contributors to peacekeeping operations during the Cold War were Australia, Austria, Canada, Denmark, Fiji, Finland, Ghana, India, Ireland, Nepal, New Zealand, Norway, Pakistan, Senegal and Sweden.

32. For a reform proposal along similar lines, see Richard Butler, "Bewitched, Bothered, and Bewildered: Repairing the Security Council,"*Foreign Affairs*, vol. 78, no. 5, September/October 1999, pp. 9–12. Several States, including Denmark and Germany, advocated such changes during their opening addresses at the General Assembly's 54th session in September–October 1999.

33. Jeremy Ginifer, "Emergent African Peace-keeping: Self-help and External Assistance" in Anthony McDermott, ed., *Humanitarian Force*, PRIO Report 4/97 (Oslo: International Peace Research Institute, 1997), pp. 123–41.

Postscript

In his article, Peter Jakobsen addresses those who argue that the United Nations is in danger of becoming marginalized in the face of recent challenges. In cases such as Kosovo in 1999, the use of force was delegated to other bodies like NATO. Thus, Jakobsen examines reforms that would help the United Nations develop more effective peacekeeping operations.

Krauthammer's critique of peacekeeping is rooted in a much deeper skepticism than any UN reforms are likely to address. His analysis stems from the realist assumption that international order can be established only through the actions of a strong, hegemonic power that is willing to enforce international rules and punish offenders, even if it means taking unilateral action. His critique strikes at the core concept of collective security, upon which the United Nations was founded.

For a more detailed realist critique of collective security see John Mearsheimer, "The False Promise of International Institutions," *International Security,* vol. 19, no. 3 (Winter 1994–95): 5–49.

Infotrac Keyword Search

"peacekeeping"

Suggested Additional Readings

Burk, James. "What Justifies Peacekeeping?" *Peace Review* 12, no. 3 (September 2000): 467–77.

Chopra, Jarat. *Politics of Peace-Maintenance.* Boulder: Rienner, 1998.

Griffin, Michéle. "Blue Helmet Blues: Assessing the Trend Towards 'Subcontracting' UN Peace Operations," *Security Dialogue* 30, no. 1, (March 1999) 43–60.

Neack, Laura. "UN Peace-Keeping: In the Interest of Community or Self?" *Journal of Peace Research* 32 (May 1995): 181–96.

"Non-Traditional Missions and the Use of Force: The Debate Over Peacekeeping, Peace Enforcement, and Related Operations." *Fletcher Forum of World Affairs,* 18 (Winter–Spring 1994): entire issue.

Paris, Roland. "Blue Helmet Blues: The End of the UN as a Security Organization?" *Washington Quarterly* 20, no. 2 (Winter 1997): 191–207.

Pugh, Michael, ed. *The UN, Peace, and Force.* London: Frank Cass, 1997.

Thakur, Ramesh Chandra. *A Crisis of Expectations: UN Peacekeeping in the 1990s.* Boulder: Westview Press, 1995.

Website Resources

Pearson Peacekeeping Centre   Canada's leading centre for peacekeeping training has a range of available resources.

Research Guide to International Law on the Internet: Peacekeeping Operations   An excellent list of peackeeping resources.

United Nations Dag Hammarskjöld Library: Peace-keeping Operations: A Bibliography   Detailed list of peacekeeping resources published before 1996.

United Nations Peacekeeping Department   Homepage of the United Nations has a collection of maps and other documents related to UN peacekeeping.

Yale University Library: Internet Access to UN Information by Research Topic: Peacekeeping   Good list of peacekeeping resources.

PART
FOUR

INTERNATIONAL
POLITICAL
ECONOMY

*Does globalization cheat the
world's poor?*

Should the WTO be abolished?

*Was the "Battle in Seattle" a
significant turning point in the
struggle against globalization?*

*Will debt relief address the needs of
highly indebted countries?*

*Would a Tobin tax on international
trade be detrimental to the global
economy?*

Does Globalization Cheat the World's Poor?

✔ **YES**
Michel Chossudovsky, "Global Poverty in the Late 20th Century," *Journal of International Affairs* 52, no. 1 (Fall 1998): 293–312

✗ **NO**
Gautam Sen, "Is Globalisation Cheating the World's Poor?" *Cambridge Review of International Affairs* xiv, no. 1 (Autumn/Winter 2000): 86–106 (revised)

There is little doubt that the globalization of the world's economy is taking place at an extraordinarily rapid pace. World merchandise exports have expanded at an average annual rate of approximately 6 percent since 1950, compared with a 4.5 percent rate in world output. In 1913 the entire flow of goods in world trade totalled only $20 billion. In contrast, in 1994, international trade in goods and services stood at $4.3 trillion a year. Foreign direct investment (FDI) has been growing at an even faster pace than trade. During recent decades, FDI has been reported to have expanded by 27 percent per year, representing an average growth of $205 billion a year. Today there are more than 2,000 larger multinational corporations (operating in six or more countries) and well over 8,000 smaller ones. Together, these 10,000 multinationals are estimated to control over 90,000 subsidiaries.

At the same time, technology has been undergoing a similar process of globalization. Miniaturization and computerization have speeded up communications and transportation times while reducing costs. Rapid developments in communications, when combined with the globalization of financial markets, have led to a sharp increase in the movement of capital. Together, these developments have helped propel an expansion of the global economy, which is not limited by traditional geographical constraints. Factors such as geography and climate no longer give a particular region a comparative advantage.

For some observers, the rapid pace of globalization is a welcome trend. The lowering of economic barriers, greater openness to competitive market forces, and the reduction of artificial market restraints are seen as promoting higher economic growth and prosperity. Consumers have access to cheaper, more diverse, and more advanced products. Expansion of trade and investment generates jobs. At the same time, globalization is said to generate positive political dividends. States that adjust to the changing market are able to generate higher rates of economic growth and technological innovation. They have more resources to deploy in the international arena to both promote and defend their interests. Countries that are linked by economic ties, and have a mutual interest in promoting economic growth, are more likely to seek stable, peaceful, and cooperative ties with other states. Similarly, firms and workers with a stake in trade advancement and economic growth are likely more supportive of active and constructive foreign policies that are aimed at maintaining these benefits. Edward Mansfield, in *Power, Trade, and War* (Princeton, NJ: Princeton University Press, 1994), suggests that the data clearly support the contention that war and peace are closely related— higher levels of trade are usually associated with lower levels of international hostility and antagonism.

Despite this optimistic picture, economic globalization clearly has its downside. An increasingly liberalized economic world imposes severe adjustment burdens on certain segments of workers and firms. The distribution of wealth, both within and between states, has become more unequal. Exposure to the uncertainties and insecurities of foreign competition have led to demands for protectionist measures and the abandonment of multilateral cooperation. Critics are concerned that unfettered global competition creates overwhelming pressures to abandon domestic social policies, environmental regulations, and human rights protections.

Such concerns have in turn given rise to a growing backlash against globalization itself. Globalization for many people, it is argued, has become a "race to the bottom." At the heart of globalization is growing poverty and inequality, which can be reversed only if the forces of globalization themselves are curtailed. As the massive demonstrations at several international summits have shown, anti-globalization movements have grown significantly in recent years.

These essays examine the implications of globalization, particularly for global poverty. Michel Chossudovsky examines the various forces that have contributed to the globalization of poverty and famine in recent decades. Gautam Sen argues that globalization itself need not cheat the world's poor. In fact, economic growth and globalization are important to the economic and social progress of the poor. While rejecting the arguments of anti-globalization theorists and activists, Dr. Sen argues for more attention to ways that the benefits of globalization can be more effectively redistributed to marginalized segments of society.

✔ YES
Global Poverty in the Late 20th Century
MICHEL CHOSSUDOVSKY

THE GLOBALIZATION OF POVERTY

The late 20th century will go down in world history as a period of global impoverishment marked by the collapse of productive systems in the developing world, the demise of national institutions and the disintegration of health and education programs. This "globalization of poverty"—which has largely reversed the achievements of post-war decolonization—was initiated in the Third World, coinciding with the onslaught of the debt crisis. Since the 1990s, it has extended its grip to all major regions of the world including North America, Western Europe, the countries of the former Soviet block and the Newly Industrialized Countries (NICs) of South East Asia and the Far East.

In the 1990s, famines at the local level have erupted in sub-Saharan Africa, South Asia and parts of Latin America; health clinics and schools have been closed down; and hundreds of millions of children have been denied the right to primary education. In the Third World, Eastern Europe and the Balkans, there has been a resurgence of infectious diseases including tuberculosis, malaria and cholera.

IMPOVERISHMENT—AN OVERVIEW

Famine Formation in the Third World

From the dry savannah of the Sahelian belt, famine has extended its grip into the wet tropical heartland. A large part of the population of the African continent has been affected: 18 million people in Southern Africa (including 2 million refugees) are in "famine zones" and another 130 million in 10 countries are seriously at risk.[1] In the Horn of Africa, 23 million people (many of whom have already died) are "in danger of famine" according to a United Nations estimate.[2]

In the post-independence period extending through the 1980s, starvation deaths in South Asia had largely been limited to peripheral tribal areas. But in India today, there are indications of widespread impoverishment among both the rural and urban populations following the adoption of the 1991 New Economic Policy under the stewardship of the Bretton Woods institutions. More than 70 percent of rural households in India are small marginal farmers or landless farm workers, representing a population of over 400 million people. In irrigated areas, agricultural workers are employed for 200 days a year and in rain-fed farming for approximately 100 days. The phasing out of fertilizer subsidies—an explicit condition of the International Monetary Fund (IMF) agreement–and the increase in the prices of farm inputs and fuel is pushing a large number of small- and medium-sized farmers into bankruptcy.

A micro-level study conducted in 1991 on starvation deaths among handloom weavers in a relatively prosperous rural community in Andhra Pradesh sheds light on how local communities have been impoverished as a result of macroeconomic reform. The starvation deaths occurred in the months following the implementation of the New Economic Policy: with the devaluation and the lifting of controls on cotton yarn exports, the jump in the domestic price of cotton yarn led to a collapse in the pacham (24 meters) rate paid to the weaver by the middle-man (through the putting-out system). "Radhakrishnamurthy and his wife were able to weave between three and four pachams a month, bringing home the meagre income of 300 to 400 rupees (U.S. $12 to 16) for a family of six; then came the Union Budget of 24 July 1991, the price of cotton yarn jumped and the burden was passed on to the weaver. Radhakrishnamurthy's family income declined to 240 to 320 rupees a month (U.S. $9.60 to 13.00)."[3] Radhakrishnamurthy of Gollapalli village in Guntur district died of starvation on 4 September 1991. Between 30 August and 10 November 1991, at least 73 starvation deaths were reported in only two districts of Andhra Pradesh.[4] There are 3.5 million handlooms throughout India supporting a population of some 17 million people.

Economic "Shock Therapy" in the Former Soviet Union

When assessing the impact on earnings, employment and social services, the post-Cold War economic collapse in parts of eastern Europe appears to be far deeper and more destructive than that of the Great Depression. In the former Soviet Union (starting in early 1992), hyperinflation triggered by the downfall of the ruble contributed to rapidly eroding real earnings. Economic "shock therapy" combined with the privatization program precipitated entire industries into immediate liquidation, leading to lay-offs of millions of workers.

In the Russian Federation, prices increased one hundred times following the initial round of macroeconomic reforms adopted by the Yeltsin government in January 1992. Wages, on the other hand, increased tenfold. The evidence suggests that real purchasing power plummeted by more than 80 percent in the course of 1992.[5]

The reforms have dismantled both the military-industrial complex and the civilian economy. Economic decline has surpassed the plunge in production experienced in the Soviet Union at the height of the Second World War, following the German occupation of Byelorussia and parts of the Ukraine in 1941 and the extensive bombing of Soviet industrial infrastructure. The Soviet gross domestic product (GDP) had by 1942 declined by 22 percent in relation to pre-war levels.[6] In contrast, industrial output in the former Soviet Union plummeted by 48.8 percent and GDP by 44.0 percent between 1989 and 1995, according to official data, and output continues to fall.[7] Independent estimates, however, indicate a substantially greater drop and there is firm evidence that official figures have been manipulated.[8]

While the cost of living in eastern Europe and the Balkans was shooting up to western levels as a result of the deregulation of commodity markets, monthly minimum earnings were as low as ten dollars a month. "In Bulgaria, the World Bank and the Ministry of Labor and Social Assistance separately estimated that 90 percent of Bulgarians are living below the poverty threshold of U.S.$4 a day."[9] Old age pensions in 1997 were worth two dollars a month.[10] Unable to pay for electricity, water and transportation, population groups throughout the region have been brutally marginalized from the modern era.

Poverty and Unemployment in the West

Already during the Reagan-Thatcher era, but more significantly since the beginning of the 1990s, harsh austerity measures are gradually contributing to the disintegration of the welfare state. The achievements of the early post-war period are being reversed through the derogation of unemployment insurance schemes, the privatization of pension funds and social services and the decline of social security.

With the breakdown of the welfare state, high levels of youth unemployment are increasingly the source of social strife and civil dissent. In the United States, political figures decry the rise of youth violence, promising tougher sanctions without addressing the roots of the problem. Economic restructuring has transformed urban life, contributing to the "thirdworldization" of western cities. The environment of major metropolitan areas is marked by social apartheid: urban landscapes have become increasingly compartmentalized along social and ethnic lines. Poverty indicators such as infant mortality, unemployment and homelessness in the ghettos of American (and increasingly European) cities are in many respects comparable to those prevailing in the Third World.

Demise of the "Asian Tigers"

More recently, speculative movements against national currencies have contributed to the destabilization of some of the world's more successful "newly industrialized" economies (Indonesia, Thailand, Korea), leading virtually overnight to abrupt declines in the standard of living.

In China, successful poverty alleviation efforts are threatened by the impending privatization or forced bankruptcy of thousands of state enterprises and the resulting lay-offs of millions of workers. The number of workers to be laid off in state industrial enterprises is estimated to be on the order of 35 million.[11] In rural areas, there are approximately 130 million surplus workers.[12] This process has occurred alongside massive budget cuts in social programs, even as unemployment and inequality increase.

In the 1997 Asian currency crisis, billions of dollars of official central bank reserves were appropriated by institutional speculators. In other words, these countries are no longer able to "finance economic development" through the use of monetary policy. This depletion of official reserves is part and parcel of the process of economic restructuring leading to bankruptcy and mass unemployment. In other words, privately held capital in the hands of "institutional speculators" far exceeds the limited reserves of Asian central banks. The latter acting individually or collectively are no longer able to fight the tide of speculative activity.

GLOBAL FALSEHOODS

Distorting Social Realities

The increasing levels of global poverty resulting from economic restructuring are casually denied by G7 governments and international institutions (including the World Bank and the IMF); social realities are concealed, official statistics are manipulated, economic concepts are turned upside down. In turn, public opinion is bombarded in the media with glowing images of global growth and prosperity. As expressed in one *Financial Times* article, "Happy days are here again ... a wonderful opportunity for sustained and increasingly global economic growth is waiting to be seized."[13]

The world economy is said to be booming under the impetus of "free market" reforms. Without debate or discussion, so-called "sound macroeconomic policies" (meaning the gamut of budgetary austerity, deregulation, downsizing and privatization) are heralded as the key to economic success. In turn, both the World Bank and the United Nations Development Programme (UNDP) assert that economic growth in the late 20th century has contributed to a remarkable reduction in the levels of world poverty.

Defining Poverty at "A Dollar a Day"

The World Bank framework departs sharply from established concepts and procedures for measuring poverty.[14] It arbitrarily sets a "poverty threshold" at one dollar a day, labeling population groups with a per capita income above one dollar a day as "nonpoor."

This subjective and biased assessment is carried out irrespective of actual conditions at the country level.[15] With the liberalization of commodity markets, the domestic prices of basic food staples in developing countries have risen to world market levels. The one-dollar-a-day standard has no rational basis: population groups in developing countries with per capita incomes of two, three or even five dollars remain poverty stricken (i.e., unable to meet basic expenditures on food, clothing, shelter, health and education).

Arithmetic Manipulation

Once the one-dollar-a-day poverty threshold has been set, the estimation of national and global poverty levels becomes an arithmetic exercise. Poverty indicators are computed in a mechanical fashion from the initial one-dollar-a-day assumption. The data is then tabulated in glossy tables with forecasts of declining levels of global poverty into the 21st century.

These forecasts of poverty are based on an assumed rate of growth of per capita income; growth of the latter implies pari passu a corresponding lowering of the levels of poverty. For instance, according to the World Bank's calculations, the incidence of poverty in China should decline from 20 percent in 1985 to 2.9 percent by the year 2000.[16] Similarly, in the case of India (where according to official data more than 80 percent of the population (1996) have per capita incomes below one dollar a day), a World Bank "simulation" (which contradicts its own "one-dollar-a-day" methodology) indicates a lowering of poverty levels from 55 percent in 1985 to 25 percent in the year 2000.[17]

The entire framework built on the one-dollar-a-day assumption is tautological; it is totally removed from an examination of real life situations. No need to analyze household expenditures on food, shelter and social services; no need to observe concrete conditions in impoverished villages or urban slums. In the World Bank framework, the "estimation" of poverty indicators has become a numerical exercise.

The UNDP Framework

While the UNDP Human Development Group has in previous years provided the international community with a critical assessment of key issues of global development, the 1997 *Human Development Report* devoted to the eradication of poverty conveys a viewpoint similar to that advanced by the Bretton Woods institutions. According to the UNDP, "the progress in reducing poverty over the 20th century is remarkable and unprecedented.... The key indicators of human development have advanced strongly."[18] The UNDP's "human poverty index" (HPI) is based on "the most basic dimensions of deprivation: a short life span, lack of basic education and lack of access to public and private resources."[19]

Based on the above criteria, the UNDP Human Development Group comes up with estimates of human poverty which are totally inconsistent with country-level realities. The HPI for Colombia, Mexico and Thailand, for instance, is around 10 to 11 percent (see Table 1). The UNDP measurements point to achievements in poverty reduction in sub-Saharan Africa, the Middle East and India which are totally at odds with national estimates of poverty.

The human poverty estimates put forth by the UNDP portray an even more distorted and misleading pattern than those of the World Bank. For instance, only 10.9 percent of Mexico's population is categorized by the UNDP as "poor." Yet this estimate contradicts the situation observed in Mexico since the early 1980s: a collapse in social services, the impoverishment of small farmers and a massive

TABLE 1

THE UNDP HUMAN POVERTY INDEX, SELECTED DEVELOPING COUNTRIES

Country	
Trinidad and Tobago	4.1
Mexico	10.9
Thailand	11.7
Colombia	10.7
Philippines	17.7
Jordan	10.9
Nicaragua	27.2
Jamaica	12.1
Iraq	30.7
Rwanda	37.9
Papua New Guinea	32.0
Nigeria	41.6
Zimbabwe	17.3

Source: Human Development Report 1997, Table 1.1, p. 21.

decline in real earnings triggered by successive currency devaluations. According to one report:

> [R]eal income [in Mexico] fell between 1982 and 1992 [following the adoption of IMF prescriptions]. Infant deaths due to malnutrition tripled. The real minimum wage lost over half its value; and the percentage of the population living in poverty increased from just under one-half to about two-thirds of Mexico's 87 million people.[20]

A recent OECD study confirms unequivocally the mounting tide of poverty in Mexico since the signing of the North American Free Trade Agreement (NAFTA).[21]

Double Standards in the "Scientific" Measurement of Poverty

Double standards prevail in the measurement of poverty The World Bank's one-dollar-a-day criterion applies only to "developing countries." Both the Bank and the UNDP fail to acknowledge the existence of poverty in Western Europe and

North America. Moreover, the one-dollar-a-day standard contradicts established methodologies used by western governments and intergovernmental organizations to define and measure poverty in "developed countries."

In the West, methods for measuring poverty have been based on minimum levels of household spending required to meet essential expenditures on food, clothing, shelter, health and education. In the United States, for instance, the Social Security Administration (SSA) in the 1960s set a "poverty threshold" which consisted of "the cost of a minimum adequate diet multiplied by three to allow for other expenses." This measurement was based on a broad consensus within the U.S. Government.[22] The U.S. "poverty threshold" for a family of four (two adults and two children) in 1996 was U.S.$16,036. This figure translates into a per capita income of U.S.$11 a day (compared to the one-dollar-a-day criterion of the World Bank used for developing countries). In 1996, 13.1 percent of the U.S. population and 19.6 percent of the population in central cities of metropolitan areas were below the poverty threshold.[23]

Neither the UNDP nor the World Bank undertakes comparisons in poverty levels between "developed" and "developing" countries. Comparisons of this nature would no doubt be the source of "scientific embarrassment," as the poverty indicators presented by both organizations for Third World countries are in some cases of the same order of magnitude as (or even below) the official poverty levels in the United States, Canada and the European Union. In Canada, which occupies the first rank among all nations according to the same 1997 Human Development Report published by the UN, 17.4 percent of the population is below the national poverty threshold, compared to 10.9 percent for Mexico and 4.1 percent for Trinidad and Tobago, according to UNDP's HPI.[24]

Conversely, if the U.S. Bureau of Census methodology (based on the cost of meeting a minimum diet) were applied to the developing countries, the overwhelming majority of the population would be categorized as "poor." While this exercise of using "Western standards" and definitions has not been applied in a systematic fashion, it should be noted that with the deregulation of commodity markets, retail prices of essential consumer goods are not appreciably lower than in the United States or Western Europe. The cost of living in many Third World cities is higher than in the United States. Moreover, household budget surveys for several Latin American countries suggest that at least 60 percent of the population in the region does not meet minimum calorie and protein requirements. In Peru, for instance, according to household census data, 83 percent of the Peruvian population was unable to meet minimum daily calorie and protein requirements following the 1990 IMF sponsored "Fujishock."[25] The prevailing situation in Sub-Saharan Africa and South Asia is more serious, where a majority of the population suffers from chronic undernourishment.

Poverty assessments by both organizations take official statistics at face value. They are largely office-based exercises conducted in Washington and New York with insufficient awareness of local realities. For example, the 1997 UNDP Report points to a decline of one-third to one-half in child mortality in selected countries of sub-Saharan Africa, despite declines in state expenditures and income levels. What it fails to mention, however, is that the closing down of health clinics and massive lay-offs of health professionals (often replaced by semi-illiterate health volunteers) responsible for compiling mortality data has resulted in a de facto decline in recorded mortality.

Vindicating the "Free" Market System

These are the realities which are concealed by the World Bank and UNDP poverty studies. The poverty indicators blatantly misrepresent country-level situations as well as the seriousness of global poverty. They serve the purpose of portraying the poor as a minority group representing some 20 percent of world population (1.3 billion people).

Declining levels of poverty including forecasts of future trends are derived with a view to vindicating free market policies and upholding the "Washington Consensus" on macroeconomic reform. The "free market" system is presented as the most effective means of achieving poverty alleviation, while the negative impact of macroeconomic reform is denied. Both institutions point to the benefits of the technological revolution and the contributions of foreign investment and trade liberalization, without identifying how these global trends might exacerbate rather than abate poverty.

THE CAUSES OF GLOBAL POVERTY

Global Unemployment: "Creating Surplus Populations"[26] in the Global Cheap-Labor Economy

The global decline in living standards is not the result of a scarcity of productive resources as in preceding historical periods. The globalization of poverty has indeed occurred during a period of rapid technological and scientific advance. While the latter has contributed to a vast increase in the potential capacity of the economic system to produce necessary goods and services, expanded levels of productivity have not translated into a corresponding reduction in levels of global poverty.

On the contrary, downsizing, corporate restructuring and relocation of production to cheap labor havens in the Third World have been conducive to increased levels of unemployment and significantly lower earnings to urban workers and farmers. This new international economic order feeds on human poverty and cheap labor: high levels of national unemployment in both developed and developing countries have contributed to the depression of real wages. Unemployment has been internationalized, with capital migrating from one country to another in a perpetual search for cheaper supplies of labor. According to the International Labor Organization (ILO), worldwide unemployment affects one billion people, or nearly one third of the global workforce.[27]

National labor markets are no longer segregated: workers in different countries are brought into overt competition with one another. Workers' rights are derogated as labor markets are deregulated. World unemployment operates as a lever which "regulates" labor costs at a world level. Abundant supplies of cheap labor in the Third World (e.g., China with an estimated 200 million surplus workers) and the former Eastern bloc contribute to depressing wages in developed countries. Virtually all categories of the labor force (including the highly qualified, professional and scientific workers) are affected, even as competition for jobs encourages social divisions based on class, ethnicity, gender and age.

PARADOXES OF GLOBALIZATION

Micro-Efficiency, Macro-Insufficiency

The global corporation minimizes labor costs on a world level. Real wages in the Third World and Eastern Europe are as much as seventy times lower than in the United States, Western Europe or Japan: the possibilities of production are immense given the mass of cheap impoverished workers throughout the world.[28]

While mainstream economics stresses efficient allocation of society's scarce resources, harsh social realities call into question the consequences of this means of allocation. Industrial plants are closed down, small and medium-sized enterprises are driven into bankruptcy, professional workers and civil servants are laid off and human and physical capital stand idle in the name of "efficiency." The drive toward an "efficient" use of society's resources at the microeconomic level leads to exactly the opposite situation at the macroeconomic level. Resources are not used "efficiently" when there remain large amounts of unused industrial capacity and millions of unemployed workers. Modern capitalism appears totally incapable of mobilizing these untapped human and material resources.

Accumulation of Wealth, Distortion of Production

This global economic restructuring promotes stagnation in the supply of necessary goods and services while redirecting resources toward lucrative investments in the luxury goods economy. Moreover, with the drying up of capital formation in productive activities, profit is sought in increasingly speculative and fraudulent transactions, which in turn tend to promote disruptions on the world's major financial markets.

In the South, the East and the North, a privileged social minority has accumulated vast amounts of wealth at the expense of the large majority of the population. The number of billionaires in the United States alone increased from 13 in

1982 to 149 in 1996. The "Global Billionaires Club" (with some 450 members) has a total worldwide wealth well in excess of the combined GDP of the group of low-income countries with 56 percent of the world's population.[29]

Moreover, the process of wealth accumulation is increasingly taking place outside the real economy, divorced from bona fide productive and commercial activities. As noted in *Forbes Magazine*, "Successes on the Wall Street stock market [meaning speculative trade] produced most of last year's [1996] surge in billionaires."[30] In turn, billions of dollars accumulated from speculative transactions are funneled toward confidential numbered accounts in the more than 50 offshore banking havens around the world. The U.S. investment bank Merrill Lynch conservatively estimates the wealth of private individuals managed through private banking accounts in offshore tax havens at U.S. $3.3 trillion.[31] The IMF puts the offshore assets of corporations and individuals at U.S. $5.5 trillion, a sum equivalent to 25 percent of total world income.[32] The largely ill-gotten loot of Third World elites in numbered accounts is placed at U.S. $600 billion, with one-third of that held in Switzerland.[33]

Increased Supply, Reduced Demand

The expansion of output in this system takes place by "minimizing employment" and compressing workers' wages. This process in turn backlashes on the levels of consumer demand for necessary goods and services: unlimited capacity to produce, limited capacity to consume. In a global cheap labor economy, the very process of expanding output (through downsizing, layoffs and low wages) contributes to compressing society's capacity to consume. The tendency is therefore toward overproduction on an unprecedented scale. In other words, expansion in this system can only take place through the concurrent disengagement of idle productive capacity, namely through the bankruptcy and liquidation of "surplus enterprises." The latter are closed down in favor of the most advanced mechanized production. Entire branches of industry stand idle, the economy of entire regions is affected and only a part of the world's agricultural potential is utilized.

This global oversupply of commodities is a direct consequence of the decline in purchasing power and rising levels of poverty. Oversupply contributes in turn to the further depression of the earnings of the direct producers through the closure of excess productive capacity. Contrary to Say's Law of Markets, heralded by mainstream economics, supply does not create its own demand. Since the early 1980s, overproduction of commodities leading to plummeting (real) commodity prices has wreaked havoc, particularly among Third World primary producers, but also (more recently) in the area of manufacturing.

Global Integration, Local Disintegration

In developing countries, entire branches of industry producing for the internal market are eliminated while the informal urban sector—which historically has played an important role as a source of employment creation—has been undermined as a result of currency devaluations and the liberalization of imports. In sub-Saharan Africa, the informal sector garment industry has been wiped out and replaced by the market for used garments, imported from the West at U.S. $80 a ton.[34]

Against a background of economic stagnation (including negative growth rates recorded in Eastern Europe, the former Soviet Union and sub-Saharan Africa), the world's largest corporations have experienced unprecedented growth and expansion of their share of the global market. This process, however, has largely taken place through the displacement of pre-existing productive systems, i.e., at the expense of local-level, regional and national producers. Expansion and profitability for the world's largest corporations is predicated on a global contraction of purchasing power and the impoverishment of large sectors of the world population.

Survival of the fittest: the enterprises with the most advanced technologies or those with command over the lowest wages survive in a world economy marked by overproduction. While the spirit of Anglo-Saxon liberalism is committed to "fostering competition," G-7 macroeconomic policy (through tight fiscal and monetary controls) has in practice supported a wave of corporate mergers and acquisitions as well as the bankruptcy of small- and medium-sized enterprises.

In turn, large multinational companies (particularly in the U.S. and Canada) have taken control of local-level markets (particularly in the service economy) through the system of corporate franchising. This process enables large corporate capital ("the franchiser") to gain control over human capital, cheap labor and entrepreneurship. A large share of the earnings of small firms and/or retailers is thereby appropriated, while the bulk of investment outlays is assumed by the independent producer (the "franchisee").

A parallel process can be observed in Western Europe. With the Maastricht Treaty, the process of political restructuring in the European Union increasingly heeds dominant financial interests at the expense of the unity of European societies. In this system, state power has deliberately sanctioned the progress of private monopolies: large capital destroys small capital in all its forms. With the drive toward the formation of economic blocks both in Europe and North America, the regional- and local-level entrepreneur is uprooted, city life is transformed, individual small scale ownership is wiped out. "Free trade" and economic integration provide greater mobility to the global enterprise while at the same time suppressing (through non-tariff and institutional barriers) the movement of small, local-level capital.[35] "Economic integration" (under the dominion of the global enterprise), while displaying a semblance of political unity, often promotes factionalism and social strife between and within national societies.

THE ONGOING INTERNATIONALIZATION OF MACROECONOMIC REFORM

The Debt Crisis

The restructuring of the global economic system has evolved through several distinct periods since the collapse of the Bretton Woods system of fixed exchange rates in 1971. Patterns of oversupply started to unfold in primary commodity markets in the second part of the 1970s, following the end of the Vietnam War. The debt crisis of the early 1980s was marked by the simultaneous collapse of commodity prices and the rise of real interest rates. The balance of payments of developing countries was in crisis, and the accumulation of large external debts provided international creditors and "donors" with "political leverage" to influence the direction of country-level macroeconomic policy.

The Structural Adjustment Program

Contrary to the spirit of the Bretton Woods agreement of 1944, which was predicated on "economic reconstruction" and stability of major exchange rates, the structural adjustment program (SAP) has, since the early 1980s, largely contributed to destabilizing national currencies and ruining the economies of developing countries.

The restructuring of the world economy under the guidance of the Washington-based international financial institutions and the World Trade Organization (WTO) increasingly denies individual developing countries the possibility of building a national economy. The internationalization of macroeconomic policy transforms countries into open economic territories and national economies into "reserves" of cheap labor and natural resources. The state apparatus is undermined, industry for the internal market is destroyed, national enterprises are pushed into bankruptcy. These reforms have also been conducive to the elimination of minimum wage legislation, the repeal of social programs and a general diminution of the state's role in fighting poverty.

"Global Surveillance"

The inauguration of the WTO in 1995 marks a new phase in the evolution of the post-war economic system. A new "triangular division of authority" among the IMF, the World Bank and the WTO has unfolded. The IMF has called for more effective "surveillance" of developing countries' economic policies and increased coordination among the three international bodies, signifying a further infringement on the sovereignty of national governments.

Under the new trade order (which emerged from the completion of the Uruguay Round at Marrakesh in 1994), the relationship of the Washington-based institutions to national governments is to be redefined. Enforcement of IMF-World Bank policy prescriptions will no longer hinge upon ad hoc country-level loan agreements (which are not "legally binding" documents). Henceforth, many of the mainstays of the structural adjustment program (e.g., trade liberalization and the foreign investment regime) have been permanently entrenched in the articles of agreement of the WTO. These articles set the foundations for "policing" countries (and enforcing "conditionalities") according to international law.

The deregulation of trade under WTO rules combined with new clauses pertaining to intellectual property rights will enable multinational corporations to penetrate local markets and extend their control over virtually all areas of national manufacturing, agriculture and the service economy.

Entrenched Rights for Banks and MNCs

In this new economic environment, international agreements negotiated by bureaucrats under intergovernmental auspices have come to play a crucial role in the remolding of national economies. Both the 1997 Financial Services Agreement under the stewardship of the WTO and the proposed Multilateral Agreement on Investment under the auspices of the OECD provide what some observers have entitled a "charter of rights for multinational corporations."

These agreements derogate the ability of national societies to regulate their national economies. The Multilateral Agreement on Investment also threatens national-level social programs, job creation policies, affirmative action and community-based initiatives. In other words, it threatens to lead to the disempowerment of national societies as it hands over extensive powers to global corporations.

CONCLUSION

Ironically, the ideology of the "free" market upholds a new form of state interventionism predicated on the deliberate manipulation of market forces. Moreover, the development of global institutions has led to the development of "entrenched rights" for global corporations and financial institutions. The process of enforcing these international agreements at national and international levels invariably bypasses the democratic process. Beneath the rhetoric of so-called "governance" and the "free market," neoliberalism provides a shaky legitimacy to those in the seat of political power.

The manipulation of the figures on global poverty prevents national societies from understanding the consequences of a historical process initiated in the early 1980s with the onslaught of the debt crisis. This false consciousness has invaded all spheres of critical debate and discussion on the "free" market reforms. In turn, the intellectual myopia of mainstream economics prevents an understanding of the actual workings of global capitalism and its destructive impact on the livelihood of millions of people. International institutions including the United Nations follow suit, upholding the dominant economic discourse with little assessment of how economic restructuring backlashes on national societies, leading to the collapse of institutions and the escalation of social conflict.

TABLE 2
POVERTY IN SELECTED DEVELOPED COUNTRIES, BY NATIONAL STANDARDS

Country	Poverty Level
United States (1996)(*)	13.7
Canada (1995)(**)	17.8
United Kingdom (1993)(***)	20.0
Italy (1993)(***)	17.0
Germany (1993)(***)	13.0
France (1993)(***)	17.0

(**) Center for International Statistics, Canadian Council on Social Development

(***) European Information Service

Source: (*) U.S. Census Bureau

NOTES

1. See Food and Agricultural Organization of the United Nations, *Food Supply Situation and Crop Prospects in Sub-Saharan Africa, Special Report*, no. 1 (April 1993). While there are no data at a regional level, one can infer from country-level figures that at least a quarter of Sub-Saharan Africa's population is at risk of famine. Ten million peasants in the Sertao region of Northeast Brazil suffer from famine and lack of water according to official figures. See "Dix millions de paysans ont faim et soif," *Devoir*, 16 April 1993, p. B5.

2. For further details see Claire Brisset, "Risque de famine sans precedent en Afrique," *Monde Diplomatique* (July 1992), pp. 24–25, and Claire Brisset, "Famines et guerres en Afrique subsaharienne," *Monde Diplomatique* (June 1991), pp. 8–9.

3. K. Nagaraj, et al., "Starvation Deaths in Andhra Pradesh," *Frontline*, 6 December 1991, p. 48.

4. Ibid.

5. See Michel Chossudovsky, *The Globalization of Poverty* (London: Zed Books, 1997), chapter 11.

6. World Bank, *World Development Report 1997* (Washington, DC: World Bank, 1997), Fig. 2.1, p. 26.

7. United Nations *Economic Commission for Europe, Economic Survey of Europe, 1995–96* (Geneva: UNECE, 1996).

8. Interviews conducted by the author with academic economists and international organizations based in Moscow, November 1992.

9. Jonathan C. Randal, "Reform Coalition Wins Bulgarian Parliament," *Washington Post*, 20 April 1997, p. A21.

10. "The Wind in the Balkans," *Economist*, 8 February 1997, p. 12.

11. Eric Ekholm, "On the Road to Capitalism, China Hits a Nasty Curve: Joblessness," *New York Times*, 20 January 1998.

12. Ibid.

13. "Let Good Times Roll," *Financial Times*, 1 January 1995 (editorial commenting on OECD economic forecasts), p. 6.

14. For a methodological review on the measurement of poverty see Jan Drewnowski, *The Level of Living Index* (Geneva: United Nations Institute for Social Research and Development (UNRISD), 1965). See also the extensive research on poverty thresholds conducted by the U.S. Bureau of the Census.

15. See World Bank, *World Development Report, 1990* (Washington, DC: World Bank, 1990).

16. See World Bank (1997), table 9.2, chapter 9.

17. Ibid.

18. United Nations Development Programme, *Human Development Report, 1997* (New York: United Nations, 1997), p. 2.

19. Ibid., p. 5. Introduced in the 1997 *Human Development Report*, the human poverty index (HPI) attempts "to bring together in a composite index the different features of deprivation in the quality of life to arrive at an aggregate judgement on the extent of poverty in a community." A high HPI indicates a high level of deprivation. See www.undp.org/undp/hdro/anatools.htm#3.

20. Soren Ambrose, "The IMF Has Gotten Too Big for Its Riches," *Washington Post*, 26 April 1998, p. C2.

21. See Clement Trudel, "Le Mexique subit le choc de l'internationalization," *Devoir*, 28 March 1998, p. A4.

22. See U.S. Bureau of the Census, *Current Population Reports, Series P60-198, Poverty in the United States: 1996* (Washington, DC: U.S. Bureau of the Census, 1997).

23. Ibid., p. 7.

24. According to the official definition of Statistics Canada (1995). For country ranks based on the UNDP's Human Development Index, see United Nations Development Programme (1997), table 6, p. 161.

25. See Chossudovsky, *El Ajuste Economico: El Peru bajo el Dominio del FMI* (Lima: Mosca Azul Editores, 1992), p. 83.

26. See Leonora Foerstel, *Creating Surplus Populations* (Washington, DC: Maisonneuve Press, 1996).

27. International Labour Organization, *Second World Employment Report* (Geneva: International Labour Organization, 1996).

28. See Saulma Chaudhuri and Pratima Paul Majumder, *The Conditions of Garment Workers in Bangladesh, An Appraisal* (Dhaka: Bangladesh Institute of Development Studies, 1991). According to this study, monthly wages in the garment industry were on the order of U.S.$20 a month (including overtime) in 1992—less than ten cents an hour.

29. "International Billionaires, the World's Richest People," *Forbes Magazine*, 28 July 1997.

30. Charles Laurence, "Wall Street Warriors Force their Way into the Billionaires Club," *Daily Telegraph*, 30 September 1997.

31. "Increased Demand Transforms Markets," *Financial Times*, 21 June 1995, p. II.

32. "Global Investment Soars," *Financial Times*, 7 June 1996, p. III.

33. See Peter Bosshard, "Cracking the Swiss Banks," *Multinational Monitor*, November 1992.

34. Based on the author's research and interviews in Tunisia and Kenya, December 1992.

35. For instance, while the large multinational enterprises move freely within the North American free trade area, non-tariff restrictions prevent small-scale local capital in one Canadian province from extending into another Canadian province.

✗ NO

Is Globalisation Cheating the World's Poor?
GAUTAM SEN

INTRODUCTION

Globalisation pertains to integration between economies of all types, at different levels of development and encompasses developed and developing countries. The discussion below is principally concerned with the absorption of developing economies into the wider world economy, dominated by developed countries. Some radical critics of globalisation consider it the contemporary manifestation of Western expansionism and cultural hegemony. As a corollary, globalisation is held to conceal the mundane imperatives of exploitation and dominance in the language of economic determinism and progress.[1] The key concepts underpinning globalisation are, first and foremost, economic progress itself as well as its unspoken, but universally acknowledged, correlate, the international division of labour. The second set of references pertains to the vehicles for their attainment, which are export orientation, the import of technology and transnational corporations, the crucial institutional conduit for wider economic interaction with the outside world. Finally, two contextual elements, good governance and structural adjustment, or transition in the former planned economies have come to be associated with globalisation. They are invariably presented as the preconditions that enable the instruments for achieving the putative goals to operate. These goals, means and preconditions are embodied in the so-called "Washington consensus," shared by the IMF, the World Bank and US official agencies.

The radical riposte to this depiction is that, in reality, the global economy is characterised by a growing concentration of wealth and inequality owing to exploitation, equalling plunder, as well as revolutionary new methods for generating wealth denied to developing countries.[2] Thus, globalisation is condemned as a neo-imperial ideology, a self-serving obfuscation that cajoles and ensures the consent of subordinate peoples. The dichotomy is between the promise of escape from dire material necessity and improved living standards through global economic integration and the failure to achieve it. And the discourse on globalisation supposedly diverts attention from the failure to promote its ostensible aim of welfare and, perhaps, the autonomy of its intended beneficiaries, to a self-absorbed intellectual teleology of economic integration.

This "Washington consensus" could be regarded as an ideology in the Marxist sense because it conceals social contradictions, but nevertheless aspires to the progressive historical outcome of economic advancement.[3] However, while a Marxist perspective could agree that the goals are progressive, the role and dynamics of the means for achieving it are questioned, as are the conception of governance and adjustment, suggested as necessary. Nevertheless, it is pertinent to note that these disagreements about globalisation now occur within the categories and assumptions of conventional economic analysis rather than some materialist conception of social contradictions that require different issues to be addressed. In relation to the Gramscian notion of ideology, to the extent that the victims of globalisation do not accept the ideological discourse on globalisation, but acquiesce in the prescriptions of its protagonists, the issue becomes one of power, or more exactly their lack of it.[4] A contrasting liberal view would question the idea that globalisation and economic integration are primarily conflictual or a failure. In this view, if globalisation is an ideology it is a useful symbolic representation for simplifying complex reality, by compressing its multi-dimensional character in a form of shorthand. The pro-market ideology of globalisation could then be regarded as both a convenient generalisation and a source of "satisficing" action in the face of uncertainty and the absence of a complete knowledge of options and consequences or their comprehension within a meaningful time frame. For example, the standard explanation of gains from trade can be allowed to settle policy questions when the general equilibrium outcome of a situation is difficult to predict.

The contention of the present discussion is that, firstly, globalisation is positive for the economic welfare of the majority, including the poor. Indeed, it is judged to be a precondition for it, even if the benefits are not immediate. Secondly, the only vehicle for easing poverty and deprivation in the short run is redistribution, which requires political decisions and specific programmes. However, there is little evidence of political support for effective and meaningful redistributive measures, either in the advanced or developing countries. Thirdly, on the contrary, not only are the poor ignored, they are the victims of various forms of discrimination in the market place because they only possess a weak political voice. Such discrimination occurs because the politicisation of markets primarily benefits the powerful and acts against the interests of the vulnerable, especially those in developing countries. Thus, it is argued that it is the political character of globalisation that distorts economic development and hurts the poor rather than any features inherent in the economic dynamics of globalisation, per se, which is the world-wide spread of capitalism.

Globalisation has multiple empirical dimensions, but both those who question its novelty or assert that it is an uniquely important contemporary phenomenon, if not altogether new, agree that globalisation is primarily an economic phenomenon.[5] Critics of globalisation condemn its economic consequences as well as many of its socio-political manifestations. But the issue of its economic configuration remains a critical nodal point that needs to be outlined in order to comprehend the differing views of globalisation. In order to appreciate globalisation as a historical phenomenon it needs to be situated in relation to an older intellectual tradition and the ideas of classical political economists, like Adam Smith and David Ricardo on the one hand and Karl Marx and his followers on the other. It is also necessary to identify the protagonists in the globalised economy and their interests in order to understand how the political economy of globalisation impacts on developing countries. The main actors are governments, domestic interests within them, transnationals (who likely have a political role in more than one national society) and inter-governmental organisations, who reflect government preferences but, perhaps, not with symmetric correspondence.

THE EMPIRICAL ECONOMIC DIMENSIONS OF GLOBALISATION

Economic interaction in the contemporary global economy contains both familiar and novel forms of interaction. It particularly highlights the enhanced importance of new institutional forms and the role of non-state actors, principally, the transnational corporation. The most important economic relationships are trade and investment, which overlap and encompass different types of capital as well as technology flows. There is also a rapid growth of international trade in services that is integrating global production and consumption distinctively as well as on a bigger scale.[6]

The most spectacular manifestations of globalization are capital mobility and the Internet. There has been a huge increase in the turnover of global capital, especially in foreign exchange markets. In 1998 $1.5 trillion of foreign exchange was swapped daily, an amount equal to one-sixth of annual US output and more than 50 times the value of trade in goods and services. The number of Internet hosts world wide increased from around 2 to 45 million between 1993 and 1999. There has also been steady growth of international trade, as measured by trade/GDP ratios. The ratio of trade to output has doubled since 1950, with a significant increase in the past decade. In fact, its impact has been greater because non-tradable services have contributed a large share of the growth in output during this period. Price changes in fuel also understate the magnitude of increased interdependence during the period. Tariff barriers on imports of manufactured goods were expected to fall to 3% after the Uruguay Round, as compared to 47% in 1947.[7]

Between 1995 and 1998 alone foreign direct investment flows rose from $315 to $644 billion, more than a rise by a factor of twelve since 1981–5. Although the share of developing countries fell in the aftermath of the Asian financial crisis in 1997, it had been growing steadily to reach 37% of total inward flows by then.[8] Transnational corporations (TNCs) are also responsible for a quarter of total international trade and a fifth of world output. Intra-firm trade is estimated to account for a third of all merchandise trade and a further third of it occurs between different TNCs. A high degree of monopoly and oligopoly therefore prevails in two thirds of all international trade transactions. It suggests that the architecture of the world economy has become institutionalized and acquired deeper roots than would be the case if international trade were dominated by arms-length, third-party transactions, which lack a similar "internalized" character. To the extent that the world economy exhibits elements of structural institutionalisation and continuity, similar to that which exists at the national level, globalisation can be said to have occurred.

CLASSICAL POLITICAL ECONOMY AND GLOBALISATION

Classical political economists like Adam Smith and David Ricardo considered the international division of labour and capitalism inextricable, though obviously not a phenomenon exclusive to capitalism because, historically, the former precedes the latter. The logic of the division of labour for Smith and comparative advantage for Ricardo created gains from trade and highlighted the compelling rationale for participation in it.[9] The diffusion of economic transformation and advancement was a potential corollary, though not exclusively dependent on it. Their critic Karl Marx considered the international division of labour to arise out of the internal contradictions of capitalism, leading to the extended reproduction of capital, and he described it as imperialist because it entailed relations of domination and subordination between capitalist and pre-capitalist societies. However, as Shlomo Avineri and Ernst Gellner have pointed out, Marx's philosophy of history denies subjectivity to non-European cultures, regarding them, like Hegel, as societies in stagnant equilibrium.[10] He assumes, rather startlingly for a theorist of the dialectical nature of change, that there was no internal catalyst that would propel an autonomous path of development in the backward colonial world. In his view, this transformation of the colonial world would occur through its encounter with European imperialism. The outward expansion of capital was expected to postpone the end of the capitalist mode of production, but only until its global limits had been reached, an issue emphasised by Immanuel Wallerstein.[11]

Classical political economists and Marx therefore viewed the international division of labour positively, although he was conscious of the human drama of conquest and plunder associated with both mercantile capitalism and the subsequent archetypal capitalist expansion, which combined conquest with the drive to export and the quest for profit.[12] Nevertheless, in terms of Marx's theoretical assumptions about the non-European world, contemporary globalisation can be deemed unremarkable as well as politically benign. Marx's analysis is not a counterpoint to the reviled "Washington Consensus," which, in comparison, is embarrassingly insouciant.[13]

The developmental logic of capitalism has also been the subject of critiques by Friedrich List who, inspired by Alexander Hamilton, insisted on the need for infant industry protection because, he argued, the spread of industrialisation would otherwise be hindered by distortions in the marketplace. However, although List had a holistic view of the nation, in which he thought the citizen should not be regarded as mere producer and consumer, and asserted the legitimacy of a balanced economy, he did not reject capitalist development. Lenin denied the capacity of late-nineteenth and early-twentieth century capitalist-imperialism to usher in economic progress in the colonial world, but did not deny the historic transformative mission of capitalism itself. In his analysis, capitalism in the advanced countries had reached a financial monopoly phase and was incapable of completing the historic task associated with capitalist-imperialism, which was the industrialisation of less advanced economies and especially the backward colonial world, largely associated today with the so-called third world.[14]

In terms of the concerns of classical political economy of Smith and Ricardo, globalisation could be interpreted as a continuation of capitalist development and therefore the path for its eventual world-wide spread. By contrast, the catalytic stimulus for the capitalist development of the non-industrial world could instead originate internally rather than due to an external "globalising" dynamic that Lenin rejected, because capitalist-imperialism in its monopoly phase no longer possessed transformative potential. This might be seen as the ideological precursor to the post-WWII advocacy of inward economic developmental strategies. It is possible to pose a further Listian qualification that national capitalist development cannot occur under conditions of free trade, which is likely to prevent or distort it. And allied to the Listian infant industry argument are the contributions, at some remove, of modern new trade theories that also justify some departures from the classical open economy approach that informed conventional debate until recent decades.[15]

Finally, there is a traditionalist rejection of both modernity and industrial life, which also has nineteenth-century roots. In the present context, it is deemed to entail the added disadvantage of being damaging to the few remaining traditional communities in the developing world, e.g., Amerindians in Brazil.[16] However, recent discussions on globalisation, inspired by this ontology and epistemology, reach mutually inconsistent insights. For example, contemporary globalisation is perceived to perpetuate a self-serving "otherness," whose antecedents can be traced to the Spanish conquest of the Americas, that progressed from "Christianisation," to a colonial Anglo-French "civilising mission" in the nineteenth century, followed by a post-WWII US ideology of "modernisation and development." Although globalisation is felt to exploit and homogenise, it is also imputed to give voice to the local and therefore liberate, exhibiting contradictory tendencies.[17] Yet, this rejectionist view essentially constitutes a critique rather than a clearly specified normative alternative and basically implies autarchy, although that does not necessarily mean the rejection of capitalism.

POLICY OPTIONS AND GLOBALISATION

The debate about the impact of the economic dynamics of globalisation concerns the nature and origins of capitalist development in latecomer countries. Classical political economy, as already indicated, assumed that economic advance would occur because of the division of labour as well as international trade. The mainstream tradition, deriving from classical political economy, therefore advocates more serious adherence to market rules and outcomes because they are considered to serve the interests of all concerned, at least in the long run.[18] And it is worth stressing the variable-sum character of the view favouring market-led outcomes. Marx, who ignored the potential for internal capitalist development in the colonial world, can be deemed to have identified a more narrowly "global" causality, since he argued that the advanced European core would be the ultimate catalyst of industrialisation beyond it. The Listian prescription for protecting infant industry and the Leninist preference for national capitalist development, implied by the conclusion that the economic stimuli could not be external, can be regarded as unavoidably convergent, although there are differences because List did not think that all societies were capable of economic development. Ultimately, the problem they both identified is a form of market failure. So, the issue needs to be assessed, firstly, in terms of how industrialisation spreads successfully. Secondly, is the catalyst for it either globalisation, which, in the contemporary world, effectively, implies the expansion of capitalism from the advanced economies, or policies dominated by inward development, i.e., import substituting industrialisation?[19] Another variant questions the wisdom of unconstrained market outcomes, and prefers shallow globalisation to the deeper international economic integration imposed by contemporary globalisation.[20] It should be noted that this is the preference of some interest groups within advanced countries, especially organised labour and ecological NGOs rather than decision-makers in developing countries.

The policy orientation highlighting market failure favours intervention to correct them and finds its post-WWII expression in the notion of special and differential treatment, embodied in the GATT system, as well as in the ideas of other international forums like the UNCTAD. It permits departures from internationally agreed norms and rules of liberal trade, enshrined in the GATT. This view derives from scepticism towards the ability of unfettered global capitalism to instigate the socio-economic transformation of less advanced economies, echoing Lenin and List. It represents an important intellectual tradition that also includes Raul Prebisch's structuralist analysis and dependency ideas, associated with Paul Baran and Andre Gunder Frank that arose as a critique of structuralism.[21] These views are not mutually exclusive, although there are essential differences in assumptions about how the world economy functions and appropriate policies to achieve, in fact, the common goal of development. The approaches to economic development, contrasted as "globalisation" or market-led versus import substitution, actually have a great deal in common, although there are distinct emphases on how sectoral growth should be sequenced. But the critical factors determining success are initial conditions and whether or not the economy is subjected to indicative or resource planning.[22]

The option of exiting the world market that the dependency theorists advocated has almost never been espoused by governments. Perhaps the former socialist Albania was a partial exception, but it cannot be regarded as a model for emulation. China itself, which inspired its political orientation, has progressively embraced the capitalist path of modernisation. Certainly, permanent economic isolation has no justification in Marx's philosophy of history and his analysis of the transformative role of capitalism. Socialist Cuba, which has suffered economic isolation because of its political estrangement from the US, its adjacent natural trading partner, would choose differently if it were possible. All sensible policy options for developing societies are located within a vector that intersects the world economy and its advanced elements. The need for imports of technology and investment finance as well as markets for exports to service the resulting debt lead back to it. Socio-economic transformation can, in principle, occur in complete isolation, but its cost would be prohibitive and impossible to sustain. Participation in international economic relations is therefore the starting point. The question is under what conditions and on what terms, since it can be agreed that both theory and practice offer a range of potential paths and outcomes. The conditions and terms lie along a spectrum bounded by pure markets on one side and high levels of intervention at the other.

The question for the opponents of globalisation would be to explain in what respects it differs from pre-existing international economic relations that makes it less attractive. There are obviously many similarities and, indeed, some critics dismiss its novelty for that very reason. Hirst and Thompson as well as other researchers have sought to demonstrate that it is an unremarkable phenomenon, which departs little from nineteenth-century experience, except in the intensity of regional economic interaction in its contemporary incarnation.[23] However, there is undoubtedly something more to it than these critics are prepared to admit. At the very least, two phenomena in contemporary globalisation are sufficiently extensive in their quantitative manifestation to merit apprehension as qualitatively unique. The first is the growing internationalisation of production, otherwise described as vertical integration that leads to intra-firm trade and more durable inter-locking of different national economies. The second is the significance of private international finance as a factor in socio-economic outcomes.[24] Critics have not, so far, argued that these two features are sufficiently disadvantageous for developing countries to call into question the entire phenomenon of globalisation. The failure of growth in many developing countries, though with some important exceptions, during most of the 1980s and 1990s was due to their indebtedness and the economic slowdown in the advanced countries.[25] The solution to it does not suggest less globalisation, since the slowdown was caused by a setback to economic interdependence, prompted by lower foreign demand, and indebtedness, which highlighted the need of better mechanisms for assessing credit-worthiness, monitoring and adjustment to illiquidity or insolvency.

Thus, globalised capitalism cannot be regarded, ipso facto, as any more problematic for socio-economic welfare than the less integrated international capitalism whose identity it has been transforming. If globalisation is to be rejected on welfare grounds, consistency dictates so should international capitalism and the heritage of classical political economy that first highlighted its merits. The reason for welcoming it remains Smithian. Greater specialisation and diffusion through globalisation increases total global wealth and the situation of the vast majority absolutely, even if it worsens relative income distribution, although there are some important caveats to these inferences, as argued below. Exactly the same arguments about specialisation and market-size hold for a single country that is experiencing economic growth, although the extent of absolute improvement for the poorest and the associated extent of relative inequality varies between countries (e.g., Republic of Korea and Taiwan as compared to Brazil or South Africa).

However, it needs to be recognised that while globalisation is both a formal and substantive phenomenon it need only entail, as a matter of logic, the former. The existence of a legally constituted single global market place, comparable to a domestic market (via treaty and practice) does not mean that economic transformation will automatically spread across space and into the developing world, in particular. Just as it is possible for underdeveloped regions to survive indefinitely within countries it is possible for them do so across legally integrated national economies, comprising the global economy. Indeed, a wide variety of entry barriers within such a global market make underdevelopment more likely to persist. The empirical outcome, ultimately, depends on the relative strength of the disadvantage of a likely weakening of state sponsorship of industrial transformation in a global market versus the positive advantage of price and productivity convergence, when high capital mobility is combined with free trade in goods. The historical evidence, so far, has pointed to a slow change of underdeveloped conditions.

A distinctive insight about the preconditions for successful economic development suggests that political stability resulting from the security and self-confidence of a ruling order is a prerequisite for such socio-economic transformation. The objective is to lengthen the shadow of the future and affect the self-interested calculations of local elites, in order to make them less shortsighted. It downgrades the significance of global factors and economic variables as the crucial explanation for economic growth. It should also be noted that the analytic division between an advanced core and a less advanced periphery is arbitrary in some important respects. It is not clear on what socio-economic basis the disadvantaged within advanced countries should be ignored in analysing the impact of globalisation.[26] This qualification needs to be borne in mind, although the main interest is the relationship between rich and poor countries that globalisation is believed to encapsulate.

ECONOMIC ANALYSIS AND GLOBALISATION

Ultimately, there is no coherent alternative economic analysis for the international division of labour that might be counterposed to the classical political economy tradition that reaches back to Adam Smith and culminates with modern neo-classical economists like, Eli Hecksher, Bertil Ohlin and Paul Samuelson.[27] The infant industry argument and more recent departures, deriving from the issue of market imperfections, arising from technology gaps and highlighting increasing returns, do not either completely controvert or reject the older tradition, but seek to account for anomalies in the patterns of international specialisation.[28] The functioning of the globalising economy can therefore be judged theoretically in relation to a spectrum that ranges from an idealised free market model rooted in classical political economy, of which Milton Friedman is one of its purest modern adherents, and an interventionist one associated with both List and Keynes.[29] The characterisation is itself idealised because prescriptions for economic policy can contain disparate elements that belong to alternative ideological traditions. Thus, the phenomenon of globalisation, which represents the expansion of capitalism, albeit a distinctive variant dependent on contingent circumstances, needs to be judged in relation to a set of goals that are both economic and philosophical, concerning notions about what is the "good life."[30]

The idealised market of general equilibrium belongs to the realm of logical possibilities, but the alternative of routine economic intervention also largely occurs within a context of markets and private property. The analysis of socio-economic transformation therefore pertains to the functioning of markets. However, it might be argued that markets may tend towards equilibrium, but remain imperfect at any given point in time. More specifically, factor rewards are not always at marginal cost and, indeed, innovation and growth in modern economies, according to new theoretical insights, require important departures like monopolistic competition that prevent pure profit from being competed away.[31] A crucial related issue for judging the impact of globalisation is the extent to which political intervention alters economic outcomes, i.e., income redistribution (not necessarily in a progressive direction) and/or institutional features that create privileges like rent.

The economic consequences of globalisation for the disadvantaged, the key ethical question, can be evaluated according to three criteria. The first is its association with reductions in absolute poverty, the second, its relationship with inequality, the issue of relative deprivation, and third, its impact on political systems, which either gain greater autonomy or remain excessively vulnerable to events beyond their own boundaries that affect the poor. Subsumed under these specific questions are issues like economic growth and the socio-political transformation of individual and community life, including their cultural identity and autonomy. But clearly, being left out of the globalised economy is worse than the failure to get a larger share of the fruits of world economic growth, as Africans have been discovering for more than two decades.[32] As a first approximation, the relevant unit of analysis remains the international system and therefore the fate of its component units, states, although some judgements require the isolation of subjects at lower levels of socio-political aggregation.

A further set of socio-political issues arises in relation to the economics of globalisation. These are questions that economists have tended to ignore because much of modern economic theory is based on abstractions that require heroic assumptions about individual behaviour and the institutional framework within which it takes place, e.g., the need for labour markets to clear speedily in response to market signals. The issue might be approached at a high level of generality in order to highlight the problem. One of the consequences of the globalisation of markets is to alter the nature of the changes that society and governments have to deal with. To the extent that markets are global, citizens of the individual countries that comprise it are subject to a variety of forces of change that originate outside their own borders and impact more frequently. Governments also need to respond to external forces that potentially limit their ability to cater to the needs and demand of their own citizens. Thus, poorer citizens with limited political salience are likely losers when governments respond to capital market volatility in order to placate very much wealthier foreigners.

POLITICAL POWER IN THE GLOBAL ECONOMY: INTERNATIONAL TRADE AND STRUCTURAL ADJUSTMENT

Economists spend a great deal of time demonstrating the existence of efficient outcomes and the conditions necessary for their achievement. The issue of market failures leads to policy prescriptions designed to minimise welfare losses. Yet the governance of the world economy has never occurred on the basis of efficiency criteria alone and certainly not according to its implied teleology of global welfare.[33] The reasons for government policies that fail to optimise global welfare have been subjected to analytical scrutiny, as have the possibility of trade-offs between global and national welfare.[34] The rules and regulations that govern the operations of the globalised market do not issue immaculately out of economic models designed to maximise global welfare. They are intimately connected to the politics of national interest and the parochial aspirations of constituents within them. As far as the analysis of globalisation and its consequences are concerned, the main interest is in actual outcomes and their causes rather than the demonstration of the technical possibility of maximising long-run global welfare, by adopting appropriate policies. It is this nexus that explains the pay-off for developing societies as well as the disadvantaged of affluent countries in the context of globalisation.

INTERNATIONAL TRADE

The impact of the global economy on developing countries is substantially a product of politicised markets, excluding the significance of the initial distribution of national and private assets. Domestic labour in advanced countries resists and curtails market access for their exports. Contemporary environmental and human rights lobbies, despite tenuous economic justification for their demands, are reinforcing this resistance. In fact, both sources of resistance to exports from developing countries ultimately stem from the desire to protect employment. The history of protectionist policies need not be recounted in detail here, except to note that developing countries only have circumscribed access to the markets of advanced economies in sectors especially crucial for their economic development. The export of labour-intensive goods like clothing, shoes and light consumer goods, critical for the livelihood of surplus labour, released by rising agricultural productivity or demographic change, has been subject to detailed regulation and persistent barriers in the form of quotas and tariff peaks.[35] Protectionist practices, as noted below, are institutionalised in the agricultural sector of the principal advanced economies and cause great harm to the prospects of a large number of Asian, African and Latin American developing countries, especially large economies like Indonesia and Argentina that enjoy a singular comparative advantage in agriculture. Genuine markets, the perceived expression of globalisation, would require the end of political intervention and free trade in these products, which are sold at marginal cost by developing countries since they do not wield market power in them.

The oligopolistic structure of retail markets in advanced countries also militates against a fair distribution of the final prices of mass-produced, non-branded products, originating in poor countries. Intermediaries resident in advanced countries capture the largest share of the final selling price. Competition policies that place poor countries at less of a disadvantage in dealings with oligopolistic agents in advanced countries would therefore be justifiable on welfare grounds. However, the blatant interference by the governments of advanced countries in favour of their own citizens highlights clear conflicts of interest with producers in poor countries that asymmetrical political power and regulatory practices are intended to perpetuate.

The history of international trade negotiations during the post-WWII period under the aegis of the GATT reflects these political imperatives. Politically weak countries usually fail to achieve their objectives and often depend on the calculated goodwill of powerful countries, which recognise that unbridled ruthlessness in translating their power capabilities into the norms and operating procedures of the regime would be counterproductive because the disenfranchised might revolt, despite costs to them. A further unhappy perversity arises because liberalisation can impose prolonged adjustment costs on the most vulnerable countries, since increased competition often eliminates their existing opportunities, for example, the loss of export quotas under the multi-fibre arrangement.[36]

The two sectors of particular interest to developing countries, clothing and agriculture, remained outside the purview of the GATT trade order until the recent Uruguay Round, although their future is not yet unambiguously clear. Paradoxically, their inclusion within the multilateral framework of international trade may be attributed to the success of globalisation, since the growing prominence of developing countries made some concessions to them unavoidable. In order to secure their agreement on other issues like the General Agreement on Trade in Services (GATS), trade-related intellectual property services (TRIPS) and trade-related investment measures (TRIMs) a negotiated quid pro quo was thought necessary. By contrast, during earlier rounds of GATT advanced countries were indifferent to tariff reductions in sectors that would have benefited developing countries, since the latter were exempted from offering reciprocity and the principal supplier rule disqualified them from taking the initiative, because of their modest shares in the relevant sectors. Once again, asymmetric political influence rather than economic criteria explains the result.

The scope and time horizon for intellectual property protection embodied in the TRIPS regime are also the product of the political power wielded by advanced economies rather than a balance between the interests of producers of intellectual property and the generality of users. The rationale for the rigidity of the regime is justified by the analytical insight that it is in the national interest of producing countries to limit the diffusion of technology beyond their own borders.[37] Once again, the economics of globalisation don a national mask. The major defeat for developing countries at the Uruguay round was to be deprived, on weak intellectual grounds, of the critical policy tool of infant industry protection, which remains a thorny issue that has not been disavowed by either compelling economic logic or policy experience. A considerable body of economic analysis continues to highlight the disadvantages of being a latecomer country, owing to the relevance of learning by doing, market size, etc.[38] These arguments are evident in the advocacy of strategic trade policies and the arbitrary nature of specialisation due to temporary technological leads rather than relative national factor endowment. But this debate was largely conceded during the Uruguay round by developing countries, on the anvil of insistent assertion by powerful national interests, rather than reasoned persuasion.

The importance of the dynamics of relative power, including the preferences of influential national constituents, as opposed to the calculus of global welfare, has thus been in sustained evidence in the outcomes of the Uruguay round negotiations. The precise contours of various agreements on most issues reflect the scope for discretion in moulding market outcomes and the historic salience of transnational corporations in guiding much of the agenda; for example, on the GATS, TRIPS and TRIMs. The most blatant was the reaffirmation of national autonomy in determining anti-dumping and countervailing actions, which most observers acknowledge to be capricious.[39] Their misuse against the exports of developing countries has less to do with maximising welfare than national and parochial interests. Significantly, protestors against globalisation from the advanced countries, frequently associated with trade unions, wish to strengthen such malpractice in the name of international brotherhood and justice. Many of them were present at the demonstrations against the WTO Ministerial meeting at Seattle. The importance of power politics, as opposed to the cogency of welfare arguments and notions of sovereign equality, was underlined by the exclusion of developing countries from the Green Room discussions at Seattle in December 1999. It was this miscalculation rather than the protesters outside in the streets that precipitated the Seattle debacle, because the debarred countries consequently decided to oppose any private understanding, as a matter of principle.[40]

STRUCTURAL ADJUSTMENT

Structural adjustment programmes (SAPs) have been another important issue for the critics of globalisation and do indeed constitute a specific and important historic crossover point for developing countries. They embody policies that are dictated by external agencies and enforce a form of globalisation on them. Quite clearly, many, if not most, developing countries would have been unlikely to adopt the retrenchment and liberalisation required by SAPs voluntarily, if only because the resulting domestic political fall-out is costly. At the same time, the harsh medicine of SAPs is administered in less potent doses to politically well-connected regimes and fuels resentment even further, since mitigated application is obviously not available to all. Recently, the most important adviser on development policy in Washington, the distinguished chief economist of the World Bank, Joseph Stiglitz, denounced SAPs as frequently ill-conceived and their architect, the IMF, as mediocre.[41] It may well be, however, that the IMF is a prisoner of circumstances, seeking to square the circle and constrained by powerful private economic interests from rich countries who are in a position to press their preferences through the US Treasury. Their concern is to retrieve local currency assets before exchange rate depreciation makes them worthless, which prompts advocacy of orthodox macroeconomic measures under the aegis of the IMF.

SAPs highlight two distinctive issues that go to the heart of the difficulties posed by globalisation for developing countries, irrespective of its economic merits and historical inevitability. The first is the problem of financial volatility in global markets that arises from the intrinsic difficulty of exchange rate management, for which policy prescription remains uncertain. For example, the circumstances in which fixed or floating exchange rates are appropriate, given the degree of exposure to international trade, etc., are far from self-evident. These novel conditions were the permissive background for the widespread corruption and mismanagement highlighted by the crisis in financial liquidity in Southeast Asia during 1997.[42]

A more intractable issue is the reality that the increase in objective global economic interdependence has not been accompanied by greater subjective societal integration that could underwrite the cost of volatility. Thus, the emerging global world economy lacks the corresponding social structures that cushion economic vicissitudes within domestic society.[43] The absence for indebted countries of the equivalent of Chapter 11 of US law, which protects agents facing bankruptcy, illustrates this dilemma. The failure of IMF SAPs to substantially mitigate their especially harsh impact on the poor adequately also reflects the inability, of wealthy governments, to protect citizens of other societies from the painful consequences of adjustment, required for participation in the world market. In fact, in recent decades the largesse of the richest countries has been diminishing, and, indeed, the US has withheld and, then, arranged for forgiveness of some of its UN dues.

The issue of good governance highlights complex problems that cannot be comprehended by slogans about the exploitative character of globalisation. It cannot be automatically assumed that the reason for the failure of socio-economic transformation in much of the developing world, and its painfully slow progress in yet other parts, is primarily economic as well as external in origin, i.e., globalisation. A passing acquaintance with the functioning of governments and bureaucracies in many Asian, African and Latin American countries cannot fail to underline the deep indigenous roots of corruption and mismanagement, independent of any external fortification.[44] The phenomenon of state capture and the theft of investment funds—which therefore ends up in consumption—as well as transfer payments intended for the poor are routine and involve many at the highest levels of government. However, blaming globalisation for the consequences diverts attention from such criminal misdeeds and also misdirects analysis of their underlying causes. The absence of good governance in a significant number of countries can undoubtedly be blamed on external factors, but these reasons were essentially political in character rather than economic.

The prolonged survival of kleptocracies in countries like Zaire, the Philippines, Indonesia and much of Latin American can be blamed on the Cold War rather than the imperatives of the global market place. The fact that Western economic interests often benefited through association with such regimes is more a consequence rather than a cause of their being in power, a by-product of narrow Cold War imperatives to maintain friendly regimes in power regardless of the wider consequences for the countries concerned. It is no coincidence that most of these kleptocratic regimes are now out of power in the aftermath of the Cold War. However, globalisation is altering the context of state action by imposing powerful constraints of external origin that can crowd out responses to local needs. The capacity for exit of external agents and its severe and immediate disruptive impact on the functioning of economies results in neglect of local constituents, especially those without a voice.[45] This is the reason for the failure to cater adequately to the needs of the poor during economic crises that impose budgetary cuts.

GLOBALISATION AND POVERTY

The causes of poverty are complex and require both careful conceptual analysis and empirical examination.[46] However, the obvious questions that can be posed are: does globalisation cause, intensify or relieve poverty? There is little evidence that globalisation, per se, causes poverty or intensifies it, unless population growth, capital market volatility and SAPs, which are usually the immediate causes of increased poverty, are primarily attributed to globalisation rather than policy failure. On the contrary, globalisation does indeed relieve poverty, albeit only slowly and, according to conventional wisdom, it worsens inequality, though these are dissimilar phenomena, because growth is likely to be associated with greater income differentials. However, recent studies challenge the inference that adjustment and globalisation either worsen poverty or increase inequality.[47] A major reason for the prevalence of poverty in the first place, as opposed to periodic variations owing to the impact of globalisation, is the absence of political will to redistribute income and assets and no amount of theorising about epistemology can obscure this stark reality.[48]

Three general issues need to be borne in mind before rushing to judgement. The first is how economic benefits can accrue to the poor. Second, the fact that although globalisation has historical antecedents, it is a phenomenon that is still at an early stage of evolution. An assessment of its eventual consequences therefore justifies some caution, for the present. Third, economic growth is a precondition for the alleviation of poverty, although whether or not globalisation inhibits development, as compared to inward development strategies, remains a separate question.

The situation of the poor improves through employment, redistributive measures or increases in the value of any assets they possess. The latter cannot be regarded as significant because subsistence at the margin for the very poor (under $1 per day) implies that such assets are liquidated quickly to ensure physical survival. Redistributive measures in regions like South Asia and especially Latin America, where a numerical majority of the world's poor live, are not significant, except during crises, though there are notable exceptions within them. Meaningful redistributive measures would first need to address the problem of unequal land ownership, which persists because the dominant elites are the landed minority. The paucity of land availability should also be borne in mind (e.g., Bangladesh), although the salience of the issue of political power is the principal explanation for skewed ownership and landlessness. The only realistic long-term solution to poverty is therefore improved employment opportunities, generated by economic growth. Such growth needs to be labour-intensive and may possess other redistributive spin-offs, but cannot be sustained in isolation from the global economy.

Recent changes in poverty indices, in the context of the increased globalisation of national economies, are ambiguous. They suggest that the largest single geographical concentration of the poor, located in the South Asian region, has experienced little or no improvement in their living standards.[49] The debate as to whether or not their numbers have grown slightly, as one recent survey seems to suggest, does not refute the main inference that the poor have benefited little from liberalisation, the precursor of globalisation, in the recent past. However, it needs to be borne in mind that the period under purview is relatively short and an enduring resolution to the long-standing historical problem of poverty is unlikely to be speedy. The relief of dire poverty, which is the outcome of the vulnerability of the very poor to economic volatility, requires periodic public intervention that depends on political will and humanitarian endeavour. Experience also shows that economic growth and the greatest recent historical successes in combating poverty have taken place in economies, like the Republic of Korea, Taiwan and now evident in the rapid socio-economic transformation of China, that have internationalised.[50] In the case of the Republic of Korea and Taiwan, substantial economic development had occurred in the first half of the twentieth century during colonial rule and the subsequent redistribution of land under US occupation ensured a critical condition for the alleviation of poverty.[51]

Thus, although globalisation, the contemporary manifestation of engagement with the international economy, may not be the ultimate catalyst of economic advance, it accompanies economic growth, as the association of rises in percapita incomes with successive increments to international trade and foreign investment demonstrates. However, the first necessary step for economic advance is political stability, the protection of property rights and the rule of law. They may be inimical for the sharpening of contradictions, as a prelude to the revolutionary seizure of power by a vanguard on behalf of the masses, labouring under false consciousness, but it is essential for capitalist development. These conditions are absent in large swathes of Africa and only weakly enforced in much of South Asia and Latin America and are a powerful reason for faltering economic performance, as potential investors, both domestic and foreign, shy away and urgent infrastructure remains undeveloped or is misapplied.

CONCLUSION

The rejectionist critics of globalisation have sought to locate it historically by engaging in metaphysical socio-political speculation at high levels of abstraction. Their preoccupation with the apocalyptic, meta-historical implications of globalisation, as well as proneness for opportunistic critiques of it on behalf of displaced labour in advanced countries, has deflected a more pragmatic assessment. It might account for their failure to give adequate attention to some of its serious negative consequences for the most vulnerable. For example, one of the meta-historical characteristics of globalisation has been the communications revolution, transporting ideas, goods and people in large volumes across space and instituting unprecedented integration of the global economy and society. Even its critics regard this phenomenon as largely positive because it has empowered them by allowing the NGOs, through which they operate, to organise opposition over the Internet. The latter is the quintessential expression of globalisation and increasingly defining its economic scope in the phenomenon of e-commerce.[52] However, it has also ensured rapid transmission of diseases like AIDS that many politically incoherent and weak administrative systems cannot cope with, as its dramatic incidence in Africa and Asia shows. This is surely a more urgent issue for those affected, requiring international intervention, than the bemoaned indignity of economic dependence or cultural homogeneity? Climate change, whose causes are still imperfectly understood, also requires global endeavour to mitigate its negative impact on poor societies that do not possess the resources to overcome recurrent floods or droughts, for example. In fact, the world is now undergoing a historic transformation that is simultaneously a centripetal economic force and a centrifugal political one. It is the source of negative feedback that needs considered attention.

The rejection of globalisation, for being supposedly inimical to the emancipation of the poor, implies a paradoxical consequent espousal of a nationalist and territorial basis for addressing their situation, the unavoidable historical alternative to it. The affirmation of such a normative outlook might be regarded as incongruous from an ideological perspective that implicitly rejects capitalism as well. Instead, it might have been expected that the privileged place of the state might also be counterposed to a potentially more radical, however weakly articulated, and cosmopolitan alternative. A further irony of the politics of rejection is the simultaneous affirmation of interests that are clearly in conflict. The protest against so-called "social dumping" (i.e., cheap imports) to protect jobs in the advanced countries cannot serve the interests of those in the third world whose livelihoods depend on it, both purported victims of a globalised market, integrated by footloose multinationals. However, one of the key complaints against globalisation that turn out to possess serious normative implications, perhaps inadvertently, is the criticism of the social cost of economic adjustment in general and its structural variety in particular. In effect, such a critique asserts the cosmopolitan character of the political right to be protected against adjustment, for all affected. The policy implication, from which its protagonists may well recoil when its true costs are known, would, in fact, entail international redistribution, depriving their own fellow citizens, who are creditors, to benefit debtors who are not.

Markets are inherently political because agents deploy their differential access to political and military resources to influence economic outcomes. In slave societies and during the feudal-mercantilist period such politicisation was unambiguous because forced labour and physical control were self-evident in determining economic outcomes. In capitalist markets, prices play a critical role in integrating the economic system as well as the distribution of income and political interference to influence economic outcomes is pervasive, but not universal. It almost certainly serves the less well-off better than previous historical alternatives as well as socialist central economic planning. "Exploiting classes," in Marxist terms, extract relative rather than absolute surplus because competition between capitalists makes it unavoidable. But there is more direct political intervention in the globalised economy than within the domestic economic sphere. The advocates of greater international economic integration systematically underrate its durability, while the critics of globalisation seek more of it without reflecting on the likelihood that it will be captured by the powerful. The political nature of such neo-mercantilist interference would merely add to the disadvantage of participation in markets without adequate human or physical assets. However, globalisation cannot provide the conditions for its own efficient operation by providing public goods like good governance and installing infrastructure.

Thus, the greatest enemies of the poor are those who wish to politicise the world economy further, because the resulting policies will be captured by dominant groups, however lofty the motives for their promulgation. The immediate alleviation of poverty requires significant redistribution of income and assets, particularly land. In the long run international economic integration constitutes the unavoidable basis for the alleviation of poverty, although globalisation can instigate negative political feedback, by privileging the voices of the newer global factors in the calculations of governments in developing countries. Such an outcome is likely to weaken the relative political salience of existing policies that benefit the poor. However, if it can be agreed that the worst drawbacks of globalisation stem from its politicisation the appropriate response to it cannot be the halting of capitalist development, but the curbing of politicisation, because it favours the powerful. The economics of the marketplace may not reduce poverty quickly, but, unlike the marketplace for political activity, it is not inherently biased against the poor.

NOTES

1. Walter D. Mignolo, "Globalization, Civilization Process and the Relocation of Languages and Cultures," in Fredric Jameson and Masao Miyoshi, eds., *The Cultures of Globalization*, Durham and London, Duke University Press, 1998, pp. 32–53.

2. See for example, Serif Hetata, "Dollarization, Fragmentation and God" in Frederic Jameson and Masao Miyoshi, pp. 273–90.

3. Jorge Larrain, *Marxism and Ideology*, London and Basingstoke, The Macmillan Press Ltd., 1983, pp. 1–45, esp.

4. For a brief summary see Antonio Gramsci, "Culture and Ideological Hegemony," in Jeffrey C. Alexander and Steven Seidman, eds., *Culture and Society Contemporary Debates*, Cambridge, UK Cambridge University Press, 1990, pp. 47–54.

5. Paul Hirst and Grahame Thompson, G*lobalisation in Question: The International Economy and the Possibilities of Governance*, Oxford, Polity Press, 1995. Robert Boyer and Daniel Drache, eds., *States Against Markets: The Limits of Globalisation*, London, Routledge, 1996.

6. World export of services grew by 25% between 1994 and1997. "Entering the 21st Century," The World Bank, *World Development Report*, Oxford, Oxford University Press, 2000, p. 64.

7. *World Development Report; UNDP Human Development Report*, UNDP, Oxford, Oxford University Press, 1997, p. 83.

8. UNCTAD, *Overview World Investment Report 1999*, New York, UN 1999, pp. XXI–XXXIV. *Human Development Report 1997* and *UNDP Human Development Report*.

9. Samuel Hollander, *Classical Economics*, Oxford, Basil Blackwell, 1987, pp. 166–70. Douglas A. Irwin, *Against the Tide*, An Intellectual History of Free Trade, Princeton, New Jersey, Princeton University Press, 1996, pp. 75–98.

10. For an incisive summary of Marx's relevant writings see Shlomo Avineri, "Karl Marx on Colonialism and Modernization," in M.C. Howard and J.E. King, eds., *The Economics of Marx,* Harmondsworth, Middlesex, 1976, pp. 235–57. For a trenchant critique of the implications of Marx's ontology cf. Ernest Gellner, "Forward," in Brendan O'Leary, *The Asiatic Mode of Production*, Oxford, Basil Blackwell, 1987, pp. VII–XII.

11. Immanuel Wallerstein, *The Politics of the World-Economy,* Cambridge: Cambridge University Press, 1984.

12. Karl Marx, "The British Rule in India" in *Selected Works,* volume One, Moscow, Progress Publishers, 1966, pp. 494–99.

13. For a robust reaffirmation of the original Marxist position, though it has been over-stated in the draft edited by John Sender, see Bill Warren, *Imperialism, Pioneer of Capitalism*, London: NLB, Verso, 1980.

14. Lenin, *Imperialism, the Highest Stage of Capitalism*, Peking, Foreign Language Press, 1973.

15. Elhanan Helpman, "The Structure of Foreign Trade," *Journal of Economic Perspectives*, Volume 13, Number 2, Spring 1999, pp. 121–44.

16. The question is analysed in Richard F. Salisbury and Elisabeth Tooker, eds., *Affluence and Cultural Survival,* 1981 Proceedings of the American Ethnological Society, Washington D.C., American Ethnological Society, 1984.

17. Enrique Dussel, "Beyond Eurocentrism: The World-System and the Limits of Modernity"; also Frederic Jameson, "Preface" and "Notes on Globalization as a Philosophical Issue" in Frederic Jameson and Masao Miyoshi, eds., 1998, op. cit. pp. 3–31; XI–XVII; 54–77.

18. Ricardo's interesting caveat regarding the abolition of the Corn Laws is worth noting. Cf. Samuel Hollander, 1987, op. cit. pp. 334–35.

19. The complexity and multiplicity of the sources of economic growth are underlined by Robert J. Barro, *Determinants of Economic Growth: A Cross-Country Empirical Study,* Cambridge, Mass., The MIT Press, 1997.

20. Dani Rodrik, "Globalisation and Labour, or: If Globalisation Is a Bowl of Cherries, Why Are There So Many Glum Faces Round the Table," in Richard E. Baldwin et al., eds., *Market Integration, Regionalism and the Global Economy,* Centre for Economic Policy Research, Cambridge, UK, Cambridge University Press, 1999, pp. 117-52.

21. Raul Prebisch, "Five Stages in My Thinking" in Gerald M. Meier and Dudley Seers, eds., *Pioneers in Development,* Oxford, Oxford University Press, 1984, pp.173-204. It is important to note that Prebisch was an advocate of infant industry protection rather than autarchy; cf. final paragraph in p. 179. Andre Gunder Frank, *Capitalism and Underdevelopment in Latin America: Historical Studies of Chile and Brazil,* New York, Monthly Review Press, 1967.

22. Gustav Ranis, "Toward a Model of Development," in Lawrence B. Krause and Kim Kihwan, *Liberalization and the Process of Economic Development,* Berkeley, California, 1991, pp. 59-101; and Robert Wade, *Governing the Market,* Princeton, New Jersey, Princeton University Press, 1990.

23. Hirst and Thompson, 1995, op. cit. and Alfred Kleinknecht and Jan ver Wengel, "The Myth of Economic Globalisation," *Cambridge Journal of Economics,* 1998, 22, pp. 637-47.

24. "Globalization Opportunities and Challenges," World Economic Outlook, *The IMF,* Washington D.C. May 1997, pp. 66-69 for a standard economic conceptualisation of globalisation.

25. William Easterly, "The Lost Decades: Explaining Developing Countries' Stagnation 1980-1998," *The World Bank,* January 2000, www.worldbank.org/research/growth/wpauthor.htm

26. For an account of the impact of globalisation on wages and employment in advanced countries see Gary Burtless, "International Trade and the Rise in Economic Inequality," *Journal of Economic Literature,* June 1995, Volume XXXIII Number 2, pp. 800-16.

27. Douglas A. Irwin, 1996, op. cit.

28. Paul R. Krugman, ed., *Strategic Trade Policy and the New International Economics,* Cambridge, Mass., The MIT Press, 1988.

29. Milton Friedman, *Capitalism and Freedom,* Chicago, University of Chicago Press, 1962; and J.M. Keynes, "The Postulates of the Classical Economics and the Principle of Effective Demand," (General Theory, chapters 1-3) in Alvin H. Hansen, *A Guide to Keynes,* New York, McGraw Hill Book Company Inc., 1953, pp. 3-35.

30. Alan Ryan, "John Rawls," in Quentin Skinner, *The Return of Grand Theory in the Human Sciences,* Cambridge, UK, Cambridge University Press, 1985, pp. 101-20; and Partha Dasgupta, *An Inquiry into Well-Being and Destitution,* Oxford, Oxford University Press, 1993; also Roger Tooze and Craig N. Murphy, "The Epistemology of Poverty and the Poverty of Epistemology in IPE: Mystery, Blindness, and Invisibility," *Millennium Journal of International Studies,* Special Issue Poverty in World Politics: Whose Global Era? Winter 1996, Volume 25, Number 3, pp. 681-708.

31. Paul R. Krugman, "Increasing Returns and the Theory of International Trade," *Rethinking International Trade,* Cambridge, Mass., The MIT Press, 1996, pp. 63-89.

32. The paltry share of foreign investment is more of a complaint than the prospect of being exploited as a result of gaining a larger proportion of it. Cf. UNCTAD, New York, UN 1999. op. cit. pp. XXIII–XXIV.

33. On the political constraints faced by governments in allowing unhindered market outcomes see James Mayall, *Nationalism and International Society,* Cambridge, UK: Cambridge University Press, 1990, pp. 108-10. Also see Strange, Susan, *States and Markets*, London, Pinter Publishers, 2nd edition, 1994.

34. Ronald Rogowski, *Commerce and Coalitions: How Trade Affects Domestic Political Alignments*, Princeton, New Jersey Princeton University Press, 1989 and an extension to it by Paul Midford, "International Trade and Domestic Politics: Improving on Rogowski's Model of Political Alignments," *International Organization*, 47, 4 Autumn 1993, pp. 535–64.

35. Sam Laird, "Multilateral Approaches to Market Access Negotiations," Staff Working Paper, Trade Policy Review Division, 98-102, Geneva, Switzerland, May 1998, WTO, pp. 1–21. On the scale of income losses for developing countries owing to textile quotas see UNDP, 1997, p. 86.

36. UNDP, 1997, ibid. calculated that overall the least developed countries would lose $600m and Sub-Saharan Africa $1.2 billion as a result of the Uruguay Round, p. 82.

37. On the logic for curbing the diffusion of technology, which the stringent trade-related intellectual property services regime that the Uruguay Round Agreement embodies cf., "A 'Technology Gap' Model of International Trade," in Paul R. Krugman, 1996. op. cit. pp. 152–64. For a critique of the current WTO intellectual property rights regime see Jagdish Bhagwati, *A Stream of Windows*, Cambridge, Mass., The MIT Press, 1998, pp. 77–82. On the importance of technology, as opposed to factor accumulation, for economic growth, cf. William Easterly and Ross Levine, "It's Not Factor Accumulation: Stylized Facts and Growth Models," Policy Research Group, *The World Bank*, January 2000, pp. 1–50, www.worldbank.org/research/growth/wpauthor.htm.

38. The idea that an efficient capital market, mainly evidenced by its absence in a majority of developing countries, can finance industries with a comparative advantage suggests a degree of wilful disingenuosness on the part of professionals.

39. Anne O. Krueger, editor, "Introduction" in *The WTO as an International Organization*, Chicago, Chicago University Press, 1998, pp.1-30.

40. See the comments of the Indian official at Seattle, Mr. N.K. Singh, in "The Seattle Ministerial Conference: Road Ahead for Developing Countries," *ICRIER*, December 1999, pp. 3-4. www.icrier.res.in/public.panel13.dec.html.

41. Joseph Stiglitz's scathing account is titled, "What I Learned at the World Economic Crisis: The Insider," *The New Republic*, 17–24, April, 2000.

42. Paul R. Krugman, "What Happened to Asia," January 1998, web.mit.edu/krugman/www/. Also Steven Radelet and Jeffrey Sachs, "The East Asian Financial Crisis: Diagnosis, Remedies, Prospects," Harvard Institute for International Development, Paper presented to the Brookings Panel, Washington, D.C. March, 1998.

43. For a clutching at straws that merely underlines the grievous weakness of a functioning global civil society that might mitigate the consequences of interdependence, see Jan Aart Scholte, "Global Civil Society," in Ngaire Woods editor, *The Political Economy of Globalization*, Basingstoke, Hants., The Macmillan Press, 200, pp. 173-201.

44. For a graphic account of the situation in Africa see "Africa," *The Economist*, Volume 355, Number 8170, March 13–19, 2000, pp. 23–25.

45. Albert O. Hirschman, *Essays in Trespassing, Economics and Politics and Beyond*, Cambridge, UK, Cambridge University Press, 1981, pp. 209–45.

46. For an exhaustive discussion see Michael Lipton and Martin Ravallion, "Poverty and Policy," in J. Behrman and T. N. Srinivasan, *Handbook of Development Economics, Volume III*, Elsevier Science, 1995, pp. 2553–657.

47. For a thorough review denying that globalisation causes poverty see David Dollar and Aart Kraay, "Growth *Is* Good For You," Development Research Group, *The World Bank*, March 2000, www.worldbank.org/research/growth/wpauthor.htm Also IMF Staff, "Globalization: Threat or Opportunity?" *IMF*, April, 2000, www.imf.org./external/gifs/space.gif.

48. Mary Durfee and James N. Rosenau, "Playing Catch-UP: International Relations Theory and Poverty," Julian Saurin, "Globalisation, Poverty and the Promises of Modernity," *Millennium*, 1996, op. cit. pp. 521–46; 657–80.

49. "Indian Poverty and the Numbers Game," *The Economist*, Volume 355, Number 8168, April 29–5 May 2000, pp. 69–70.

50. Gautam Sen, "Post-Reform China and the International Economy Economic Change and Liberalisation Under sovereign Control," *EPW*, Volume XXXV, Number 11, March 11 2000.

51. On the development of Taiwan during the first half of the nineteenth century see Christopher Howe, *The Origins of Japanese Trade Supremacy*, London, Hurst & Company, 1996, pp. 335–65. An account of the US-sponsored redistribution of land in Japan, Korea and Taiwan in the aftermath of WWII is provided by Gary L. Olson, *US Foreign Policy and the Third World Peasant*, New York, US, Praeger, 1974.

52. See Danny Quah, "The Weightless Economy in Economic Development," London: *Centre for Economic Policy Research*, Discussion Paper Number 417, 1998.

Postscript

The authors take the term globalization for granted, assuming that it is in fact taking place. Not everyone has accepted this fundamental assumption. Michael Veseth, for example, has questioned whether globalization is as far developed as analysts generally assume. In examining a number of "global" firms, Veseth found that their actual behaviour often was not genuinely global in nature. This leads him to conclude that "actual global firms are relatively rare and the process of globalization is far less developed than most people imagine." Instead, he notes that globalization as a focus of discussion has become popular because it is vague and as such a variety of policies and projects can be attached to the concept. (See Michael Veseth, *Selling Globalization: The Myth of the Global Economy*, available at www.ciaonet.org/book/veseth.) As a useful background to the above debate, it would be worthwhile for students to examine further the meaning of the term "globalization" and the various forms that it takes. Jan Aart Scholte's *Globalization: A Critical Introduction* (New York: St. Martin's Press, 2000) is a good starting point for doing this.

Infotrac Keyword Search

"globalization" + "poverty"

Suggested Additional Readings

Bello, Walden. *The Future in the Balance: Essays on Globalization and Resistance.* San Francisco: Food First and Focus on the Global South, 2001.

Birdsall, Nancy. "Life is Unfair: Inequality in the World," *Foreign Policy* 111 (Summer 1998).

Brecher, Jeremy and Tim Costello. *Global Village or Global Pillage: Economic Reconstruction from the Bottom Up.* New York: South End Press, 1994.

Chossudovsky, Michel. *The Globalisation of Poverty–Impacts of IMF and World Bank Reforms.* London: Zed Books, 1997.

_____, Gerry Mander, and Edward Goldsmith, eds, *The Case Against the Global Economy– And a Return to the Local.* San Francisco: Sierra Club Books, 1998.

Friedman, Thomas L. *The Lexus and the Olive Tree.* New York: Farrar, Straus and Giroux, 1999.

Grieder, William, *One World, Ready or Not–The Manic Logical of Global Capitalism.* New York: Simon and Schuster, 1997.

Martin, Hans-Peter and H. Schumann. *The Global Trap: Globalization and the Assault on Prosperity and Democracy.* London: Zed Books, 1997.

Scott, Bruce R. "The Great Divide in the Global Village," *Foreign Affairs* 80, no. 1 (January–February 2001): 160–77.

Website Resources

University of Warwick, Centre for the Study of Globalisation and Regionalization A leading academic research centre on globalization hosts this site, which contains a collection of working papers on various dimensions of globalization.

ELDIS The "electronic gateway to development information" hosted by the Institute of Development Studies (University of Sussex) provides access to an extensive range of materials relating to trade, development, and globalization. Look for its very useful research subject guides.

International Monetary Fund The official website of the IMF contains a number of papers examining the relationship between trade and poverty. Both the World Bank and IMF sites give helpful insight into the "Washington consensus."

Róbinson Rojas Archive The Róbinson Rojas website archives a voluminous collection of material on various aspects of globalization and international political economy.

The World Bank, Poverty Net This subsection of the official website of the World Bank includes a number of papers and studies relating to poverty and development. Especially useful is the annual *World Development Report,* with statistics on economic growth and world poverty.

Globalisation Guide The site poses a number of questions that relate to the relationship between global poverty and globalization. Also contains numerous links and other resources.

ISSUE**THIRTEEN**

Should the WTO Be Abolished?

✔ YES AND ✘ NO

Walden Bello and Philippe Legrain, "Should the WTO Be Abolished?"
An Exchange, *The Ecologist* 30, no. 9 (December 2000): 20ff

At the end of World War II, the Allied powers created a set of institutions that built an international economic order to avoid trade wars and prevent economic depression. Three principal institutions were envisioned: the International Monetary Fund (IMF), to deal with balance-of-payments problems and currency fluctuations; the International Bank for Reconstruction and Development (IBRD or World Bank), to provide loans for reconstruction and economic development; and the International Trade Organisation (ITO), to regulate trade policies.

As a result of these negotiations, the IMF and World Bank, commonly referred as the Bretton Woods Institutions, came into operation in 1945. They quickly became the key agencies for stimulating global economic recovery after the war. However, plans to create an International Trade Organization failed when the Americans decided not to support the organization, fearing that the idea of an international organization to regulate trade smacked too much of managed trade.

However, the framework that was set out as the basis for developing the Charter of the ITO continued to provide the basis for international trade policies. It became the General Agreement on Trade and Tariffs (GATT), which came into effect in 1947. The GATT was not formally an international organization; instead, it functioned more like a negotiating forum. From 1947 until 1994, the GATT was the primary vehicle for promoting freer trade on a multilateral basis. Through a series of rounds of negotiations, the member nations successfully lowered tariffs and other barriers seen as a hindrance to trade. In addition, the GATT helped to clarify the rules of trade and provided a mechanism to arbitrate disputes.

In 1995, the GATT was converted into a new organization, called the World Trade Organisation (WTO). The existing GATT agreements on trade in manufactured goods were subsumed into the WTO framework. These were then extended to include trade in services and intellectual property. The stated objectives of the WTO are to (i) help trade flow as freely as possible; (ii) encourage further liberalization of trade through negotiations; (iii) provide an impartial means of dispute settlement; and (iv) reduce the use of protectionist measures. In order to achieve this, the WTO has a staff of some 500 people in its headquarters in Geneva, Switzerland. By mid-2001, the WTO had 142 members. Almost all of the major trading nations of the world have joined the WTO and some dozen further countries have applied to join, including Russia and China.

The WTO continues GATT's role as a negotiating forum to reduce trade barriers on a multilateral basis. However, as the negotiations have moved beyond manufactured goods to such issues as services, intellectual property, telecommunications, and agriculture, they have become more complex and controversial. Any commitment to reduce barriers in these areas inevitably carries economic, social, and political costs.

The growing difficulties became evident at the 1999 Seattle WTO conference. This meeting of trade ministers was intended as the launch for a new round of negotiations to be known as the "Seattle Round." But the tensions within the membership of the organization quickly became evident. The industrialized nations of the North wanted to include discussions on such issues as environmental protection and child labour. Members for the South were critical of the North's slowness to respond to their concerns about access to Northern markets and accused the industrialized nations of seeking to maintain their trade advantages. The members could also not agree on an acceptable Director–General for the 1999–2005 term, finally accepting a compromise by splitting the five-year term between a New Zealander and a politician from Thailand. Nor could they agree on a new agenda for future talks.

Perhaps of greater significance, however, were the events taking place outside the conference halls in Seattle. Thousands of protestors from a broad political spectrum joined in street protests against the WTO meeting. Trade talks that once were carried on in relative obscurity now have became the focus of massive demonstrations. It was clear that the WTO had become the focus of a range of discontents associated with the rapidly moving globalization process. While some advocated more openness for trade talks, others made it clear that they wanted to "shut down" the WTO. Peaceful demonstrations soon turned into violent confrontations between anarchists and the Seattle police.

In this Issue, Walden Bello and Phillippe Legrain give us insight into the controversies surrounding the WTO. Walden Bello is a prolific author and political activist who has been a strong critic of the WTO, the World Bank, and the IMF. Phillipe Legrain is an official with the WTO.

✔ YES AND ✗ NO
Should the WTO Be Abolished?
An Exchange
WALDEN BELLO AND PHILIPPE LEGRAIN

Dear Philippe,

The idea that the world needs the World Trade Organisation (WTO) is one of the biggest lies of our time. The WTO came about, in 1995, mainly because it was in the interest of the US and its corporations. The European Union, Japan and especially the developing countries were mostly ambivalent about the idea; it was the US which drove it on.

Why? Because though the US, back in 1948, blocked the formation of an International Trade Organisation (ITO), believing that, at that time, the interests of its corporations would not be served by such a global body, it had changed its mind by the 1990s. Now it wanted an international trade body. Why? Because its global economic dominance was threatened. The flexible GATT (General Agreement on Tariffs and Trade) system, which preceded the WTO, had allowed the emergence of Europe and East Asia as competing industrial centres that threatened US dominance even in many high-tech industries. Under GATT's system of global agricultural trade, Europe had emerged as a formidable agricultural power even as Third World governments concerned with preserving their agriculture and rural societies limited the penetration of their markets by US agricultural products.

In other words, before the WTO, global trade was growing by leaps and bounds, but countries were using trade policy to industrialise and adapt to the growth of trade so that their economies would be enhanced by global trade and not be marginalised by it. That was a problem, from the US point of view. And that was why the US needed the WTO.

The essence of the WTO is seen in three of its central agreements: the Agreement on Trade Related Intellectual Property Rights (TRIPs), the Agreement on Agriculture (AOA), and the Agreement on Trade Related Investment Measures (TRIMs).

The purpose of TRIPs is not to promote free trade but to enhance monopoly power. One cannot quarrel with the fact that innovators should have preferential access to the benefits that flow from their innovation for a period of time. TRIPs, however, goes beyond this to institutionalise a monopoly for high-tech corporate innovators, most of them from the North. Among other things, TRIPs provides a generalised minimum patent protection of 20 years; institutes draconian border regulations against products judged to be violating intellectual property rights; and—contrary to the judicial principle of presuming innocence until proven guilty—places the burden of proof on the presumed violator of process patents.

What TRIPs does is reinforce the monopolistic or oligopolistic position of US high tech firms such as Microsoft and Intel. It makes industrialisation by imitation or industrialisation via loose conditions of technology transfer—a strategy employed by the US, Germany, Japan and South Korea during the early phases of their industrialisation—all but impossible. It enables the technological leader, in this case the US, to greatly influence the pace of technological and industrial development in the rest of the world.

The AOA is all about consolidating the monopolistic competition between the US and the EU for third country markets. The agreement does provide for cuts in certain subsidies, but these cuts are relatively small measured against the tremendous overall level of subsidization in the US, EU and other developed countries. Moreover, the AOA exempts a very important channel of subsidization: direct income payments to farmers, which in the US comes to one-fifth to one-third of farm income.

The subsidization of agricultural production in the US, EU and other developed countries is now nothing short of scandalous. OECD figures show that instead of decreasing under the WTO regime, overall subsidization has increased tremendously, from around $182 billion in 1995 to $362 billion in 1998! Naturally, this situation creates conditions of overproduction and a huge need for export markets to relieve surplus. These markets are in the developing countries, which the AOA mandates to remove agricultural quotas, bind agricultural tariffs, accept "minimum access volumes" of agricultural commodities and prevent from significantly raising their minimal levels of subsidization. Food insecurity and the displacement of millions of families who cannot compete with subsidization from elsewhere are among the bitter harvests of the AOA.

Trade-Related Investment Measures (TRIMs), such as trade-balancing mechanisms or local content policies, had been used by many Third World countries to build up industrial sectors by pushing transnational firms to source components and inputs within the country. However, these measures interfered with the inter-subsidiary trade of transnational corporations. Alongside the banning of quotas and the binding of tariffs, the TRIMS agreement, by outlawing trade-balancing and local content policies, effectively eliminates the use of trade policy for industrialisation and development.

These agreements provide just three examples of the fact that the WTO is fundamentally flawed; and fundamentally flawed agreements resist reform.

So why does the line about the necessity of the WTO keep on being repeated despite the empirical evidence? Because Washington has learned from the Nazi propaganda master Joseph Goebbels that a lie repeated often enough might ultimately attain the status of truth. Fortunately, after Seattle, people now see through this Big Lie. The world does not need the WTO. The US corporate elite does.

Walden Bello

Dear Walden,

A convincing case for the WTO's abolition must show two things. First, that the world would be better off without the WTO. Second, that the WTO's abolition is preferable to any politically feasible reform. You fail to show either.

Abolishing the WTO would not destroy globalisation, capitalism, or US corporate power. But it would wipe out a forum for governments to negotiate multilateral trade rules and a mechanism for holding them to those rules. That would make every country worse off, but the biggest losers would be the poor and the weak.

One benefit of rules is that they apply to big, rich countries as well as small, poor ones. When America blocked imports of Costa Rican underwear, Costa Rica appealed to the WTO. It won, and America lifted its restrictions. Do you honestly think Costa Rica would have such clout in Washington without the WTO? Granted, the dispute-settlement mechanism is not perfect: America has a battery of lawyers to fight in its corner, whereas small countries scrimp. It should be improved. But it is already much better than the alternative: the law of the jungle, where might makes right.

Another merit of WTO rules is that they tie governments' hands. Once countries open their markets to foreign trade and investment, they cannot close them again at whim. Without this stability, companies would be reluctant to invest abroad, particularly in developing countries with a protectionist or politically unstable record. Abolishing the WTO would further marginalise developing countries.

If there were no prospect of further multilateral liberalisation and no body to enforce existing rules, trade barriers would creep up as protectionists gain the upper hand. The world might split into hostile regional blocks, with rich-country exporters seeking captive markets in developing countries. Developing countries, which need access to rich-country markets more than rich countries need access to theirs, would have to join on unfavourable terms or be left out in the cold.

In any case, there would be less trade. And less trade means slower economic growth, stagnating living standards, and more people trapped in poverty—like in the Great Depression. Over the past 50 years, the fifteen-fold rise in world trade has driven a seven-fold rise in world output. Thanks to trade, Japan and South Korea are no longer developing countries. Jeffrey Sachs and Andrew Warner of Harvard University found that developing countries with open economies grew by 4.5 per cent a year in the 1970s and 1980s, while those with closed economies grew by 0.7 per cent a year. At that rate, open economies double in size every 16 years, while closed ones must wait a hundred. Of course, in the short term, some people lose from trade liberalisation. But in the long run, everyone gains: even the poorest South Koreans today are much richer than their counterparts 30 years ago.

Let me briefly address your specific points.

If the WTO mainly serves US corporate interests, why have 139 countries freely joined? Why are 30 others, including China, trying to join? Why is Castro, hardly a US stooge, a big WTO supporter? Presumably, they think WTO membership benefits them. Moreover, if the WTO mainly serves US corporate interests, why do America's steelmakers oppose WTO membership? And how come the US lost the biggest WTO case ever, when its foreign-sales corporations, worth some $4 billion a year to US companies, were judged to be illegal export subsidies?

On TRIPs, you recognise that innovators should have some rights over their inventions. So why shouldn't high-tech corporate innovators, such as Microsoft and Intel? True, intellectual-property rights give companies market power: that is how innovators are rewarded. But as recent US antitrust cases involving Intel and Microsoft show, patent protection does not prevent the exercise of competition law.

It is simplistic to think that countries can industrialise by copying or reverse-engineering foreign technology. Most technology can only be used effectively with the co-operation of the companies that developed it, which have associated secret know-how. Such technology transfer is more likely with a functioning intellectual-property system. Research shows that strong patent protection is positively correlated with FDI, technology licensing, and international trade. Contrary to your claim, patent protection was built into the American constitution and has a long history in Germany, Japan, and South Korea.

On agriculture, you cannot blame the WTO for US and EU subsidies: they existed before the WTO. I agree they should be cut. So you should welcome the current WTO negotiations on agriculture, which aim to reduce agricultural protectionism. How would abolishing the WTO reduce farm subsidies?

The TRIMs agreement does not effectively eliminate the use of trade policy for industrialisation and development. Yes, it outlaws trade-balancing and domestic-content requirements, which in any case research shows are ineffective. But governments can still use investment measures such as technology-transfer requirements. Moreover, developing countries can invoke exceptions to promote economic development, and have a five-year transition period (seven for least-developed countries). Nine developing countries have requested a further extension, but most have not needed to.

The WTO is not perfect. But it is still a powerful force for good in the world.

Philippe Legrain

Dear Philippe,

Your method of arguing is to set up a straw man: opponents of the WTO are opponents of the growth of trade. This is silly. Trade can be good or bad for national development—it all depends on the rules that guide it. The relative flexibility of the old GATT has disappeared under the WTO, which imposes policies that advance the interests of superpowers.

Your most prominent example of the benefits of liberalisation—South Korea—proves the opposite. Far from being a paragon of free trade, South Korea systematically subordinated trade to developmental goals. The recent paucity of foreign cars in Korea was a key condition for the emergence of its car industry. The "South Korean miracle" was based on protectionist/mercantilist trade practices, not on the doctrinaire free trade principles that undergird the WTO.

I had expected a more reasoned reply than a doomsday scenario asserting that without the WTO, the international economic order would degenerate into anarchy or hostile regional blocs. The history of the international economy in the last 55 years refutes this hysterical contention. The seventeen-fold increase in global trade between 1948 and 1997 took place without a powerful trade bureaucracy, without an all-encompassing system of trade rules.

Five years into the WTO, hardly any developing countries claim it has benefited them. Just look at the record: US and EU dumping of subsidized grain and meat is destroying agricultural industries, like the poultry industry in the Philippines. The US and other trade superpowers have scarcely implemented the lifting of quotas on textile and garment imports of interest to the developing countries, as stipulated by the Agreement on Textiles and Clothing. The Ministerial Decision approved at Marrakech in 1994 to take measures to counteract the negative effects of trade liberalisation on the net food importing countries (NFID) has never been implemented. These are among the reasons why the majority of developing countries oppose a new trade round.

So why are they in the WTO? In the case of most, it is not from the prospect of gain but out of fear that the rate at which they are being marginalised would increase if they were not members. You can hardly blame them: in 1994, Washington stampeded Third World governments to ratify the WTO by saying they would otherwise be isolated "like North Korea."

You say that the function of the WTO is to provide rules to protect the weak from the strong. Do you really believe this? It is power, Philippe, not justice, which is the currency of unequal international economic arrangements like the IMF, World Bank, and WTO. The main rationale for the WTO's existence is to reduce the cost of policing the less powerful and less developed economies that would be incurred by the hegemonic power if there were no system of rules backed up by a bureaucracy with coercive powers. This is the reason Washington's academic point man on trade, C. Fred Bergsten, could tell the US Senate that what was not possible under GATT was possible under the WTO: "[W]e can now use the full weight of the international machinery to go after those trade barriers, reduce them, get them eliminated."

The WTO is the incarnation of a paradigm that subordinates almost every other good—environment, development, food security, culture—to free trade. Shot through with this fundamental flaw, it cannot be reformed. Instead, it must be disempowered, if not abolished, and replaced by a system of global economic governance that regards the market as a mechanism to be controlled and guided to achieve social priorities.

Walden Bello

Dear Walden,

I'm disappointed that you seem not to have read my letter carefully. I didn't say that "opponents of the WTO are opponents of the growth of trade." I said trade would be lower without the WTO. Nor did I say the world "would degenerate into anarchy or hostile regional blocs" without the WTO. I said protectionism would creep up and the world might split into hostile regional blocs. Do you disagree? If so, you haven't said why. If not, you haven't shown how the reduced trade and increased protectionism that would result would benefit the world.

My position is clear. The WTO is good for the world because it helps lower trade barriers and keep them down, which boosts trade and thus economic growth. Countless country studies show this. Moreover, a rules-based system is of particular benefit to weaker countries. Of course, with or without the WTO, America is much more powerful than Cuba or Costa Rica. But equally clearly, WTO rules constrain America's ability to act unilaterally. Surely this is a big benefit for weak countries? What I'm saying is not inconsistent with your statement that WTO rules benefit America. The multilateral trading system is not a zero-sum game, where one country gains at another's expense, but a positive-sum game, where everyone can gain.

You claim most developing countries are in the WTO because they "fear that the rate at which they are being marginalised would increase if they were not members." Even accepting your premise, this means they are not as badly off in the WTO as outside. In fact, developing countries benefit from WTO membership, by opening their domestic markets and gaining better access to foreign ones. That is why none has left the WTO. I agree rich countries have been slow to lift textile-import barriers. But they will do so by 2005. Without the WTO, that would not happen. Moreover, a new WTO round could bring even bigger benefits. The Tinbergen Institute estimates developing countries would gain $155 billion a year from further trade liberalisation—over three times the $43 billion in average annual overseas aid.

You also claim the WTO "subordinates almost every other good—environment, development, food security, culture—to free trade." Not so. WTO rules allow governments to protect human, animal or plant life and health however they want so long as their measures are not arbitrarily or unjustifiably discriminatory and are not disguised protectionism. Take the recent asbestos case. Although a WTO panel found that France's ban on white asbestos discriminates against Canada, it upheld the ban on health grounds. WTO rules also give developing countries plenty of flexibility, as I described in my first letter. The Agreement on Agriculture makes allowances for non-trade concerns, such as food security and environmental protection. Perhaps more importantly, by fostering trade, the WTO raises economic growth, which is the only long-term route to development. Growth also generally helps the environment, because when people get richer they usually want a cleaner environment and are able to pay for it.

From the false premise that WTO subordinates everything to free trade, you leap to the conclusion that it "cannot be reformed." Yet the GATT became the WTO. So why couldn't the WTO change? Reform of the dispute-settlement mechanism is already being discussed. Moreover, a new WTO round will have to address developing countries' agendas or they will not agree to its launch.

It is a pity that you blame the WTO for everything you dislike. Your prejudice blinds you to the fact that, in an unequal world, the WTO makes people richer, freer, and safer.

Philippe Legrain

Dear Philippe,

Before you muddy things further, let me say this: I am for fair trade—trade that is subordinated to priorities such as development, the environment, and food security. You are for free trade—trade that is liberated from such restraints in the belief that some "invisible hand" will bring about "the greatest good for the greatest number." The WTO institutionalises this paradigm, which has brought about the opposite of the global prosperity that you touchingly have faith in.

Statistical projections are only as good as the assumptions that determine the numbers. I prefer historical evidence. The latest World Bank Development Report shows that, in the '90s, poverty and inequality increased in Eastern Europe, Latin America, the Caribbean, Sub-Saharan Africa, and South Asia. All these areas were subjected to SAPs that embodied the IMF-WTO free-trade paradigm.

If we must forecast, let us rely on universally respected sources such as the UN Development Programme. The UNDP estimates that, under the WTO, in the period 1995–2004, the 48 least developed countries will actually be worse off by US$600 million a year and Sub-Saharan Africa by US $1.2 billion a year! Seventy per cent of the gains of the Uruguay Round are expected to go to developed countries.

We cannot conclude without touching on one of the WTO's biggest flaws: its undemocratic decision-making process. Shortly after Seattle, even US Trade Representative Charlene Barshefsky conceded that the "Consensus/Green Room" method was "a rather exclusionary one," where "all meetings were held between 20 and 30 key countries, and 100 countries were never in the room." But barely

10 weeks later, Director-General Mike Moore said that the Consensus/Green Room method was "non-negotiable." So much for Mr. Moore's reform agenda.

Add all this up, Philippe, and it might finally dawn on you why the case for disempowering the WTO is so compelling.

Walden Bello

Dear Walden,

Whether you or I believe in free or "fair" trade is beside the point. It is simply incorrect to assert that the WTO subordinates development, the environment, and food security to trade. Read the GATT and Uruguay round texts. It is also ridiculous to blame the WTO for world poverty, which existed long before the WTO was set up. As for the IMF's structural-adjustment programmes, they have nothing to do with the WTO.

We are debating whether the WTO should be abolished, not whether there is injustice or misery in the world. Our question can only be answered by comparing the state of the world with the WTO (or a plausibly reformed WTO) with the likely state of the world without it. You say 70 per cent of the gains of the Uruguay round are expected to go to developed countries. That means 30 per cent go to developing countries. So, even by your figures, both developed and developing countries gain from the Uruguay round.

I am glad you brought up the alleged lack of democracy in WTO decision-making. The WTO operates by consensus. This means every country, however small, has a veto. How is that undemocratic? It is this consensus principle, not the Green Room process, which Mike Moore said was non-negotiable.

One of the myths about Seattle is that there were no Africans and hardly any developing-country representatives in the Green Room. In fact, there were six Africans and a majority from developing countries. Moreover, any deal reached in a Green Room must still be approved by all WTO members. In any case, the WTO is changing. More General Council meetings, where all members can put forward their case, were held this year than ever before. Proceedings take longer, but every country has a chance to participate. Perhaps you should come to Geneva and see.

Postscript

Walden Bello represents those critics who would like to see the WTO either significantly disempowered or abolished altogether. Bello does not believe that serious reforms to the WTO are likely. Legrain counters by suggesting that the WTO is inherently democratic since it makes decisions by consensus, meaning that "every country, however small, has a veto." In examining this debate, one's assessment of the potential for reform within the WTO is important. This issue is examined in Gerald K. Helleiner's "Markets, Politics, and Globalization: Can the Global Economy be Civilized?" *Global Governance* 7, no. 33 (July–September 2001): 243-64. Helleiner notes that process is of vital importance in discussing the role of the WTO in regulating trade. He notes that the various WTO processes may involve as many as forty-five meetings a week on highly technical and legalized issues. Thus, smaller countries, especially from the developing world, are at a serious disadvantage in participating fully in decision-making. As a result, Helleiner suggests that they are often "rule-takers" rather than "rule-makers." Rather than abolishing, or seriously disempowering, the WTO as Bello suggests, Helleiner calls for the Secretary-General of the United Nations to convene an independent commission to examine reforms to the WTO.

Infotrac Keyword Search

"WTO" or "World Trade Organization"

Suggested Additional Readings

Bagwell, Kyle and Robert Staiger. "National Sovereignty in the World Trading System," *Harvard International Review* 22, no. 4 (Winter 2001): 54-60.

Hawkins, William. "The WTO as Battleground—A Realist Revival," *World and I* 16, no. 1 (March 2001): 280ff.

Levi, Margaret and David Olson. "The Battles in Seattle," *Politics & Society,* 28, no. 3 (September 2000): 309-30.

McMichael, Philip. "Sleepless Since Seattle: What Is the WTO About?" *Review of International Political Economy* 7, no. 3 (September 2000): 466-75.

Moore, Mike. "Back on Track," *Harvard International Review* 22, no. 4 (Winter 2001): 84-85.

Sampson, Gary P. "The World Trade Organisation After Seattle," *World Economy* 23, no. 9 (September 2000): 1097-2017.

Sutherland, Peter D. "Reality Check," *Harvard International Review* 22, no. 1 (Winter/Spring 2000): 20-25.

Website Resources

Focus on the Global South   The research and lobby organization headed by Walden Bello. Contains a number of Bello's articles critiquing the WTO and other Bretton Woods Institutions.

Global Policy Forum   While covering a range of international issues, this website has a good selection of WTO articles and links.

Public Citizen, Global Trade Watch   An American NGO focusing on trade issues with a number of papers and links on trade and the WTO.

LLRX Interactive Briefs   Contains a research guide on the WTO and GATT, with a particular focus on legal issues.

World Trade Organization   The official website of the WTO has access to a range of materials geared for the general public, including some responses to criticisms leveled at it.

WTO Watch   An NGO which monitors the WTO. This site has a useful collection of resources and links.

ISSUE**FOURTEEN**

Was the "Battle in Seattle" a Significant Turning Point in the Struggle against Globalization?

✔ **YES**

STEPHEN GILL, "Toward a Postmodern Prince? The Battle in Seattle as a Moment in the New Politics of Globalisation," *Millennium: Journal of International Studies* 29, no. 1 (2000): 131–40

✘ **NO**

JAN AART SCHOLTE, "Cautionary Reflections on Seattle," *Millennium: Journal of International Studies* 29, no. 1 (2000): 115–21

Significant turning points in history have come to be symbolized by a particular event or set of events. The Boston Tea Party became identified as the beginning of the American Revolution, and the Storming of the Bastille is still celebrated as the spark of the French Revolution. In more recent times, specific events have also been interpreted as significant signposts in a changing world order. The dismantling of the Berlin Wall symbolically marked the end of the Cold War. The launch of the Persian Gulf War was seen by some as a harbinger of a "New World Order."

For many, the "Battle in Seattle" has come to symbolize one such critical turning point. The immediate context was the Third Ministerial conference of the World Trade Organization (WTO), which was scheduled to meet in Seattle from November 30 to December 3, 1999. Two previous ministerial conferences had taken place in Singapore in 1996 and Geneva in 1998, with little public fanfare. But, as delegates from 130 nations descended on Seattle for deliberations, the conference took on a totally different character.

Thousands of demonstrators took to the streets of Seattle, virtually shutting down the city and seriously disrupting WTO deliberations. As demonstrators and police clashed in increasingly violent confrontations, the "Battle in Seattle" captured headlines around the world. When the conference ended without agreement on a new Millennium Round of talks to further liberalize world trade, activists declared that they had achieved a significant victory.

The "Battle in Seattle" was in many ways reminiscent of the anti-Vietnam and anti-nuclear demonstrations of the 1960s and 1970s. However, unlike these movements, which focused on issues relating to war and peace, the Seattle demonstrations focused on issues of economic justice, corporate power, and inequality. Unlike the anti-Vietnam demonstrations of the 1960s, which were driven more by disillusioned youth, the anti-globalization demonstrations in Seattle have been described as multi-generational, multi-class, and multi-issue—environmentalists, animal-rights supporters, union members, human-rights activists, and anarchists represented a broad spectrum of causes and goals.

Since Seattle, it has become virtually impossible to hold a significant meeting of world leaders to discuss global economic issues without triggering massive demonstrations. Subsequent international meetings in Quebec City and Genoa featured similarly dramatic confrontations between demonstrators and policy-makers.

Why has the arcane world of international economics and trade become the focus of popular mass protest? Some see these events as signifying an important setback for globalization. As resistance to globalization deepens, we are entering a new phase of de-globalization. But others suggest that we are seeing a significant shift in the politics of globalization as new voices and forces, which have been excluded from global economic governance, demand access to decision-making structures. What we are witnessing is the emergence of a "global civil society." This term refers to growth in independent NGOs, social movements, and other non-profit sector actors that increasingly operate across national borders. It is argued that these actors are increasingly seeking access to international policy discussions, including those involving trade and finance. As a result, a process that was once the exclusive domain of power elites is being democratized.

In these readings we encounter two different interpretations of the meaning of Seattle. Stephen Gill of York University sees the events in Seattle as a harbinger of new political alignments and forces that are seeking to "develop a global and universal politics of radical (re)construction around values such as democratic human development, human rights, and intergenerational security." Jan Aart Scholte of Warwick University is more cautious in his interpretation of these same events. Although Scholte is hopeful that a more humane global economic order will emerge, he emphasizes that the concept of global civil society has serious limits and that developments in Seattle could be ephemeral.

✔ YES
Toward a Postmodern Prince? The Battle in Seattle as a Moment in the New Politics of Globalisation
STEPHEN GILL

The modern prince, the myth-prince, cannot be a real person, a concrete individual. It can only be an organism, a complex element of society in which a collective will, which has already been recognised and has to some extent asserted itself in action, begins to take concrete form.[1]

This essay analyses recent protests against aspects of neoliberal globalisation, as for example at the World Trade Organisation (WTO) Ministerial Meeting in Seattle in late 1999 and in Washington, DC, in spring 2000 to coincide with the IMF and World Bank Annual Meetings. I first examine the reason for the failure of the Seattle talks, and secondly, evaluate the protests and their political significance. Finally, I analyse some emerging forms of political agency associated with struggle over the nature and direction of globalisation that I call the "the postmodern Prince." This concept is elaborated in the final section of this essay. It is important to stress at the outset, however, that in this essay the term "postmodern" does not refer, as it often does, to a discursive or aesthetic moment. In my usage, "postmodern" refers to a set of conditions, particularly political, material, and ecological, that are giving rise to new forms of political agency whose defining myths are associated with the quest to ensure human and intergenerational security on and for the planet as well as democratic human development and human rights. As such, the multitude and diverse political forces that form the postmodern Prince combine both defensive and forward-looking strategies. Rather than engaging in deconstruction, they seek to develop a global and universal politics of radical (re)construction.

The battle in Seattle took place both inside and outside the conference centre in which the meetings took place; the collapse of the discussions was partly caused by the greater visibility of trade issues in the everyday lives of citizens and the increasing concern over how international trade and investment agreements are undermining important aspects of national sovereignty and policy autonomy, especially in ways that strengthen corporate power. These concerns—expressed through various forms of political mobilisation—have put pressure upon political leaders throughout the world to re-examine some of the premises and contradictions of neoliberal globalisation.

WHY THE TALKS FAILED

Why specifically did the Seattle talks fail? The first and most obvious reason was US intransigence, principally in defence of the status quo against demands for reform by other nations concerned at the repercussions of the liberalisation framework (the built-in agenda) put in place by the GATT Uruguay Round.[2] The GATT Uruguay Round was a "Single Undertaking," a generic all-or-nothing type of agreement that meant signatories had to agree to all its commitments and disciplines, as well as to the institutionalisation of the WTO. The wider juridical-political framework for locking in such commitments can be called the new constitutionalism of disciplinary neoliberalism. This encompasses not only trade and investment, but also private property rights more generally (and not just intellectual property rights). It also involves macroeconomic policies and institutions (for example independent central banks and balanced budget amendments) in ways that minimise, or even "lock out" democratic controls over key economic institutions and policy frameworks in the long term.[3]

In this context, the US mainly wanted to sustain commitments to existing protections for intellectual property rights and investment and stop any attempts to weaken the capacity of existing agreements to open new markets for American corporations. The US position was based on intelligence work by government agencies, academics, and corporate strategists co-ordinated by the CIA.[4]

So it would be easy to say that protests outside the Seattle Convention Centre and confronted by the Seattle riot police, the FBI, and the CIA had little or no effect on the failure of the talks, other than the fact that many delegates could not get into the building because of the disruptions outside. However, this would be to misunderstand the link between public concern and the negotiating positions of states in the WTO. Indeed, it is becoming clear that the central reasons for the failure of the Seattle Ministerial were linked to the fact that the establishment of the WTO has gone well beyond the traditional role of the GATT in ways that have begun not only increasingly to encroach on crucial domestic policy areas and national sovereignty, but which also have repercussions for international law. In addition, key areas of concern to the public such as food safety, biotechnology, the environment, labour standards, and broader questions of economic development add to the popular disquiet and mobilisation over cultural, social, and ethical questions linked to the globalisation project.

In this regard—and this is very relevant to the concerns of the protesters as well as many governments—the new services negotiations that will occur in Geneva as a result of the Single Undertaking have a wide mandate and the new trade disciplines will have potentially vast impact across major social institutions and programs, such as health, education, social services, and cultural issues. This will allow for wider privatisation and commercialisation of the public sector and indirectly, of the public sphere itself, for example in social programs and education.[5] The logic of the negotiations will likely inhibit many government programs that could be justified as being in the public interest, unless governments are able to convince WTO panels that these programs are not substantially in restraint of trade and investment on the part of private enterprise. Indeed, because the built-in agenda will proceed in Geneva, many divisions among governments, especially between North and South, are emerging. The North-South divisions also revolved around dissatisfaction on the South's part at concessions made in the earlier GATT Uruguay Round, coupled with their frustration in failing to open Northern markets for their manufactured and agriculture exports.

With this agenda in mind, the protesters—although drawn from a very diverse range of organisations and political tendencies—believe there is centralisation and concentration of power under corporate control in neoliberal globalisation, with much of the policy agenda for this project orchestrated by international organisations such as the WTO, the IMF, and the World Bank. Thus, it was not surprising that the battle in Seattle moved to Washington, DC, in mid-April where the same set of progressive and environmental activists and organisations, including trade unions, protested the role of the IMF, the World Bank, and the G-7.

What is significant here is that the new counter-movements seek to preserve ecological and cultural diversity against what they see as the encroachment of political, social, and ecological mono-cultures associated with the supremacy of corporate rule. At the time of writing, the protests were set to move on to lay siege to the headquarters of Citicorp, the world's biggest financial conglomerate.

THE CONTRADICTIONS OF NEOLIBERAL GLOBALISATION AND THE SEATTLE PROTESTS

Implicitly or explicably, the failure of the talks and indeed much of the backlash against neoliberal globalisation is linked to the way that people in diverse contexts are experiencing the problems and contradictions linked to the power of capital and more specifically the projects of disciplinary neoliberalism and new constitutionalism. So what are these contradictions and how do they relate to the Seattle protests?

The first is the contradiction between big capital and democracy. Central here is the extension of binding legal mechanisms of trade and investment agreements, such as the GATT Uruguay Round and regional agreements, such as NAFTA. A counter-example, which pointed the way towards Seattle in terms of much of its counter-hegemonic political form, was the failed OECD effort to create a Multilateral Agreement on Investment. The MAI was also partly undermined by grass-roots mobilisation against corporate globalisation, as well as by more conventional political concerns about sovereignty. The protesters viewed agreements such as NAFTA and organisations such as the WTO as seeking to institutionalise ever-more extensive charters of rights and freedoms for corporations, allowing for greater freedom of enterprise and world-wide protection for private property rights. The protesters perceived that deregulation, privatisation, and liberalisation are a means to strengthen a particular set of class interests, principally the power of private investors and large shareholders. They are opposed to greater legal and market constraints on democracy.

Put differently, the issue was therefore how far and in what ways trade and investment agreements "lock in" commitments to liberalisation, whilst "locking out" popular-democratic and parliamentary forces from control over crucial economic, social, and ecological policies.

The second set of contradictions are both economic and social. Disciplinary neoliberalism proceeds with an intensification of discipline on labour and a rising rate of exploitation, partly reflected in booming stock markets during the past decade, whilst at the same time persistent economic and financial crises have improvished many millions of people and caused significant economic dislocations. This explains the growing role of organised labour—for example American- based trade unions such as the Teamsters—in the protests, as well as organisations representing feminists, other workers, peasants, and smaller producers world-wide. In this regard, the numbers do not lie: despite what has been the longest boom in the history of Western capitalism, the real incomes of average people have been falling. So if this happens in a boom, what happens in a bust? This question has been answered already in the East Asia crisis when millions were impoverished.

Third, for a number of years now, discipline has become linked to the intensification of a crisis of social reproduction. Feminist political economy has shown how a disproportionate burden of (structural) adjustment to the harsher, more competitive circumstances over the past twenty years has fallen on the shoulders of the less well-paid, on women and children, and on the weaker members of society, the old and the disabled. In an era of fiscal stringency, in many states social welfare, health, and educational provisions have been reduced and the socialisation of risk has been reduced for a growing proportion of the world's population. This has generated a crisis of social reproduction as burdens of adjustment are displaced into families and communities that are already under pressure to simply survive in economic terms and risk becomes privatised, redistributed, and generalised in new forms.[6]

The final set of contradictions are linked to how socio-cultural and biological diversity are being replaced by a social and biological mono-culture under corporate domination, and how this is linked to a loss of food security and new forms of generalised health risk. Thus, the protesters argued that if parts of the Seattle draft agenda were ratified, it would allow for a liberalisation of trade in genetically modified crops, provisions to allow world water supplies to be privatised, and the patenting of virtually all forms of life including genetic material that had been widely used across cultures for thousands of years. The protesters also felt particularly strongly about the patenting of seeds and bio-engineering by companies like Novartis and Enron, and other firms seen to be trying to monopolise control over food and undermine local livelihood and food security.[7]

Hence protesters opposed the control of the global food order by corporate interests linked to the new constitutionalism. These interests have begun to institutionalise their right "to source food and food inputs, to prospect for genetic patents, and to gain access to local and national food markets" established through the GATT Uruguay Round and WTO.[8] Transnational corporations have managed to redefine food security in terms of the reduction of national barriers to agriculture trade, ensuring market rule in the global food order. The effect is the intensification of the centralisation of control by "agri-food capital via global sourcing and global trading," in ways that intensify world food production and consumption relations through

> unsustainable monocultures, terminator genes, and class-based diets [in ways] premised on the elimination of the diversity of natural resources, farm cultures, and food cultures, and the decline of local food self-suffi-ciency and food security mechanisms.[9]

Together, these contradictions contribute to what might be called a global or "organic crisis" that links together diverse forces across and within nations, specifically to oppose ideas, institutions, and material power of disciplinary neoliberalism. Much of the opposition to corporate globalisation was summed up by AFL-CIO President John Sweeny, who alongside President Clinton, was addressing the heads of the 1,000 biggest transnational corporations at the annual meeting of the self-appointed and unelected World Economic Forum in Davos in February 2000. Sweeny stated that the protests from North and South represented "a call for new global rules, democratically developed" to constrain "growing inequality, environmental destruction, and a race to the bottom for working people," warning that if such rules were not forthcoming "it will generate an increasingly volatile reaction that will make Seattle look tame."[10] Indeed, Clinton's remarks made at Davos

> seemed designed as a reminder that these fears—even expressed in unwel-come and sometimes violent ways, as they were in Seattle—have a legiti-macy that deserves attention in the world's executive suites and government ministries.[11]

We know by now, of course, that the violence in Seattle was almost completely carried out by the heavily armed police militias who took the battle to the pro-testers. In Washington, in April 2000, police pre-emptively arrested hundreds of demonstrators, in actions justified by the local police chief as a matter of prudence. Another example of this was the repression of peaceful protests at the Asia-Pacific Economic Co-operation meeting in Vancouver in 1998. The protests focused on the contradiction of separating free trade from political democracy, dramatised by the presence of the Indonesian dictator, President Suharto. In sum, state authorities will quickly act to restrict basic political rights and freedoms of opposition by alternative members of civil society—rights supposedly underpinned by the rule of law in a liberal constitutional framework—when business interests are threatened.

At Seattle, the anonymous, unaccountable, and intimidating police actions seemed almost absurd in the light of the fact that the protests involved children dressed as turtles, peaceful activists for social justice, union members, faith groups, accompanied by teachers, scientists, and assorted "tree huggers," all of whom were non-violent. Indeed, with the possible exception of a small number of anarchists, virtually none of the protesters was in any way violent. In Washington, the police protected the meetings wearing heavy armour from behind metal barricades, in the face of protesters carrying puppets and signs that read "spank the Bank." Moments such as these, however, illustrate not only comedy of the absurd but also the broader dialectic between a supremacist set of forces and an ethio-political alternative involved in a new inclusive politics of diversity.

Indeed, since the Seattle debacle the protesters have been able to extend their critique of what they see as the political mono-culture by showing how one of its key components, the "quality press" and TV media, reported what occurred. In the US, for example, the mainstream media found it impossible to represent the violence as being caused by the authorities in order to provoke and discredit the opposition as being Luddite, anti-science, and unlawful. Seen from the vantage point of the protesters, "the *Washington Post* and the *New York Times* are the keepers of 'official reality,' and in official reality it is always the protesters who are violent."[12]

TOWARD A POSTMODERN PRINCE?

In conclusion, I advance the following hypothesis: the protests form part of a world-wide movement that can perhaps be understood in terms of new potentials and forms of global political agency. And following Machiavelli and Gramsci, I call this set of potentials "the postmodern Prince," which I understand as something plural and differentiated, although linked to universalism and the construction of a new form of globalism, and of course, something that needs to be understood as a set of social and political forces in movement.

Let us place this hypothesis in some theoretical context. Machiavelli's *The Prince* addressed the problem of the ethics of rule from the viewpoint of both the prince (the *palazzo*, the palace) and the people (the *piazza*, the town square). Machiavelli sought to theorise how to construct a form of rule that combined both *virtù* (ethics, responsibility, and consent) and fear (coercion) under conditions of *fortuna* (circumstances). *The Prince* was written in Florence, in the context of the political upheavals of Renaissance Italy. Both Machiavelli and later Gramsci linked their analyses and propositions to the reality of concrete historical circumstances as well as to the potential for transformation. These included pressing contemporary issues associated with the problems of Italian unification, and the subordinate place of Italy in the structures of international relations. And it was in a similar national and international context that Gramsci's *The Modern Prince* was written in a Fascist prison, a text that dealt with a central problem of politics: the constitution of power, authority, rule, rights, and responsibilities in the creation of an ethical political community. Nevertheless, what Gramsci saw in *The Prince* was that it was "not a systematic treatment, but a 'live' work, in which political ideology and political science are fused in the dramatic form of a 'myth.'"[13] The myth for Machiavelli was that of *condottiere*, who represented the collective will. By contrast, for Gramsci *The Modern Prince* proposed the myth of the democratic modern mass political party—the communist party—charged with the construction of a new form of state and society, and a new world order.

In the new strategic context (*fortuna*) of disciplinary neoliberalism and globalisation, then, a central problem of political theory is how to imagine and to theorise the new forms of collective political identity and agency that might lead to the creation of new, ethical, and democratic political institutions and forms of practice (*virtù*). So in this context, let me again be clear that by "postmodern Prince" I do *not* mean a form of political agency that is based on postmodern philosophy and the radical relativism it often entails. What I am intending to communicate is a shift in the forms of political agency that are going beyond earlier modernist political projects. So the "postmodern Prince" involves tendencies that have begun to challenge some of the myths and the disciplines of modernist practices, and specifically resisting those that seek to consolidate the project of globalisation under the rule of capital.

Thus, the battles in Seattle may link to new patterns of political agency and a movement that goes well beyond the politics of identity and difference: it has gender, race, and class aspects. It is connected to issues of ecological and social reproduction, and of course, to the question of democracy. This is why more than 700 organisations and between 40,000 and 60,000 people—principally human-rights activists, labour activists, indigenous people, representatives of churches, industrial workers, small farmers, forest activists, environmentalists, social justice workers, students, and teachers—all took part collectively in the protests against the WTO's Third Ministrial on 30 November 1999. The protesters seem aware of the nature and dynamics of their movement and have theorised a series of political links between different events so that they will become more than what James Rosenau called "distant proximities" or simply isolated moments of resistance against globalisation."[14]

In sum, these movements are beginning to form what Gramsci called "an organism, a complex element of society" that is beginning to point towards the realisation of a "collective will." This will is coming to be "recognised and has to some extent asserted itself in action." It is beginning to "take concrete form."[15] Indeed the diverse organisations that are connected to the protests seek to go further to organise something akin to a postmodern transitional political party, that is one with no clear leadership structure as such. It is a party of movement that cannot be easily decapitated. This element puzzled mainstream press reporters at

Seattle since they were unable to find, and thus to photograph or interview, the "leaders" of the protests. However, this emerging political form is not a signal of an end to the protests. It is also not a signal of an end to universalism in politics as such, since many of the forces it entails are linked to democratisation and a search for collective solutions to common problems. It seeks to combine diversity with new forms of collective identity and solidarity in and across civil societies. Thus, the organisers of the April 2000 Washington demonstrations stated that "Sweeny's prediction" made at Davos was in fact a description of events that were going on right now, but that are largely ignored by the media:

> The Zapatista uprising in Mexico, the recent coup in Ecuador, the civil war in the Congo, the turmoil in Indonesia, and the threat of the U'Wa people to commit mass suicide, are all expressions of the social explosion that has arisen from the desperation caused by the politics of the World Bank, IMF, and their corporate directors.... Fundamental change does not mean renaming their programs of other public relations scams. Fundamental reform means rules that empower the people of the world to make the decisions about how they live their lives—not the transitional CEO's or their purchased political leaders.[16]

In this regard, the effectiveness of the protest movements may well lie in a new confidence gained as particular struggles come to be understood in terms of a more general set of inter-connections between problems and movements world-wide. For instance, the Cartagena Protocol on Biosafety on genetically modified life forms was signed in late January 2000 in Montreal by representatives from 133 governments pursuant to the late 1992 UN Convention on Biological Diversity for the trade and regulation of living modified organisms (LMOs). The draft Protocol ensures that sovereign governments have rights to decide on imports of LMOs provided this is based on environmental and health risk assessment data. The Protocol is founded on the "precautionary principle," in effect meaning that where scientific uncertainty exists, governments can refuse or delay authorisation of trade in LMOs. Apart from pressure from NGOs, the negotiations were strongly influenced by scientists concerned about genetic and biological risks posed by the path of innovation. The process finally produced a protocol with significant controls over the freedoms of biotechnology and life sciences companies. Indeed, linkages and contradictions between environmental and trade and investment regulations and laws are becoming better understood by activists world-wide, for instance, how the Biosafety Protocol and the rules and procedures of the WTO may be in conflict.

Nevertheless, it must be emphasised that, although they may represent a larger proportion of the population of the world in terms of their concerns, in organised political terms the protest groups are only a relatively small part of an emerging global civil society that includes not only NGOs but also the activities of political parties, churches, media communication corporations, and scientific and political associations, some progressive, others reactionary. Transnational civil society also involves activities of both transnational corporations, and also governments that are active in shaping a political terrain that is directly and indirectly outside the formal juridical purview of states. Indeed, as the UN Rio conference on the environment and its aftermath illustrated, corporate environmentalism is a crucial aspect of the emerging global civil society and it is linked to what Gramsci called *transformismo* or co-optation of opposition. For example, "sustainable development" is primarily defined in public policy as compatible with market forces and freedom of enterprise. When the global environment movement was perceived as a real threat to corporate interests, companies changed tack from suggesting the environmentalists were either crackpots or misguided to accepting a real problem existed and a compromise was necessary. Of course a compromise acceptable to capital was not one that would fundamentally challenge the dominant patterns of accumulation.

I have not used the term postmodern in its usual sense. Rather, I apply it to indicate a set of conditions and contradictions that give rise to novel forms of political agency that go beyond and are more complex than those imagined by Machiavelli's *The Prince* or Gramsci's *The Modern Prince*. Global democratic collective action today cannot, in my view, be understood as a singular form of collective agency, for example, a single party with a single form of identity. It is more plural and differentiated, as well as being democratic and inclusive. The new forms of collective action contain innovative conceptions of social justice and solidarity, of social possibility, of knowledge, emancipation, and freedom. The content of their mobilising myths includes diversity, oneness of the planet and nature, democracy, and equity. What are we discussing is, therefore, a political party as well as an educational form and a cultural movement. However, it does not act in the old sense of an institutionalised and centralised structure of representation. Indeed this "party" is not institutionalised as such, since it has a multiple and capillary form. Moreover, whilst many of the moments and movements of resistance noted above are at first glance "local" in nature, there is broad recognition that local problems may require global solutions. Global networks and other mobilizing capabilities are facilitated with new technologies of communication.

A new "postmodern Prince" may prove to be the most effective political form for giving coherence to an open-ended, plural, inclusive, and flexible form of politics and thus create alternatives to neoliberal globalisation. So, whilst one can be pessimistic about globalisation in its current form, this is perhaps where some of the optimism for the future may lie: a new set of democratic identities that are global, but based on diversity and rooted in local conditions, problems, and opportunities.

NOTES

I would like to thank Cemal Acikgoz, Isabella Bakker, Adam Harmes, and Ahmed Hashi for their comments and help in preparing this essay.

1. Antonio Gramsci, *Selections from the Prison Notebooks of Antonio Gramsci*, trans. Quintin Hoare and Geoffrey Nowell Smith (New York: International Publishers, 1971), 129.

2. Scott Sinclair, "The WTO: What happened in Seattle? What's Next in Geneva?" *Briefing Paper Series: Trade and Investment* 1, no. 2 (Ottawa: Canadian Centre for Policy Alternatives, 2000), 6.

3. Stephen Gill, "Globalisation, Market Civilisation, and Disciplinary Neoliberalism," *Millennium: Journal of International Studies* 23, no. 3 (1994): 399–423.

4. See "CIA Spies Swap Cold War for Trade Wars," *Financial Times*, 14 August 1999, 1.

5. Editorial, "New Trade Rules Education," *Canadian Association of University Teachers Bulletin*, 7 September 1999, 1. The *Bulletin* added that Educational International representing 294 educational unions and associations world wide expressed great concern about how WTO initiatives would undermine public education.

6. See the essays in Isabella Bakker, ed., *The Strategic Silence: Gender And Economic Policy* (London: Zed Books, 1994).

7. Paul Hawken, "The WTO: Inside, Outside, All Around The World," [http://www.co-intelligence.org/WTOHawken.html] (26 April 2000.)

8. Phillip McMichael, "The Crisis of Market Rule in the Global Food Order" (paper presented at the British International Studies Annual Meeting, Manchester, 20–22 December 1999).

9. Ibid., 2.

10. John Sweeny, "Remember Seattle," *Washington Post*, 30 January 2000, B7.

11. Ann Swardson, "Clinton Appeals for Compassion in Global Trade; World Forum Told Don't Leave 'Little Guys' Out," *Washington Post*, 30 January 2000, A18.

12. Posted on http://www.peoples@psot4.tele.dlk (26 April 2000) on behalf of the NGO network "Mobilization for Global Justice" that organised the Washington protests. Their website [http://www.a16.org] passed 250,000 visitors at the time of the protests.

13. Gramsci, *Selections from the Prison Notebooks*, 125.

14. James Rosenau, "Imposing Global Order: A Synthesised Ontology for a Turbulent Era," in *Innovation and Transformation on International Studies*, Stephen Gill and James H. Mittleman, eds. (Cambridge: Cambridge University Press, 1997), 220–35.

15. Gramsci, *Selections from the Prison Notebooks*, 129.

16. Posted by the NGO network "Mobilization for Global Justice" on http://www.peoples@post4.tele.dk (26 April 2000).

✘ NO

Cautionary Reflections on Seattle
JAN AART SCHOLTE

"The Battle of Seattle": stage one on a global popular revolution? Nail in the coffin of neoliberalism? Harbinger of a more secure, equitable, and democratic world order? While I count myself a proponent of far-reaching reform of globalisation, my reactions to recent events in the city of my youth are somewhat cautious.[1]

The demonstrations of late 1999 in Seattle against the World Trade Organisation (WTO) are the latest in a string of street protests against prevailing global economic regimes. The windows of McDonald's in Geneva suffered a similar fate to the panes of Pike Street when the WTO Ministerial Conference met on the shores of Lac Leman in 1998. Most of the Annual and Spring Meetings of the International Monetary Fund (IMF) and the World Bank have witnessed opposition rallies since several thousand people crowded the squares of Berlin in 1988. Throughout the 1990s, protesters also raised their voices outside the yearly summits of the Group of Seven (G7), most notably when tens of thousands of campaigners for the cancellation of Third World debt encircled the Birmingham G7 Summit in 1998. In early 2000, the annual Davos gathering of the World Economic Forum (WEF) became the latest occasion for "civil society" to raise the banners against "globalisation."

This popular mobilisation has made an impact. The launch of the Millennium Round in Seattle was abandoned in part due to public unease as expressed in the streets. Similarly, co-ordinated opposition from many non-governmental organizations (NGOs) played an important role in halting moves toward a Multilateral Agreement on Investment (MAI) in late 1998. Grassroots pressure for debt relief has helped prompt some reductions of bilateral and multilateral claims on poor countries. Lobbying by NGOs, trade unions, and reform-oriented think tanks has also encouraged greater attention by global and regional institutions to alleviating the social costs of economic restructuring in the face of globalisation. In 1999 the IMF even went so far as to recast its "Enhanced Structural Adjustment Facility" as the "Poverty Reduction and Growth Facility." Following pressure from civil society, the IMF, the Organisation for Economic Cooperation and Development (OECD), the WTO, and the World Bank have all intensified public relations efforts, including marked increases in disclosure about their decisions and policy processes.

These developments are welcome. Civic action has pushed issues of social justice and democracy high up the agenda of global economic governance. We may hope that these new priorities retain and indeed increase their current prominence and generate concrete benefits.

Yet "victory" in the "Battle of Seattle" is no occasion for exuberance or complacency about the future of globalisation or the role of civil society in shaping its course. Halting a new round of trade liberalisation is not the same thing as building a better world order. Nor have civic initiatives in the Seattle scenario provided full confidence in the contributions of civil society to progressive global politics.

The following comment elaborates three cautionary notes. First, we should not overestimate the significance of Seattle in terms of policy change. Second, when assessing Seattle we should not romanticise civil society as an inherently powerful and progressive force. Third, we should look beyond the dismantlement of neoliberal globalisation to the construction of something better.

SMALL HARVESTS

My first cautionary note relates to the scale of change represented by the disruption of the proceedings in Seattle. The Millennium Round has only been deferred, not dropped altogether. Social movements have sought major reform of the WTO since its inception in 1995. Development activists pursued change in the General Agreement on Tariffs and Trade (GATT) for several decades before that. These long efforts have booked only modest gains to date. Thanks in good part to pressure from certain civic groups, the WTO has since 1996 added competition issues, development concerns, environmental problems, and labour standards to its agenda. However, little has happened on these matters beyond occasional meetings of committees and working groups.[2] The core mission of the WTO has remained that of the widest and fastest possible liberalisation of cross-border flows of goods and services.

Thanks in part to pressure from churches, NGOs, and trade unions, the Bretton Woods institutions have in recent years made some greater policy revisions than the WTO; nonetheless, so far, they too have retained a mainly neoliberal orientation.[3] The IMF's recent stress on poverty has brought a striking change of rhetoric, as the World Bank's adoption in 1999 of the so-called Comprehensive Development Framework. However, we have yet to see what concrete improvements in social and environmental conditions these changes will bring. To date, "structural adjustment" in a globalising world economy has for the Bretton Woods agencies continued in the first place to mean liberalisation, privatisation, and deregulation.

Meanwhile, civic campaigns for change have had little to say—let alone achieved much—in respect of global finance. The previously mentioned campaigns for debt reduction in the South constitute an exception in this regard, though the actual sums of relief have thus far remained fairly small. Following crises in Asia, Latin America, and Russia, much discussion spread in the late 1990s regarding a new global financial architecture, but present prospects point toward emergency rewiring rather than major reconstruction.

In short, social movements of the kind represented on the streets of Seattle have achieved only marginal reforms of global economic governance to date. Instead of the unadulterated neoliberalism that prevailed in the 1980s and early 1990s, we now have neoliberalism with some fringes of social and environmental policy. Advocates of change have succeeded in placing neoliberal approaches to globalisation under more critical public scrutiny, but the supertanker is slow to turn.

LIMITS OF CIVIL SOCIETY

My second cautionary note relates to limitations in the practices of civil society regarding global economic governance.[4] Many civic activists have assumed rather uncritically that civil society efforts inherently contribute to human betterment. Some academic accounts of global civil society have reinforced these presumptions. Such romanticism does little to advance actual reform of globalisation and indeed can encourage detrimental complacency. Measured—and at times even sceptical—assessments of global civil society are needed to maximise its contributions and sustain its integrity.

By no means does this sober stance deny the significant positive potentials of civil society for progressive global politics. For one thing, community-based organizations, labour unions, and NGOs can play substantial roles in citizen education about globalisation. Civic groups can also give voice to stakeholders who tend not to be heard through official channels. Actors in global civil society can furthermore fuel policy debates by advancing alternative perspectives, methodologies, and proposals. Pressure from civic circles can thus increase transparency and accountability in the governance of globalisation. Moreover, at a time when official channels do not provide adequate mechanisms for democracy in globalisation, civic activism can help legitimise (or delegitimise) prevailing rules and governance institutions. In all of these ways, civil society can strengthen social cohesion, countering various other aspects of contemporary globalisation that have tended to weaken it. In principle, then, a lot of good can come out of global civic mobilisation.

Events in Seattle bore out these potential benefits in a number of ways. With regard to civic education, for example, the commotion (and more particularly the media attention that it attracted) made a larger public aware of the WTO and some of the downsides of the current neoliberal global trade regime. In terms of giving voice, the streets of Seattle (briefly) handed the microphone to grassroots associations that are not often heard in policy processes surrounding global trade. With respect to fuelling debate, the demonstrations in Seattle made it plain that alternatives to currently prevailing regimes are conceivable and perhaps desirable. This pressure has also compelled proponents of the neoliberal trading order to formulate their own case more clearly, precisely, and—we may hope— self-critically. The activists of Seattle have also impressed on regulators of world trade the need to open up and be accountable to citizens. Finally, the "Battle of Seattle" illustrated the importance of civil society in legitimating—or in this case delegitimating—multilateral laws and institutions. Global economic governance cannot rest on technocratic expertise alone: it requires popular consent as well.

Yet, events in Seattle also illustrated various limitations on civil society involvement in global economic governance. For one thing, we must not exaggerate the scale of the benefits just mentioned. Much more civic education is needed about the WTO and globalisation in general. We have yet to see whether Seattle will have launched a lasting, searching, inclusive public debate about the nature of the global economy and its governance. While the managers of global economic institutions have clearly been shaken by the Seattle episode, this experience does not so far appear to have substantially raised their attention to direct public accountability.

The coalition of resistance forces in Seattle may have also proved to be ephemeral. Does this movement have the necessary levels of resources and commitment for a long-haul campaign of global economic reform and/or transformation? A core of activists has devoted itself to the cause full-time, but wider public backing has to date generally been episodic and shallow. For example, a flurry of civic actions has surrounded the IMF/World Bank Annual and Spring Meetings for the last dozen years, but between these gatherings the day-to-day pressure for change (occasional upsurges in one or the other programme country aside) has been largely restricted to a handful of professional NGO campaigners.

In Seattle, as elsewhere, campaigners for change in the global economy have faced major resource disadvantages in their struggle with forces for neoliberal continuity. Oxfam and Fifty Years Is Enough have not begun to match the World Economic Forum and the Institute of International Finance in terms of staff, funds, equipment, office premises, and access to information. Thus far, proponents of change in the global economic order have also rarely developed effective symbolic capital, that is, ideas, images, and slogans that can mobilise a large constituency in a sustained way.

Nor should we forget that most of the nonofficial actors in Seattle did not subscribe to the street protesters' rejection of neoliberal global trade. As at earlier WTO meetings in Geneva and Singapore, far and away the largest sector of civil society present in Seattle was the business lobby. Likewise, bankers have far outnumbered other non-governmental groups at meetings of the multilateral financial institutions. Business associations and individual firms have influenced the shape of contemporary global economic governance much more than reformers and radicals in other quarters. If we take the scope of civil society to include commercial lobbies and policy think tanks as well as trade unions, NGOs, and community groups, then organised non-governmental forces have on balance actually *favoured* the neoliberal status-quo, not opposed it.

This situation points to a more general problem of equitable and democratic representation in global civil society as it has developed to date. In terms of class, for instance, the non-state actors that influence global economic governance have drawn disproportionately from propertied, professional, computer-literate, and English-speaking circles. In terms of countries, the people who have congregated in Seattle, Geneva, and Washington have come disproportionately from the North. In terms of civilisational inputs, most organized civic engagement with global economic institutions has come from Western circles, with Buddhist, Hindu, Islamic, and other cultures largely left out of the loop. In terms of gender and race, women and people of colour have been severely underrepresented in the academic, business, and trade union sectors of global civil society. In addition, urban residents have tended to obtain far easier access to civic campaigns on global economic governance than people from the countryside.

In short, there is a significant danger that global civic activism can reproduce the exclusions of neoliberal globalisation, even in campaigns that mean to oppose those inequities. How can we ensure that civil society indeed gives voice to all, and not just to those who speak the right language and can afford an airfare to Seattle?

Other deficits in democratic practice can also undermine the credentials of civic campaigners for global economic change. For example, global associations—no less than a government department or a business corporation—can be run with top-down managerial authoritarianism. In addition, policy making in global civic organizations can be quite opaque to outsiders: who takes the decisions, by what procedures, and for what reasons? Civic groups may be further deficient in respect to transparency when they do not publish financial statements or even a declaration of objectives, let alone full-scale reports of their activities. Moreover, the leadership of many NGOs is self-selected, raising troubling questions of accountability and potential conflicts of interest. In short, there is nothing inherently democratic in global civil society, whether we are talking about the WEF or the demonstrators of Seattle.

LOOKING AHEAD

My final cautionary note regarding recent events in Seattle concerns the way forward. Regrettably, campaigners for change in the global economy have on the whole held underdeveloped visions of the alternative worlds that they desire. Thus far, the energies of anarchists, consumer advocates, development campaigners, environmentalists, trade unions, and women's movements have, on balance, concentrated far more on undermining the neoliberal agenda than on mapping a different course. To be sure, certain critics have articulated some fairly specific ways forward, but many opponents have not moved beyond protest to proposal, offering reconstruction as well as destruction, specifying what they are for as well as what they are against. The demonstrators of Seattle spoke forcefully about what they rejected, but they offered comparatively few details about what they wanted in place of the Millennium Round, the WTO regime, and the current global economy more generally.

In particular, calls for "deglobalisation" have not been satisfactory in this regard. Many critics of neoliberalism have sought to unravel globalisation and to regain a purportedly better pre-global past. These circles have included economic nationalists (among them some old-style socialists) and a number of environmentalists. Many religious revivalists and xenophobic groups have also wanted to turn back the clock on globalisation.

These negative stances are understandable in light of the pains of neoliberal economic restructuring for many social circles. However, calls to reverse gear are misguided. For one thing, proponents of deglobalisation have greatly romanticised the local community and national sovereignty, neither of which have produced utopia in the past. Reactive opponents of neoliberalism have also tended to discount some of the benefits of globalisation, including indeed the possibility of developing transborder solidarities of the oppressed in global civil society. Moreover, deglobalisation is impracticable. The ideational, productive, regulatory, and technological forces behind globalisation have reached such magnitude that any return to a pre-global status quo ante is currently out of the question.[5]

The challenge, then, is to reorient globalisation, to steer the process in a different direction. Like many critics, the demonstrators in Seattle, Davos, and elsewhere have often conflated globalisation with neoliberalism. They have denounced "globalisation" when their actual target is the neoliberal approach to globalisation. Other policy frameworks could handle global economic governance in more effective, equitable, and democratic ways. The problem is not globalisation, but the way we handle it.

Progressive elements in global civil society therefore face a far greater challenge than disrupting summits on global economic governance. If neoliberal globalisation has unacceptable adverse consequences, and deglobalisation is not a viable option, then new forms of globalisation need to be developed. Fortunately some academic and civil society practices are beginning to explore these potentials.[6] If the energy of protest could be coupled with the inspiration of innovation, than more humane global futures could result.

NOTES

1. See Jan Aart Scholte, *Globalization: A Critical Introduction* (Basingstoke: Macmillan, 2000), especially chap. 12.

2. Jan Aart Scholte, Robert O'Brien, and Marc Williams, "The WTO and Civil Society," *Journal of World Trade* 33, no 1 (1999): 107–24.

3. See Paul J. Nelson, *The World Bank and Non-Governmental Organizations: The Limits of Apolitical Development* (Basingstoke: Macmillan, 1995); Jonathan A. Fox and L. David Browns, eds., *The Struggle for Accountability: The World Bank, NGOs and Grassroots Movements* (Cambridge, MA: MIT Press, 1998); and Robert O'Brien et al., *Contesting Global Governance: Multilateral Economic Institutions and Global Social Movements* (Cambridge: Cambridge University Press, 2000).

4. The following points draw on Jan Aart Scholte, "Global Civil Society," in *The Political Economy of Globalization*, Ngaire Woods, ed. (Basingstoke: Macmillan, 2000), 173–201.

5. This assessment is elaborated in *Globalization: A Critical Introduction*, chap. 4.

6. See, for instance, Samir Amin, *Capitalism in the Age of Globalization: The Management of Contemporary Society* (London: Zed Books, 1997); James H. Mattelman, *The Globalization Syndrome: Transformation and Resistance* (Princeton, NJ: Princeton University Press, 2000); Jan Nederveen Pieterse, ed., *Global Futures: Shaping Globalization* (London: Sage, 2000); and Michael Edwards and John Gaventa, eds., *Global Citizen Action: Perspectives and Challenges* (Boulder, CO: Lynne Rienner, forthcoming).

Postscript

One problem in understanding the significance of events such as the "Battle in Seattle" is sorting out the diverse range of groups participating in the demonstrations and their wide range of tactics and strategies. The more radical anti-globalization groups seemed primarily concerned with disruptive techniques aimed at bringing the work of the WTO to a halt. Others were concerned with finding ways to hold the WTO accountable by demanding a greater popular voice in decision-making processes surrounding trade policies.

Events such as those in Seattle have led some to draw attention to the "dark side" of global civil society. In an article cited below, David Robertson argues that if NGOs want to hold institutions like the WTO accountable to the public and make their work more transparent, then NGOs must be prepared to do the same. He notes that many NGOs do not hold elections for officers and do not reveal their sources of funding or their expenditures. What makes them, he asks, any more representative of the population than the governments participating in WTO negotiations? Robertson suggests that NGOs should sign a code of conduct before they are given greater accessibility and participation. What would such a code of conduct look like? Would it even be feasible or desirable?

Infotrac Keyword Search

"WTO" or "World Trade Organization"

Suggested Additional Readings

Bhagwati, Jagdish. "Responding to Seattle," *Challenge* 44, no. 1 (January–February 2001): 6–19.

Clarke, Tony. "Taking on the WTO: Lessons from the Battle of Seattle," *Studies in Political Economy* 62 (Summer 2000): 7–16.

Hoad, Darren. "The World Trade Organisation: The Events and Impact of Seattle 1999," *Environmental Politics* 9, no. 4 (Winter 2000): 123–29.

Kaldor, Mary. "'Civilising' Globalisation? The Implications of the 'Battle in Seattle,'" *Millennium: Journal of International Studies* 29, no. 1 (2000): 105–14.

Kiely, Ray. "Globalization: From Domination to Resistance," *Third World Quarterly* 21, no. 6 (December 2000): 1059–71.

Levi, Margaret and David Olson. "The Battles in Seattle," *Politics & Society,* 28, no. 3 (September 2000): 309–30.

McMichael, Philip. "Sleepless Since Seattle: What is the WTO About?" *Review of International Political Economy* 7, no. 3 (September 2000): 466–75.

Robertson, David. "Civil Society and the WTO," *World Economy* 23, no. 9 (September 2000): 1119–35.

Website Resources

The Nation: The Battle in Seattle   A collection of articles and audio clips on the events in Seattle prepared by *The Nation*.

BBC News: Battle for Free Trade   A collection of written and audio-visual reports on the events in Seattle as covered by the BBC.

Global Action   A collection of reports and analyses of Seattle from the viewpoint of anti-globalization activists.

Global Issues, Free Trade and Globalization: WTO Protests in Seattle   A collection of resources on the Seattle protests, with special emphasis on the media coverage of the events.

ISSUE**FIFTEEN**

Will Debt Relief Address the Needs of Highly Indebted Countries?

✔ **YES**

WILLIAM PETERS AND MARTIN J. DENT, "Grass Roots Mobilization for Debt Remission: The Jubilee 2000 Campaign," paper presented at the annual meetings of the International Studies Association, San Diego, April 1996

✗ **NO**

DENISE FRONING, "Will Debt Relief Really Help?" *The Washington Quarterly* 24, no. 3 (Summer 2001): 199–211

For many in the developing world, particularly in Africa and Latin America, the 1980s has come to be referred to as the "lost decade." By the beginning of the decade, it was evident that the call for a new international order, launched with much fanfare in the late 1960s, had become bogged down in fruitless debate. Instead of moving toward a more prosperous and hopeful future, many in the developing world found themselves facing deepening economic crises, deteriorating environmental conditions, and, in Africa, recurring famines. But the main story of the decade became the mounting debt crisis faced by a growing number of less-developed countries (LDCs). By the end of the 1980s, this debt was estimated to be about $1.4 trillion (US). Efforts to repay it have led to a net transfer of resources from the South to the North. In 1988 alone, $32.5 billion (US) more was transferred to the North, mostly in the form of debt service payments, than was received in the South in aid and loans. Instead of moving toward a new and more equitable international economic order, North-South relations in the 1980s became preoccupied with crisis management and the politics of debt.

The international response to the debt crisis can best be described in terms of two phases, labelled after two successive American secretaries of the treasury who took leadership of the North's reaction to the debt crisis. The first phase, the Baker Plan, unveiled by then-U.S. Treasury Secretary James Baker, called for an additional $40 billion (US) to be lent to the fifteen largest, mostly middle-income, debtors. Half of the funds would come from the World Bank and regional development banks, while the other half would come from "voluntary" loans from commercial banks. Access to these loans would be conditional on acceptance of International Monetary Fund-approved (IMF) programs. New sources of funding were also promised for the smaller, lower-income African states whose debts, owed mainly to donor governments and international financial institutions (IFIs) were in many cases more onerous.

However, the Baker Plan soon lost momentum, and support from many donors fell short of promised levels. Private financial flows dropped, as commercial banks withdrew from all but the most risk-free loans. Resentment in the South mounted as governments struggled with the political consequences of implementing many of the austerity measures demanded by the IMF. LDC governments complained that the IMF-imposed structural adjustment programs, which typically included sharp cuts in government services and subsidies, undermined their political legitimacy without really resolving their economic crisis. Throughout the 1980s, "IMF riots" became commonplace in many LDCs. More countries were falling into arrears, not only to banks, governments, and their export credit agencies, but also to the IFIs, such as the IMF and the World Bank, whose debt payments cannot be rescheduled.

In 1989, James Baker's successor, Nicholas Brady, launched a new initiative to deal with the debt crisis. The centerpiece of the Brady Plan was to make up to $35 billion (US) available to finance debt-reduction deals negotiated between selected debtor countries and their creditor banks. The plan was adopted by the IFIs and the G-7 industrialized countries as their primary approach to the debt crisis. But from the beginning, critics charged that the plan was fundamentally flawed and woefully inadequate. The South Commission, chaired by the former President of Tanzania, Juilius Nyere, pointed out that the plan dealt only with debt owed to commercial banks, and that reduction of even this debt was still up to those banks. Further, the commission argued that the pool of funds available under this plan was clearly inadequate to achieve any real measure of debt reduction. In reviewing Northern efforts to deal with the debt crisis, the commission's report, *The Challenge to the South* (Oxford University Press, 1990), concluded: "The upshot is that debt has become a form of bondage, and the indebted economies have become indentured economies—a clear manifestation of neo-colonialism. This state of affairs cannot go on. The debt and its service must be reduced to a level that allows growth to proceed at an acceptable pace" (p. 227).

At the end of the 1990s, it is increasingly evident that the fears of the South Commission have come true, especially in the case of African countries. In its 1986 *World Development Report*, the World Bank predicted with confidence that by the mid-1990s developing-country debt would, in the worst-case scenario, amount to about $864 billion, and that the amount owed by African low-income countries would be only about $29 billion. However, by 1994, according to the World Bank's own figures, the external debt of all developing countries stood at nearly $2 trillion, while the debt of sub-Saharan African countries was $210 billion (Susan George, "Rethinking Debt," *Development 2* [1996]: 54).

The continuing debt crisis has led some people to question whether more radical debt-relief measures are needed to address the problems facing developing countries. One voice in this movement has been the Jubilee 2000 campaign, a grass-roots movement started in the United Kingdom to mobilize support for debt remission. The co-founders of Jubilee 2000, William Peters and Martin Dent, liken their campaign to the struggle against slavery in an earlier century. They set out their case for debt relief, drawing on the Hebraic concept of the jubilee as a model for debt forgiveness today.

In part as a result of the work of the Jubilee campaign, debt forgiveness has become a major international issue in recent years; the Pope and celebrities such as Bono of the pop band U2 have become spokespeople for the cause. There has also been a number of promising developments recently. One of these is the World Bank's Highly Indebted Poor Countries (HIPC) Initiative. Announced in 1996 and implemented in September 1997, HIPC aims debt-relief funding at the poorest and most heavily indebted countries. After a number of initial projects in Uganda and Bolivia, the World Bank expanded the initiative; it is now known as the Enhanced Highly Indebted Poor Countries Initiative. The overall goal is to combine HIPC with more traditional forms of debt forgiveness and forgive up to $55 billion, a little more than half the total outstanding debt of these countries. Mozambique qualified for an additional $600 million of debt relief in April 2000, bringing its total to $4.3 billion of debt forgiven. Burkina Faso was approved for an additional $700 million in June 2000 after meeting previous guidelines. The World Bank has also established a Trust Fund for the HIPC to assist multilateral development banks with the costs they incur when forgiving debt. Since then a number of individual countries have announced measures to forgive a substantial portion of developing-country debt.

However, these measures have not always achieved the hoped-for results. Some people suggest that debt relief alone will not address the problems faced by indebted nations. Denise Froning examines some of the problems with reliance on debt forgiveness. She addresses the internal problems of developing countries, which need to be addressed, and looks at the changes needed in the policies of industrialized nations.

✔ YES
Grass Roots Mobilization for Debt Remission: The Jubilee 2000 Campaign
WILLIAM PETERS AND MARTIN J. DENT

1. INTRODUCTION

Nongovernmental organizations (NGOs) have sprung to center stage in contemporary development policy debates. NGOs often give voice to a vision quite distinct from those of academics, politicians, or bureaucrats. When these visions resonate with a substantial constituency or, more directly, with senior decision-makers, they can exert considerable influence over the politically determined course of policy.

This paper offers an insider account of the motivations and methods of Jubilee 2000, a UK-based NGO working for debt forgiveness for poor countries, including some detail of the modalities for debt forgiveness the group recommends. What is distinctive about Jubilee 2000, as its name suggests, is its emphasis on the jubilee principle of extraordinary forgiveness. This is manifest in the explicit attention its leadership has paid to articulating clear moral guidelines for debt forgiveness as well as in the close parallels the Jubilee movement draws to the Abolitionist movement to eradicate slavery from the British Empire in the first half of the 19th century. Other, more traditional participants in the development policy debate may argue the empirical and theoretical basis for debt forgiveness from within the social sciences. Jubilee 2000 feels it important to articulate and emphasize the moral principles that may well prove more important than economic or technical concerns in ultimately resolving this pressing humanitarian and political issue.

2. THE JUBILEE 2000 MOVEMENT

Jubilee 2000 is an educational charity in the UK. It addresses a nonspecialist audience, mainly in churches and NGOs. It seeks to explain how, in its present form, the global financial system works to the detriment of a considerable number of countries in the Third World, reducing the poorer segments of their populations to acute poverty. Jubilee 2000 works alongside Campaign Jubilee 2000, a charitable company. The dual purpose of Jubilee 2000 is, first, to gather strong popular support at the grass roots level for changes in the global financial system, particularly the remission of the unpayable parts of the state debt of highly indebted poor countries (HIPCs);[1] and, second, to persuade opinion formers, academics, politicians, and international financial bureaucrats that the unpayable parts of the debt can and should be remitted on a once-for-all and comprehensive, case-by-case basis, with exit packages working out for each debtor country.

The basis thesis of Jubilee 2000 is a simple one, namely that the backlog of the unpayable debt of governments of poorer countries can never be removed, except by an agreed remission on the part of the creditors.[2] For the sake of creating a new and disciplined beginning in financial relations between richer and poorer countries, it is important that this act of remission be completed by the year 2000, so as *not* to create any expectations of "remission on demand." It can, of course, start before 2000; the sooner the better. The bottom line, however, is that we aim to have it completed before the end of that year. We need the remission to be achieved as part of one carefully planned Jubilee, arranged for the benefit of the human family by both rich and poor nations in serious, balanced, and detailed negotiation with one another.

The name Jubilee 2000 was coined in 1990 as part of the campaign working to develop effective ways to help poorer nations. We realized that aid, fairer terms of trade, and a number of other things were necessary, but we also concluded that without a radical answer to the problem of the backlog of unpayable debt, all other remedies might be of no effect. We had to maintain the general principle that debts should be honored, on which all commerce and banking depend, and at the same time we had to correct the present monstrous imbalance by which most of the poorer nations in the human family owe unpayable debt to the richer ones. We could only do this by designating a special time by which, and in association with which, to complete an adequate, planned act of debt forgiveness. This removal of the detritus of past inert debts, no longer balanced by any continuing productive capacity, has to be sufficient to free debtor nations from the insolvent situation of having to seek repeated debt rescheduling.

Jubilee 2000 bases its case as an educational charity on three premises:

1. The HIPCs cannot pay.

2. Creditors will not remit without substantial material benefits from doing so.

3. There are strong nonmaterial and moral reasons for removing or massively reducing the debt burden. These can stand on their own but also draw strength from Christian texts and the sacred writings of other faiths.

The first premise needs little elaboration. It is undoubted fact that a number of HIPCs, especially in Africa, but also in parts of Asia, Latin America, and the Caribbean, are unable to meet the cost of paying the interest on or repaying the principal of loans (stock) which they accepted during the late 1970s and early 1980s. Later in this paper we detail the criteria by which countries are judged to be unable to repay their debt. Papers prepared for the Spring Meeting of the Development Committee—the Joint Ministerial Meeting of the Boards of Governors of the World Bank (WB) and the International Monetary Fund (IMF)—by WB and

IMF staff provisionally identify 41 countries as HIPCs, up to 20 already noted as potential beneficiaries of remission (World Bank, 1996). Jubilee 2000 concentrates on the poorest countries but suggests that some remission beyond the 41 identified should be accorded to less-distressed debtor countries, tapering to zero in step with rising GNP.

Here a few examples may suffice. Tanzania is one of over 20 African countries unable to service their debts. The ratio between Tanzania's debt overhang and its exports of goods and services (XGS) is 1219%. Apart from one brief conflict with Uganda, Tanzania has suffered none of the catastrophes which pushed a number of others into the most overburdened category. For three in that category, Sudan, Namibia, and Mozambique, the ratios are 3263% (1992), 2599% (1990), and 1416%. Not all African countries have unmanageable debts. Botswana, with rich mineral resources including diamonds, has a debt to XGS ratio of only 26%. The average wealth per capita ratio between the whole of the Third World and the First World was 1:30 in 1960; by 1989 it had risen to 1:60. In the quest for budget savings to meet debt payments, most HIPC governments are forced to cut services such as health, education, and social support. In 1990, the average per capita expenditure of African governments on health was US$2 per head per annum, of which $0.07 only went on H.I.V., although the continent has the greatest and most rapidly increasing H.I.V. incidence. These figures have worsened since 1990. Deprivation in HIPCs has reached unconscionable levels, calling for an international effort for substantial alleviation.

The second premise of Jubilee 2000's case is that, self-evidently, if creditors are to agree to comprehensive remission of the debt repayments due to them, they need strong arguments mostly of a practical kind to persuade them all at the same time to contemplate such sacrifices. There must be reasons over and beyond the hardship suffered through debt servicing by the poorest segment of the debtor countries' population (which creditors might blame on the governments incurring the debts for lacking prudence, honesty, or discipline). There are at least 10 such arguments.

a) Since 1985, creditor banks, governments, and the IFIs have tried several methods of relieving the debt burden: through London and Paris Club reschedulings, debt conversions mediated through secondary markets for commercial debt, the World Bank's so-called Fifth Dimension facility, etc. All these processes are palliatives. For virtually all the HIPCs, the total burden of remaining debt stock and interest due is greater than it was before the start of these measures (Dent, 1994). For Sub-Saharan Africa, the debt stock has grown from US$192 billion at end-1990 to $211 billion at end-1994 (World Bank, 1995). The first benefit for creditors from comprehensive remission would, therefore, be that it would replace and fulfill the partial efforts of the last 12 years to return HIPCs to viable debt management by a process which had a reasonable prospect of doing so.

b) The removal of the backlog of debt on agreed formulae would mean that investors in the creditor countries who wish to do so could restart capital flows to the former debtors.

c) With the reduction of debt servicing to manageable proportions, the governments of the beneficiaries would be able to restore cuts in health, education, and social services forced on them by structural adjustment programs. General easing of economic conditions would enable the former debtor countries to resume imports of industrial products with beneficial effects for trade balances and employment in the creditor countries. This would be consolidated when the debtors returned to a condition in which they could resume self-sustaining development.

d) The debtor countries have learned hard lessons from the debt crisis. After substantial remission, they would not readily fall into unmanageable debt (nor presumably would creditors encourage them to do so). There are many indications that loan discipline would be self-imposed. For example, after independence, Namibia was most loath to take loans from the IMF, World Bank, and bilateral lenders. They were strongly advised by all African governments represented in Windhoek to refrain to the maximum possible degree from borrowing. Post-apartheid South Africa is adopting the same line.

e) Remission would, to some extent, offset the almost universal shortfalls in aid-giving by industrialized countries below the UN-recommended guideline of 0.7% of GNP.

f) The urge to economic migration from impoverished countries would lessen as economic conditions improve, removing a global irritant in North/South relations.

g) Similarly, improved economic conditions, by reducing hardship, would lower some internal pressures and this, in time, would lessen the risks of low intensity conflict and the concomitant demand for arms or peace-keeping efforts.

h) The creditors, in working out remission packages, could find opportunities for and acceptance of bolstering terms against clandestine capital flight relating to future loans, and tie them specifically to identified, income-earning development projects.

i) Cases against the Duvaliers of Haita, the Marcos family of the Philippines, and two former presidents of South Korea, Chun Do-Whum and Rioh Tae-Woo, over claims on their private fortunes brought by the states of which they were heads, open a distinct possibility that legal methods may be found for recovering from corrupt or criminal rules improper gains sequestered from state funds. This clearly has a relevance for certain African states. From them suggestions are now made that, in settling state debts, the ill-gotten gains of certain politicians should be seized by appropriate western authorities, using whatever powers may prove valid for the Philippines and South Korea, and deducted from the total debt owed.

Should the legal cases not provide a valid method of dealing with such ill-gotten gains, it would become necessary to withhold a relief package from countries like Zaire. The people of the country would therefore continue to suffer, but broad awareness that neighbors in contiguous countries were forging ahead economically might well stir up strong movements to remove corrupt leaders. The eventual remission package would include provision for state accountability and democratic choice.

j) There is very little likelihood that much more of the debts can be repaid. The old saw "You can't get blood out of a stone" is apposite. If the notional sums still due are no more than book entries—and most of them have already been heavily reduced in real terms through the operation of the secondary market in debt—there is little advantage for the creditors in retaining them, while the psychological and practical effects on the debtors are a major obstacle to movement towards self-sustaining development.

The benefits for the debtor countries are obvious, like the removal just mentioned of obstacles to self-sustaining development. That also clearly has beneficial potential for the global economy. But the remission has to be seen to be fair to debtor countries among themselves. For example, the government of a country which has applied strict rules of austerity to its domestic expenditure in order to meet its debt-servicing obligations would expect to be treated more favorably than one which, in its present form or that of a predecessor, has been prodigal in spending domestically beyond its means and careless of debt-service obligations. This is one form of the arguments from moral hazard frequently used against debt remission. The answer is that such differences must be reflected in the terms and conditions of the remission package. Similarly (see (i) above), special attention will be needed for countries which have been pillaged for personal benefits and that of close associates by dictatorial rulers or oligarchies, resulting in severe falls in living standards.

The third premise is perhaps the most distinctive point of the Jubilee 2000 campaign. The international financial community has been bogged down for more than a decade in technical debate over what have proved mere palliatives to a crisis of mounting human dimensions. Clear guiding moral principles are needed to focus the attention and accelerate the activity of decision-makers in this arena. Professor Tony Thirlwall[3] has expressed succinctly a strong underlying argument for a balanced plan of remission. He holds that

> shared blame requires shared sacrifice ... the burden of debt should be shared three ways: by the creditors, the debtors, and by the whole world

community that derived a benefit from the debt creation process in the sense that the world economy would have collapsed in the 1970s (rather like in the 1930s) had international capital flows not taken place from the developed to the developing countries.

Thirlwall recalls John Maynard Keynes' analysis of the transfer problem arising from reparations for Germany imposed by the Treaty of Versailles. "Keynes mocked the folly and futility (of reparations) on the grounds that it would be likely to be self-defeating, and so it turned out to be."

In their reappraisal of economic theory in the light of globalization and the intergenerational need to protect the environment (reducing pollution risks including the long-term nuclear ones), many economists now recognize that the place accorded to short-term self-interest in economic theory from Adam Smith onwards is perhaps too prominent. We are reminded that Adam Smith wrote *The Theory of Moral Sentiments* as well as *The Wealth of Nations*. Margaret Thatcher enunciated, in her address to the Church of Scotland's General Assembly in September 1987, the view that the creation of wealth is essentially amoral, and that, once created, questions concerning its distribution should be treated as matters for private, residual conscience. But Brian Griffiths (1984), for several years a close Thatcher adviser, argues that markets cannot function effectively without a clear basis for individual rights and notions of obligations to others. He goes on to trace some of the required moral ingredients to elements of Judaeo-Christian thought, such as obligations to one's neighbors, especially the weak and disadvantaged, and the consequences of believing that human beings are created in the image of a compassionate God. The question of whether markets need a moral framework is high on several politico-economic agenda. Hay (1995) concluded that markets do not need a moral framework, but only if the conditions are right. Those conditions include a continuing market about which sufficient information is widely available to allow suppliers to establish a reputation among consumers. Where the conditions were not right, it is necessary to rely on either statutory or self-regulation. But, he points out, regulation can be costly, sometimes ineffective, sometimes inimical to good behavior. So "perhaps a moral code is not such a bad idea after all: at the very least, honesty is cheaper."

The Jubilee concept is firmly rooted in Judaeo-Christian thought. First mentioned in the book of Leviticus, Chapter 25, it prescribes remission of unpayable debts as rare acts of grace on special occasions, consonant with God's mercy (forgiveness) towards human failure. Initially, the intervals were a mere seven years, later extended to seven times seven, and the beneficiaries were fellow Israelites only. The purpose was to permit some levelling of the grosser inequalities which inevitably arise among people in any society through the misfortunes of war, natural disaster or disease, as well as variations in personal endowment. This was considered necessary, partly because extreme inequality was socially dangerous and partly because of the sense of wrong in situations where patently the actual distribution of the good things of the earth left some in acute deficit while others enjoyed great surpluses.

Duchrow (1995) provides a thorough historical and textual analysis of the biblical passages which describe and evolve the Jubilee concept. From this it emerges that Jubilee was originally invoked after the escape of the Israelites from bondage in Egypt at the time when Israel was consolidating itself as a "just" society in a state subject only to Yahweh, cushioned between the empires and city kingdoms of the Near East (c. 1250–1000 BC). As kingship developed, the "justice" in that society eroded despite periodic rescue efforts, recorded in terms of returns to obedience to Yahweh. After the cesura when Jerusalem was destroyed by Nebuchadnezzar and the deportation to Babylon or flight to Egypt of the majority of the Israelite elite (585 BC), the remainder had partial autonomy, which enabled them, later joined by returning exiles, to devise social forms which looked back to the "just" society of patriarchal times (Deuteronomy 25). The onset of the Hellenistic–Roman era (333 BC–312 AD) led to a "period of active rejection (by minority groups) of an economically, politically and ideologically totalitarian system and of attempts to create small scale alternatives." This was the context of Jesus and the early Christians. By this analysis, Duchrow seeks to establish that jubilee is a concept of great antiquity with an authority some would regard as sacred, which has reappeared from time to time as part of succeeding attempts to reform contemporary systems perceived to be "unjust" and unworkable.

Duchrow outlines a root and branch reform of societies and economies, emphasizing the need for coalitions of small-scale organizations such as cooperatives and voluntary societies. Henley (1991) is less sweeping. He considers that the Jubilee regulations in Leviticus 25 "point to important normative issues that are of contemporary relevance to the formulation of Christian applied economics." He deals with gaps in recent discussions of a Christian ethical framework for economics which "have not addressed the question how to progress to a Christian analysis of contemporary economic life." Although he has welcomed the outline program in Jubilee 2000, he does not, in his writings, specifically address the question of international debt but says that in modern conditions such issues as homelessness, unemployment, training, housing, and land ownership yield positively to analysis based on the jubiliary principle. Per contra, he says, with unmodified policies of the Thatcherite type, "the modern capital market threatens the economic viability of the basic social block of our modern economy."[4]

The writers of Leviticus saw the jubilee as a time not only for levelling inequities but also for rejoicing and celebrating the start of a new phase with past obstacles to community swept away. Jesus, in his first sermon in Nazareth (Luke 4), quotes Isaiah on His mission to "proclaim the acceptable year of the Lord." This is a synonym for Jubilee. In his encyclical "Tertio Millenio Adveniente"[5] Pope

John Paul II looks forward to the celebration of 2000 as a Jubilee in which all people can rejoice together in their common humanity. He says,

> If we recall that Jesus came to preach the good news to the poor (Mt 11:5; Lk 7:22), how can we fail to lay greater emphasis on the Church's preferential option for the poor and the outcast? Indeed, it has to be said that a commitment to justice and peace in a world like ours, marked by so many conflicts and intolerable social and economic inequalities, is a necessary condition for the preparation and celebration of the Jubilee. Thus, in the spirit of the Book of Leviticus (25:8-12), Christians will have to raise their voice on behalf of all the poor of the world, proposing the Jubilee as an appropriate time to give thought, among other things, to reducing substantially, if not cancelling outright, the international debt which seriously threatens the future of many nations.

Christianity may be the religion with the largest support in most of the creditor countries, although in the biggest, Japan, Christians are a small minority. This need not reduce the force of Judaeo-Christian sacred texts as signposts to global debt relief. They are paralleled in the sacred writings of almost all faiths where the concepts of concern for the poor and compassion for suffering are prominent. Buddhists recognize the names of Avaloketisvara or Sakyamuni as patterns of compassion. The Koran excludes charging interest. Modern texts, such as the social doctrines of Mahatma Gandhi, reinforce them and make them accessible to a wide range of people, especially in the Third World. For atheists, agnostics, and humanists, the purely economic arguments for remission can and do stand on their own, as do some moral arguments without the backing of sacred texts. 2000, the second millennium of the birth of Christ, is of immense significance for Christians; but it is also a date which is numerically distinctive within a calendar system which is now accepted virtually everywhere.

3. MOBILIZATION FOR DEBT REMISSION

Based on the above three premises, Jubilee 2000 has begun seeking public support, primarily in creditor countries where resistance to remission is greatest, but not forgetting opinion in debtor countries, where the poorest segments of the population, unlike some in the more prosperous segments, wholeheartedly long for remission. The model for turning to a broad public for support is the abolitionist movement, which campaigned for the abolition of slavery in Britain in the early part of the 19th century. That campaign began in liberal political circles but was defeated in Parliament by a coalition of vested interests, especially plantation owners, slave shippers, and merchants in the triangular trade, together with conservatives opposed to change led by the Duke of Wellington. Leaders of the abolitionists—Wilberforce, Buxton, and others—realized they needed wide popular backing and sought it through the churches. At that time, the churches, much stronger than at present in Britain and in touch with a very wide proportion of the population, caught their fervor. The demand for abolition grew and eventually enabled the leaders to overcome the political opposition in Parliament. Among the opponents of abolition were doomsayers who warned that it would undermine the current economic and financial system with catastrophic effect, words which are being heard again in relation to debt forgiveness. A key turning point in the campaign was the meeting of the Anti-Slavery Movement in Exeter Hall in 1832, when the goal was decisively changed from the amelioration of slavery and its gradual extinction, to complete and immediate abolition. This has its parallel in Jubilee 2000, which seeks remission of the unpayable backlog of debt faced by poorer countries, and not its reduction to "sustainable levels."

In present conditions, the churches in many countries do not have sufficient popular support to propel a charity like Jubilee 2000 to success. But voluntary movements in most OECD countries are nowadays a major sociopolitical feature: they have elaborated techniques for winning popular support and applying it to specific objectives. The charity's proponents, therefore, decided that they should aim for a coalition of church groups and NGOs. The first overt step was taken by Martin Dent at Keele University, who encouraged students to sign a petition to the UN Secretary General to declare the year 2000 a UN Year of Jubilee, for the remission of the unpayable parts of Third World debt. The Secretary General responded in encouraging terms, advising that the first step should be to find a state member of the UN willing to propose at the UN General Assembly a resolution for 2000 to be adopted as a UN Year of Jubilee as proposed in the petition. Action, on Dr. Boutros-Ghali's suggestion, has so far succeeded in interesting two OECD governments, the Norwegian and the Irish, in drafting a resolution. Several African delegates have also expressed their support. Further, in private correspondence, the campaign has gained the support of, among many others, the Vice-President of the European Union (Sir Leon Brittan), the Commonwealth Secretary General (Chief Emeka Anyaoku), and the Anglican House of Bishops in the UK. Jubilee 2000's patrons include Archbishop Desmond Tutu and Sir David Steel, recently retired from leadership of the British Liberal Party. In the UK, it has support from all the political parties.

Meanwhile, a group of NGOs in Britain, focused on problems in the Third World, formed a Debt Crisis Network led by the New Economics Foundation and with the material support of the major charity, Christian Aid. Jubilee 2000 is one of over 40 NGOs belonging to the Debt Crisis Network. To spearhead its work the Network has engaged a lobbyist and an information officer. In February 1996, they arranged a tour of Britain by seven well-known African politicians, churchmen, economists, and businessmen who, from the African point of view, drew the attention of as wide a public as possible to the consequences of African debt overhang.

In its current state, UK charity law does not allow a charity to be registered (and so become eligible for tax concessions) if it participates in political processes relating to its objectives in a way which "encroaches too far into the sphere of politics." Obviously, a charity, if it is to receive taxpayers' money, cannot be aligned with a political party. But, beyond that, if its objectives could lead to changes in the law in either the home or any other country, it cannot have charitable status. Part of Jubilee 2000's purpose is to bring about changes in the management by the WB and IMF of the funds within their control, with particular reference to money lent to HIPCs. Those changes could well lead to a requirement for changes for changes in the law of several countries, depending on how they have framed legislation dealing with their role vis-à-vis the IFIs. So it is proving necessary for Jubilee 2000, as indicated at the beginning of this article, to separate its charitable, educational work and its campaign to bring about changes in the international financial structure.

4. MODALITIES FOR DEBT FORGIVENESS

We have, to a large extent, won the battle of the concepts, for it is now accepted, as it was not 10 years ago, that remission of debt is not only permissible but necessary. We now have to go on to win the battle of implementation. The devil is in the details, for those with a vested interest to defend will tend to agree to a liberative principle in theory but deny it in practice. For instance, a very senior official in the British Foreign Office said to one of us, "Why are you talking about Jubilee 2000? We have almost achieved it already in our Trinidad Terms." In fact, these terms relate only to a fairly small fraction of the backlog of unpayable debt, provide too low a percentage of remission, and leave many important low-income countries outside the boundaries of debt forgiveness.

Thus, in order to implement Jubilee 2000, we need to know the details, country by country, of the debts to be remitted, and to sketch in the conditionalities which should accompany the remission. In this way we seek to ensure that once the debtor countries are freed from the burden of past, inert debts, they do not fall into unpayable debt again. The message to the debtors who are granted remission must be "go your way, and waste no more," and that to the creditors "go your way, and create fairer relations in international trade and finance in order to allow poorer, former debtor countries to achieve sustainable development. Wherever possible, substitute grants for loans, and negotiate terms of trade less unfavorable to the products of poorer nations, or build in schemes to compensate for abnormal price fluctuations." Furthermore, the necessary emphasis on conditionalities for remission is directed to the simple task of ensuring that those countries forgiven their debts do not fall into unpayable debt again.

The experience of programs of partial debt relief indicates that a deadline is needed. Hence, Jubilee 2000's incorporation of a terminal date, which is reinforced by the historical pattern of Jubilee (see above). It is instructive to examine the genesis and progress of actual remission programs. For example, elements of the Paris Club's so-called Naples Terms—which involve the remission of parts of the bilateral, government-to-government debts of a number of the poorest countries— were being discussed in the British Treasury and Foreign Office, whence they orig- inated, as early as 1984. It was not until the G7 meeting in Naples in July 1994 that they appeared for the first time to have support from all G7 members. Yet even now legal and political obstacles, particularly in the United States, obstruct the full application of the Naples Terms and their endorsement by the Paris Club (which coordinates governmental debt transactions) is partial only. When the British Chancellor, Kenneth Clarke, put forward a proposal for dealing with mul- tilateral debt at the Commonwealth Finance ministers' Meeting in Valetta in September 1994, there were some in finance ministries and IFIs who claimed with optimism that the battle for relief was over. There was no further need, they said, to pore over solutions. Clarke's proposal is that a proportion of the IMF's gold reserves should be sold and the proceeds invested, providing noninflationary income to subsidize easier repayment terms for the poorest countries for their multilateral debt. But the Naples Terms, not wholly adopted after more than a decade, are simple compared with the Clarke formula. On that analogy we shall be well into the first century of the third millennium before practical results begin to flow regarding multilateral debt. The World Bank's accounts for 1994–95 show cumulative retained earnings of $15.5 billion, and a general reserve of $20 bil- lion (World Bank, 1996). Surely, at least some of this money should be available for debt remission.

The basic logic that underlies the figures of suggested debt presented in this paper is that after the debt forgiveness, all the poorer nations must be left only with a residue of debt which can reasonably be expected to repay in the medium term. For the low-income countries, with GNP per head below $700 per annum,[6] this implies total forgiveness, since the incomes of their governments are so low that any diversion of funds to debt servicing or repayment would deprive the poor of essential services. For the countries which are poor, but not among the poorest, with GNP per head between $700 and $2,000 per annum, this implies forgiveness of all debt above a certain figure, which we have taken to be 20% of GNP or eight months' exports of goods and services (XGS), whichever is the least. We thus leave this latter category with a residue of debt, small enough to be repaid without causing a level of suffering which no honorable creditor would exact.

We have to settle upon a suitable cut-off date for remission, since no one would make further loans to likely beneficiaries if such credit would likely be included in the debt stock to be remitted. We have taken the year 1993 so that the for- giveness would apply to all debt more than seven years old at the time of the Jubilee. One would also forgive any interest accruing on those principal sums between 1993 and 2000. It must, however, be emphasized that the year 1993 is not a sacrosanct milestone for this purpose. If it is found more suitable, the write-off of debts proposed for the year 2000 could apply to those outstanding rather nearer to the Jubilee year.

The two factors needing overwhelming emphasis in deciding on which countries should benefit from debt remission and at what level are the ratio of the debt owed to annual XGS, and the GNP per head of the country concerned. The first measures the physical ability of the debtor country to pay, and the second measures the need of that country. If the XGS is so low that there are no funds to repay the debt, it is in an obvious sense unpayable, unless resources can be shifted from other purposes to export promotion. This is likely to involve unfavorable results for the poorer people in the country concerned.

There are two reasons why a debt may be unpayable. It may be that there are no possible resources to pay it, owing to insufficient earnings from XGS. Alternatively, it could be possible to repay, but only at a cost in human suffering, which no honorable creditor would impose. If the GNP per head of a country is below the $700 limit for low-income countries, one can surely assume that any funds diverted from essential government expenditure on services and infrastructure to the repayment of a long outstanding debt, or of interest upon it, will cost too much in human suffering. It is for this reason that the GNP per head is the prime criterion for deciding which countries should get remission.

The outstanding example of the repayment of a debt in a way which caused so much human suffering that one wishes that it had not occurred is that of Romania. Ceausescu had such an obsession with the prompt extinction of Romania's debt that he almost extinguished the Romanian people in the process of reducing that debt from $5,653 million in 1986 to $199 million in 1989—a reduction of 96% in three years! The result was that so much suffering was caused to the Romanian people, both by his tyranny and by the overrapid debt repayment, that he was overthrown and executed in the revolution. The Romanian people have still hardly recovered from the aftereffects of their privation.

Any reductions already made under Brady deals applying to commercial debt must, of course, also be taken into account. This is of particular importance in Latin America. Where a deal has been made, granting a certain percentage of debt write-off in exchange for putting the remaining part of the debt into some sort of prioritized bonds, the debtor country may well feel a moral obligation to honor those bonds in full, since the honoring of the whole of the remaining bank debt was a part of the Brady deal.

A further factor is the extent to which a major part of the indebtedness arises from the corrupt activities of the present or former heads of government and their immediate associates. (See point (i) in Section 2.) In Africa, Nigeria needs mention, as well as Zaire and others. A specific exception from the remission could be made for an estimate of the holdings abroad, in the name of past or present heads of state and their immediate entourage, insofar as these holdings have derived from corrupt practices while in government. The new Nigerian Constitution, for application after the return to civilian rule, accepts the justice of attempting to obtain the restitution of stolen funds, and sets up a special "Committee for the Recovery of Ill-Gotten Wealth" (section 290). Swiss law has now been changed to remove some of the secrecy of numbered accounts. There is a fairly strong opinion in some international financial circles in support of recovering wrongfully acquired overseas deposits, thus transferring this part of the debt liability from the country as a whole to the corrupt leaders concerned.

Such restitution of funds is essential for disciplinary reasons, as well as for the political consideration of presenting a case which creditors will be able to accept. No taxpayer wishes to make sacrifices to forgive debts which are matched by overseas holdings of corrupt and fabulously rich foreign heads of state. In Nigeria, for instance, a lot of ordinary people insist that the necessary process of radical debt remission must be accompanied by action to recover stolen funds invested abroad. This does not, of course, mean that all overseas holdings of Nigerians should be confiscated to pay the debt, but rather that a limited, clearly focused process should be instituted as part of the debt remission package. At the same time, it is essential to construct, by mutual agreement between creditor and debtor countries, an effective system of audit and accountability to prevent further massive misappropriation of funds.

It is for this reason that the Nigerian case needs special attention. One person in four in Africa south of the Sahara lives in Nigeria. Nigeria owes $29 billion out of the $165 billion long-term debt owed by Africa south of the Sahara. Furthermore, Nigeria is the only country in the area whose interest payments on debt have exceeded grants received. In the period 1986–93, grants to Nigeria have totalled $1.248 billion, whereas Nigeria's interest payments during the same period have been nine times this figure. Its projected debt repayment for 1995 was put at $1.495 billion by the Minister of Finance, Chief Ani. It is clear, therefore, that any detailed proposal for debt remission which omits Nigeria leaves untouched one of the major debt burdens of the continent and fails to help a quarter of the population of Sub-Saharan Africa.

We must, therefore, use the powerful lever of projected debt remission to obtain both a more efficient system of audit and also a recovery of at least some of the stolen funds. Whether this is to be achieved by judicial action in Nigeria, or in the countries where the funds are held, remains to be determined. Alternatively, some procedure analogous to the present South African "Truth Commission" might be used to grant immunity from prosecution, on condition that half or a third of the stolen funds are voluntarily repatriated by the official concerned, and donated to a special fund for development and debt repayment. Failure to make a truthful declaration would result in prosecution and a demand for 100% of all the official's funds. A return to elected civilian rule should also be part of the package. Such an approach would be more constructive for the creditors to offer than a rigid refusal ever to consider remission for Nigeria, on the fallacious grounds that the country and government are incurably corrupt.

It is held by some that the granting of debt remission should be conditional upon the debtor country concerned having kept punctually to its debt service obligations. Clearly, this corresponds to the view of a number of people that one should reward financial virtue and penalize financial irresponsibility. It may also be a guide to the likelihood of the debtor country adopting responsible financial policies after the remission, but this is by no means certain. This approach is influential in the case-by-case scenario so popular with creditors and policy makers in the Paris Club and the IFIs. Clearly, this factor must have some weight, but it should not be dominant. It is difficult to assess relative levels of moral hazard for different countries. Almost all African countries have had to reschedule their debt service payments, and it is clear that no low-income or low-middle income country, except Romania, has been able to make a substantial reduction in long-term debt. Apart from Romania, the highest percentage of debt reduction achieved in the years 1985–92 was the 25% reduction effected by Yugoslavia, and this has been a contributory factor to the subsequent troubles there.

It is as if all the poorer debtor countries were imprisoned at the bottom of a well. Only one had ever climbed out, and in that case, the effort had left the country gasping and incapacitated. It is, therefore, unrealistic to base the debt remission on the comparison of how far the country concerned has succeeded in climbing up the wall of the well. Since none of the African countries (apart from the richer ones of Libya, Botswana, and Gabon) are able to escape from unpayable debt through their own efforts, it is unrealistic to place too much reliance on the moral hazard argument. In any case, the criteria on which one might base the moral hazard argument often contradict one another.

Furthermore, if one examines the record of African countries looking for examples of financial mismanagement or corruption, and of failure to meet debt obligations on time, one will find few states which pass the examination. Debt remission should not be made dependent on exact compliance with IMF recommendations. Indeed, some of these recommendations are ones which, if implemented, would produce benefit to the economy of the debtor country and to its population as a whole. But some involve undue suffering to the more vulnerable members of the country concerned. Furthermore, other IMF recommendations, such as the removal of import duties or restrictions, seem to be more in the interests of the richer exporting countries than of the poorer importing debtor countries. There is also a danger that a case-by-case approach can degenerate into a "political ally by political ally" approach, where remission is granted (as in the case of Egypt) to countries that support the policies of the western powers, rather than to those most in need. Clearly, unless there is a countervailing economic rationale, political considerations will always determine remission policy.

The overwhelming concern in Africa is with official debt, not private. In any case, we find that sometimes banks offer terms at least as generous as those offered by government. For instance, Nigeria in 1991 owed $5,590 million to commercial banks, but in 1992 was able to make a deal with her bank creditors to remit the bank debt, plus a considerable quantity of overdue interest payments, in exchange for creating $2,051 million of prioritized bonds. The write-off element in this deal was about 80%, apparently the highest of any Brady type deal so far negotiated. This bargain was clinched with the banks at 3 o'clock in the morning, after prolonged negotiation by Alhaji Abubakar Alhaji, the Nigerian Minister for Finance. The Nigerian government has kept up its payments on the bonds in a punctual and conscientious way since making the deal. The exact motivation of the banks is not clear; it may have been a mixture of realism and generosity and is in contrast to the more rigid way in which they have so far dealt with South American debt, where the remission on Brady type deals has generally been in the region of 35%.

The problem of remission of bilateral debt is the most simple one since, given the political will, it generally requires only the stroke of a number of governmental pens for implementation. The remission of Japanese debt presents a peculiar procedural problem, since the loans have been made from a fund which, according to Japanese law, prohibits their cancellation. However, there are simple procedural means for the Japanese government, given the political will, to provide from elsewhere the funds for the necessary remission.

The remission of World Bank debt has, until recently, been prevented by that institution's questionable insistence that its charter forbids debt forgiveness. Perhaps more importantly, remission would remove much of the World Bank's present power to dictate economic policy to these countries. To those who regard the bank as a firm governess for unruly and foolish children, the disappearance of this power would be a disappointment. However, to those who believe that the sovereignty of independent nations in economic policy is important, and that self-reliance is enhanced by making your own decisions, the emancipation of poorer countries from obligatory World Bank control would be a positive advantage. The World Bank could thus fulfill a beneficial role on a voluntary, consultative basis, and as a provider of new funds. The remission itself must be accompanied by strict conditionalities, as explained earlier. In general, this is best envisaged on a once-for-all basis rather than a continuing tutelage; however, it could possibly prove advantageous, in some cases, to make the remission in principle in the great Jubilee 2000, but to provide that the remission will be confirmed at a date to be determined, some three or four years after the Jubilee. This would provide a way of ascertaining that countries with a reputation for extravagance or corruption have actually made the necessary changes.

The World Bank presents an unrealistic view of the value in its balance sheet of debts owed to it by countries which are almost bankrupt. In fact, these debts have no more real value than would a debt owed to a London shop by a person who is now sleeping on the Embankment, unable (without begging) to afford even the price of a cup of tea. The only reason that World Bank debts owed by very poor countries can be quoted at face value by the Bank as part of its assets is that it is the creditor with the first claim on any resources which the debtor country possesses. Therefore, funds paid to the debtor country by other aid givers can be diverted to the World Bank. This is an unreal, as well as an exploitative, debt situation. Fortunately, the World Bank is now considering ways to write off unpayable debts, and it is imperative that these efforts should produce substantial results.

The advantages to debtors are threefold: the great psychological sense of liberation, the improved credit rating of countries no longer insolvent, and the actual gain in terms of remission from the burden of debt servicing. In the case of Sub-Saharan Africa, the volume of interest payments made in the last seven years to 1993 has been fairly moderate. The average interest repayment has been $6 billion per year, while the average excess of disbursement of principal over principal repayment has been $3.7 billion. Average annual grants received over this period have been $10.4 billion, not to mention additional annual technical cooperation grants of $5 billion.[7] These facts emphasize the categorical moral imperative of aid, from richer countries to poorer, as a kind of tithe imposed upon us by common membership of the human family. Aid is not to be considered as part of the debt equation.

If debt remission were to be accompanied by a cessation of grants, the cash flow position of countries in Sub-Saharan Africa would be much worse. It is essential, therefore, that debt remission is regarded not as a final step, but as a way of introducing a series of other measures to help poorer countries in Africa. This means that the sacrifice required of creditor nations and institutions to eradicate African debt is a relatively small one, but conversely, the debt forgiveness will not be of great net value unless accompanied by other measures. These must include new grants and loans at the present level or better. If these remain constant, Sub-Saharan Africa would benefit by some $6 billion per year, a substantial but not gigantic sum.

5. CONCLUSION

NGOs are increasingly important actors on the international development policy-making stage. It is important to understand the motivations, methods, and proposals of these movements. This paper explains the three basic premises which serve as the foundation for the Jubilee 2000 campaign for debt forgiveness for HIPCs. It is clear that HIPCs cannot repay their full debts and that creditors stand to benefit materially from forgiven HIPC debts. Moreover, there is a moral imperative to remission, one for which the jubilee concept serves as a uniquely relevant and powerful guide.

Clear principles, implementable guidelines, and a deadline are needed to move swiftly and productively toward a resolution of the continuing debt crisis among poor countries. The penultimate section outlines one such proposal in the hope that this will help foster serious debate among policymakers, as well as scholars, on the modalities of debt remission.

In sum, the debt remission Jubilee 2000 advocates is balanced (in the sense of being evenhanded, with benefits to creditors as well as debtors), unique (in that it will occur by or in 2000 once for all, not to be repeated), and comprehensive (because it covers all the state debts of the HIPCs involved: commercial, bilateral, and multilateral). This last point is important. It is insufficient to remit only one or two types of debt. Countries' ability to resume unstressed economic life rests on their freedom from all types of unpayable state debt. Their multilateral debt, the type now beginning to be tackled, takes priority for service as well as repayment over the other two types, and default in it has more serious consequences than defaults in the other two—a total halt to multilateral borrowing and thus loss of access to the most concessional funds.

NOTES

1. Third World debtor countries were known to the World Bank as Severely Indebted Low Income Countries (SILICs), Severely Indebted Lower-Middle Income Countries (SILMICs), and Severely Indebted Middle Income Countries (SIMICs). The Jubilee 2000 campaign is concerned primarily with the first group, more recently known as Highly Indebted Poor Countries (HIPCs). A country becomes severely indebted when the principal and interest of its total accumulated debt amount to more than 200% of its GNP or 800% of the value of its annual exports. Continued inability to service debts indicates that a country has become severely indebted.

2. This was clearly demonstrated in the analysis of the reductions in the totals of debt owed by Third World countries from 1985 to 1992 in Dent (1994). Only 10 of 116 countries reduced their debt over that period, all of them for special reasons, and all except Romania and Yugoslavia by less than 20%.

3. Private communication. See also Thirlwall (1990).

4. See also Schluter (1986).

5. See also Pontifical Council for Justice and Peace (1986): "She (the Church) restates the priority to be granted to people and their needs, above and beyond the constraints of financial mechanisms often advanced as the only imperatives." For a parallel Anglican exposition, see Gorringe (1994).

6. The World Bank (1995), Vol. II, page xxv note introduces a dividing line of $695 GNP per head, to distinguish low-income countries from middle-income.

7. The Nigerian case is an exception to the general rule of net inflow of aid and debt resources (total grants and loans received less total principal and interest payments made). It has paid interest at a rate of 3.5% above that for the rest of Sub-Saharan Africa from 1985–92. Furthermore, Nigeria has received much smaller grants and, in

consequence, has experienced a new outflow of $6 billion. The rest of Sub-Saharan Africa has benefited from a net inflow of $72 billion during this period; however, this was counterbalanced by worsening terms of trade.

REFERENCES

Dent, Martin J. *Jubilee 2000 and Lessons of the World Debt Tables (1992-3 and 1993-4)* (Keele: University of Keele, 1994).

Duchrow, Ulrich. *Alternatives to Global Capitalism.* English translation (Utrecht: International Books, 1995).

George, Susan. *A Fate Worse Than Debt* (London: Penguin Books, 1989).

Gorringe, Timothy J. *Capital and the Kingdom: Ethics and Economic Order* (New York: Orbis Books, 1994).

Griffiths, Brian. *The Creation of Wealth* (London: Hodder & Stoughton, 1984).

Hay, Donald. "Do Markets Need a Moral Framework?" *Association of Christian Economists Journal* 19 (1995).

Henley, Andrew. "Applying the Jubilee: Biblical Ethics and Asset Accumulation." *Association of Christian Economists Journal* 11 (1991): 1-21.

Mistry, Percy. *African Debt Revisited: Procrastination or Progress?* (The Hague: FONDAD, 1991).

Mistry, Percy. *Multilateral Debt: An Emerging Crisis* (The Hague: FONDAD, 1994).

Pontifical Council for Justice and Peace. "At the Service of the Human Community: An Ethical Approach to the International Debt Question" (Vatican: December 27, 1986).

Pontifical Council for Justice and Peace. *Social and Ethical Aspects of Economics* (Vatican: 1992).

Pontifical Council for Justice and Peace. *Tertio Millenio Adveniente* (Vatican: November 10, 1994).

Schluter, Michael. *Family Roots of Mobility* (Cambridge: Jubilee Centre, 1986).

Thirlwall, Anthony P. "How to Escape the Debtors' Prison." *Samizdat Foreign Focus* (March-April 1990): 23-24.

Thirlwall, Anthony P. "An Analysis of Changes in the Debt Service Ratio for 96 Countries, 1986-1990." *Banco del Lavoro Quarterly Review* 84 (1993).

World Bank. *World Debt Tables 1994/95* (Washington: World Bank, 1995).

World Bank. "Frameworks of Action to Resolve the Debt Problems of the HIPCs," Sec. M96-340/a (Washington: April 12, 1996).

World Bank. *Annual Report* (Washington: World Bank, 1996).

✗ NO
Will Debt Relief Really Help?
DENISE FRONING

In 2000, debt relief for what the International Monetary Fund (IMF) and World Bank term Heavily Indebted Poor Countries (HIPCs) was the cause of the moment in development theory, attracting international attention and broad agreement that it was the single most important piece of the poor-country development puzzle. Widespread consensus emerged that international lenders must forgive the HIPCs' debt burden. In the ebb and flow of development trends, debt relief thus had its moment in the sun, and rich countries rightly agreed to forgive some of the debt—although the World Bank and the IMF did not.

This relief, although limited to bilateral debt, will help. But when the G-7 and other advocates of development move on to the latest fad in the quest for solutions to the problems of the world's poorest countries—whether disease, education, or some yet unmentioned ill—all the attendant causes of debt relief will still need to be addressed.

All of these problems are long-term concerns. None of these countries will be wealthy tomorrow, nor will they solve all their troubles immediately. For G-7 nations, perhaps especially the United States, accustomed to focusing on the next quarter's profits rather than long-term returns, the temptation will likely be to give up too soon. That decision would be a mistake.

The fact is that these poor countries face far too many problems in addition to overwhelming debt, many of which are precisely what caused the debt accumulation in the first place. Many factors—disease, poverty, lack of education, lack of institutions, lack of transportation infrastructure, lack of food, lack of business, lack of security, lack of foreign investment, and lack of prospects—continue to stifle the economic growth of these countries, and they will continue to do so after debt relief. Without a change in these circumstances, debt relief will be only a short-term palliative, and these countries will find themselves back in the same predicament that they now face.

WHAT IS THE PROBLEM?

Bad policies and their attendant outcomes, both within and outside these countries, contribute to the "problem of poverty." Poor countries must improve domestically in a number of areas; their poverty cannot be attributed entirely to external factors. Although these countries face some valid domestic woes, many of the excuses for poverty are invalid. A lack of natural resources, for instance, does not fully account for the poverty the HIPCs face. Africa, where most of the world's 41 HIPCs are located, is awash in natural wealth, from diamonds, gold, and oil to arable agricultural land.[1] As George Ayittey observes, the continent has abundant natural potential. This potential, however, remains largely unrealized. Citing examples such as Russia, some have argued that such resources are more a curse than a blessing, but that argument does not explain the lack of development. Country after country has become rich based on these very resources.

Some maintain that lack of progress among HIPCs is due in part to geographical location and the affliction of disease that accompanies that location. The impact of disease, from malaria to cholera to AIDS, is indeed debilitating; but even if disease were entirely eliminated, the lack of institutions (or the persistence of corrupt ones) would keep the people of these countries poor.

I do not belittle the effects of disease or suggest that people should abandon attempts to mitigate the health crisis in the HIPC countries. Rather than quibble about which cause of poverty should be considered paramount, however, we must first acknowledge that the troubles of these countries are legion and that each must be addressed for lasting development to take place. For example, a couple of years ago, before the debt-relief craze, corruption was the cause du jour. The World Bank and other august institutions held conferences, everyone nodded their heads sagely, and learned people everywhere agreed that corruption was corrosive and that something must be done. Although work to address this particular problem undoubtedly continues, the international focus on corruption has shifted to other contributing factors of poverty; yet corruption's effects remain as debilitating as ever.

The construction of sound institutions, as one example, ought not to be abandoned because other problems exist. In fact, admitting that the impediments are many and related reduces the risk of "fad" development, in which whatever currently fashionable panacea that captures popular attention reigns while other crucial issues are forgotten.

Bad leaders

Ayittey makes the important distinction between the African people and the leaders of African nations. It is not the African people who squander development opportunities. Too often, it is African leaders, as Ayittey has observed, who seize both native wealth and foreign aid while plunging their countries into war and plundering their money, both through the exploitation of resources like diamonds and by stealing massive amounts of foreign aid.[2] As the Freedom House annual survey of political freedom points out, "Only 21 African countries (40 percent) are electoral democracies."[3] The African people do not choose these leaders, but they must suffer the consequences of these leaders' poor decisions.

Corruption

Despite its trendiness as an issue, corruption is a truly debilitating factor in the poorest countries. Indeed, much of Africa reflects the results of corruption undermining efforts to foster emerging market economies. Corruption is a cancer on the most legitimate efforts at development in many African countries, affecting regulation as well as property rights and discouraging economic progress. Although hardly unique to Africa or to developing nations, corruption is all the more damaging to them; it creates obstacles to development that an already established, large-scale economy might survive but that can prove fatal to fledgling efforts at market development in small economies.

Part of Africa's development problem, as economist John Mukum Mbaku writes, is bureaucrats who are often

> members of the politically dominant group and have significant influence over the allocation of resources. Under these conditions, civil servants behave like interest groups whose primary objective is to put pressure on the political system in an effort to redistribute wealth to themselves. "In countries with poorly constructed, inefficient, and non–self-enforcing constitutional rules, opportunistic behavior (including rent seeking) [is] usually quite pervasive.... Excessive regulation of economic activities creates many opportunities for rent seeking, including bureaucratic corruption.[4]

Mukum Mbaku's solution: reform the laws to remove the state from direct control over the economy—a system which leads to profit skimming, if not outright profit seizure.

Corruption compounds itself. Sometimes because of profit seizure, lower-level bureaucrats themselves are underpaid and regard taking bribes as necessary for their survival. The whole system becomes rotten in layers, with the entire structure threatening to tumble down if one attempts to reform one part of it.

Bad institutions

Ayittey delineates four institutional pillars[5] that are essential for lasting development in Africa: an independent judiciary, an independent central bank, free media, and neutral armed forces. In HIPCs and other poor countries, these pillars are often missing, which is why foreign assistance—even by those agencies whose sole purpose is giving aid—has proved ineffective overall. World Bank analysis of past loans and credits concludes that assistance "has a positive impact on growth [only] in countries with good fiscal, monetary, and trade policies."[6] In countries with poor policies, aid has had a negative impact. Robert Barro's analysis reveals that countries with "good fiscal, monetary, and trade policies" are more likely to experience positive economic growth whether they receive assistance or not.[7] Meanwhile, regardless of how much assistance they have received, countries with poor economic policies have not experienced sustained economic growth.[8] Clearly, sound economic policies, not foreign assistance, are the key to development.

HOW RICH NATIONS EXACERBATE THE PROBLEM

For poor countries to succeed in the international economy, they must have access to the markets of developed countries. Yet the United States levies the most onerous of its tariffs—as high as 45 percent—against some of these impoverished nations.

The U.S. weighted-average tariff rate of only 2 percent on worldwide imports is low by global standards,[9] but rather than apply this rate evenly among nations, the United States applies tariffs according to the type of product imported. The goods that face the highest U.S. tariffs are precisely those that the poorest countries produce: agricultural goods, textiles, and apparel. Combined with the impact of quotas, the U.S. tariff structure presents a significant obstacle to any country struggling to create even an initial presence in the world economy.

U.S. weighted-average tariff rates vary widely when plotted along lines of the exporting countries' economic wealth. Countries whose inhabitants earn an annual per capita gross domestic product (GDP) of more than $25,000 face an average U.S. tariff rate of 2 percent. Twenty-five countries with annual per capita GDPs of less than $1,000—approximately the amount that a minimum-wage worker in the United States earns in one month—face tariff rates greater than the U.S. average.

This disparity in U.S. tariff rates exists because poor countries tend to export many of the commodities that are subject to high tariffs in the United States and other wealthy markets. Low-income nations develop industries in which they have a comparative advantage and which provide goods and services that meet the basic needs of their people. The agricultural, textile, and apparel industries are labor-intensive and do not require sophisticated machinery or large amounts of capital to make a profit. The resource they do require, and the resource—sometimes the only resource—that developing countries have, is people.

The United States imposes absurdly high duties on the very goods for which poor countries most need a market, effectively pricing HIPCs out of the market. For example, Gambia, which has a GDP per capita of about $325 per year, faces duty rates on exports to the United States ranging from 8.8 percent on woven cotton fabrics to 11.8 percent on textile outerwear to 15.4 percent on women's clothing; the tariff on women's clothing is almost eight times the U.S. average tariff rate of 2 percent. The notion that women's skirts from Gambia are going to flood the U.S. market, overwhelm American textile factories, and send Ann Taylor out of business is clearly preposterous. In fact, if Gambia exported its entire economy to the United States, it would amount to less than 0.005 of 1 percent of total U.S. GDP.

Other examples of U.S. protectionism against HIPCs are just as absurd and needlessly damaging. Burkina Faso, a landlocked nation subject to droughts and desertification (both of which make agriculture a difficult endeavor, to say the least), has an annual GDP per capita of about $215. Its main exports are cotton and gold, and the United States is not one of its principal markets. Nonetheless, Burkina Faso faces a 33.3 percent tariff on whatever outerwear it might attempt to send to the United States. If Burkina Faso—which faces high costs in exporting everything because of its poverty and landlocked nature—somehow manages to get a coat to the United States, that coat is instantly taxed at a third against its cost.

Likewise, Malawi produces a total GDP of only $1.8 billion—just 0.02 percent the size of the U.S. economy—but faces a U.S. tariff rate of 32.8 percent on exports of suits and coats (raincoats excluded). Presumably, raincoats fall under "outerwear," which faces a 15.3 percent tariff when entering the U.S. market.

Ironically, the United States has said it wants to help these very countries! The entire economies of these HIPCs, much less their total exports, are a raindrop in the ocean of the U.S. economy. The same situation is true for other wealthy nations like those of the European Union (EU). It would cost nothing for developed nations such as the G-7 countries to eliminate all duties and quotas on HIPCs, but that act could mean a lot to the Malawian who can expect to earn $160 this year—the proverbial "less than a dollar a day."

An opportunity to use the resources they do possess—people—to build the sort of labor-intensive industries that are the only comparative advantage of poor countries could lead to long-term development. These high tariffs and continuing quotas, however, discourage development of such industries. Who in these poorest countries can afford to risk precious money to build a factory producing goods for which no market exists?

On the other hand, by gaining access to the world market, where the demand and remuneration are much higher than in domestic markets, poor countries can acquire more capital. This capital in turn fuels further production, increases savings, and fosters the development of new industries that can create further economic growth.

WHAT IS THE SOLUTION?

Breaking the cycle of indebtedness will require several actions.

Forgive debt

Among those actors who must act on debt forgiveness are the World Bank and IMF, which refuse to forgive the debt HIPCs owe to them even though multilateral debt accounts for as much as 80 percent of overall debt in some of these countries. The policies of these lenders perpetuate the debt cycle, forcing indebted countries to continue to depend on new aid in order to pay off old debts. This situation will never lead to sustainability.

The debt crisis in poor countries is real. A long-term solution requires total forgiveness of existing bilateral and multilateral debt, which is unlikely to be repaid in any event, and ending the debt cycle by eliminating bilateral and multilateral assistance. Countries must foster their own economic policies that attract private-sector credit and investment and that have proven to be the best means of achieving long-term, sustainable economic growth.

Remove barriers to globalization

Dani Rodrik cites "a long list of admission requirements" imposed on countries that try to join the world economy today.[10] He's right: a thicket of protectionist policies has sprung up around the global market, impeding developing countries' progress toward wealth. Of course, regardless of the protectionist behavior of other nations, rich or poor, it is crucial to HIPC development that the HIPCs themselves unilaterally lower their own barriers to trade and foster sound institutions internally. These measures will benefit the HIPCs regardless of what other countries do.

Nonetheless, the impediments to which Rodrik refers do exist. Therefore, rich countries should give the HIPCs time to implement the Uruguay Round obligations to which they have committed themselves in the World Trade Organization (WTO), recognizing that poor countries face very high costs in their efforts to liberalize. Among the WTO's 140 members are 109 developing or transition economies. The cost of implementing just three WTO agreements—the sanitary and phytosanitary measures, the customs valuation, and the TRIPS (Trade-Related Aspects of Intellectual Property Rights) agreements—is $150 million for each developing country.[11]

For such countries where, as Rodrik remarks, $150 million may amount to a full year's development budget, implementation is a huge task. Clearly, for these countries to comply with the TRIPS or other agreements in any reasonable amount of time (reasonable from any perspective, rich or poor), they need some assistance. Thus, wealthy countries should increase their commitment to providing educational advice on how to implement such agreements and should be receptive to creative alternatives with respect to implementation by those countries that may lack the infrastructure developed countries take for granted. Also, rich countries must be patient and recognize that obstacles will have to be resolved along the way.

Encourage trade through regional customs arrangements

Encouragement can include strengthening the free-trade role of such existing customs unions as the Southern African Development Community (SADC). For many of the HIPCs, multilateral agreements on the WTO scale may simply be too big an aspect of modern globalization to undertake at present. Without giving up on the multilateral endeavors to which they have already committed, they may need to focus on more manageable liberalization, through bilateral or regional negotiations.[12] Multilateral advancement of free trade is ideal, but in an imperfect world, the perfect often must give way to the achievable.

Establishing a common trading system such as a regional trade union will allow these poor countries to pool their limited resources to establish a customs framework. At the same time, each country can gain expertise in building the institutional elements of a modern economy without bearing the cost of modernizing on its own. Regional customs arrangements also alleviate the trade burden for landlocked countries, including some HIPCs, which face dramatically higher trading costs because they must transport goods through a neighboring country to reach a port.

Notably, however, these regional customs unions often have not met their own trade liberalization commitments for various reasons. Sometimes, members delay pledged liberalization due to war or the fear that trade constitutes a threat to their own industries—as Tanzania did when withdrawing from COMESA (the Common Market for Eastern and Southern Africa). In such circumstances, the HIPCs and other poor countries must take responsibility for their own actions and honor the free-trade commitments they have already made, which will foster economic growth in the long run even if trade flows do not rise significantly in the short term.

Eliminate all tariffs and quotas on HIPCs

Rich countries should lower the entry fees HIPCs pay to join the global economy by removing trade barriers imposed on these countries. Both the United States and the EU have passed legislation intended to increase market access for developing countries. The EU recently proposed duty-free access to its market for 48 poor countries in its "Everything But Arms" plan; the United States enacted the Trade and Development Act of 2000 to increase access to the U.S. market for poor African and Caribbean countries.

Both of these initiatives, however, offer only limited market access improvements in sectors that would most benefit these developing countries: textiles and some agricultural goods in the U.S. market; sugar, rice, and bananas in the EU. Moreover, both efforts serve domestic protectionist interests far more than they promote economic development in poor countries. For example, under the EU's proposal, tariff reductions on rice and sugar would not even begin until 2006. Because 2006 is also the year in which the EU's agricultural subsidy program, or Common Agricultural Policy (CAP), is due for its next review, the likelihood that those tariffs will be eliminated or even reduced is questionable.

Aside from denying market access to developing countries, the CAP is very costly to the world economy, around $75 billion annually.[13] Two-thirds of the cost ($49 billion) is borne by Europeans in the form of higher prices, inefficient production, and economic distortions. The remaining $25 billion—roughly equal to the total output of Burkina Faso, Gambia, Malawi, Cameroon, Guinea-Bissau,

Madagascar, Mali, and Mozambique—falls on countries outside the EU in the form of lost agricultural export opportunities in Europe.

The United States also maintains barriers in the textile and apparel sector that impose enormous costs on U.S. citizens as well as on developing countries. The annual cost imposed on foreign countries by U.S. textile and apparel barriers ranges from $4 billion to $15.5 billion.[14]

The European CAP and U.S. textile and apparel barriers impose a significant burden on the world economy and are clearly an impediment to trade liberalization. As illustrated above, the cost to rich nations of eliminating these barriers for HIPCs is minimal; but for many low-income countries, agricultural and textile exports are a vital source of income and an important path to development.

Institute economic freedom

Ultimately, establishing sound institutions is crucial to development. For development to take place, a country must first establish a rule of law on which its people can rely. Laws must ensure protection of personal property rights, as Barro established in his studies.

Other actions to maximize economic freedom are also essential, including minimizing the level of corruption and reducing the regulation that stifles economic development and hinders individual liberty. Hernando de Soto details the very real way in which red tape can prevent the legal purchase of property in some developing countries, requiring a number of steps that can reach into the hundreds through a number of agencies and last for years.[15] Free-trade flows are also a key component of development.

The benefits of economic freedom are not just ivory-tower musings. They appear as tangible evidence in the real world. Regardless of geography or culture or the unique conditions of different nations and regions, economic freedom, and through it the seeds of prosperity, can develop globally. Examples include Chile in Latin America, Hong Kong and Singapore in the Asian tropics, and Estonia among the former Communist republics of Eastern Europe, not just the already vibrant Western economies.

Critics often dismiss such examples of success as isolated incidents that are exceptions to the rule. They say, for example, that Hong Kong and Singapore are too small to be representative, or that Taiwan and South Korea succeeded economically in a different era, and so on. These criticisms are excuses, not reasoned arguments. The fact that so few countries in the tropics have developed is indeed a sign of more things wrong than right in the region, but to dismiss Hong Kong and Singapore is counterproductive when examples of success are needed instead. In addition, the notion of an "exception proving a rule" is scientifically backward: theories are proven wrong when an exception is found, not vice versa. The development of Hong Kong and Singapore, two tropical countries, disproves the theory that development of the Western kind cannot occur in the tropics.

The next argument that inevitably arises about Hong Kong and Singapore—that they are not viable tropical success stories because of their territorial size—is equally invalid. As Jagdish Bhagwati observes,

> The exceptionalism cited to explain away the East Asian performance has taken some strange forms. For instance, it used to be asserted that Hong Kong and Singapore were small "city states" and therefore somehow not subject to the economic laws applying to other "normal" nations. Of course, many nations around the world are even smaller on dimensions such as population.[16]

Such exceptionalism was likewise applied to "exceptionally large" countries like India to justify development failures without regard to the success of the United States, a large country in every sense of the word.[17] Is the economic growth of the United States then to be regarded as an exception? Where does one draw the line? Is Switzerland too small to be anything other than an exception to development success? Is Chile? Or Estonia?

In truth, countries will succeed or fail regardless of their size. Their performance depends far more on implementing successful institutions and addressing their unique problems, as well as taking advantage of the unique attributes that each finds in its own situation. In a variation on the Anna Karenina principle,[18] each troubled country is troubled in its own way.

The standard excuses for lack of HIPC development, then, fall short. Tropics are not the reason: there are examples of tropical success stories. Lack of resources is not the reason: the tropics possess abundant natural resources, far more in fact than many other regions. Countries in the tropics do have the problem of disease. Along with the admitted problems of their tropical location, however, their natural wealth offers a potential solution. A country like Nigeria that has an abundance of oil could spend all its petroleum proceeds on vaccines if its government so chose. But it does not. Instead, the money vanishes into private bank accounts. Why? Corruption and lack of sound institutions, as well as the lack of a viable rule of law that could, if present, minimize the siphoning of profits into private hands.

REASON TO HOPE

Success stories exist, often in places few would predict. Upon its establishment in 1949, the Republic of China on Taiwan had a poor, agricultural economy that was inefficient and overregulated, and its people were not politically free. In the 1960s, however, the government began to institute economic reforms. It guaranteed private property and set up a legal system to protect it, reformed the banking and financial sectors, stabilized taxes, gave public lands to private citizens, and allowed the free market to expand. Taiwan has become one of the world's fastest growing economies in recent years; in the 1990s, its growth rate was 11 percent.

Taiwan also has developed a functional democracy and has conducted successful multiparty elections in both the legislative and executive branches of government after years of rule by a repressive, one-party system. It is proof that a nation that was under an authoritarian regime little more than a quarter-century ago can evolve into an economically thriving democracy.

For those who are convinced by the argument that Taiwan's development took place at a time in which the costs of globalization were lower, Chile, whose GDP per capita has grown steadily since the government imposed economic reforms (except during a recession in the mid-1980s), offers a more recent example. Although the costs of this economic liberalization were often high, Chile demonstrates that institutions of economic freedom can impel political liberalization as well, for it was Augusto Pinochet's military regime that first began to institute the reforms that continued and intensified under subsequent democratic governments. Today, Chile has a market-oriented economy characterized by a high level of foreign trade.

An even more recent example of poor-country growth took place in the 1990s, when the costs of joining the world economy were about as high as they are now: Estonia, which emerged from half a century of Soviet domination in 1991 only to find that its standard of living, which in 1939 had been on par with Scandinavian cousin Finland, now lagged far behind. (Even today, Estonia's GDP per capita is one-seventh the level of Finland's.) Lacking an education in Western-style economic or political theory and having been taught in the Soviet system, Estonians began building sound economic institutions, privatizing state-owned industries, establishing a sound legal framework to attract foreign investment, liberalizing trade barriers, balancing the budget, and stabilizing the currency (by tying it to the German mark). In 10 short years, Estonia has become a model of economic development.

Of course, some could argue that Estonia's location—near its Scandinavian neighbors, which were already developed countries—has eased its progress; certainly, having a high volume of trade with Finland has proven beneficial. Yet some could also argue that Estonia's location—next to an unpredictable giant that just 50 years earlier overran it and destroyed its economic prosperity along with its sovereignty—is a distinct liability. Fundamentally, Estonia, like Chile, Singapore, Taiwan, and the rest of the world's economic success stories, has maximized its assets and sought to minimize its liabilities. All countries must do the same, no matter how insurmountable the liabilities may seem, in order to develop.

Three countries in three distinct regions, with three different cultural backgrounds, and in three different time frames: all examples of the possibilities of growth through sound institutional reform. Addressing the plight of the HIPCs may seem an overwhelming endeavor, but that does not mean it cannot be done. Far from it; anyone who sees a solution to a particular HIPC problem should be encouraged to tackle it, for these countries need assistance in many areas.

I myself advocate the fundamental necessity of institution building. Economic freedom is vital and, in the end, the only truly humane solution, for history demonstrates that only under such a system do people have the chance to use free will to achieve maximum prosperity. But creating economic freedom also means building sound, corruption-resistant, independent institutions that minimize the ability of anyone, native or foreign, rich or poor, to meddle in individual lives. Only then will debt relief really help.

NOTES

1. George Ayittey, *Africa in Chaos* (New York: St. Martin's Press, 1998).

2. Ayittey, "How the West Compounds Africa's Crisis," *Intellectual Capital*, June 29, 2000, located at <http://207.87.15.232/issues/Issue387/item9858.asp>.

3. Adrian Karatnycky, *Freedom in the World: 2000–2001*, located at <http://www.freedomhouse.org/research/freeworld/2001/essay1.htm>.

4. John Mukum Mbaku, "Bureaucratic Corruption in Africa: The Futility of Cleanups," *Cato Journal* 16, no. 1, located at <http://www.cato.org/pubs/journal/cj16n1-6.html>.

5. Ayittey, "How the West Compounds Africa's Crisis."

6. Craig Burnside and David Dollar, "Aid, Policies, and Growth," World Bank, Policy Research Department, Macroeconomic and Growth Division, June 1977.

7. See Robert J. Barro, "Rule of Law, Democracy, and Economic Performance," in Gerald P. O'Driscoll, Kim R. Holmes, and Melanie Kirkpatrick, eds., *2000 Index of Economic Freedom* (Washington, D.C.: Heritage Foundation and Dow Jones & Co., 2000), 31–51.

8. David Dollar and Lant Pritchett, "Assessing Aid: What Works, What Doesn't and Why," *World Bank Policy Research Report*, 1998, 2.

9. U.S. International Trade Commission, information available at <http://www.usitc.gov>.

10. Dani Rodrik, "Trading in Illusions," *Foreign Policy* (March/April 2001), located at <http://www.foreignpolicy.com/issue_marapr_2001/rodrick.html>.

11. J. Michael Finger, remarks at workshop on "Developing Countries and the New Round of Multilateral Trade Negotiations," Harvard University, November 5–6, 1999.

12. Traci Phillips, "Copyrights and Wrongs," *Marquette Intellectual Property Law Review* 4 (2000), in *Foreign Policy* (January–February 2001), located at <http://www.foreignpolicy.com/issue_janfeb_2001/gnsjanfeb2001.html>.

13. Brent Borell and Lionel Hubbard, "Global Economic Effects of the EU Common Agricultural Policy" in *Reforming the CAP* (Institute of Economic Affairs, 2000), 21.

14. Robert Feenstra, "How Costly Is Protectionism?" *Journal of Economic Perspectives* 6, no. 3 (Summer 1992): 163. See also Laura Baughman et al., "Of Tyre Cords, Ties and Tents: Window-Dressing in the ATC?" *World Economy* 20, no. 4, 409.

15. Hernando de Soto, *The Mystery of Capital* (New York: Basic Books, 2000).

16. Jagdish Bhagwati, *The Wind of the Hundred Days* (MIT Press, 2000), 31.

17. See generally Bhagwati, *The Wind of the Hundred Days*.

18. The opening line of Leo Tolstoy's *Anna Karenina*: "Happy families are all alike; every unhappy family is unhappy in its own way."

Postscript

An interesting dimension of the issue of debt relief has been the success of the Jubilee 2000 movement in winning some concessions on the issue. In the past, advocacy campaigns on more complex technical issues like international trade and finance have met with limited results. Campaigns like the Global Ban on Landmines have been successful because they focus on an issue of physical harm that is readily identifiable; as well, the link between cause and effect can be more easily drawn. In the case of debt relief, the framing of the issue as a form of "debt bondage" and the analogy to the anti-slavery movement seems to have worked well in rallying popular support for the issue. However, after examining both of the readings, do you feel the "debt bondage" imagery is sound? It what ways might it also obscure some issues in the debate? With whom does responsibility for the problem of debt lie?

While many people are sympathetic to the notion of debt relief, like Denise Froning, they are concerned about whether the monies saved in forgiving debts will actually be used in a productive way. Some of the issues involved in ensuring the proper use of debt-relief are discussed in the article by M.A. Thomas, cited below.

Infotrac Keyword Search

"debt relief" or "debt forgiveness" or "Jubilee 2000"

Suggested Additional Readings

Bulow, Jeremy and Kenneth Rogoff. "Cleaning up Third World Debt Without Getting Taken to the Cleaners." *Journal of Economic Perspectives*, Vol. 4, No. 1 (Winter 1990), 31–42.

Carole Collins et al. "Jubilee 2000: Citizen Action Across the North-South Divide." In Michael Edwards and John Gaventa, eds., *Global Citizen Action*. Boulder: Lynne Rienner, 2001.

Dent, Martin and Bill Peters. *The Crisis of Poverty and Debt in the Third World*. Aldershot: Ashgate, 1999.

Garg, Ramesh C. "The Case for Debt-Forgiveness for Latin America and the Caribbean Countries." *Intereconomics*, Vol. 28, No. 1 (Jan–Feb 1993), 30–4.

Keet, Dot. "The International Anti-Debt Campaign: A Southern Activist View for Activists in 'the North'...and 'the South.'" *Development in Practice* 10, no. 3/4 (August 2000): 461–78.

Thomas, M.A. "Getting Debt Relief Right." *Foreign Affairs* 80, no. 5 (September/October): 36–45.

Website Resources

Debt Relief International Debt Relief International runs a program to build the capacity of the governments of the Heavily Indebted Poor Countries (HIPCs) to manage their own debt strategy and analysis, without having to rely on international technical assistance.

Global Policy Forum This site has a large number of documents and articles relating to debt relief.

Jubilee 2000 This site is the homepage for the British-based Jubilee campaign. It has extensive documentation and links to many of the other national Jubilee campaigns around the world.

OneWorld: Debt Guide This guide to the debt issue, prepared by the UK-based OneWorld, is a good starting point for understanding debt issues.

The World Bank Group: HIPC The HIPC site maintained by the World Bank has a number of official documents and reports relating to debt relief.

Would a Tobin Tax on International Trade Be Detrimental to the Global Economy?

✔ **YES**

A.R. RIGGS AND TOM VELK, "The Tobin Tax: A Bad Idea Whose Time Has Passed," *Policy Options* 20, no. 6 (July/August 1999): 53–57

✘ **NO**

ALEX C. MICHALOS, "The Tobin Tax: A Good Idea Whose Time Has Not Passed," *Policy Options* 20, no. 8 (October 1999): 64–67

In 1972, a Princeton University economics professor proposed a levy on international currency transactions as a way to "preserve some possibilities of autonomy in national or continental monetary policies" that were wracked by the instability of money markets. He stated that a one percent tax on currency conversions should be considered as a way to deter rampant quick-turnaround currency speculation, and, secondarily, generate significant revenues by way of a relatively small penalty.

Although it provoked contentious debate at the time, the idea was widely perceived to be impractical. As other issues came to the fore, interest in it wained. In recent years, however, there has been renewed interest in the idea. Advocacy networks in Canada, the United States, and several European countries have been formed to promote the Tobin tax concept.

Renewed interest in the Tobin tax has surfaced because of the continuing globalization of financial markets and the series of financial and economic crises, including the so-called "Asian meltdown," that rocked the 1990s. When Tobin first proposed his tax in the 1970s, about $18 billion a day was traded on international currency markets. By the end of the 1990s, this figure had reached $1.5 trillion.

What has concerned many observers is that, as currency transactions have grown, so to has the volatility of markets resulting from rampant speculation on the markets. An estimated 95 percent of currency transactions are of a speculative nature—short-term trading aimed at capitalizing on fluctuations in the markets. Shrewd bankers and investors are able to take advantage of market volatility to make multi-million dollar profits.

But some observers have been concerned about the cost that such speculative trading has, both on national economies and on individuals. Critics argue that globalized currency speculation transforms local economic shocks into major financial crises, which often spread to other countries. The result is rising unemployment, wage cuts, inflation, and reductions in public spending. Vulnerable sectors of society—including women, children, and the elderly—often suffer most from the economic fall-out. Governments, fearing to take any actions that might unsettle foreign currency speculators, feel that their control over economic policy is hampered.

The financial crises of the 1990s gave new impetus to the Tobin tax idea. Simply put, the Tobin tax would essentially be a simple sales tax on all currency sales across borders. It would be equivalent to the payment-processing costs currently paid on each currency transaction. The tax would amount to only 0.1 to 0.5 percent of the cost of the total transaction. Some people have also proposed a higher level of taxation that might kick in during periods of volatility.

The aim of the tax would be twofold. First, it is argued that it would discourage short-term market speculation while leaving long-term productive investments untouched. This would diminish the adverse negative affects that the global financial markets have on poorer populations in countries experiencing financial crises.

Second, it is argued that the Tobin tax would generate much-needed funding for global projects that could be used to promote economic development and underwrite humanitarian projects. It is estimated that the Tobin tax could generate $150–300 billion in revenue a year. Given that the United Nations estimates that it would need $40 billion a year to ensure access to basic social services for all the world's population, proponents of the idea see immense benefits. The Tobin tax could be used, for example, to supply the $25 billion that is estimated to be needed to clear away the millions of mines strewn through war-torn societies.

On March 23, the House of Commons lent its support to the Tobin tax notion by passing Motion M-239, which read: "That, in the opinion of the House, the government should enact a tax on financial transactions in concert with the international community."

However, many people still oppose the concept. They believe that the Tobin tax is simply not practicable. The market for trading in foreign exchange is decentralized, unregulated, and highly mobile. If any particular country tries to impose the tax, trading of its currency will simply move offshore, they say. To work, a globally coordinated tax would be required. But it would be hard to achieve the necessary political consensus for that, especially as there are strong incentives for individual countries to opt out and offer a tax-free haven. Even if a global tax were successfully implemented, it would be hard to collect the tax on the many financial and foreign-exchange assets that can be used to mediate a foreign-exchange transaction. And there would be no guarantee that the funds collected would go towards those global causes that advocates hope would benefit.

When the issue came up in the House of Commons, there was renewed discussion within Canada about the Tobin tax. Tom Velk, an economist, and A.R. Riggs, an historian, outline why they think that nearly 30 years later, the Tobin tax is still a bad idea. In response, Alex C. Michalos, a political scientist, outlines why he thinks that the time has come for the Tobin tax to be implemented.

✔ YES
The Tobin Tax: A Bad Idea Whose Time Has Passed
A.R. RIGGS AND TOM VELK

The Asian financial crisis that hit financial markets hard last summer gave rise, as all recent financial crises have, to renewed interest in the "Tobin tax," a small tax on short term capital flows proposed by Nobel economist James Tobin of Yale almost 30 years ago. The worst of the Asian crisis now seems to have passed—and so, we hope, has this cycle's interest in Prof. Tobin's statist monetary scheme. In our view, his proposal to, as its proponents say, "throw a little sand in the wheels of the international capital markets" is a bad idea whose time has passed.

At bottom, the Tobin tax is an attempt to reduce the harm done by what are popularly known as "currency speculators." These speculators, hoping to earn short-term profits based on their belief that they have correctly foreseen price trends, or thinking their actions will cause desired price changes in the foreign exchange market, are persons, firms, or even (we suppose) governments who buy and sell currencies. (It is difficult to distinguish them from persons who buy and sell currencies for other reasons, of course.) Tobin-tax advocates believe these "speculators" distort and aggravate foreign exchange price movements. They claim that a small universal tax on short-term capital movements would improve economic efficiency by diminishing unhealthy price gyrations. Arguing that, world-wide, the tax would collect over 1.5 trillion US dollars annually, they want the world's governments to agree upon a sharing formula to split this tax windfall among themselves, as well as with several *supra*-national claimants, including the IMF, the UN, and the World Bank. They conclude that the removal of this vast sum from the pockets of world-class traders and investors would have little effect upon the volume of world trade. Critics, on the other hand, often worry about where the true tax burden will fall, and what effect it may have on the incentives to locate, work, save, invest, and trade. Another formidable criticism is the destructively high rate of the Tobin tax against the net gains earned by the aggregate of all currency traders.

We prefer to call persons who make short-run trades in currency markets "specialists" rather than speculators, because the outcome they achieve—quite without intending it—is the same as that achieved by other specialists in stock markets. On a trading floor, orders to buy may come when no sellers are offering securities; at other times, sellers may not find buyers. In the absence of specialists, this bad timing would cause large price fluctuations—or trades could fail to be consummated at all. In the stock market, specialists have existed to cure this technical problem for as long as exchanges have operated. Many times in each trading day, so many it makes them look like "speculators," they step in to buy when no one else will, and sell when orders might otherwise go unfilled. Their management of buffer inventories prevents undue price fluctuations and maintains an orderly market. Over the long run, they make money for themselves, since they can take a small advantage out of the "missing half" situation to buy a bit cheaper, and sell a bit dearer than would be likely if the missing halves were as fully attentive to market movements as are the specialists.

If a Tobin tax were to be applied to currency market specialists, the small margin they subtract from their bid price or add to their asked price would have to be larger—for the Tobin rate is upon the value of the trade, not the margin earned by the trader. A Tobin tax might well drive specialists out of the market altogether, with undesired results for all traders. So the sand that Prof. Tobin wants to pour into the gears and wheels of the foreign exchange markets will make the machine run less well, particularly when one notes that the Tobin tax revenues would exhaust currency specialists' total profits many times over.

The world-wide Tobin scheme has never been implemented, and is unlikely ever to be so. Even if universal agreement could be momentarily reached to implement such a tax, the trillion-dollar-a-year pot of gold would be more than enough to induce any number of governments to cheat, to set themselves up as tax-cut havens, or to insist upon more payout than is their due. A cartel with many members, each with a different degree of financial need, some with a cynical disregard of their agreements, and others with substantial capacity for subterfuge, requires not just good faith from its members, but a degree of generosity toward co-conspirators verging on the saintly.

Even without the connivance of governments, currency traders themselves will devise evasions and financial innovations allowing them to move from one nation's money to another's, not by taxed open purchase, but by hard-to-observe internal-to-one-market swaps—whether of treasury bills or other contractual derivatives, any one of which will give counter-party traders claims on equivalent-to-foreign goods or financial instruments, denominated in each party's preferred currency. To put the point simply: If you want foreign money, you need not go to a foreign person or market to get it. You find a fellow-citizen or financial institution willing to create, for a fee, a financial instrument for you denominated in the desired foreign currency, and in all other respects built to your specifications. Any gains or losses you experience because of exchange rate changes are "settled in cash" in terms of your domestic currency. Your needs are met, you have neither "crossed any border," nor have you exposed yourself to any but the most intrusive and expensive-to-administer Tobin tax.

You have not actually put your hands on any foreign currency in such a transaction, nor have the counter-parties who supply your needs. You are merely betting, in a side market, on the price of a currency, without yourself entering the main market for the currency. It has been said that such bets cannot change the "real" currency price, anymore than betting on a horse makes it run faster (the exception being our betting history: Our picks clearly run slower for it, when they don't get scratched). But in the securities market, betting does change the race's outcome. Options on stocks are "mere bets" on the underlying stock. The options are priced in their own, separate market. But the price there can change the price of the related stock by a process of arbitrage. If the cost of acquiring rights to buy a stock (which immediately translates into a cost for the stock) gets out of line with the price of that stock when bought directly, options buyers or writers shift to the "real" market, while "real" players shift the other way. Many players will hedge the bets they make in the real market with option-type insurance, guaranteeing a minimum selling price for persons long in the real market, and likewise setting a maximum buy-back cost for persons short in the real market. And this insurance play works equally well for the options players, too. These insurance possibilities link real and options markets even more closely.

The basic rule for all connected markets—and all open markets are connected—is that only one price for any one commodity may rule at one time. Options, futures, derivatives, and synthetic securities are just different paint for the same underlying horse, but the paint doesn't change the horse's ability to run.

At bottom, it isn't even obvious which market, real or derivative, is the more important. Farmers the world over have long cursed options and futures "speculators," the volume of whose trading is claimed to be large enough to "wag the dog." High-volume options, futures, and derivative markets exist for all major currencies, and it is hard to say which market—real or "casino"—dominates the other. Nor does the options/real link introduce novel elements in the determination of equilibrium prices for the securities involved. Real prices for future earnings are determined by real events—profits, risks, interest rates, and their distribution over time. It is entirely possible, however, that information about these real determinants sometimes might appear first in the options market and at other times in the "real" market, in each case afterwards flowing to the lagging market and changing prices there.

Thus in modern financial markets traders can separate the unit of account, the means of settlement and the standard of value and so frustrate Prof. Tobin. Claims and contracts can be drawn up whose value is driven by observed exchange-rate changes, without the need to actually take possession of any of the currencies involved, just as profits in copper (mined in Africa) and pork bellies (raised in Quebec) can be earned by Wall Street day-traders, who, always seated at their keyboards, will never soil their powder-white buck shoes in a mine or pig farm.

Financial innovation is sure to evolve further under added pressure from taxes and regulations. Profits go up if a tax or other artificial cost laid upon otherwise desirable trading can be avoided. Regulators react by expanding the range, reach and complexity of the tax apparatus. The process ends when the marginal costs of private innovators and public regulators completely exhaust the marginal gains earned by trading or preventing trade. This end point is no kind of regulatory optimum. It may occur only after substantial resources have been consumed in a circular pattern of regulation, evasion, and re-regulation. The final tax design is unlikely to be the simple one that Prof. Tobin claimed for his system. Moreover, today's "day-trader" speculators profit from an hour-to-hour volatility, not so much in foreign exchange markets but also in foreign securities markets they wish to access. When Prof. Tobin first suggested the tax, he did not anticipate a stock market where hourly volatility is measured in tens of percentage points for hot securities. Even random stock selection gives record-setting annual rates of return and risk. In such an environment, the low rate of the Tobin tax (as distinguished from the vast sum that it would actually collect) means that the most active stock and currency "speculators" are not likely to be dissuaded from trading by a Tobin tax. If speculation is "wrong" because it aggravates volatility, or generates "false prices" and other kinds of misinformation, then speculators lose money over the long run. In the very long run they disappear altogether, since bottom-line unprofitable speculation is a black hole for capital. And so if speculation persists in any market it must be stabilizing, buffering shocks, and generating better information.

Prof. Tobin made his suggestion in hopes of giving central banks greater power to manipulate floating exchange rates. A standard policy prescription of the 1960s, managed floating rates were thought to be a good way to control national income, prices, and employment. But fixed exchange rates are now in favor—the Euro is an example—and many economists believe politically controlled central banks lack the wisdom, the means, and the freedom of action required to manage exchange rates.

Political leaders have always been interested in managing money, and not always for the best. Henry VIII debased England's currency, as Caesar did Rome's. But money was not thought of as, nor could it be, a legitimate tool of government before this century's changes in political institutions and in the composition of the securities market. Today's citizenry allows government officials a degree of authority over money, credit, and banking that the authors of the American Constitution specifically denied to the legislature, and that David Hume, not to mention Tacitus, warned against in the strongest terms. Not until government debt, taxes, and spending reached the high levels created by the wars and statist experiments of this century did governments possess the instrument—government debt large enough to affect general credit conditions—and the equation (tax, spend and then elect) that finally added up to Prof. Tobin's idea.

But its moment has passed. Technical developments in private markets for information and communication allow public and private cheaters, evaders, innovators, and fine-liners a range of instruments and strategies sufficient to get around virtually any tax or regulation. The monopoly power upon which rested the logic of Tobin-style monetary policy is gone. Domestic financial markets are no longer hidden behind insurmountable political barriers. Governments and central banks cannot establish prices and quantities for money and credit different from those existing internationally. Government domination over financial markets is a thing of the past. There are today over one hundred national governments capable of issuing money, or having an ambition to do so, but far larger than any one of them is the private market that moves money and credit across national borders at the click of a mouse, or the murmur of a telephoned command.

The aggregate buying and selling capacity of the largest and healthiest government central banks is measured in the tens of billions, or at most one or two hundred billion US dollars. And that amount, once spent, could not easily or quickly be regathered for another onslaught of market-making or price-fixing. On the other hand, private trading in the aggregated, unified currency, and securities markets of the world, amounting to about 1.5 trillion American dollars a day, is immense and constantly replenished. No government, nor any politically stable coalition of governments, wishing to establish a price for some security different than the price the market dictates, has the international reserves, the overseas borrowing power, or the unencumbered tax base needed to change that price from the value the private marketeers judge it should have.

Diminished monopoly power also means no government may take an action without consideration of backlash. Policy makers in small, open, trading societies who change the quantity of money, generate inflation or deflation, redirect the flow of loans and credits from one industry to another, or change the tax and subsidy environment, must consider reciprocal changes other governments might make. They must calculate the likelihood that private international and domestic entities may shift the locus of their activity away from costly exposures and toward more preferred ones, perhaps crossing international borders in so doing. Thus the range of actions a government may take to control monetary prices and quantities is limited by the short reach of its laws and regulations, by governments of other nations acting in energetic opposition, and by the literal and figurative mobility of private economic actors. Instead of paying Prof. Tobin's tax, or being satisfied with their share of it, players on the economic stage will take advantage of money's omnipresent and malleable qualities, and, with a good lawyer's help, claim that the true locus of their wealth, their deal-making activity, their cost and profit experience, or their sovereign power is wherever the tax-hungry cartel cannot go.

Economists who favor the market believe that governments no longer have (if ever they did) the power to establish conditions for money, credit, interest rates, tax, and spending levels that are significantly at odds with what private players subject to their laws approve. Note that this does not imply that monetary and fiscal conditions are everywhere identical, or should be driven to some lowest common denominator. We do not say that governments cannot undertake meaningful economic policy affecting money markets. Constitutional design that: protects property rights and contract; treats all citizens uniformly; guarantees due process without institutionalizing an overly litigious spirit in the people; and, to the extent possible in a democratic state, disallows a strategy of tax and tax, spend and spend, elect and elect—a design that does all these is for long-run private prosperity. But money and credit are such powerful instruments at the ballot box, so easily manipulated in ways beyond the average citizen's understanding, so frequently mismanaged in human history, that we are overcome with awe at the shameless manner in which politicians claim for themselves sovereignty over an industry they have so frequently mismanaged into total breakdown. Arguments like that of Prof. Tobin's, calling for an international government monopoly over a key dimension of the market for money and credit, should be rejected. If education, fire and police protection, mail service and garbage collection are all too complicated and important to be left to government, money clearly is, too.

✗ NO
The Tobin Tax: A Good Idea Whose Time Has Not Passed
ALEX C. MICHALOS

The collection of essays on world capital in *Policy Options* July/August 1999 was timely and provocative, but unbalanced: There was no defence of Tobin taxes to match the critical essay of A.R. Riggs and Tom Velk (hereafter "RV"). Although Professor Tobin assured us in the last paragraph of his essay that he still believes in his idea, the rest of the essay concerned other things. In the interest of bringing balance to the discussion, I would like to provide some basic information about Tobin taxes. I will also try to show that RV's problems with Tobin taxes are misguided, but my main aim is constructive rather than critical. A more thorough account may be found in my monograph *Good Taxes: The Case for Taxing Foreign Currency Exchange and Other Financial Transactions* (Science for Peace and Dundurn Press, 1997).

To begin with, take RV's assertion that the Tobin tax is *passé*. Of many examples that one could give showing that Tobin's idea is alive and probably has a bright future, I will mention only three.

- On March 23 of this year, by a vote of 164 to 83, the Canadian House of Commons endorsed a private member's motion "that, in the opinion of the House, the government should enact a tax on financial transactions in concert with the international community." Such taxes are precisely the sort that Professor Tobin, following Keynes by some years, has recommended.

- A group called ATTAC (Association pour une Taxation des Transactions financières pour l'Aide aux Citoyens), which was founded in 1998 has, as I write these lines, over 100 chapters in France with a total membership of over 10,000 people. ATTAC chapters now also exist in Argentina, Austria, Belgium, Brazil, Greece, Ireland, Italy, Quebec, Senegal, Spain and Switzerland. It is worth remembering that France's withdrawal in October 1998 from OECD negotiations on the Multilateral Agreement on Investment (MAI) was the result of NGO activity of the same sort as that undertaken by ATTAC (and by many of the same people) and that it was sufficient to prevent the MAI from going forward. ATTAC organized massive demonstrations at the World Economic Forum in Davos earlier this year and issued the Davos Declaration endorsing, among other things, Tobin taxes.

- In Helsinki, a coalition of over 200 national and international NGOs joined forces to launch the new publication *The Tobin Tax: How to Make it Real* by Heikki Patomaki and Katerina Sehm. The government of Finland is promoting Tobin taxes and the prime minister is chair of the European Union for the rest of 1999.

In short, the Tobin tax is alive and well and by all indications gaining in popularity and acceptance.

And not a moment too soon. The Bank for International Settlements' estimate of daily foreign currency exchange trading was over $1,300 billion in 1995, including derivative contracts (i.e., contracts involving assets "derived" from others, as for example, financial futures and options contracts to buy or sell foreign currency at a future time). When derivatives are excluded, the trading figure dropped slightly to $1,230 billion a day. Multiplying the $1,300 billion daily figure by 240 business days yields a yearly figure of $312 trillion. RV mistakenly asserted that a Tobin tax "would collect over 1.5 trillion US dollars annually," presumably because they confused the estimated current daily trading figure with the tax collectible from such trading. The most conservative estimates of the annual amount of revenue that a tax of 0.05 per cent (five basis points) might have attracted on a global basis in 1995 ranged from $90 billion to $97 billion. Most likely, that range would still be appropriate today.

It is crucial to understand that only about two per cent of all global foreign currency exchange activity is connected to the export and import of real goods. The vast majority of activity is simply not connected to the world's real economy. This is very important for Canadians to remember. Gordon Thiessen, Governor of the Bank of Canada, reported to the Standing Senate Committee on Banking, Trade and Commerce earlier this year that, as an exporting country, Canada would suffer from a Tobin tax. On the contrary, since Canada would share global revenues from the $50 worth of foreign exchange activity that is currently not taxed for every $1 worth of activity connected to exports and imports of real goods, Canadians would clearly be net gainers by a wide margin.

Over 80 per cent of the foreign exchange transactions in question are for round trips of seven days or less. Eighty per cent also happens to be the share of total transactions handled in the seven leading financial countries (the UK, the USA, Japan, Singapore, Switzerland, Hong Kong, and Germany). Nearly three quarters of global spot transactions are inter-dealer exchanges made through a few central clearing-houses using increasingly carefully monitored electronic systems. Institutions that deal in such transactions might have 3,000 to 4,000 trades on an average day, with quoted prices changing 20 times a minute for the most important currencies. The dollar-deutsche mark rate might change as many as 18,000 times in a day, and trades worth from $200 million to $500 million are not unusual.

At the moment, no taxes are levied on foreign currency exchange transactions. On the other hand, many countries—including France, Switzerland, Japan and the United Kingdom—impose excise taxes on intranational financial transactions; e.g., taxes on the sale and/or purchase of stocks and/or bonds within a country. Some other countries have had such taxes and phased them out (e.g., Germany and the United States).

The wide variety of taxes on intranational financial transactions is remarkable in itself. Different policymakers have selected different instruments to suit the special conditions of their own countries. For example, some countries have maximum tax levels (Australia and France) and some do not (Japan). Some countries tax only new security issues (Sweden); some tax no new issues (Denmark); and some tax both new security issues and transfers (Austria). Some tax only transfers of shares (Argentina) while others tax transfers of shares, bonds and securities (Belgium). Some tax only banks and financial institutions (Australia); some tax no financial institutions (Denmark). Some tax their own citizens anywhere (Austria) while others tax their own citizens trading outside their country (Italy and Japan). Some tax borrowers and buyers of securities or foreign currency (Brazil); others tax only stock transactions (China). Some tax all banking transactions (Brazil, temporarily); some tax all checks (New Zealand); and some tax all financial transactions (Portugal). Some tax only resident sellers of shares (Denmark) while others tax only resident buyers and sellers of stocks (France, Malaysia). Some tax buyers of their own securities less than buyers of foreign securities (Switzerland). Some tax government bonds less than shares and some tax government money market securities not at all (Japan).

For countries such as Canada and the United States, which currently have no excise taxes on financial transactions, the idea of introducing a Tobin tax may seem very whimsical, indeed. But from the point of view of most other industrialized countries, which do have some form of financial transactions excise taxes, the idea of a Tobin tax is not at all fantastic.

In the last paragraph of their essay, RV make clear their view of the possible role of governments in this area of policy. They do not believe governments have "the power to establish conditions for money, credit, interest rates, tax, and spending levels that are significantly at odds with what private players subject to their laws approve." They do believe that governments have the power to "undertake meaningful economic policy affecting money markets" in the form of "constitutional design that: protects property rights and contract; treats all citizens uniformly; guarantees due process without institutionalizing an overly litigious spirit in the people; and, to the extent possible in a democratic state, disallows a strategy of tax and tax, spend and spend, elect and elect." In their view, a design that does all these will permit long-run private prosperity.

As a matter of principle they believe

> ... money and credit are such powerful instruments at the ballot box, so easily manipulated in ways beyond the average citizen's understanding, so frequently mismanaged in human history, that we are overcome with awe at the shameless manner in which politicians claim for themselves sovereignty over an industry they have so frequently mismanaged into total breakdown. Arguments like that of Prof. Tobin's calling for an international

government monopoly over a key dimension of the market for money and credit, should be rejected. If education, fire and police protection, mail service and garbage collection are all too complicated and important to be left to government, money clearly is, too.

Regarding the factual matters they raise, while it is true that governments have the power that "private players" grant, RV do not fully appreciate the fact that in democratic societies *all* private citizens are "private players" when they are educated and organized and actively pursue their interests in an enlightened fashion. RV assume instead that in the realm of financial transactions the real "private players" are people with significant real wealth and that, therefore, a necessary condition of successful government activity is that such people be kept happy. In fact, the necessary condition of successful government activity is that a majority of voters be kept happy, and sometimes that requires making many or most people with significant real wealth unhappy. It is worth remembering that during much of the 30 years prior to the Reagan-Thatcher-Mulroney period RV's "private players" were typically less happy than they subsequently became and that such a state of affairs may occur again.

RV evidently do not believe that passing and enforcing laws protecting property rights and contracts, however important that may be, can prevent the sort of foreign currency exchange evasions described in the paper. Indeed, virtually all writers who enumerate the sorts of tax-evasive maneuvers RV describe fail to realize how much infrastructure support and protection financial traders need. Without the full support of governments, laws, licencing, police, courts and so on, foreign exchange activity would simply be impossible. But such support can be withheld, reduced or expanded, depending on the political will of voters. Paul Martin was certainly right when he said that "our efficient domestic markets are the result of sound regulation" (p. 7 of the summer issue of *Policy Options*), and so was Joseph Stiglitz when he wrote "Governments play a large role in all of the most successful financial markets. Wall Street, the international emblem of free markets, is one of the most highly regulated markets in the United States" (p. 25).

By contrast, David Henderson was certainly wrong in arguing: "... the main lesson to be learned from the events of the past few years is that unchecked government power causes human tragedy and that to reduce the size and frequency of these tragedies, we need to eliminate the vast majority of powers that various governments have over innocent people" (p. 33).

Clearly unchecked power is always dangerous, whether in the hands of governments or private individuals or corporations. However, the appropriate solution to the problem of mismanaged power is not to abandon but to improve management. Whether in public or private organizations, management can be improved by more enlightened and active participation by all stakeholders, and by holding people responsible and accountable for their actions.

Regarding the matters of principle raised by RV, their position is plainly anti-democratic. They simply do not trust elected representatives to manage much of anything, but especially money and credit. Here again, RV show an incredible ignorance and/or lack of appreciation of the history of money and banking. For most of the past 2,000 years it has been a history of socialization brought about as a direct result of the failures of private financial industry. For example, the Bank of Canada was created in 1935 precisely because of the mess made by RV's "private players" in the 1920s. If it were not for our Canada Deposit Insurance Corporation, the private banking industry would have gone and stayed belly-up many years ago. Of course deposit insurance increases moral hazard, as Henderson said, but the solution to the problem of increased moral hazard is, as Stiglitz argued, the introduction of appropriate taxes and regulation. Insurance companies put higher premiums on accident-prone drivers and in extreme cases governments simply deny them driver's licences. Similarly, Tobin taxes put higher premiums on short-term trading that is typically not connected to the real economy, while in extreme cases dealers who insist on evading such taxes may be denied licences to trade. There is no good reason for allowing any financial trader to enjoy the benefits of a stable international financial system while taking a free ride on every other stakeholder.

Monetary systems have never been successfully self-regulating. The question is: In whose interest shall they be regulated? Unfortunately, in Canada since the 1970s our system has been regulated primarily in the interest of the rentier class. The evidence for this is, first, that the Bank of Canada allows commercial banks to create most of the new money required to keep our economy growing—and to create debt at the same time—even though the Bank has the authority to create the same amount of new money without creating debt, and, second, that real interest rates are allowed to continue to be two to three times their traditional, pre-1970s levels. Both of these facts can and I think will be changed when there is both the will and the political intelligence in the Canadian electorate to do so.

The last point I want to make regarding RV's essay concerns their misguided faith in the efficient market hypothesis (EMH) with respect to the churning that characterizes foreign currency exchange markets. They expressed their faith when they wrote "the short-term capital movements that are blamed for market volatility often serve to keep markets functioning and stable." I have already emphasized that 98 per cent of short-term capital movements are unrelated to the real economy. It is therefore a red herring to suggest that reducing such movements would have a distorting effect on real economy markets. But aside from this argument there are four good reasons for thinking that the EMH does not hold in securities markets:

- If the EMH were true, then observed market prices would give good estimates of the actual cash flows from securities. But they do not; rather, market speculation makes market prices much more variable than earnings (cash flows).

- If the EMH were true, then there should be no speculative booms and busts, and no cyclical fluctuations in securities market prices. But such fluctuations obviously occur.

- If the EMH were true, then irrational investing, noisy trading, fads, herd behaviour and over-speculation would tend to disappear, as trading came to be dominated by rational exchanges based on fundamental values. But securities trading is notorious for its signs of irrational investing.

- If the EMH were true, then there would be some relatively objective basis on which the future value of securities rested. But there is no such objective basis. Rather, the future value of securities rests on diverse and transient human assumptions, perceptions, judgments, expectations and behaviour.

Given the failure of the EMH, it would be unreasonable for governments to behave as if it were true. Those who continue to insist on liberalizing capital accounts, as RV do, are basing destructive public policies on patently false theories. The only reasonable course now is to consider appropriate sorts of regulation for securities markets. In the case of foreign currency exchange markets, the most promising instrument is some sort of Tobin tax. It cannot be the only or entire solution to the variety of problems generating increasingly frequent monetary crises in the world today, but it can certainly be an important part of a solution.

Good taxes should generate enough revenue to pay for public goods and services that not only provide a social safety net for relatively underprivileged or unlucky people but also provide the resources to create sustainable human communities with a good quality of life. Good taxes should be levied roughly in proportion to people's ability to pay, and should be administratively manageable and cost effective. In this as in most other areas of life, what is good or bad, right or wrong, can only be decided pragmatically, by carefully weighing all the likely benefits and costs involved. I think Tobin taxes would be good and I hope my comments on the essays from the July/August issue will motivate others to undertake their own investigations to confirm or deny my assessments.

Postscript

As globalization makes national borders less relevant, governments in both developed and developing countries are finding that their tax base is eroding. Many NGOs supporting the Tobin tax advance an ethical argument in support of this idea. The tax is beneficial because the revenues accrued could be used to finance development and humanitarian projects in developing countries and underwrite United Nations programs. But since the tax is being collected in wealthier countries, governments could be tempted to retain a significant portion of the funds to assist their own dwindling budgets. How could a Tobin tax be structured in such as way as to ensure that the benefits would be redistributed in ways that its advocates desire?

The Tobin tax is intended to benefit developing countries in two ways: It would generate revenues for worthy development projects, but it would also reduce currency speculation, thereby helping those economies buffeted by the inflow and rapid outflow of funds. However, like many policies, the impact of the tax could be double-edged. While the Tobin tax may discourage speculation, it could mean a slowing of financial capital into developing economies. Would the benefits of the tax outweigh such potential side effects?

Infotrac Keyword Search
"Tobin Tax" or "Tobin" + "tax"

Suggested Additional Readings

Johnson, Robert. "The Tobin Tax: Another Lost Opportunity?" *Development in Practice* 7, no. 2 (May 1997).

Mendez, Ruben P. "Paying for Peace and Development." *Foreign Policy* 19 (September 22, 1995).

Singh, Kavaljit. "Tobin Tax: An Idea Whose Time Has Come." *Economic and Political Weekly* (May 1, 1999): 1019–20.

Stotsky, Janet G. "Why a Two-Tier Tobin Tax Won't Work." *Finance & Development* 33, no. 2 (June 1996): 28–29.

Tobin, James. "A Proposal for International Monetary Reform." *Eastern Economic Journal* 4 (1978): 153–59.

Wachtel, Howard. "Tobin and Other Global Taxes." *Review of International Political Economy* 7, no. 2 (Summer 2000): 335–352.

Walker, Martin. "Global Taxation: Paying for Peace." *World Policy Journal* 10, no. 2 (Summer 1993): 7–12.

Website Resources

ATTAC France (Association pour une Taxation des Transactions financières pour l'Aide aux Citoyens). The largest French initiative on the Tobin Tax. It has extensive documentation in French.

Halifax Initiative A Canadian initiative to promote the Tobin tax.

Oxfam Great Britian Note the discussion paper. "Time for a Tobin tax? Some Practical and Political Arguments."

Tobin Tax Initiative An American advocacy group promoting the Tobin tax. Contains extensive materials including a detailed bibliography and links to other major Tobin tax sites.

PART FIVE

GLOBAL COOPERATION AND HUMAN SECURITY

Do we need an international criminal court?

Can international law eliminate the problem of child soldiers?

Should states pursue an open border policy toward migrants?

Should political and civil rights always take priority over economic and social rights?

Can economic sanctions mitigate conflict and halt human-rights abuses?

Does Africa pose a threat to global environmental security?

ISSUE**SEVENTEEN**

Do We Need an International Criminal Court?

✔ **YES**
DOUGLAS CASSEL, "Why We Need the International Criminal Court," *Christian Century* 116, no. 15 (May 12, 1999)

✘ **NO**
ALFRED P. RUBIN, "Some Objections to the International Criminal Court," *Peace Review* 12, no. 1 (March 2000)

How are notions of justice and human security to be implemented in a world composed of nation-states? One answer to that question is the argument that the state should remain the primary arena where issues such as justice, human rights, and civil liberties are defined and protected. The best hope for pursuing justice then is in the maintenance of orderly and stable relations between states. In a society of states, this order can best be achieved by observance of two fundamental legal and moral principles: respect for national sovereignty of all states and nonintervention in the domestic affairs of another sovereign state. These principles were largely built on the belief, rooted in the turmoil of the sixteenth and seventeenth centuries, that the greatest threat to peace and the pursuit of justice stemmed from the widespread intervention in the affairs of other states. They assumed that the priority should be placed on promoting peace and justice between states rather than addressing the issues of peace and justice within states; issues of domestic justice are placed beyond the concerns of the international community.

However, this way of thinking has had an important impact on the way that human justice has been viewed in the international system. As Hedley Bull notes, "the basic concept of coexistence between states, expressed in the exchange of recognition of sovereign jurisdiction, implies a conspiracy of silence entered into by governments about the rights and duties of their respective citizens" (*The Anarchical Society: A Study of Order in World Politics* [London: Macmillan, 1977], p. 83). It is this conspiracy of silence that has increasingly come to bother many people. While some have seen in the notion of sovereignty the promise of security and protection from the wanton harm of outsiders, others have experienced sovereignty as a cloak of protection for oppression and injustice. The worst crimes against humanity and the most oppressive human-rights abuses, they argue, have taken place under the legal protection of national sovereignty. In fact, studies of contemporary conflicts show that in this century, more people have been killed in intrastate fighting than interstate wars. For many people, the greatest threat to personal security is not a foreign military force, but their own government.

How do we address this situation? Some have suggested that the world needs a permanent International Criminal Court. Such an idea is not new. As long ago as 1474, Peter van Hagenbach was tried by the Court of the Holy Roman Empire for the torture of civilians. At the Congress of Vienna in 1815, states debated whether there should be trials for those engaged in the slave trade. And, in 1872, the "Peace Society of the United States" made the first effort to outline the jurisdiction of an international criminal court by drawing up an International Criminal Code.

Although discussions of the concept of an international criminal court continued in the twentieth century, actual efforts at implementing such a plan proceeded largely on an ad hoc basis. Following the atrocities of World War II, the International Military Tribunal at Nuremburg and the International Military Tribunal for the Far East were established to prosecute war criminals. But these efforts have long been subject to criticism for being driven by political imperatives rather than representing a triumph of the rule of law. Some critics argued that they were nothing more than "victor's tribunals."

During the Cold War, the ideological struggle between the East and the West created little political will to move forward with the idea of an international criminal court. However, the end of the Cold War and the experience of conflicts in Yugoslavia and Rwanda with devastating civilian casualties and human-rights abuses created new momentum for such a project. In 1994, an Ad Hoc Committee for the Establishment of the International Criminal Court, composed of state representatives, was set up to begin working on a draft statute. This work eventually led to the convening in Rome of a UN Diplomatic Conference of Plenipotentiaries on the Establishment of an International Criminal Court in June 1998. These negotiations in turn led to the adoption of a treaty in July 1998 calling for the creation of an International Criminal Court (ICC). A total of 120 countries voted in favour, 21 abstained, and 7 were opposed. The United States and Israel joined China, Iran, Iraq, Libya, and Sudan in opposing the treaty.

The Rome Statute declares that the signatories recognize that international crimes "threaten peace and security" and affirms that these crimes "must not go unpunished." At the same time, signatory states promise to ensure "an end to impunity" for individual perpetrators. Proponents of the treaty see its provisions as a significant advancement of the norms of human justice in the international system. The ICC would provide a means of non-military intervention to protect the welfare of individuals. Advocates argue that it is a significant advancement in the development of cosmopolitan values. However, the Rome Statute has strong critics who are skeptical about whether anything like a commonly understood notion of international criminal law exists between nations. Further, the growing intrusion into national sovereignty is seen as having potentially dangerous side effects in the future.

In the first essay, Douglass Cassel, a professor of international law, makes the case for an International Criminal Court. Then Alfred P. Rubin, also a professor of international law, argues against implementing the ICC.

✔ YES
Why We Need the International Criminal Court
DOUGLAS CASSEL

This has been a good century for tyrants. Stalin killed millions but was never even charged with a crime. Pol Pot slaughtered well over 1 million but never saw the inside of a prison cell. Idi Amin and Raoul Cedras are comfortably retired. Despite recent legal complications, Chile's General Augusto Pinochet, too, will probably escape trial. Ditto for Slobodan Milosevic, who has chosen to close out the century by brutalizing Kosovo.

There have been few exceptions to this pattern of impunity. The most notable exceptions are the Nazis who faced judgment at Nuremberg. Joining the short list of adjudged are the Greek colonels, the Argentine junta, the genocidal regime in Rwanda and some leaders in the former Yugoslavia. But the odds have overwhelmingly favored those who commit atrocities. Will the 21st century be any better?

The answer may well depend in large part on the success—or failure—of the world's first permanent court with global jurisdiction over the most serious international crimes. Last summer in Rome, by a vote of 120 nations in favor, seven opposed and 21 abstentions, a United Nations diplomatic conference adopted a treaty to establish an International Criminal Court (ICC) in The Hague in the Netherlands. It will hear cases of genocide, war crimes and crimes against humanity that national governments are unable or unwilling to prosecute.

The ICC will differ from the existing World Court, officially called the International Court of Justice, also located in The Hague. The World Court hears only lawsuits between governments and cannot prosecute individuals. As a permanent global court, the ICC will likewise differ from the special International Criminal Tribunals created by the UN Security Council to address atrocities in the former Yugoslavia and Rwanda.

Nearly all the world's democracies—Europe plus such countries as Argentina, Australia, Canada, Costa Rica, South Africa and South Korea—supported the Rome treaty. Seventy-eight nations have now signed the treaty, indicating their intention to join it. Once 60 countries complete the ratification process (to date only Senegal has done so), the treaty will go into effect and the ICC will be created.

Late blooming 20th-century tyrants have little to fear; the ICC will have power to try only crimes committed after it is established. The current carnage in Colombia, Congo and Sierra Leone, for example, will either go unpunished or be addressed in some other way.

Only two democracies—Israel and the United States—opposed the ICC, thereby joining a rogue's gallery of regimes like China, Iran, Iraq, Libya and Sudan. Israel's opposition is regrettable but understandable: the Jewish state has lost so many lopsided UN votes that it fears giving power to an international prosecutor.

The U.S., too, professes to fear frivolous or politically motivated prosecutions of American soldiers and officials. However, the ICC has so many built-in safeguards against unwarranted prosecutions that the odds of abuse are minimal. Otherwise, the ICC would hardly have garnered support from Britain, France and other countries with extensive military and peacekeeping forces overseas.

Washington's real grievance is that it cannot control the court. In 1995, on the 50th anniversary of the Nuremberg trials, President Clinton became the first U.S. president to announce support for an ICC. But the U.S. insisted on an ICC that would be an arm of the UN Security Council, which would make prosecutions subject to a U.S. veto and insulate Washington from unwanted trials.

The rest of the world found this vision uninspiring. Still, in a fruitless effort to induce U.S. participation, backers of the ICC at Rome offered numerous concessions, including a significant role for the Security Council. The council will be empowered to refer cases to the ICC. Indeed, at least in the early years, council referral is likely to be the primary route by which cases reach the court. While cases can also be referred by states that are party to the treaty or by the prosecutor, the obstacles to doing so will initially be so high that the ICC will depend heavily on the council. The council can also block investigations by voting to defer them for one year, renewable indefinitely.

But these and other concessions were not enough to dispel Washington's fears that if American troops commit war crimes in another country, that country could have those troops tried in The Hague (unless the U.S. would agree to investigate the case itself). Also, other nations with veto power on the Security Council could block a resolution to defer a case. In short, U.S. control is less than fully assured under the ICC, which pleased neither the Pentagon nor Senate Foreign Relations Committee Chair Jesse Helms, who declared that any treaty to create a court that could conceivably prosecute Americans would be "dead on arrival" on Capitol Hill.

U.S. opposition to the ICC is of a piece with its vote a year earlier against the treaty to ban antipersonnel landmines, its refusal to pay UN dues, its economic sanctions on allies that do business in Cuba and its implicit foreign policy of demanding a "superpower exemption" from international rules. It lends further support to the views held by "elites of countries comprising at least two-thirds of the world's people," according to Harvard scholar Samuel Huntington, writing in *Foreign Affairs*, that Uncle Sam is "intrusive, interventionist, exploitative, unilateralist, hegemonic, hypocritical, and applying double standards." Small wonder that following the 120-7 humiliation of the U.S. in Rome, delegates applauded for 15 minutes.

U.S. opposition to the ICC not only undermines American credibility and diplomacy but also strains the human rights banner Washington purports to carry. The rest of the world cannot fail to notice that the U.S. supports the prosecution of Yugoslavs and Rwandans for human rights crimes but not the prosecution of

Americans. If human rights is no more than a flag of convenience, its rallying power diminishes.

But American participation, while important, is not indispensable. The world's democracies are likely to go ahead without us. Americans who care more for the dignity of humanity than for the color of their passports should support the ICC, despite its shortcomings, as a first step toward international justice for crimes against humanity.

But does "justice" for atrocities require a court, let alone a criminal court, much less an international criminal court? Volumes have been devoted to defining justice. For ICC purposes, however, we can focus on an operational definition. Justice calls for identification, exposure, condemnation and proportionate punishment of individuals who violate fundamental norms recognized internationally as crimes, and it calls for reparations to victims, by means of fair investigations and fair trials by an anthorized judicial body. Thus defined, justice requires criminal courts, including—as experience has shown—at least the possibility of prosecution before international courts.

Like other efforts to capture "justice" in words, this account covers both too little and too much. As Martha Minow has observed, some crimes are so horrific or massive that no amount of punishment can be proportional. And no form of court-ordered reparation can truly repair the loss of even a single loved one, much less of an entire people. At best, successful prosecutions can deliver only a measure of justice.

On the other hand, criminal punishment may not always contribute to a just society. As argued eloquently by Donald Shriver in these pages (August 26, 1998), "living with others sometimes means that we must value the renewal of community more highly than punishing, or seeking communal vengeance for, crimes." And while "some forms of justice sow the seeds of justice, some do not. Without peaceful public acceptance of their decisions, courts risk irrelevance at best and social chaos at worst."

The case for an ICC must acknowledge the wisdom of such insights. Yet these comments do not so much counsel against the existence of the ICC as remind us of its inherent limitations. Criminal justice is not, by itself, sufficient to heal either victims or societies.

Still, without at least the credible prospect of criminal punishment, victims and societies are unlikely to wield the leverage necessary to pry out the truth, which is an essential prerequisite to genuine repentance, forgiveness and reconciliation. Pervasive impunity is therefore the enemy of justice in all its dimensions.

How might the ICC contribute to justice?

First, in particular cases, it may identify, expose, condemn and punish perpetrators and provide reparations to victims. It may do so either by its own prosecutions or by stimulating prosecutions in national courts, brought by governments reluctant to see their officials and soldiers hauled off to The Hague for trial. Either way, an effective ICC could lift the blanket of impunity that now covers atrocities almost everywhere. By so doing, it could provide a measure of justice to some victims. That by itself would justify creation of the ICC.

But such a court would have even broader impact. It would serve to reinforce moral norms. There is no more powerful social condemnation of evil than to label it as a serious crime, for which serious punishment may be imposed. The preamble adopted in Rome elevates ICC crimes to the status of the "most serious crimes of concern to the international community as a whole." The ICC's every indictment, arrest, conviction and sentence may serve to remind governments, the media and the public that there is "zero tolerance" for crimes against humanity.

The pedagogical and practical import of such moral messages is illustrated by the current case of General Pinochet. In strictly legal terms, he has suffered no more than deprivation of liberty and freedom of movement for some months. He may never actually be prosecuted. But his hopes of becoming a respected senior statesman and to go down in history as his country's savior have been dashed. He will now be remembered, above all, as a torturer who got nabbed. Not only has he suffered loss of honor and reputation, but Chile will now understand its history differently. In Chile and elsewhere, a generation of youth has been taught that his alleged crimes, most of which took place before they were born, are so unconscionable that he is pursued for them even today.

Such messages sensitize global consciousness. This, in turn, has practical consequences. Governments may find it more difficult to grant visas, confer political asylum or otherwise treat alleged torturers as if their crimes could be forgotten. Voices of conscience may be empowered; their demands to treat future Pinochets as pariahs will be legitimized. Of course, to the extent the ICC proves to be ineffective, its moral message will be undermined. An impotent ICC may serve merely to stoke the fires of cynicism. This is one reason why the extensive compromises made at Rome are troubling.

To succeed, however, the court need not be perfect. Consider the case of former Bosnian Serb leader Radovan Karadzik. In 1995 he was indicted for genocide by the International Criminal Tribunal for the former Yugoslavia. Yet he remains at large, because NATO troops in Bosnia to date have not dared to arrest him. Does his case show that genocide is tolerated in practice?

Prior to the Dayton peace agreements, that may indeed have been the message. Until then, few of the suspects indicted by the International Tribunal had been arrested. Karadzik still strutted the world stage as head of the Bosnian Serb "government." But he was barred from Dayton, because he had been indicted and would have to be arrested if he left Yugoslavia. The agreements reached at Dayton also excluded him from any future position in government because, again, he had been indicted. Since then he has lost his official position, and remains hunkered down in Serb territory, unable to travel. Dozens of other suspects have now been arrested or have surrendered.

A similar point may be made on the question of the court's deterrent value. The prospect of prosecution will not deter a Pol Pot or a Slobodan Milosevic. But not all dictators are fanatics like Pol Pot. And at times, calculating manipulators like Milosevic may be restrained by the threat of indictment. How often this happens may depend on how credible the threat is. That, in turn, depends on how the compromises made at Rome play out in practice.

Two of the Rome compromises are especially troublesome. The first imposes a "state consent" requirement on the ICC's jurisdiction (except in cases referred by the Security Council). In cases referred by states or by the prosecutor on his or her own motion, the ICC will not be free to prosecute crimes regardless of where they are committed. It will have jurisdiction only by consent of either the state where the crime was committed or the state in which the accused is a citizen. States that ratify the Rome treaty are parties to the court and automatically consent to its jurisdiction. Other states may consent on a case-by-case basis.

The treaty negotiations suggest the significance of this limitation. Germany proposed that the ICC have "universal" jurisdiction, that is, be able to prosecute crimes wherever they are committed. This made legal sense. For centuries individual states have had the right to prosecute piracy, regardless of where it takes place. Treaties now allow states to prosecute genocide, torture and serious war crimes—all within ICC jurisdiction wherever they are committed. If individual states have universal jurisdiction over such heinous international crimes, why can they not agree to delegate it to an international court?

This legally sensible proposal did not, however, attract much diplomatic support. Most states were unwilling to give the court a worldwide license to prosecute.

South Korea proposed a compromise: Let the ICC hear any case that has the consent of any one of four states—the state where the crime took place, the state of nationality of the defendant, the state of nationality of the victim, or the state having custody of the suspect. While far short of universality, this proposal would have given the ICC jurisdiction in most cases. But the U.S. strenuously objected. Allowing so many states to invoke ICC jurisdiction would allow the court to bypass the Security Council.

In a last-ditch effort to bring the U.S. on board without gutting the court's jurisdiction, the Canadian chair of the Rome conference whittled the four states in South Korea's proposal down to two: the territorial state and the state of nationality of the accused. Over U.S. objections, this proposal became part of the final text of the treaty.

To understand the effect of this provision, consider a hypothetical case involving Saddam Hussein. If he commits atrocities in Kuwait, either of two states could consent to ICC jurisdiction: Kuwait, where the crimes were committed, or Iraq, the state of Saddam's nationality. Since Kuwait would be likely to consent, in such cases—international wars—state consent is not a major obstacle.

But suppose Saddam commits atrocities against Kurds or political dissidents inside Iraq. Then the territorial state and the state of his nationality are one and the same: Iraq, which he controls. In such cases—regimes that repress ethnic minorities or others within their own borders—the ICC may be unable to act.

This kind of situation poses a serious threat to the effectiveness of the court. Except on referral by the Security Council, the ICC could not, for example, prosecute Milosevic for atrocities committed in Kosovo, nor Pol Pot for killing Cambodians, nor Pinochet for "disappearing" Chileans.

Another potentially crippling compromise allows the ICC to hear cases (again, except for those referred by the Security Council) only when the states involved are unable or unwilling to do so. The U.S. likes this provision; it can avoid ICC jurisdiction simply by conducting its own good-faith investigation—even if the result is a decision not to prosecute, or an acquittal.

But what if, say, a Milosevic promises to investigate alleged war crimes by his troops in Kosovo? Unlike the International Criminal Tribunal for Yugoslavia, which has primary jurisdiction, the ICC would have to defer to a Yugoslav national investigation unless the ICC prosecutor can prove that it is a sham. But how can the prosecutor impeach a national investigation before it starts? In most cases, the ICC will have to wait until the individual nation has a chance to show its true colors. In the meantime, what may happen to fingerprints, blood samples, autopsies and witnesses? ICC prosecutor and judges will have to keep careful watch lest national prosecutors merely go through the motions, stall and possibly ruin the ICC's case.

Despite such weaknesses and uncertainties, the agreement on the ICC reached in Rome is the best we are likely to get for the foreseeable future. It deserves support as an essential first step. Once created, it will have a chance to prove itself. If it fails, the need to strengthen it will be demonstrated.

Neither the Clinton administration nor the U.S. Senate is likely to accept the ICC. This is no reason, however, for American supporters to sit on their hands.

It should be stressed that the ICC has significant safeguards against abuse. For example, its judges must have expertise in criminal or international law, and can be elected only by a two-thirds majority of states which are parties to the treaty, most of which will be democracies. Its prosecutor cannot begin an investigation of an American without first notifying the U.S. and allowing it to take over the investigation and any prosecution. Even if the U.S. consents, the ICC prosecutor still cannot begin an investigation without reasonable grounds and the prior approval of a three-judge panel, which may be appealed to a five-judge panel. Once the investigation is complete, no trial can be held without another prior approval by the three-judge panel. Even then there are extensive fair-trial safeguards. No judicial system is airtight, but this one comes close.

Supporters can also dispel Pentagon claims that because American troops undertake so many overseas missions they are uniquely exposed to ICC prosecution.

In Bosnia as of mid-1998, for example, our troops represented less than 20 percent of NATO forces and only 10 percent of the International Police Task Force.

Bringing international criminals to justice is no easy task. But the ICC gives humanity in the coming century a chance to administer justice that wasn't available in the 20th century. Let us not miss the opportunity.

THE PINOCHET PRECEDENT

Chile's General Augusto Pinochet would be a prime candidate for trial before the International Criminal Court—if the court existed. Since it does not, a makeshift substitute—extraditing him from Britain for trial in Spain—has been attempted.

In 1973, assisted by the U.S., Pinochet overthrew the democratically elected government of socialist Salvador Allende. His military regime then set out to eliminate and terrorize its political opponents. According to reports based on official Chilean investigations, Pinochet's regime was responsible for over 2,000 assassinations, more than 1,000 disappearances and countless cases of torture.

Numbers cannot tell the full story. As noted by Lord Steyn in the British extradition proceedings, "The case is not one of interrogators acting in excess of zeal." Rather, as Lord Steyn described the alleged torture, "The most usual method was the "grill," consisting of a metal table on which the victim was laid naked and his extremities tied and electrical shocks were applied to the lips, genitals, wounds or metal prosthesis."

Nor is Pinochet accused merely of failing to prevent crimes by underlings. Chile's intelligence agency responsible for torture, the notorious DINA, "was directly answerable to General Pinochet rather than to the military junta." According to the Spanish charges, DINA killed, disappeared and tortured victims "on the orders of General Pinochet."

To date Pinochet has enjoyed both de facto and de jure impunity in Chile. In 1978, after the worst was over, he awarded himself and his men an amnesty for any crimes that might have been committed by their regime. When he finally restored civilian rule in 1990, he warned against "touching a hair on the head of one of my men." The new constitution also made him senator for life, immune from prosecution. For added insurance, military courts retain jurisdiction over any alleged crimes by the military.

Pinochet was so safe from prosecution in Chile that he presumed he was safe anywhere. He was wrong. Assisted by human fights activists, Spanish Judge Baltasar Garzon has in recent years accumulated enough evidence to charge the general not only for murdering Spanish citizens but also for committing crimes against a far larger number of Chileans.

As Pinochet recuperated from back surgery in London last October, Judge Garzon asked British authorities to arrest him for extradition to Spain. Britain obliged. As of this writing, the general has been under house arrest in England for six months. Three British courts have now ruled on the case. Most recently a committee of Law Lords, Britain's highest court, voted six to one against the general's claim that as a former head of state he is immune from prosecution. The United Nations Convention Against Torture, they ruled, requires member states either to extradite or prosecute alleged torturers. Sitting heads of state are immune, but former heads are not.

Since Britain did not join the convention until 1988, however, the lords authorized the government to extradite Pinochet only for torture committed after 1988. British Home Secretary Jack Straw decided in April that the post-1988 cases submitted by the Spanish judge justify extradition. However, lengthy legal proceedings, followed by a final opportunity for Straw to reconsider, could take months or even years.

Whatever the ultimate outcome, the rulings in this case by the highest courts of Britain and Spain make clear that international law now permits third countries to prosecute torturers whose home country is unwilling or unable to bring them to court. But the case also shows the unreliability of this approach. What if Britain had not joined the torture convention? Or if Downing Street were still occupied by Tories and not Tony Blair? Would Britain have arrested Pinochet? Whatever the outcome, the Pinochet case thus underlines the need for an ICC.

✗ NO
Some Objections to the International Criminal Court
ALFRED P. RUBIN

Perhaps it is unwise to comment on the structure of the proposed International Criminal Court (ICC) while the negotiations to define it still continue. Nevertheless, there are underlying inconsistencies between the dominant conceptions of the ICC's operations and the realities of the international legal (and political and economic) order. These inconsistencies cannot be remedied by tinkering with the details. As currently conceived by its supporters, the ICC cannot work as envisaged without massive changes in the international legal order. But those changes cannot be accomplished without losses that nobody realistically expects and few really want.

The ICC assumes there is such a thing as international criminal law. But what is its substance? Who exercises law-making authority for the international legal community? Who has the legal authority to interpret the law once supposedly found?

While ample precedents for the international equivalent of common law can be found in the claims and property areas, the criminal law is different. Some acts by individuals have been historically deemed to violate it, whatever it is—piracy, war crimes, international traffic in slaves, and now genocide and perhaps aggression and other atrocities. But until now those "crimes" have not been defined by international law as such. They have been defined instead by the municipal laws of many states and in a few cases by international tribunals set up by victor states in an exercise of positive law making. Thereby, the tribunal's new rules were "accepted," under one rationale or another, by the states in which the accused were nationals.

Some Nazis were convicted at Nuremberg of planning aggressive war, but the Nazi attack on Poland in 1939 was preceded by the Molotov-Ribbentrop Pact. The notion that the Soviets did not help plan the "aggressive war" was regarded by many as hopelessly unconvincing, so it was agreed among the Nuremberg prosecutors not to allow any mention of that treaty at the trial. As to "war crimes," Grand Admiral Doenitz, Hitler's successor in Germany, was convicted at Nuremberg among other things of authorizing unrestricted submarine warfare in violation of a 1936 treaty. Admiral Nimitz, the American hero, sent a letter to the tribunal pointing out that he had issued almost identical orders in the Pacific on December 7, 1941. Of course, Nimitz was not tried for anything by anybody.

As for "crimes against humanity," it was agreed to define those as acts connected with Word War II itself. Thus, the Soviet Union's deliberate starvation of the Ukraine and the establishment of the Gulag Archipelago were not within the

Nuremberg charge. Nor were American acts of wartime hysteria, such as the mass displacement of Americans of Japanese heritage from the three West Coast states but not from Hawaii. The nuclear bombing of Nagasaki was not mentioned either, although it could be said to have raised serious questions about American observance of the laws of war even assuming the Hiroshima bomb was a legitimate wartime act. In sum, the victors did not apply to themselves the rules they purported to find in the international legal order. The deeper question is whether rules asserted by victors and applied only to losers represent "law" at all.

Another theory has been that if all or nearly all "civilized" states define particular acts as violating their municipal criminal laws, then those acts violate "international law." Far from being new to the international arena, that conception attempts to revive jus gentium theory, which failed when Lord Mansfield, Sir William Scott, and Joseph Story, among many others, developed conflict-of-law and choice-of-law theory in a civil claims context so as to make it unnecessary to determine which states are "civilized" and which rules are universal.

Occasionally, the same theory has been urged under the argument that some acts violate "general principles of law recognized by civilized states," and thus violate general international law. But to define states that agree with us as "civilized" and those that disagree as not worth considering would eliminate most of the human race from the rubric "civilized." That might be correct as far as we are concerned, but it will not likely represent any universal "law." And it does not make even acknowledged wicked acts "criminal" in any known sense.

Suppose it was possible to define as universal crimes acts defined and punished as criminal by various municipal legal orders. If that were done it still would not confer "standing" in the international community to expand any single state's municipal jurisdiction, to create a "universal" jurisdiction over the acts of foreigners abroad, no matter how horrendous.

Early attempts to resolve these problems abound. For example, in the United States, the first statute criminalizing "piracy" was enacted in April 1790. It made criminal by U.S. law any "offense which if committed within the body of a county, would by the laws of the United States be punishable by death" and various lesser acts such as running away with goods "to the value of $50" (not saying whether lesser valuations or greater valuations would be included in the definition), yielding up a "vessel voluntarily to any pirate" (not defining "pirate"), or mutiny (without using the word). The statute was found defective in early cases and was supplemented with another in 1819 which made criminal by U.S. law "the crime of piracy as defined by the law of nations" and apparently asserted universal jurisdiction over those committing "piracy" as so defined by subjecting them to the American criminal process if they were "afterwards ... brought into or found in the United States," even if they were foreigners acting solely against foreign interests or persons.

That statute was upheld by the Supreme Court in 1820, but reduced in its effect, as to both definition and jurisdiction, and eventually abandoned, although it still appears in the U.S. Code. The principal problem was that Joseph Story and some other judges felt they knew how the "law of nations" defined "piracy" but very few others did. Despite Story's objections, in all but "piracy cases," "common law crimes" were abandoned in the United States federal courts because prosecutors refused to bring such cases.

A similar fate met attempts to establish an international criminal court to hear cases involving the international traffic in slaves. When such a court was proposed by the British in the 1830s and 1840s, it was rejected by the U.S. A close examination of the British proposal showed how it would authorize British warships to arrest vessels of any nationality in only some parts of the world, but did not authorize American or other warships to arrest British vessels near the British Isles. Indeed, when Haiti established its own anti-slave-trade legislation based on identical assertions of universal jurisdiction in 1839, the British objected, claiming that the universal law of the sea allowed no universal jurisdiction in any case outside of the exercise of belligerent fights in wartime.

Turning to attempts to incorporate universal jurisdiction in an ICC by treaty construction, consider that the Genocide Convention and the four 1949 Geneva Conventions on the protection of the victims of armed conflict leave the traditional jurisdictional arrangements of general international law untouched. All four Geneva Conventions refer to some "grave breaches," generally acts that individuals might commit or order that seem to harm persons or property that need not be harmed in order for the conflict to proceed in the usual miserable ways. The obligation is on the High Contracting Parties severally to enact municipal legislation. The Conventions provide in identical language in each Convention that "The High Contracting Parties undertake to enact any legislation necessary to provide effective penal sanctions for persons committing, or ordering to be committed, any of the grave breaches of the present Convention defined [sic] in the following Article."

In fact, the various wicked acts are not "defined" in the Geneva Conventions. For example, each of the Conventions lists "willful killing" as such a "grave breach." But soldiers routinely "willfully kill" the enemy. All known legal orders excuse or authorize "willful killing" in self-defense or to defend a protected class of others, such as family members. The 1949 Conventions do not attempt to draw the necessary distinctions between a "willful killing" that is legally a "grave breach" to be made the subject of criminal sanctions in all contracting states, and one that remains legally within a soldier's privilege.

Nor do they define who is a "soldier" for those purposes. The attempt to define who is entitled to prisoner-of-war treatment if captured by an enemy might be interpreted as such a definition, but not necessarily, and itself leads to serious complications. Indeed, in the Prisoners of War Convention itself (Convention III of 1949), questions about status are to be resolved by "a competent tribunal" (Article 5) with no clue as to who should convene the tribunal or determine its criteria. And there is much more that is doubtful about the interpretation of the key provisions of this part of the Prisoners of War Convention, indeed of all four Conventions.

Similarly, the Genocide Convention of 1948, although calling "genocide" a "crime under international law," restricts the definition and enforcement of this "crime" to the municipal tribunals of the various parties who alone are "to provide effective penalties for persons guilty of genocide." And persons charged with genocide "shall be tried by a competent tribunal of the State in the territory of which the act was committed, or by such international penal tribunal as may have jurisdiction with respect to those Contracting Parties which shall have accepted its jurisdiction." Clearly those who sought to establish in 1948 a universal jurisdiction by means of the positive law failed.

It has been argued that at least the 1949 Geneva Conventions resolve the universal jurisdiction issue by providing that "[e]ach High Contracting Party shall be under the obligation to search for persons alleged to have committed, or to have ordered to be committed, such grave breaches, and shall bring such persons, regardless of their nationality, before its own courts." But there are many problems with this interpretation. First, so severe have been the practical difficulties that there have been no cases in the 50 bloody years since 1949 in which any High Contracting Party has fulfilled that "obligation." Second, even if the "obligation" were taken seriously, it would be impossible in many cases for the accused to defend themselves. How could General Schwarztkopf, for example, produce the evidence to show that before he ordered the bombing during the Gulf War of what later appeared to be a civilian bomb shelter, his best intelligence—derived from intercepts and possibly infiltrators or other eye-witnesses—was that the supposed bomb shelter was actually an illegal overlay of civilians above a military communications site?

It can be argued that the law has progressed from the days of Nuremberg and the 1948 and 1949 Conventions: that universal jurisdiction is now an accepted custom. But is it? What states, under what circumstances, have accepted the custom? Even where it has been enacted, has it been accepted outside of a positive commitment? Accepted as law? We should have serious doubts about the assertions of customary law that are occasionally used in this context.

What about the ICC Convention itself as a positive law document under which states agree to submit to the Court and to have it exercise jurisdiction over specified offenses? That would seem to fit the caveat in the Genocide Convention and make the "world community" the "victor," setting up a victor's tribunal for which Nuremberg and Tokyo would be the precedents. Indeed, similar tribunals with non-combatant "victors" were set up regarding events in the former Yugoslavia and Rwanda. But that has not and would still not solve the deeper problems as they appear on the surface.

To illustrate the difficulties, let us agree that to be "law" the rule to be applied must be applied universally. Some villains will escape, of course, as they do in municipal legal orders' criminal subsets. But are the jurisdictional rules and the substantive rules themselves applicable? Would they apply, for example, to Russian soldiers in

Chechnya? To Chechens who infiltrate Russia and blow up civilian housing? If conceptually the rules did apply regardless of Russian or Chechen legislation defining their soldiers' status and privileges, which might otherwise exempt their own personnel from liability, the next question is whether Russian or Chechen officials would agree that American or other police have the authority to investigate or make arrests in Russian or Chechen controlled territory. Is their agreement necessary?

In East Timor it was thought to be necessary, and the formal government of Indonesia did agree to the introduction of foreign forces in its territory, apparently to apply some notion of law (although precisely what law, how it is to be applied and by whom are open questions) while East Timor remained part of the Indonesian state. If so, then this returns us to the world of positive law and national discretion. If not, before what forum is the point to be argued? By whom? What if the Russians or Chechens still disagree? Would Americans agree to Russian or Chechen investigators or police, unauthorized by American law, making arrests of American military personnel in U.S. territory and placing them before their own or some "international" tribunals to be tried under their concept of "criminal law"?

But, it may be argued, we are not speaking of Russian or Chechen officials. We are speaking of representatives of the international community. Surely we cannot object to an evolution of the international legal order to allow international inspectors and police to make arrests for offenses defined by positive law. But Iraq has made exactly that objection to the United Nations. And Iraq turns out not to be friendless, regardless of the American notion of the Iraqi legal argument and however villainous Saddam Hussain may be. We are left with the notion that positive submission is probably required both to define the evil acts and to enforce their proscription against individuals. But that positive submission has not yet been given by anybody outside various victors' or similar situations (such as with the former Yugoslavia). As a matter of positive law, once the agreement has been given it is subject to interpretation and it cannot be reasonably supposed that the state whose leaders are accused of violating the undefined law will agree with those officials of any institution on all their interpretations of the "law."

These theoretical difficulties obviously arise in practice, and no amount of new theory can resolve the problems as I see them. The issue is not the politicization of tribunals. It is the value systems in the minds of honorable judges. For example, in 1970 Mohammed Bedjaoui, later President of the International Commission of Jurists, argued that newly independent states retain a discretion to renounce their debts and nationalize foreign-owned property based on the primacy of national self-determination over property rights in the international legal order. Who can say definitively that he was wrong? Despite the ringing assertions of "reasonableness" we have heard on all sides since the days of Cicero, arguments over value systems, about which reasonable people do in fact disagree, are not the same as having political biases.

In practice, the issues arise in yet another form. Not only are the value systems in the minds of the ICC's officials very much in question, but the questions extend to the entire process. For example, when is an indictment to be handed down or carried out? If it is to be immediately upon discovering convincing evidence of an indictable atrocity, then is a general to be arrested in the midst of a battle? By whom? And what of the battle? Assuming, as I suppose we must, that Article 2.4 of the United Nations Charter makes international armed conflict itself unthinkable, what about internal battles? Or have we reached a stage in world development in which all existing constitutions are to be protected by the international community from revolutionary change? Who is to determine that rebels, using the best tools available to them, are to fail because there are legal questions surrounding the use of some of those tools that seem to outside parties to be disproportionate in the death and destruction they bring to innocents?

Is war and revolution to be reduced to the status of a game with an impartial umpire blowing a whistle when his or her conception of the rules is violated? Then is the world supposed to stop while the case is brought to a tribunal that might in fact find that the umpire blew the whistle prematurely? And if the umpire blows the whistle after the battle ends, is the victorious military leader to be tried? Was Admiral Nimitz or President Truman or "Bomber" Harris or Josef Stalin responsible for the transgressions of which they have been accused?

The notion that any society should be ruled by the "best," regardless of the will of ordinary folks, has been with us since at least the days when Plato wrote his Republic. But who is to discover the "best"? Who is to convince the traditional holders of authority to yield that authority to others whom yet others regard as the "best"? I forbear to cite examples when this approach has been tried, including the attempt by Dionysus II to apply it in his Kingdom of Sicily with Plato himself present. It has always failed.

The reasons why it has failed were eloquently illustrated in a naively arrogant book by Sherard Osborn, a British Navy Captain publishing in 1857 about events during the 1830s when he served British interests in the Malay Peninsula:

> Such are the cruelties perpetrated by these wretched native monarchies ... and yet philanthropists and politicians at home maunder about the unjust invasion of native rights, and preach against the extension of our rule. As if our Government, in its most corrupt form, would not be a blessing in such a region, and as much if not more, our duty to extend, as a Christian people, than to allow them to remain under native rulers, and then to shoot them for following native habits.

Those who agree with the moral rationales for 19th-century European imperialism and ignore the other things that went with it, such as the exercise of force to implement that fancied moral and political superiority, might support the ICC. I cannot.

Postscript

Critiques of the International Criminal Court concept, especially in the United States, are concerned with the threat such an institution poses to national sovereignty. Is there an alternative that would address issues of international justice while not being overly interventionist?

Some people have suggested that countries recovering from conflicts may follow South Africa's model in using a Truth and Reconciliation Commission. In South Africa, the Commission focused on information-gathering and exposing the horrors of the past without assigning guilt. It is argued that this approach may allow for speedier national and ethnic healing. But such an approach lacks an element of punishment. Furthermore, it requires a stable, credible government to operate it, which may not be present. In addition, some internationalists worry that the actions of such a commission serve only to protect the guilty from having to take responsibility for their crimes.

Another alternative to the ICC would be to continue the use of ad hoc tribunals similar to those operating in Rwanda and the former Yugoslavia. The greater flexibility of these tribunals would allow international intervention to bring perpetrators to justice. However, the tribunals in Rwanda and the former Yugoslavia have not been problem-free, and those opposing the ICC often cite these tribunals to support their positions.

Another alternative to the ICC that would help preserve national sovereignty while addressing the pertinent crimes would be to allow states to handle such prosecutions domestically. The United Nations could help developing countries create judicial systems that are credible within the scope of national law. Yet it might be very difficult for such national tribunals to respond in cases where the individual perpetrators are high-level government officials. Thus, each of the possible alternatives to the ICC poses its own set of challenges.

Infotrac Keyword Search

"international criminal court" or "war crimes" or "war crimes tribunal"

Suggested Additional Readings

Anderson, John B. "An International Criminal Court—An Emerging Idea." *Nova Law Review,* 15 (1991): 433–47.

Arsanjani, Mahnoush. "The Rome Statute of the International Criminal Court." *American Journal of International Law* 93, no. 1 (1999): 22–43.

Bass, Gary J. *Stay the Hand: The Politics of War Crimes Tribunal.* Princeton: Princeton University Press, 2000.

Bassiouni, Cherif. "From Versailles to Rwanda in Seventy-Five Years: The Need to Establish a Permanent Internationl Criminal Court." *Harvard Human Rights Law Journal* 10 (1997): 11–62.

Gallarotti, Giulio M. and Arik Y Preis. "Toward Universal Human Rights and the Rule of Law: The Permanent International Criminal Court." *Australian Journal of International Affairs* 53, no. 1 (April 1999): 95–112.

Rieff, David. "Court of Dreams." *New Republic* 219, no. 10 (1998): 16–18.

Rubin, Alfred P. "Challenging the Conventional Wisdom: Another View of the International Criminal Court." *Journal of International Affairs* 52 (Spring 1999): 783–95.

Tucker, Robert W. "The International Criminal Court Controversy." *World Policy Journal* 18, no. 2 (Summer 2001): 71–82.

Website Resources

Coalition for an International Criminal Court   Website established by a coalition of NGOs supporting the ICC. Contains not only textual material, but audio documentaries and extensive links.

Human Rights Watch: International Criminal Court   This is the home page for the NGO Human Rights Watch's campaign, which supports the ICC.

Lawyers Committee for Human Rights   This lawyers' site is concerned about human rights and has a good collection of materials on the ICC and other international tribunals.

Rome Statute of the International Criminal Court   Official UN website for the ICC contains the text of the statute, information regarding current status of ratification, and related documentation.

University of Chicago Library   The page entitled "International Criminal Court: Resources in Print and Electronic Format" gives updated coverage on materials and conferences on the ICC.

ISSUE**EIGHTEEN**

Can International Law Eliminate the Problem of Child Soldiers?

✔ **YES**

ROSS SNYDER, "The Optional Protocol on the Involvement of Children in Armed Conflict," from Rob McCrae and Don Hubert, *Human Security and the New Diplomacy: Protecting People, Promoting Peace* (Montreal: McGill-Queen's University Press, 2001)

✘ **NO**

ANANDA S. MILLARD, "Children in Armed Conflicts: Transcending Legal Responses," *Security Dialogue* 32, no. 2 (2001): 187–200

During the past several decades, armed conflict has taken a very deadly turn for civilians. Analysts point out that between twenty-five and thirty-five intrastate wars have been fought every year since the collapse of the Berlin Wall. The casualties in these internal conflicts have been, overwhelmingly, civilians, mostly women and children. Rather than being incidental victims, however, children are often part of a deliberate strategy of total war, in which adversaries terrorize, dominate, or destroy civilians as a way to achieve control. Children are not simply caught in the crossfire; they are all too often the direct targets.

In 1993, the U.N. General Assembly commissioned a global study on the impact of war on children. The resulting report, published in 1996, documented widespread abuses including attack, sexual violence, displacement, loss of parents, destruction of homes and property, and witnessing by children of deaths, executions, tortures, and rapes. In the past decade some two million children have been killed and more than four million disabled. More than one million have been orphaned, and twenty million have been displaced from their homes. An estimated ten million children have been psychologically scarred by the traumatic events they have witnessed. Over 300,000 are believed to be serving in armies, acting not only as fighters, but also as sex slaves, spies, minelayers, and bomb carriers.

The engagement of children in military activity is not a new phenomenon. Selected youths have often been groomed during various historical periods to be knights, samurai warriors, and raiders. What *is* new is the widespread availability of lightweight, relatively inexpensive weapons, including AK-47 assault rifles, which has enabled young teenagers and even ten-year-olds to be effective combatants. This fact has not been lost on field commanders, who are desperate to fill their ranks. In fact, many have come to prefer young people as soldiers because they are easy to manipulate, subject to indoctrination and intimidation, and often agree to take on very dangerous assignments.

Some United Nations agencies such as UNICEF have taken up the cause of these children. Each year, the agency publishes a report on the state of the world's children. In September 1997, the UN General Assembly appointed Olara Otunnu as a Special Representative to the Secretary-General for Children and Armed Conflict. The role of the Special Representative has been to act as a global advocate, to keep the issue of war-affected children before the international community.

As concerns about the global welfare of children rose on the international agenda, individual countries gave the issue increased attention. In Canada, as the Liberal government moved the concept of human security to the centre of Canadian foreign policy, children were given special emphasis. Help for war-affected children, child labourers, and sexually exploited youth was increasingly integrated into Canadian aid programming. The Canadian International Development Agency (CIDA) allocates some $25 million in humanitarian and development programming for war-affected children in countries such as Angola, Liberia, Sierra Leone, Rwanda, and Uganda.

As international agencies, national governments, and non-governmental organizations (NGOs) have increasingly focused on the needs of children, the debate has shifted to how best to address these needs. One view is that problems like child soldiering are grounded in the structural violence of poverty and social inequities. Environmental degradation, failed states, poverty, and social injustice are the root causes of most armed conflicts today. In situations of armed conflict, it is mostly poor children living in difficult circumstances who are at risk of being recruited as child soldiers. Within a community, poor children are most likely to be the orphans, the unaccompanied, or the marginalized, and therefore are at greatest risk of abduction because they lack basic protection. Further, impoverished communities are most likely to be attacked and used as pawns by unscrupulous leaders who routinely exploit young people as soldiers. Even where youths join the military on a presumably voluntary basis, it is overwhelmingly children in poor and marginalized communities who are likely to be the recruited. For many, military life may actually appear more attractive than their current situation, offering excitement, the power of the gun, and a way to achieve status, wealth, and a sense of control. In some cases, families have actually encouraged their children to go off to war in the hope that they gain income or a better future, or in order to maintain family and ethnic honour. In such circumstances, poverty reduction, accompanied by more equitable resource allocation, is critical to addressing the problem of child soldiers.

Others have argued, however, that attention also needs to be placed on the construction of more comprehensive and effective legal and human rights standards. For example, the International Coalition to Stop the Use of Child Soldiers, a coalition of NGOs, advocates for the establishment under international law of a universal minimum age (of eighteen) for military recruitment. The argument behind this approach is that there already exists a body of international law embodied in the UN Convention on the Rights of Child, which deals with the rights of children and sets out standards for human rights behaviour in this area. The task should be to strengthen this body of law. One way to do this would be to add an Optional Protocol to the Convention of the Rights of the Child, which would make it a violation to recruit children under eighteen. In response to these calls, the UN established a Working Group on the Optional Protocol to draft such a document.

In the first reading, Ross Synder discusses the Optional Protocol, the role of the Canadian government and Canadian NGOs in its drafting, and its potential in addressing the problem of child soldiers. Ananda Millard then examines the implications of taking a legalistic approach to addressing problems like child soldiers. She examines both the limites of international law and the need to take a broader approach to resolving such complex issues.

✔ YES
The Optional Protocol on the Involvement of Children in Armed Conflict

ROSS SNYDER

The plight of war-affected children is one of the most devastating tragedies of our time. The pictures are haunting: children who suffered physical and psychological injury, with fear and desperation on their faces. By now, the statistics are well known: millions of children caught up and scarred by the emotional, physical, sexual, psychological brutality of war and conflict. This includes children who have lost their parents, their homes, their schools, and the ability to play. It also compromises an estimated 300,000 who have served fighting factions—whether as soldiers, sexual slaves, or water carriers. Still others have witnessed inhuman acts against their families and carry the memories with them. The human security agenda challenges us to examine the issue of war-affected children from the perspective of those children. The problem is multifaceted, and the solutions must also be multifaceted.

Among the strategies to address the problem of war-affected children, the strengthening of international norms and standards has been one of the more high-profile efforts in the past several years. A broad range of countries and organizations have argued that work in this area, indeed, can make a significant contribution by putting into place a set of standards that, if enforced, will lead to the elimination of the use of soldiers under the age of eighteen.

New international norms work at several levels. Governments that ratify the norms can change national laws in a way that allows for taking action against rebel groups that employ child soldiers. International organizations that work with children can use the new norms to negotiate, using moral and political suasion with the national governments or nonstate actors on behalf of the affected children. Of course, the impact can only be relatively limited without effective enforcement, and some have questioned the development of new norms when existing standards are routinely violated. The response must be that the strengthening of norms and improved enforcement of existing standards need to be parallel. By the same token, strengthening norms and enforcing existing norms have only limited impact without efforts in other related fields, such as the political engagement of the parties involved in conflict, along with humanitarian action and appropriate development assistance.

In January 2000, the international community completed six years of often difficult negotiations on an Optional Protocol to the Convention on the Rights of the Child on Involvement of Children in Armed Conflict. The final negotiating session attracted considerable attention, and had its own share of drama. Indeed, the agreement on a final text was not certain until almost the last minute. That an agreement was achieved against some considerable odds underlines the degree to which the issue of war-affected children in the past several years has captured the conscience of the public, of civil society, and of governments. The result was a text that substantially advances international standards in regard to the use of child soldiers. The Optional Protocol was opened for signature on 5 June 2000 and Canada was the first country to sign and ratify the instrument. It will come into force three months after the deposit of the tenth instrument of ratification or accession.

THE ORIGINS OF THE OPTIONAL PROTOCOL

The reasons that governments felt compelled to develop an Optional Protocol go back to the negotiations on the Convention on the Rights of the Child in the 1980s. Before then, international law relating to the minimum age for recruitment and participation in hostilities was largely contained in Additional Protocols I and II to the four Geneva Conventions of 1949, which set the age for involvement in armed conflict at fifteen years. This tended to mirror international practice shortly after World War Two in which the school leaving age in many countries was fifteen. The Convention on the Rights of the Child, which was adopted by the UN General Assembly in 1989 and came into force in 1990, defined a child as "every human being below the age of 18 years unless, under the law applicable to the child, majority is attained earlier."[1] A number of governments sought to have this age also apply to military recruitment and participation in hostilities, but were unable to get broad agreement on such a standard. In fact, there was considerable divisiveness on this issue. As a result, negotiators decided essentially to reiterate existing international law by including Article 38, which contains the following three provisions:

- State parties shall undertake to respect and ensure for rules of international humanitarian law applicable to them in armed conflicts which are relevant to the child.

- State parties shall take all feasible measures to ensure that persons who have not attained the age of fifteen years do not take a direct part in hostilities.

- State parties shall refrain from recruiting any person who has not attained the age of fifteen years into their armed forces. In recruiting among those persons who have attained the age of fifteen years but who have not attained the age of eighteen years, state parties shall endeavour to give priority to those who are oldest.

Within three years of the adoption of the Convention on the Rights of the Child, there were renewed efforts to address the issue of age of recruitment and participation. Initially, the Committee on the Rights of the Child, set up to monitor implementation of the Convention on the Rights of the Child, recommended in 1993 the adoption of an Optional Protocol to raise the age to eighteen. The World Conference on Human Rights in 1993 also called for action in this area. In turn, the Commission on Human Rights in 1994 established an open-ended working group (i.e., open to all countries) to develop a draft Optional Protocol. The working group first met in 1994, and continued its work until January 2000.

Old divisions did not disappear, and by early 1998, the working group had reached an impasse, not surprisingly on the key issues of age of recruitment and participation. Indeed, the February 1998 session proved to be quite contentious and ended early because of the very strong disagreements on these questions. Some countries also wished to address a number of related issues such as the applicability of age limits to military schools and the extent to which the Optional Protocol should apply to so-called nonstate actors.

KEY ISSUES AND KEY ACTORS

There were several main camps on the complex issue of age. One group held that the Optional Protocol should set the age at eighteen for both recruitment and participation (the "straight-18" position), even if it meant that a few influential governments were unlikely to ratify. This group argued that it was especially important for developed countries to set this high standard to show they were part of a coalition demonstrating moral leadership. They also noted that since the Optional Protocol was "optional" in any event, the aim should be to achieve the highest standard, that would not be diluted or compromised. Over time, others would become parties as they became convinced of its value. Another group saw the main objective as preventing the use of those under eighteen in conflict, and that the focus, therefore, should be on age of participation. A third group argued that the emphasis should be on enforcing existing standards for governments, while exacting the highest possible standards from nonstate actors. The result of the 1998 session was the tabling of a chairman's report that contained a "rolling text" of the negotiated draft text with numerous "square bracketed" sections showing areas of disagreement, and a "chair's perception text" outlining what the chairman thought could be an agreed text based on his informal discussions and sense of the negotiations. It was also agreed that rather than having a formal session in 1999, the chair should pursue informal consultations to determine if agreement was possible on Optional Protocol. As it turned out, this "recess" proved to be important in building international pressure to complete the negotiations.

During the course of 1998 and 1999, the problem of war-affected children increasingly came into the limelight. Disturbing images of child soldiers involved in conflicts in such countries such as Uganda, Sierra Leone, Burma, and Columbia haunted television screens. Following on the landmark Graça Machel report on the impact of conflict on children, the UN secretary-general appointed a new Special Representative for Children and Armed Conflict, Olara Otunnu. A number of nongovernmental organizations (NGOs) formed a new "Coalition to Stop the Use of Child Soldiers" that actively lobbied governments and international organizations. The coalition, based in Geneva, initially focused its energies in northern countries, and its core leadership and membership were largely European and North American. In time, its membership base broadened. In turn, the issue of war-affected children came increasingly onto the agendas of such international and regional organizations as the United Nations (UN), the Organization of American States (OAS), the Organization for Security and Cooperation in Europe (OSCE), and the Organization for African Unity (OAU), thanks to the work of the coalition and a number of like-minded governments, including Canada.

In virtually all cases, the problem of international norms and the unfinished business around the Optional Protocol remained at the centre stage. The coalition, with a small budget, but with a significant and active network, played a particularly important role in keeping the issue of child soldiers on the international agenda. It organized high-profile regional conferences in Mozambique, Uruguay, and Germany to highlight its agenda.

The result was to lend a sense of urgency to the negotiating session of the working group set for January 2000. A number of governments met several times informally, often with NGOs, to try to develop common approaches. Canada, for example, hosted a workshop for representatives from foreign and defence ministries in May 1999 to compare legislative practices. In November and December, 1999, there was an informal consultation in Ottawa of experts aimed at strengthening the draft text in a number of areas and adding new elements. The paper coming out of that latter meeting became the basis for much of the discussion in Geneva, and resulted in a number of additional strengthening provisions in the final text. All the while, the new chair of the Working Group, Ambassador Catherine von Heidenstam of Sweden, quietly met with governments and NGOs in Geneva and in capitals, also with the aim of determining possible outcomes. Behind the scenes political negotiations conducted sometimes at the highest levels of government were also instrumental in reaching an agreement.

THE FINAL NEGOTIATIONS

By January 2000, the key divisive issues remained the following:

- age of voluntary recruitment;
- age of participation in hostilities;

- whether there should be an exception for military schools;
- applicability to nonstate actors.

At the same time, it became clear shortly after delegates arrived in Geneva for the negotiations that there was strong political will to produce a result. The increased awareness manifested since the last round was having its effect. Governments also were conscious that in the period leading to the 2001 UN Special Session on Children, it would be politically costly to leave unfinished an important piece of legal infrastructure. The Canadian view and that of a number of others was that not having an agreement was getting in the way of focusing on other elements of the war-affected children agenda. At the outset, it was clear to delegations that agreement on the age of eighteen for recruitment was not feasible, and other ways of addressing recruitment were needed. However, there were real prospects of reaching closure on other issues, although the age for participation had the potential to be very difficult.

The spirit of compromise brought to Switzerland was initiated in a Canada-US summit between Prime Minister Chrétien and President Clinton in October 1999. Prospects for agreement on language for the Optional Protocol had been stalled in large part due to reluctance on the part of the United States to accept higher minimum ages for recruitment and deployment than were currently in place. At the summit, the two leaders recognized the importance of a compromise, and they focused on the age of deployment rather than the age of recruitment as the decisive issue. Without this personal engagement in the issue by politicians in both governments, the Optional Protocol might not have been agreed upon.

The success of this effort would also not have been possible without major efforts at coalition building within cabinet and between departments in the government of Canada. The help and cooperation of the Canadian Department of National Defence and Defence Minister Art Eggleton were essential in allowing Canada to take the active stance it did on the protocol. Minister Eggleton worked hard with Minister Axworthy to find an agreeable way forward that preserved the integrity of the protocol, while respecting certain traditions of recruitment in the Canadian Armed Forces. In the end that interaction proved decisive.

Back in Geneva, the two-week session became in large measure a classic multilateral negotiation. The use of "informals" proved to be a particularly efficient way of moving the discussions along. For each of the major issues, individual country representatives agreed to act as coordinators and met with other interested delegations to hammer out agreed texts. The chair became directly involved if there was a genuine impasse in one of the informals. This flexibility of approach allowed for considerable negotiating out of the limelight. Several countries, including Canada, played a key role in the background, including through drafting of alternative texts. This was especially important in the contentious areas of age of recruitment and participation. In the end, many delegations demonstrated considerable flexibility. For example:

- Age of volunteer recruitment was raised to sixteen, short of what many had hoped for, but there were provision for safeguards designed to ensure that those under eighteen are not sent into hostilities.
- Age of participation was raised to eighteen, a move that will require some countries, notably the US, to change operational practices. However, some of the language was not as strong as many delegations would have preferred.
- Those countries not parties to the Convention on the Rights of the Child, in particular the US (Somalia being the only other nonparty), will be allowed to become parties to the Optional Protocol, but in doing so agree to abide by those parts of the Convention on the Rights of the Child relevant to the Optional Protocol. Debate on this issue went down to the last half hour of the time allowed for the session.
- There are references to the importance of international assistance and cooperation, which some would rather have wished to contain a stronger undertaking by developed countries to provide financial assistance.

In the end, the new Optional Protocol can claim a number of significant advances in requiring state parties to:

- set eighteen as the minimum age for compulsory recruitment, and for recruitment and participation by nonstate actors;
- take all feasible measures to ensure that members of their armed forces who are under the age of eighteen years do not take a direct part in hostilities; and
- raise the minimum age for voluntary recruitment to a least sixteen years while obliging state parties to deposit a binding declaration describing safeguards undertaken to ensure that recruitment is genuinely voluntary, is done with parental consent and reliable proof of age, and that recruits are fully informed of the duties involved in military service.

Although the Optional Protocol may not fully meet the objectives of all those involved in the negotiations, the text marks significant progress in setting standards on the issue of war-affected children. It reflects the determination of many in the international community, the importance of political negotiations, and should be considered an important contribution in the effort to eliminate the use of children as combatants.

LESSONS LEARNED

As noted, the form and process of the negotiations were relatively traditional; states engaged in a working group that developed a text by consensus, with good use of informals and "informal informals" (the latter involving a small number of countries drafting texts that were then presented to the larger informal groups). The forum was also open, with the coalition and representatives from the UN system effectively full partners in many of the negotiations and development of texts. An interesting element, referred to earlier, was the extensive work by governments and the coalition that took place during the period when the formal talks were suspended. This is perhaps one of the more important lessons from the negotiations—that thorough, patient, and low-key preparation can, indeed, be central to achieving a result in difficult, divisive negotiations.

Would a different form of negotiation have produced a stronger Optional Protocol? A few governments contemplated abandoning the working group process and the Optional Protocol altogether in the absence of a straight-eighteen result, and moving to a process akin to that used for the Landmines Treaty outside the UN. This would have resulted in a new legal instrument that would have involved only governments committed to the straight-eighteen approach. Many others, however, thought that the priority should be an improved standard that gained wide acceptance. At least in theory such an approach would benefit a larger number of children, even at the cost of a straight-eighteen outcome. In the end, the purist approach did not gain broad support. In part, this may have been because many of those involved in the issue of war-affected children believed that the Optional Protocol was one in a series of political, humanitarian, and developmental measures aiming to address the problem of war-affected children. The general view was that the Optional Protocol, as finally agreed upon, represented an advance in standards and did not close out options for future improvements.

The Optional Protocol will assist the work of UNICEF, the Secretary-General's Special Representative for Children and Armed Conflict, and the Red Cross by establishing a clear international norm. A number of governments proposing to ratify the Optional Protocol will need to change existing practices on recruitment and deployment, while others, like Canada, are taking or have taken steps to entrench into law existing procedures that already comply with the Optional Protocol. Even before the instrument comes into force, there are indications that some armed groups are prepared to consider the Optional Protocol as "guidance" and to make some effort to abide by its spirit. While these are promising developments, Canada and many other governments and organizations remain committed to carrying on with work across the full range of issues related to war-affected children.

NOTES

1. *The Convention on the Rights of the Child*, November 1989.

REFERENCES

Convention on the Rights of the Child. New York, November 1989.

Optional Protocol to the Convention on the Rights of the Child on the Involvement of Children in Armed Conflict. Geneva, May 2000.

✗ **NO**
Children in Armed Conflicts: Transcending Legal Responses
ANANDA S. MILLARD

INTRODUCTION

Could legislation have prevented Eva, 14, from becoming one of the best snipers her comrades had ever seen? Could legislation have prevented her from believing that she could help liberate her people and make her country a place where they could live without fear? Eva, alongside many other child soldiers, fought for the Farabundo Marti National Liberation Front (FMLN) during the civil war in El Salvador. Being regarded as a good sniper gave her a sense of pride and accomplishment.[1]

At the present time, there are over 300,000 children participating in armed conflicts. Some, like Eva, believe that what they do is right and necessary and engage voluntarily. Others, as was often the case in Mozambique, are kidnapped from their families and forced to commit horrific acts of violence against their will. The current trend in conflicts employing children is to use younger and younger children as active participants, increasing the severity of the problem substantially.[2] Can we rely on law alone to address the horror of today's conflicts?

This article suggests that the primarily legalistic approach that dominates the international debate about child soldiers is based on a limited understanding of the issues at hand. Moreover, existing legal standards have some unintended consequences that are to the detriment of the children fighting today's wars. The above thesis is based on the following two central tenets. First, we need to recognize that identifying the use of children as active participants in war as a violation of international legal standards alone is too limited: it should also be understood as a manifestation of the evolution of warfare. Hence, in order to address the issue of child soldiers, we need to acknowledge the value of examining the dynamics of new wars. Second, we must acknowledge that the international community generally has little ability to oversee and control conflict conduct, and the illegality of some of the acts conducted in modern warfare serves as a motive to make such actions covert.[3] This should prompt us to search for a field that is better suited to examining the child soldier problem, which, for instance, could be placed within the broader framework of studies of new wars. This article presents a possible platform from which we can examine the issue from a different angle. It does not intend to provide a response to the child soldier problem.

DICHOTOMY IN THE LEGAL INSTRUMENTS

I shall first examine the evolution of the law that protects children, focusing particularly on whether it is sufficiently flexible to be applied in conflict situations. The 1989 Convention on the Rights of the Child is the first international, legally binding document which outlines the explicit rights of children, although earlier documents set precedents for its drafting and ratification.[4] Initially, documents outlining child protection were limited to concerns of economic or sexual exploitation and incorporated the assumption that children ought to rely fully on the protection and care of adults.[5] This concept was reinforced in the 1959 Declaration on the Rights of the Child and in Article 24 of the 1966 International Covenant of Civil and Political Rights. While none of these legal documents pertained specifically to children involved in armed conflict, they set the tone for documents that followed. The principal problem with these documents, however, was that they were inflexible in the way they conceptualized children, seeing them solely as passive beneficiaries of rights, not as individuals with an active relationship to those rights. Indeed, the idea that children lack the ability to have an independent perspective was an implicit tenet in all international legal documents until 1989. These documents assumed that children live in a social setting that is able to protect them and advocate on their behalf. This, as will be explored later, is at odds with the social setting of new wars, where child soldiers are increasingly employed.

Potential Tools for Prohibition

The 1989 Convention on the Rights of the Child, adopted unanimously by the General Assembly of the United Nations, was the first legal document to acknowledge that children possess rights to autonomy as well as rights to preservation and protection.[6] However, with regard to children's rights in relation to participation in armed conflict, very little is outlined by the convention; the issue is mentioned only in Articles 38 and 39,[7] where the former of these, inter alia, establishes the following:

2. State Parties shall take all feasible measures to ensure that persons who have not attained the age of fifteen years do not take a direct part in hostilities.

3. State Parties shall refrain from recruiting any person who has not attained the age of fifteen into their armed forces. In recruiting among those persons who have attained the age of fifteen years but who have not attained the age of eighteen years, State Parties shall endeavour to give priority to those who are oldest.

This article is a recapitulation of the pre-existing 1977 protocols. However, the reiteration of the minimum recruitment age is important at the international level.

The extensive ratification of the Convention on the Rights of the Child means that using children under the age of 15 in conflict has become illegal almost everywhere.[8] It is important to note, however, that although the convention, on the whole, does not limit its applicability to governments, it does not (unlike the 1977 Protocol II) make its applicability to non-state parties explicit in Article 38, so non-state parties could argue that they are not bound by its terms. This is particularly important because most conflicts employing children are civil wars. More recently, additional documents—such as the Optional Protocol to the Convention on the Rights of the Child on the Involvement of Children in Armed Conflict (2000) and the International Labour Organization (ILO) Convention 182 Concerning the Prohibition and Immediate Action for the Elimination of the Worst Forms of Child Labour (1999)—promote an increase in the minimum age of recruitment from 15 to 18 years. Nonetheless, the Convention on the Rights of the Child remains the most important document because it applies to the largest constituency.

The reference made to children and their involvement in armed conflict as outlined in these documents tends to support the tenet that children have neither the right to autonomy nor the capability for either self-protection or self-preservation. Children tend to be identified as "non-participatory victims" of armed conflict.[9] Not only do some children claim to have chosen to become active participants independently, in some cases their decision to participate has been prompted by their view of the circumstance that surround them.[10] In Sierra Leone, child soldiers explained that one of the reasons they had decided to join armed groups was that they were unable to cope with the economic realities they faced due to lack of education.[11]

An additional issue of key importance here is that of measures for implementation. The upholding and enforcement of the provisions of the Convention on the Rights of the Child depend on the good will of parties to it.[12] In the case of child soldiers, the notion of good will has been countered by the 1998 Statute of the International Criminal Court (ICC), which outlines, in Article 8, that the use of child soldiers will be regarded as a crime of war. Yet the existence of such a document does not ensure its enforcement. Inability to monitor the participation of children in armed conflict leaves the ICC statute potentially ineffective.[13] So far, no case on grounds of the violation of Article 8 has taken place, and the ICC has not been able to serve as a further deterrent to conscription. A similar analysis may be applied to the Optional Protocol and to ILO Convention 182. Neither of these documents gives due credit to the dynamics that create the space for the use of children in armed conflict; hence, they also fail to outline feasible ways of enforcement. This does not mean that the existence of these standards does not have impact at the international level. The statute can serve, for example, as a guideline for special war-crimes tribunals, as is planned for the Special Court for Sierra Leone. Whilst this is a positive move, it does not ensure the punishment of all perpetrators. Therefore, we cannot rely on the statute to serve as a deterrent.

In sum, the 1989 Convention on the Rights of the Child, despite its large reliance on the good will of ratifying parties to ensure enforcement, has succeeded in increasing the level of attention given to children's rights at the international level. Hence, irrespective of the inability to enforce legal standards as relevant to children's involvement in armed conflict, the convention is, and should be regarded as, a success in the international legal arena. This legal document, however, is inappropriate for tackling the greater question of how to prevent the use of children in war because it tries to give children "conventional modelled rights."[14] More specialized documents, such as the ILO Convention 182, the Optional Protocol and the ICC statute, also fail to recognize the contextual realities of conflict and the reasons leading to the use of child soldiers.

Governments involved in civil wars are quite often unable to ensure that their opponents uphold legal standards. Indeed, in some cases, the governments themselves violate standards they have ratified. This is done because the costs of violating the legal standards are outweighed by the benefits gained thereby.[15] As a result, these legal documents inherently undermine the prevention of the use of children in conflict at the field level. Interestingly, the only efforts that have succeeded in preventing the use of children in conflict have been localized indigenous approaches, of which little is known.[16] Indigenous approaches seem to have been able to brake the modality of conflicts, with people building on existing cultural practices to refuse to permit the use of their children in a conflict. The participation of children has also been non-existent in cases where children were not regarded as useful or effective instruments of war.[17]

[...]

THE REALITY OF NEW WARS

One alternative way to respond to the problem is to contextualize the use of child soldiers as instruments of current conflicts; this should help us to explore ways in which we can increase the costs of exploiting child soldiers, thus ensuring that it is not cost-effective. The typology of what Mary Kaldor has termed "new wars" provides a general outline of the context within which child soldiers have been used in the 1980s and 1990s.[18]

New Wars and Children

The concept of new wars, as presented by Mary Kaldor, serves to help us understand the type of environment that currently fosters the use of children as instruments of war. New wars arise from the disintegration of state structures. They are characterized by a loss of the legitimacy of political institutions, which is caused by disappointment with post-colonial nationalist regimes, despotism and/or widespread corruption, and the inability of governments to implement promises. New wars involve the breakup of state monopolies on organized violence, the fragmentation of armies and police forces, the growth of organized crime and para-military groups, and the ready availability of weapons and mercenaries.[19] Wars no longer follow the Clausewitzean model of conflicts between states, fought with clearly defined aims and leading to the absolute victory of one party over another. But nor is it correct to assert that new wars are characterized by a return to primitive and tribal practices;[20] as Kaldor argues:

> Quite apart from the fact that concepts like tribalism or ethnic nationalism are relatively recent constructions, and that so-called primitive warfare was often sophisticated and organised, the new wars have certain shared characteristics that are quite clearly contemporary and post- rather than pre-Clausewitzean.[21]

New wars are further characterized by:

- being longer and having less clear motives;
- causing greater damage to infrastructure, such as hospitals and schools;
- violating previously recognized distinctions between combatants and civilians; and
- targeting whole populations, including children, women and elders.

This type of warfare creates a state of constant and collective terror that permeates all social relations and the culture itself.[22] New wars often aim at the destruction or destabilization of the state as a way of establishing a new power-base. A good example is the conflict between the Mozambican National Resistance (RENAMO) and the Mozambican Liberation Front (FRELIMO), where RENAMO's principal aim was to destroy FRELIMO's capacity to govern the country.[23] Destruction or destabilization of the state depends on the mobilization of substantial portions of the population. Such mobilization can take a variety of forms, the most commonly used techniques in new wars being:

- undermining social trust through means such as corruption and collective fear, as was the case in Mozambique;
- employing social institutions, such as religious bodies, for mobilization purposes, as was the case in the Salvadoran conflict; and
- employing electronic media as a channel of mobilization, as was the case in the Rwandan massacre.

Another characteristic of new wars is the complexity of their sources of support. These include nationals living abroad, as was the case in Mozambique; Mafia-like structures, which exist in Angola; and regional powers, which often contribute to the expansion of the conflict across national borders. Unlike earlier wars, where armed bodies were centralized and easily recognized, new wars are characteristically fought by fragmented groups and often involve paramilitary parties and criminal groups. Additionally, they often have unclear conflict lines, with shifts in alliances occurring throughout the conflict.[24] Tactics used in the new wars involve widespread and massive atrocities, and reliance on such war methods as population displacement and famine creation leads to the destruction of key economic structures, so that economic survival is often contingent on humanitarian support. New wars rarely end in a victory for one side: they tend to slow down owing to mutual exhaustion of combatants, only to re-ignite at a later point. All of the above factors lead to situations which are very difficult to control by international law.[25]

Looking at the situation from a different perspective, actors engaged in assistance would define these scenarios as complex emergencies. Mackinlay's definition of this phenomenon presents a fairly condensed view:

> A complex emergency is a humanitarian disaster that occurs in a conflict zone and is complicated by, or results from, the conflicting interests of warring parties. Its causes are seldom exclusively natural or military: In many cases a marginally subsistent population is precipitated toward disaster by the consequences of militia action or a natural occurrence such as earthquake or drought. The presence of militias and their interest in controlling and extorting the local population will impede and in some cases seriously threaten relief efforts. In addition to violence against the civilian populations, civilian installations such as hospitals, schools, refugee centres, and cultural sites will become war objectives and may be looted frequently or destroyed.[26]

This description illustrates the inherent complexities and the all-encompassing nature of new wars. Although neither new wars nor the complex emergencies that result from them can be defined or characterized in absolute terminology, having a general idea of the types of conflicts that employ child soldiers is important. The above description allows for a greater understanding of the type of atmosphere in which children become actively embroiled in armed conflict in both armed and unarmed capacities. Indeed, it is this atmosphere that promotes the use of child soldiers.

The Scale of the Problem

While it is crucial to recognize that the severity of the child soldier problem is principally caused by the type of warfare currently being engaged in, we must not forget that child soldiers have existed for centuries, perhaps for as long as war itself. Yet it must also be recognized that the number of child soldiers has increased in recent decades.[27] The reasons for this increase can be grouped into four closely interrelated categories: political factors, including the nature of war;

technological factors; socio-psychological factors; and economic factors.[28] The latter two are important, but become irrelevant if the former two are not in place. Examining these factors is crucial for understanding the phenomena of contemporary use of child soldiers.

Political changes in the last decades have influenced the increase in the employment of child soldiers worldwide. The 20th century has embraced such strategic concepts as "total war" and "people's war," which essentially erase long-held distinctions between civilians and combatants. The embracing of these new modes of war has been a response to a perceived necessity identified by conflict parties: they believe that, in order to win a conflict, all available and cost-effective tactics and tools should be used. The end of the Cold War has also made a difference: as Washington and Moscow reduced funding to their regional military proxies, some military and guerrilla groups resorted to the employment of children as active participants in conflicts. This was partly done as an attempt to counterbalance the reduction in foreign military aid with manpower. Additionally, the reduction in monetary and hardware aid forced parties to move toward the increased employment of smaller weapons.[29]

Technology has played a principal role in revolutionizing warfare. One could argue that the increasing reliance on light weapons in new wars is one of the reasons for the increased use of child soldiers. The employment of children cannot be efficient when weapons are large, heavy and highly technical.[30] However, physical strength and stamina are no longer prerequisites for active participation in armed conflict. Such modern machine guns as the AK-47 and the M-16 are capable of firing 600 and 800 rounds per minute respectively, weigh little more than three kilograms each, do not require extensive training prior to use and are inexpensive.[31] Essentially, these types of weapons are "ideal" for children, who now become capable of mastering the technical aspects of armed fighting. This factor has allowed for the increase in the use of child soldiers as active combatants in civil wars, where the majority of weapons are small firearms.[32] In short, technology becomes an important factor once conflict parties have decided that, because of a perceived necessity, traditional norms excluding children and the general population from partaking in conflict will not be upheld.

The specific features of the socio-psychological development of children are an additional factor influencing their employment in active combat. In this respect, studies on child development and psychology have shown that children are more willing to put themselves at risk. Children are also more easily formed and disciplined, and are more loyal and docile than adults. Moreover, children are more impressionable and can be turned into fierce fighters who are willing to fight under unfavourable conditions. It is believed that individuals recruiting children have come to recognize these characteristics of child behaviour as assets because these factors make children perfect combatants.[33]

As regards economic considerations, child soldiers often place no demands for remuneration on their employers. In many cases, the economic conditions of children living in war zones are so deficient that the offer of essential food and clothing is sufficient to ensure their will to participate. Such factors, combined with a variety of innovative recruitment techniques, guarantee a rich supply of children ready for active participation in war. In addition, ideology and religious belief have been used to encourage children to participate in armed conflict, as for example in El Salvador and in the Iran-Iraq war.[34]

The Varied Use of Children as Instruments of War

Children are used an instrument of warfare not only to increase personnel numbers, but also to corrupt and terrorize populations. One of the added benefits associated with the use of children is that they are often willing to fight in ways that adults will not. Children provide warring parties with the possibility of both gaining extra manpower and breaking down a society as a way of achieving victory.[35] The following two examples serve to illustrate this. In Mozambique, children were often kidnapped to partake in conflict. Forcing children to participate in war and to take part in gruesome acts of violence against their own communities was intended to prevent these children from returning home, where they feared rejection. More generally, this practice was aimed at breaking down the social structure of the communities from which the children were "recruited." In El Salvador, the employment of children was designed to consolidate support for the revolutionary movement by involving all members of society. Children were taught to believe in the goals of the movement in a blind fashion, without questioning either the methods employed or the tangible goals that were to be achieved. From a political stance, the use of children was seen as a step in forming a generation that believed in the ideals of the revolution and was willing to enforce these ideals at any cost.

Once involved in the conflict, child soldiers are assigned duties contingent on various factors, such as age, sex and location (for instance, urban or rural setting). Although cases have been reported where children below the age of nine were frontline combatants, this is rare. In some cases, child soldiers are first given non-combat duties and only gradually become fully fledged combatants. Usually, children who have been recruited, but who have yet to commence frontline participation, are given alternative tasks, such as odd jobs in the military camps. While performing alternative duties, they often receive informal military training. Institutionalized training for small children does not seem to be a common practice, but it is known to happen on occasion.[36] Children have also performed duties as spies and couriers. In some cases, these duties have been expressly given to young children because it has been thought that they can more easily infiltrate and travel without being thought suspect. Additionally, child soldiers have also been known to perform tasks not given to adult soldiers because of their inherent dangers; for example, child soldiers have been employed to clear minefields.[37]

The difference in assigned duties is often determined by the physical strength (handling weapons and carrying equipment) and psychological capacities of a child (trustworthiness, for example).[38] Some fighting units are known to evaluate children's physical and mental capacities on a regular basis. When governments legally recruit children under 18 years of age, we often see that various special measures are taken. Finland, for instance, allows for the recruiting of children under 18, but they are not permitted to perform any combat duties before they reach 18 years of age. In other cases, governments claim to provide access to chaplains and psychologists and to monitor the use of alcohol.[39]

In some cases, duties are gender-specific or influenced by gender. In Mozambique, for example, RENAMO upheld a view that promoted gender-specific tasks and did not allow females to partake in combat. This policy was directly linked to a political stance against the FRELIMO government, which promoted equality between the sexes.[40] In contrast, in El Salvador, the revolutionary movement was characterized by its abandoning of the traditional cultural impositions on gender, and it allowed both sexes to perform similar tasks.[41] In both cases, the approach to gender was closely linked to the ideals upheld by the different parties. Whilst RENAMO was hoping to achieve a return to more traditional practices, the FMLN advocated the exact opposite. In neither case was gender at the core of the political movement, but the use of children and the labour division between the sexes served as an expression of political goals. Ensuring that children felt that these norms were upheld would aid in the consolidation of such belief systems in postwar social structures.

In urban settings, children are often involved in resistance movements and sabotage. In some cases, the duties of child soldiers include the recruitment of other children. The differentiation between urban and rural participatory roles depends on whether the conflict is being fought in both urban and rural areas, on the tactics employed in combat, and occasionally on the choice of the combatant.

All of the tasks outlined above are examples of how children are treated and used during conflicts. New wars force us to recognize the eradication of strict codes of conduct in current war situations. Children are used because the flexible codes governing new wars allow for it. From this perspective, children can be crudely referred to as an instrument of war.

CONCLUDING REMARKS

This article has reviewed some of the problems faced by the international community in trying to prevent the use of child soldiers in current conflicts. Ideally, the use of children would be eradicated; in reality, it appears that we must rather attempt to mitigate the effects of this persistent problem.

In short, we must recognize that given the types of wars currently fought, children are an invaluable asset. This requires that we re-examine the ways in which we have thus far attempted to respond to the plight of children involved in armed conflict. We must contextualize the issue of child soldiers within the types of con-flict that foster their employment, interpreting the child soldier issue as a war phenomenon rather than a legal issue. The use of child soldiers is certainly a vio-lation of children's rights and of the laws of war, but we have to focus on how it has been caused by numerous contextual factors governing the conduct of the wars in which they take part.

Because the international community is largely incapable of preventing recruit-ment through the use of international legal codes, it has become more urgent to concentrate on reintegration instead. While, in the legal context, reintegration is proposed, guidelines for operationalizing assistance are not provided. This neces-sitates the further examination of reintegration.

All of the above issues require that the child soldier question be reopened and current perceptions re-examined. We must revisit the following key questions:

- Do locally defined concepts of childhood provide, in different settings, a way of preventing the use of children in conflict?
- How can the need for children as instruments of war be minimized within the new war context?
- Can understanding the experience of children in conflict assist in providing for their reintegration?

Proposing the re-examination of the above key issues is not intended to mean that past reviews of the child soldier issue were not meaningful steps forward. We must recognize that the early analyses of the child soldier topic were aimed at providing the background for a legal response and at placing the issue on the international agenda. However, these documents are insufficient to respond to what have been identified here as the central problems associated with the use of children in war. The challenge now is to move beyond the legal response, to strengthen our analysis of the child soldier issue as an integral element of new wars. Ultimately, we need to move on to the design and implementation of new and innovative ways of preventing recruitment and assisting reintegration.

NOTES

The author acknowledges support for her research from the Norwegian Foreign Ministry and would also like to thank Kristian Berg Harpviken for his helpful comments.

1. Martin Adler, *Children of War* (newsletter, Save the Children, Sweden), no. 2, 1996.

2. Rachel Brett & Margaret McCallin, *Children: The Invisible Soldiers*, 2nd ed. (Stockholm: Save the Children, Sweden, 1998); Ilene Cohn & Guy Goodwin-Gill, *Child Soldiers: The Role of Children in Armed Conflict* (Oxford: Clarendon Press, 1997).

3. See Ian Brownlie, *Principles of Public International Law* (New York: University Press, 1990); Geoffrey Best, *War and Law Since 1945* (Oxford: Clarendon Press, 1994).

4. Geraldine Van Bueren, *International Documents on Children* (Boston, MA & London: Martinus Nijhoff & Save the Children, 1993); Geraldine Van Bueren, *The International Law on the Rights of the Child* (London: Martinus Nijhoff & Save the Children, 1995).

5. For examples, see the International Labour Conference of 1919, the 1921 International Convention on Traffic of Women and Children, and the 1924 Geneva Declaration of the Rights of the Child. See Van Bueren, 1993 (note 4 above); see also Eugeen Verhellen, *Convention on the Rights of the Child* (Leuven Apeldoorn: Garant, 1994).

6. See Van Bueren, 1993 (note 4 above); Verhellen (note 5 above).

7. See Sharon Detrick, ed., *On the Rights of the Child: A Guide to the "Travaux Préparatoires"* (Zoetermeer: Martinus Nijhoff, 1992); Geraldine Van Bueren, "The International Legal Protection of Children in Armed Conflict," *International Comparative Law Quarterly*, vol. 43, no. 4, October 1994, pp. 809–826.

8. The current prominence of the Convention within the legal arena of children's rights stems from the fact that all countries, with the exception of the United States and Somalia, are legally bound by it.

9. See Van Bueren, 1993 (note 4 above); 1994 (note 7 above).

10. Krijn Peters & Paul Richards, "Fighting with Open Eyes: Youth Combatants Talking About War in Sierra Leone," in Celia Petty & Patrick Bracken, eds., *Rethinking the Trauma of War* (London & New York: Free Association Books & Save the Children, 1998), pp. 76–111.

11. Peters & Richards (note 10 above).

12. See Article 41.3 of the Convention on the Rights of the Child; Jenny Kuper, *International Law Concerning Child Civilians in Armed Conflict* (Oxford: Clarendon Press, 1997).

13. See Brett & McCallin (note 2 above); database of Save the Children, Sweden, available at www.rb.se/childwardatabase/.

14. The term "conventional" is here employed to refer to the set of rights outlined by the 1989 Convention on the Rights of the Child.

15. Michael Howard, "Temperamenta Belli: Can War be Controlled?" in Jean Bethke Elshtain, ed., *Just War Theory* (Oxford: Basil Blackwell, 1992), pp. 22–35.

16. Field research interviews, Mozambique 1989, 2000.

17. See Howard (note 15 above).

18. Mary Kaldor, *New & Old Wars: Organised Violence in a Global Era* (Oxford: Polity Press, 1999).

19. Mary Kaldor, "Introduction," in Mary Kaldor & Basker Vashee, eds., *Reconstructing the Global Military Sector: New Wars (Vol. 1)* (London and Washington, DC: Pinter, 1997), pp. 3–33. See also Kaldor (note 18 above); Cherif Bassiouni, "Organised Crime and New Wars," in Mary Kaldor & Basker Vashee, eds., pp. 34–54.

20. For counter argument, see Kaplan, "The Coming Anarchy," *Atlantic Monthly*, no. 273, February 1994, pp. 44–76.

21. Kaldor, 1997 (note 19 above), p.3.

22. See Derek Summerfield, *The Impact of War and Atrocities on Civilian Populations: Basic Principles for NGO Interventions and a Critique of Psychological Trauma Projects*, Relief and Rehabilitation Network Paper 14 (London: Overseas Development

Institute, 1996); Carolyn Nordstrom & Jo Ann Martin, eds., *The Paths to Domination, Resistance and Terror* (Berkeley, CA: University of California Press, 1992).

23. Joseph Hanlon, *Beggar Your Neighbours* (Bloomington, IN: Indiana University Press, 1996).

24. See Robert Reich, *The Work of Nations: Preparing Ourselves for 21st Century Capitalism* (New York: Simon & Schuster, 1991); Alex De Wall, "Contemporary War in Africa," in Kaldor & Vashee, eds. (note 19 above), pp. 287–332.

25. Howard (note 15 above); Brownlie (note 3 above).

26. John Mackinlay, ed., *A Guide to Peace Support Operations* (Providence, RI: Brown University, Thomas J. Watson Jr. Institute for International Studies, 1996), pp. 14–15.

27. Brett & McCallin (note 2 above); database of Save the Children, Sweden (note 13 above); United Nations, *Impact of Armed Conflict on Children: Report of the Expert of the Secretary-General, Ms. Graça Machel, Submitted Pursuant to General Assembly Resolution 48/157* (New York: United Nations, August 1996).

28. Cohn & Goodwin-Gill (note 2 above).

29. UNICEF, *Summary: The State of the World's Children* (New York: UNICEF 1996); Mark Frankel, Joshua Hammer, Joseph Contreras, Ron Mareau & Christopher Dickey, "Boy Soldiers," *Newsweek,* 7 August 1995, pp. 10–21.

30. See John Keegan, *The Face of Battle* (New York: Penguin, 1978).

31. UNICEF, *Press Release: War Against Children* (London: UNICEF United Kingdom Committee, 11 November 1996); Major Frederick Myatt MC, *An Illustrated Guide to Rifles and Sub-Machine Guns* (London: Salamander Books, 1981).

32. Cohn & Goodwin-Gill (note 2 above).

33. United Nations (note 27 above); Brett & McCallin (note 2 above).

34. See Alison Benjamin, *Children at War* (London: Save the Children, 1994); see also Centre on War and the Child, *Iran's Child Martyrs: A Summary Report* (Eureka Springs, AR: Centre on War and the Child, 1987).

35. Brett & McCallin (note 2 above).

36. Ibid.

37. UNICEF (note 29 above).

38. Brett & McCallin (note 2 above); database of Save the Children, Sweden (note 13 above); United Nations (note 27 above).

39. Brett & McCallin (note 2 above).

40. Ruth Jacobson, Research Fellow at the Department of Peace Studies, Bradford University, unofficial interviews, Bradford, 1997.

41. Norma Vázques, Cristina Ibánez and Clara Murguialday, *Mujeres Montaña: Vivencias de Guerrilleras y Colaboradoras del FMLN* [Mountain Women: Experiences of Female Guerrillas and Collaborators in the FMLN] (Madrid: Horas y Horas, 1996).

Postscript

In her article, Ananda Millard points out that the use of child soldiers is a war phenomenon and not a legal issue. She bases this point on the argument that the use of child soldiers is very much a part of the "new wars" that have emerged, particularly in the post-Cold War era. It is worth exploring how these new wars differ from past wars and why there is a particular incentive to use child soldiers.

Millard suggests taking a more holistic approach if legal approaches alone are not sufficient. What might an aid program that focused on trying to prevent the recruitment of child soldiers look like?

Canada played an instrumental role in promoting the issue of child soldiers. We held a conference on war-affected children in Winnipeg in September 2000. The issue continues to be addressed by Canadian NGOs and by the Canadian International Development Agency. However, since then the issue has not received much attention within Canada among the general population. Does this suggest, as with the landmines issue, that governments and NGOs have had difficulty in building a constituency for addressing such humanitarian issues on a long-term basis?

Infotrac Keyword Search
"child soldiers" or "children" + "war"

Suggested Additional Readings

Brett, Rachel & Margaret McCallin. *Children: The Invisible Soldiers.* Vaxjo: Radda Barnen, 1996.

Cairns, Edward. *Children and Political Violence.* Oxford: Blackwell, 1996.

Cohn, Ilene & Guy Goodwin-Gill. *Child Soldiers: The Role of Children in Armed Conflicts.* Oxford: Clarendon, 1994.

Kaldor, Mary. *New & Old Wars: Organised Violence in a Global Era.* Oxford: Polity Press, 1999.

Malan, Mark and Deirdre van der Merwe, "Codes of Conduct and Children in Armed Conflict," *Canadian Foreign Policy* 8, no.1 (Fall 2000): 67–81.

"U.N. Study on the Effects of War on Children." *Peace and Conflict: Journal of Peace Psychology* 4, no. 4 (1998): 319–428.

UNICEF. *The State of the World's Children.* New York: UNICEF, 1996.

Wessells, Michael. "Can We Prevent Child Soldiering?" Peace Review 12, no. 3 (September 2000): 407ff.

_____. "Child Soldiers." *Bulletin of the Atomic Scientists* 53, no. 6 (1997): 32–39.

_____ & Deborah Winter. 1998. "The Graca Machel U.N. Study of the Effects of War on Children." *Peace and Conflict: Journal of Peace Psychology* 4, no. 4 (1998): 319–428.

Website Resources

Amnesty International   Amnesty International publishes its findings on the use of child soldiers and other human rights abuses.

Coalition to the Stop the Use of Child Soldiers   A coalition of NGOs working on a no-child-soldiers campaign. Contains a variety of materials and resources.

Conference on War-Affected Children   This is the official website containing much of the document relevant to the Conference on War-Affected Children hosted by Canada in September 2000.

Human Rights Watch   The homepage for Human Rights Watch's campaign on child soldiers. Has a very useful list of links.

UNICEF   Official homepage of UNICEF, with extensive materials on children and war.

ISSUE**NINETEEN**

Should States Pursue an Open Border Policy toward Migrants?

✔ **YES**

ANDREW COYNE, "The Case for Open Immigration: Why Opening Up Our Borders Would Be Good for the Country and Good for the Soul," *The Next City* (Winter 1995)

✘ **NO**

G.E. DIRKS, "Why States Are Justified in Limiting Their Entry of Migrants"

Mass migrations provoked by disasters or political upheaval have recurred throughout history. With the institutionalization of a global system of states, the acceptance of such people rests on the will of the receiving state. Historically, many states like Canada and the United States took an open-door policy toward migrants, seeing them as a potential resource in the process of nation-building. Migrants helped settle underpopulated regions of the country, brought new skills with them, and often were a source of cheap labour, especially when they were willing to take on the menial, low-paid, and frequently dangerous jobs that local populations shunned. Receiving countries like Canada advertised and actively recruited for immigrants, providing incentives to those willing to take up the offer to leave their homes and emigrate abroad. In the early part of the twentieth century Canada even took some 100 000 orphaned and destitute children from Great Britain as a source of cheap labour for its farmers.

The open-door policy of this period of history contrasts sharply with the growing hostility to many immigrants in traditional destination countries today. International migration has come to be seen by many as a potential threat that recipient countries must take steps to control. This changed perception is partly rooted in the changing patterns of migration in the 1990s. Today an estimated 125 million people live in countries not of their birth. The nature of international migration flows has become much more complex. Each year an average of one million people are admitted to traditional receiving countries as legally admitted, permanent immigrants. An estimated twenty million people are living in other countries as legally admitted seasonal labourers or contract workers. Another twenty million are classified by the United Nations High Commissioner for Refugees (UNHCR) as "refugees and other peoples of concern." These people have been displaced outside of their country because of political conflict, natural disasters, or other factors. An estimated one million are asylum-seekers asking for refugee status in foreign countries. Finally, it is estimated that there are thirty to forty million illegal, undocumented migrants.

Several factors have contributed to this dramatic rise in international migration. During the Cold War, communist regimes, fearing a mass exodus of dissatisfied citizens, prevented their residents from emigrating or even travelling abroad. Since the collapse of the USSR, Central and Eastern European countries now see emigration as a way of reducing domestic unemployment levels while generating foreign exchange from remittances of workers abroad. Economic crises and a growing gap in income and lifestyles have led to an increased flow of migrants from developing countries in the South to industrialized countries in the North. The growing number of "complex political emergencies" in regions of Africa has produced large numbers of "forced migrants," people who have been compelled to flee their homelands because of ethnic violence, political instability, or economic collapse.

As the number of migrants has grown and the situations they are leaving have become more complex, traditional distinctions between political refugees and economic migrants have become blurred. Are Haitian migrants to the United States political refugees fleeing persecution or are they economic migrants seeking a better standard of living in a wealthier neighbouring country? In addition, the traditional distinctions between sending, transit, and recipient countries are breaking down. For example, Germany, which has historically produced large numbers of migrants, is now an important transit country for migrants from Eastern Europe and the Third World. And it is under increasing pressure to permanently settle larger numbers of migrants.

As a result of this increasingly complex situation, international migration has become a sensitive political issue in many receiving states. Fears are expressed regarding the impact of migration on unemployment levels and the ability of government to maintain social and health services, which are already facing pressure from deficit-reduction measures. The growing diversity of geographical sources of migrants has raised questions about the impact of migration on national identity and the ability of societies to cope with cultural diversity. For example, in the United States, citizens of some states have been asked to vote on propositions designed to protect English as the official language of the United States and to strip illegal immigrants of any social or education benefits.

At the same time, governments have increasingly looked at ways to tighten the regulation of international migration flows by narrowing the definition of refugees, establishing stricter procedures for processing claims of asylum-seekers, and reducing the movement of illegal immigrants across the borders. Such efforts raise important questions about the role of international migration today and the rights of states to regulate their borders.

In the first article, Andrew Coyne, a noted Canadian journalist and columnist, discusses the historical role of immigration in Canada. He argues that immigration has made and continues to make a positive contribution to Canadian society. He argues that what Canada needs is not a more restrictive regulation of immigration but a policy of welcoming even larger numbers of immigrants in the future. On the other hand, Gerry Dirks of Brock University examines the reasons states are justified in seeking to regulate the flow of migrants across their borders.

✔ YES

The Case for Open Immigration: Why Opening Up Our Borders Would Be Good for the Country and Good for the Soul
ANDREW COYNE

Somewhere around the 15th century, cities began to lose their walls. Since their rebirth from the rubble of the Dark Ages four centuries before, the cities of Europe had sheltered within layers of protective fortifications, adding new ones as expansion demanded. Town and country were then separate in tradition, hierarchy and poverty; cities were dynamic, egalitarian and wealthy. It was only natural that they should be separate in a physical as well as spiritual sense.

The medieval city filled the role the New World would play in later centuries. It was a place of escape, an island of liberty, where the serf, if he could evade recapture by his lord for a year and a day, became a freeman, with the special rights and privileges that city residents enjoyed. Yet it also offered security, a sanctuary for the merchants and artisans against the depredations of the nobility—and of competitors. Cities had their own currencies, their own weights and measures, their own tolls and tariffs. Outsiders were restricted to a particular corner of the marketplace, their stay limited to a certain number of days. They were often required to register the name of their innkeeper with the authorities.

As the influx from the countryside progressed, however, and as the town was a centre of production as well as commerce, the original urban preference for autarchy gave way in succeeding centuries to a high level of trade between city and hinterland. This mutual interdependence, besides greatly enriching them both, blurred many of the distinctions between them. With the rise of the nation-state, the walls withered away. The nation-state now provided protection; a transcendent national identity bolstered the community of city life.

Social differences remained, of course. But the two tribes, urban and rural, no longer viewed each other as alien. They were, they realized, countrymen, subjects of the same king. Today, we would consider it absurd not only to put up walls, but to place virtually any barrier to the flow of people, trade or capital across city limits. The outside world starts at the international boundary, where we now place barriers.

These have grown ever fewer over the last two centuries. Since the publication of Adam Smith's *Wealth of Nations*, freedom of trade between nations has fought a slow, unsteady but still inexorable path to fruition. The 19th century's gold standard and today's electronic integration of financial markets gave us first the free and now the instantaneous flow of capital around the world.

But in one crucial respect, the movement of people, progress has curiously been reversed. Controls on immigration have multiplied. Until the 19th century, when nearly 60 million Europeans crossed the seas, their numbers were not even recorded. Immigration quotas are largely a 20th-century invention. Indeed, passports didn't exist before the First World War.

While restrictions on trade and capital flows remain only in the face of concerted intellectual attack, the notion that immigration can and should be controlled stands as unquestioned orthodoxy. Even economists, who generally agree that the free movement of people, like any other productive resource, would benefit the world economy—some studies suggest the gains would exceed those from removing all other trade restrictions combined—rarely support open immigration. Rival camps of restrictionists dominate the immigration debate. Both agree there must be a ceiling; they differ only on its level. Both accept that immigrants must be selected; they differ solely on the criteria. I propose to challenge these assumptions. I question not merely whether we should have more or less immigration, nor whether we should use this or that basis of selection, but whether the whole moral premise of the enterprise—that is, that the current inhabitants of a country may rightfully bar others from joining them—is sustained by anything more than the force of habit. I argue not merely that we liberalize immigration controls, but that we abolish them....

Any proposal to add to the population through immigration inevitably raises a wide range of fears that might be grouped together under the heading of "too many people." These fears may revolve around unemployment, wages, social programs, cultural values or the environment; they may focus on the level of population, its density or its rate of growth; but they are invariably and unshakably rooted in a belief, not only that there exists a natural level of population for Canada, but that by a remarkable coincidence, we are precisely at it.

This is most plainly stated in that most antique of complaints, that immigration adds to unemployment. If there are just so many jobs to go around, it is reasoned, and if a certain number of workers are added to the labor force, unemployment will rise in like measure. But there is no natural limit to the demand for labor. As the economist Herbert Grubel puts it, every immigrant "brings along hands and a mouth." The money immigrants earn at their jobs fuels the consumption that creates jobs.

That is why the United States, with a population of 250 million, can have a lower unemployment rate than Canada, with a population of 29 million. It is also why, in the 1950s, West Germany could absorb 13 million refugees into a prewar population of 39 million, yet emerge from the decade with the lowest unemployment rate in Europe: just one percent. The Economic Council commissioned a battery of econometric studies seeking a link between the unemployment rate and either the level of population or its growth rate, using data from many different countries, and from different periods of time in Canada. It found none.

A related concern is that immigrants tend to depress wages. With more competition for jobs, workers are forced to undercut each other. For some current residents, especially unskilled workers, the distributional consequences would seem potentially painful. That's the theory.

In practice, the very increase in profits arising from all cheap labor just as quickly attracts an offsetting flood of capital from abroad. The almost perfect mobility of international capital is one of the most widely remarked phenomena of our times. Again, empirical research supports the thesis that countries with larger or faster-growing populations have no tendency to suffer low or declining wages. China is not poor because it is populous. It may, however, be populous because it is poor. It is poor because it is communist. Now that it is getting less communist, it is getting less poor.

If anything, the effects on incomes are positive. The Economic Council estimates, on the basis of scale efficiencies alone, an increase of 0.3 percent in per capita GDP for every additional million people over current population levels, or about $71 per resident citizen in 1991 dollars, every year, forever. Put another way, that's a gift to the native-born population of almost $2,000 per immigrant per year. Capitalizing the discounted value of all future gains, that works out to a lump-sum benefit to the native-born population of $76,000 per immigrant family of four. The returns from each added million diminish at higher levels of population. At current rates of investment, the Economic Council estimates the "optimal" population for Canada to be 100 million, at which point real per capita incomes would be about seven percent higher than at present—which would seem consistent with the actual gap between Canadian and U.S. incomes.

An objection might be that the same economies of scale could be captured simply through trade with other countries. But recent research, including that by Michael Porter in his best-selling *The Competitive Advantage of Nations*, stresses the special intensity of trading activity within domestic markets. The volume of trade, and with it the opportunity for specialization, is much greater among 100 million people inside one set of borders with one set of laws than it is between two countries of 50 million each, even where these are partners in a free trade area. Not least of the gains, of course, are those that stem from the mobility of labor—a freedom enjoyed within a full-blown economic union, but not within most free trade areas.

And these are just the measured gains. Some analysts, notably Julian Simon of the University of Maryland, point to other economic benefits less easily captured in the data. Large populations, Simon notes, produce "more Einsteins," bright people with bright ideas, which can benefit the rest of the population, beyond the returns accruing to the Einsteins themselves. More firms mean more competition, more products and more choices for consumers; larger and more competitive national markets offer more scope for firms to learn how to make and sell products for a world market. Immigrants, moreover, are more likely than the general population to be in their peak saving years (nearly half arrive between the ages of 20 and 39), with still more incentive to save: The older they are on arrival, the less their eligibility for contributory pensions. Higher national savings reduce the need for foreign capital to finance domestic borrowing, including government deficits, which helps the balance of payments.

Indeed, in the decades to come, the demographic role of immigration will assume increasing importance. The fertility rate has declined to 1.7, less than half the baby boom pace of the 1950s, and well below replacement level. With no immigration (and with existing emigration of about 50,000 per year), population would peak around the year 2015, dwindling to 10 million by the end of the following century. We'll need about 200,000 immigrants a year just to keep the population from falling. Of more immediate concern, as the baby boomers age, the costs of the elderly's pensions and health care will increase dramatically. With no net immigration, the "dependency ratio"—the number of children and old people as a proportion of the working age population—would rise to more than 85 percent by 2040, from 65 percent today. True, immigration, at least at the levels most people envisage, cannot stem the aging tide. But it can't hurt. Even at a net immigration rate of 0.8 percent of the population, only slightly higher than present rates, the dependency ratio could be held to about 72 percent.

Which brings us to perhaps the most direct and tangible economic benefit from immigration: its contribution to the public purse. Yes, contribution. The most common current fear about immigrants, that they impose an intolerable burden on the rest of us through their use of welfare and other public services, is the least defensible in fact.

Research by economist Ather Akbari of Saint Mary's University in Halifax, using data from Statistics Canada's Survey of Consumer Finances, shows no significant difference between immigrants and native-born Canadians in their total consumption of public services: They use more of some services, like education, but less of others, like pensions. Of particular note, immigrants are 23 percent less likely to draw unemployment insurance than native-born Canadians. They are also less likely to be on welfare. Even among recent (1981–85) immigrants, the 1986 census shows 12.5 percent on social assistance—higher than the 6.7 percent among those in the 1976–80 cohort, but lower than the 13.8 percent of native-born Canadians. Some provinces have done better than others. While immigrants make up 22 percent of British Columbia's population, they accounted for just 2.7 percent of its social assistance caseload in 1989.

But the other side of the ledger is just as important. Akbari's research confirms what other studies have shown: Immigrants as a group earn more than native-born Canadians, and hence pay more in taxes. While recent immigrants earn less than the national average—whether because of language and other adjustment difficulties, or simply because they tend to be younger and less advanced in their careers—within a decade or so they have caught up and surpassed it. Total household earnings of immigrants in 1990 averaged between $34,125 (for those who arrived in 1981–85) and $47,366 (for arrivals in the 1966–70 period), compared to $32,127 for all non-immigrant households.

Not only does the average immigrant household pay more than twice as much in taxes as it consumes in services, but the gap between the two is wider than in native-born households: That is, immigrant families pay more than their fair share in net contributions to the public treasury. Moreover, immigration spreads the cost of "pure public goods" like defence across a larger population, which reduces the bill to the average taxpayer: according to Akbari, by about $1,215 per immigrant household in 1990.

Far from a burden, in sum, immigrants transfer income to current residents. Akbari reckons that the average immigrant family paid the native-born population a premium of $1,813 in taxes net of services in 1990: a total annual transfer on the order of $2.6 billion, or about $100 per current resident. Or to put it another way, the typical young immigrant family arriving in 1990 would generate a discounted sum of $46,695 in net fiscal transfers to the native-born population over the next 45 years, in 1990 dollars....

Those who insist on the necessity of selectivity, or fear the social costs of immigration, underestimate the high degree of self-selection involved when an immigrant, as the Confederation orator D'Arcy McGee put it, "heaves up the anchor of his heart from its old moorings." People are not normally inclined to leave their soil, their language, their culture, their family and friends, to travel 3,000 miles in the bottom of a boat to a strange and frozen land just to spend the rest of their lives on welfare. Nor is the survivor of a famine or pogrom likely to lack the basic resourcefulness required to succeed in such a land of peace and plenty as Canada. As immigration lawyer Peter Rekai has written, even the humblest immigrant brings "an intangible, immeasurable source of energy. It is a blend of hope, toil and ambition. It is the excitement generated by opportunities to break through previously impenetrable barriers of class and social standing. It is the movement generated by people on the climb: the bricklayers becoming builders, the clerks becoming supervisors, the cooks becoming restaurateurs."

That sort of human capital is not caught by such conventional measures as years of schooling–though here, too, immigrants have the edge. The median immigrant has 12.8 years of schooling, compared to 12.5 for his native-born counterpart. Indeed, a Statistics Canada review of 1991 census data, *Canada's Changing Immigrant Population*, indicates the "quality" of the immigrant population has been rising in recent years, even as the proportion passing through the points system has been falling. The obsession of so many with the supposed decline in quality of recent immigrants is out of all proportion to the available evidence. Studies purporting to show a decline generally use data from the early 1980s–a period of unusually restrictive entry–or else focus on those just off the proverbial boat, who always, in any period, underperform the average.

While immigrants form a slightly smaller proportion of the labor force than native-born Canadians, that's due to earlier arrivals, not later: Immigrants of the 1960s, 70s and 80s have higher than average participation rates. Immigrants are also, on average, more likely to be highly educated than those born in Canada: 14.4 percent have a university degree, compared with 10.5 percent among the native-born population. Of the more recent immigrants, arriving between 1981 and 1991, 17 percent had a university degree, compared with nine percent of those arriving before 1961. More than 55 percent of total immigrants are professional, skilled or semiskilled workers; that proportion has been rising steadily since the early 1980s and now stands at an all-time high.

The social characteristics of immigrants are even more striking. According to Statistics Canada, immigrants are more likely to be married than the average Canadian (66 percent to 52 percent), 22 percent less likely to be divorced. Fewer children of immigrants live with only one parent: 12 percent, in 1986, compared with more than 14 percent. Perhaps because of this stronger family structure, immigrants are, notwithstanding a few high-profile cases, less likely to land in jail than the rest of us, accounting for barely half as many penitentiary inmates in 1991 as their share of the population would warrant. (Similar results have been reported in Australia and the United States; the same trend has consistently been observed in Canada for several decades.) They are more likely to own their own home, more likely to be self-employed, save more, have higher net worths—in short, the very model of the stable, self-reliant citizen we profess to admire.

What about the cost of resettlement and language programs? The Economic Council estimated the combined cost to the federal and provincial governments to be about $20 per capita annually. The federal share this year, $271 million, includes the social assistance costs of refugee applicants, who were until recently prohibited from working while their claims were assessed. This $271 million is about a fifth as much as immigrants transfer directly to native-born taxpayers every year, not counting any gains from scale economies and the like. The difficulties of integration are wildly overstated in any case. While it is true that 40 percent to 50 percent of current immigrants speak neither English nor French on arrival, within three years that proportion has halved, and within eight years it has halved again. The 1991 census recorded only 378,000 Canadians who spoke neither official language.

Likewise, the Economic Council's research on popular attitudes towards immigrants, especially visible minorities, confirms what ought to be obvious from any reading of our own history: Familiarity breeds respect. The Council's study drew on 62 public opinion surveys between 1975 and 1990, on subjects such as the acceptability of interracial marriages and other indicators of "social distance." It found that the higher the proportion of visible minority immigrants in a community, such as one might find in Toronto or Vancouver, the more tolerant was popular opinion of racial or ethnic differences. Likewise, if found increasingly favorable attitudes over time towards both the level and composition of immigration. The exceptions were in periods of high unemployment or rapid change in the ethnic makeup of immigrants, both of which might be regarded as transitional stages.

It is often said that today's mix of immigrants differs from [that of] the past. Whatever distinctions existed among people from diverse European countries, it is argued, pale (as it were) beside the differences between Europeans and, say, Asians or Africans. But this perspective views the past through today's eyeglasses. Social differences that today seem trivial, such as between Catholic and Protestant, were once the stuff of civil wars (in some places, they still are). The charge of being unable to "fit in" has been leveled against every arriving immigrant group, in every succeeding wave: the Irish, the Germans, the Ukrainians, even the English. It was not uncommon at the turn of the century to see help-wanted ads accompanied by the admonition "No English Need Apply" since, as it was explained to a visiting English journalist, "the Englishman is too cocksure; he is too conceited, he thinks he knows everything and he won't try to learn our ways." The founder of Canadian socialism, J.S. Woodsworth, demanded that "non-assimilable elements" should be "vigorously excluded," while in Quebec, Henri Bourassa, the great French-Canadian nationalist, stormed that Canada had become "a refuge for the scum of all nations." Somehow the country survived.

Immigrants from the Third World are in fact among the most eager to participate in Canadian society, from politics to business to the arts. Asian and African immigrants apply for Canadian citizenship, for example, an average of five years after arriving, compared to the 15 years typical of American or Western European immigrants. Multiculturalism may be official policy, but in *The Illusion of Difference: Realities of Ethnicity in Canada and the United States*, University of Toronto sociologists Jeffrey Reitz and Raymond Breton show that, far from the "mosaic" of mythology, immigrants to Canada assimilate into the mainstream faster than their American counterparts. There is little tendency to ethnic segregation in Canadian cities, other studies have found, and what there is shows up less among visible minorities than other groups: "It is scarcely sensible to talk of ghettos in Canadian cities," concludes sociologist John Mercer. Rates of ethnic endogamy—marriage within the ethnic group—have been falling since 1931. Less than 10 percent of Canadians speak a language other than English or French at home. We are not Babel, and we are not about to become one. So long as we avoid minefields like multiculturism, antiracism and employment equity—which many immigrants themselves oppose—the country shows every sign of tolerating its differences tolerably well.

Nonetheless, communitarians fret that immigration will irreparably alter our national culture and identity in some indefinable fashion. Probably it will. What of it? What is the Canadian way of life? Which one should we choose? Today's? That of 50 years ago? One hundred years ago? The chauvinism this implies is not so much directed against outsiders as against anything but the here and now. It is a false conservatism, a myopic fixation on the present, the product of what G.K. Chesterton decried as "the small and arrogant oligarchy of those who merely happen to be walking about at the time." The way of life that nativists fear is in jeopardy would itself be unrecognizable to an earlier generation of nativists, who themselves struggled to preserve a way of life entirely novel to the generation before. Our culture exists not only in the present, but over time. It does not belong only to us, but to all who went before and all who will come after. It is an organic whole, a constantly evolving, living thing. When we deny that evolution, we are not preserving our culture, we are embalming it....

Ultimately, however, this issue cannot be resolved empirically. Those who believe that Canada is "full" are no more likely to be persuaded by mere statistical evidence than the chief executives of tobacco companies. No matter how many studies may conclude that the effects of immigration are on balance positive, the true nativist will not be shaken from his fundamentalist faith. And so long as the case for immigration is put in empirical terms, it remains hostage to next year's study. What if it were found that immigration's effects were negative? Would that make the case for shutting the doors?

Only if you accept the underlying premise of the restrictionists: That the existing members of a nation-state should have the power to stop others from joining them; that the right of citizenship should depend not on a willingness to assume its obligations, but on the accident of birth. "Citizenship in Western liberal democracies is the modern equivalent of feudal privilege—an inherited status that greatly enhances one's life chances," University of Toronto political scientist Joseph Carens has written. "Like feudal birthright privileges, restrictive citizenship is hard to justify when one thinks about it closely."

The true case for open immigration depends not on its advantages or otherwise to the native-born population, but rather on the simple observation that all human beings are created equal. As such, we are obliged to consider not only our losses (if any), but their gains. Immigrants typically start out much poorer than other Canadians. So each dollar in income adds more to the average immigrant's quality of life than the average native-born Canadian loses from an equivalent decline in income. If that sounds too altruistic, try this thought experiment, made famous by the philosopher John Rawls. Suppose, in deciding what immigration policy to choose, we did not yet know which ticket we ourselves would draw in the lottery of life: Canadian-born, or foreign-born. We should then be obliged to decide in a way that would be fair to all. Indeed, it would be in our own interest to ensure both groups had an equal right to live in Canada, lest we find ourselves among those left outside.

If that is the case, then it is just as wrong to keep them out as to keep us in. On what basis, then, do we distinguish between the right to emigrate and the right to immigrate? The former is unquestionably a moral absolute, one of the first points of distinction between free and unfree states. If a Canadian wishes to leave the country, we pride ourselves on his freedom to do so. It would violate his human rights, we say, to prevent him from living where he chooses. Yet that is what we do to immigrants. If it were suggested that, in order to upgrade the labor stock of the country, we subject native-born Canadians to the "points test" and deport anyone who failed, decent people would likewise recoil in horror. Yet we cheerfully put those born elsewhere through this same degrading ritual.

Immigration undoubtedly has some unpleasant social side effects. But so does emigration. If Canada were to start hemorrhaging people by the hundreds of thousands, the effect on those remaining would be bleak. Think of East Germany after the wall. If anything, emigration is more disruptive. Which is worse for society—to have too many doctors or too few?

Whatever the effects of immigration, moreover, they are surely no greater than those induced by internal population movements. Consider first the vast annual influx of newborn children. In 1960, at the height of the baby boom, the crop of new arrivals numbered 480,000—twice current immigration levels into a population barely half as large. Without doubt, this historic demographic bulge has had untold consequences, good and bad, for society. Yet no one suggested that, to avoid this disruption, women should be prevented from giving birth. At the same time, the work force was being invaded by millions of women, many of them unskilled; in 30 years, the participation rate has doubled, from 30 percent to 60 percent, causing an enormous social upheaval, at home and at work. Yet no one demanded that their numbers be restricted in line with some alchemistic calculation of "absorptive capacity."

Only when a national border is crossed does the movement of people suddenly become an issue. When hundreds of thousands of people migrate from province to province every year—British Columbia absorbed 85,000 people from other provinces in 1992, plus 37,000 immigrants from other lands, for a total per capita rate of immigration four times that of Canada—they are not put through endless hearings to divine whether they are moving for economic or political reasons. Just as when, earlier, millions of people migrated from the country to the city, they did not have to climb a wall to get in.

Why not? Because people have, we recognize, a right to live and work where they choose. But somehow, those who are not Canadian citizens are not considered to possess the same rights.

For some rights, restrictions are defensible. We would not extend the right to vote in Canadian elections to citizens of other countries. We pay the taxes, we get to vote. These are rights of citizenship. But we would not deprive someone of the right to, say, a fair trial, merely because he was not a Canadian citizen. That was confirmed in 1985, when the Supreme Court ruled that refugee claimants were protected by the Charter of Rights and Freedoms. Some rights, in other words, are portable. They inhere in the individual himself, whatever his nationality, solely by virtue of his humanity. These are human rights. The freedom to live where one likes, subject to the laws of the state in which one finds oneself, is surely one of those rights. It is not a right of citizenship in itself; it merely qualifies one to become a citizen.

I am not suggesting we impose no controls on immigration, but only that we apply the principle of "national treatment," familiar from the free trade debate. The same rules should determine which persons are fit to live and work among us, whether they were born here or elsewhere. That would permit excluding escaped criminals and other threats to society, and, in the rare cases where necessary, quarantining those with highly infectious diseases. Other than that, no special rules need apply.

Once we stop looking at immigrants as something other than ourselves, we see that many of the problems commonly identified with immigration are in fact problems of the whole society. Even if it were true, for example, that too many immigrants were trapped on welfare, that's not an immigration problem, it's a welfare problem. Fix the incentives in the system, and most people will choose to work, wherever they are from. If it is important to instil Canadian values in immigrants it is no less essential to instil those same values in Canadians born here. Indeed, an understanding of what it means to choose to be a Canadian might prove enlightening to the rest of us. How many Canadians have ever heard the oath of allegiance a new citizen learns by heart?

Perhaps there is a limit to Canada's "absorptive capacity." But no one knows what it is, much less how to calculate it. All we know is what we are used to, which is no guide to anything....

An open immigration policy invariably provokes the sovereignty argument—that open immigration denies the very legal basis of nation-states, that is, self-determination.

Certainly a state has the legal power to declare limits on immigration; only its moral right to do so is in question. A state is no less sovereign with open borders than with closed; it is no less an act of sovereignty to renounce immigration controls than it is to impose them. A state obviously has a right to defend itself against armed invasion, or to protect its citizens' property from unlawful seizure. But immigrants are not coming to take our land: They are coming to bid for it, to buy or rent property the same as anyone else. The right of self-determination, so far as it has any meaning, means only that a given people living in a given territory has the right to govern itself according to its own laws. If immigrants agree to be found by the same laws, that condition is not disturbed.

The thought of open immigration also provokes some variant of "it's our country," usually accompanied by an analogy to home ownership. This is the community argument, nicely summarized by Jack Pickersgill, Louis St. Laurent's immigration minister. "Immigration is a privilege which we have a perfect right to grant or deny as we see fit," he said. "When an alien applies for admission to Canada, he is like someone applying for membership in a club."

The property rights analogy—that our right to restrict immigration is akin to membership in a club or an individual's right to forbid entry to his house—rests on a false foundation. There cannot be a collective ownership of something called Canada. Property rights have already been assigned throughout. There is private property, and there is public property. The sum of private plus public property equals all the territory of Canada. To assert, in the name of community, a sort of overarching third right to property is to negate the first two.

Certainly a society, like a club, is entitled to dictate certain terms of membership. But whatever terms apply must apply equally to all, and all who meet these terms should have equal right to admission. The social contract cannot be so defined as to exclude a class of people from even the choice of accepting it or rejecting it.

Why not? That's what clubs do, isn't it? But what clubs may do, the state may not. A private group may use any grounds it pleases in deciding who it will allow to join it. But the state, having authority over every inhabitant of a given territory, carries with it the obligation of equal treatment, without regard to national origin. (Indeed, it is even debatable whether clubs, being neither wholly public nor wholly private organizations, may decide who to admit on just any basis: Connections, comportment, or ability to pay may be acceptable grounds, but not, increasingly, race or sex.)

"To say that membership is open to all who wish to join is not to say that there is no distinction between members and non-members," writes the University of Toronto's Carens. "Those who choose to cooperate together in the state have special rights and obligations not shared by non-citizens.... What is not readily compatible with the ideal of equal moral worth is the exclusion of those who want to join. If people want to sign the social contract, they should be permitted to do so."

So even though states obviously have the power to restrict immigration, they cannot claim a philosophical justification for it, whether in property rights or self-determination. What's left? We were here first? But if by "we" you mean anyone but the aboriginal people, we weren't. The laws we now apply to others would have kept our own grandfathers out. Far from fearing immigration, we ought to embrace it as part of our national mission. Not only was Canada founded on it, the migration of peoples is the very motive force of human history. As my *Encyclopaedia Britannica* notes, as late as A.D. 900, "there was not one German in Berlin, not one Russian in Moscow, not one Hungarian in Budapest; Madrid was a Moorish settlement; no Turks lived in Ankara, and the few in what is now Istanbul were slaves and mercenaries."

Every Canadian schoolchild knows the proud boast of Sir Wilfrid Laurier that the 20th century would be Canada's. Very few know what it was based on: immigration. "For the next 75 years, nay the next 100 years, Canada shall be the star towards which all men who love progress and freedom shall come," Laurier said in 1904. "There are men living in this audience ... who before they die ... will see this country with at least 60 millions of people." This was only a commonplace of the time. "Growing, growing, growing," Stephen Leacock saw his country, "with a march that will make us 10 millions tomorrow, 20 millions in our children's time and a 100 millions ere the century runs out."

As every schoolchild also knows, neither prediction came true. As the century winds down, Canadians are edgily aware their country has failed to live up to its potential. Could the contrast between our present timorousness and the robust self-confidence of Laurier's day be linked to the shift in immigration policy? Many of our difficulties, indeed, stem directly from the scarcity of our population. The insecurity of our position relative to the United States is only the most obvious result. It shows itself, too, in our internal imbalances, in the vast spaces between us that weaken our sense of connection to one another. To be so few in number makes us more prone to domination by narrow elites, whether in business, politics or the media. It is reflected in the parochialism of our concerns, in the mediocrity of our expectations, in our relative insignificance on the world stage. And mostly, in lost momentum.

We first began to lose our way as a nation when we rejected free trade in 1911; when we shut down mass immigration, we threw away all hope of greatness. Within the cloister of our borders, Canada retreated into self-delusion and provincialism. And of all the many myths we have spun about ourselves, the worst is this: That we have done well enough, thank you, and have nothing left to do. We have become a caretaker society, when we have much work before us.

Laurier's century is not out. In a rededication to greatness, we can rediscover our sense of common purpose. Indeed, the very act of opening the borders would be a tonic in itself. Liberty and community need not be opposed, where the community is rooted in the values of liberty. Far from weakening our sense of nationhood, free immigration offers the hope of planting it in firmer soil: a nationalism with nativism. As long as immigration is still a matter of deciding how many we should "let" in, we remain stuck in the national identity cul-de-sac, forever obsessed with defining the differences between "us" and "them." Free immigration, on the other hand, recalls Laurier's sense of the nation as a gathering, like a crowd that draws nearer to hear a speaker, its cohesion growing as its numbers swell. A nation, it says, is not something you are, it's something you join.

We might then come to see the border not as a barrier, but as a contour line, defining only where a common system of laws prevails, and no more. Like borders, nations and states would still exist. They just wouldn't define themselves by their ability to exclude others. Nations would then be understood not as immutable divisions of humanity, but as self-determined associations of free people, distinguished not by the trivial differences of race or culture, but in the diverse paths to justice they pursue. In this model, the individual, the nation and humanity are but points on a continuum; the nation is the means by which the individual is led to that wider allegiance he owes humanity.

Free immigration seems radical only because of the moral blind spot that allows us to look upon immigrants as having lesser human rights than ourselves. It may be the convention now to restrict immigration, but we should not be so vain as to think it the natural order of things. It has not "always been this way," nor need it be in future. The idea that the state should concern itself with restricting the flow of people across its borders will seem in time as quaint as the notion that cities should have walls seems today. The issue thus turns not on what we can do for immigrants or on what they can do for us, but on the simple recognition, long delayed, of our common humanity—city to nation to world, the completion of the paradigm shift begun five centuries ago.

To forbid people from spending their short time on earth in whatever place offers them the best chance for a happy and fulfilling life will then seem a peculiarly backward and selfish tyranny, the more so given the false assumption—that immigration harms, rather than helps, the host community—on which it is based. The course before us, then, is clear: It is to open our hearts, open our eyes—and open the doors.

✗ **NO**

Why States Are Justified in Limiting Their Entry of Migrants

G.E. DIRKS

Human migration is a phenomenon that stretches back to the earliest days of our species. The factors motivating ancient and contemporary migration are numerous, many of them arising from prevailing economic conditions but others reflecting chronically undesirable political and social circumstances. Today, it is estimated that more than 100 million people globally are outside their states of origin, and the number is expected to rise significantly during the next quarter-century. Some of the people on the move have travelled comparatively short distances, seeking an improved life in neighbouring countries, often in Africa, Asia, and South and Central America, regions considered by North American standards as less developed and frequently containing politically unstable governments. Yet in relative terms, such destinations are nevertheless seen by millions of people as better locations than where they are now. Other migrants, usually with a small nest egg and a greater amount of initiative than most, have travelled greater distances to destinations in the developed, affluent, and stable parts of the world, including Canada, in search of what they hope will be economic prosperity, social security, and political tranquillity. These millions of migrants, if no effective restrictive steps are taken, soon will be joined by sizable numbers of despairing relatives, friends, and acquaintances, all examples of what is labelled "chain migration." These desperate people are fleeing from such conditions as poverty, urban squalor, famine, environmental degradation, political oppression, and civil unrest. Such would-be migrants, whether seeking nearby or distant destinations, routinely possess minimal wealth, few occupational skills, and limited education. They are all pushed by intolerable conditions at home and are pulled by the expectation of improved living conditions elsewhere.

This essay contends that massive worldwide migration and its anticipated intensification in the near future demands some strong action by the governments of both sending and destination states, aimed at its management and constraint. The argument that follows asserts that international migration cannot and should not be entirely prevented or curtailed. It can and must, however, be effectively channelled and regulated. The position adopted here is not particularly derived from moral philosophy but, rather, has its basis in the widely endorsed neorealist paradigm, primarily that aspect relating to the ongoing preeminence of the principles underlying the sovereign state. While the classical concept of sovereignty may be under some challenge today from a number of factors and forces, one cannot convincingly question that the world is still organized into sovereign states, such as Canada, that possess the legitimate capacity to coerce when necessary and owe their citizens protection and security from external and internal threats to their physical, economic, social, and cultural well-being. Thus, this paper argues that governments, Canada's being no exception, continue to have the obligation to adopt policies for the overall benefit of their existing populations. The claims of outsiders wishing to enter a state are superseded by the principles of national sovereignty. There is an obligation to do what is best for the state's own citizens. One widely accepted role for governments in an effort to protect the prevailing culture and way of life of citizens is to determine who and how many newcomers will be either temporarily or permanently welcomed into their midst.

Humans are social creatures and have organized themselves into groups or communities that as early as the 17th century in Europe came to be known as sovereign states. These political entities strive to achieve and maintain control over their own affairs and protect their societies' territories, values, and culture. State communities, particularly but not exclusively ethnically homogeneous ones, are frequently closely knit entities, possessing strong emotional attachments based on a number of factors, including a common language, religion, and history. Many communities have acquired the status of sovereign states. Such states then provide their societies with the legitimate capacity to establish rules aimed at preserving overall group identity and aspects of life that are deemed desirable. Moreover, governments, acting for the state, can determine the grounds for the admission or rejection of persons wishing to gain temporary or permanent entry into the society. Community members tend to believe that outsiders—foreigners, in common parlance—may not share the prevailing culture, preferences, and value system, and thus such aliens are to be shunned or excluded. Those outsiders, however, who may ultimately be accepted into the society will need to possess characteristics the community members find to be similar to their own or believe the would-be newcomer can quickly acquire. While states like Canada have numerous purposes, the focus in this essay is on their role as agents for protecting and preserving what their societies or members consider valuable. Screening aliens so as not to endanger the prevailing general welfare of society constitutes one of the fundamental tasks the Canadian and other governments fulfill.

The impetus for communities to gain independence so as to govern themselves is extremely powerful and pervasive and is not easily neutralized, as the inexorable move to self-determination for peoples around the world this past century has indicated. Once the status of sovereignty has been attained, liberal democratic traditions call for states to be in a position to offer their societies, through responsive and accountable governments, orderliness, stability, and protection from threats, whether they emanate from within or beyond the territorial preserve of the community. With respect to discouraging immigration, the state sets out to prevent the entry of aliens perceived to be actually or potentially capable of destabilizing the community by proving to be an economic burden or by not adhering to the prevailing values and popular expectations.

The intensification of the sense of threat to what is valued has become especially apparent among those states having limited or unpleasant experiences with foreigners and whose citizens feel they have most to lose. Frequently, these are the comparatively affluent countries of the North, where a semi–siege mentality has in some instances taken root. Western and Southern European societies illustrated this first, adopting an attitude of "drawing the wagons into a circle" during the mid- and late 1980s. More latent but nevertheless still noticeable strains of this anxiety are to be found today even in states with long traditions of admitting immigrants, such as the United States, Canada, and Australia. Today, even refugees, the recipients in the past of genuine and profound humanitarian concern in many developed countries like Canada, who were offered sanctuary, sustenance, and at times permanent residence, are no longer welcome. This reticence is understandable. Migrants of all types are perceived today by formerly generous societies as an unneeded burden and a drain on social service budgets. Given the endless number of human tragedies that have followed on the heels of other tragedies, we should not be surprised to be witnessing among developed countries growing signs of compassion fatigue.

In many cases, the population constituting the society of a state places profound importance on preserving and even strengthening its sense of identity and belonging. This sense of identity has taken generations to develop and flourish and ranks high among the desired features or values shared by members of a state's society. Communities with concern for the viability and durability of their identity may perceive would-be migrants as an unwanted threat. Governments of such states will be expected to take steps through legislation and regulation to limit or eradicate threats to societal identify. While it is not a sovereign state—at least at the time this piece is written—the Canadian province of Quebec is a good example of a society that perceives itself as culturally vulnerable and where the provincial authorities strenuously work to protect the French language and other valued cultural features of the society.

Governments, acting on behalf of their citizens, confronted by actual or potential demands from aliens for entry into their communities, are, not surprisingly, compelled to choose a variety of cost-benefit analyses when evaluating the question of admission. Certainly, the positive aspects of admitting immigrants can be significant. Would-be newcomers may, in some instances, provide needed labour. Similarly, immigrants, if legally in the country, can be expected to pay taxes, thereby contributing to the public treasury. But the perception in many countries today is that the immediate and long-term costs of admitting large numbers of migrants outweigh any benefits. Here it is important to recognize the possible distinction between perceived and actual costs. It is, after all, what governments and their citizens believe, even if it is not or only partly valid, that usually prompts legislative and other action. Thus, if societies and their leaders perceive an unacceptable cost, not only a financial cost, to be the result of large-scale migrant admission, policies to prevent this are in order.

In most cases, the anticipated negative economic implications of immigrant entry, often assumed to be probable by the home society, play a major part in determining the responses of destination countries. As crucial as these anxieties are in comparatively affluent countries, they may be still more acute for less-developed states and their societies. In these latter situations, authorities may be unable to provide basic necessities for their own citizens. Permitting outsiders from neighbouring countries to freely enter their territories can only exacerbate already desperate economic and social conditions. For the "have" countries, the economic costs might be less, but for their citizens, already complaining about high taxes and large national debts, the idea of thousands of migrants being added to welfare rolls, drawing upon medical and educational services, and seeking other types of subsidization, is highly irritating and exposes responsible, accountable governments such as Canada's to the potential wrath of the electorate. In the past decade, grassroots movements in several European states, concerned about economic and social costs and not accustomed to admitting immigrants, have fuelled extremist political parties and resulted in restrictive moves against potential newcomers by those parties already in power. In North America, anti-immigrant propositions have appeared on ballots in California and other American states accommodating large numbers of legal and illegal foreigners. Similarly, in larger Canadian cities, municipal authorities and school boards have expressed alarm over the funds needed to mount language programs for non–English-speaking people already here, let alone for those yet to come.

Destination states have been the focus of this essay to this point. This reflects the prevailing circumstances whereby governments of sending states have done comparatively little to discourage population outflow. At least three considerations account for this. First, the funds or remittances migrants send back to their families and friends in the homeland are substantial, even enormous by some standards. These funds quickly enter the economies of those countries. The treasuries of such countries as Bangladesh, the Philippines, and smaller states in Africa and the Western hemisphere obtain a vast amount, in some cases the majority of their foreign exchange, usually desperately needed hard currencies, from such remittances. Second, unrestricted emigration provides a useful safety valve to release pressure in societies where high rates of unemployment can contribute to social unrest and potential political instability for the governments of such states. Third, there have been few occasions, since migration pressures have intensified, in which the governments of destination countries have meaningfully striven to involve sending-state governments in deliberations aimed at regulating and managing global migration. Thus, for these and other reasons, authorities in sending countries see little if any justification for impeding population outflow, especially as in several United Nations conventions and declarations, the freedom to exit one's homeland is considered a right. With the establishment of liberal democratic political systems in the former communist countries of Central Europe and the disintegration of the Soviet Union, governments have adopted these freedom-of-exit principles and hundred of thousands of migrants have exercised this right. There is, of course, no equivalent right of entry to another state.

Some destination countries today are treating population pressures at their frontiers and at ports of entry as a question of genuine national security. Security can be an elusive concept. Fundamentally, it calls upon government to not only protect the territory of the state but also to prevent threats to the overall well-being of society. Included in the provision of security is the task of precluding any feeling among citizens that the community is in danger of being culturally or politically overwhelmed. Under this admittedly expanded definition of security, the perceived danger is not from conventional military aggression but rather from threats to societal stability and economic well-being potentially the result of any mass entry of unwanted immigrants. Concern for the maintenance of stability within the state is a particularly high priority for governments. Unwanted cross-border population movements can create or exacerbate conflict and social disharmony. In some instances, it has proven to be easier to defend the state and its citizens against the threat of military aggression than from challenges caused by uncontrolled mass migration.

To this point, this essay has asserted that the ability to freely enter a state other than the one we are born in cannot be considered as a basic human right. The claims of outsiders wishing to enter are superseded by the principles of state sovereignty. A state's first obligation is to its own society. This essay does not question that the contemporary world contains innumerable economic, political, and social inequities and injustices. Opening borders to permit the unimpeded flow of millions of people, however, will not halt or prevent these inequities and injustices, deplorable as they may be. Conceivably, opening state frontiers in those destination countries most attractive to would-be migrants would result in horrific consequences. Unprecedented strains would be placed on every aspect of the economic, social, and political infrastructure of the so-called affluent states, causing the standards of living, measured by any criteria, to plunge. In fact, the conditions in the formerly desirable destination state would reflect those in the states of origins being evacuated by the migrants.

Individually, the citizens in liberal democratic countries such as Canada have often demonstrated their generosity toward genuine refugees and in other humanitarian causes. Individuals, in fact, may be willing to accommodate an indigent migrant or refugee in their homes, but that is not an argument for a government policy to admit unlimited numbers of people from impoverished states. Personal ethics are not an appropriate basis for making public choices because they do not take into consideration the consequences such choices impose upon others in the community. An act should be judged by its probable consequences and not by its intent. Many well-intentioned policies can have and have had unsettling, unexpected results.

States under the conventions of sovereignty, with primary obligations to their own societies, are justified in selecting and limiting the types of persons permitted to temporarily or permanently gain entry. What options then are available to governments to enable them to effectively enforce the regulations they have established to manage this restricted migration? While the idea of enforcement appears particularly negative and exclusionist, in the final analysis the only approach governments can adopt consists in explicitly indicating and executing regulations and procedures based on the number and types of migrants perceived as desirable. With this in mind, and as an example, what course has Canada adopted?

Put succinctly, Canada's approach to immigration for at least a quarter-century has been to base admissions policy on three categories of potential arrivals: family, refugee, and independent. During the 1990s, the annual number of persons accepted for permanent settlement from all categories has stood at approximately 200 000, a figure deplored by many critics who argue that Canada's absorptive capacity is far less. Efforts are made by officials to ensure that the family class does not dominate the annual intake level, although it regularly exceeds one-third of yearly arrivals. Refugees, as defined by the United Nations, constitute approximately ten to fifteen percent of annual arrivals, reflecting Canada's long-standing commitment to humanitarian and compassionate principles. The independent class is composed of persons selected because of a number of criteria weighing their attributes. Points are awarded on the basis of such aspects as education, employment skills, language capabilities, and age.

By the early 1990s, the Canadian government, reflecting growing public anxiety, adopted a series of immigration policy and regulatory modifications aimed at addressing a number of problems perceived as threats to Canada's values and self-interests. Some of the issues of concern to the public and government included the following: an enormous, unmanageable backlog of applications from would-be immigrants; the rising costs to the Canadian treasury of administering the prevailing policy; the need to avoid a migrant onslaught at Canada's ports of entry as European countries close their doors to migrants; the increase in the number of aliens seeking to enter with fraudulent identity documents or no papers at all; and the unprecedented demands on government education, health, and welfare budgets from migrants requiring language training or waiting to have claims for refugee status resolved.

In an attempt to respond to these and other factors, legislation came into force in 1993 placing a cutoff point on the number of applications for entry officials would annually accept, enabling the priority for processing applicants among the three admissible classes to be altered, and tightening controls to restrict still further the admission of illegal migrants, often people with fraudulent or no identification papers.

Canada continues to be one of the few countries that maintain an active immigration program. But as this paper has argued, increased controls on international migration, even by comparatively liberal societies such as Canada's, are essential and are being strengthened to maintain a way of life believed to be worth preserving. The Canadian regulations pale compared with restrictions adopted by countries not seeing themselves as needing or wanting foreign newcomers. By embracing rigorous control methods, governments do so with the approval of their societies as well as of the conventions of sovereignty and international law. The time when open borders become the norm in our world of sovereign states is certainly nowhere in sight.

Inequities persist throughout the world. Yet, with technological advances in communications such as television, videos, and the Internet, tens of millions of people who experience poverty and oppression are now acutely aware of the comparatively better lives led by others in Europe, North America, and parts of Australia. Moreover, improvements in transportation now facilitate the movement of people over large distances. Humanity now finds itself embroiled in a profoundly serious competition between desperate, innovative people with little to lose striving to move to more attractive destinations and the governments of those destination states doing more and more to limit if not prevent the entry of these people. The state, with its monopoly on the legitimate use of coercion to enforce laws and regulations, now stands the best chance of achieving its objectives. Nevertheless, the would-be migrants will persist in their efforts to move until circumstances in their own communities are made more tolerable. And when will that be?

BIBLIOGRAPHY

Appleyard, R. *International Migration: Challenge for the Nineties.* Geneva: International Organization for Migration, 1992.

Castles, S., and M. Miller. *The Age of Migration.* New York: Guilford Press, 1993.

Collinson, S. *Europe and International Migration.* London: Pinter Publishers, 1993.

Dirks, G.E. *Controversy and Complexity: Immigration Policy-Making in the 1980s.* Montreal and Kingston: McGill-Queen's University Press, 1995.

———. "International Migration in the Nineties: Causes and Consequences." *International Journal* 48, no. 2 (1993).

Freeman, G. "Can Liberal States Control Unwanted Migration?" *Annals of the American Academy of Political and Social Sciences* 534 (July 1994).

Jervis, R. *Perception and Misperception in International Politics.* Princeton, NJ: Princeton University Press, 1976.

Keely, C., and S. Russell. "Responses of Industrialized Countries to Asylum-Seekers." *Journal of International Affairs* 47, no. 2 (Winter 1994).

Loescher, G. *Beyond Charity: International Cooperation and the Global Refugee Crisis.* New York: Oxford University Press, 1993.

Weiner, M. "Ethics, National Sovereignty and the Control of Immigration." *International Migration Review* 30, no. 1 (Spring 1996).

———. *The Global Migration Crisis: Challenge to States and Human Rights.* New York: HarperCollins, 1995.

Weiner, M. (ed.). *International Migration and Security.* Boulder, CO: Westview Press, 1993.

Postscript

The issue of immigration poses a number of difficult dilemmas. Is immigration a fundamental human right? The United Nations Universal Declaration of Human Rights and the Helsinki Accords assert the universal right of emigration. If emigration is a fundamental human right, how do we reconcile this with claims of states to national sovereignty and the right to control immigration? If governments have the right to determine whom they will admit and to whom they will grant citizenship, what criteria should be used to make these decisions? Whom exactly do states have an obligation to admit? Refugees? Migrants from poor countries? Only those who have the skills and cultural background deemed necessary to contribute to society? Should those who want to reunite with family members already in Canada be given preference?

This issue cannot be discussed without some reference to the increased concerns about terrorism and the need for stricter border controls. Since Canada has been an immigrant nation, its future vitality, as Coyne argues, depends on maintaining fairly high levels of immigration. How can this necessity be reconciled with fears that immigration must be more tightly regulated in order to keep out suspected terrorists?

Infotrac Keyword Search
"immigration policy"

Suggested Additional Readings

Carens, Joseph. "Aliens and Citizens: The Case for Open Borders." *The Review of Politics* 49, no. 2 (Spring 1987): 251–73.

_____. "Realistic and Idealistic Approaches to the Ethics of Migration." *International Migration Review* 30, no. 1 (Spring 1996): 156–69.

Dirks, Gerald E. *Controversy and Complexity: Canadian Immigration Policy During the 1980s.* Montreal: McGill-Queen's University Press, 1995.

Hawkins, Freda. *Canada and Immigration: Public Policy and Public Concern.* Montreal: McGill-Queen's University Press, 1998.

Knowles, V. *Strangers at Our Gates: Canadian Immigration and Immigration Policy, 1540–1997.* Toronto: Dundurn, 1997.

Weiner, Myron. "Ethics, National Sovereignty and the Control of Immigration." *International Migration Review* 30, no. 1 (Spring 1996): 171–97.

_____. *The Global Migration Crisis.* New York: HarperCollins, 1995.

_____ and Rainer Münz. "Migrants, Refugees and Foreign Policy: Prevention and Intervention Strategies." *Third World Quarterly* 18, no. 1 (1997): 25–51.

Website Resources

Center for Immigration Studies According to its homepage, the Center for Immigration Studies "is animated by a pro-immigrant, low-immigration vision which seeks fewer immigrants but a warmer welcome for those admitted." Has a variety of resources on immigration issues available.

Centre for Refugee Studies (York University) Houses a good collection of resources on refugee issues in particular.

Center for Migration Studies (New York) Although more American-focused, this site houses much useful information on population migration issues.

Citizenship and Immigration Canada Contains the document, "Building on a Strong Foundation for the 21st Century: New Directions for Immigration and Refugee Policy and Legislation," which sets out the Canadian government's current position on immigration.

ISSUE**TWENTY**

Should Political and Civil Rights Always Take Priority over Economic and Social Rights?

✔ **YES**

GEORGE WEIGEL, "The New Human-Rights Debate," *Idealism Without Illusions: U.S. Foreign Policy in the 1990s* (Grand Rapids, MI: Eerdmans, 1994)

✘ **NO**

RON DART, "The New Human Rights Debate: A Reply to George Weigel"

In 1954, when the United Nations Charter was drafted, a number of participants felt strongly that the new organization should deal with the question of universal human rights. They believed that the rise of European fascism and Asian militarism had demonstrated the need for the international community to seek more rigorous means of protecting human rights. U.S. president Franklin Roosevelt had already stressed the importance of four freedoms, including the freedom from "want," as the basis for international peace and security, and First Lady Eleanor Roosevelt had become a prominent proponent for human rights, including the rights of women. In addition, a growing number of intellectuals and nongovernmental organizations campaigned in support of a clearer commitment on the part of the international community to human rights.

As negotiations surrounding the UN Charter unfolded, a growing number of leaders, including Joseph Stalin of the Soviet Union, accepted the inclusion of human rights provisions in the new document. The preamble to the Charter, in its second clause, states that a principal purpose of the United Nations is to "affirm faith in fundamental human rights." And Article 1 of the Charter goes on to state that one of the purposes of the Charter is to promote "respect for human rights and for fundamental freedoms for all without distinction as to race, sex, language, or religion." Later, in Article 55, the Charter states that the United Nations will promote:

a. higher standards of living, full employment, and conditions of economic and social progress and development;
b. solutions of international economic, social, health, and related problems; and international cultural and educational cooperation; and

    c. universal respect for, and observance of, human rights and fundamental freedoms for all without distinction as to race, sex, language, or religion.

Although the wording suggests a fairly broad view of what constitutes human rights, the phrasing of the Charter was still deliberately vague. In making it that way, the framers of the Charter succeeded in codifying a commitment of member countries to human rights without clearly defining what constituted human rights or providing a comprehensive list of them. It was left to the United Nations to spell out more specifically what human-rights principles the Charter would cover.

The first step in the process was the General Assembly's adoption of the Universal Declaration of Human Rights in 1948. Since then more than twenty-five conventions and protocols have covered a range of issues, from political and social rights to economic and cultural rights to the rights of women and a prohibition against slavery.

Although broad in scope, these treaties cover what scholars have identified as three broad clusters of rights. *First-generation negative rights* are those civil and political rights that Western societies take as being fundamental to democratic society. They define the limits of public interference in the lives of private individuals by guaranteeing such rights as freedom of thought, speech, religion, privacy, and assembly. *Second-generation positive rights* deal more with the material needs of populations, obligating governments to take "positive" steps to ensure that their citizens have adequate food, shelter, and health care. *Third-generation solidarity rights* have been increasingly promoted to ensure collective rights, not just the rights of individuals. In some more recent formulations, a right to peace, development, and a healthy environment have been cited as the common heritage of humankind.

As the United Nations has attempted to specify what these rights entail, member states have increasingly been at odds with one another concerning how these rights should be defined and which ones have priority. Western states most readily identify with first-generation civil and political rights, since they are seen as the cornerstone of building a democratic civil society. Third World and socialist countries have long argued for the need to emphasize social, economic, and collective rights as a fundamental basis for economic development and nation-building, even if political and civil rights may have to be given a lower priority.

In the 1970s, the Carter administration placed human rights at the centre of American foreign policy. As a result, the American government appeared to give at least rhetorical support for economic and social rights as an integral part of a global human rights regime. But in the 1980s, with the rise of a more conservative orientation in American politics, the Reagan administration rejected the notion that social, economic, cultural, and collective rights were genuine human rights at all. The call for a narrower definition of human rights that focuses principally on civil and political rights has been heavily influenced by the rise of neo-conservatism as a political force in Western countries.

Representative of this school of thought is George Weigel, former president of the Ethics and Public Policy Center in Washington, DC. The following selection is drawn from his book *Idealism without Illusions: U.S. Foreign Policy in the 1990s.* In this collection of essays, Weigel contends that he wants to go beyond cynical realism and naive idealism to outline "a realistic social ethic of idealism without illusions." He then presents a series of essays to show how such an ethic can be applied to concrete policy issues. In the essay "The New Human-Rights Debate," Weigel critically examines recent United Nations efforts to spell out in clearer detail second- and third-generation rights. He views the effort to give greater priority to economic and social rights as a direct assault on the fundamental principles that underlie a free and democratic society. He calls on the United States to exercise greater leadership by reasserting its tradition of commitment to political and social rights. Ron Dart, a political theorist and former Amnesty International official, critiques Weigel's position while setting out the case for giving social and economic rights increased importance.

✔ YES
The New Human-Rights Debate
GEORGE WEIGEL

In spite of, or perhaps because of, the horrors of the twentieth century, the cause of "human rights" has become one of the most powerful forces in contemporary world politics. Evidence for this is not only to be found in decent societies with a long record of protecting civil rights and political freedoms, or in the recent triumphs of human-rights activists in Solidarity and Charter 77. Compelling proof also lies in the tribute that vice pays to virtue: in the fact that virtually every tyranny in the world today tries to justify its repressions in the name of an "alternative" understanding of "human rights."

The modern human-rights movement has various roots, some of them reaching deep into the cultural subsoil of Western civilization. As Peter L. Berger once put it, a long view of human-rights advocacy today would find evidence of the movement's origins in some of the defining locales and experiences in the history of the West: "in the Temple in Jerusalem, in the *agora* of Athens, in the schools of Jewish rabbis, among Roman jurists and medieval moral philosophers."[1] The deepest of these roots is, I believe, the biblical vision of man as created in the image and likeness of God, as a moral agent with intelligence and free will, and thus endowed (to adopt Mr. Jefferson's language) with a certain "inalienable" dignity. This moral claim—that the individual has an irreducible value and dignity *prior* to his or her "public" status (as citizen, or slave, or indentured servant, or freedman, or member of the aristocracy)—is the sturdiest possible foundation for any scheme of "human rights" that seeks to protect human beings from arbitrary (and often brutal) state power.

Mediated through the reflections of political philosophers during the English and Scottish Enlightenments, this great Western moral understanding shaped the revolution of 1776 and 1787–89 in the United States; its influence is palpable in the most important political self-expressions of the American founders and framers, the Declaration of Independence, the Constitution, and the Bill of Rights. And in this historical tradition, "human rights" meant two thing: *civil liberties*, understood as personal liberties that state power may not abrogate (thus the "right" to freedom of religion, of speech, of association, and of assembly); and *political freedoms*, such as the right to vote, to organize a political opposition, to petition for redress of grievances, and to be judged by a jury of one's peers. "Human rights," on the Anglo-Scottish-American model, meant a societal (and constitutional) recognition that certain spheres of personal and communal activity are to be protected from the tendency of all states (but especially modern states) to expand the reach of their power.

On the other side of the Atlantic, the European discussion of "human rights" was confused by two historical phenomena, not unrelated. The first was the proto-totalitarianism of the Jacobin wing of the French Revolution, which interpreted Rousseau's doctrine of the "general will" to mean that the state had the power (and even the obligation) to trump individual claims to civil rights and political freedoms. The second was the use of the language of "rights" by various Marxist theoreticians to ascribe a thick moral content to their social and economic goals. (An interesting European attempt to employ elements of the human-rights tradition that shaped the American Revolution was the Polish Constitution of May 3, 1791—a tragically short-lived experiment that came to grief just months later.)

In Europe, the older human-rights tradition—the tradition of civil liberties and political freedoms—was revivified by the French philosopher Jacques Maritain in response to the threat of Fascism in the 1930s and the 1940s (a development that would have a profound effect on the human-rights thinking of the Roman Catholic Church, and that helped give birth to post-war Christian Democracy in western Europe and Latin America). But the newer Marxist notion of "social and economic rights" would prove to have considerable staying power in the post–World War II period: among intellectuals and politicians of the Left, and later among various post-colonial Third World leaders.

A TROUBLESOME DECLARATION

That staying power derived in part from the follies committed by Eleanor Roosevelt when she led the drafting of the United Nations' 1948 Universal Declaration of Human Rights, the basic international legal text on the subject. While the Universal Declaration does give priority to civil liberties or civil rights and political freedoms, it also uses the language of "rights" to describe a vast array of social and economic *desiderata*, such as jobs, health care, and education. The historian Arthur M. Schlesinger, Jr., once described the politics of the Declaration in these terms: "The Universal Declaration of Human Rights included both 'civil and political' rights and 'economic, social, and cultural rights,' the second category designed to please states that denied their subjects the first"— which is, perhaps, too charitable an interpretation of the role of Mrs. Roosevelt, who was not unsympathetic to the notion that social and economic goods ought to be described as "rights."[2]

But however responsibility is assigned, the fact remains that the Universal Declaration, for all the good its norms have helped accomplish, has also fostered the confusion, and in some respects the debasement, of the human-rights debate. By using the same language to describe both the immunities an individual holds *against* the state (civil rights) and the claims that an individual is putatively justified in making *on* the state (economic "rights"), the Universal Declaration created an image of moral equivalence that dozens of tyrants turned to their advantage. How many times, during the Cold War, did we hear it said, "Well, *they* just have a different concept of human rights—they think it's more important to provide free health care and to guarantee everybody a job than to have regular elections and a free press"? Too many times, and not by cranks but by presumably serious people. The human-rights curriculum approved by the National Council for the Social Studies in the early 1980s, for example, used precisely this tactic to suggest that the citizens of the oxymoronic People's Republic of China enjoyed a large, if different, range of "human rights."

An American Argument, a European Revolution

These definitional arguments—and the ways in which they were manipulated by dictators of all stripes, but pre-eminently by Communists and their Western apologists—shaped the foreign-policy debate in the United States for a generation. In the 1976 presidential primaries, Senator Henry M. Jackson of Washington, in a challenge to the détente policies of Henry Kissinger, argued that the classic American conception of civil rights and political freedoms had universal applicability and ought to be a central concern of U.S. foreign policy. Jimmy Carter picked up the theme, but once in office his administration distorted it badly: the human-rights bureau in the Carter State Department not only argued for "economic, social, and cultural rights" but seemed to give them priority over civil rights and political freedoms. Moreover, the Carter team showed too little interest in how human rights are institutionalized in societies: which is to say, the Carterites paid very little attention to the linkage between human rights and democracy.

The Reagan administration is typically portrayed as having ignored human rights in its conduct of foreign affairs. But in fact it saved U.S. human-rights policy from terminal silliness—largely through the efforts of two superb appointees to the post of assistant secretary of state for human rights, Elliott Abrams and Richard Schifter. Under Abrams and Schifter, and with strong support from the president and from Secretary of State George Shultz, the priority of civil rights and political freedoms was vigorously asserted; Communist doubletalk about "alternative" human-rights "traditions" was dismissed, correctly, as self-serving propaganda; and the linkage between effective protection of human rights and transitions to democracy became a driving force on policymaking. Though this approach was all too often savaged by the prestige press and by many Democrats, its efficiency is now on display throughout Latin America and in central and eastern Europe.

The latter, of course, was the scene of the contemporary human-rights revolution *par excellence*. Ideologically, strategically, and tactically, the Revolution of 1989 was a direct result of human-rights activism, in many cases inspired by the "Basket Three" provisions of the 1975 Helsinki Final Act. Moreover, in the Revolution of 1989 the prerogatives of genuine democracy were boldly asserted against the hoary Marxist fiction of "people's democracies" and their emphasis on "economic, social, and cultural rights." The transnational and ecumenical resistance community composed of central and eastern European human-rights activists plus kindred spirits and friendly governments in the West was also evidence that "human rights" were not a concern within one political-cultural tradition alone. And during the decade-long run-up to the Revolution of 1989, another institutional actor of great power came onto the scene: led by Pope John Paul II, and drawing on the teachings of the Second Vatican Council, the Roman Catholic Church became perhaps the world's foremost institutional defender of basic human rights, with important results in venues as various as Chile, the Philippines, South Korea, Poland, and what was then Czechoslovakia.

BACK TO SQUARE ONE

The Revolution of 1989 and the New Russian Revolution of 1991 might have been thought to have settled the debate about "human rights." These non-violent revolutions embodied the priority of civil rights and political freedoms: they were revolutions *against* regimes that located no small part of their legitimacy in their putative provision of "economic, social, and cultural rights." The truth, of course, was that there were no "rights," economic, cultural, civil, or otherwise, in Communist societies. Jobs, educational opportunities, and health care were linked to political conformity; literature and art were rigorously policed; and the ubiquity of the secret police gave the lie to any notion of enforceable "civil rights." After the 1989 and 1991 upheavals, it should have been perfectly clear that regimes defending their records on the basis of "alternative" conceptions of human rights are to be viewed with the greatest skepticism.

Alas, it was not to be. The World Conference on Human Rights, held in Vienna under U.N. auspices in June 1993, demonstrated in painful detail how the old rationalizations for tyranny are being recycled: now in the guise of "multiculturalism," but with the same result—people treated as chattels (and worse) by their governments. And, regrettably, the United States did far less than it should have done to reverse this backsliding trend.

The Bangkok Conspirators

The bad guys at Vienna were not exactly shy about what they were up to. Two months before the Vienna conference got under way, they blatantly telegraphed their punch.

At an Asian regional meeting held in Bangkok in April, an unholy alliance of Communists (China and Vietnam), anti-Communists (Indonesia), Middle Eastern despots (Iran and Syria), old-fashioned military thugs (Burma), and the gung-ho capitalist micro-state of Singapore decided that they all had something in common, after all: contempt for the classic notion of "human rights" as civil rights and political freedoms. The "Bangkok Declaration" denied the universality of human rights; such rights, it said, "must be considered in the context of ... national and regional particularities and various historical, cultural, and religious backgrounds."

On its face, and to those unschooled in the arcana of U.N.-speak, this assertion might not seem unreasonable. The cause of human rights surely requires a careful consideration of how different religious and philosophical systems provide moral ground for human-rights claims. And effective protection of such rights over the long haul requires the exercise of common sense when the fragile institutions of a nascent civil society are threatened by fanaticism of one kind or another.

But the bad guys gave the real game away when the Bangkok Declaration went on to "[reaffirm] the interdependence and indivisibility of economic, social, cultural and civil and political rights and the need to give equal emphasis to all categories of human rights," while concurrently insisting that, as the Chinese representative baldly put it, "only when state sovereignty is fully respected can the implementation of human rights really be assured."

Decorous translation: We'll define what we mean by "human rights"; we'll implement that definition however we see fit; and nobody else has any standing to object.

Street translation: Get outta my face.

But not so far out that they can't reach our wallets, for the Bangkok Declaration also made a great to-do about the "right to development," another bit of U.N. argot. Here is the "economic rights" notion turned into an international shakedown: by "right to development," Third World despots have meant the putative "right" to draw Western foreign aid from a virtually unlimited account. The claimants place all the blame for the widespread poverty and suffering of Third World peoples on the greedy hegemons of "the North," blithely ignoring the political, social, economic, and cultural depredations wrought by the post-colonial kleptocracies that have run these societies into the ground.

The "right to development" is the international equivalent of welfare pimping, and the Bangkok Declaration not only endorsed it but gave it another twist by condemning "any attempt to use human rights as a conditionality for extending development assistance." Translation: The fact that Sudan is committing genocide against its Christian population in no way affects its claims to vast sums of development aid money. Ditto for Burma and political dissidents, China and its colonized Tibetans, and so on.

GETTING IT LESS-THAN-HALF RIGHT

The Bangkok Declaration was, among other things, a gauntlet thrown down before the Clinton administration. The Vienna Conference would be the first major international human-rights meeting in which the new administration participated; how would the new kids on the block react?

The policy process leading up to Vienna left much to be desired. Conflicting ideological claims to the mind and soul of the State Department's human-rights bureau had buffeted the administration from start, and the new assistant secretary of state for human rights, John Shattuck, was confirmed only a week before the conference began. More than a few Democrats wanted to revive the Carter approach to human-rights issues; this would have led to a policy in which the United States looked benignly on the "right to development," and might even have resulted in a tacit acceptance of the Bangkok Declaration's denial of the universality of human rights. Others, notably Joshua Muravchik of the American Enterprise Institute (author of *The Uncertain Crusade*, the most telling critique of Carter-administration human-rights policy), argued that the Clintonistas should build on the success of the Abrams/Schifter approach and stress the linkage between human rights and democratization, on one hand, and successful economic and social development, on the other, while avoiding Bushbaker pusillanimity toward such Olympic-class human-rights violators as China.

Because the new administration took so long to staff the State Department (and because State itself has little institutional interest in human-rights matters—leadership on this front comes almost exclusively from political appointees), the United States went to the World Conference on Human Rights in damage-control mode. There were some things we wanted to stop (like a retreat from universality); there were some bones we were willing to throw to our adversaries to get what we wanted; there was some interest in distancing the new administration from its predecessors' policies; but there were no long-term policy goals to guide U.S. participation at Vienna.

The result was an American performance that, viewed from one angle, hit .500 (no mean average in any league), but viewed from another, barely made it over the Mendoza Line (.200).

Secretary of State Warren Christopher's speech to the conference—the defining moment for U.S. policy at Vienna—included a strong defense of the universality of basic human rights. Americans, Christopher noted, "respect the religious, social, and cultural characteristics that make each country unique." But, he immediately continued, "we cannot let cultural relativism become the last refuge of repression." Thus the United States "reject[s] any attempt by any state to relegate its citizens to a lesser standard of human dignity."

Christopher also nailed the hypocrisy of the Bangkok declaration in sharp and uncompromising terms: "There is no contradiction between the universal principles of the [Universal] Declaration and the cultures that enrich our international community. The real chasm lies between the cynical excuses of oppressive regimes and the sincere aspirations of their people." Not bad, that.

Moreover, the Administration backed off from its previous commitment to seek Senate ratification of the "International Covenant on Economic, Social, and Cultural Rights"—a step that would have further damaged the idea of "human rights" by dulling the edge of the claims embedded in civil rights and political freedoms. Christopher also emphasized the linkage between human-rights protections and democracy, and if his rhetoric was less compelling than Ronald Reagan's, the point was nevertheless made.

So why not award Christopher and the U.S. delegation full marks?

Because what the United States asserted in Christopher's speech it then significantly undercut by accepting a conference Final Document that contradicts the secretary's key points in several crucial respects.

The Vienna Declaration

The Vienna Declaration of the World Conference on Human Rights is not reading material for the faint of heart or the stylistically squeamish. Thirty-three densely packed pages of rhetoric—divided into the standard "preambular" ("Considering ... recognizing ... re-affirming ... emphasizing ..." etc., etc.), a thirteen-page statement of principles, and a sixteen-page "action plan"—were agreed to by 183 nations on the basis of "consensus."

A "consensus" process in international meetings is one in which everybody has to agree on everything for anything at all to get done. (One Helsinki Accord's review conference was held up for weeks because Malta—Malta!—got into a snit and "refused consensus.") In Vienna, "consensus" meant that the final vote had to be 183–0 or there would be no final document. The consensus process often sets up negotiating dynamics in which countries whose governments could be criticized by their publics for "wrecking the conference"—by digging in their heels, for example, on points of moral or political principle—are at a serious disadvantage. Syria, Burma, Vietnam, and China can be as obscurantist and difficult as they want, secure in the knowledge that their people will hear only what the rulers want them to know about the conference. But open, democratic societies are placed in a different and difficult position by the consensus procedure.

Most democracies—especially those eager not to appear harsh toward the Third World—are afraid of being charged with conference-wrecking. Moreover, while many western European chanceries take exercises such as the Vienna conference— or 1992's world environmental summit—with a large grain of salt, Americans tend to think that the language of an international agreement ought to reflect at least a modicum of reality, and that commitments undertaken because of such agreements ought to be serious commitments. These points tend to put the United States at a disadvantage in these situations, and the disadvantage is magnified when the United States has a new team that is unclear about its policy goals, unfamiliar with the curve balls thrown in this particular league, and eager to get a document it can live with so that it can claim a major international success.

"Consensus" caused its usual headaches at Vienna. But the real problem, the enduring problem, of the Vienna Declaration was not the way it was produced but what it did and didn't say.

THE DOGS THAT DIDN'T BARK

The most important part of the Vienna Declaration is Part II, the statement of principles. And the key to grasping the grave problems of Part II is to notice, like Sherlock Holmes, the dog that didn't bark—in this case, the affirmations that were *not* made.

The Vienna Declaration affirms the "right to self-determination," the "right to development," and the "right to enjoy the benefits of scientific progress," while hinting broadly at a Third World "right" to debt relief (meaning debt cancellation). It condemns the toxic-waste dumping in Third World sites (no doubt a problem) as a human-rights violation. And it finds ample room in which to praise indigenous peoples, disabled people, migrant workers, and refugees: all of whom are, to be sure, frequently abused.

But the Vienna Declaration contains no clear articulation of the basic human rights of:

- religious freedom, or
- freedom of association, or
- freedom of assembly, or
- freedom of the press.

Which is to say, the Vienna Declaration is not serious business.

The entire experience of the twentieth century testifies to the fact that civil rights and political freedoms are the bedrock of any meaningful scheme of human rights. For there can be no effective protection of basic human rights without transparency in government, without a constitutional codification of the fundamental and inalienable rights of persons, and without a clear, unambiguous recognition that society exists prior to state, and that the state exists to serve society, not vice versa. Yet this historical experience, in societies that are both the most free and the most prosperous in human history, was virtually ignored in the Vienna Declaration.

A "human rights declaration" that fails to reaffirm the priority of basic civil rights and political freedoms is, at best, a confession of ignorance and a self-consignment to irrelevance. But the Vienna Declaration took shape not in a political vacuum but in the political and ideological context established by the Bangkok Declaration, which was nothing less than a declaration of war against the Universal Declaration of Human Rights. For the Vienna Final Document to take so accommodating a position toward the agenda embedded in the Bangkok Declaration makes it worse than irrelevant: the Vienna Declaration must be considered dangerous, an actual threat to the protection of human rights.

THE INDICTMENT

Some examples will help establish this point.

• Paragraph 3 of the Vienna Declaration's statement of principles reads: "All human rights are universal, indivisible, and interdependent and inter-related. The international community must treat human rights globally in a fair and equal manner, on the same footing, and with the same emphasis."

This is simply the Bangkok Declaration tarted up for public display. What is conceded by the statement of "universality" is immediately denied on the basis of "indivisibility, interdependence, and inter-relatedness," These three nouns may sound unobjectionable; but do not think that they are "neutral" terms. In the current U.N. context, they have very explicit meanings. To get down to specific cases: according to this formulation, the putative right to "periodic holidays with pay, as well as remuneration for public holidays" is as basic a "human right" as freedom of religious belief.

This pernicious and demeaning approach reduces human life to a (slightly) higher form of animal life. It denies a basic anthropological truth: that certain innate human aspirations reflect a quality of transcendent nobility that radically distinguishes man from his pet dog and other sentient creatures. Moreover, we have had a long, hard experience of what happens in countries whose regimes blather on about their commitment to "economic, social, and cultural rights": they tend to be poor, absolutely or relatively, and to be ruled by dictators. For the United States to agree to a human-rights declaration in which the alleged "indivisibility, interdependence, and inter-relatedness" of human rights were given equal footing, morally and legally, with the universality of basic human rights was a serious error.

• Paragraph 6 reaffirms the "right to development" as a "universal and inalienable right and an integral part of fundamental human rights."

In the days when he was representing the United States at the U.N. Human Rights Commission in Geneva, Michael Novak used to ask whether, if there was a "right to develop," there was not a corresponding "responsibility to develop." And if there *was* such a responsibility (as the notion of such a "right" would seem to imply), then what should we say about governments whose corruption, malfeasance, and economic wrong-headedness were the primary causes of their nations' underdevelopment? Would there not be, in these instances, something like a "right to get government out of the way of development"?

These would have been useful questions to pose during the Vienna debate. For, however much confusion there may have been about various schemes of economic development at the time when the Universal Declaration of Human Rights was drafted, the world has had forty-five years of experience since then, and the verdict is in. There is no general positive correlation between levels of "development assistance" and real economic development; therefore demands for "development assistance" on the basis of a rights claim take on the ever more ugly character of international extortion. Moreover, countries that want to create wealth and to distribute its benefits equitably will opt, not for state-sponsored and state-directed development assistance (which is what is implied by the "right to development"), but for market-based economic modernization (which can, to be sure, be furthered at key moments by external assistance—primarily investment).

The choice is not between "concern for the Third World" and economic realism. To be concerned—*seriously* concerned—about gross poverty and deprivation of the Third World is to advocate those policies of market-oriented economic (and democratic political) reform that are most likely to empower the poor and to lead to real economic growth. We know, now, what those policies are, at least in general orientation. And it is long past time for the United States to do some essential economic truth-telling in international forums, and to respond, sharply and with facts and figures, to the charge that such truth-telling constitutes hegemonism or "insensitivity."

But that would require a settled American policy (one that transcends changes of administration) that we shall, publicly, in and out of season, argue that the "right to development," as it has come to be understood by the majority of states in the United Nations, is dangerous nonsense.

• Paragraph 19–2 of the Vienna Declaration is a Castroite plea for an end to the U.S. economic embargo of Cuba. Paragraph 19–3 brings us right back to the agenda of the Bangkok Declaration.

Again, the U.N.-ese may seem, at first blush, unobjectionable: "The World Conference reaffirms the importance of ensuring the universality, objectivity, and non-selectivity of the consideration of human rights issues." But what do "objectivity" and "non-selectivity" mean in the linguistic fantasy-land that is the current U.N.? Well, "non-selectivity" means that there can be no special human-rights rapporteurs (investigators, really) appointed for specific *countries*; there can only be special rapporteurs for *issues* (like religious freedom). Thus despotic governments (Cuba, for instance) can further seal themselves off from international scrutiny. And "objectivity" means that, for example, in the case of a special rapporteur's criticism of the state of religious freedom in, say, Sudan, the

Sudanese government can reject the report as being "non-objective," insensitive to cultural differences, biased, and so forth. Orwell lives, indeed.

• Paragraph 26 of the Vienna Declaration was another victory for the Bangkok Declaration sensibility. The preceding paragraph, on non-governmental organizations (NGOs), had stated that human-rights monitors and other NGOs should "be free to carry out their human rights activities, without interference, within the framework of national law and the Universal Declaration of Human Rights." Fine. But Paragraph 26, on the media, merely states that the press should be guaranteed "freedom and protection ... within the framework of national law"—there is no mention of the Universal Declaration and its principled affirmation of freedom of the press. This has serious implications, not only for press access to countries run by despotic regimes, but for international broadcasting services like the Voice of America, Radio Marti, and Vatican Radio. Jamming these sources of information does not, according the Vienna Declaration, constitute a serious breach of human rights. Indeed, a clever lawyer (Ramsey Clark? William Kunstler?) could probably turn Paragraph 26 into an argument for the international illegality of Radio Marti (the U.S.-sponsored, Radio Free Europe-style "surrogate radio" for Cuba).

Thus it appears that the U.S. damage-control effort was, at best, only minimally successful. "Universality" was reaffirmed: but at the price of acquiescing to a host of silly, mendacious, or downright dangerous affirmations that may well subject the claim of universality (and the protections it has afforded dissidents) to the death of a thousand cuts.

BOONDOGGLES

The Vienna Declaration's action plan also included a couple of dubious proposals for expanding the U.N. human-rights bureaucracy. The first is the creation of a U.N. High Commissioner for Human Rights, to coordinate U.N. human-rights activity and to serve as a kind of universal ombudsman for human rights—much as the U.N. High Commissioner for Refugees has done for the victims of war, famine, and natural disasters. The proposal, attractive in the abstract, becomes far less so in the light of current U.N. politics.

The position of High Commissioner would, like the Secretary-Generalship, almost certainly have to rotate among various regions of the world. This would virtually guarantee bad choices, or High Commissioners who could be counted on not to rock the boat. Moreover, the office of the High Commissioner for Human Rights would add yet another layer of bureaucracy to a U.N. system that is already choking to death on red tape. The money required for this initiative might be better spent on strengthening the system of special rapporteurs responsible to the U.N. Human Rights Commission. The United States supported the idea of a High Commissioner at the Vienna conference, presumably out of a concern that we be seen as "serious" about human rights; but it is not at all clear that the cause of human-rights protection will be advanced by the addition of another blizzard of paper.

The United States did oppose the establishment of a "Working Group on the Right to Development," a truly Brobdingnagian boondoggle whose creation was supported by our increasingly unserious western European allies. But the Yanks lost the argument, and another bureaucratic black hole was created into which hundreds of thousands of dollars will be sucked.

The Necessity of Hardball

Although the Clinton administration publicly claimed great success at the Vienna conference, its more candid members were likely to argue, privately, that given the consensus procedure, the United States made the best it could out of a bad set of circumstances. But why did we agree to a consensus-driven conference in the first place?

The U.S. delegation believed it could "solve" the problem of the Bangkok Declaration in Vienna by the discreet application of some muscle and a wide range of concessions behind the scenes: this would avoid a public quarrel (which a vote on issues like "universality" would surely have provoked) and preserve the image of unanimity that now surrounds the Universal Declaration of Human Rights. But why is this a priority? Why should we *want* to maintain a fiction of unanimity with despots—unless the West in general, and the United States in particular, is leery of being seen as pushing its weight around? As the conference opened in mid-June, Joshua Muravchik proposed a tougher strategy, based on a more assertive understanding of the position of the United States and its democratic friends in world politics today:

> The end of the Cold War has brought down many barriers, including, it seems, the barrier that used to divide communist and anti-communist tyrants. On the other side of the coin, advocates of human rights and democracy are united across the political spectrum as never before. Why shouldn't the democracies accept the challenge thrown down by the dictators? Who needs false unanimity? Why not declare that the new dividing line in global politics is between those who honor and practice human rights and democracy and those who do not? Why not have a vote?[3]

Why not, indeed?

But such assertiveness requires leadership. That means the United States would have to accept responsibility for spearheading a reconception of human-rights work in international political and legal institutions today. The Europeans will do nothing unless the United States takes the lead, and much of the heat. And one has to wonder, sadly, whether the United States could gather itself to such a task, just now. Our people are in an isolationist mood (which in no small part reflects a failure of political leadership). The Clinton administration really seems to believe that its Republican predecessors "dismantled" America's human-rights policy, showed gross insensitivity to the Third World, and paid too little attention to the agenda that flies under the flag of "economic, social, and cultural rights." (The first two judgments are profoundly mistaken, and the third ought to be celebrated, not deplored.)

But the United States does the cause of human rights no favor when it takes the advice of former President Carter, who argued in Vienna that the democracies should be "understanding" about the "frustrations" of the countries that signed the Bangkok Declaration.[4] The United States has no shortage of problems; but it is ludicrous to suggest that we enter a discussion of human rights on an equal moral footing with the signatories of the Bangkok Declaration.

What the cause of human rights needs is an assertive United States, unashamed of its own human-rights traditions, committed to the notion that civil rights and political freedoms are the basic building blocks of decent societies, and willing to challenge the shibboleths that have fouled international human-rights discourse for two generations now. That is not, unfortunately, the United States that showed up at the World Conference on Human Rights. And the real losers were the victims of human-rights abuse throughout the world.

NOTES

1. Peter L. Berger, "Are Human Rights Universal?" *Commentary*, September 1977, 60.

2. Arthur M. Schlesinger, Jr., cited in Joshua Muravchik, "Why Accept the Hubris of Tyrants?" *Los Angeles Times*, June 15, 1993.

3. Ibid.

4. This was, in fact, one of the least objectionable of Carter's sundry Vienna pronouncements. After being shouted down by Latin American radicals at an NGO forum in Vienna, Carter said that he only wanted these "frustrated" people to know that "I was not [at the forum] representing my country because I have strongly disagreed [with] and condemned the human rights policy of my country for the past twelve years." The Georgia sage also condemned the "selfish attitudes of the nations of the North who control the economic, political, and cultural power in the world," trotted out the old tyrants' saw that a family starving to death wouldn't be interested in freedom of speech, and claimed that, while the United States has invested "billions of dollars" in the Salvadoran military, none of this has benefited "ordinary people."
   Plus ça change ...

✗ **NO**

The New Human Rights Debate: A Reply to George Weigel
RON DART

In the tradition of John Courtney Murray and Rheinhold Niebuhr, George Weigel has become one of the outstanding social critics of our time.
- Eugene Rostow

I don't want educated people, I want oxen.
- Anastasio Somoza

We should cease to talk about vague and—for the Far East—unreal objectives such as human rights, the raising of living standards and democratization. The day is not far off when we are going to have to deal in straight power concepts. The less we are then hampered by idealistic slogans, the better.
- George Kennan

THE CONTEXT: G. WEIGEL AND NEOCONSERVATISM

George Weigel, President of the Ethics and Public Policy Center (EPPC) in Washington, DC, is very much on the cutting edge of the neoconservative movement in the United States. There are many wealthy and influential neoconservative thinktanks in the United States, such as the Heritage Foundation (Reagan's oracle), M. Novak's American Enterprise Institute (AEI), R.J. Neuhaus's Institute on Religion and Public Life, the Rand Foundation, the Hoover Institute, and the Manhattan Institute, to name a few. Publications such as W. Buckley's *National Review*, Podhoretz's *Commentary,* and the ongoing work of Irving Kristol and his wife, Gertrude Himmelfarb, have done much to give credibility and depth to the neoconservative movement. Populist and popular neoconservatism reached many through W. Bennett's *The Devaluing of America, The Book of Virtues,* and *The Moral Compass,* and the New Christian Right (NCR) of Ralph Reed. Newt Gingrich's *To Renew America* has drawn the applause and support of many. So George Weigel stands within a tradition, a tradition that in its more sophisticated forms draws from the insights of E. Voegelin, L. Strauss, R. Kirk, A. Bloom, and R. Nisbet, and, in its cruder forms, from Rush Limbaugh.

Canadian groups such as the Fraser Institute (founded in 1973 by Patrick Boyle of MacMillan Bloedel), the C.D. Howe Institute, and the Business Council on National Issues (founded in 1976 by various corporations) mirror many of the significant concerns of the neoconservative groups in the United States. Recent Canadian publications such as M. Coren's *Setting It Right* (1996) and D. Frum's *What's Right? The New Conservatism and What It Means for Canada* (1996) reflect and articulate the neoconservative outlook that George Weigel inhabits. An analysis of Weigel's *The New Human Rights Debate* will reveal to us some of the strengths and limitations of neoconservatism.

VILLAINS AND HEROES: COMIC BOOK POLITICS

Most comic books have a hero and a villain; the roles are clearly defined, the contest between them is raised to a melodramatic level, and usually the hero emerges the victor. Weigel's article "The New Human-Rights Debate" has its villains and heroes; there are no shades of grey, no pockets of doubt or ambiguity in this article. Weigel sees himself as St. George doing necessary battle with the dragon. Who are these villains that our modern St. George feels so compelled to treat as dragons, as enemies? Weigel has done us the honour of articulating, in the clearest manner possible, who these dragons are and why we must do battle with them.

There are four major villains in Weigel's short essay. First, Eleanor Roosevelt is targeted because she, while playing a significant role in drafting the Universal Declaration of Human Rights (1948), dared to concern herself with such issues as "jobs, health care, and education." Weigel was pleased that Roosevelt prioritized "civil rights" and "political freedoms," but he was rather annoyed when she argued that social and economic goods should also be seen as legitimate rights. Much hinges on the role and responsibilities of the state in all this. Weigel seems to think the state has little or no responsibility for citizens' social or economic needs. The Universal Declaration of Human Rights front-stages political, civil, and legal rights while subordinating economic, social, and cultural rights. But this is not good enough for Weigel; he would like to see economic, social, and cultural rights not only subordinated but redefined away as rights. Eleanor Roosevelt's blunder was to, at least, include economic, social, and cultural needs as rights; Weigel's more exclusive perspective tends to isolate and upstage political, civil, and legal rights.

The second group of villains in "The New Human-Rights Debate" are Rousseau, the French Jacobins, and Marxism. Rousseau's notion of the "general will" is seen as a sort of precursor to totalitarianism and the French Jacobins are proto-totalitarians. There is no doubt Rousseau's "general will" can be interpreted, when forced and twisted out of context, into a totalitarian mould, but Rousseau is much more complex then Weigel is willing to acknowledge. Weigel also tends to generalize about French Jacobins; there were many moderate Jacobins from the Jacobin Club, the Cordelier Club, and the Girondins who opposed the violence and ideology of the terrorist Jacobins. In short, the French Revolution, in its concerns for freedom, equality, and fraternity, and the role of the state in facilitating these principles, had various means before it. Weigel is right in condemning the violence of Robespierre and tribe, but he errs when he assumes there are no options other than violence to protect social, economic, and cultural rights. Abuse does not prohibit use. A careful thinker would recognize that many French revolutionists distorted and twisted the meaning of economic, social, and cultural rights. The task is to cut through the distortions and discover the white heat of insight.

The third villain comprises the Bangkok Declaration (April 1993) and the Vienna Declaration (June 1993). Weigel is right when he argues that the "Communists (China and Vietnam), anti-communists (Indonesia), Middle Eastern despots (Iran and Syria), old-fashioned military thugs (Burma), and the gung-ho capitalist micro-state of Singapore" tried at the Bangkok conference to define rights in a culturally sensitive and relativist way. Weigel is also right when he says that this form of viewing human rights, when decoded, often goes like this:

> Decorous translation: We'll define what we mean by "human rights"; we'll implement that definition however we see fit; and nobody else has any standing to object.
> Street translation: Get outta my face.

Weigel is spot on when he perceives how some Third World states redefine rights to justify brutal treatment of their citizens. But again abuse does not prohibit use. Just because the language of rights is distorted does not mean we toss out the language of social, economic, and cultural rights. The best antidote to bad thought is not no thought; it is good thought. The best antidote to a bad discussion of rights is not no discussion of rights, but a critical discussion of social, economic, and cultural rights. Weigel goes on to discuss how the Vienna Declaration does not include, in an explicit and specific way, "religious freedom," "freedom of association," "freedom of assembly," and "freedom of the press." But anyone familiar with the post–World War II process of threading together political, civil, legal, social, economic, cultural, and environmental rights knows that the Vienna Declaration does not stand alone; it was the roof put on the edifice of the International Bill of Human Rights (IBHR) and the foundation of the Universal Declaration of Human Rights (UDHR). The Vienna Declaration merely corrected and complemented the uneven development, since World War II, of political, civil, and legal rights by insisting that the "right to development" include other substantive rights. It seems that Weigel's reactive perspective distorts his perception.

The fourth villain in this melodrama, as can be expected, is J. Carter–B. Clinton. Both presidents were too soft on political and civil rights while being eager to broaden the rights mandate to social and economic rights. The debate between Weigel and Carter–Clinton, of course, is the Democratic–Republican debate and the role of the state in protecting certain inalienable, fundamental, and universal rights.

The villains in this tale, now exposed, clearly point out to us where St. George stands. The heroes in this epic are those who battle communism and any form of socialism. Those who gave their lives to free Central-Eastern Europe are given many kudos; the crucial work of Solidarity and Charter 77 is much applauded. The pivotal events of 1989 and 1991 are warmly welcomed, of course. Weigel's concern for political, civil, and legal rights in communist states should be acknowledged; men such as Lech Walesa and Václav Havel have demonstrated much courage. There is no doubt, and it would be foolish to deny, that Communist states have wreaked havoc on all sorts of basic rights. This being said, though, we need to ask, on the one hand, why Weigel so obstinately refuses to accept social, economic, and cultural rights as legitimate, and why, on the other hand, he fails to see the inconsistencies and hypocrisy in American practice of political and civil rights. It does not take much political insight to realize that the United States, in its support of many authoritarian states, such as Guatemala (R. Montt), Indonesia (Suharto), Chile (Pinochet), Nicaragua (Somoza), Philippines (Marcos), Iran (Shah), Saudi Arabia (Saud family), El Salvador, and many other states in the Middle East, Africa, the Americas, and Asia, has persistently violated all those rights Weigel claims to uphold. In fact, since Weigel holds Reagan and clan in such high esteem, it would be very simple to point out how Reagan's foreign policy, in many countries, led to the suppression of most civil and political rights. But more on this later.

HUMAN RIGHTS THEORY: AN INTEGRATED OR SEGREGATED MODEL?

There are two approaches to the theory of rights, both of which are rooted in the Western political tradition. These two traditions can be called the integrated and fragmented perspectives; Weigel belongs to the latter tradition.

Samuel Kim, in his article "Global Human Rights and World Order," although strongly differing from Weigel in his understanding of how rights co-inhere, agrees that the language of rights has evolved in its most distinct and articulate form since World War II. Kim's approach is integrated, whereas Weigel's is segregated. Weigel would argue that political, civil, and legal rights are essential for a democratic society to thrive and flourish. Weigel would further argue that the state has a responsibility to protect these basic rights. So far so good. Weigel, as I have mentioned above, distinguishes clearly between political, civil, and legal rights, which he thinks antedate social, economic, and cultural rights, but are also more essential to a democratic and liberal society. On the other hand, Kim and many of his tribe would argue that the seven major rights are interdependent, indivisible, universal, and fundamental. This more organic or integrated approach to human rights, I would argue, is much closer to the heart of the Western political tradition than Weigel's segregated, exclusive, and fragmentary approach.

Weigel argues that the front-staging of social, economic, and cultural rights is somehow new to the Western tradition. I would strongly disagree. Weigel pits the Anglo-Scottish-American tradition against the French-Marxist-Communist tradition, arguing that the former perspective is primarily concerned with political, civil, and legal rights, whereas the latter tradition regularly and predictably stomps and crushes those rights for the purpose of protecting social, economic, and cultural rights. I think Weigel has distorted the Anglo-Scottish-American tradition to suit his ideological purposes. A brisk reading of *The Peasant Revolt 1381* (P. Lindsay and R. Groves, 1950), M. Walzer's *The Revolution of the Saints: A Study in the Origin of Radical Politics* (1965), Coleridge's *Bristol Lectures* (1795), S. MacCoby's *The English Radical Tradition: 1763–1914* (1952), G. Claey's *The Politics of English Jacobinism: Writings of John Thelwall* (1995), Goodwin's *The Friends of Liberty* (1979), or any of Christopher Hill's writings will dispel the notion that social, economic, and cultural rights come before political, social, and legal rights either in time or worth.

Weigel, I fear, is not dealing with a new human rights debate; he is dealing with an old debate within the Western tradition, and he has chosen the segregated and exclusive model to work from; this means he is selective in what he chooses and how he chooses it. We need, I think, as we near the end of this century, to be much more rooted in an organic and inclusive model; when we do this, we will be less inclined to ignore the very real needs of those who lack basic social and economic needs. Medical care, employment, and education are essential to a just society—so are political, civil, and legal rights. We need not think in an either–or way. It does little good to pick the excesses and worst examples of those who have priorized social, economic, and cultural rights while idealizing political, civil, and legal rights. We need to catch the integrated vision that is basic and essential to our Western political tradition.

COLERIDGE, THE ENGLISH JACOBINS, AND THE BRISTOL LECTURES: CRITICAL THEORY AND THE NEED FOR REFLECTIVE PATRIOTS AND CITIZENS

Weigel was quick to condemn the French Jacobins while welcoming the Anglo-Scottish-America tradition of rights. But there is an English tradition that Weigel has ignored. The English Jacobins were as critical as Burke of the excesses of the French Revolution, but unlike Burke and kin they realized there were some affinities between the French and English concerns. S.T. Coleridge delivered three impassioned speeches at Bristol in 1795: *Conciones Ad Populum, Lectures on the Slave Trade,* and *On the Present War.* The key to unlocking Coleridge's insights can be found in his critical patriotism; it is this critical patriotism that Weigel lacks in a substantive way.

Coleridge lived at a time when the excesses of the French Revolution were playing themselves out. Many Tories, led by Burke, condemned both the revolutionary excesses and the underlying vision of the French Revolution while lifting up, rather uncritically, the British ideal. Coleridge would have none of this hypocrisy and inconsistency. Coleridge, as an English Jacobin, stood by the side of the Tories and Whigs when they publicly denounced the folly and foolishness of Robespierre and tribe. But Coleridge, unlike Burke and many Tories, refused to blind himself to the way his state justified and supported many of the same atrocities in other countries and within England itself. Coleridge pointed out in the clearest terms that England was not innocent. It was England, he reminded his fellow patriots, that profited enormously from the slave trade; it was England that supported Catherine the Great (who brutalized the Poles) and Frederick William II (who invaded Poland); it was England that concluded a treaty with the Dey of Algiers in 1795 that legitimated piracy. It was England, also, in the "new world" that paid a handsome price for scalps taken in war and the massacres of many indigenous peoples. Coleridge vehemently protested, also, against Pitt's Gagging Bills, which claimed to protect political and civil rights while denying these rights to English dissidents. Many of the English Jacobins such as Priestly, Frend, Wordsworth, Coleridge, Thelwall, Gerald, Muir, Palmer, and Margarot were either imprisoned, spied on, or sent to Botany Bay for questioning the English misuse of power. Coleridge's hesitations about naively goose-stepping before any party can be seen in his two poems "France: An Ode" and "Fears in Solitude."

Coleridge was a critical patriot who refused to salute at the flagpole of either Whig or Tory; our modern Whigs or Tories are Democrats or Republicans. It does little to help the political process when devotees insightfully assault other parties but go numb and mute at the weaknesses within their own tribe. Weigel, who seems to have an appreciation for the English tradition, could learn something from the critical patriotism of Coleridge and the English Jacobins; these men did not marginalize social, economic, or cultural rights. In fact, many of them could be seen as forerunners of the environmental movement also.

THE UNITED STATES AND HUMAN RIGHTS: INCONSISTENCIES AND HYPOCRISY WITHIN NEOCONSERVATISM

Weigel is right, of course, when he announces that political, civil, and legal rights are a legitimate and essential part of the Western political tradition; he is also right when he criticizes those who would subvert these rights. But Weigel fails to see (a predictable American shortcoming) that the very rights he claims to represent and honour are ones that his country frequently violates on an international level. We need to turn some of Weigel's arguments on him. Yes, we can agree with Weigel that many who claim to uphold social, economic, and cultural rights distort the very ideals they claim to uphold; in short, there is a credibility gap between the ideal and its implementation. This same process can be seen at work in the foreign policy of the United States and most of Weigel's comrades; Weigel, I suspect, needs to befriend Coleridge for a season.

G. Kennan once said, "The day is not far off when we are going to have to deal in straight power concepts." Weigel, and many neoconservatives like him, fail to acknowledge Nietzsche's *wille zur macht* (will to power) that shapes American foreign policy rather than some consistent policy of political and civil rights. The United States since World War II has consistently supported some of the most authoritarian states in the world. The American support of Tsaldares (Greece), Rhee (South Korea), Duvalier (Haiti), Batista (Cuba), Suharto (Indonesia), Somoza (Nicaragua), Pinochet (Chile), Ubico-Mont (Guatemala), Salazar (Portugal), Franco (Spain), Phibun (Thailand), Zia (Pakistan), and authoritarian regimes in Zaire, Argentina, Israel, Turkey, Vietnam, Laos, and Cambodia speak volumes about its consistent commitment to political and civil rights. The United States has sub- verted constitutional governments in Guatemala (Arbenz), British Guyana (Jagan), Iran (Mossadegh), Dominican Republic (Bosch), Indonesia (Sukarno), Brazil (Goulart), and Chile (Allende). The reply to this, of course, is that no state is per- fect, and the United States, when push comes to shove, would rather support a right-wing fascist state than a left-wing totalitarian state. But at a certain point this becomes a case of special pleading, a case of denying the very ideals that are held so high in the name of protecting such ideals.

Jeanne Kirkpatrick made the distinction between "authoritarian" and "totali- tarian" regimes. But this distinction unravels when the threads are pulled with a minimal level of exertion. Kirkpatrick claimed that totalitarian regimes were much more brutal than authoritarian regimes; she is right, of course, in some instances. There are many instances, though, when rightist authoritarian regimes have been more brutal than leftist regimes. Cuba and the Sandinistas, in the 1980s, had a much better track record than Guatemala (125 000 killed), El Salvador (75 000 killed), or Honduras; the United States backed Guatemala, El Salvador, and the Contras in Nicaragua, even though any minimal semblance of basic rights was obviously absent. A cursory sampling of reports from Amnesty International, Human Rights Watch, Humana Report, Freedom House, or the United Nations Development Program would clearly highlight how the United States has con- sciously and consistently supported violent rogue states. The School of the Americas at Fort Benning, Georgia, has a proven track record of training tyrants and assassins; such tyrants have served America's interests in the Caribbean and Meso and Latin America.

Weigel's friends Kirkpatrick and Reagan, although claiming to defend political and civil rights, have often played a crucial role in negating them. The sooner the neoconservatives acknowledge this obvious fact, the sooner a more meaningful and honest dialogue can begin. It is difficult to dialogue with those who deny the facts or, worse yet, justify them, in Machiavellian style, under the guise of liberty and democracy. The language of liberty and democracy, when it is honestly decoded, means liberty for the military-corporate-academic elite to do as they please. Power, in short, is what it is all about. At least Kennan was honest enough to acknowledge *realpolitik* as the motive for substantive decisionmaking.

A CONCLUSION: THE NEED FOR TWO EYES

Our modern neoconservatives are rightly concerned about the decay and unravelling of the West; the West has been tempted and, in many ways, has grown soft and given in. Neoconservatives, rightly, long to claim standards; the obvious interest in such language as nature, natural law, and the classical virtues (rather than values) needs to be heeded. But there is more than one way to interpret natural law and the language of virtues. The neoconservatives, in their longing to retrieve and recover standards, are often selective in the issues they front-stage; it is this selectivity that makes their agenda highly suspect. Needless to say, the liberals and progressives do much the same thing. If we are ever going to authentically retrieve a meaningful and consistent understanding of natural law and the virtues, we need to accept their organic nature in theory and practice. Weigel has failed to do this, and this is his weakness and limitation. In short, we need to see with two eyes; single vision makes us myopic, and all the ideologies (including Weigel's neoconservatism) are based on a myopic outlook. A responsible, just, equitable, and consistent outlook that is rooted in the best of the Western political tradition will include political, civil, legal, social, economic, cultural, and environmental rights in theory and practice.

Postscript

George Weigel focuses most of his criticism on the World Conference on Human Rights held in Vienna in 1993. The Vienna Conference was the largest gathering ever held on human rights and the UN's second conference dealing with this issue. Some 171 states and 800 non-governmental agencies participated in the discussions. Preparations for the conference, which began in 1989 and included four preparatory meetings and numerous regional consultations, revealed the deep divisions between countries on the issue of human rights.

A particularly contentious issue leading up to the conference was the universality of human rights. Asian countries, such as China, Indonesia, North Korea, and Malaysia, argued that human rights were essentially a Western construct and that because of social and cultural differences in their countries, they should not be held to the same standards. Western attempts to interfere in their internal affairs would inhibit their economic and social development.

At the conference, the United States argued strongly against any definition of human rights that takes regional and cultural differences into account. Despite prolonged wrangling that threatened to scuttle the conference, a consensus was reached and the Vienna Declaration and Programme of Action was adopted. While many saw the declaration as a victory for the notion of the universality of human rights, others, like Weigel, were unhappy with the willingness of Western states to recognize the validity of social and economic rights and to recognize their interdependence with civil and political rights. This compromise, they believe, was too high a price for achieving a declaration. What do you think?

Infotrac Keyword Search
"international human rights"

Suggested Additional Readings

Alston, Philip. "The UN's Human Rights Record: From San Fransisco to Vienna and Beyond." *Human Rights Quarterly* 16 (1994): 375–90.

Boyle, Kevin. "Stock-taking on Human Rights: The World Conference on Human Rights, Vienna, 1993." *Political Studies* 43 (1995): 79–95.

Brown, Seyom. *Human Rights In World Politics*. New York: Longman, 2000.

Cerna, Christina M. "Universality of Human Rights and Cultural Diversity: Implementation of Human Rights in Different Socio-Cultural Contexts." *Human Rights Quarterly* 16 (1994): 740–52.

Donnelly, Jack. *International Human Rights*. Boulder: Westview, 1993.

Gomez, Mario. "Social and Economic Rights and Human Rights Commissions." *Human Rights Quarterly* 17 (1995): 155–69.

Vincent, R.J. *Human Rights and International Relations*. Cambridge: Cambridge University Press, 1986.

Website Resources

Cambridge University Search here to find a collection of legal essays on human rights.

Human Rights International This NGO-supported site provides a gateway to resources on international human-rights issues.

Institute of Asian Affairs, Hamburg This site has a collection of links related to the Vienna Conference on Human Rights, which highlights the perspective of Asian countries.

Office of the High Commissioner for Human Rights Contains a large collection of official UN materials on human rights, including the final report of the World Conference on Human Rights and other follow-up materials.

Can Economic Sanctions Mitigate Conflict and Halt Human-Rights Abuses?

✔ **YES**

ELIZABETH ROGERS, "Economic Sanctions and Internal Conflict," in Michael E. Brown, ed., *The International Dimensions of International Conflict* (Cambridge, Mass.: MIT Press, 1996): 411–34

✗ **NO**

KIM RICHARD NOSSAL, "The False Promise of Economic Sanctions"

Economic sanctions have provoked ongoing interest throughout the twentieth century. With the growth of international trade and communication in the early part of the century, world leaders increasingly believed that a strategy of economic denial should play an essential role in any new collective-security system that was developed. In the aftermath of World War I, international sanctions were included as a key component of the new League of Nations. Article 16 of the League Covenant gave extensive powers to the new organization to diplomatically and economically ostracize any nation bent on international aggression. The assumption was that the threat of international ostracism itself would be a sufficient deterrent to prevent future acts of international aggression.

Despite the high hopes of its founders, the League of Nations experiment with international sanctions was largely a failure. The League had limited membership (which did not include the United States) and relied on only voluntary actions in enforcement of sanctions. The only major case of sanctions, imposed against Italy after its invasion of Ethiopia, proved to be largely ineffectual. The failure of these sanctions played a significant role in discrediting the League and contributing to its eventual demise.

Although the experience with sanctions under the League was ultimately disappointing, the Charter of the United Nations placed significant importance on the role of sanctions as a response to international aggression. According to provisions of Chapter VII of the Charter, the United Nations Security Council was empowered to respond to acts of aggression with a variety of actions. Article 41 outlines a series of diplomatic, communication, and economic measures that the Security Council could implement. The underlying assumption is that in applying a series of escalating measures—first diplomatic, then cultural, and finally economic—the Security Council would be able to inflict sufficient harm on an aggressor nation that collective military action could be avoided.

Despite these expectations, economic sanctions remained an underutilized instrument of the Security Council during the Cold War years. The only case of comprehensive sanctions applied by the United Nations during the Cold War was against Rhodesia. In 1966, the Security Council determined that the unilateral declaration of independence (UDI) declared by the white regime of Ian Smith in Rhodesia, over the protestations of the United Kingdom and other members of the Commonwealth, constituted a "threat to the peace." Selected measures, including a ban on the export of armaments and petroleum and an embargo on imports of key Rhodesian commodities, were imposed in December 1966. In 1968 these measures were extended to include a total economic boycott of Rhodesia. These economic sanctions remained in place until 1979, when an agreement leading to the emergence of a majority-governed Zimbabwe was reached. Although observers generally agree that the sanctions did play some role in weakening the capacity of the Rhodesian regime, most believe that the growing intensity of the guerrilla war was the major factor in bringing about a change in government.

The United Nations also imposed a series of measures against the South African government, attempting to bring pressure to bear on the apartheid regime. In 1977 the Security Council placed an arms embargo on South Africa. South Africa was also expelled or forced to withdraw from several UN agencies, including the World Health Organization (WHO) and the Food and Agricultural Organization (FAO). However, the United Nations never imposed broader sanctions on the South African regime. Although a wide variety of sanctions was imposed against South Africa by a number of governments and organizations, such as the Commonwealth and the Organization of African Unity (OAU), these measures were never coordinated and their consistency of implementation was widely acknowledged to be uneven.

Instead of being an instrument of multilateral diplomacy, economic sanctions during the Cold War were used primarily in the context of bilateral foreign policy relations. David Cortright and George A. Lopez note—in *Economic Sanctions: Panacea or Peacebuilding in a Post-Cold War World?* (Boulder, CO: Westview, 1995), p. 9—that between 1945 and 1990, sanctions of one kind or another were imposed by one nation on others more than sixty times. Although some sanctions were imposed within the framework of a regional organization, such as the Organization of American States' (OAS) sanctions against Cuba, most sanctions during this period reflected a clear preference for unilateralism, especially on the part of the United States. This is illustrated by the U.S.-led sanctions against Iran, the Soviet Union, and Poland. Cortright and Lopez note that between 1945 and 1990, more than two-thirds of international sanctions episodes were initiated and maintained by the United States. In three-quarters of these cases, the United

States was acting alone. However, lest one think that sanctions are only a preoccupation of the major powers, a recent study by Kim Nossal shows that "middle powers" such as Canada and Australia also have a strong interest in the use of economic sanctions and have participated in many of the major sanctions episodes of the Cold War.

However, since the end of the Cold War a significant shift in the use of economic sanctions has taken place. The number of sanctions episodes has increased dramatically, averaging more than one new episode per year. Significantly, virtually all of the major sanctions episodes have taken place in a multilateral forum. Since 1990 the UN Security Council has applied multilateral sanctions against Iraq, Libya, Somalia, Sudan, Liberia, Haiti, the former Yugoslavia, and the Khmer Rouge-held areas of Cambodia. Although the writers of the UN Charter anticipated that sanctions would be used primarily as an instrument of collective security against states carrying out aggressive wars against other states (matters of interstate justice), the majority of sanctions episodes have addressed primarily internal situations (matters of intrastate justice). Sanctions have increasingly been seen as an instrument that can be used to promote a range of issues, such as improving human-rights situations, encouraging a transition to democracy, or mitigating international conflicts.

The renewed interest in economic sanctions has reignited the debate over the effectiveness of such sanctions as an instrument of statecraft. In the first essay below, Elizabeth Rogers makes the case for using economic sanctions as a means of mitigating the growing number of internal conflicts. In contrast, Kim Richard Nossal of McMaster University questions the effectiveness of economic sanctions, whether to address human-rights abuses or to solve internal conflicts.

✔ YES
Economic Sanctions and Internal Conflict
ELIZABETH ROGERS

Can international coalitions use economic sanctions, or the threat of economic sanctions, to prevent, manage, or resolve internal conflicts?[1] If so, under what conditions will sanctions be most successful? What kinds of sanctions will be most successful and how should they be applied?

These are the questions this chapter addresses. Two recent developments lend them importance. First, the need to address the problems posed by internal conflicts has grown clearer as post–Cold War disorder has deepened, with wars unfolding in the former Yugoslavia, the Caucasus, the Middle East, Somalia, Sudan, Tajikistan, Liberia, and elsewhere. If uncontained, such conflicts could injure Western interests and those of other powers. Second, the U.S. public has grown increasingly leery of risking U.S. troops in overseas adventures. This often precludes the use of military force to dampen internal conflicts.[2] Can economic sanctions offer an alternative to force, serving as an instrument that allows international powers to sustain or impose peace without exposing their troops to danger?

I advance six main arguments. First, economic sanctions could help to prevent, manage, or resolve internal conflicts in many cases. The historical record supports this conclusion: sanctions often worked when they were applied seriously and systematically. Past studies of sanctions understate their effectiveness by deriving their conclusions in part from cases of half-hearted or partial sanctions. If forceful sanctions are considered alone and are assessed against a reasonable standard of success, the record shows sanctions succeeding much more often than these studies suggest, and fairly often overall.[3] It follows that economic sanctions could be an effective tool for preventing or dampening internal conflicts.

Second, economic sanctions will enjoy more success in containing than in stopping or preventing internal conflicts. The control of internal conflict can be subdivided into three tasks: preventing the outbreak of civil wars; containing the international spread of civil wars after they have broken out (which falls under the heading of conflict management); and halting civil wars (or inter-state wars, if they have already spread). Economic sanctions will be most effective in the area of conflict management, somewhat effective with respect to conflict prevention, and least effective with regard to conflict resolution. However, sanctions could produce worthwhile results even in the area of conflict resolution, and should be applied toward all three goals.

Third, economic sanctions are often more cost-effective than military force. They are usually less effective than military options, but are also less costly and therefore are competitive alternatives to force.

Fourth, conditions are now more auspicious for using sanctions than they were during the Cold War. Most important, the collapse of the Soviet Union removed the "black knight" that broke Western sanctions in the past.[4] Sanctions are far more effective when applied by most or all major states. Before and during the Cold War, unanimity was seldom possible. Unanimity will be possible more often in the post–Cold War era. Hence, sanctions will be more effective.

Fifth, in order to succeed, post–Cold War sanctions efforts must be led by the United States. Sanctions cannot succeed without leadership by a great power, and the United States now stands alone as a superpower.[5]

Sixth, sanctions success requires that sanctioning governments (especially the U.S. government) fully commit to the enterprise. A full commitment entails several special policies. The broadest possible range of sanctions should be applied early on. (Conversely, partial sanctions or slowly tightened sanctions should be avoided.) A broad international coalition must be assembled under U.S. leadership. Sanctions must be married to political programs that clearly frame what the international coalition wants local actors to do in order to have sanctions lifted. Finally, sanctions should be joined to strong declarations shaped to persuade target states or parties that the international coalition has the resolve to maintain sanctions until they comply.

If these policies are adopted, economic sanctions can often prevent or contain internal conflicts. If they are not adopted, sanctions will likely fail. Preventing, managing, and resolving internal conflicts are demanding tasks, and economic sanctions are not all-powerful. The key is getting U.S. leaders to fully commit to the enterprise.

I infer these conclusions from a worldwide survey of economic sanctions efforts since 1914. This record includes 130 cases: 115 instances of sanctions used by the United States and other powers from the pre–Cold War and Cold War eras (1914–89), and 15 post–Cold War (1989–95) cases. For sanctions imposed prior to 1989, I used the data compiled by Gary Hufbauer, Jeffrey Schott, and Kimberly Elliott.[6] I compiled data on 15 post–Cold War cases from press accounts.

A cursory look at this record suggests pessimistic conclusions, since most of these sanctions efforts failed. However, a closer look suggests the opposite. The track record includes many cases of half-hearted, partial, or unilateral sanctions, and sanctions efforts that were undercut by the Soviet Union during the Cold War. Such cases say little about the efficacy of U.S.-led multilateral sanctions firmly applied in the post–Cold War era. In very few of these 130 cases were the full range of economic sanctions actually employed.

This chapter addresses the efficacy of U.S. and U.S.-led sanctions. I do not explore efforts led by other states or institutions in detail, because only U.S.-led efforts stand much chance of success in the post–Cold War era....[7]

U.S.-LED SANCTIONS EFFORTS AFTER THE COLD WAR

How have U.S.-led economic sanctions fared in the post–Cold War era? A sanctions optimist might expect that the disappearance of the Soviet Union, a perennial Cold War black knight, will enhance the prospects for success. A sanctions pessimist might expect that, without the alarming specter of an enemy superpower, building and maintaining sanctions coalitions will be more difficult, thus decreasing their efficacy.[8]

Which view is correct? The post-1989 record is brief, but supports the optimistic view. No black knight has frustrated U.S.-led sanctions efforts since 1989, coalition problems have not developed, and U.S.-led sanctions have succeeded at a high rate when they have been firmly applied.

The United States has employed economic sanctions fifteen times since 1989. (See Table 1.) The U.S. government pursued most of these actions half-heartedly, but in three cases—Iraq, Haiti, and Yugoslavia—it made very determined efforts. The breadth of its tactics reflects its seriousness of purpose in these three cases: in each case the U.S. government sought broad international support for its campaign; used the full spectrum of economic sanctions (i.e., trade cutoffs, aid cutoffs, and financial sanctions); and used sanctions in conjunction with other policy instruments (e.g., military force or the threat to use force). These cases, in which the United States placed a high priority on success, are more revealing than other cases, since they show what sanctions can accomplish when they are seriously applied.[9]

Lack of Opposition

No determined sanctions-buster emerged in these three cases, or in any of the other twelve post–Cold War cases. In both Yugoslavia and Iraq, one might have expected Moscow to play the role of black knight. Russia and Serbia have historic ties based on culture and ethnicity. However, although Russia has given some diplomatic support to the Yugoslav position on Bosnia-Herzegovina, it has not undercut sanctions sponsored by the United Nations (UN). The Soviet Union also had an intermittent friendship with Iraq during the Cold War, but Moscow has supported UN-sponsored sanctions on Iraq and has not undercut them.

In some cases, China has come close to undercutting U.S.-led sanctions, but has not done so openly or aggressively. China sold M-11 missiles, or at least the technology to make them, to Pakistan; helped Algeria build a nuclear power plant; and assisted Iran's nuclear and chemical weapons programs.[10] China also blocked agreement on using economic sanctions to compel North Korea to halt its nuclear program.[11] However, China has not taken steps to undercut any U.S. or UN sanctions directly.

The absence of a powerful black knight in the post–Cold War world is a major development that should make sanctions much more effective.

TABLE 1

POST–COLD WAR U.S. ECONOMIC SANCTIONS

Year	Target State	Official Purpose	Type of Sanction	Result
1990	Iraq	Punish/reverse invasion of Kuwait	Aid, trade, financial	Ongoing but some success; sanctions damage Iraqi economy, weaken Iraqi military
1990	Pakistan	Halt nuclear program	Aid	Failure; nuclear program continues
1990	Guatemala	Reverse coup	Aid (trade threatened)	Success; coup reversed
1991	Jordan	Punish for pro-Iraq stance	Aid	Success; Jordan punished, later adopts friendly stance
1991	Yugoslavia	Support Croatian secession	Trade	Failure; Yugoslavia does not recognize Croatia
1991	Haiti	Restore Jean-Bertrand Aristide to power	Aid, trade, financial	Partial success; sanctions softened by Haitian elite
1991	Kenya	Improve human rights, compel elections	Aid	Partial success; elections held
1992	Peru	Reverse martial law	Aid	Success; elections held
1992	Libya	Punish for Pan Am 103 bombing; force extradition of suspects	Trade	Partial success; economic damage inflicted but no suspects are delivered
1992	Iran	Halt nuclear program	Trade	Failure; nuclear program continues
1992	Yugoslavia (Serbia & Montenegro)	Support Bosnian secession	Trade	Partial success; Bosnia recognized and Serb economy damaged
1993	Nigeria	Punish for annulment of elections	Aid	Ongoing; no new elections yet
1993	China	Punish for weapons exports to Pakistan	Trade	Success; PRC promises not to export in future
1993	Pakistan	Punish for import of weapons from China	Trade	Partial success; no new evidence of weapons imports
1994	Rwanda	Halt genocide	Financial	No result; sanctions applied too late

Sources: Compiled by author from press accounts.

Continued Coalition Cohesion

The emerging evidence does not support the proposition that international coalitions will be harder to form and maintain in the post–Cold War world, where there is no superpower enemy to rally against. When the United States has sought to create and preserve a tight coalition—in Iraq, Haiti, and Yugoslavia—it has succeeded. It achieved unprecedented levels of cooperation in its campaign against Iraq.[12] The United States and other Organization of American States (OAS) members cooperated effectively in imposing sanctions on Haiti. The United States and its North Atlantic Treaty Organization (NATO) allies have disagreed on Bosnian policy, but their disagreements have been over the use of NATO military forces, maintaining the arms embargo, and peace plans—not on economic sanctions policy. In short, when the United States has been serious about gaining and maintaining international cooperation for economic sanctions efforts, it has been able to do so.[13]

Assessing Success and Failure in Iraq, Haiti, and Yugoslavia

The forgoing suggests that the conditions for employing economic sanctions are auspicious in the post–Cold War world. However, have post-Cold War sanctions efforts in fact produced results? Iraq, Haiti, and Yugoslavia may seem at first glance to be cases where sanctions have failed. Yet, in all three cases, economic sanctions had considerable impact.

In the Iraqi case, economic sanctions have crushed the Iraqi economy—Iraq's gross national product (GNP) has fallen by more than fifty percent since sanctions were imposed[14]—and weakened the financial position of the Iraqi elite. Iraqi president Saddam Hussein has been forced to exhaust his large cash reserves secretly held in foreign banks.[15] Economic constraints have slowed the rebuilding of the Iraqi military and strengthened UN efforts to prevent Iraq from acquiring weapons of mass destruction.[16] They have also contributed to Iraq's decision to recognize Kuwait. Finally, the vast economic harm that sanctions have inflicted on Iraq serves as a powerful warning to other potential aggressors: it shows that a U.S.-led coalition can devastate an aggressor's economy.

Critics make two main observations to support their claim that sanctions have failed in Iraq. First, Saddam remains in power. Second, sanctions failed to induce Iraq to withdraw from Kuwait during the 1990–91 crisis. Their first argument measures sanctions against an unduly high standard of performance. National leaders who are firmly in power, as Saddam was in 1990, are very hard to unseat. Achieving their overthrow is perhaps the hardest task one could demand of sanctions. Economic sanctions have failed to overthrow Saddam, but military and covert action have also failed at the same task. The failure of economic sanctions to bring about Saddam's political demise means their success in Iraq is only partial. However, this should not obscure the successes they have achieved.[17]

The second observation, that sanctions failed to remove Iraq from Kuwait, is true but remains a weak indictment of sanctions efficacy because sanctions were not left in place long enough to accomplish the task. U.S. President George Bush decided not to wait to see if sanctions would work, but instead moved ahead with the military option six months into the crisis. Sanctions do not work overnight. During the Gulf crisis, sanctions advocates forecast that sanctions would take at least a year to force a change in Iraqi policy.[18] Sanctions were not given a full trial in Iraq and, therefore, cannot be judged a failure.

In Haiti, the United States got the policy outcome it wanted. President Jean-Bertrand Aristide is back in power. The question is whether or not economic sanctions contributed to this result. The case against sanctions is that sanctions were ineffective for three years and that the military junta stepped aside only when a U.S. military invasion was imminent.

In fact, sanctions were ineffective because they were first imposed in a tentative, half-hearted manner. The sanctions imposed in 1991 were partial, not total. Sanctions were targeted on Haitian elites only in the latter stages of the three-year confrontation.[19] Since the 1991 coup that ousted Aristide was sponsored by Haitian elites, sanctions would have to be targeted against the elites to bring about a policy change; this was a serious omission. Strong sanctions were imposed only in May–June 1994. Moreover, sanctions at first contained loopholes for U.S. businesses operating in Haiti, were loosened prematurely during the crisis before Haiti fully complied with U.S. and UN demands, and were accompanied by weak U.S. declarations and visible signs of U.S. irresolution.[20] In short, sanctions were implemented in a very hesitant manner, especially in early phases of the crisis. Thus, it is not surprising that these sanctions were initially ineffective.

In the end, sanctions had an impact because they were toughened and targeted on Haitian economic and military elites. The junta's decision to step aside in September 1994 was undoubtedly triggered by the U.S. military forces on their way to Haiti, but economic sanctions had set the stage for their surrender by weakening their ability and their will to resist military action. Once sanctions were toughened to include a total trade embargo and a freeze of assets, they crippled the Haitian economy and hurt the elites.[21] This helped to convince Haiti's political elites to accept the idea of Aristide's return.[22] This, in turn, left the military leadership without its base of support, and unwilling to resist the U.S. invasion force. Economic sanctions made Haiti's military junta more willing to leave power peacefully when the United States threatened to use force.

Thus, despite being badly implemented at first, economic sanctions eventually injured the Haitian elites and thereby eased Aristide's restoration to power. These sanctions also serve as a powerful example that may deter militaries and elites elsewhere from considering anti-democratic coups.

The United States and the United Nations imposed aid, trade, and financial sanctions on Yugoslavia (Serbia and Montenegro) in 1992 with the goal of persuading it to rein in its Bosnian Serb clients and thus bring an end to the war in Bosnia.[23] These sanctions devastated the Yugoslav economy and helped to persuade Serbian leader Slobodan Milosevic to end his war for a "Greater Serbia." In late 1995, Milosevic accepted a U.S.-brokered peace agreement reached in Dayton, Ohio, and pressed the Bosnian Serbs to accept it as well. Without the U.S.–UN sanctions, it seems very unlikely that the Serb side would even have considered the terms of the Dayton accord, let alone accepted them.[24]

Using economic instruments to end a war is extremely difficult. However, in this case, achieving peace has been made even more difficult because the United States has immoderate goals. Specifically, the United States has formally rejected a partition settlement, insisting that Bosnia must be maintained as a unitary state.[25] This requires the Bosnian Serbs to surrender sovereignty over all of their territory and abandon their goal of national independence—things they are very unlikely to do. The sanctions effort might have succeeded in achieving peace sooner if its goal had been more modest.

In short, economic sanctions have had a substantial impact on policy in Yugoslavia. Their failure to bring peace in Bosnia has been due mainly to U.S. political aims.

These three cases show that when a U.S.-led coalition has had the will to impose tough, comprehensive sanctions, it has achieved positive results. At a minimum, the economic damage done by these sanctions warns the world that the United States in coalition with other international powers can impose high economic costs on miscreant states and regimes. In addition, sanctions brought about important changes in the behavior of three targeted states. In the absence of sanctions, Saddam Hussein would have withheld his concessions on weapons of mass destruction, the Haitian elites would not have accepted Aristide's return, and Milosevic would not have pressured Bosnian Serbs to make concessions for peace.

In sum, economic sanctions work better than the academic literature or the conventional public wisdom suggests. The post–Cold War experience to date suggests that the prospects for U.S.-led sanctions are bright. No black knight has emerged to undercut sanctions efforts, and U.S.-led coalitions have remained cohesive. Sanctions are not surefire weapons, but they can help to bring about important changes in policy if they are firmly applied. They regularly work as well or better than other foreign policy instruments.

THE COSTS OF IMPOSING SANCTIONS

Some skeptics argue that sanctions are poor foreign policy instruments because their use imposes exorbitant costs on sender states. According to this line of thinking, sanctions are not worthwhile: the price of success is excessive even if sanctions eventually succeed.[26] The high costs of sanctions make them less likely to succeed, because these costs weaken the senders' resolve. Seeing this, targets are emboldened to hold out, which further weakens the senders' will and eventually leads to the campaign's collapse. Finally, some critics argue that sanctions impose a moral cost on senders that outweighs their value.

In fact, the high economic costs that are cited by critics are largely mythical: sanctions seldom impose high economic costs on sender states. The case that costs are high has four shortcomings.

First, even the numbers used by skeptics do not indicate that economic costs to sender states are high. The National Foreign Trade Council, an anti-sanctions organization, has estimated that economic sanctions cost the United States $7 billion in lost exports to target states in 1987.[27] Even if this is true, $7 billion was only a very small fraction of U.S. gross domestic product (GDP) and total U.S. exports for 1987.[28] Moreover, the actual losses from these sanctions were undoubtedly lower because some portion of the exports not sent to sanctioned states were exported to other markets.

Second, many economic sanctions are cost-free to senders. Reducing or terminating bilateral foreign aid costs nothing, and will usually provide a net economic and domestic political gain. Similarly, financial sanctions, such as freezing assets and slowing or halting World Bank and International Monetary Fund (IMF) assistance impose almost no costs on senders. Even trade sanctions, which usually stir the greatest opposition, can give an economic boost to domestic businesses by providing protection from foreign competitors. Hufbauer, Schott, and Elliott concluded that 85 percent of U.S. unilateral and U.S.-led economic sanctions produced a net gain to the senders or had little effect on the senders.[29]

Third, sanctions imposed with broad international support avoid the cost that businesses are most averse to paying: relative loss of market share to foreign competitors. When export restrictions are imposed, the pain and complaint level varies depending on whether the costs are relative or absolute.[30] Absolute costs occur when a sanctions effort has widespread support, such as the 1990 sanctions against Iraq. Under these conditions, firms lose business but do not lose market share to their foreign competitions because the competition is also participating in the embargo. Relative costs are incurred when countries impose unilateral sanctions or when only a small number of other states participate in the campaign. Under these conditions, businesses are likely to lose market share to foreign competitors.[31] However, with prospects for broad cooperation on sanctions efforts brightened by the Cold War's end, this problem will probably arise less often in the future.

Fourth, the costs to senders of imposing sanctions are far smaller than the costs of threatening or using force. Although sanctions cost the United States $7 billion in lost exports in 1987, the defense budget that year cost $283.5 billion.[32] It is also clear that the use of force has not been cost-free to the United States 85 percent of the time, as economic sanctions have been.[33] Moreover, sanctions do not risk U.S. lives.

Finally, some critics condemn sanctions because they hurt innocent civilians in the target country, and thus violate a moral proscription on injuring political innocents.[34] Two main points need to be made in response. First, injury to innocents is a real drawback to sanctions use. However, this cost should be measured against the benefits that sanctions provide. The value of avoiding injury to innocents is not an absolute, and should give way if the benefits of sanctions are greater. It is important to note that innocent civilians often welcome the imposition of sanctions against their countries when they share the goals of outside powers; Haiti is a case in point.[35] Sanctions should, of course, be targeted as much as possible at the government in question and its key supporters. Second, the alternative policy instrument—military force—would also, in most cases, cause significant and more grievous harm to ordinary citizens.

IMPLICATIONS FOR THE PREVENTION, MANAGEMENT, AND RESOLUTION OF INTERNAL CONFLICT

What role can U.S.-led economic sanctions play in helping to prevent, manage, or resolve internal conflict in the future? How should they be applied? I argue that sanctions can be an effective instrument for controlling internal conflict, and should be used for that purpose far more than in the past. Sanctions are most likely to succeed when used to manage or contain internal conflicts, less likely to succeed when used to prevent conflicts, and least likely to succeed when used to resolve conflicts. When they are used, sanctions should be total and should be imposed early in the conflict. The United States must win widespread cooperation from other states, and must show resolve to the target state. This, in turn, requires building domestic support for the sanctions policy, and clearly committing the relevant governments to maintaining the sanctions until the target complies with the demands being made of it.

Using Sanctions to Prevent Internal Conflict

Outside powers could use economic sanctions to prevent internal conflicts if they could foresee impending civil wars and could pressure one or more colliding parties to adopt more peaceful policies. For example, governments could be pressured to adopt reforms that would defuse impending rebellions. Such reforms might include implementing democratic changes, granting autonomy to or sharing power with national minorities, land reform, redistribution of wealth, or refraining from disseminating hate propaganda. The sanctions that pressured South Africa to end apartheid could be considered a successful example of conflict prevention.

International financial institutions such as the World Bank and the IMF could tie economic assistance to a government's domestic policies—a procedure known as conditionality—for the same purpose.[36] Although not a traditional economic sanction, tying economic assistance to a government's domestic policies (e.g., respect for minority rights) is a way of using leverage to bring about peaceful political change.[37]

Sanctions efforts of this sort are worth attempting because conflict prevention is far easier than conflict resolution. If a conflict can be caught early, the effort required to avert it will be far less than the effort to halt it once it begins. The parties are not yet politically mobilized for war. Hence, they are more tractable.

There are, however, three serious impediments to using economic sanctions for conflict prevention. First, violent internal conflict is hard to predict. This makes it hard to identify cases where conflict prevention measures are needed. Second, the causes and preventives of internal conflicts can be difficult to distinguish. For example, pressuring repressive regimes to reform can cause either peace or war, depending on the situation. The trick lies in knowing which situation one faces. U.S. pressures to reform sparked civil conflicts in both Nicaragua and Iran in the 1970s. Neither Anastasio Somoza Debayle nor the Shah Muhammed Reza Pahlavi ever enacted meaningful reforms, but the pressure to do so may have galvanized opponents by convincing them that the United States would not intervene to prop up the regime.[38] If sanctions are to be used for conflict prevention, a good understanding of the roots of internal conflict is needed in order to avoid such mistakes.

Third, it is difficult to impose sanctions against opposition groups and forces. In so many cases, no clearly delineated borders separate the opposition from the government, making trade sanctions problematic. In addition, opposition groups are generally not direct recipients of foreign economic aid. This reduces outside leverage. Finally, freezing assets is often not an option because members of opposition groups are not wealthy enough to have assets in foreign banks, or because secrecy makes it difficult to identify those individuals whose assets should be frozen.

Thus, the prospects for using economic sanctions to prevent internal conflict are mixed. The fact that conflict prevention involves deterrence rather than compellence bodes well for success. The greatest difficulty with using sanctions to prevent civil conflict lies not with the power of the tool, but with the wisdom of its user. There are limits to our ability to recognize when civil war is imminent, and to distinguish the conditions in which pressure to reform will prevent war (as in South Africa) from the conditions in which pressure will trigger war (as in Nicaragua and Iran). To use sanctions effectively for conflict prevention in the future, excellent intelligence and a better understanding of the roots of war will be needed.

Using Sanctions to Manage the Spread of Internal Conflict

Outside powers can become involved in internal conflicts in two ways. First, outside powers can intervene in civil wars. Examples include the German and Italian interventions in the Spanish civil war, and the U.S. intervention in the Vietnamese civil war. Second, belligerents in civil wars can attack outside powers. Examples include Sandinista attacks on Honduras in the 1970s, and Vietnamese communist intrusions into Cambodia in the 1960s and 1970s.

Hypothetically, economic sanctions can play a role in averting both kinds of problems. A coalition could avert the first scenario by threatening to sanction any outside powers that intervene in a civil war. It could avert the second scenario by threatening to sanction any belligerent in a civil war that attacks neighboring states.

Economic sanctions and the threat of sanctions are well suited to efforts to limit outside intervention in civil wars. First, one is attempting to deter contemplated action rather than compel an actor to reverse steps already taken. Second, identifying the outside powers that might intervene in a civil war is relatively easy. The target of the threat (and of the sanction) would be clear.

Preventing belligerents from lashing out at neighboring states may be more difficult, because these belligerents are highly motivated, and therefore less likely to be swayed by sanctions or the threat of sanctions. However, even here a U.S-led coalition may have leverage if its aid or trade is critical to a belligerent's war effort, or to its postwar rebuilding effort. If all else fails, a threat to assist the belligerent's enemies could deter it from attacking neighboring states.

Using Sanctions to Resolve Internal Conflict

Outside powers could adopt one of two strategies to terminate ongoing civil conflicts. One option is to choose a side and aid it in gaining a decisive victory. A second option is to coerce the parties to accept a compromise.[39] Regardless of which strategy the United States and its coalition partners adopt, using economic sanctions to end wars is difficult. First, the coalition members must reach agreement on a plan for peace—something they could not do with respect to Bosnia until the war was over three years old. Without a clear policy goal, no instrument, including economic sanctions, can be effective. Agreements on goals, however, can be difficult to forge. Second, even when a peace plan is in place, it can be difficult to verify compliance.[40] But unless one knows which party is in greatest breach of the plan, one will not know whom to sanction. Determining who should be targeted for sanctions is a problem that must be solved. However, this can be difficult. Third, ending wars is harder than preventing wars because compellence is harder than deterrence: it is always harder to coerce actors to reverse policies already adopted than to eschew policies not yet embraced. Acts of war are among the hardest policies to reverse because the stakes are high and reversals leave elites politically exposed.

Finally, turning sanctions on and off, as iterated coercion of the parties may require—as one side, then the other, might need encouragement to comply with a peace plan—is problematic. The pain that sanctions produce can lag behind the imposition of sanctions by months or years. As a result, the sanctioner cannot locate the punishment close in time to the transgression, robbing the punishment of its deterrent effect. Turning sanctions on and off also allows the parties to stockpile goods while sanctions are not in effect. This will undercut the efficacy of future rounds of sanctions.

In sum, economic sanctions are less well suited to the task of stopping wars than to conflict prevention. However, sanctions still have some prospects of success at this task, and often remain the best instrument for the job. The United States can impose sanctions at little cost. This cost is nearly always less than the cost of using military force. Hence, it is worthwhile to try using economic sanctions to resolve internal conflicts.

How to Apply Economic Sanctions

How should economic sanctions be applied in order to maximize their efficacy for conflict prevention, management, and resolution? Policymakers should embrace four main operating principles: imposing total sanctions, imposing sanctions immediately, obtaining the cooperation of all key states, and demonstrating resolve.

First, the full range of available economic instruments should be threatened and used. A combination of aid, trade, and financial sanctions is markedly more effective than any lesser combination. Iran (1979), Iraq (1990), Haiti (1991), and Yugoslavia (1992) are all cases where total sanctions produced positive results. When the United States and other international powers have shown the will to impose total sanctions, they have usually achieved results.

Second, total sanctions should be imposed as soon as decisions to impose sanctions are taken. A slow, incremental tightening of sanctions is far less effective. Incrementalism allows the target time to adjust and take steps (e.g., stockpiling supplies and moving money) that make sanctions less effective. Incremental sanctions may also cause the target to question the resolve of the United States and other coalition partners.

Third, in order to maximize the chances for success, the United States must acquire and maintain the cooperation of key states. The states whose cooperation is most necessary are the neighbors and major trading partners of the target. Not coincidentally, these are the states, in addition to the target, which are most likely to suffer from the imposition of economic sanctions. Therefore, gaining their cooperation may not be easy. However, it is possible to build a coalition if the United States and other powers provide carrots and sticks to induce cooperation from key states. Carrots could include compensation for the loss of revenue from trade with the target. Sticks could include threats to reduce aid or trade. Carrots will seldom induce perfect compliance—even if neighboring state governments cooperate, some smuggling is likely—but perfect compliance is not required. As Iraq and Haiti have demonstrated, a little leakage does not prevent sanctions from devastating the target's economy.

Fourth, the coalition must convince the target that it will continue to impose the sanctions until they are successful. This is extremely important because sanctions can take months, even years, to produce results.[41] Two steps are required to create this impression. First, if the United States leads the coalition, the U.S. government must commit itself, in a highly visible way, to maintaining sanctions until the target complies. Such a commitment will make a retreat more difficult. Second, the U.S. government must build broad domestic support for the sanctions policy. A lack of strong domestic support could lead the target to believe that it could wait out the sanctions. To do this, Washington must identify domestic interests that will be hurt by the sanctions in question. It then must decide to pay the political price of standing up to them, or persuade them not to work for the sanctions' repeal. This may involve providing compensation (political or economic) to offset the negative effects of the sanctions.

CONCLUSIONS

The conditions for using economic sanctions for conflict prevention, management, and resolution are generally auspicious and should remain so for the foreseeable future. Sanctions are better suited for these purposes than they were during the Cold War for two reasons. First, the Soviet black knight has vanished, and no replacement has emerged. This makes all Western uses of sanctions more likely to succeed. Second, there is a growing awareness in the United States and Western Europe that regional wars pose real costs and risks to the major industrial states. The world is consequently more willing to support U.S.-led efforts to prevent or contain such wars. One concern is that these conflicts will produce refugees who will head for the West. The war in Vietnam created a refugee crisis that is still not fully resolved. More recently, Haitian refugees forced the United States to deal with that country's political problems. The conflicts in Algeria and Bosnia have created refugee problems for Western Europe. These refugee crises have made Western powers more willing to act to stop the wars that produce them.

The United States has never used economic sanctions explicitly for preventing, managing, or resolving internal conflicts. It should do so. Sanctions are underrated, more effective than most analysts suggest, and they could be an effective damper on internal conflict. This conclusion clashes with the conventional view on sanctions, which holds that sanctions are seldom effective. However, past studies understate the effectiveness of sanctions by including cases of half-hearted sanctions and by defining success in narrow terms. Direct extrapolations from these studies would lead one to understate the likely success of U.S.-led sanctions in the post–Cold War era.

The efficacy of sanctions is also underrated because, unlike other foreign policy instruments, sanctions have no natural advocates or constituency. Business leaders dislike sanctions because they disrupt international commerce. Within the

U.S. government, the State Department, the Central Intelligence Agency, and the Defense Department are natural advocates for diplomacy, covert action, and the use of military force, respectively. Economic sanctions have no equivalent champion. As a result, their successes go unreported while their failures are exaggerated by those with an interest in either avoiding the use of sanctions, or in using other instruments.

The main impediments to the success of economic sanctions stem from domestic political and intellectual concerns. The problem lies not with the weakness of the sanctions instrument—it is a strong and effective instrument, if wielded properly, firmly, and in a timely manner—but with the political indecisiveness and intellectual weaknesses of its users. To use sanctions for the prevention, management, and resolution of internal conflicts, we must develop a grasp of the roots of these wars, learn to predict their occurrence more accurately, and become better able to decide what solutions to impose. The United States and other international powers must also be willing to maintain sanctions for months or years if necessary, to stand up to (or buy off) domestic interests injured by sanctions, and to lead allies to cooperate. If these conditions are met, economic sanctions stand a good chance of producing results.

NOTES

1. Economic sanctions involve the threat or use of economic punishment (e.g., trade embargoes, aid reductions or cutoffs, and asset-freezing) by one state or a coalition of states to produce a change in the political behavior of another state. Not included are military sanctions such as arms embargoes.

2. The limits of the U.S. public's tolerance for U.S. casualties were shown in Somalia in 1993, where a total of thirty U.S. combat deaths triggered a U.S. decision to withdraw. For more on this argument, see Harvey M. Sapolsky, "War without Killing," in Sam C. Sarkesian and John Mead Flanagin, eds., *U.S. Domestic and National Security Agendas* (Westport, Conn.: Greenwood, 1994), pp. 27–40.

3. Success should be measured by asking: would those who applied them be closer to their policy goals, farther from them, or at the same point if sanctions had never been imposed? Sanctions are successful if they bring these powers closer to policy goals.

4. Gary Clyde Hufbauer, Jeffrey J. Schott, and Kimberly Ann Elliott use the term "black knight" to refer to a power that counters another's sanctions by providing offsetting aid and trade to the target state. See their *Economic Sanctions Reconsidered*, Vol. 1, 2nd ed. (Washington, D.C.: Institute for International Economics, 1991), p. 12.

5. Sanctions efforts by medium powers against very weak states can sometimes succeed, and thus form exceptions to this generalization.

6. See Hufbauer, Schott, and Elliott, *Economic Sanctions Reconsidered*, Vol. 1, pp. 16–27. They warn that their list may omit some cases of sanctions imposed by small states (see Vol. 1, p. 4), but I believe it includes all major sanctions episodes involving great powers.

7. Some might argue that the United Nations plays a major role in leading sanctions efforts, but this view rests on an overestimate of its autonomy from the great powers. When the United Nations acts, it acts as an arm of the great powers. In short, the concept of "UN-led sanctions" is a myth: sanctions led by great powers are implemented under the auspices of the United Nations: Rhodesia (1966), South Africa (1977), Iraq (1990), Yugoslavia (1991), and Libya (1992). Concurring with this view are Hufbauer, Schott, and Elliott, *Economic Sanctions Reconsidered*, Vol. 1, pp. 10–11.

   Discussing and debunking the importance of international institutions in general is John J. Mearsheimer, "The False Promise of International Institutions," *International Security* Vol. 19, No. 3 (Winter 1994/95), pp. 5–49.

8. I thank Samuel Huntington for suggesting this argument.

9. I have also focused on the Iraqi, Haitian, and Yugoslav cases because U.S. goals in these cases included the prevention, management, and resolution of internal conflict.

10. Nicholas D. Kristof, "The Rise of China," *Foreign Affairs*, Vol. 72, No. 5 (November/December 1993), p. 71.

11. Nicholas D. Kristof, "China Opposes Sanctions in North Korea Dispute," *New York Times*, March 24, 1993, p. A8.

12. France, Russia, and China have favored lifting the sanctions on Iraq. As of late 1995, however, the United States has been able to keep the coalition together and get the necessary votes in the UN Security Council to maintain the sanctions. See "France Starts to Open the Doors," *Economist*, January 14, 1995, pp. 41–42; Barbara Crossette, "Iraq Hides Biological Warfare Effort, Report Says," *New York Times*, April 12, 1995, p. A8.

13. For more on international cooperation and economic sanctions, see Lisa L. Martin, *Coercive Cooperation: Explaining Multilateral Economic Sanctions* (Princeton, N.J.: Princeton University Press, 1992).

14. Iraq's GNP fell from $35 billion in 1989 to $15 billion in 1991 and $17 billion in both 1992 and 1993. See International Institute for Strategic Studies (IISS), *The Military Balance*, 1994–1995 (London: IISS, 1994), p. 129. The economic damage that sanctions inflict on targets is an indirect but nevertheless useful measure of their success. A target state may defy a sender's wishes even if it suffers economically, but the odds of compliance generally increase with the severity of the damage. Moreover, the damage that sanctions inflict directly measures their capacity to weaken the target (thereby reducing its capacity for mischief) or punish the target (thereby deterring it and others from future mischief). As discussed above, this can serve a valuable purpose.

15. Youssef Ibrahim, "Iraq Said to Sell Oil in Secret Plan to Skirt U.N. Ban," *New York Times*, February 16, 1995, p. A6.

16. UN monitor Rolf Ekeus described Iraq as in compliance with respect to nuclear and chemical weapons, but not biological weapons. Crossette, "Iraq Hides Biological Warfare Effort, Report Says."

17. It also bears mention that Saddam's overthrow is not a formal goal of the sanctions campaign. UN Security Council Resolution 687, passed in April 1991, required only that Iraq renounce all weapons of mass destruction—chemical, biological, and nuclear—and missiles with ranges above 150 kilometers, and that Iraq pay compensation and war reparations from the proceeds of future oil sales. See Alan Dowty, "Sanctioning Iraq: The Limits of the New World Order," *Washington Quarterly*, Vol.

17, No. 3 (Summer 1994), p. 180. Overthrowing Saddam became an informal U.S. sanctions goal shortly after the Gulf War.

18. See Gary C. Hufbauer and Kimberly A. Elliott, "Sanctions Will Bite—and Soon," *New York Times*, January 14, 1991, p. A17; and Les Aspin, "The Role of Sanctions in Securing U.S. Interests in the Persian Gulf," in U.S. Congress, House Committee on Armed Services, *Crisis in the Persian Gulf: Sanctions, Diplomacy and War*, Hearings Before the Committee on Armed Services, 101st Cong., 2nd sess., 1990, pp. 862–863.

19. Most strikingly, the financial assets of Haitian military leaders in the United States were not frozen until January 1994, more than two years into the crisis. See "U.S. Extends Economic Sanctions on Haiti," *New York Times*, January 28, 1994, p. A7.

20. The half-hearted and tentative nature of U.S. sanctions is reflected in the slow and meandering chronicle of their imposition. Shortly after Aristide's overthrow, in October and November of 1991, the United States suspended aid, trade, and all transactions with the Haitian government. OAS sanctions followed shortly. But in February 1992 the Bush administration created exemptions for U.S. businesses operating in Haiti. Only in June 1992 was the embargo broadened to deny U.S. ports to ships engaged in commerce with Haiti. Only in June 1993, nineteen months into the confrontation, did the United Nations impose an oil embargo on Haiti. This embargo was suspended in August after the Haitian junta signed the Governors Island Agreement; the embargo was reimposed in October 1993 when the junta reneged on the deal. Also in October 1993—two years into the confrontation—the United States froze the assets of forty-one government supporters. Only in January 1994 did the United States freeze the assets of members of the Haitian military and prohibit transactions with them. Commercial air service with Haiti was banned and financial transactions were further restricted only in June 1994. See Erin Day, *Economic Sanctions Imposed by the United States against Specific Countries: 1979 through 1992* (Washington, D.C.: Congressional Research Service, August 10, 1992), pp. 513–524, 523–525; "U.S. Extends Economic Sanctions on Haiti," *New York Times*, January 28, 1994, p. A7; Paul Lewis, "U.N. Again Imposes Sanctions on Haiti after Pact Fails," *New York Times*, October 14, 1993, p. A1; Heather M. Fleming, "Give Sanctions Time to Bite, Gray Tells Lawmakers," *CQ Weekly Report*, Vol. 52 (June 11, 1994), p. 1540.

21. Howard W. French, "Haiti's Poor Feeling the Pinch as Sanctions Ruin Economy," *New York Times*, November 15, 1993, p. A7; "Tightening the Stranglehold," *Economist*, August 6, 1994, p. 35.

22. "Sanctions Work," *Economist*, September 4, 1993, p. 41; Rick Bragg, "Many of Haiti's Elite Resign Themselves to Aristide's Return," *New York Times*, September 25, 1994, p. 16.

23. "Wide-Ranging Sanctions Imposed against Yugoslavia," *UN Chronicle*, Vol. 28, No. 3 (September 1992), pp. 5–12; Day, *Economic Sanctions Imposed by the United States Against Specific Countries*, pp. 425–428.

24. "Feeling the Pinch," *Economist*, October 8, 1994, pp. 54–55; Roger Cohen, "An Imperfect Peace," *New York Times*, November 22, 1995, p. A1.

25. David Binder, "U.S. Policymakers on Bosnia Admit Errors in Opposing Partition in 1992," *New York Times*, August 29, 1993, p. 10; Chuck Sudetic, "Clinton Writes to Reassure Bosnian Government of Support," *New York Times*, December 5, 1994, p. A12.

26. On this argument, see Mary H. Cooper, "Economic Sanctions," *CQ Researcher*, Vol. 4, No. 40 (October 28, 1994), pp. 941, 943.

27. Gary Hufbauer, "The Impact of U.S. Economic Sanctions and Controls on U.S. Firms," report to the National Foreign Trade Council, April 1990, p. 23. The National Foreign Trade Council describes itself as an anti-sanctions organization. See Hufbauer, p. iii.

28. Total U.S. exports for 1987 were $250.4 billion and GDP was $4.46 trillion. Thus, $7 billion was 2.8 percent of total exports and 0.16 percent of GDP. Moreover, two-thirds of the $7 billion in losses resulted from Coordinating Committee for Multilateral Export Controls (COCOM) sanctions against the Soviet bloc, which have since been lifted. See Hufbauer, "Impact of U.S. Economic Sanctions," p. 44; IISS, *The Military Balance 1988–1989* (London: IISS, 1988), p. 18; U.S. Arms Control and Disarmament Agency (ACDA), *World Military Expenditures and Arms Transfers 1988* (Washington, D.C.: ACDA, 1989), p. 107.

29. Of the seventy-three cases involving the United States, forty-eight percent resulted in a net gain, thirty-seven percent had little effect on the sender, fourteen percent resulted in a modest loss to the sender, and only one percent (one case) caused a major loss to the sender. This single case was Iraq (1990), and the negative effects fell mainly on U.S. allies rather then the United States itself. Thus, the United States has never suffered a major economic loss from a sanctions effort. Data calculated from tables in Hufbauer, Schott, and Elliott, *Economic Sanctions Reconsidered*, Vol. 1, pp. 84–90.

30. The concepts of relative and absolute costs are inspired by Joseph Grieco, who uses the concepts of relative and absolute gains to explain state behavior. See Joseph M. Grieco, *Cooperation among Nations* (Ithaca, N.Y.: Cornell University Press, 1990).

31. This explains the growing U.S. corporate opposition to the COCOM sanctions in the 1980s. See Beverly Crawford, *Economic Vulnerability in International Relations: East-West Trade, Investment, and Finance* (New York: Columbia University Press, 1993), pp. 31–36; and Kevin F.F. Quigley and William J. Long, "Export Controls: Moving beyond Economic Containment," *World Policy Journal*, Vol. 7, No. 1 (Winter 1989–90), pp. 175–178.

32. IISS, *The Military Balance 1988–1989*, p. 18.

33. A full comparison of the costs of economic sanctions and force requires assessing the cost of preparing to use each instrument and the actual cost of their use. Economic sanctions are usually far cheaper on both dimensions. Preparation for economic sanctions costs very little, requiring at most some stockpiling of goods. Preparation for force involves the cost of training, maintaining, and arming the military. Like sanctions, the cost of force will vary from case to case. For example, preparation for the Gulf War cost the United States $68 billion, and the war itself cost another $52 billion. Because of unique circumstances, the entire $52 billion was paid by allies. However, even this relatively cheap war cost the United States far more than the $7 billion total cost of all the economic sanctions in place during the year 1987. See Ann Markusen, "Mixed Messages: The Effects of the Gulf War and the End of the Cold War on the American Military-Industrial Complex," in John O'Loughlin, Tom Mayer, and Edward S. Greenberg, eds., *War and Its Consequences: Lessons from the Persian Gulf Conflict* (New York: HarperCollins, 1994), p. 165.

34. For more on this issue, see Lori Fisler Damrosch, "The Civilian Impact of Economic Sanctions," in Lori Fisler Damrosch, ed., *Enforcing Restraint: Collective Intervention in Internal Conflicts* (New York: Council on Foreign Relations, 1993), pp. 274–315.

35. See Pamela Constable, "Dateline Haiti: Caribbean Stalemate," *Foreign Policy,* No. 89 (Winter 1992/93), pp. 175–176, 183; "Still Embargoed," *Economist,* October 10, 1992, p. 54.

36. For an analysis of the issues surrounding conditionality by international financial institutions, see Wolfgang H. Reinicke, "Cooperative Security and the Political Economy of Nonproliferation," in Janne E. Nolan, ed., *Global Engagement: Cooperation and Security in the 21st Century* (Washington, D.C.: Brookings Institution, 1994), pp. 175–234.

37. Milada Vachudová argues, along similar lines, that the possibility of membership in the European Union and NATO has had a positive effect on the economic, social, and foreign policies of Central European countries. Thus, Western conditioning of membership in these institutions on political criteria such as maintaining democracy has dampened the potential for conflict in Central and Eastern Europe.

38. Perhaps having learned from those experiences, the United States helped ease another dictator, Ferdinand Marcos, out of power in the Philippines without a civil war or a takeover by a hostile regime.

39. Discussing these options are Richard K. Betts, "The Delusion of Impartial Intervention," *Foreign Affairs,* Vol. 73, No. 6 (November/December 1994), pp. 20–33; and Barbara F. Walter, "The Resolution of Civil Wars: Why Negotiations Fail," Ph.D. dissertation, University of Chicago, 1994.

40. Bosnia is a case in point. It has often proven impossible to ascertain who first broke cease-fire agreements between Serbs and Muslims.

41. The average duration of sanctions coded as successes by Hufbauer, Schott, and Elliott was 2.9 years. See their *Economic Sanctions Reconsidered,* Vol. 1, p. 101.

✔ **NO**
The False Promise of Economic Sanctions
KIM RICHARD NOSSAL

Economic sanctions continue to be one of the most popular tools of statecraft in the post–Cold War era. In response to human rights abuses, or the outbreak of civil conflict, or some violation of international norms, a common response has been to call for sanctions against the offending country. For example, when the Nigerian regime of Sani Abacha executed Ken Saro-Wiwa and eight other Ogonis in November 1995, sanctions were clearly the preferred response. Sanctions will work to restore democracy, Senator Nancy Kassebaum argued in the introduction to legislation she introduced in the United States Senate, symbolically titled the Nigeria Democracy Act. It is time to get serious with Nigeria, Tony Lloyd, the foreign affairs spokesman of the British Labour Party said; sanctions *are* serious, he claimed, and they will force Abacha out. The refrain was echoed by Canada's foreign minister, Lloyd Axworthy: sanctions, he claimed, will make the regime in Lagos sit up and take notice.

The enthusiasm for sanctions in the Nigerian case is by no means unusual. Sanctions have become the instrument of choice for responding to human rights violations, international norms, and outbreaks of internal conflict. In the post–Cold War era, sanctions have been imposed against a number of states— including Cuba, Haiti, Iraq, Kenya, Libya, Nigeria, Rwanda, Sudan, and the former Yugoslavia—and advocated against a number of others.

In each case, reasoning about the effectiveness of sanctions proceeds along markedly similar lines. Some take a straight instrumentalist position: sanctions, by causing harm to the target economy, will bring an end to whatever prompted these measures in the first place: the invasion of a neighbour will be reversed, the violation of human rights will cease, the results of an election will be recognized.

Others, by contrast, argue that regardless of the effectiveness of sanctions, violations of international norms need to be punished in some way, if only in order to encourage the development of norms in the international community. Others are more cynical: sanctions are the best response to such violations of norms because they give the appearance of firm action in the face of evil, but in fact they give policymakers a solid excuse to avoid taking harsher (and likely more effective) measures, such as military intervention, subversion, or assassination.

However, whatever the wellsprings of the enthusiasm for sanctions, it can be argued that resorting to this tool of statecraft is highly questionable, politically and ethically. My skepticism for sanctions derives from three observations.

First, the long history of sanctions reveals that such measures do not have a solid track record of success. Now it is true that students of sanctions love to quarrel with one another over how to define success and failure, and which cases of sanctions count as "successes."[1] However, even enthusiasts of sanctions acknowledge that there are relatively few success stories, if they can be called that, where sanctions, threatened or actually imposed, produced the political change sought by those imposing these measures. The successes would include American threats of sanctions against Israel in 1956, the sanctions imposed by the Soviet Union against Finland in 1958–59, the South African sanctions against Lesotho in the early and mid-1980s, French threats of sanctions against New Zealand in 1986, global sanctions against South Africa in the late 1980s, and aid sanctions against Kenya in 1991. Perhaps the key success story for many sanctions enthusiasts are the global sanctions imposed against South Africa in the late 1980s, a case that is commonly said to demonstrate beyond any doubt that sanctions can bring about political change.

The case of South Africa is indeed an important one, and the impact of sanctions in this case needs further analysis of the kind that Neta Crawford and Audie Klotz and their colleagues have done.[2] However, lessons about the success of sanctions in this case should be drawn with care. For it should be noted that in the South African case—and indeed all others with the exception of Lesotho—the "success stories" involved political communities where there was a well-established electoral procedure for removing governments. It can be argued that the governments of Israel, Finland, Kenya, New Zealand, and South Africa bowed to the pressures of economic sanctions because of the prospect of electoral retaliation.

But what of countries where the regime holds on to power through terror, coercion, corruption, or co-optation? These are manifestly not regimes that bend to peaceful domestic pressures. And yet the theory of sanctions employed by so many sanctions enthusiasts depends on fundamentally liberal democratic assumptions about the ability to use economic pressure on the governed to squeeze the governors.

The standard response to such objections in particular cases is always the same: this time, the sanctions enthusiasts say, it will be different. This time we will design the sanctions package right so it squeezes correctly. This time the objective conditions are just right. This time the regime is weak or vulnerable. This time the correlation of international forces will be on the side of the sanctioners. This time there will be no "black knight" like the Soviet Union to disrupt the sanctioning process. We heard this refrain in the cases of Iraq after its invasion of Kuwait, Haiti after the 1991 coup, Nigeria after the execution of Saro-Wiwa, and Cuba after the Cessna shootdown in February 1996.

Sanctions enthusiasts, in short, tend to live in hope; they deny or selectively forget the past; they reinterpret the present in order to paint a rosy future where sanctions work just like South African measures did against Lesotho in January 1986 (within three weeks the economy collapsed and the regime was ousted in a bloodless coup). By contrast, many students of sanctions have heard the mantra of hope too many times to be anything but depressed about how little sanctions enthusiasts appear to have learned from history.

One of the reasons for being depressed is that if sanctions have a poor track record of changing the behaviour of regimes, they have a very good track record of doing considerable damage to national economies, and, in the process, people's lives, which is a second reason for skepticism about the wisdom and the morality of embracing sanctions as a way of responding to internal conflicts, human rights abuses, or other violations of international norms.

For sanctions *do* work. They *do* hurt: they cause deprivation, shortages, and disruptions. They distort the economic lives of communities. They play havoc with foreign exchange and the regular supply of imported goods and services on which most communities have come to rely. Instead, they encourage black markets—and the gangsterism and corruption that tend to go with them. They produce sudden large-scale unemployment and longer-term underemployment, and all the social and familial dysfunctions that accompany such economic dislocation. Because they affect supplies of fuel, food, and medicine, sanctions can have grave effects on public health.

The post–Cold War sanctions against Haiti, or Serbia, or Iraq—or the longer-lived sanctions against Vietnam, or Cuba, or North Korea—demonstrate nicely how well sanctions can and do destroy the lives of ordinary people, but without producing the kind of political change that would allow these measures to be lifted and normalcy restored. These cases show, in other words, how well sanctions work—while they aren't working at all.

The third objection to sanctions is that although these measures are targeted at an entire economy, they affect groups within that community very differently. Thanks to the efforts of UNICEF and other agencies, the international community is slowly beginning to recognize that sanctions, because they disrupt normal economic activity, tend to have a proportionately more devastating effect on children than others in society, making access to both food and medicine more difficult.

But what is rarely acknowledged is that sanctions are one of the more gendered instruments of statecraft. In other words, when sanctions are imposed, women are affected by these measures very differently than men. Sanctions are measures that tend to be advocated by men, targeted against governments dominated by men, by governments dominated by men. There is usually little recognition that the tasks of actually coping with the deprivations and disruptions caused by sanctions tends to fall disproportionately on the shoulders of women—the very members of society who are already often in a marginalized position in many countries in the South.[3]

Likewise, the governors and the wealthy elites in a country hit by sanctions are always going to fare better in times of deprivation than the governed. Supposedly "smart" or "surgical" sanctions targeted at elites—such as curbs on international travel or access to funds—invariably do little more than challenge the ingenuity of the rich to find new and imaginative ways around the games governments play with one another. Rarely are such sanctions more than a trifling annoyance, particularly in an era when funds can be moved electronically between countries almost instantaneously and elites often have multiple passports.

Government elites, for their part, do not have to worry either, for governments, after all, control access to goods and services and resources. Generals never have to stand in line for cooking oil; they never have to worry about medical attention for their children, or where their next meal is going to come from. The governors of a sanctioned country will always manage to ensure that they, their families, and the security forces are fed, clothed, sheltered, entertained first, with the governed left to fend for themselves.

In short, when one looks at sanctions as a policy option, one is hard-pressed to see much to recommend them. On the contrary: sanctions might appear attractive, particularly if one is looking for something that will give the appearance of *doing* something about internal conflict, or human rights abuses, or violations of international norms.

But when one examines what sanctions actually do—and, as importantly, what they don't do—one might be forgiven for wondering why this instrument of statecraft continues to be the first thing that both policymakers and ordinary folk reach for to respond to human rights violations.

Of course, such skepticism begs an obvious question: what, then, should one do when confronted with internal conflict, or human rights abuses, or violations of international norms? Besides economic warfare, one only has so many options: force, coercion, persuasion, inducement, and of course doing nothing.

Most would probably agree that the options at either end of this spectrum should be eliminated. The nastier, if more effective, forms of statecraft—the use of force, or removing leaders by either assassination or extraterritorial kidnapping—are measures not likely to command widespread support.

Likewise, at the other end of the spectrum, governments should not do nothing. Bluntly put, to be silent or to do nothing in the face of wrongdoing is to condone it, and thus to become *particeps criminis*.

Rather, a multifaceted policy that combined elements of punishment, persuasion, and inducement—similar to the kind of tactics used against apartheid in South Africa in the 1980s—would probably be more effective at achieving political change than a sanctionist policy. Moreover, such a mix would not subject ordinary—and innocent—citizens of the target country to the "double punishment" of having to suffer not only abuses of their governors, but the deprivations visited on them by well-meaning folks in the international community.

First, such an approach would demand that governments continue some punitive tactics: speaking out on violations of norms, rejecting contentions by human rights abusers that the international community has no place or right to comment on these matters. Banning arms sales would be an appropriate measure, even though entirely symbolic given the relative ease with which arms can be purchased on the open market. Refusing to take any measure that would increase the offending regime's legitimacy would be another measure, as would refusing to increase its "comfort level," or to engage in the niceties of "friendly relations."

However, such an approach would also stress staying involved rather than seeking to break ties. Keeping diplomatic representatives in these countries, rather than bringing them home. Working with the diplomatic representatives of other like-minded states to maintain an obvious presence at public events, trials, funerals. Providing funds to local groups seeking political change and to international groups who work for human rights—such as Amnesty International, for example—that would allow them to expand their advocacy for prisoners of conscience. Keeping human rights-abusing regimes in international organizations rather than throwing them out. Keeping aid organizations and NGOs actively engaged in the country, instead of forcing them to leave. Keeping the issue of human rights before the international community, internationalizing it as much as possible.

More controversially, one could, in partnership with other like-minded states, engage in what are euphemistically called "positive sanctions." In other words, openly induce human rights abusers to accelerate transitions to democracy and acceptance of norms. Most people have difficulty with this approach, since it involves "doing business" with regimes accused of wrongdoing, sends unwanted signals about what behaviour is punished and what behaviour is rewarded, and has an equally uncertain track record.

These represent small and incremental measures. But whatever the policy mix, a multifaceted response is likely to be more ethical, if not more effective, in its consequences than the blunt instrument of sanctions usually advocated.

NOTES

1. An excellent survey of sanctions can be found in Margaret Doxey, *International Sanctions in Contemporary Perspective*, 2nd ed. (New York: St. Martin's Press, 1996).

2. See Neta Crawford and Audie Klotz, eds., *How Sanctions Work: South Africa* (New York: St. Martin's Press, forthcoming).

3. For an elaboration of this argument, and its application to the case of Iraq, see Kim Richard Nossal, Lori Buck, and Nicole Gallant, "Sanctions as a Gendered Instrument of Statecraft," British International Studies Association, December 1996.

Postscript

Proponents of sanctions frequently argue that sanctions are a morally preferable instrument of statecraft because they are essentially non-violent in nature. As should already be clear from the Nossal article, this assumption is suspect. Albert Pierce and Joy Gordon, in articles cited below, carry this argument even further. They attempt to apply traditional just-war criteria to the use of economic sanctions and find that the moral case for comprehensive economic sanctions is weak. Using Haiti as a case study, Pierce shows how sanctions clearly violate the just-war prohibition against deliberately targeting civilian populations. Gordon uses sanctions against Iraq as a case study and concludes that economic sanctions are nothing more than "a bureaucratized, internationally organized form of siege warfare." If this is the case, it is useful to discuss whether a sanctions policy can be developed that minimizes the harm done to civilian populations. To explore this question further it is helpful to examine recent efforts to develop "smart sanctions" or "targeted sanctions," which are designed to attack the financial capacity of government and ruling elites rather than impose harm on the general population.

Infotrac Keyword Search
"economic sanctions" or "targeted sanctions" or "smart sanctions"

Suggested Additional Readings

Alerassool, Mahvash. *Freezing Assets: The USA and the Most Effective Economic Sanction.* New York: St. Martin's Press, 1993.

Center for Economic and Social Rights. *UN Sanctioned Suffering in Iraq.* New York: CESR, 1996.

Cortright, David and George A. Lopez, eds. *Economic Sanctions: Panacea or Peacebuilding in a Post-Cold War World?* Boulder: Westview, 1995 .

——. *The Sanctions Decade: Assessing UN Strategies in the 1990s.* Boulder: Lynne Rienner, 2000 .

Doxey, Margaret P. *International Sanctions in Contemporary Perspective.* New York: St. Martin's Press, 1987.

Elliott, Kimberly Ann. *Towards a Framework for Multilateral Sanctions.* Atlanta: Carter Center, 1996.

Gordon, Joy. "Economic Sanctions, Just War Doctrine, and the "Fearful Spectacle of the Civilian Dead." *Crosscurrents.* Available at www.crosscurrents.org/gordon/htm.

Minear, Larry, David Cortright, Julia Wagler, George A. Lopez and Thomas G. Weiss. *Toward More Humane and Effective Sanctions Management: Enhancing the Capacity of the United Nations System.* Providence, RI: Watson Institute, Occasional Paper #31, 1998.

Nossal, Kim Richard. *Rain Dancing: Sanctions in Canadian and Australian Foreign Policy.* Toronto: University of Toronto Press, 1994.

Pierce, Albert. "Just War Principles and Economic Sanctions." *Ethics and International Affairs* 10 (1996): 99–113.

Weiss, Thomas G., David Cortright, George A. Lopez, and Larry Minear. *Political Gain and Civilian Pain: Humanitarian Impacts of Economic Sanctions.* Lanham, MD: Rowman and Littlefield, 1997.

Website Resources

Center for Strategic and International Studies (CSIS)   The Unilateral Economic Sanctions Project examines policy implications of the unilateral use of sanctions by the United States government.

Heritage Foundation   Conservative American think tank website contains *A User's Guide to Economic Sanctions,* prepared by Robert O'Quinn.

Institute for International Economics   Contains a range of articles and resources on economic sanctions. It is especially useful for a discussion of the effectiveness of sanctions.

Institute for National Strategic Studies   Contains book-length study on sanctions by Richard E. Hull–*Imposing International Sanctions: Legal Aspects and Enforcement by the Military.*

USA Engage   A coalition of American business and agricultural groups opposed to economic sanctions.

Voices in the Wilderness   An advocacy organization campaigning for an end to sanctions against Iraq.

Watson Institute for International Studies   Material on using targeted financial sanctions as an alternative to comprehensive economic sanctions.

Does Africa Pose a Threat to Environmental Security?

✔ **YES**

ROBERT D. KAPLAN, "The Coming Anarchy: How Scarcity, Crime, Overpopulation, Tribalism, and Disease Are Rapidly Destroying the Social Fabric of Our Planet," *The Atlantic Monthly* 273, no. 2 (February 1994): 44–76

✘ **NO**

CYRIL OBI, "Globalised Images of Environmental Security in Africa," *Review of African Political Economy* 27, no. 83 (March 2000): 47–63

In 1994, Robert Kaplan published an article in the *Atlantic Monthly* entitled "The Coming Anarchy." Having recently returned from a tour of Africa, Kaplan wrote a vivid account of how the scarcity of resources, disease, overpopulation, refugee migrations, unprovoked crime, and tribalism were rapidly destroying the social and political fabric of many African countries. He suggested that the future of Africa is a bleak one in which "the coming upheaval, in which foreign embassies are shut down, states collapse, and contact with the outside world take place through dangerous, disease-ridden coastal trading posts, will loom large in the century we are entering." More ominously, Kaplan contended that his vision of Africa foreshadows what is in store for the rest of the planet in the coming decades, as environmental degradation contributes to a downward spiral of ethnic and political conflict.

President Clinton is said to have been captivated by Kaplan's analysis, making extensive notes in the margins of his personal copy. Soon members of his cabinet were quoting Kaplan in testimony before Congress. Kaplan's article came at a time when the American administration was dealing with the fall-out of the American intervention in Somalia, including the gruesome sight of dead American airmen being dragged through the streets of Mogadishu. At the same time, the Americans were contemplating what their next move should be in response to the growing number of refugees fleeing by boat from the repressive military regime in Haiti. Extensive media coverage of an outbreak of ebola in Zaire gave further credence to the perception of the developing world as a cauldron of disease and poverty, an ecological time bomb waiting to contaminate the rest of the world.

Although writing as a journalist and drawing on anecdotal evidence, Kaplan claims his analysis is confirmed by recent academic research. In particular, he cites the work of Thomas Homer-Dixon at the University of Toronto. Homer-Dixon has headed up a multi-year research project on environmental change and acute conflict. This project attempts to identify the linkages between environmental degradation, population migrations, and social conflict. The model developed suggests that environmental conflict can lead to other conflicts through several stages. Environmental degradation contributes to a reduction in the quality and quantity of resources, thus producing scarcity. Population growth further reduces the availability of resources by dividing them among an ever-growing number of people. As dwindling resources become concentrated in the hands of fewer people, competition and social conflict intensify. As scarcities increase, populations are forced to migrate, creating new conflict over scarce resources in receiving areas. The work of this research group has led to the publication of books such as Thomas Homer-Dixon and Jessica Blitt, *Ecoviolence: Links among Environment, Population, and Security* (Rowan and Littlefield, 1998).

The writings of journalists like Kaplan and scholars like Homer-Dixon have been influential in stimulating debate over the need to broaden the traditional notion of security to include a focus on environmental threats. If these authors are correct, then states should take issues like environment degradation and climate change more seriously, since future conflicts could be rooted in environmental causes. By seeing the environment as a security issue, states are encouraged to devote the attention and resources needed to addressing these new "threats" as they have done to military threats in the past. The language of "environmental security" quickly caught on within elite decision-making circles in capitals such as Washington, DC. By 1998, the United States government's National Security Strategy was citing rapid population growth, new infectious diseases, and uncontrolled refugee migration as issues having important implications for American security.

Is this "securitization" of the environment a positive trend? Will it help governments deal with environment problems in a more urgent and holistic manner? Critics of the concept of environment security are not so certain. Analysts argue that the construction of security threats is not a neutral enterprise, but instead reflects existing biases and interests. Critics of the concept of environmental security suggest that the very ambiguity of the concept leaves it open to several dangers. First, there is a high risk that turning environmental issues into a security concern will result in the militarization of environmental policy, which will have a detrimental effect on society and hinder efforts to find solutions. Second, environmental security policies may actually reduce security, especially if they increase conflict rather than promote peaceful relations among nations. Third, the examination of environmental issues through a security lens could lead to new distortions in identifying the root causes of contemporary problems.

One such critic of the environmental security approach is Cyril Obi, a research fellow at the Nigerian Institute of International Affairs. In the reading, Obi responds to analysts like Kaplan who have given particular attention to the problems of environmental degradation on the African continent. Rather than creating a better understanding of Africa's environmental problems, Obi argues that the environmental security perspective has unfairly "criminalized" the African continent. Moreover, the environmental security perspective has tended to overlook how both Africa's interaction with capitalist markets and the impact of structural adjustment have had a negative impact on the environment. Instead, Obi argues, environmental security is a value-laden term that has been used to justify maximizing Western interests and supporting market-driven policies. This in turn has made it more difficult for Africans to get their own global environmental politics right.

YES

The Coming Anarchy: How Scarcity, Crime, Overpopulation, Tribalism, and Disease Are Rapidly Destroying the Social Fabric of Our Planet

ROBERT D. KAPLAN

The Minister's eyes were like egg yolks, an after effect of some of the many illnesses, malaria especially, endemic in his country. There was also an irrefutable sadness in his eyes. He spoke in a slow and creaking voice, the voice of hope about to expire. Flame trees, coconut palms, and a ballpoint-blue Atlantic composed the background. None of it seemed beautiful, though. "In forty-five years I have never seen things so bad. We did not manage ourselves well after the British departed. But what we have now is something worse—the revenge of the poor, of the social failures, of the people least able to bring up children in a modern society." Then he referred to the recent coup in the West African country Sierra Leone. "The boys who took power in Sierra Leone come from houses like this." The Minister jabbed his finger at a corrugated metal shack teeming with children. "In three months these boys confiscated all the official Mercedes, Volvos, and BMWs and willfully wrecked them on the road." The Minister mentioned one of the coup's leaders, Solomon Anthony Joseph Musa, who shot the people who had paid for his schooling, "in order to erase the humiliation and mitigate the power his middle-class sponsors held over him."

Tyranny is nothing new in Sierra Leone or in the rest of West Africa. But it is now part and parcel of an increasing lawlessness that is far more significant than any coup, rebel incursion, or episodic experiment in democracy. Crime was what my friend—a top-ranking African official whose life would be threatened were I to identify him more precisely—really wanted to talk about. Crime is what makes West Africa a natural point of departure for my report on what the political character of our planet is likely to be in the twenty-first century.

The cities of West Africa at night are some of the unsafest places in the world. Streets are unlit; the police often lack gasoline for their vehicles; armed burglars, carjackers, and muggers proliferate. "The government in Sierra Leone has no writ after dark," says a foreign resident, shrugging. When I was in the capital, Freetown, last September, eight men armed with AK-47s broke into the house of an American man. They tied him up and stole everything of value. Forget Miami: direct flights between the United States and the Murtala Muhammed Airport, in neighboring Nigeria's largest city, Lagos, have been suspended by order of the U.S. Secretary of Transportation because of ineffective security at the terminal and its environs. A State Department report cited the airport for "extortion by law-enforcement and immigration officials." This is one of the few times that the

U.S. government has embargoed a foreign airport for reasons that are linked purely to crime... In Abidjan, effectively the capital of the Côte d'Ivoire, or Ivory Coast, restaurants have stick- and gun-wielding guards who walk you the fifteen feet or so between your car and the entrance, giving you an eerie taste of what American cities might be like in the future. An Italian ambassador was killed by gunfire when robbers invaded an Abidjan restaurant. The family of the Nigerian ambassador was tied up and robbed at gunpoint in the ambassador's residence. After university students in the Ivory Coast caught bandits who had been plaguing their dorms, they executed them by hanging tires around their necks and setting the tires on fire. In one instance Ivorian policemen stood by and watched the "necklacings," afraid to intervene. Each time I went to the Abidjan bus terminal, groups of young men with restless, scanning eyes surrounded my taxi, putting their hands all over the windows, demanding "tips" for carrying my luggage even though I had only a rucksack. In cities in six West African countries I saw similar young men everywhere–hordes of them. They were like loose molecules in a very unstable social fluid, a fluid that was clearly on the verge of igniting.

"You see," my friend the Minister told me, "in the villages of Africa it is perfectly natural to feed at any table and lodge in any hut. But in the cities this communal existence no longer holds. You must pay for lodging and be invited for food. When young men find out that their relations cannot put them up, they become lost. They join other migrants and slip gradually into the criminal process...."

A PREMONITION OF THE FUTURE

West Africa is becoming the symbol of worldwide demographic, environmental, and societal stress, in which criminal anarchy emerges as the real "strategic" danger. Disease, overpopulation, unprovoked crime, scarcity of resources, refugee migrations, the increasing erosion of nation-states and international borders, and the empowerment of private armies, security firms, and international drug cartels are now most tellingly demonstrated through a West African prism. West Africa provides an appropriate introduction to the issues, often extremely unpleasant to discuss, that will soon confront our civilization. To remap the political earth the way it will be a few decades hence–as I intend to do in this article–I find I must begin with West Africa.

There is no other place on the planet where political maps are so deceptive–where, in fact, they tell such lies–as in West Africa. Start with Sierra Leone. According to the map, it is a nation-state of defined borders, with a government in control of its territory. In truth the Sierra Leonian government, run by a twenty-seven-year-old army captain, Valentine Strasser, controls Freetown by day and by day also controls part of the rural interior. In the government's territory the national army is an unruly rabble threatening drivers and passengers at most checkpoints. In the other part of the country units of two separate armies from the war in Liberia have taken up residence, as has an army of Sierra Leonian rebels. The government force fighting the rebels is full of renegade commanders who have aligned themselves with disaffected village chiefs. A pre-modern formlessness governs the battlefield, evoking the wars in medieval Europe prior to the 1648 Peace of Westphalia, which ushered in the era of organized nation-states.

As a consequence, roughly 400,000 Sierra Leonians are internally displaced, 280,000 more have fled to neighboring Guinea, and another 100,000 have fled to Liberia, even as 400,000 Liberians have fled to Sierra Leone. The third largest city in Sierra Leone, Gondama, is a displaced-persons camp. With an additional 600,000 Liberians in Guinea and 250,000 in the Ivory Coast, the borders dividing these four countries have become largely meaningless. Even in quiet zones none of the governments except the Ivory Coast's maintains the schools, bridges, roads, and police forces in a manner necessary for functional sovereignty. The Koranko ethnic group in northeastern Sierra Leone does all its trading in Guinea. Sierra Leonian diamonds are more likely to be sold in Liberia than in Freetown. In the eastern provinces of Sierra Leone you can buy Liberian beer but not the local brand.

In Sierra Leone, as in Guinea, as in the Ivory Coast, as in Ghana, most of the primary rain forest and the secondary bush are being destroyed at an alarming rate. I saw convoys of trucks bearing majestic hardwood trunks to coastal ports. When Sierra Leone achieved its independence, in 1961, as much as 60 percent of the country was primary rain forest. Now six percent is. In the Ivory Coast the proportion has fallen from 38 percent to eight percent. The deforestation has led to soil erosion, which has led to more flooding and more mosquitoes. Virtually everyone in the West African interior has some form of malaria.

Sierra Leone is a microcosm of what is occurring, albeit in a more tempered and gradual manner, throughout West Africa and much of the underdeveloped world: the withering away of central governments, the rise of tribal and regional domains, the unchecked spread of disease, and the growing pervasiveness of war. West Africa is reverting to the Africa of the Victorian atlas. It consists now of a series of coastal trading posts, such as Freetown and Conakry, and an interior that, owing to violence, volatility, and disease, is again becoming, as Graham Greene once observed, "blank" and "unexplored." However, whereas Greene's vision implies a certain romance, as in the somnolent and charmingly seedy Freetown of his celebrated novel *The Heart of the Matter*, it is Thomas Malthus, the philosopher of demographic doomsday, who is now the prophet of West Africa's future. And West Africa's future, eventually, will also be that of most of the rest of the world....

The fragility of these West African "countries" impressed itself on me when I took a series of bush taxis along the Gulf of Guinea, from the Togolese capital of Lome, across Ghana, to Abidjan. The 400-mile journey required two full days of driving, because of stops at two border crossings and an additional eleven customs stations, at each of which my fellow passengers had their bags searched. I had to change money twice and repeatedly fill in currency-declaration forms. I had to bribe a Togolese immigration official with the equivalent of eighteen dollars before he would agree to put an exit stamp on my passport. Nevertheless, smuggling across these borders is rampant. The *London Observer* has reported that in 1992 the equivalent of $856 million left West Africa for Europe in the form of "hot cash" assumed to be laundered drug money. International cartels have discovered the utility of weak, financially strapped West African regimes.

The more fictitious the actual sovereignty, the more severe border authorities seem to be in trying to prove otherwise. Getting visas for these states can be as hard as crossing their borders. The Washington embassies of Sierra Leone and Guinea—the two poorest nations on earth, according to a 1993 United Nations report on "human development"—asked for letters from my bank (in lieu of prepaid round-trip tickets) and also personal references, in order to prove that I had sufficient means to sustain myself during my visits. I was reminded of my visa and currency hassles while traveling to the communist states of Eastern Europe, particularly East Germany and Czechoslovakia, before those states collapsed.

Ali A. Mazrui, the director of the Institute of Global Cultural Studies at the State University of New York at Binghamton, predicts that West Africa—indeed, the whole continent—is on the verge of large-scale border upheaval. Mazrui writes, "In the 21st century France will be withdrawing from West Africa as she gets increasingly involved in the affairs [of Europe]. France's West African sphere of influence will be filled by Nigeria—a more natural hegemonic power.... It will be under those circumstances that Nigeria's own boundaries are likely to expand to incorporate the Republic of Niger (the Hausa link), the Republic of Benin (the Yoruba link) and conceivably Cameroon."

The future could be more tumultuous, and bloodier, than Mazrui dares to say. France will withdraw from former colonies like Benin, Togo, Niger, and the Ivory Coast, where it has been propping up local currencies. It will do so not only because its attention will be diverted to new challenges in Europe and Russia but also because younger French officials lack the older generation's emotional ties to the ex-colonies. However, even as Nigeria attempts to expand, it, too, is likely to split into several pieces. The State Department's Bureau of Intelligence and Research recently made the following points in an analysis of Nigeria: "Prospects for a transition to civilian rule and democratization are slim.... The repressive apparatus of the state security service ... will be difficult for any future civilian government to control.... The country is becoming increasingly ungovernable.... Ethnic and regional splits are deepening, a situation made worse by an increase in the number of states from 19 to 30 and a doubling in the number of local governing authorities; religious cleavages are more serious; Muslim fundamentalism and evangelical Christian militancy are on the rise; and northern Muslim anxiety over southern [Christian] control of the economy is intense ... the will to keep Nigeria together is now very weak."

Given that oil-rich Nigeria is a bellwether for the region—its population of roughly 90 million equals the populations of all the other West African states combined—it is apparent that Africa faces cataclysms that could make the Ethiopian and Somalian famines pale in comparison. This is especially so because Nigeria's population, including that of its largest city, Lagos, whose crime, pollution, and overcrowding make it the cliché par excellence of Third World urban dysfunction, is set to double during the next twenty-five years, while the country continues to deplete its natural resources.

Part of West Africa's quandary is that although its population belts are horizontal, with habitation densities increasing as one travels south away from the Sahara and toward the tropical abundance of the Atlantic littoral, the borders erected by European colonialists are vertical, and therefore at cross-purposes with demography and topography. Satellite photos depict the same reality I experienced in the bush taxi: the Lome-Abidjan coastal corridor—indeed, the entire stretch of coast from Abidjan eastward to Lagos—is one burgeoning megalopolis that by any rational economic and geographical standard should constitute a single sovereignty, rather than the five (the Ivory Coast, Ghana, Togo, Benin, and Nigeria) into which it is currently divided.

As many internal African borders begin to crumble, a more impenetrable boundary is being erected that threatens to isolate the continent as a whole: the wall of disease. Merely to visit West Africa in some degree of safety, I spent about $500 for a hepatitis B vaccination series and other disease prophylaxis. Africa may today be more dangerous in this regard than it was in 1862, before antibiotics, when the explorer Sir Richard Francis Burton described the health situation on the continent as "deadly, a Golgotha, a Jehannum." Of the approximately 12 million people worldwide whose blood is HIV-positive, 8 million are in Africa. In the capital of the Ivory Coast, whose modern road system only helps to spread the disease, 10 percent of the population is HIV-positive. And war and refugee movements help the virus break through to more-remote areas of Africa. Alan Greenberg, M.D., a representative of the Centers for Disease Control in Abidjan, explains that in Africa the HIV virus and tuberculosis are now "fast-forwarding each other." Of the approximately 4,000 newly diagnosed tuberculosis patients in Abidjan, 45 percent were also found to be HIV-positive. As African birth rates soar and slums proliferate, some experts worry that viral mutations and hybridizations might, just conceivably, result in a form of the AIDS virus that is easier to catch than the present strain.

It is malaria that is most responsible for the disease wall that threatens to separate Africa and other parts of the Third World from more-developed regions of the planet in the twenty-first century. Carried by mosquitoes, malaria, unlike AIDS, is easy to catch. Most people in sub-Saharan Africa have recurring bouts of the disease throughout their entire lives, and it is mutating into increasingly deadly forms. "The great gift of Malaria is utter apathy," wrote Sir Richard Burton, accurately portraying the situation in much of the Third World today. Visitors to malaria-afflicted parts of the planet are protected by a new drug, mefloquine, a side effect of which is vivid, even violent, dreams. But a strain of cerebral malaria resistant to mefloquine is now on the offensive. Consequently, defending oneself against malaria in Africa is becoming more and more like defending oneself against violent crime. You engage in "behavior modification": not going out at dusk, wearing mosquito repellent all the time.

And the cities keep growing. I got a general sense of the future while driving from the airport to downtown Conakry, the capital of Guinea. The forty-five-minute journey in heavy traffic was through one never-ending shantytown: a nightmarish Dickensian spectacle to which Dickens himself would never have given credence. The corrugated metal shacks and scabrous walls were coated with black slime. Stores were built out of rusted shipping containers, junked cars, and jumbles of wire mesh. The streets were one long puddle of floating garbage. Mosquitoes and flies were everywhere. Children, many of whom had protruding bellies, seemed as numerous as ants. When the tide went out, dead rats and the skeletons of cars were exposed on the mucky beach. In twenty-eight years Guinea's population will double if growth goes on at current rates. Hardwood logging continues at a madcap speed, and people flee the Guinean countryside for Conakry. It seemed to me that here, as elsewhere in Africa and the Third World, man is challenging nature far beyond its limits, and nature is now beginning to take its revenge.

Africa may be as relevant to the future character of world politics as the Balkans were a hundred years ago, prior to the two Balkan wars and the First World War. Then the threat was the collapse of empires and the birth of nations based solely on tribe. Now the threat is more elemental: nature unchecked. Africa's immediate future could be very bad. The coming upheaval, in which foreign embassies are shut down, states collapse, and contact with the outside world takes place through dangerous, disease-ridden coastal trading posts, will loom large in the century we are entering. (Nine of twenty-one U.S. foreign-aid missions to be closed over the next three years are in Africa—a prologue to a consolidation of U.S. embassies themselves.) Precisely because much of Africa is set to go over the edge at a time when the Cold War has ended, when environmental and demographic stress in other parts of the globe are becoming critical, and when the post-First World War system of nation-states—not just in the Balkans but perhaps also in the Middle East—is about to be toppled, Africa suggests what war, borders, and ethnic politics will be like a few decades hence.

To understand the events of the next fifty years, then, one must understand environmental scarcity, cultural and racial clash, geographic destiny, and the transformation of war. The order in which I have named these is not accidental. Each concept except the first relies partly on the one or ones before it, meaning that the last two—new approaches to mapmaking and to warfare—are the most important.

They are also the least understood. I will now look at each idea, drawing upon the work of specialists and also my own travel experiences in various parts of the globe besides Africa, in order to fill in the blanks of a new political atlas.

THE ENVIRONMENT AS A HOSTILE POWER

For a while the media will continue to ascribe riots and other violent upheavals abroad mainly to ethnic and religious conflict. But as these conflicts multiply, it will become apparent that something else is afoot, making more and more places like Nigeria, India, and Brazil ungovernable.

Mention the environment or "diminishing natural resources" in foreign-policy circles and you meet a brick wall of skepticism or boredom. To conservatives especially, the very terms seem flaky. Public-policy foundations have contributed to the lack of interest, by funding narrowly focused environmental studies replete with technical jargon which foreign-affairs experts just let pile up on their desks.

It is time to understand the environment for what it is: the national-security issue of the early twenty-first century. The political and strategic impact of surging populations, spreading disease, deforestation and soil erosion, water depletion, air pollution, and, possibly, rising sea levels in critical, overcrowded regions like the Nile Delta and Bangladesh—developments that will prompt mass migrations and, in turn, incite group conflicts—will be the core foreign-policy challenge from which most others will ultimately emanate, arousing the public and uniting assorted interests left over from the Cold War. In the twenty-first century water will be in dangerously short supply in such diverse locales as Saudi Arabia, Central Asia, and the southwestern United States. A war could erupt between Egypt and Ethiopia over Nile River water. Even in Europe tensions have arisen between Hungary and Slovakia over the damming of the Danube, a classic case of how environmental disputes fuse with ethnic and historical ones. The political scientist and erstwhile Clinton adviser Michael Mandelbaum has said, "We have a foreign policy today in the shape of a doughnut—lots of peripheral interests but nothing at the center." The environment, I will argue, is part of a terrifying array of problems that will define a new threat to our security, filling the hole in Mandelbaum's doughnut and allowing a post-Cold War foreign policy to emerge inexorably by need rather than by design.

Our Cold War foreign policy truly began with George F. Kennan's famous article, signed "X," published in *Foreign Affairs* in July of 1947, in which Kennan argued for a "firm and vigilant containment" of a Soviet Union that was imperially, rather than ideologically, motivated. It may be that our post-Cold War foreign policy will one day be seen to have had its beginnings in an even bolder and more detailed piece of written analysis: one that appeared in the journal *International Security*. The article, published in the fall of 1991 by Thomas Fraser Homer-Dixon, who is the head of the Peace and Conflict Studies Program at the

University of Toronto, was titled "On the Threshold: Environmental Changes as Causes of Acute Conflict." Homer-Dixon has, more successfully than other analysts, integrated two hitherto separate fields—military-conflict studies and the study of the physical environment.

In Homer-Dixon's view, future wars and civil violence will often arise from scarcities of resources such as water, cropland, forests, and fish. Just as there will be environmentally driven wars and refugee flows, there will be environmentally induced praetorian regimes—or, as he puts it, "hard regimes." Countries with the highest probability of acquiring hard regimes, according to Homer-Dixon, are those that are threatened by a declining resource base yet also have "a history of state [read 'military'] strength." Candidates include Indonesia, Brazil, and, of course, Nigeria. Though each of these nations has exhibited democratizing tendencies of late, Homer-Dixon argues that such tendencies are likely to be superficial "epiphenomena" having nothing to do with long-term processes that include soaring populations and shrinking raw materials. Democracy is problematic; scarcity is more certain.

Indeed, the Saddam Husseins of the future will have more, not fewer, opportunities. In addition to engendering tribal strife, scarcer resources will place a great strain on many peoples who never had much of a democratic or institutional tradition to begin with. Over the next fifty years the earth's population will soar from 5.5 billion to more than nine billion. Though optimists have hopes for new resource technologies and free-market development in the global village, they fail to note that, as the National Academy of Sciences has pointed out, 95 percent of the population increase will be in the poorest regions of the world, where governments now—just look at Africa—show little ability to function, let alone to implement even marginal improvements. Homer-Dixon writes, ominously, "Neo-Malthusians may underestimate human adaptability in today's environmental-social system, but as time passes their analysis may become ever more compelling."

While a minority of the human population will be, as Francis Fukuyama would put it, sufficiently sheltered so as to enter a "post-historical" realm, living in cities and suburbs in which the environment has been mastered and ethnic animosities have been quelled by bourgeois prosperity, an increasingly large number of people will be stuck in history, living in shantytowns where attempts to rise above poverty, cultural dysfunction, and ethnic strife will be doomed by a lack of water to drink, soil to till, and space to survive in. In the developing world environmental stress will present people with a choice that is increasingly among totalitarianism (as in Iraq), fascist-tending mini-states (as in Serb-held Bosnia), and road-warrior cultures (as in Somalia). Homer-Dixon concludes that "as environmental degradation proceeds, the size of the potential social disruption will increase...."

"We need to bring nature back in," he argues. "We have to stop separating politics from the physical world—the climate, public health, and the environment."

Quoting Daniel Deudney, another pioneering expert on the security aspects of the environment, Homer-Dixon says that "for too long we've been prisoners of 'social-social' theory, which assumes there are only social causes for social and political changes, rather than natural causes, too. This social-social mentality emerged with the Industrial Revolution, which separated us from nature. But nature is coming back with a vengeance, tied to population growth. It will have incredible security implications...."

We are entering a bifurcated world. Part of the globe is inhabited by Hegel's and Fukuyama's Last Man, healthy, well fed, and pampered by technology. The other, larger, part is inhabited by Hobbes's First Man, condemned to a life that is "poor, nasty, brutish, and short." Although both parts will be threatened by environmental stress, the Last Man will be able to master it; the First Man will not.

The Last Man will adjust to the loss of underground water tables in the western United States. He will build dikes to save Cape Hatteras and the Chesapeake beaches from rising sea levels, even as the Maldive Islands, off the coast of India, sink into oblivion, and the shorelines of Egypt, Bangladesh, and Southeast Asia recede, driving tens of millions of people inland where there is no room for them, and thus sharpening ethnic divisions.

Homer-Dixon points to a world map of soil degradation in his Toronto office. "The darker the map color, the worse the degradation," he explains. The West African coast, the Middle East, the Indian subcontinent, China, and Central America have the darkest shades, signifying all manner of degradation, related to winds, chemicals, and water problems. "The worst degradation is generally where the population is highest. The population is generally highest where the soil is the best. So we're degrading earth's best soil."

China, in Homer-Dixon's view, is the quintessential example of environmental degradation. Its current economic "success" masks deeper problems. "China's fourteen percent growth rate does not mean it's going to be a world power. It means that coastal China, where the economic growth is taking place, is joining the rest of the Pacific Rim. The disparity with inland China is intensifying." Referring to the environmental research of his colleague, the Czech-born ecologist Vaclav Smil, Homer-Dixon explains how the per capita availability of arable land in interior China has rapidly declined at the same time that the quality of that land has been destroyed by deforestation, loss of topsoil, and salinization. He mentions the loss and contamination of water supplies, the exhaustion of wells, the plugging of irrigation systems and reservoirs with eroded silt, and a population of 1.54 billion by the year 2025: it is a misconception that China has gotten its population under control. Large-scale population movements are under way, from inland China to coastal China and from villages to cities, leading to a crime surge like the one in Africa and to growing regional disparities and conflicts in a land with a strong tradition of warlordism and a weak tradition of central government—again as in

Africa. "We will probably see the center challenged and fractured, and China will not remain the same on the map," Homer-Dixon says....

A NEW KIND OF WAR

To appreciate fully the political and cartographic implications of postmodernism—an epoch of themeless juxtapositions, in which the classificatory grid of nation-states is going to be replaced by a jagged-glass pattern of city-states, shanty-states, nebulous and anarchic regionalisms—it is necessary to consider, finally, the whole question of war.

"Oh, what a relief to fight, to fight enemies who defend themselves, enemies who are awake!" André Malraux wrote in *Man's Fate*. I cannot think of a more suitable battle cry for many combatants in the early decades of the twenty-first century. The intense savagery of the fighting in such diverse cultural settings as Liberia, Bosnia, the Caucasus, and Sri Lanka—to say nothing of what obtains in American inner cities—indicates something very troubling that those of us inside the stretch limo, concerned with issues like middle-class entitlements and the future of interactive cable television, lack the stomach to contemplate. It is this: a large number of people on this planet, to whom the comfort and stability of a middle-class life is utterly unknown, find war and a barracks existence a step up rather than a step down.

"Just as it makes no sense to ask 'why people eat' or 'what they sleep for,'" writes Martin van Creveld, a military historian at the Hebrew University in Jerusalem, in *The Transformation of War*, "so fighting in many ways is not a means but an end. Throughout history, for every person who has expressed his horror of war there is another who found in it the most marvelous of all the experiences that are vouchsafed to man, even to the point that he later spent a lifetime boring his descendants by recounting his exploits." When I asked Pentagon officials about the nature of war in the twenty-first century, the answer I frequently got was "Read Van Creveld." The top brass are enamored of this historian not because his writings justify their existence but, rather, the opposite: Van Creveld warns them that huge state military machines like the Pentagon's are dinosaurs about to go extinct, and that something far more terrible awaits us.

The degree to which Van Creveld's Transformation of War complements Homer-Dixon's work on the environment, my own realizations in traveling by foot, bus, and bush taxi in more than sixty countries, and America's sobering comeuppances in intractable-culture zones like Haiti and Somalia is startling. The book begins by demolishing the notion that men don't like to fight. "By compelling the senses to focus themselves on the here and now," Van Creveld writes, war "can cause a man to take his leave of them." As anybody who has had experience with Chetniks in Serbia, "technicals" in Somalia, Tontons Macoutes in Haiti, or soldiers in Sierra Leone can tell you, in places where the Western Enlightenment has not penetrated and where there has always been mass poverty, people find liberation in violence. In Afghanistan and elsewhere, I vicariously experienced this phenomenon: worrying about mines and ambushes frees you from worrying about mundane details of daily existence. If my own experience is too subjective, there is a wealth of data showing the sheer frequency of war, especially in the developing world since the Second World War. Physical aggression is a part of being human. Only when people attain a certain economic, educational, and cultural standard is this trait tranquilized. In light of the fact that 95 percent of the earth's population growth will be in the poorest areas of the globe, the question is not whether there will be war (there will be a lot of it) but what kind of war. And who will fight whom?

Debunking the great military strategist Carl von Clausewitz, Van Creveld, who may be the most original thinker on war since that early-nineteenth-century Prussian, writes, "Clausewitz's ideas ... were wholly rooted in the fact that, ever since 1648, war had been waged overwhelmingly by states." But, as Van Creveld explains, the period of nation-states and, therefore, of state conflict is now ending, and with it the clear "threefold division into government, army, and people" which state-directed wars enforce. Thus, to see the future, the first step is to look back to the past immediately prior to the birth of modernism—the wars in medieval Europe which began during the Reformation and reached their culmination in the Thirty Years' War.

Van Creveld writes, "In all these struggles political, social, economic, and religious motives were hopelessly entangled. Since this was an age when armies consisted of mercenaries, all were also attended by swarms of military entrepreneurs.... Many of them paid little but lip service to the organizations for whom they had contracted to fight. Instead, they robbed the countryside on their own behalf....

"Given such conditions, any fine distinctions ... between armies on the one hand and peoples on the other were bound to break down. Engulfed by war, civilians suffered terrible atrocities."

Back then, in other words, there was no politics as we have come to understand the term, just as there is less and less politics today in Liberia, Sierra Leone, Somalia, Sri Lanka, the Balkans, and the Caucasus, among other places.

Because, as Van Creveld notes, the radius of trust within tribal societies is narrowed to one's immediate family and guerrilla comrades, truces arranged with one Bosnian commander, say, may be broken immediately by another Bosnian commander. The plethora of short-lived ceasefires in the Balkans and the Caucasus constitute proof that we are no longer in a world where the old rules of state warfare apply. More evidence is provided by the destruction of medieval monuments in the Croatian port of Dubrovnik: when cultures, rather than states, fight, then cultural and religious monuments are weapons of war, making them fair game.

Also, war-making entities will no longer be restricted to a specific territory. Loose and shadowy organisms such as Islamic terrorist organizations suggest why borders will mean increasingly little and sedimentary layers of tribalistic identity and control will mean more. "From the vantage point of the present, there appears every prospect that religious ... fanaticisms will play a larger role in the motivation of armed conflict" in the West than at any time "for the last 300 years," Van Creveld writes. This is why analysts like Michael Vlahos are closely monitoring religious cults. Vlahos says, "An ideology that challenges us may not take familiar form, like the old Nazis or Commies. It may not even engage us initially in ways that fit old threat markings." Van Creveld concludes, "Armed conflict will be waged by men on earth, not robots in space. It will have more in common with the struggles of primitive tribes than with large-scale conventional war." While another military historian, John Keegan, in his new book *A History of Warfare*, draws a more benign portrait of primitive man, it is important to point out that what Van Creveld really means is re-primitivized man: warrior societies operating at a time of unprecedented resource scarcity and planetary overcrowding.

Van Creveld's pre-Westphalian vision of worldwide low-intensity conflict is not a superficial "back to the future" scenario. First of all, technology will be used toward primitive ends. In Liberia the guerrilla leader Prince Johnson didn't just cut off the ears of President Samuel Doe before Doe was tortured to death in 1990—Johnson made a video of it, which has circulated throughout West Africa. In December of 1992, when plotters of a failed coup against the Strasser regime in Sierra Leone had their ears cut off at Freetown's Hamilton Beach prior to being killed, it was seen by many to be a copycat execution. Considering, as I've explained earlier, that the Strasser regime is not really a government and that Sierra Leone is not really a nation-state, listen closely to Van Creveld: "Once the legal monopoly of armed force, long claimed by the state, is wrested out of its hands, existing distinctions between war and crime will break down much as is already the case today in ... Lebanon, Sri Lanka, El Salvador, Peru, or Colombia."

If crime and war become indistinguishable, then "national defense" may in the future be viewed as a local concept. As crime continues to grow in our cities and the ability of state governments and criminal-justice systems to protect their citizens diminishes, urban crime may, according to Van Creveld, "develop into low-intensity conflict by coalescing along racial, religious, social, and political lines." As small-scale violence multiplies at home and abroad, state armies will continue to shrink, being gradually replaced by a booming private security business, as in West Africa, and by urban mafias, especially in the former communist world, who may be better equipped than municipal police forces to grant physical protection to local inhabitants.

Future wars will be those of communal survival, aggravated or, in many cases, caused by environmental scarcity. These wars will be subnational, meaning that it will be hard for states and local governments to protect their own citizens physically. This is how many states will ultimately die. As state power fades—and with it the state's ability to help weaker groups within society, not to mention other states—peoples and cultures around the world will be thrown back upon their own strengths and weaknesses, with fewer equalizing mechanisms to protect them. Whereas the distant future will probably see the emergence of a racially hybrid, globalized man, the coming decades will see us more aware of our differences than of our similarities. To the average person, political values will mean less, personal security more. The belief that we are all equal is liable to be replaced by the overriding obsession of the ancient Greek travelers: Why the differences between peoples?

THE LAST MAP

In *Geography and the Human Spirit*, Anne Buttimer, a professor at University College, Dublin, recalls the work of an early-nineteenth-century German geographer, Carl Ritter, whose work implied "a divine plan for humanity" based on regionalism and a constant, living flow of forms. The map of the future, to the extent that a map is even possible, will represent a perverse twisting of Ritter's vision. Imagine cartography in three dimensions, as if in a hologram. In this hologram would be the overlapping sediments of group and other identities atop the merely two-dimensional color markings of city-states and the remaining nations, themselves confused in places by shadowy tentacles, hovering overhead, indicating the power of drug cartels, mafias, and private security agencies. Instead of borders, there would be moving "centers" of power, as in the Middle Ages. Many of these layers would be in motion. Replacing fixed and abrupt lines on a flat space would be a shifting pattern of buffer entities, like the Kurdish and Azeri buffer entities between Turkey and Iran, the Turkic Uighur buffer entity between Central Asia and Inner China (itself distinct from coastal China), and the Latino buffer entity replacing a precise U.S.-Mexican border. To this protean cartographic hologram one must add other factors, such as migrations of populations, explosions of birth rates, vectors of disease. Henceforward the map of the world will never be static. This future map—in a sense, the "Last Map"—will be an ever-mutating representation of chaos....

Not only will the three-dimensional aspects of the Last Map be in constant motion, but its two-dimensional base may change too. The National Academy of Sciences reports that "as many as one billion people, or 20 per cent of the world's population, live on lands likely to be inundated or dramatically changed by rising waters.... Low-lying countries in the developing world such as Egypt and Bangladesh, where rivers are large and the deltas extensive and densely populated, will be hardest hit.... Where the rivers are dammed, as in the case of the Nile, the effects ... will be especially severe...."

Issues like West Africa could yet emerge as a new kind of foreign-policy issue, further eroding America's domestic peace. The spectacle of several West African nations collapsing at once could reinforce the worst racial stereotypes here at home. That is another reason why Africa matters. We must not kid ourselves: the sensitivity factor is higher than ever. The Washington, D.C., public school system is already experimenting with an Afrocentric curriculum. Summits between African leaders and prominent African-Americans are becoming frequent, as are Pollyanna-ish prognostications about multiparty elections in Africa that do not factor in crime, surging birth rates, and resource depletion. The Congressional Black Caucus was among those urging U.S. involvement in Somalia and in Haiti. At the Los Angeles Times minority staffers have protested against, among other things, what they allege to be the racist tone of the newspaper's Africa coverage, allegations that the editor of the "World Report" section, Dan Fisher, denies, saying essentially that Africa should be viewed through the same rigorous analytical lens as other parts of the world.

Africa may be marginal in terms of conventional late-twentieth-century conceptions of strategy, but in an age of cultural and racial clash, when national defense is increasingly local, Africa's distress will exert a destabilizing influence on the United States.

This and many other factors will make the United States less of a nation than it is today, even as it gains territory following the peaceful dissolution of Canada. Quebec, based on the bedrock of Roman Catholicism and Francophone ethnicity, could yet turn out to be North America's most cohesive and crime-free nation-state. (It may be a smaller Quebec, though, since aboriginal peoples may lop off northern parts of the province.) "Patriotism" will become increasingly regional as people in Alberta and Montana discover that they have far more in common with each other than they do with Ottawa or Washington, and Spanish-speakers in the Southwest discover a greater commonality with Mexico City. (*The Nine Nations of North America*, by Joel Garreau, a book about the continent's regionalization, is more relevant now than when it was published, in 1981.) As Washington's influence wanes, and with it the traditional symbols of American patriotism, North Americans will take psychological refuge in their insulated communities and cultures.

Returning from West Africa last fall was an illuminating ordeal. After leaving Abidjan, my Air Afrique flight landed in Dakar, Senegal, where all passengers had to disembark in order to go through another security check, this one demanded by U.S. authorities before they would permit the flight to set out for New York. Once we were in New York, despite the midnight hour, immigration officials at Kennedy Airport held up disembarkation by conducting quick interrogations of the aircraft's passengers—this was in addition to all the normal immigration and customs procedures. It was apparent that drug smuggling, disease, and other factors had contributed to the toughest security procedures I have ever encountered when returning from overseas.

Then, for the first time in over a month, I spotted businesspeople with attaché cases and laptop computers. When I had left New York for Abidjan, all the businesspeople were boarding planes for Seoul and Tokyo, which departed from gates near Air Afrique's. The only non-Africans off to West Africa had been relief workers in T-shirts and khakis. Although the borders within West Africa are increasingly unreal, those separating West Africa from the outside world are in various ways becoming more impenetrable.

But Afrocentrists are right in one respect: we ignore this dying region at our own risk. When the Berlin Wall was falling, in November of 1989, I happened to be in Kosovo, covering a riot between Serbs and Albanians. The future was in Kosovo, I told myself that night, not in Berlin. The same day that Yitzhak Rabin and Yasser Arafat clasped hands on the White House lawn, my Air Afrique plane was approaching Bamako, Mali, revealing corrugated-zinc shacks at the edge of an expanding desert. The real news wasn't at the White House, I realized. It was right below.

✗ NO

Globalised Images of Environmental Security in Africa

CYRIL OBI

Since the end of the Cold War in the late 1980s, there has been a pronounced concern in academic and policy circles with global environmental change, and its implications for global security (Speth, 1990; Brock, 1991; Renner, 1996; Brown, 1994; Obi, 1997a, 1997b, 1998b; Leach & Mearns, 1996; Hyden, 1999). At the heart of this shift has been the expansion of the notion of security to include the containment of non-military, extra-state threats. Thus, issues such as poverty, environmental degradation, crisis, wars, drug-trafficking and even migration were included in the emerging perspective to security. Also, globalisation meant that threat-perception in the West began to take on board the linkages between environmental crisis in the third world, with its strategic needs for stability, markets, resources, and even, leisure. At the same time, there was the concern among some policymakers and scholars of the implications of globalisation for the post-colonial African state, which was experiencing various forms and intensities of crisis. Such fears were based on the belief that a crisis-ridden Africa would pose a serious threat to global peace and security. This concern is most pronounced in the surviving Cold War superpowers, particularly the United States, which is the undisputed global hegemon in the post-Cold War order.

Increasingly, more interest is being paid to the implications of global interdependence, the revolution in communications and technology, conflicts, and the deepening entrenchment world-wide of market relations, for global, but in particular, Western and American security (Klare & Thomas, 1994; Simmons, 1995; Porter, 1995; Homer-Dixon, 1996). In the absence of the pronounced military threat to the West following the collapse of the Warsaw Pact, more attention has focused on non-military, especially environmental threats. Out of this approach, which has posed the problem within a sociology of science that is reflective of the "broader historical, political and institutional context" (Leach & Mearns, 1996:4) of the western capitalist knowledge production system, has emerged the "globalised" image of Africa as the greatest source of environmental threat to global security. It has thus become commonplace to label Africa a site of overpopulation and violent ethnic or tribal wars, both of which lead to environmental degradation and conflict. This has unfairly shifted the blame for environmental insecurity to Africa, leaving out the external economic agents that deepen the contradictions within the continent. Such analysis almost usually seeks to generalise or draw conclusions for the whole of Africa based on one or two local cases, which are often distorted to "fit the model" of the environmental-security nexus. Furthermore, they are based on second-hand accounts or at best casual observations by "intellectual tourists" who then elevate their biased deductions to the level of treatises on Africa. Since these are more often than not based on faulty or slanted assumptions, they invariably arrive at wrong conclusions, which when fed into the policy process invariably compound Africa's environmental problems.

Perhaps the greatest source of the exaggeration of, or outright falsehood about the nature of Africa's environmental crisis and conflict is the global mass media, supported by environmental security analysts and policy makers operating within the geopolitical and ideological frameworks of strategic think-tanks and right-wing foundations based in the advanced market-economy countries (Obi, 1998b: 15–16). The role of the media in constructing a negative, horrific image of the African environment, which is then flashed to all parts of the world simultaneously, is well captured by Binns (1995:1):

> The mass media so often portray Africa as a dismal, gloomy and unhappy place, plagued with civil war, drought, famine and poverty. Africa's people are frequently accused of degrading their own environment.

The image of Africa as a source of environmental degradation, overpopulation and conflict has much wider implications, when we consider the trends in global environmental change, development and security studies. Africa is wrongly pictured as an undifferentiated whole, alongside an equally homogenous picture of environmental degradation across the continent in the construction of the global image of how environmental stresses generated within the continent threaten global security. In this calculus, there is hardly a unified African response to the debates on the implications of global environmental change for global security. Furthermore, the imperatives of addressing the specificities of Africa's environmental security are obscured by the emphasis on the national security of the United States masked as "global security."

It is to the interrogation of the construction and implications of distorted global images of the African threat to global security, at a mainly conceptual level, and other related considerations that this article is directed. Beyond this, it critiques the "conventional wisdom" about the African environment (Leach & Mearns, 1996:1), and suggests how its fundamental shortcomings can be exposed and transcended.

In order to set about its task, this article is divided into four broad parts: the Introduction, which sets out the background and main issues in the article. The section that follows is on Globalisation and Environmental Security: The Linkages. It examines the connections between globalisation and global environmental security, and its broad implications for Africa. The third and analytical fulcrum of the article is on the Main Themes in Environmental Security: a critique. This part, for convenience is broken down into three sub-themes: image, causality and implications. It is then followed by the conclusion, which ties up the arguments, and proffers a way towards deconstructing the negative globalised image of how stresses generated from the African environment pose a potent threat to global security now, and in the 21st century.

Globalisation and Environmental Security: The Linkages

In order to capture the linkages between globalisation and environmental security, it would be appropriate to analyse both concepts. This would enable us to grapple with how global forces fuel, and seek to benefit from the African environmental crisis, while at the same time nursing fears that the fall-outs of this crisis may spill over into the industrial North.

GLOBALISATION

Globalisation is perhaps one of the most fashionable but controversial terms in international relations discourse today. Like environmental security, it assumed an unprecedented profile at the end of the Cold War, and is part of the neo-liberal ideology of moulding the world in the image of market forces. As a concept, it is the historical outcome of a global capitalist project of an integrated world market that is several centuries old, even if this "market" is one in which the few powerful rich fleece the majority poor, in a world characterised by wide differences in development, wealth, resources and power. In terms of political economy, globalisation is a complex and contested notion. The debate is broadly between those who see globalisation as a transformatory capitalist project that is "dissolving international borders, and rendering the nation-state and traditional concepts of sovereignty irrelevant and obsolete" (Ohmae, 1995; Drenzer, 1998), and those who insist, that it is "far from a linear, uniform or homogenising process" (Boyer & Drache, 1996; Zyman, 1996; Saurin, 1996). Perhaps it is most rewarding to understand globalisation in terms of an ongoing project of global capital that "points at expanding market interconnections in the form of investments, financial networks and trade" (Zyman, 1996:157). Tandon (1998:2) gives an excellent description of a central feature of globalisation, when he notes that:

> The contemporary globalisation's specific feature is financial liberalisation. It seeks to remove all national and cultural barriers to the free movement of international capital, and to secure for it privileged treatment within the economic domain of emend country.

It is very important to understand the nature of power relations and the role of hegemonic economic forces based in, and controlled by the West (the main beneficiaries) in the processes of globalisation. This means that for those who are the underdogs, or come late to the globalisation table, they are either left with nothing, or risk becoming the dinner of the club of global powers!

From the foregoing it is clear that globalisation is neither uniform in its reach or impact, nor addresses the inequities in the international political economy. What this implies is that there are winners and losers in globalisation. Its processes thrive on the deepening of global inequities, and the increased exploitation and marginalisation of the developing world, especially Africa. The lesson in all this is that any analysis of globalisation must be rooted in its political economy, and related to the specificity of a concrete setting.

The impact of globalisation on Africa, though not uniform, has economically speaking been a disaster, with wider adverse social ramifications. The continent's share of global trade has shrunk further. Foreign aid and foreign direct investments have reduced to a trickle, while the entrenchment of market forces through structural adjustment programmes and neo-liberal reforms have severely worsened the crises in which most African states have been immersed in the last two decades (Mkandawire & Olukoshi, 1995; Olukoshi, 1998). Apart from the fact that Africa has been more of an observer and victim than a participant in the drawing up of the new global trading regime on which globalisation partly rests (the World Trade Organisation [WTO]), a lot of the rules of the game discriminate against the resource-rich but poor members of the "global village." Emphasis on trade liberalisation, economic deregulation and the retrenchment of the state simply lay open the resources and economies of third-world countries for the picking by the powerful multinationals and financial speculators from the Industrial North, and their local allies. Thus, Tandon's (1998:6) observation that globalisation has contributed to de-industrialisation, the further weakening of African states vis-a-vis foreign capital, ring true. Africa's position in the global division of labour as an exporter of primary commodities and resources also means that the continent is short-changed in the global drive toward financial liberalisation. Even worse, the contradictions unleashed by the global expansion of capital within the continent are sharply refracted into a range of state and domestic crises, with dire consequences for governance and environmental sustainability.

ENVIRONMENTAL SECURITY

Environmental security deals with the containment of a range of "threats," or contradictions emanating from the interaction between human beings and nature. This can either be in the form of the extraction of natural resources or their transformation into food, goods and services for livelihood purposes, or for profit. Where rates of extraction exceed the rate of recovery of "renewable" resources (natural capital), or non-renewable resources are depleted, it is perceived as a threat. The transformation of natural capital also has another consequence—the generation of waste which usually pollutes or degrades the ecosystem. The degradation of the ecosystem arising from extraction and transformation is also seen as a threat, as it may lead to a fall in quality, or a depletion of resources. Issues of extraction and transformation are hinged on access, control, ownership and power and are therefore linked to political economy and security. At once we are able to glean two contradictory perspectives of security, one which privileges the interests of those who have power, access and control over the ecosystem, and marginalises those who do not.

The second strand of environmental security, which is directly relevant to this article, revolves around a global perspective. This is because the reality of global economic and environmental interdependence has ensured the expansion of the concept beyond narrow statist boundaries of military (external) threats (Obi, 1997a:1–3). Dabelko & Dabelko (1995) provide a basic definition of environmental security from a global perspective as a:

> ... transnational idea, the core of which holds that environmental degradation and depletion, largely human-induced, pose fundamental threats to the physical security of individuals, groups, societies, states, ecosystems and the international system.

This does not mean that the issue of environmental security is a settled matter as the debate continues to rage between those Hyden (1999:151–62) describes as "the realists, the liberals, the moralists and the populists" over the notion of the security-environment nexus. There is no doubt, and this can be gleaned from the literature coming out of Washington (and Toronto), that the realist and neo-realist perspectives are still the most fashionable. There is the tradition established by the pioneering works of Ullman (1983), Myers (1989) and Mathews (1989), in which they argued that environmental degradation and resource-wars in areas of strategic US interest could hurt American national interests. In spite of the effort of others, who are of the opinion that the claims of proponents of environmental security are spurious (Deudney, 1990, 1991; Levy, 1995; Deudney & Matthew, 1996), the notion of environmental security has continued to gain ground. A lot of its focus has been on the security of human beings within local, national, regional and global contexts. Of particular concern is the impact of rapidly growing populations on the environment. Threat perception in environmental terms is either in the form of "increasing stresses on the earth's life support system and renewable resources (that) have profound implications for human health and welfare" (Porter, 1995), or the "new dimensions and driving forces behind stress and insecurity" (Hjort af Ornas and Lundqvist, 1999:5).

If it is understood that global environmental change is largely the outcome of the impact of the globalisation of capital on the global environment, it will become clearer that capitalism has been largely responsible for the "production" of environmental degradation (and conflict) on a global scale (Saurin, 1996). As such, it is understandable that there is a concern for preventing the contradictions spawned by the depletion (and pollution) of resources on a global scale from coming home to roost in the industrial North, while further opening up other regions of the world to "market forces."

LINKAGES

From the foregoing, it is not difficult to fathom the linkages between capital-led globalisation and environmental security. In the first place, globalisation has intensified the pressures on the global ecosystem in its expanding quest for raw materials, cheap energy (oil and gas), markets and profits; and receptacles for its (non-bio-degradable and toxic) waste. As such these growing pressures are feeding into concerns in the industrialised world on the need to protect itself from repercussions from the violent explosion of contradictions spawned in the ecosystems of the developing world. In the second place, the further entrenchment of market relations in the third world has meant the further commodification of its renewable and non-renewable resources, as the countries are further integrated into global capitalism and grapple with export-led growth in a context of worsening economic and external debt crises. It among other things means that those with money and power can gain access to, and control more resources, while those without money and power are marginalised and dispossessed. In reality, it is the environmental security of the poor and marginalised that is at stake.

There should be a clear understanding that globalisation is feeding the relative scarcity of resources, and worsening inequities in relation to access and power over resources. It is also devaluing the resources of developing countries as they open up further to market forces. Third, is the concern in certain circles that struggles over shrinking resources will explode into violent conflict in the developing world which are capable of destabilising sources of supply for raw materials and markets for finished goods and services. There is also the fear that such conflicts generate eco-refugees, some of who cross international borders and provoke inter-state wars, or migrate to the West, where they can pose all kinds of threat to security.

What the preceding shows is that globalisation is one of the greatest threats to global environmental security. This is largely due to the ways it produces resource scarcities and degradation, and sharpens social contradictions in the environment. However, the distribution of threat is felt more in the poorer parts of the world and lesser in the more prosperous parts. The implication of the globalisation-environment nexus for Africa, one of the richest resource-wise, but economically impoverished parts of the world marks it out among the most threatened by this linkage. Why then has orthodox environmental security discourse in protecting its "privileges" turned logic on its head by blaming the victim, Africa, for generating environmental stresses that threaten the security of the West? Who gains from this distorted image of Africa's environmental security; how?

Main Themes in Environmental Security: A Critique

In certain circles, the environment is seen as the main security issue in the post-Cold War world. The main themes of environmental security discourses can be identified as image, causality and the implications. Taken together, they pose a problematic of the African environmental crisis and its implications for global security. In order to convince the Western audience—academics, strategists and policy-makers—a shocking image of Africa as a source of growing threat is constructed to press home the point on the need in the national interest, to "act now before it becomes too late."

IMAGE

Perhaps the most hideous image of environmental stresses emanating from Africa is that constructed by Kaplan (1994, 1997). But he is by no means the only one concerned with how Africa threatens global security. However, the fact that Kaplan's works have been taken seriously in policy circles in the United States make it one case that must be addressed. According to Kaplan, in his extensively cited piece, "The Coming Anarchy," Africa features prominently in the world of "Hobbes's First Man." To him "the last man healthy, well fed and pampered by technology will be able to master environmental stress, but the first man cannot." He goes on to describe the African "threat":

> West Africa is becoming *the* symbol of world-wide demographic, environmental, and societal stress, in which criminal anarchy emerges as the real "strategic" danger. Disease, overpopulation, unprovoked crime, scarcity of resources, refugee migrations, the increasing erosion of nation-states and international borders, and the empowerment of private armies, security firms, and international drug cartels are most tellingly demonstrated through a West African prism. West Africa provides an appropriate introduction to the issues, often extremely unpleasant to discuss, that will soon confront our civilisation.

The implication of the foregoing quote from Kaplan's "treatise"—copies of which were reportedly faxed to US embassies across the world—underscore the image of the African threat based in part on Kaplan's "experiences" during a tour through a couple of African countries, on which basis he first extrapolated for Africa, and then the rest of the world. This follows the trend in the works of Homer-Dixon, Percival and others, who are of the opinion that resource-scarcity arising from the pressures of overpopulation on renewable resources are at the heart of (environmental degradation) violent conflict in the continent, and are consequently a threat to western security. Invariably such environmental conflicts according to this logic take the form of ethnic, religious or "tribal" wars, which are "natural" to Africa (Furley, 1995:1–18).

The same thread can be gleaned in the way policy towards Africa—either in terms of environmental or development "aid"—has been influenced by this image of an Africa waiting to explode under the weight of overpopulation, ethnic wars and violent struggles over "scarce resources" As Leach & Mearns (1996:1) are quick to point out:

> The driving force behind much environmental policy in Africa is a set of pow-
> erful, widely perceived images of environmental change. They include over-
> grazing, and the "desertification" of drylands, the widespread existence of a
> "woodfuel" crisis, the rapid and recent removal of once pristine forests, soil
> erosion, and the mining of resources caused by a rapidly growing population.

The ease with which the image of the African stereotype is constructed—crisis-ridden, and threatening—is hardly surprising given the epistemological stakes in obscuring the external roots of the African crises. What is relevant at this stage is that a critical part of the agenda of subordinating Africa further into the world of globalised capital is to give the impression that Africans left on their own cannot manage their environmental resources. This opens the door for global intervention in order to "stop" Africa from threatening the "Civilisation of the world of the Last Man." Yet, it is important not to gloss over an extreme position that Africa, on the basis of its "natural habit of conflict," is not really worth it, and that globalisation should seek much safer and stable havens (Asia and the Pacific Rim). But the reality of global trade and financial flows has made this choice a most unattractive one, hence the move towards promoting Western models of environmental management and conflict resolution in Africa as a way of protecting Western interests on the continent, and preventing conflicts in Africa from threatening the world.

CAUSALITY

At the heart of the global environmental security discourse is the issue of causality or those elements identified as the causes of environmental conflict. Basically, a neo-Malthusian perspective heavily influences mainstream discourse on environmental security. This is hinged upon the connections between over-population and resource scarcity and that between resource scarcity and violent conflict. It is assumed that when the rate of population growth exceeds the "carrying capacity" or threshold of a given ecosystem, it feeds into stresses that directly or indirectly provoke conflict (Brown & Jacobson, 1986; Homer-Dixon, 1994; Klare, 1996). Thus, the demographic trap becomes a principal culprit of environmental conflict (Obi, 1997b). A lot of premium is placed on environmental stress or resource scarcity as the trigger of conflict. This is linked to the ways in which scarcities arising from overuse, misuse or degradation feed into environmental stresses and lead to violent struggles or conflict over what is left. According to Homer-Dixon (1996:359):

> Scarcities of environmental resources—in particular cropland, freshwater, and forest—are contributing to mass violence in several areas of the world. While these environmental scarcities do not cause wars between countries, they do sometimes aggregate stresses within countries helping stimulate ethnic clashes, urban unrest, and insurgencies.

Homer-Dixon also observes that there is an emphasis on "resource-wars" within countries, and is concerned about the threats these pose to "western national interests by destabilising trade and economic relations, provoking migration, and generating complex humanitarian disasters that divert militaries and absorb huge amounts of aid." The same position re-echoes in the work of Swain (1993), and particularly that of Klare (1996), where it is noted that:

> High growth rates in crisis-ridden LDC's is likely to produce high rates of rural-urban migration, and from poor and low income ones to affluent countries.

From the foregoing, several things are clear from the perspective of environmental security discourses on causality. There is a cause-effect relationship between overpopulation and environmental stresses, which lead to conflict. Secondly, environmental degradation can also worsen scarcities, which feed stresses and finally conflict. Third, environmental conflicts in the third world (including Africa) are a cause of threat to the prosperous, Western world. In order to arrest these trends in Africa and elsewhere, the West has introduced a policy mix made up of market-based reforms, birth (population) control, technologically driven, top-heavy, western models. At the heart of all these is the desire by the West to place Africa's resources at the easy disposal of extractive global forces, while attempting to insulate itself from the contradictions arising from extraction, expropriation and degradation in the continent. In order to convince Western policy-makers of the urgency of dealing with the "African threat" in the national interest, it would seem that the temptation of the worst-case scenario, riddled with deliberately distorted conclusions and terrifying images, have become too powerful to ignore.

THE IMPLICATIONS

The implications of the foregoing are varied, but revolve around the distorted image of the causes of environmental crises and conflict in Africa, and how these threaten the industrial North. There is also a heavy dose of cultural prejudice in the way that non-Western societies are stereotyped in the literature as overpopulated, prone to environmental degradation and stresses, resource wars and the resurgence of violent primordial hatreds. At the end, there is always the hidden agenda of "modernisation." That Africa will forever be condemned to overpopulation, natural disasters, wars, crime, disease, failed states, etc. if it refuses to modernise, or what is in real terms an unconditional African surrender to the forces of the global marketplace. Yet, the implications of the current "global" onslaught against Africa cannot be fully grasped outside of a critique of the globalised image of environmental security, which in its nudity is a caricature of the truth, denying any Western responsibility for the African crisis, masking the ways it benefits from the crisis, and seeking to reinforce its hegemony over the resources of the so-called "First Man."

Before going into the critique proper, several clarifications need to be made. This article is not a refutation of the fact of an environmental crisis in Africa. It does not deny that Africa has had more than its fair share of natural and man-made disasters over the years; neither is it an attempt to downplay the escalation of intra-state wars on the continent since the onset of the economic and debt crisis and the end of the Cold War. What it does object to is the way these occurrences have been selectively and subjectively distorted. It is an implicit rejection of bias and fright-mongering masquerading as scientific knowledge or informed analysis. And it is a call for the need for more responses to the African challenge in environmental security and conflict discourse, beyond the designs of neo-Malthusian orthodoxy which "persists in academic, national policy-making, or international financial institution circles" (Bush, 1997:503). Clearly, there is a need for a more balanced approach to the study of international relations, without rubbing salt into the historical and current injuries and injustices being inflicted on Africa.

THE CRITIQUE

The image of a global Armageddon extrapolating from the anarchy in Africa has been challenged even within the United States as "racist uniculturalism" (Cockburn, 1994) and "incorrect" (Lancaster, 1994). Binns (1995), Leach & Mearns (1996) and many others have invested a lot of energy in deconstructing Kaplan's terrifying image of Africa, and its looming threat to the United States. The fact that Kaplan's work came out shortly before the Rwandan genocide did confer upon it, in the mood of that time, with some credibility in official circles. But when put to closer scrutiny, Kaplan's image is about Africa as viewed from a "unicultural" monocle, but it is definitely not of Africa. The basis on which he arrives at his conclusion is at best fleeting and at worst a grotesque distortion of both history and reality. It ignores the fact that the Africa he is dealing with is both a historical construct and a product of a global political economy that is basically structured against it. Though Kaplan's piece has been criticised extensively, it cannot be separated from the image of Africa largely cast in the looming shadow of Afro-pessimism. As Olukoshi (1999:452) has observed:

> But even in otherwise respectable intellectual and policy circles, including the World Bank, few were able to resist the prognosis that Africa had been "hemmed in," with its societies sliding back to precolonial and early-colonial enclave arrangements, its states undergoing a "freefall," and its people increasingly abandoned to a Hobbesian law of nature amid a growing disorder.

What comes out of this is that the image of the African threat had been a paradigmatic preoccupation and had a captive policy audience and a global agenda and message: "adapt (to the global market), or perish" (Olukoshi, 1999:453). In order to pursue this agenda on the environmental front, the image of an Africa hopelessly incapable of managing its environment, and eternally bogged down by environmental degradation or ravaging hordes fighting over scarce resources has become a critical part of environmental security discourse. Because of its clearly instrumentalist ends, it has had to rely more on distortions of the African reality, drawing on scientific methodologies that are selective, and are based on partial or very weak empirical evidence. Furthermore, the role of actors, and policies from the West in worsening scarcities, degradation and conflict in Africa as the cases of the Niger Delta (Rowell, 1996, Obi, 1997a) and the Sudan (Suliman, 1999) clearly show, are ignored.

The shortcomings of mainstream "Afro-pessimist" environmental security discourse are further exposed when one revisits the issue of causality. As noted earlier, violent conflicts in Africa have been blamed on stresses placed on the environment by exploding populations who then trigger fights (ethnic, religious, etc.) over "scarce" renewable resources. Three inter-linked fundamental questions need to be raised: How are scarcities constructed? Is scarcity the inescapable outcome of "overpopulation"? Who gains from scarcity?

While it is true that relative scarcity is one of the facts of nature—as natural endowments and resources are unevenly dispersed at all levels—there is a way that scarcity, in the socio-economic sense, can be "constructed." In the first place, the environment itself is socially constructed, underpinned by social relations of political and social power (Redclift & Benton, 1994), which then define issues of culture, access and control over the environment. Hence scarcity can equally be the product of the "distribution of economic and political power within society" (Hildyard, 1999:12).

In all class societies, the few who control power invariably can control access and exclude the majority, thus creating scarcity for them in the midst of plenty! In a capitalist society or world, scarcity becomes the outcome of a socio-economic system that commodifies nature and excludes the producer from the social surplus, placing such a group in a weak position from which they are structurally incapable of commanding resources which become "scarce." As Hildyard (1999:13), further explains, "where common regimes give way to state or market-based regimes, the experience of scarcity is different. With the commodification or state appropriation of land, for example, control over subsistence is assigned to actors outside the community, almost always to the detriment of those whose bargaining power is weak." Going further, the point is made that, "the deliberate manufacture of scarcity now provides one of the principal means through which powerful state and private interests monopolise resources, control markets and suppress the demographic majority" (Hildyard, 1999:13). This concretely represents the current paradox of Africa's poverty in the midst of plenty.

From the foregoing, it is clear that there is more than one form of scarcity, and it can be caused by other factors apart from the size of the population or environmental degradation. This is not to deny the obvious impact that a large population can have on finite natural resources, but to point out that contradictions over scarce resources equally reflect the inequitable relations of power in which the environment is immersed. This leads to the exclusion of the "demographic majority" who are then forced to fight over the little that is left, or the little they can get in order to survive. Such exclusion can also sharpen existing contradictions along the lines of class and ethnic identity, and undermine the social basis of welfare and citizenship. In such conditions in which the state largely functions to repress mass opposition to expropriation and rising poverty, conflict becomes emblematic of protest and the quest for survival, equity and liberation.

The foregoing has become more obvious in Africa under the conditions of economic crisis and structural adjustment, and the crisis of state legitimacy. Several studies have clearly documented the increase in resource wars across Africa as a result of the deepening of social contradictions over the environment, and the increasing expropriation and degradation of peasant land (and waters) by the state, private foreign (multinationals) and local interests operating under industrial or "green revolution" projects (Obi, 1998a). Specific examples of such "manufactured" scarcities are replicated with varying degrees of intensity across the Sahelian belt of sub-Saharan Africa, the volatile Niger Delta where the people have been up in arms against oil multinationals (Ibeanu, 1999; Robinson, 1996; Obi, 1999a, 1999b) and the state, since the late 1980s. Other examples are the Great Lakes region (Uvin, 1996), and the Sudanese civil war, intensified by the expropriation and degradation of peasant land by large scale mechanised agriculture in some of the most populous and fertile parts of the country (Suliman, 1999:27–28).

The scarcities bred by adjustment, the alienation of people followed by repression and further pauperisation has fuelled conflict as the people seek to survive, and local and global interests continue to exercise monopoly over resources. The impact of IMF/World Bank policies towards the African environment is not lost to analysis. Such Western policies clearly designed to advance the globalisation agenda have worsened scarcities and deepened contradictions. As Suliman (1999: 27) explains further:

Their loan conditionalities have accelerated considerably the restructuring of resource utilisation from local needs and the local market towards the demands of the international market. Despite the rapid increase in the area of land in use and increased export capacity, the overall effect of the new export-oriented policies was negative. The value of primary commodities in the international market steadily declined and poverty worsened in the urban slums and in rural Africa.

It is then obvious that while overpopulation may lead to scarcity, the relationship between high population rates and environmental conflict is more complex, and is mediated by the prevalent relations of power over the environment. Thus scarcities can be created, or worsened outside of the "demographic trap," as demonstrated with the impact of structural adjustment in deepening contradictions in the African environment. It therefore shows that the stereotyping of environmental conflict as ethnic or tribal wars (in which global capital constricts access as it expands its control over Africa's resources) is bound to end up with grossly distorted and diversionary analysis.

It also shows that a lot more needs to be done to demonstrate how the interaction between capital and the environment in Africa has bred a relation of power that disempowers the majority. This is the product of a system which alienates and marginalises them, in ways that lead to conflicts within the "excluded" (intra-class, pastoralists versus farmers, ethnic minorities versus dominant majorities, intra- and inter-communal, sectarian), and between them and their expropriators—usually the state, and local elite in partnership with foreign capital. The phenomenon of "dispossessed" ethnic groups is a particularly explosive issue, as can be gleaned from the case of the Ogoni (Robinson, 1996; Naanen, 1995; Obi, 1999b), those of the Dinka, Ngoni, Hadedowa and Fulani (Salih, 1999:181–98), and the deployment of identity politics in the struggle for "national liberation." It will be wrong therefore to see all environmental conflicts in the light of a primordial or atavistic throw-back to an imagined state of nature, rather than focus on the conflictive relations: repression/resistance, exclusion/inclusion, all embedded in the African environment. Issues of access/non-access lead to violent conflict over claims, entitlements and survival. This invariably opens up the issue of who benefits from these "manufactured scarcities," and how they seek to reproduce their gains within the context of globalisation.

Powerful extractive global and national interests benefit from the "manufactured scarcities." If it is well understood that in the context of adjustment the state in Africa has been weakened both by its own internal contradictions and all forms of conditionalities being hurled at it by the Bretton Woods twins and the G-7 countries, then it becomes clear that the global has a lot of leverage in the continent. In order to adapt to globalisation, survive and broadly serve the interests of both local and global factions of capital, the state in Africa has adopted the agenda of the global market, even if state mediation of global-local relations is done in such a way as not to compromise the class interests of the statist elite: military, bureaucratic and business factions.

The state through legislation, its policies and at times naked force, has broadly moved in the direction of an environmental governance that pays less attention to local needs, and places more premium on the global market and the interests of those who have "privatised" the state in Africa. They are the ones who get prime land with state subsidies, and win contracts to construct the gigantic dams and irrigation projects, dredge the rivers, and mine the forests of precious timber, the oceans for fish and the land for non-renewable resources: oil and gas, gold, bauxite, etc.

The wholesale adoption of the market principle in tackling the African economic crisis has had its most deleterious impact on the environment. For one thing, the opening up of economies has meant exporting more resources for less money (due to devaluation, and declining global prices for primary products). The degradation of Africa's fragile soils, increased pressures on its forests and waters by inappropriate technology especially in large-scale agriculture, and the urge to earn more foreign exchange to service debts have further altered the African political ecology.

More people are displaced from their land by the state and foreign big business, lose their livelihoods and are severely pauperised, leaving them with little choice than to migrate in search of jobs in the capitals, or to remain in the countryside and fight it out, either among themselves, against their neighbours, the state or big business. The state in Africa—hamstrung by its own internal contradictions: instability or fragility as a result of elite rivalry, or the quest to consolidate democracy, crises of accumulation and legitimacy arising partly from the massive erosion of post-colonial welfare gains by adjustment—is often not placed in a position to equitably mediate the struggles for power over the environment. The artificial nature of Africa's borders and the growing informalisation of cross-border transactions also implies that goods and services are exchanged with the global market in ways that could undermine the environment without the "formal" notice of the state. At the end of the day, the state is as much a contestant in the environment as the other stakeholders, as it struggles to advance its own interests (not the people's) alongside that of global capital. Thus, just as Africa loses out economically in the process of globalisation, it is increasingly losing control over its natural wealth, with very serious implications for sustainability, and the future of the continent.

The analysis so far reinforces the position expressed earlier, that the imagery and causal linkages on which mainstream environmental security discourse is based is flawed, and amount to "the lie of the land" (Leach & Mearns, 1996). Its attempt to make Africa a "scapegoat" for the security fallouts of global environmental change seek to seize upon the historical moment of Afro-pessimism, to shift attention from the ways globalisation is eroding the social glue binding the African environment and the people.

CONCLUSION: RECONSTRUCTION THROUGH DECONSTRUCTION

From the onset, it was fairly obvious that the same forces that today blame Africa for threatening global environmental security are the same ones that have historically through their economic power (capital), deepened environmental stresses and benefited from the transformation of the continents' resources into cheap commodities for the world market. How does the African populace threaten the global environment in a context where

> the United States with only 5% of the planets population consumes nearly 30% of the planets natural resources and where industrial countries generate 75% of the world's pollutants and waste (One Earth).

If global scarcity is greater because a small proportion of the people on the planet control and consume most of its resources, and then generate most of the waste, how just is it then to tag one of the "dispossessed" and marginalised regions of the world the main culprit without connecting the poverty of the latter to the prosperity of the former?

Thus, there is a clear case for the reconstruction of the globalised image of environmental security in Africa, away from the current distorted form. Fortunately this effort has been going on for a while, and can be gleaned from the pioneering work of Hjort af Ornas and Salih (1989), both of whom are still very much in the struggle. Yet a lot more needs to be done to establish a space within African political science, social science and international relations for environmental conflict and security studies. If we must reconstruct a truly African perspective to global environmental security, our intellectuals must be the critics, moulders and shapers of the paradigmatic shift. From there, policy-makers, and the people who are the stakeholders must be joined in resisting the wholesale abandonment of our environmental heritage to global market forces.

At a conceptual level, it is important to deconstruct the neo-Malthusian and monocausal scarcities' perspective to environmental security, and reject its criminalisation of Africa in orthodox global environmental change discourse. The limited analytical value of such approaches and their value-laden agenda of maximising Western interest, promoting modernisation and market-led policies, should be exposed. Rather, focus should be re-directed at critically interrogating their assumptions, and demonstrating that the roots of violent conflict lie in the way the capitalist-led global system interacts with the African environment and the contradictory social and power relations arising from that process. The challenge is to stand logic on its feet and reconstruct the notion of African environmental security. As noted elsewhere (Obi, 1998a),

> The path to transcendence lies in recognising the link between the dominant mode of production in Africa and the rapid depletion of resources, the

role of the state as an actor in, and mediator of relations between the people, global capital and the environment, and the conflictual relations of inclusion and exclusion in terms of access and control over "scarce" resources.

Beyond the conceptual, Africa needs to get its global environmental politics right. There is no strong pan-African response to the inequities embedded in the ongoing processes of globalisation. More critical is the absence of a concerted regional or continental effort at reducing environmental conflict on the continent. In most cases, policy-makers and militaries in Africa are yet to come to terms with the social and politico-ecological roots of conflict. Thus, their approaches have broadly followed the ineffective managerial, top-down, capital-intensive, or repressive approach to environmental management and security. These have basically worsened the problem and filled the pockets of local bureaucrats, warlords, and elite, donor-countries, expatriate consultants and suppliers of military weapons to Africa.

It is important that a blueprint stating an African position on the environment, environmental conflict and security be drawn up and popularised within all member-states of the OAU as a matter of urgency. There should be a shift away from peace-enforcement from the top, to peace-building from the bottom upwards based on democratic participation, equitable access of the majority to resources, popular sovereignty and the tenets of the sustainable management of environmental resources.

Finally, the security of the African environment can best be assured only within an equitable global economic and political system that is sensitive to the welfare and development of all Africans. True, some may see this as an El Dorado, given the sorry economic state of the continent, partly the "gift" of the ravaging forces of the global market: adjustment, speculators and multinationals, and the outcome of the treachery of local gatekeepers of the state and global capital. Yet others would be more correct to say that it is a more viable alternative on which to build a just and peaceful world. More fundamentally, it addresses the environmental security of the African rather than the caricature which globalised orthodox environmental security discourse seeks to force-feed us.

REFERENCES

Binns, T (ed.) (1995), *People and the Environment*, Chichester, New York: Brisbane, Toronto and Singapore: John Wiley and Sons.

Boyer, R & D Drache (1996), *State Versus Markets: The Limits of Globalisation*, New York: Routledge.

Brock, L (1991), "Peace Through Parks: The Environment on the Peace Research Agenda," *Journal of Peace Research*, 28.

Brown, L (1994), "World Interests and the Changing Dimensions of Security," in M Klare & D Thomas (eds.), *World Security: Challenges for a New Century*, New York: St. Martins Press.

Brown, L & J Jacobson (1986), "Our Demographically Divided World," *World Watch Paper*, no. 74.

Bush, R (1997), "African Environmental Crisis: Challenging the Orthodoxies," *Review of African Political Economy*, vol. 24, December.

Claussen, E (1995), "Environment and Security: The Challenge of Integration," in P Simmons (ed.), *Environmental Change and Security Report*, Washington DC: The Woodrow Wilson Center, Issue 1, Spring.

Cockburn, A (1994), "The Horror," *The Nation*, 28 March.

Dabelko, G & D Dabelko (1995), "Environmental Security: Issues of Conflict and Security," in P Simmons (ed.), *Environmental Change and Security Report*, Washington DC: The Woodrow Wilson Center, Issue 1, Spring.

Deudney, D (1990), "The Case Against Linking Environmental Degradation With National Security," *Millennium: Journal of International Studies*, 19; (1991) "Environment and Security: Muddled Thinking," *Bulletin of Atomic Scientists*, April.

Deudney, D & R Matthew (eds.) (1996), *Contested Ground: Security and Conflict in the New Environmental Politics*, New York: Suny Press.

Drezner, D (1998), "Globalizers of the World Unite," *Washington Quarterly*, vol. 21, no. 1.

Englund, H (1996), "Culture, Environment and the Enemies of Complexity," *Review of African Political Economy*, no. 76.

Furley, O (1995), "Africa: The Habit of Conflict," in O Furley, *Conflict in Africa*, London and New York: I B Taurin Publishers.

Hildyard, N (1999), "Blood, Babies and Social Roots of Conflict," in Mohamed Suliman (ed.) *Ecology, Politics and Violent Conflict*, London and New York: Zed Books.

Hjort af Ornas, A & J Lundqvist (1999), "Life, Livelihood, Resources and Security-Links, and a Call for a New Order," in Tiiarita Granfelt (ed.), *Managing the Globalised Environment*, London: IT Publications.

Hjort at Ornas, A & M Salih (ed.) (1989), Ecology and Politics: *Environmental Stress and Security in Africa*, Uppsala: SAIS.

Homer-Dixon, T (1991), "On the Threshold: Environmental Changes as Causes of Acute Conflict," *International Security*, 16, (2); (1994), "Environmental Scarcities and Violent Conflict: Evidence from Cases," *International Security*, 19 (1); (1995), "Strategies for Studying Causation in Complex Ecological Systems," University of Toronto; (1995-6), "Environmental and Security—Homer-Dixon to Marc Levy," *International Security*, 20 (3); (1996), "Environmental Scarcity, Mass Violence, and The Limits to Ingenuity," *Current History*, vol. 95, no. 604.

Hyden, G (1999), "Environmental Awareness, Conflict Genesis and Governance," in Tiiarita Granfelt (ed.), *Managing the Globalised Environment*, London: IT Publications.

Ibeanu, O (1999), "Ogoni-Oil, Resource Flow and Conflict in Rural Nigeria," in Tiiarita Granfelt (ed.), *Managing the Globalised Environment*, London: IT Publications.

Kaplan, R (1994), "The Coming Anarchy: How Scarcity, Crime, Overpopulation, Tribalism, and Disease are Rapidly Destroying the Social Fabric of our Planet," *Atlantic Monthly*,

February; (1997), *The Ends of the Earth: A Journey at the Dawn of the 21st Century*, London: Papermac.

Klare, M (1996), "Redefining Security: The New Global Schisms," *Current History*, vol. 95, no. 604.

Klare, M & D Thomas (eds.) (1994), *World Security Challenges for a New Century*, New York: St. Martins Press.

Lancaster, C (1994), "The Coming Anarchy," *CSIS Africa Notes*, no. 163, August.

Leach, M & R Mearns (eds.) (1996), *The Lie of the Land, Challenging Received Wisdom on the African Environment*, London: Oxford, New Hampshire: International Institute, James Currey and Heinemann.

Levy, M (1995), "Is the Environment a National Security Issue?" *International Security*, Fall.

Mathews, J (1989), "Redefining Security," *Foreign Affairs,* 68 (2), Spring.

Mathew, R (1995), "Environmental Security: Demystifying the Concept, Clarifying the Stakes," in P Simmons (ed.), *Environmental Change and Security Report*, Washington DC: The Woodrow Wilson Center, Issue 1, Spring.

Mkandawire, T & A Olukoshi (eds.) (1995), *Between Liberalization and Repression: The Politics of Structural Adjustment in Africa*, Dakar: CODESRIA Books.

Myers, N (1995), "Redefining Security," *Foreign Affairs*, 68 (29), Spring.

Naanen, B (1995), "Oil-Producing Minorities and the Restructuring of Nigerian Federalism: The Case of the Ogoni," *Journal of Commonwealth and Comparative Studies*, vol. 32, no. 1.

Obi, C (1997a), "Oil, Environmental Conflict and National Security in Nigeria: Ramifications of the Ecology-Security Nexus for Sub-Regional Peace," University of Illinois at Urbana-Champaign: *ACDIS Occasional Paper*, January; (1997b), "Resources, Population and Conflicts: Two African Case Studies," Lead Paper presented to Laureates of the CODESRIA Institute of Governance on the Theme: the Political Economy of Conflicts in Africa, Dakar, 18–22 August; (1998a), "Environmental Security in Africa: Some Theoretical Concerns and Emerging Issues," *Africa Insight*, vol. 28 no. 1/2; (1998b), "The Environment-Security Nexus: Is it Real?, *CODESRIA Bulletin*, no. 2; (1999a), "Globalisation and Environmental Conflict in Africa," *African Journal of Political Science* (New Series), vol. 4, no. 1; (1999b), "The Changing Forms of Identity Politics in Nigeria Under Structural Adjustment: The Case of the Oil Minorities Movement of the Niger Delta," Seminar Paper presented to the Department of Political Science, University of Helsinki, 11 May.

Ohmae, K (1995), T*he End of the Nation-State: The Rise of Regional Economies*, London: Harper Ellis.

Olukoshi, A (1998), "The Elusive Prince of Denmark: Structural Adjustment and the Crisis of Governance in Africa," Uppsala, *NAI Research Report* no. 104; (1999), "State, Conflict and Democracy in Africa: The Complex Process of Renewal," in, Richard Joseph (ed.), *State, Conflict, and Democracy in Africa*, Boulder and London: Lynne Rienner.

Percival, V (1997), "Environmental Scarcity and Violent Conflict: Case of South Africa and Rwanda" in Alex Morrison et al. (eds.), *Refugees, Resources and Resoluteness*, Clementsport: Canadian Peacekeeping Press.

Percival, V & T Homer-Dixon (1995), "Environmental Security and Violent Conflict: The Case of Rwanda," American Association for the Advancement of Science and the University of Toronto.

Porter, G (1995), "Environmental Security as a National Security Issue," *Current History*, vol. 94, no. 592, May.

Redclift M & T Benton (eds.) (1994), *Social Theory and the Environment*, London and New York: Routledge.

Rennet, M (1996), *Fighting for Survival: Environmental Decline, Social Conflict and the New Age of Insecurity*, New York and London: W W Norton and Company.

Richards, P (1996), *Fighting for the Rainforest: War, Youth and Resources in Sierra Leone*, Oxford: James Currey, in association with the International Africa Institute.

Robinson, D (1996), *Ogoni: The Struggle Continues*, Geneva and Nairobi: World Council of Churches and All Africa Conference of Churches.

Rowell, A (1996), "A Shell-Shocked Land," in *Green Backlash: Global Subversion of the Environmental Movement*, London and New York: Routledge.

Salih, M (1999), *Environmental Politics and Liberation in Contemporary Africa*, Dordrecht, Boston and London: Kluwer Academic Publishers.

Saurin, J (1996), "International Relations, Social Ecology and the Globalisation of Environmental Change," in J Vogler & M Imber (eds.), *The Environment and International Relations*, London: Routledge.

Speth, G (1990), "Environmental Security for the 1990s," *Development: Journal of the Society for International Development*, vol. 3/4.

Suliman, M (1999), "The Rationality and Irrationality of Violence in Sub-Saharan Africa," in, Mohammed Suliman (ed.), *Ecology, Politics and Violent Conflict*, London and New York: Zed Books.

Swain, A (1993), "Environment and Conflict: Analyzing the Developing World," *Report no. 37*, Department of Peace and Conflict Research, Uppsala University.

Tandon, Y (1998), "Globalisation and Africa's Options," *AAPS Newsletter*, January–April, and May–August.

Timberlake, L (1985), *Africa in Crisis: The Causes, The Cures of Environmental Bankruptcy*, London and Washington DC: Earthscan Publications.

Ullman, R (1983), "Redefining Security," *International Security* (8).

Uvin, P (1996), "Development, Aid and Conflict: Reflections from the Case of Rwanda," *Research for Action*, 24, United Nations University/ WIDER, Helsinki

www.OneEarth.org.

Wilken, P (1996), "New Myth for the South: Globalisation and The Conflict Between Private Power and Freedom," *Third World Quarterly*, vol. 17, no. 2.

William, M (1996), "International Political Economy and Global Environmental Change," in J Vogler & M Imber (eds.), *The Environment and International Relations*, London: Routledge.

Zyman, J (1996), "The Myth of the "Global" Economy: Enduring National Foundations and Emerging Regional Realities," *New Political Economy*, vol. 1, no. 2.

Postscript

In discussing this issue, it should be noted that the definition of environmental security used here focuses on a narrower concept of security that links it to military threats. The main concern of writers like Robert Kaplan and Thomas Homer-Dixon is whether environmental degradation, population pressures, or access to natural resources lead to violent conflict. More recently, other analysts have argued for a greater focus on the notion of global environmental security. Their suggestion is that environmental degradation is an issue demanding attention on its own merits, whether or not there is an immediate threat of conflict. This encourages a more holistic and less militarized approach to environmental issues. Those promoting the concept of human security have argued that environmental issues should be seen as but one dimension in a more comprehensive definition of security. For a discussion of how the meaning of environmental security has been constructed differently, see the web-based article, "Facing Environmental Security" by Heather Smith, at www.stratnet.ucalgary.ca/journal/article3.html.

Infotrac Keyword Search

"environmental security" or "environment" + "Africa"

Suggested Additional Readings

Deudney, Daniel. "The Case Against Linking Environmental Degradation and National Security." *Millennium* 19: 3 (1990): 461–76.

_____. "Environment and Security: Muddled Thinking." *Bulletin of Atomic Scientists* (April 1991): 22–28.

Gleick, Peter. "Environment and Security: The Clear Connections." *Bulletin of Atomic Scientists.* (April 1991): 17–21.

Homer-Dixon, Thomas F. and M.A. Levy. "Environment and Security, Correspondence." *International Security* 20: 3 (1995): 189–98.

_____ "Environmental Scarcities and Violent Conflict." *International Security* 19: 1 (1994): 5–40.

_____, J. H. Boutwell, and G. W. Rathjens. "Environmental Change and Violent Conflict." *Scientific American* (1993): 38–44.

Levy, Marc A. "Is the Environment a National Security Issue?" *International Security* 20: 2 (1995): 35–62.

Litfin, Karen. "Constructing Environmental Security and Ecological Interdependence." *Global Governance* 5, no. 3 (July–September 1999): 359–78.

Matthew, Richard A. "Environmental Security: Demystifying the Concept, Clarifying the Stakes." *Environmental Change and Security Project,* Report Issue 1 (Spring 1995): 14–23.

Salih, M. *Environmental Politics and Liberation in Contemporary Africa.* Boston: Kluwer Academic Publishers, 1999.

Website Resources

Center for Environmental Security   Has a large number of papers and links on the environment as a security issue.

The Environmental Change and Security Project (ECSP)   This website is sponsored by The Woodrow Wilson International Centre for Scholars in Washington, DC.

Environmental Security Database   The Environmental Security Database contains information on books, journal articles, papers, and newspaper clippings relating to the study of the links between environmental stress and violent conflict in developing countries. Much of the material was gathered as part of the research program undertaken by Thomas Homer-Dixon.

Globe South Africa   Contains the papers from a conference on environmental security in Africa.

United Nations Environment Programme (UNEP)   Official UN site of the UNEP based in Nairobi, Kenya. Contains a number of speeches and papers on environmental security.

APPENDIX

HOW TO WRITE AN ARGUMENTATIVE ESSAY

LUCILLE CHARLTON

Argumentative essays are written to convince or persuade readers of a particular point or opinion. Whether the point is to change the public's mind on a political issue or to convince a person to stop smoking, all argumentative essays have common elements: a well-defined, convincing argument, credible evidence, and a rebuttal of criticism. While most points of general essay writing apply to argumentative essays, there are several special guidelines the writer of a good persuasive essay must consider. The following sections introduce students to six basic steps in writing an argumentative or persuasive essay.

STEP 1: DEFINE THE ARGUMENT

It is easy to point out that there are two sides to every discussion; however, it is difficult to define precisely one's own opinion on a subject and write about it. First, the writer must be certain that there is, in fact, something to disagree about. For example, Castro is the President of Cuba: no one can dispute that fact. However, if I claim in my essay that Castro's policies have benefited the Cuban nation, many people would disagree with me. There must be room for disagreement with whatever position is taken, so an argumentative essay has to be more than an affirmation of acknowledged facts. In this way, argumentative writing differs from descriptive or journalistic writing. Also, the writer must state the argument in a precise thesis statement that will act as a controlling idea for the entire essay. All ideas expressed in the essay must relate to the thesis statement.

Second, an argumentative essay is more than a restatement of the two sides of the question. A simple recounting of opposing arguments does not give the reader any clear indication of how the writer feels about the subject, and is not really a persuasive statement. For example, a court transcript contains every word spoken by the witnesses at a trial. These statements are entered as evidence in the court, but it is up to the lawyers for both sides to interpret the evidence and present it in a persuasive manner to the jury, leaving no doubt about which side they are on. In the same way, the writer first carefully defines the subject, examines the evidence, and then interprets that evidence by writing a precise opinion. An argumentative essay takes one side of a controversial issue; there should be no doubt in the reader's mind where the writer stands on that issue.

STEP 2: GATHER THE EVIDENCE

Arguments need credible supporting evidence, and good persuasive writers assemble a variety of information from different sources. This evidence can be found in statements from authorities, statistics, or personal experience, or can be interpreted from research data. The authors in this book have chosen one or more of these types of evidence to support their positions. These four types of evidence can also be used by student writers in their argumentative essays.

When researching evidence to support a particular position, the writer needs to keep in mind the four *R's*: *reliable, relevant, recent,* and *referenced.*

First, all authorities used for supporting evidence need to be reliable—that means an acknowledged authority published in a recognized source. Evidence can be suspect if it is published only in unreliable sources, or if a researcher is unable to independently verify the statements. A good writer recognizes acceptable sources and is knowledgeable of the biases normally found in newspapers, magazines, journals, and Internet sources.

Because of the vast amount of material now available through electronic sources, writers must become skilled in evaluating the information presented. Newspaper and journal articles go through a process of editing and evaluation before publication. This acts as a check on information from unreliable sources. Electronic sources are not subjected to such scrutiny, so it is advisable to independently verify information from Internet sources. Consult the web address at the end of the appendix for information on evaluating the reliability of electronic sources.

Reference librarians can assist students in finding a variety of trustworthy sources for essays. Using suspect information will damage the credibility of the writer. A variety of reliable sources adds credibility to the writer's arguments.

Second, sources need to be relevant; that is, they have something to contribute on the immediate topic. The Economic Council of Canada has expertise in the area of the Canadian economy, but scholars know that it is an unlikely source for information on the status of Pakistan's nuclear weapons. Writers can easily lose unity in their essays by adding irrelevant quotes or paraphrases just to sound authoritative.

Third, a good writer looks for recent information on the topic. Using outdated information could affect the outcome of the argument. For example, if I were arguing for increased funding for AIDS victims in sub-Sahara Africa, I would not base my essay on statistics from 1995, when fewer cases of HIV were reported. The writer should be familiar with the effects of recent changes on the topic: politicians can reverse their positions, new statistics can change the writer's perspective, and new research can add to the evidence. Internet access greatly enhances a writer's ability to access updated statistics, and instructors expect student initiative in this area.

In addition, a writer must also know how much background research needs to be done to introduce the topic to the reader. Background information may be necessary to show how events have progressed over the last few years. For example, any serious discussion of the terrorist events of September 11, 2001, needs background information on the previous attack at the World Trade Center and the two United States embassy bombings.

Finally, all sources need to be carefully quoted and referenced in an acceptable citation form. There are a few basic rules to follow when using someone else's material:

1. Quotations are the exact words of the original author, and they must always be referenced. Consult one of the reference books or web sites listed at the end of this article for correct formats. If you are unsure how to reference a particular source, consult with your instructor or a reference librarian.

2. Paraphrases are your restatement of the original author's ideas. Paraphrases keep the same idea, but are restated in your own words. All paraphrases must be referenced. Scholars and researchers frequently use both quotations and paraphrases from a variety of sources to make their arguments.

3. Be careful when using quotations. Do not take either quotations or paraphrases out of context, thereby misquoting a source. Make sure you do enough research to know the writer's position on a topic. Use quotations sparingly, only when you want to emphasize an important point. Double check all quotations to make sure you haven't missed anything in transcribing the words.

4. Give credit whenever using information that did not originate with you, except for general information or well-known facts. For example, you do not need to acknowledge that India became independent from Britain in 1947. However, you must acknowledge statistical data taken from census or research reports used to support your arguments. The contributors to this volume have acknowledged their sources at the end of their articles in notes or references.

In gathering the evidence, keep careful notes and records of all your sources. Make sure to acknowledge all of your sources. The reference manuals and web sites listed at the end of this article have helpful information on how to cite your sources. Avoid plagiarism. If you are not certain what constitutes plagiarism, ask your instructor for assistance and consult your school's policy on plagiarism. All colleges and universities have serious penalties for plagiarism.

STEP 3: REFUTE THE OPPOSITION

In order to be convincing, writers have to support their argument while defusing criticism of the position taken. When researching the arguments, the writer also anticipates opposing viewpoints, researches them thoroughly, and is ready to refute them in the essay. Casting doubt on another writer's position or reasoning can clinch your support. This can be done in several ways. First, the writer can cite authorities that hold opposing views, then refute their arguments by quoting other sources or different statistics. Second, rebuttals of arguments can be constructed through differing personal experiences. A third method is to attack the opposition's interpretation of documents and facts.

Writers often concede some of the arguments an opponent makes, then challenge the opponent with a strong conclusion. Concessions should be included early in the argument. The strongest points should be left for the last, leaving no doubt in the reader's mind of the writer's intentions. Avoiding all mention of the opposing position is not a good strategy.

Whether building support for their own arguments or refuting criticism of their positions, writers must be careful to avoid argumentative fallacies, or mistakes in reasoning or argument. The most common fallacies that appear in essays are overgeneralization, faulty cause and effect, and misrepresentation of the opposition. Various writing manuals contain complete discussions of argumentative fallacies.

STEP 4: OUTLINE YOUR ESSAY

Good essay writers start with an outline that incorporates their key ideas into the body of the essay. All argumentative essays begin with an attention-getter: the writer quotes an interesting fact, makes a dramatic statement, or even illustrates with the opposite opinion. In Issue 19, Ananda Millard asks an intriguing question to begin her article on child soldiers. Once the reader is hooked into reading the essay, the writer continues with a thesis statement and proceeds with the arguments.

The body of an argumentative essay can be organized in two ways:

Pattern I

Introduction
Thesis statement
Background (if needed)
Listing of all your arguments with supporting evidence
A refutation of all your opponent's points
A reminder of your strongest arguments
Conclusion, including a strong opinion statement

Pattern II

Introduction
Thesis statement
Background (if needed)
Statement of your opponent's first argument, with concession or refutation
Statement of your opponent's second argument, with concession or refutation
Continued refutation of your opponent's arguments, in order
Conclusion, with a strong statement of your own opinion

Many of the contributors to this volume follow Pattern II, which is more effective for longer essays. Pattern I is acceptable for shorter essays with fewer points of supporting evidence, because the reader will not get lost following the train of thought from argument to refutation. In both patterns, concessions are made early in the argument, and a strong opinion statement concludes the essay.

STEP 5: DECIDE TONE AND STYLE

The tone and style of your essay will depend on your audience. Most writers assume that they are writing for intelligent people who have open minds on the topic. Therefore, the tone of the essay cannot be insulting or pejorative. Treat your opposition and your readers with respect.

Examples:

Wrong: As every intelligent person knows...
Better: Many people believe...

Wrong: Only children would assume that...
Better: I do not agree with this position...

The essay must also be readable. Using language that is either hard to understand or too casual for the audience will not win converts to your point of view. The language used in an essay must be clear, direct, understandable, and free of gender, racial, or other biases.

Examples:

Wrong: Legitimized concerns on this matter were postponed by the committee.
Better: The committee delayed discussion.

Wrong: Those guys really messed up on this one.
Better: The politicians made mistakes in their analysis.

Wrong: A cabinet minister is accountable for his decisions.
Better: Cabinet ministers are accountable for their decisions.

Most academic essays are written in a formal tone, making minimal use of the pronoun "I." However, be sure to know what your audience expects. Sometimes persuasive essays or speeches are directed at a particular group, and the writer can then use a less formal style of presentation.

STEP 6: CHECK AND DOUBLE CHECK

After writing a draft of an essay, follow this basic checklist of items. By working through the list, you can catch errors in your essay.

Argumentative essay checklist:

1. Have I defined the argument?

2. Do I have a well-stated opinion on the topic?

3. Is my thesis statement clear? Does it have sufficient support?

4. Is my essay unified? Do all parts of the essay relate to the thesis statement?

5. Have I avoided argumentative fallacies?

6. Are my tone and style consistent and appropriate?

7. Have I varied my sentence structure and vocabulary?

8. Have I concluded with a strong statement?

9. Does the opening paragraph grab the reader's attention?

10. Have I checked for spelling errors and misused words and expressions?

11. Have I cited all sources in an acceptable style?

12. Have I correctly punctuated my sentences?

SOURCES TO CONSULT ON ESSAY WRITING

Buckley, Joanne. *Fit to Print: The Canadian Student's Guide to Essay Writing.* 5th ed. Toronto: Harcourt Brace Canada, 2000.

Finnbogason, Jack, and Al Valleau. *A Canadian Writer's Guide.* Toronto: Nelson Canada, 1997.

Gibaldi, Joseph. *MLA Handbook for Writers of Research Papers.* 5th ed. New York: Modern Language Association, 1999.

Heckman, Grant. *Nelson Guide to Web Research 2001-2002.* Toronto: Nelson Thomson Learning, 2001.

For ESL Students

Hall, Ernest, and Carrie S.Y. Jung. *Reflecting on Writing: Composing in English for ESL Students in Canada.* Toronto: Harcourt Brace Canada, 1996.

Websites

The Internet has now become the best source for up-to-date information on essay writing. Listed below are several key sites which contain information useful for citation styles, evaluation of electronic sources, and general writing guidelines.

Modern Language Association

Simon Fraser University, Department of Political Science: Guidelines for Citing Electronic Source Materials

Purdue University's Online Writing Lab (OWL)

Writing at the University of Toronto, Standard Documentation Formats

General Resources on Political Science

Political Resources on the Net

Academic Info: Political Science

The University of British Columbia Library, Political Science: A Net Station

CONTRIBUTOR ACKNOWLEDGMENTS

The editors wish to thank the publishers and copyright holders for permission to reprint the selections in this book, which are listed below in order of appearance.

Issue 1
John Mueller, "The Obsolescence of Major War," reprinted with permission from *Security Dialogue* 21: 3 (2001), 321–328.

Michael O'Hanlon, "Coming Conflicts: Interstate War in the New Millenium," reprinted with permission from *Harvard International Review* 23: 2 (Summer 2000), 42–47.

Issue 2
Susan Strange, "The Erosion of the State." Reprinted with permission from *Current History* magazine 96: 613 (November 1997). © 1997, Current History, Inc.

Martin Wolf, "Will the Nation-State Survive Globalization?" Reprinted by permission of *Foreign Affairs* (January/February 2001). Copyright 2001 by The Council on Foreign Relations, Inc.

Issue 3
Samuel Huntington, 'The Clash of Civilizations? The Next Pattern of Conflict." Reprinted by permission of *Foreign Affairs* (Summer 1993). Copyright 1993 by The Council on Foreign Relations, Inc.

Douglas Ross, "Despair, Defeatism, and Isolationism in American 'Grand Strategy': The Seductive Convenience of Huntington's 'Civilizational Clash' Thesis," © Nelson, a division of Thomson Canada Ltd., 1998.

Issue 4
Lloyd Axworthy, "Human Security: Safety for People in a Changing World." Ottawa: Department of Foreign Affairs and International Trade, 1999. Reproduced with the permission of the Minister of Public Works and Government Services Canada, 2002.

William W. Bain, "Against Crusading: The Ethics of Human Security and Canadian Foreign Policy," reprinted with permission from *Canadian Foreign Policy* 6: 3 (Spring 1999), 85–98.

Issue 5
Reprinted with permission of the publisher from Andrew Cooper, Richard Higgott, and Kim Richard Nossal, *Relocating Middle Powers: Australia and Canada in a Changing World Order.* © University of British Columbia Press, 1993. All rights reserved by the publisher.

Mark Neufeld, "Hegemony and Foreign Policy Analysis: The Case of Canada as a Middle Power," reprinted with permission from *Studies in Political Economy* 48 (Autumn 1995), 7–29.

Issue 6
Evan H. Potter, "Niche Diplomacy as Canadian Foreign Policy," reprinted with permission from *International Journal* LII (Winter 1996–1997), 25–38.

Heather A. Smith, "Caution Warranted: Niche Diplomacy Assessed," reprinted with permission from *Canadian Foreign Policy* 6: 3 (Spring 1999), 57–72.

Issue 7
Caleb Carr, "Terrorism as Warfare: Lessons of Military History." Reprinted by permission of International Creative Management, Inc. Copyright © 1996 and Caleb Carr.

Bruce Hoffman, "Terrorism: Who is Fighting Whom?" *World Policy Journal* 14: 1 (Spring 1997), 97–105. Reprinted with permission of the author.

Issue 8
Michael Klare, "An Anachronistic Policy: The Strategic Obsolescence of the 'Rogue Doctrine'," reprinted with permission from *Harvard International Review* 22: 2 (Summer 2000), 46–52.

Thomas Henriksen, "The Rise and Decline of Rogue States: Dividing Patrons from Rogue Regimes," *Vital Speeches* 67: 10 (March 1, 2001), 292ff. Reprinted with permission of the author.

Issue 9
Ernie Regehr, "Missile Proliferation, Globalized Insecurity, and Demand-Side Strategies," Waterloo: Project Ploughshares, Ploughshares Briefing, 01/4 (March 2001). Reprinted with permission.

Frank P. Harvey, "The International Politics of National Missile Defence: A Response to the Critics," reprinted with permission from *International Journal* 55: 4 (Autumn 2000); 545–66.

Issue 10
Francis Fukuyama, "Women and the Evolution of World Politics." Reprinted by permission of *Foreign Affairs* (September/October 1998). Copyright 1998 by The Council on Foreign Relations, Inc.

J. Ann Tickner, "Why Women Can't Run the World: International Politics According to Francis Fukuyama," reprinted with permission from *International Studies Review* 1: 3 (Fall 1999).

Issue 11

Charles Krauthammer, "Peacekeeping Is for Chumps," reprinted with permission from *Saturday Night* (November 1995), 73–76.

Peter Viggo Jakobsen, "Overload, Not Marginalization, Threatens UN Peacekeeping," reprinted with permission from *Security Dialogue* 31: 2 (June 2000), 167–178.

Issue 12

Michel Chossudovsky, "Global Poverty in the Late 20th Century," *Journal of International Affairs* 52: 1 (Fall 1998), pp. 293–312. Published by permission of *The Journal of International Affairs* and the Trustees of Columbia University, New York.

Gautam Sen, "Is Globalisation Cheating the World's Poor?" *Cambridge Review of International Affairs* XIV, no. 1 (Autumn/Winter 2000), pp. 86–106. Reprinted with permission of the author.

Issue 13

Walden Bello and Philippe Legrain, "Should the WTO Be Abolished?" reprinted with permission from *The Ecologist* 30: 9 (December 2000), 20ff.

Issue 14

Stephen Gill, "Toward a Postmodern Prince? The Battle in Seattle as a Moment in the New Politics of Globalisation," reprinted with permission from *Millennium: Journal of International Studies* 29: 1 (2000), 131–140.

Jan Aart Scholte, "Cautionary Reflections on Seattle," reprinted with permission from *Millennium: Journal of International Studies* 29: 1 (2000), 115–121.

Issue 15

William Peters and Martin J. Dent, "Grass Roots Mobilization for Debt Remission: The Jubilee 2000 Campaign," reprinted by permission of the authors.

Denise Froning, "Will Debt Relief Really Help?" *The Washington Quarterly* 24: 3 (Summer 2001), 199–211. © 2001 by The Center for Strategic and International Studies (CSIS) and the Massachusetts Institute of Technology.

Issue 16

A.R. Riggs and Tom Velk, "The Tobin Tax: A Bad Idea Whose Time Has Passed," reprinted with permission from *Policy Options* 20: 6 (July/August 1999), 53–57.

Alex C. Michalos, "The Tobin Tax: A Good Idea Whose Time Has Not Passed," reprinted with permission from *Policy Options* 20: 8 (October 1999), 64–67.

Issue 17

Douglass Cassel, "Why We Need the International Criminal Court," *Christian Century* 116:15 (May 12, 1999). Copyright 1999 Christian Century Foundation. Reprinted with permission from the May 12, 1999 issue of the *Christian Century*. Subscriptions: $49/yr. from P.O. Box 378, Mt. Morris, IL 61054.

Alfred P. Rubin, "Some Objections to the International Criminal Court," reprinted with permission from *Peace Review* 12: 1 (March 2000), www.tandf.co.uk/journals.

Issue 18
Ross Snyder, "The Optional Protocol on the Involvement of Children in Armed Conflict," from Rob McCrae and Don Hubert, *Human Security and the New Diplomacy: Protecting People, Promoting Peace* (Montreal: McGill-Queen's University Press, 2001). Department of Foreign Affairs and International Trade. Reproduced with the permission of the Minister of Public Works and Government Services, 2002.

Millard, Ananda S., "Children in Armed Conflicts: Transcending Legal Responses," reprinted with permission from *Security Dialogue* 32: 2 (2001), 187–200.

Issue 19
Andrew Coyne, "The Case for Open Immigration: Why Opening Up Our Borders Would Be Good for the Country and Good for the Soul," reprinted from *The Next City* (Winter 1995), by permission of the author and the publisher.

G.E. Dirks, "Why States Are Justified in Limiting Their Entry of Immigrants," © Nelson, a division of Thomson Canada Ltd., 1998.

Issue 20
George Weigel, "The New Human-Rights Debate." From George Weigel, *Idealism Without Illusions: US Foreign Policy in the 1990s*, © 1994 The Ethics and Public Policy Center, published by Wm. B. Eerdmans Publishing Company, Grand Rapids, MI. Used by permission; all rights reserved.

Ron Dart, "The New Human Rights Debate: A Reply to George Wiegel," © Nelson, a division of Thomson Canada Ltd., 1998.

Issue 21
Elizabeth Rogers, "Economic Sanctions and Internal Conflict," reprinted from Michael E. Brown, ed., *The International Dimensions of Internal Conflict* (Cambridge, Mass.: MIT Press, 1996), 411–434, by permission of the publishers.

Kim Richard Nossal, "The False Promise of Economic Sanctions," © Nelson, a division of Thomson Canada Ltd., 1998.

Issue 22
Robert D. Kaplan, "The Coming Anarchy: How Scarcity, Crime, Overpopulation, Tribalism, and Disease Are Rapidly Destroying the Social Fabric of Our Planet," reprinted with permission from *The Atlantic Monthly* 273, no. 2 (February 1994), 44–76.

Cyril Obi, "Globalised Images of Environmental Security in Africa," reprinted with permission from *Review of African Political Economy* 27: 83 (March 2000), 47–63.